OXFORD STUDIES IN BYZANTIUM

Editorial Board

JAŚ ELSNER   CATHERINE HOLMES
JAMES HOWARD-JOHNSTON   INE JACOBS
ELIZABETH JEFFREYS   HUGH KENNEDY
MARC LAUXTERMANN   PAUL MAGDALINO
MARLIA MANGO   CLAUDIA RAPP
JEAN-PIERRE SODINI   JONATHAN SHEPARD

OXFORD STUDIES IN BYZANTIUM

Oxford Studies in Byzantium consists of scholarly monographs and editions on the history, literature, thought, and material culture of the Byzantine world.

John Zonaras' *Epitome of Histories*
A Compendium of Jewish-Roman History and Its Reception
Theofili Kampianaki

Symeon Stylites the Younger and Late Antique Antioch
From Hagiography to History
Lucy Parker

Depicting Orthodoxy in the Russian Middle Ages
The Novgorod Icon of Sophia, the Divine Wisdom
Ágnes Kriza

The Beginnings of the Ottoman Empire
Clive Foss

Church Architecture of Late Antique Northern Mesopotamia
Elif Keser Kayaalp

Byzantine Religious Law in Medieval Italy
James Morton

Caliphs and Merchants
Cities and Economies of Power in the Near East (700–950)
Fanny Bessard

Social Change in Town and Country in Eleventh-Century Byzantium
Edited by James Howard-Johnston

Innovation in Byzantine Medicine
The Writings of John Zacharias Aktouarios (c.1275–c.1330)
Petros Bouras-Vallianatos

Emperors and Usurpers in the Later Roman Empire
Civil War, Panegyric, and the Construction of Legitimacy
Adrastos Omissi

The *Universal History* of Stepʻanos Tarōnecʻi
Introduction, Translation, and Commentary
Tim Greenwood

Theodoros Prodromos:
Miscellaneous Poems

An Edition and Literary Study

NIKOS ZAGKLAS

Great Clarendon Street, Oxford, OX2 6DP,
United Kingdom

Oxford University Press is a department of the University of Oxford.
It furthers the University's objective of excellence in research, scholarship,
and education by publishing worldwide. Oxford is a registered trade mark of
Oxford University Press in the UK and in certain other countries

© Nikolaos Zagklas 2023

The moral rights of the author have been asserted

First Edition published in 2023

All rights reserved. No part of this publication may be reproduced, stored in
a retrieval system, or transmitted, in any form or by any means, without the
prior permission in writing of Oxford University Press, or as expressly permitted
by law, by licence or under terms agreed with the appropriate reprographics
rights organization. Enquiries concerning reproduction outside the scope of the
above should be sent to the Rights Department, Oxford University Press, at the
address above

You must not circulate this work in any other form
and you must impose this same condition on any acquirer

Published in the United States of America by Oxford University Press
198 Madison Avenue, New York, NY 10016, United States of America

British Library Cataloguing in Publication Data

Data available

Library of Congress Control Number: 2022948232

ISBN 978–0–19–288692–7

DOI: 10.1093/oso/9780192886927.001.0001

Printed and bound by
CPI Group (UK) Ltd, Croydon, CR0 4YY

Links to third party websites are provided by Oxford in good faith and
for information only. Oxford disclaims any responsibility for the materials
contained in any third party website referenced in this work.

In memory of Wolfram Hörandner

Acknowledgements

Theodoros Prodromos has been a wonderful companion in the last few years, from the first stages of my PhD dissertation to its transformation into the current book. However, it would have been impossible to delve into his fascinating literary world and grasp many of its complexities and particularities without the help of various colleagues and friends. Andreas Rhoby was kind enough to take me on as his first doctoral student and devote enormous time and energy to training me as a Byzantinist. His constant support, continuing advice, and consistent guidance have provided me with the necessary strength to carry out this project and master its various challenges. Our endless discussions have determined many aspects of this book. Theodora Antonopoulou and Andreas Müller acted as co-supervisors, offering insightful suggestions and corrections at various stages of the doctoral process. The former has been a devoted teacher since my undergraduate studies at the University of Patras. My doctoral studies in Vienna were supported by the Greek State Scholarship Foundation (*IKY*) and its European scholarship programme. A short-term predoctoral residency at Dumbarton Oaks Research Library and Collection in March 2014 allowed me to finish writing up the dissertation. I am most grateful to Margaret Mullett and all the fellows of that academic year for their interest in my project and our stimulating discussions. I also thank Ingela Nilsson and Marc Lauxtermann for acting as the external reviewers of my dissertation and offering much constructive feedback, ranging from suggestions for improvement to various corrections. Both of them provided a lot of the impetus which has led to the dissertation being turned into a book.

A short talk with Elizabeth Jeffreys during a seminar in Katowice was the first step towards setting in motion the process of publishing the book with OUP. I am most grateful to her for guiding me through the first stages of the publication process. During this period of revision, I was fortunate enough to receive support from various institutions. A fund from project UMO-2013/10/E/HS2/00170 of the National Science Centre of Poland and a fellowship at Dumbarton Oaks Research Library and Collection provided me with the necessary means and conducive environments to progress with the production of the book. A grant from the Faculty of Historical and Cultural Studies of the University of Vienna covered a range of expenses towards the final stages of the book production. I am also grateful to various libraries for allowing me to consult much of the material *in situ*: the Biblioteca Apostolica Vaticana, the Biblioteca Nazionale Marciana in Venice, the Bodleian Library, the US Library of Congress, the National Library of Greece in Athens, and the Österreichische Nationalbibliothek in Vienna.

During the transitional period from PhD student to early-career scholar, Ingela Nilsson and Przemek Marciniak helped me become more confident in my abilities. They also helped me acquire a more nuanced understanding of twelfth-century literature. Krystina Kubina has been a wonderful colleague and friend. Our regular conversations over the last few years have given shape to many of the ideas expressed in this book. Claudia Rapp constantly encouraged me to finish the project, especially at moments when my motivation was flagging. Special thanks also to Nate Aschenbrenner for reading an earlier draft of my translations and offering many excellent suggestions for improvements.

My work has also benefited from conversations with a series of friends and colleagues: Eirene Afentoulidou, Panagiotis Agapitos, Manolis Bourbouhakis, Carolina Cupane, Kristoffel Demoen, Ivan Drpić, Antonia Giannouli, Eleni Kaltsogianni, Marina Loukaki, Ekaterini Mitsiou, András Nemeth, Ilias Nesseris, Eva Nyström, Cosimo Paravano, Anneliese Paul, Dimitris Skrekas, and Foteini Spingou. I am particularly grateful to Marc Lauxtermann and Floris Bernard for reading through the penultimate draft of the book. Their sharp eyes have saved me from a lot of mistakes, inconsistencies, and inaccuracies. Their comments have improved the quality of the English translations immensely. I am also grateful to Judith Ryder who did the final proofreading of the entire book, contributing a great deal to the final result. Special thanks also to Klidi Abazaj for helping me with the indices. Needless to say, all mistakes remain mine.

I would like to dedicate this book to the memory of the late Professor Wolfram Hörandner. When I arrived in Vienna, he was already retired. However, he informally assumed the role of a co-supervisor, introducing me to the enchanting world of Theodoros Prodromos, and Byzantine literature in general. I received many different kinds of help from him, ranging from advice about a number of challenging aspects of the edition to full access to his personal library and collection of microfilms. I will never forget our long conversations and our shared enthusiasm for Prodromos' work. During one of our conversations he even offered me as a gift a rare copy of the sixteenth-century Basel edition by Hieronymus Guntius, which he had acquired from a second-hand bookstore in the DDR in the 1970s. Unfortunately, he did not survive to see the publication of this book, but I hope its dedication to him will be a small recompense.

Finally, I would like to thank my parents, Georgios and Antonia, my brother, Stamatis, and all my friends (especially Dimitris and Eleni), who encouraged me throughout this long process. Above all, I want to thank my partner for life, Steffi, for her support, especially at moments when I most needed it.

Vienna,
December 2021

Contents

List of Figures   xiii
List of Abbreviations   xv
Note to the Reader   xvii

SECTION 1

1. Introduction   1
   1.1 *Status Quaestionis*   1
   1.2 *Miscellaneous Poems*   10
       1.2.1 Some Perils of Authorship   11
       1.2.2 Poems and Epigrams: Functional Ambiguity and Genre Elasticity   15
       1.2.3 Veiled Occasions: Poems 1–6 and the Orphanotropheion of St Paul   24

2. A Writer on Command and His Strategies   31
   2.1 Theodoros Prodromos and His Professions   32
   2.2 Complaints and the Futility of Letters: Tangled Mosaics of Reality and Fictionality   43
   2.3 The Court, *Theatron*, and Classroom as 'Communicating Vessels'   53

3. Formal Features: Metre and Prosody   71
   3.1 Accentual metres   72
       3.1.1 Dodecasyllables   72
       3.1.2 Political Verse   75
   3.2 Dactylic Metres: A Strong Revival in the Twelfth Century   77
       3.2.1 Pentameters   79
       3.2.2 Hexameters: A Quantitative Survey   80
   3.3 Prosody   84
       3.3.1 Attic Correption   85
       3.3.2 Epic Correption   86
       3.3.3 Duplication of Consonants   86
   3.4 Hiatus   87

4. Manuscript Transmission   88
   4.1 Description of the Manuscripts   88
   4.2 *Vaticanus Graecus* 305 and Its Prodromean Collection   122
   4.3 Dissemination in the Twelfth Century and Beyond   130
   4.4 The Relationships between the Manuscripts   140
       4.4.1 Manuscript V   140
       4.4.2 The Remaining Manuscripts   146

xii CONTENTS

5. Previous Editions and Prolegomena   155
   - 5.1 From Hieronymus Guntius to the Present Edition   155
   - 5.2 The Present Edition   160
     - 5.2.1 Accentuation of the Clitics   163
     - 5.2.2 Punctuation   166

SECTION 2

Greek Text and Translation   169

Commentary   290

Bibliography   339
Index Locorum   361
Index of Works   370
General Index   375
Index of Manuscripts   381

List of Figures

2.1	Vat. Reg. gr. PP Pii II 54, fol. 409^{r-v}. © 2022 Biblioteca Apostolica Vaticana.	64
4.1	Vat. gr. 305, fol. VIII^r. © 2022 Biblioteca Apostolica Vaticana.	124
4.2	Chios, church of Panagia Krina, 18th c., inscription (Prodromos' poem 55). Courtesy of Anneliese Paul. Used with permission.	138
5.1	Vat. gr. 305, fol. 121^v. © 2022 Biblioteca Apostolica Vaticana.	168

List of Abbreviations

AHG	=	G. Schirò, *Analecta Hymnica Graeca e codicibus eruta Italiae inferioris*, 13 vols. (Rome 1966–83)
AnBoll	=	*Analecta Bollandiana*
AP	=	H. Beckby, *Anthologia Graeca*, 4 vols. (Munich 1957–58)
BF	=	*Byzantinische Forschungen*
BMGS	=	*Byzantine and Modern Greek Studies*
BS	=	*Byzantine Studies*
BSl	=	*Byzantinoslavica*
Byz	=	*Byzantion*
BZ	=	*Byzantinische Zeitschrift*
DOP	=	*Dumbarton Oaks Papers*
ΕΕΒΣ	=	*Ἐπετηρὶς Ἑταιρείας Βυζαντινῶν Σπουδῶν*
GRBS	=	*Greek, Roman and Byzantine Studies*
IRAIK	=	*Izvestiia Russkogo arkheologicheskogo institutav Konstantinopole*
JÖB	=	*Jahrbuch der Österreichischen Byzantinistik*
LBG	=	E. Trapp [et al.], *Lexikon zur byzantinischen Gräzitat besonders des 9.–12. Jahrhunderts*, 2 vols. (Vienna 1994–2017)
LSJ	=	H. G. Liddell – R. Scott – H. S. Jones—R. McKenzie, *A Greek-English lexicon*. With a Revised Supplement, Supplement ed. by P. G. W. Glare (Oxford 1996)
MEG	=	*Medioevo Greco*
NE	=	*Νέος Ἑλληνομνήμων*
ODB	=	A. Kazhdan (ed.), *The Oxford Dictionary of Byzantium*. 3 vols. (Oxford 1991)
PG	=	J. P. Migne, *Patrologia cursus completus. Series graeca*, 161 vols. (Paris 1857–66)
PGL	=	G. W. H. Lampe, *A Patristic Greek Lexicon* (Oxford 1961)
PLP	=	E. Trapp [et al.], *Prosopographisches Lexikon der Palaiologenzeit*, 15 vols. (Vienna 1976–96)
RbK	=	*Reallexikon zur byzantinischen Kunst*
REB	=	*Revue des Études Byzantines*
RGK	=	E. Gamillscheg, D. Harlfinger, and H. Hunger, *Repertorium der griechischen Kopisten, 800–1600*, 3 vols. (Vienna 1981–97)
RSBN	=	*Rivista di Studi Bizantini e Neoellenici*
SBN	=	*Studi Bizantini e Neoellenici*
Script	=	*Scriptorium*

Symm = Βυζαντινά Σύμμεικτα
TLG = *Thesaurus Linguae Graecae*
VV = *Vizantijskij Vremennik*
WSt = *Wiener Studien*
ZRVI = *Zbornik Radova Vizantološkog Instituta*

Note to the Reader

One of the main aims of this book is to mark a new step forward in our understanding of Prodromos' work and to make this as widely accessible as possible. For this reason, all the editions of Prodromos' poems presented here are accompanied by translations into English. The same goes for most of the Greek cited in the main body of the page. The only exceptions are some quotations in the footnotes and the commentary. Unless indicated otherwise, all translations in this book are my own.

I have chosen not to use Anglicized forms of names for authors and other individuals who were active in the middle and late Byzantine periods (e.g. Theodoros Prodromos instead of Theodore Prodromos, Ioannes Tzetzes instead of John Tzetzes). By contrast, I have stuck to well-established Anglicized forms in the case of the church fathers and some other saints (e.g. Gregory of Nazianzus instead of Gregorios Nazianzos, John Chrysostom instead of Ioannes Chrysostom). The same principle applies to ancient Greek authors (e.g. Homer, Hesiod). Although this mixed system of transliteration results in some inconsistencies (e.g. Gregory of Nazianzus versus Gregorios of Corinth), it is aimed at striking a balance between the use of original forms and clarity.

1
Introduction

1.1. *Status Quaestionis*

'Theodoros Prodromos ist einer der bekanntesten und fruchtbarsten byzantinischen Autoren des 12. Jahrhunderts.';[1] '...a Professor of Philosophy, a poet, orator and intellectual leader in twelfth-century Byzantium';[2] '...among the best known of Byzantine poets, and he is certainly one of the most popular with Byzantinists';[3] '...the poet laureate of his time';[4] '...one of the most prolific and well-known writers of the twelfth century';[5] '...the most versatile, inventive and prolific of the writers functioning in the first half of the twelfth century';[6] 'un auteur se trouve pendant une longue période au centre de cette production littéraire de la cour comnène et il peut même être regardé comme une personnification du courtisan type...'.[7]

Unlike many other Byzantine authors, whose works have been treated with suspicion by modern scholars, Theodoros Prodromos has attracted sustained interest from those with an interest in the history of Byzantine literature, receiving many flattering appraisals of his literary pursuits, and often being described as the leading intellectual of the second quarter of the twelfth century, or even the 'superstar author' of the entire Komnenian period. Something else that becomes clear from the enthusiastic assessments quoted above is that his poetry occupies a special place in his work. His surviving corpus comprises approximately 17,000 authentic verses in all possible metres, both ancient and Byzantine, ranging from hexameters, elegiac couplets, and anacreontics, to dodecasyllables and the fifteen-syllable 'political' verse, securing

---

[1] See the introductory note by Herbert Hunger in W. Hörandner, *Theodoros Prodromos: Historische Gedichte* (Vienna 1974), 7.
[2] M. J. Kyriakis, 'Professors and Disciples in Byzantium', *Byz* 43 (1973), 108–19, here at 109–10.
[3] A. Kazhdan, 'Theodore Prodromus: A Reappraisal', in: A. Kazhdan and S. Franklin (eds), *Studies on Byzantine Literature of the Eleventh and Twelfth Centuries* (Cambridge/Paris 1984), 87–114, here at 87.
[4] M. D. Lauxtermann, 'The Velocity of Pure Iambs: Byzantine Observations on the Metre and Rhythm of the Dodecasyllable', *JÖB* 48 (1998), 9–33, 13.
[5] M. Bazzani, 'The Historical Poems of Theodore Prodromos, the Epic-Homeric Revival and the Crisis of Intellectuals in the Twelfth Century', *BSl* 65 (2007), 211–28, 211.
[6] E. Jeffreys, *Four Byzantine Novels* (Liverpool 2012), 3.
[7] I. Nilsson, *Raconter Byzance: la littérature du 12e siècle* (Paris 2014), 36.

him a place among the most prolific and versatile poets of the Byzantine Middle Ages. Many of his verses were addressed to or commissioned by various members of the imperial family, aspiring aristocrats, high-ranking bureaucratic and ecclesiastical officials, and intellectual peers, meaning that his poetry reflects the vibrant diversity of the sociocultural *milieu* of twelfth-century Constantinople. Although he did not author a historical account or epic, his poetry offers significant fragments of historical information to the modern student of twelfth-century Byzantium. Although one may say that the historical value of much of his poetry is the main reason it has continued to be of interest to modern scholarship, in a field that still pursues the extraction of historical evidence at any cost, nevertheless some of his poems have also been discussed for their literary features: their conspicuous rhetorical opulence and their 'poetic' qualities,[8] the authorial self-praise and pride usually partially masked by a veil of self-deprecation and humility,[9] or even their highly satirical overtones, which share many features with various ancient satirical strands.[10]

Working on commission, as did many writers of his day, Prodromos produced a wide array of texts, both in prose and verse—from lengthy narratives (a novel and a hagiographical vita) to fully fledged rhetorical texts (letters, orations, and monodies), satires, educational exercises (the so-called *schede*), along with philosophical, theological, and grammatical texts. These works employ various modes (encomiastic, narrative, self-referential etc.) and revolve around different themes (friendship, love/eros, death, vanity, pleasure, envy etc.). However, a feature that makes Prodromos exceptional as an author is his keenness to experiment with forms to subvert the traditional expectations of a given genre. For example, he is very keen on bestowing verse form on genres with a long-established tradition in prose. The most telling example might be his novel *Rhodanthe and Dosikles*, written in the style of

---

[8] See, for instance, M. Bazzani, 'Theodore Prodromos' Poem LXXVII', *BZ* 100 (2007), 1–12. For the contrast between Byzantine and modern appreciation of the poetic characteristics of this poem, see F. Bernard, *Writing and Reading Byzantine Secular Poetry, 1025–1081* (Oxford 2014), 33.

[9] For example, Prodromos constantly presented himself as a have-not panegyrist by appropriating the image of Homer as poor eulogist of gods; see E. Cullhed, 'The Blind Bard and "I": Authorial Personas and Homeric Biography in the Twelfth Century', *BMGS* 38 (2014), 49–67, at 50–58; cf. also I. Drpić, *Epigram, Art, and Devotion in Later Byzantium* (Cambridge 2016), 35.

[10] Most of the work on the study of Prodromos' satirical poetry has been conducted by Przemysław Marciniak: P. Marciniak, 'Prodromos, Aristophanes and a Lustful Woman: A Byzantine Satire by Theodore Prodromos', *BSl* 73 (2015), 23–34; P. Marciniak, 'It Is Not What It Appears to Be: A Note on Theodore Prodromos' *Against a Lustful Old Woman*', *Eos* 103 (2016), 109–15; J. Kucharski and M. Marciniak, 'The Beard and Its Philosopher: Theodore Prodromos on the Philosopher's Beard in Byzantium', *BMGS* 41 (1) (2017), 45–54; P. Marciniak and K. Warcaba, 'Theodore Prodromos' *Katomyomachia* as a Byzantine Version of Mock-Epic', in: A. Rhoby and N. Zagklas (eds), *Middle and Late Byzantine Poetry: Texts and Contexts* (Brepols 2018), 97–110.

ancient novels. Unlike its predecessors, which are in prose, Prodromos' text is composed of 4,614 dodecasyllabic lines,[11] making it the first verse novel in the long history of the genre in the Greek tradition. On other occasions, Prodromos even combines verse with prose. Apart from his numerous *schede*, which usually open with a prose section and conclude with verses, some of his satirical works are also a mixture of prose and verse. Good examples are the two satirical works in the Lucianic style: *Amarantos, or the passions of an old man*, and *Sale of the political and poetical lives*. The former combines prose with elegiac couplets and anacreontics,[12] the latter is a blend of prose and hexameters.[13] The mixture of diverse metres within the very same poem is a further characteristic of his versatility and resourcefulness as an author. For example, historical poem 56, addressed to the *Orphanotrophos* Alexios Aristenos and described as a metrical *tour de force*,[14] consists of sixty-one dodecasyllables, fifty hexameters, twenty-four pentameters, and twenty-eight anacreontics. Such quasi-prosimetric and multimetric texts are evidence of a major technique in Prodromos' work, which enjoyed widespread popularity in the twelfth century and beyond;[15] and this mixture of various forms reflects a constant shift in the relationships between genre and occasion throughout his long career, affording him a leading place among his peers.

In addition to the distinctive literary features—as well as the historical value—of his writings, Prodromos has become a household name among modern Byzantinists for yet another reason: namely, the question of the relationship between the 'three Prodromoi', Theodoros Prodromos, Manganeios Prodromos, an anonymous author of 148 poems, and (Ptocho)prodromos, another anonymous author of four vernacular poems.[16] Though it was already

---

[11] The only exception is an embedded oracle in hexameters: see *Rhodanthe and Dosikles* 9.196–204.

[12] The prose text includes two epithalamia sung during the wedding of Amarantos' teacher Stratocles. For the text, T. Migliorini, 'Teodoro Prodromo: Amaranto', *MEG* 7 (2007), 183–247, at 193–95. For some further comments, see N. Zagklas, 'Experimenting with Prose and Verse in Twelfth-Century Byzantium: A Preliminary Study', *DOP* 71 (2017), 229–48, at 233.

[13] This applies mainly to the sections in which ancient poets such as Homer and Aristophanes speak, with most of the passages being quotations taken from their works; see Zagklas, 'Prose and Verse', 234–36.

[14] Lauxtermann, 'Velocity', 13.

[15] Zagklas, 'Prose and Verse', and Zagklas, 'Metrical *Polyeideia* in Twelfth-Century Poetry: Multimetric Poetic Cycles as a Medium for Generic Innovation', in: A. Rhoby and N. Zagklas (eds), *Middle and Late Byzantine Poetry: Texts and Contexts* (Brepols 2018), 43–70.

[16] In addition to these four vernacular poems, there is the so-called Maiuri poem, another vernacular poem ascribed to Prodromos. This poem was never edited together with the four (Ptocho)prodromika poems. When the edition of the (Ptocho)prodromika by Dirk C. Hesseling and Hubert Pernot was published they were not aware of its existence. On the other hand, Eideneier decided not to include this poem in his edition because he claimed that it is very different from the other four texts. In my view, this distinction is not necessary and for this reason I prefer to call it 'fifth ptochoprodromic poem'; for the editions of Prodromos' vernacular poems, see below p. 8.

clear from the beginning of the twentieth century that Theodoros Prodromos and Manganeios Prodromos are two different authors,[17] the relationship between Theodoros Prodromos and (Ptocho)prodromos is much more uncertain.[18] The complexity of this question is reflected in the vehement debate among various well-known scholars, especially since the 1970s. Hans-Georg Beck argued that the works attributed to (Ptocho)prodromos may well have been written by Prodromos, but he did not exclude the possibility that they are vernacular versions of his learned poetry, written by an unknown poet.[19] Unlike Beck, who was more flexible concerning the authorship of these poems, many other scholars either accepted or rejected Prodromos' authorship. On the basis of style, metre, language, and manuscript transmission, Wolfram Hörandner, Stylianos Alexiou, and Margaret Alexiou have argued in favour of identification with Theodoros Prodromos, while others such as Hans Eideneier have argued against it. In recent years, the debate has taken a rather surprising turn, since it has even been suggested that (Ptocho)prodromos might be the same person as Manganeios Prodromos.[20] However, in one of the most recent studies on this issue, Panagiotis Agapitos credited Theodoros Prodromos anew with the authorship of the (Ptocho)prodromika, even going as far as arguing that the first poem was presented together with the learned poem 24 to the emperor Ioannes II Komnenos in 1141/42.[21]

It is true that the (Ptocho)prodromika pose challenges to modern scholars, especially in the absence of a comprehensive study examining them alongside each other. There even seem to be differences between them, casting some doubts on the attribution of all of them to Prodromos. For example, when compared with the first three, the fourth poem possesses some syntactic and metrical idiosyncrasies.[22] Moreover, on the basis of numismatic evidence and

---

[17] S. Papadimitriou, 'Ὁ Πρόδρομος τοῦ Μαρκιανοῦ κώδικος XI 22', *VV* 10 (1903), 102–63; W. Hörandner, 'Theodoros Prodromos und die Gedichtsammlung des Cod. Marc. XI 22', *JÖB* 17 (1967), 91–99; and M. Jeffreys, 'Rhetorical Texts', in: E. Jeffreys (ed.), *Rhetoric in Byzantium* (Aldershot 2003), 87–100, at 87, note 1.
[18] For good overviews of this debate, see. A. Rhoby, 'Verschiedene Bemerkungen zur Sebastokratorissa Eirene und zu Autoren in ihrem Umfeld', *Nea Rhome* 6 (2009), 305–336, at 330; cf. also M. Kulhánková, '"…For Old Men Too Can Play, Albeit More Wisely So": The Game of Discourses in the Ptochoprodromika', in: P. Marciniak and I. Nilsson (eds), *Satire in the Middle Byzantine Period: The Golden Age of Laughter?* (Leiden-Boston 2020), 304–23, at 305–12.
[19] H.-G. Beck, *Geschichte der byzantinischen Volksliteratur* (Munich 1971), 104.
[20] Rhoby, 'Eirene Sebastokratorissa', 330–34, and M. Kulhánková, 'Figuren und Wortspiele in den Byzantinischen Bettelgedichten und die Frage der Autorschaft', *Graeco-Latina Brunensia* 16 (2011), 29–39.
[21] See P. A. Agapitos, 'New Genres in the Twelfth Century: The *Schedourgia* of Theodore Prodromos', *Medioevo Greco* 15 (2015), 1–41, 29–33.
[22] M. C. Janssen and M. D. Lauxtermann, 'Authorship Revisited: Language and Metre in the Ptochoprodromika', in: T. Shawcross and I. Toth (eds), *Reading in the Byzantine Empire and Beyond* (Cambridge 2018), 558–84.

historical references, poems 3 and 4 may have been written after 1160, when Prodromos was already dead.[23] That said, the marked reluctance of some modern scholars, particularly Hans Eideneier,[24] to accept that these poems were written by Prodromos owes much to the opposition—artificial, I would say—imposed by some modern scholars between learned and vernacular linguistic registers.[25] This reluctance has denied Prodromos' oeuvre layers of its rhetorical style and has cast doubts on his distinctive technique of alternating between one linguistic register and another. To understand this technique better, we should view it as an analogue to the blending of prose and verse, the metrical heterogeneity, and the shift in terms of genre and style briefly discussed above, which, as Antonio Garzya has pointed out, is 'sehr byzantinisch...vielmehr sehr tzetzianisch und sehr prodromisch'.[26] As with his alternation between prose and verse, or even between different metres, the composition of poems both in learned and vernacular Greek is another means of demonstrating his range and versatility. In other words, Prodromos' practice of using different linguistic registers, metres, and stylistic forms should be considered as a kind of literary experiment, aimed at achieving the rhetorical variation which was highly appreciated by the Byzantines. Moreover, it was his bold literary experimentations which helped him to shape his own authorial trademark and establish himself within the fiercely competitive twelfth-century literary market.

Needless to say, a study that would examine Prodromos' work in its entirety and further enhance our understanding of all these aspects remains a desideratum. Although the secondary literature on Theodoros Prodromos and his work has grown significantly in recent years, no one has so far attempted to piece together the entire puzzle of his literary activity and discuss him as an author working on commission in twelfth-century Constantinople. This shortcoming in current scholarship on Prodromos matches the general inadequacy of available monographs looking at the full output of individual Byzantine authors to construct the protean authorial persona across various

---

[23] See M. Alexiou, 'The Poverty of Écriture and the Craft of Writing: Towards a Reappraisal of the Prodromic Poems', *BMGS* 10 (1986), 1–40, at 25–28; cf. also Janssen and Lauxtermann, 'Ptochoprodromika', 563–4.

[24] See H. Eideneier, 'Tou Ptochoprodromou', in: M. Hinterberger and E. Schiffer (eds), *Byzantinische Sprachkunst: Studien zur byzantinischen Literatur gewidmet Wolfram Hörandner zum 65. Geburtstag* (Berlin/New York 2007), 56–76, and H. Eideneier, *Πτωχοπρόδρομος* (Herakleion 2012), 93–99 and 138–42.

[25] Karl Krumbacher was the first modern scholar to impose this dichotomy, in his history of Byzantine literature: see P. A. Agapitos, 'Karl Krumbacher and the History of Byzantine Literature', *BZ* 108 (2015), 1–52.

[26] A. Garzya, 'Literarische und rhetorische Polemiken der Komnenenzeit', *BSl* 34 (1973), 1–14, at 14.

text types and their varying contexts of performance.[27] To undertake such a study for Prodromos and his huge literary oeuvre would first demand some painstaking philological work.

A good number of Prodromos' writings—especially those with grammatical, theological, and philosophical focus—still require basic editorial work. Prodromos' *exegesis* on the canons of Kosmas and Ioannes of Damascus still awaits a new edition and study, since Stevenson's nineteenth-century edition includes only the preamble, the first five of the seventeen canons, and a small portion of the sixth canon.[28] Prodromos' grammatical treatise for Eirene the Sevastokratorissa is still only available in an outdated and unreliable edition by Carolus Goettling, published approximately two hundred years ago, which does not even take into consideration Panaghiou Taphou 52, a codex produced during Prodromos' lifetime.[29] Similarly, it must be regretted that Prodromos' commentary on Aristotle's *Posterior Analytics* 2 has been entirely overlooked by modern Byzantine philologists, no doubt because Michel Cacouros' doctoral dissertation with an edition of the text was never published as a book.[30] Instead, it has only been used as a source for the study of the reception of Aristotle in twelfth-century Byzantium.[31] A modern critical edition by Michiel D. J. Op de Coul of Prodromos' prose letters and orations is expected to be published soon,[32] while most of Prodromos' satirical writings have been edited in a dissertation by Tommaso Migliorini, which remains unpublished.[33] Just as most Byzantine *schede* remain unedited and thus

---

[27] Two very good exceptions are S. Papaioannou, *Michael Psellos: Rhetoric and Authorship in Byzantium* (Cambridge 2013), and I. Nilsson, *Writer and Occasion in Twelfth-Century Byzantium: The Authorial Voice of Constantine Manasses* (Cambridge 2020).

[28] H. M. Stevenson, praefatus est I. B. Pitra, *Theodori Prodromi Commentarios in Carmina Sacra Melodorum Cosmae Hierosolymitani et Ioannis Damasceni* (Rome 1888). For some introductory remarks on this work, see P. Cesaretti and S. Ronchey, *Eustathii Thessaloncensis Exegesis in Canonem iambicum pentacostolem* (Munich/Boston 2014), 63*–67*.

[29] C. G. Goettling, *Theodosii Alexandrini Grammatica* (Leipzig 1822). For a brief discussion of this work, see N. Zagklas, 'A Byzantine Grammar Treatise Attributed to Theodoros Prodromos', *Graeco-Latina Brunensia* 16 (2011), 77–86.

[30] M. Cacouros, *Le commentaire de Théodore Prodrome aux Analytiques postérieurs, livre II d'Aristote: Texte (editio princeps, tradition manuscrite), étude du commentaire de Prodrome*, unpublished PhD thesis (Paris IV-Sorbonne 1992).

[31] M. Cacouros, *Recherches sur le commentaire inédit de Théodore Prodrome sur le second livre des Analytiques Postérieurs d'Aristote* (Naples 1990); cf. also M. Cacouros, 'La tradition du commentaire de Théodore Prodrome au deuxième livre des Seconds Analytiques d'Aristote: quelques étapes dans l'enseignement de la logique à Byzance', Δίπτυχα Ἑταιρείας Βυζαντινῶν καὶ Μεταβυζαντινῶν Μελετῶν 6 (1994–95), 329–54.

[32] For the time being see M. D. J. Op de Coul, *Théodore Prodrome. Lettres et Discours. Édition, Traduction, Commentaire*, 2 vols., unpublished PhD thesis (Paris 2007). The edition is being prepared for *Corpus Christianorum*.

[33] Migliorini, *Teodoro Prodromo*. Editions of *Amarantos* and *Bion Prasis* have been published separately: for the former text, see Migliorini, 'Amaranto', for the latter, see the edition by Eric Cullhed in P. Marciniak, *Taniec w roli Tersytesa: Studia nad satyrą bizantyńską* [A Dance in the Role of Thersites: Studies on Byzantine Satire] (Katowice 2016).

insufficiently studied, so too do most schedographical texts by Prodromos.[34] Finally, a number of rhetorical, theological, satirical, and philosophical works are to be found only in old and poorly accessible editions.[35]

If we focus on Prodromos' poetic work, it is clear that there has been a lot of progress in this area over the last seven decades. In the mid-1950s, Ciro Giannelli published an edition of the cycles of tetrastichs on the great martyrs[36]—Theodoros, Georgios, and Demetrios—as well as an edition of the calendar, also written in the form of tetrastichs.[37] In 1968, Herbert Hunger produced a modern edition of the *Katomyomachia*,[38] heralding the leading role that the Viennese school of Byzantine Studies would play in the *Editionsgeschichte* of Prodromos' poetry, reinforced by the publication of Wolfram Hörandner's edition of Prodromos' *Historical poems* six years later, in 1974. Hörandner's edition signified a turning point in our understanding of Prodromos' work and its prominent place in Komnenian literary culture, since it includes all the poems that permit reconstruction of Prodromos' activity in the courtly and intellectual life of the capital. Eighty poems (6,912 verses) with divergent genre types and themes are grouped under the broad title 'historische Gedichte' (*Historical poems*).[39]

---

[34] For a list of Prodromos' *schede*, see I. Vassis, 'Graeca sunt, non leguntur: Zu den schedographischen Spielereien des Theodoros Prodromos', *BZ* 86/87 (1993/94), 1–19; cf. also I. Vassis, 'Τῶν νέων Φιλολόγων Παλαίσματα. Η συλλογή σχεδῶν του κώδικα Vaticanus Palatinus gr. 92', *Hell* 52 (2002), 37–68. For some editions of his *schede*, see S. D. Papadimitriou, *Feodor Prodrom*, Odessa 1905, 422–24 and 429–35; Vassis, 'Theodoros Prodromos', 14–19; I. D. Polemis, 'Προβλήματα τῆς βυζαντινῆς σχεδογραφίας', *Hell* 45 (1995), 277–302; and I. Nesseris, *Η Παιδεία στην Κωνσταντινούπολη κατά τον 12ο αιώνα*, unpublished PhD thesis (Ioannina 2014), 407 with the edition of an unknown *schedos* by Prodromos from codex *Neapol. Branc. IV A 5*; for the *schede tou Myos*, J.-T. Papadimitriou, 'Τὰ σχέδη τοῦ μυός: New Sources and Text', *Classical Studies presented to B. E. Perry by his students and colleagues at the University of Illinois, 1924-1960*, Illinois Studies in Language and Literature 58 (1969), 210–22; cf. also M. Papathomopoulos, 'Τοῦ σοφωτάτου Θεοδώρου τοῦ Προδρόμου τὰ σχέδη τοῦ μυός', *Παρνασσός* 21 (1979), 377–99; for the question of authorship and its attribution to Konstantinos Manasses, see M. D. Lauxtermann, 'Of Cats and Mice: The *Katomyomachia* as Drama, Parody, School Text, and Animal Tale', in: B. van den Berg and N. Zagklas (eds), *Byzantine Poetry in the Twelfth Century (1081-1204)* (forthcoming).

[35] Hörandner, *Historische Gedichte*, nos. 113, 135, 136, 145, 150, and 151.

[36] C. Giannelli, 'Epigrammi di Teodoro Prodromo in onore dei senti megalomartiri Teodoro, Giorgio e Demetrio', in: *Studi in onore di Luigi Castiglioni* (Florence 1960), 333–71 = *SBN* 10 (1963), 349–78. A new edition is necessary because Giannelli included only the tetrastichs which were unedited until that time. The remaining tetrastichs are still to be found in Miller's edition among texts by Manuel Philes: E. Miller, *Manuelis Philae carmina*, 2 vols. (Paris 1855–57; repr. Amsterdam 1967), vol. 1, 438 and vol. 2, 294–306.

[37] C. Giannelli, 'Tetrastici di Teodoro Prodromo sulle feste fisse e sui santi del calendario bizantino', *AnBoll* 75 (1957), 299–336 = *SBN* 10 (1963), 255–89. For a discussion of the work, see C. Giannelli, 'Un altro "calendario metrico" di Teodoro Prodromo', *ΕΕΒΣ* 25 (1955), 158–69 = *SBN* 10 (1963), 203–13.

[38] H. Hunger, *Der byzantinische Katz-Mäuse-Krieg* (Graz/Vienna/Cologne 1968).

[39] Hörandner, *Historische Gedichte*; cf. the later critical studies by A. Kambylis, *Prodromea* (Vienna 1984), and G. Papagiannis, *Philoprodromica: Beiträge zur Textkonstitution und Quellenforschung der historischen Gedichte des Theodoros Prodromos* (Vienna 2012). Moreover, the historical poem 78 was

After the edition of the 'historische Gedichte', other major compositions by Prodromos, in the field of religious poetry, found their way into modern editions. In 1983, Augusta Acconcia Longo produced the *editio princeps* of Prodromos' iambic calendar,[40] while in 1997 Grigorios Papagiannis presented the first solid edition of Prodromos' iambic and hexametric tetrastichs on the Old and New Testaments.[41] In the 1990s, Hörandner undertook the edition of some poems by Prodromos which were not included in the 'historische Gedichte'. In 1990, he published the first edition of two figured poems (no. 157 from his list), which form a poetic diptych consisting of an admonitory poem together with another centring on the theme of envy,[42] and in 1997, he published no. 126, a small epigram of fourteen iambics about the Last Supper.[43]

More recently, Mario D'Ambrosi published an edition of Prodromos' tetrastichs on the life of Gregory of Nazianzus.[44] In addition, D'Ambrosi is currently working on the tetrastichs on the life of John Chrysostom. A new edition of Prodromos' tetrastichs on the life of Basil the Great had been promised by Acconcia Longo, but the fate of this editorial project is uncertain following her death. The vernacular poems ascribed to Prodromos are also available in modern editions: the so-called 'fifth' (Ptocho)prodromic poem was edited as early as 1913,[45] while a modern edition with a German translation of the four (Ptocho)prodromika, by Hans Eideneier, appeared in 1991.[46] In 2012, Eideneier's edition of the (Ptocho)prodromika was reprinted with some minor textual corrections and a new comprehensive introduction in modern Greek.[47]

But for all this significant progress, a good deal of Prodromos' poetry has been overlooked by modern philologists and literary scholars. An examination of the long list of Prodromos' works that prefaces Hörandner's

---

re-edited in M. Tziatzi-Papagianni, *Theodoros Prodromos, Historisches Gedicht LXXVIII*, BZ 86–87 (1993-94), 363–82.

[40] A. Acconcia Longo, *Il calendario giambico in monostici di Teodoro Prodromo* (Rome 1983).

[41] G. Papagiannis, *Theodoros Prodromos: Jambische und hexametrische Tetrasticha auf die Hauptterzählungen des Alten und des Neuen Testaments*, 2 vols. (Wiesbaden 1997).

[42] W. Hörandner, 'Visuelle Poesie in Byzanz: Versuch einer Bestandaufnahme', *JÖB* 40 (1990), 1–43, at 30–37.

[43] W. Hörandner, 'Zu einigen religiösen Epigrammen', in: U. Criscuolo and R. Maisano (eds), *Synodia: Studia humanistica Antonio Garzya septuagenario ab amicis atque discipulis dicata* (Naples 1997), 431–42, at 433–35.

[44] M. D'Ambrosi, *I tetrastici giambici ed esametrici sugli episodi principali della vita di Gregorio Nazianzeno, Introduzione, edizione critica, traduzione e commento* (Rome 2008). For a monostich prefacing the tetrastichs on the lives of the Three Hierarchs, see M. D'Ambrosi, 'Un monostico giambico di Teodoro Prodromo per i ss. Tre Gerarchi', *Bollettino dei Classici* 33 (2012), 33–46.

[45] A. Maiuri, 'Una nuova poesia di Theodoro Prodromo in greco volgare', *BZ* 23 (1914-19), 397–407.

[46] H. Eideneier, *Ptochoprodromos: Einführung, Kritische Ausgabe, deutsche Übersetzung, Glossar* (Cologne 1991).

[47] Eideneier, *Πτωχοπρόδρομος*.

Historische Gedichte reveals that many of them remain scattered in outdated and completely unreliable editions.[48] They mostly belong to three main categories according to Hörandner's classification list: religious epigrams (nos. 120, 121, 122, 123, 124, 125, 127, 129, 130, 131, 132, and 133), rhetorical/satirical works (nos. 142 and 143), and works on various themes (nos. 153, 154, 155, 156, 158, 160, 161, and 162). Many of these works are poetic cycles of several poems,[49] resulting in a corpus of 1,002 verses. Because they do not contain historical information, they have never been properly edited or analysed. It is the principal goal of this book to rescue these texts from this state of oblivion, study them, and present them in a modern critical edition.

However, it should be emphasized from the outset that the present corpus does not include all the poems from Hörandner's list of the poems that have not so far been presented in a modern edition. First, it does not include any poems from Hörandner's list of Prodromos' dubious works,[50] with the single exception of no. 164.[51] The evidence for the remaining eight poems (nos. 173–180) is sparse and does not allow us to attribute them safely to Prodromos. Second, it does not include genuine poems for which new editions are currently being prepared by other scholars. As we remarked above, new editions have been announced for the iambic and hexametric tetrastichs on the lives of Basil the Great and John Chrysostom, which, with the recent edition of tetrastichs on the life of Gregory of Nazianzus, will complete the poetic cycle for the three Hierarchs. Third, the edition omits the poems *Against a lustful woman* and *Against a man with a long beard*, nos. 140 and 141 from Hörandner's list, because they were edited with Prodromos' satirical writings by Tommaso Migliorini.[52]

Despite the omission of these poems, this book aspires to bring us significantly closer to having modern editions of all of Prodromos' poetic works and contribute to a more nuanced understanding of his entire literary corpus and its place within the literary tradition of its time. It is arranged in two main parts. The second part includes the edition of the poems, accompanied by translations and commentaries. The first part is made up of five chapters, which aim to approach the texts from the perspective of both literary interpretation and traditional philology. The remaining three sections of Chapter 1 examine more closely the poems' authorship and their thematic features and genre characteristics, as well as the original function of the first six poems

---

[48] For a complete list of all these editions, see pp. 155-60.
[49] See pp. 160-61.
[50] Hörandner, *Historische Gedichte*, 57-61.
[51] For the authorship of this poem, see below p. 12.
[52] See Migliorini, *Teodoro Prodromo*, 3-7 and 19-21.

which form a poetic cycle. They seek to demonstrate the ambiguity regarding many aspects of these poems, and attempt to resolve some of them. Building upon the first chapter, Chapter 2 constitutes a study of the intellectual pursuits of Theodoros Prodromos, looking at his social professions as teacher and court orator, the complaints that pervade many of his writings, and the multifunctionality of many of his works. Chapter 3 shifts our attention to more philological aspects of the corpus by discussing the metre and prosody of the poems. Chapter 4 lists and describes the manuscripts and includes the first detailed analysis of the main manuscript, Vaticanus gr. 305, and a survey of the dissemination of the poems across the centuries. Chapter 5 includes a complete list of all previous editions and presents the editorial principles employed here.

1.2. Miscellaneous Poems

Before we embark upon the study of these poems, it is necessary first to find an appropriate title to describe them as a single group. Whereas certain links can be drawn between many of the poems of the present corpus, no uniform thematic nexus can be established which unites all of them. Unlike the *Historical poems*, very few of these poems were composed for an identifiable occasion or are addressed to a specific individual. They were not composed at one particular point in time or for a single event, but were written at different times over Prodromos' long career. They are not all transmitted together in a single Byzantine poetry book; instead, they are dispersed across numerous manuscripts. Thus, the selected corpus cannot be traced back to a single collection assembled by the author himself or a later scribe. All these peculiarities pose various challenges to the description of this corpus, and this has consequences for our methodological approach. Designations with strong overtones, such as 'neglected' or 'minor' poems, have been avoided because they would tend to undermine the value of these poems. Instead, inspired by the title 'Στίχοι διάφοροι' of the miscellaneous poetry books by Ioannes Mauropous in Vat. gr. 676 and Christophoros Mitylenaios in Grottaferrata Z a XXIX, I have opted for the subtitle *Miscellaneous poems*.[53]

---

[53] While Prodromos' *Miscellaneous poems* is a modern compilation, 'Στίχοι διάφοροι' in Vat. gr. 676 is a collection put together by Mauropous himself, since the manuscript is a master copy; on this issue, see D. Bianconi, ' "Piccolo assaggio di abbondante fragranza": Giovanni Mauropode e il Vat. gr. 676', *JÖB* 61 (2011), 89103. Similarly, *Grottaferrata Z a* XXIX probably goes back to an earlier collection put together by Mitylenaios himself; see E. Kurtz, *Die Gedichte des Christophoros Mitylenaios* (Leipzig 1903), xvi. For a discussion of both collections and their various thematic cycles and structure, see Bernard, *Poetry*, 128-53.

1.2.1. Some Perils of Authorship

Few other Byzantine writers have been the subject of as much scholarly dispute over authorship as Prodromos, with the (Ptocho)prodromic poems at the centre of such discussions.[54] As I have discussed, many scholars have argued in favour of or against the attribution of these four vernacular poems to Prodromos. These, however, are not the only works for which Prodromos' authorship has been contested. What should be emphasized first is that issues of authorship are difficult to resolve, especially when it comes to works written by contemporaries. Many of their works written under similar historical and literary conditions tend to resemble each other in vocabulary and thematic focus, and even when there are some rare words or *hapax legomena* it is not easy to discern whether they were written by a particular author or by one of his peers. In this respect, it is hardly surprising that some works by other twelfth-century authors have been spuriously attributed to Prodromos. A good example is the astrological poem for Eirene the Sevastokratorissa, which was long considered a work of Prodromos.[55] Only in recent years has its authorship by Konstantinos Manasses gained scholarly consensus.[56]

The scarcity of manuscript evidence can also challenge the authorial attributions of some Byzantine texts, and in the case of Prodromos the manuscript transmission has cast doubt even on some of his most well-known works. Prodromos' authorship of the *Katomyomachia*, for example, is documented only in a single manuscript (Marcianus gr. 524) out of twenty copies, strengthening the perception among early scholars that it was an anonymous work, a position espoused in its first edition by Arsenios Apostoles, published in Venice around 1495.[57] Another issue is the pseudonymity which permeated Byzantine literary culture: that is, the tendency to attribute anonymous texts or texts by lesser-known writers to well-known figures. This served a number of needs, such as the intensive preoccupation of the Byzantines with authority and their eagerness to associate certain texts with well-known individuals. This is another reason why authorship of some Byzantine texts is doubted.[58]

---

[54] See the discussion on pages 3–4.
[55] See Hörandner, *Historische Gedichte*, 48–49. It may be worth noting that modern scholars have often tried to attribute to Prodromos even poems for which the evidence is very scarce; see M. Alexiou, 'Of Longings and Loves: Seven Poems by Theodore Prodromos', *DOP* 69 (2015), 209–24, and U. Kenens and P. van Deun, 'Some Unknown Byzantine Poems Preserved in a Manuscript of the Holy Mountain', *MEG* 14 (2014), 111–18.
[56] Rhoby, 'Eirene Sebastokratorissa', 321–29.
[57] For the reasons behind its anonymity, see Lauxtermann, 'Of Cats and Mice' (forthcoming).
[58] S. Papaioannou, 'Voice, Signature, Mask: The Byzantine Author', in: A. Pizzone (ed.), *The Author in Middle Byzantine Literature: Modes, Functions, and Identities* (Berlin/Boston 2014), 21–40, at 24.

Even middle Byzantine authors were credited by later scribes with the authorship of works produced much later than their lifetime. Michael Psellos stands out as an author to whom dozens of later works are falsely attributed.[59] Such is also the case for Prodromos, who in the late Byzantine period became a model poet, together with Gregory of Nazianzus and Georgios of Pisidia;[60] his popularity was immense in Byzantine book culture throughout the last three centuries of the empire.[61] All these issues pose a series of challenges for modern readers, who have become very cautious—occasionally perhaps too cautious—when discussing issues of Prodromean authorship.

This caution becomes all the more evident when we look at the introduction to the modern edition of Prodromos' *Historical poems*. Wolfram Hörandner tried to group the works attributed to Prodromos into three separate groups: 'echte' (genuine), 'zweifelhafte' (dubious), and 'unechte' (false). Even though Hörandner in most cases draws safe conclusions about their authenticity, there are some poems which are, in my view, incorrectly excluded from the list of the authentic poems. These are therefore included in the edition at hand. Poem 67, a short dedicatory poem for an icon made in honour of the Holy Virgin, is a case in point. This poem—no. 164 in Hörandner's list—is arbitrarily grouped among the dubious works. However, evidence both internal and external to the text suggests that the poem was written by Prodromos. The internal evidence is that the wording of the fourth verse, 'ἐξαγόρασον ταῖς λιταῖς σου, παρθένε', is very similar to the final verse 'ἀνταγόρασον σαῖς λιταῖς πρὸς τὸν Λόγον' of poem 25, a dedicatory epigram for the Holy Virgin, indisputably by Prodromos. Both epigrams are also permeated with similar vocabulary associated with the slave trade. In addition to sharing phraseology with another genuine poem by Prodromos, the text is preserved with other works of Prodromos, on fol. 183ʳ of manuscript Vind. Suppl. 125.

But Hörandner should not be blamed for the insufficient investigation into the poem's authorship which led to its exclusion from the list of Prodromos' genuine works. As has been mentioned already, the authorship of many Byzantine works was far from secure; once circulated, be it in oral or written form, their links to their author could gradually become looser. Even some of the *Miscellaneous poems*, which are grouped among Prodromos' authentic works in Hörandner's list, are attributed to multiple authors in the manuscript tradition. This is the case for poems 29–54, a cycle of epigrams on virtues and

---

[59] See Papaioannou, *Michael Psellos*, 2.
[60] Ps. Gregorios Korinthios, *On the Four Parts of the Perfect Speech*, 108, 162–65.
[61] See also the remarks on pages 130–39.

vices. The twenty-five manuscripts which transmit this work do not establish a consensus on the issue of authorship. In addition to Theodoros Prodromos, two other possible authors are named. The most interesting case is arguably that of 'Paniotes', named in the rubrics of the cycle in both Vat. Chis. gr. R.IV.11 and Laur. San Marco 318, copied in the thirteenth and fourteenth centuries, respectively. Nicola Festa, the most recent editor of the poem, noted that the designation 'τοῦ Πανιώτου' does not stand for a real author, arguing that it is simply a mistake which emanated from the sloppy copying of the word 'πανι(ερ)ω(τά)του' during the dissemination of the work.[62] However, a recent study has shown that Paniotes was indeed a twelfth-century author (perhaps even Konstantinos Manasses), whose social and intellectual achievements caused annoyance for Ioannes Tzetzes.[63]

But the picture of the cycle's authorship becomes even more blurred because a second cluster of post-Byzantine manuscripts suggests that the author of these twenty-six iambic couplets was Michael Psellos. The earliest codex presenting Psellos as the author of these epigrams is Paris. gr. 3058.[64] This codex was copied by Arsenios Apostoles at the beginning of the sixteenth century, certainly before 1519, when a printed version of the manuscript appeared with the poems under discussion.[65] It is, however, hardly likely that Psellos was the author of these verses, especially in view of the length of time—approximately four centuries—between Psellos' period (mid-eleventh century) and the oldest manuscript bearing his name as author of the poems. It seems more likely that Arsenios copied the epigrams from a manuscript in which they were ascribed to Paniotes. It is even possible that he considered the designation 'Paniotes' as a sort of familiar name for Michael Psellos, since Arsenios' manuscript shares two 'binding errors' with Vat. Chis. gr. R.IV.11,[66] one of the two manuscripts that bear the name of Paniotes.[67] One should also bear in mind that the attribution of spurious works on similar topics to Psellos is not uncommon. For instance, on fol. 198ᵛ of the manuscript Berol. Phil. 214

---

[62] N. Festa, 'Nota sui versiculi in vitia et virtutes', in: *Miscellanea Ceriani: Raccolta di scritti originali* (Milan 1910), 569–76, at 572.

[63] A. Rhoby and N. Zagklas, 'Zu einer möglichen Deutung von Πανιώτης', JÖB 61 (2011), 171–77.

[64] All the later mss that preserve the poem—seventeen manuscripts in total—repeat the attribution to Psellos, but they are all merely apographs of Paris. gr. 3058.

[65] A. Apostoles, Ἀποφθέγματα φιλοσόφων καὶ στρατηγῶν, ῥητόρων τε καὶ ποιητῶν συλλεγέντα παρὰ Ἀρσενίου ἀρχιεπισκόπου Μονεμβασίας (Rome c. 1519).

[66] Cf. p. 153.

[67] The other manuscript is Laur. San Marco 318. Both Vat. Chis. gr. R.IV.11 and Laur. San Marco 318 were copied in the same scriptorium in southern Italy. Thus, scribes from this region may be responsible for the attribution of the poetic cycle to Paniotes.

we read τοῦ σοφωτάτου Ψελλοῦ περὶ ἀρετῶν καὶ κακιῶν,[68] as the title of a prose work that is, in fact, from the anthology of Stobaeus. In the case of the cycle of Prodromos' epigrams, their authorship is secured by two of the earliest manuscripts: the thirteenth-century Vat. gr. 307 and fourteenth-century Laur. Conv. Soppr. 48. The manuscript Paris. gr. 854 is further evidence in favour of Prodromos' authorship: although it transmits the cycle anonymously, it is to be found together with ten other authentic poems by Prodromos.[69]

Poems 22–23, two short epigrams on the *Dodekaorton*, are also attributed to more than one author. In the fourteenth-century Vind. Hist. gr. 106, the poem survives under the name of Ioannes Mauropous, the eleventh-century poet, probably because the scribe had in mind Mauropous' collection of epigrams describing the Dominical feasts.[70] In the late thirteenth-century manuscript Vat. gr. 1126, the poems are preserved under the name of Manuel Philes, and the same happens in the mid-fourteenth-century Bodl. Roe 18, with a later hand adding next to the rubric of the epigrams 'Τοῦ Πτωχοπροδρόμου'. Once again, Prodromos' authorship should be considered certain, especially if we take into account that the manuscript Vat. gr. 1126 dates before 1283, while Philes was born around the year 1270.[71] Moreover, the designation of (Ptocho)prodromos stands for Theodoros Prodromos in late Byzantine book culture.[72]

Another poem claimed for several authors is poem 26, a short epigram on St Peter. In ms. Göttingen phil. 29, the poem survives under the name of Christophoros Mitylenaios, while the modern editor of Kallikles' poetry lists it among Kallikles' dubious works, because in Marc. gr. 524 it is transmitted with poems of Kallikles, but without any attribution to this author in the title. Although Prodromos' authorship is only indicated in the thirteenth-century manuscript Vat. gr. 305, it should be considered sound. This manuscript is the richest collection of Prodromos' prose and verse works that has come down to us.[73] The poem is found on fol. 128ᵛ τοῦ αὐτοῦ (i.e. Θεοδώρου Προδρόμου) εἰς τὸν ἅγιον Πέτρον σταυρούμενον, immediately following Prodromos'

---

[68] W. Studemund and L. Cohn, *Verzeichnisse der griechischen Handschriften der Königlichen Bibliothek zu Berlin*, 2 vols. (Berlin 1890), vol. 1, 93.

[69] See Rhoby and Zagklas, 'Πανιώτης', 172.

[70] Migne even published this poem along with other religious poems of Mauropous dedicated to Christological feasts; cf. *PG* 120, col. 1197 A–B.

[71] See more recently K. Kubina, *Die enkomiastische Dichtung des Manuel Philes: Form und Funktion des literarischen Lobes in der Gesellschaft der frühen Palaiologenzeit* (Berlin/Boston 2020), 4.

[72] W. Hörandner, 'Autor oder Genus? Diskussionsbeiträge zur "Prodromischen Frage" aus gegebenem Anlass', *BSl* 54 (1993), 314–24, at 316–17.

[73] For a discussion of the manuscript, see pp. 122–30.

poem 'Farewell Verses to Byzantium' (historical poem 79), and before an epitaph for Konstantinos Kamytzes (historical poem 64).

The Prodromean authorship of some of the *Miscellaneous poems* edited here was frequently disregarded throughout their dissemination in the late Byzantine and post-Byzantine period. Many of them are attributed to several other Byzantine poets, including Christophoros Mitylenaios, Michael Psellos, Nikolaos Kallikles, and a certain Paniotes, who, as mentioned earlier, may well have been Konstantinos Manasses. This is hardly surprising, since some of these authors were active around the same time. As noted, their works include individual features, but they also share with Prodromos' poems many similarities in form and style, motifs and themes, metrical and genre characteristics, and especially wording. Take, for example, poem 6, a hexametric poem for St Nicholas. Unlike the other *Miscellaneous poems*, the Prodromean authorship of this text is beyond question because it only survives in Vat. gr. 305, with other works by Prodromos. Were this not the case, one might have attempted to resolve the issue of authorship on the basis of the seemingly rare word γλυκύρροος in verse 5. However, the modern reader would soon notice that this word seems to have been particularly popular in the twelfth century, used by Prodromos, Tzetzes, and Manasses,[74] all of whom belonged to closely connected intellectual circles, and occasionally even shared the same patron, Eirene the Sevastokratorissa. This case suggests the circulation of shared vocabulary in the works of twelfth-century peers, partly explaining the multiple claims of authorship for some of the *Miscellaneous poems* (and other twelfth-century works) advanced by both Byzantines and Byzantinists.

1.2.2. Poems and Epigrams: Functional Ambiguity and Genre Elasticity

Just like the collection of Christophoros Mitylenaios in the Grottaferrata manuscript,[75] the collection of Prodromos' *Miscellaneous poems* consists of poems on various themes written in a wide range of genres. However, to avoid imposing modern perceptions of issues of genre, which would ill serve these texts, it is appropriate to look to the twelfth century to see how Prodromos

---

[74] Cf. *LBG* s.v.
[75] See, for example, K. Demoen, '*Phrasis poikilē*: Imitatio and Variatio in the Poetry Book of Christophoros Mitylenaios', in: A. Rhoby and E. Schiffer (eds), *Imitatio—Aemulatio—Variatio: Akten des internationalen wissenschaftlichen Symposions zur byzantinischen Sprache und Literatur* (Vienna 2010), 103–18.

and other contemporary authors imagined the boundary lines between their works. In a funerary work for his teacher, Niketas Eugenianos praised Prodromos for his poems intended to adorn works of art or tombs, and for his imperial panegyrics in hexameters.[76] Eugenianos thus hints at a taxonomy of genre distinguishing between the inscriptional and performative functions of Prodromos' poetry, making this an excellent example of pre-modern literary criticism. This implicit classification of Prodromos' works by Eugenianos has been the basis of many modern approaches to issues of genre in Byzantine poetry-writing, and especially for the seminal distinction between epigrams and poems proper.[77] Similarly, the poems in the present corpus can be viewed as relating to these two broad categories, though I make no clear-cut distinction between their inscriptional and performative function in each case.[78]

Epigrammatic poetry makes up the lion's share of *Miscellaneous poems*.[79] Many of them have a religious theme, celebrating the Virgin Mary (poems 24, 25, and 67) and various saints, such as the three Hierarchs (poems 2–4), and Sts Gregory of Nyssa (poem 5), Nicholas (poem 6), Barbara (poems 11–21), Paul (poem 1), and Peter (poem 26). Some of the poems are even concerned with well-known Christian feasts: poems 27–28 are dedicated to Crucifixion, while poems 22–23 deal with the entire festal cycle of the life of Christ. Poems 7–8 are concerned with the hospitality of Abraham. But there are also texts with a more secular focus: poems 55–56 could be used as inscriptions for a depiction of Life (*Bios*); poems 29–54 form a cycle of twenty-six epigrams on virtues and vices; and poems 57–61 consist of five iambic couplets concerned with the representation of two tangled trees springing from the breasts of a pair of lovers.

But since all these texts survive exclusively in manuscripts, their epigrammatic features and their use as inscriptions can only be reconstructed with the help of various indications, such as deictic elements, the naming of a donor, or reference to the iconography or a material object.[80] For example, poem 67

---

[76] See M. D. Lauxtermann, *Byzantine Poetry from Pisides to Geometres: Texts and Contexts*, 2 vols. (Vienna 2003–19), vol. 1, 34.
[77] See Lauxtermann, *Byzantine Poetry*, vol. 1, 34.   [78] See, for example, below, pp. 28–29.
[79] We have come a long way since Alan Cameron's words, 'No one has yet written the history of the Byzantine epigram or of the classical epigram at Byzantium': see A. Cameron, *The Greek Anthology from Meleager to Planudes* (Oxford 1993), 329. We are now much better informed about this type of text: see Lauxtermann, *Byzantine Poetry*, vol. 1; the monumental four-volume work of A. Rhoby, *Byzantinische Epigramme in inschriftlicher Überlieferung*, 4 vols. (Vienna 2009–2018); and the excellent study on the symbiosis of epigrammatic poetry and art in later Byzantium by Ivan Drpić: Drpić, *Epigram*.
[80] See E. van Opstall, 'Verses on Paper, Verses Inscribed? A Case Study, with Epigrams of John Geometres', in: W. Hörandner and A. Rhoby (eds), *Die kulturhistorische Bedeutung byzantinischer Epigramme: Akten des internationalen Workshop (Wien, 1.-2. Dezember 2006)* (Vienna 2008), 55–60; cf. also Bernard, *Poetry*, 112–17.

was written on commission for George of Antioch for an icon of the Virgin Mary. Its structure is typical of Byzantine dedicatory epigrams: the donor asks the Virgin Mary to intercede with Christ to offer him deliverance from the sins he has committed. Similarly, the text of poems 24 and 25 is based upon negotiations for a reciprocal exchange between the donor and the sacred recipient. In both poems, the anonymous donors put forward a request for remission of their sins by offering material goods. Other texts contain some deictic indications for their possible use as inscriptions. Take, for example, poem 28, which opens as follows: 'Here Jesus, the giver of breath, yields his last breath'.[81] The word ἐνθάδ' helps us to understand that the viewer is addressed and encouraged to pay attention to the iconography of an object, without specifying its exact nature. In some other poems, however, we can determine the object. The rubric of poems 57–61 informs us that they were intended to be inscribed on a ring. The rubric and the main text of poem 25 include evidence that it was an epigram written for an icon which was restored by an anonymous donor.

The epigrammatic style of some other texts does not entail their use as inscriptions, or even if it does, the original occasion is so well camouflaged that it makes it almost impossible for the modern reader to reconstruct it. One of the most challenging cases is the cycle of five poems under the title 'ἐπὶ κήπῳ' (poems 62–66). The title does not refer to the location for which it was intended, but instead signifies their subject matter. All five texts abound in strong allegorical connotations revolving around the concept of the garden and ideas of consumption, pleasure, and moderation. They should therefore not be viewed as *ekphraseis* of a real garden, although they contain ekphrastic elements. Take, for example, the second epigram:

Ὁρῶν σε, κῆπε, καὶ τὰ δένδρα σου βλέπων,
ἐκπλήττομαι μὲν τῇ θέᾳ τὴν καρδίαν,
φαντάζομαι δὲ τῆς Ἐδὲμ τὸ χωρίον,
καὶ βούλομαι μὲν τοῖς φυτοῖς προσεγγίσαι.
5 Πλὴν τοῦ φυτοῦ τὴν γεῦσιν εἰς νοῦν λαμβάνω,
ἐξ οὗ φαγὼν ὤλισθον εἰς ἁμαρτίαν·
θέλω τρυγῆσαι καὶ φαγεῖν, ἀλλὰ τρέμω,
μὴ γνώσεως τὸ ξύλον ἐκφαγὼν θάνω.

---

[81] *Miscellaneous poems*, 28.1 Πνοιὴν πνοιοδότης μὲν ἐρεύγεται ἐνθάδ' Ἰησοῦς.

> Beholding you, garden, and looking at your trees
> I am overwhelmed in my heart at the sight,
> I imagine you to be the place of Eden,
> and I wish to approach your plants.
> 5 But the tasting of the fruit comes to my mind,
> the fruit from which I ate and fell into sin;
> I wish to gather and eat, but I tremble in fear
> lest I die eating from the Tree of Knowledge.

The I-person articulates a strong desire to approach the garden and partake of its delights, but soon a sense of anxiety arises when the garden and its fruits are compared to the Garden of Eden and the Tree of Knowledge. The question at stake for the modern reader is: what do the garden and its delightful flowers stand for? The figurative language and the ambiguity that governs the narrative of all five texts, together with the absence of any extratextual evidence whatsoever, make a definite answer to this question impossible.

In discussing the fourth poem of the cycle, Ingela Nilsson has highlighted its metapoetic function: 'it is also an implicit—or in this case perhaps rather explicit—invitation to pick the fragrant flowers of literature and create a garland or a garden of your own'.[82] The texts can indeed be described as invitations, permeated with a subtle sense of eroticism, reminiscent of the central theme of the Song of Songs. Additionally, as in the Song of Songs, which is a dialogue between two lovers, these epigrams form a sort of dialogue between the garden and its beholder. If we accept that these five texts are epigrams and we stick to the premise that most epigrams in Byzantium are *Gebrauchstexte*,[83] perhaps the most appropriate genre designation for them is that of book epigrams. In other words, one could argue that the garden probably stands for an anthology of literary works prefaced by these five poems. This would not be the only text by Prodromos with such a function: historical poem 61 was used to preface a book containing the *schede* of a certain Ioannikios. What is more, in a short epigram that prefaces the so-called Ἰωνιά—an anthology of sayings put together for Pope Leo X—in Paris. gr. 3058, Arsenios Apostoles exhorts his addressee(s) to select from the material he has included in the book, using a phraseology strongly resembling that of Prodromos: σύ δ' οὖν τρύγησον

---

[82] See I. Nilsson, 'Nature Controlled by Artistry: The Poetics of the Literary Garden in Byzantium', in: H. Bodin and R. Hedlund (eds), *Byzantine Gardens and Beyond* (Uppsala 2013), 14–29, at 23–24.

[83] Although I make use of the term, it seems to be somewhat elusive, since many other types of Byzantine texts have an utilitarian function. For the term, see A. Garzya, 'Literarische Gebrauchsformen: Testi letterari d'uso strumentale', *JÖB* 31 (1981), 263–87, and W. Hörandner, 'Customs and Beliefs as Reflected in Occasional Poetry: Some Considerations', *BF* 12 (1987), 235–47, 236. See also the discussion in Kubina, *Manuel Philes*, 163–64 and Nilsson, *Constantine Manasses*, 4–13.

τῶν ἴων, ὅσ' ἂν θέλῃς, / κρίνον, κρόκον, νάρκισσον, θύρσον ἢ ῥόδον.[84] I am not saying that there is a direct influence of Prodromos on Apostoles' text, but it is very likely that the metaphor of the garden and the invitation to pluck its flowers used by Apostoles goes back to the tradition of ancient and Byzantine epigrams prefacing literary anthologies,[85] a tradition to which Prodromos' garden poems may belong.

However, in the absence of any firm reference, the question that inevitably presents itself is: how sure can we be that this poetic cycle goes back to a real-life occasion (a *Sitz im Leben*)? Although there is a clear tendency among Byzantinists to impose certain practical purposes on epigrams, we should also consider the possibility that these five texts may simply be purely literary compositions.[86] The five texts read like epigrams, but this does not necessarily indicate that they were written for a specific object or a real-life occasion. In my view, we need to leave the possibility open that these works were philosophical allegories in verse, hence literary reflections rather than purely functional texts.

If we now turn to non-epigrammatic poetry, *Miscellaneous poems* may not include imperial panegyrics in the heroic metre (such as those praised by Eugenianos), but it does contain texts that are quite diverse in terms of theme and genre. The rubrics of some of the poems in the manuscripts hint at their shared genre identity.[87] Poem 68, for example, survives under the title Ἀΐνιγμα εἰς τὴν νεφέλην, which not only signifies the genre of the poem but also gives away the solution to the riddle.[88] Even more interesting are poems 69 and 70–72. In both cases, the rubric immediately attracts the attention of the reader, since it anticipates the peculiarity of the poems' subjects.

Ὑποθετικοὶ ἐπί τινι ἐκβρασθέντι τῆς θαλάσσης ἄχειρι νεκρῷ

Hypothetical verses about a dead body without hands washed up by the sea

Ὑποθετικοὶ εἰς Παυσανίαν ἀπολιθωθέντα διὰ τὸν θάνατον τοῦ υἱοῦ αὐτοῦ Πέτρου

Hypothetical verses about Pausanias petrified by the death of his son Peter

---

[84] Arsenios, *Metrical preface to Ionia*, ed. C. Walz, *Arsenii violetum*: Ἀρσενίου Ἰωνίαν (Stuttgart 1832), 10, lines 3–4.
[85] The most authoritative text about the concept of 'flowers of words' is Meleager's introductory poem to his poetic garland (*AP* IV.1).
[86] See the extremely interesting discussion in Bernard, *Poetry*, 110–12.
[87] For a study on the rubrics of Byzantine poems, see A. Rhoby, 'Labeling Poetry in the Middle and Late Byzantine Period', *Byzantion* 85 (2015), 259–83.
[88] This is quite common in the Byzantine book tradition; see also Lauxtermann, *Byzantine Poetry*, vol. 2, 254.

The word ὑποθετικοί is also of great interest, since these appear to be the only two poems in Prodromos' corpus—indeed, in the entire Byzantine tradition— that contain this word in their rubrics. Although impossible to determine whether these rubrics were shaped by Prodromos himself or added by a later scribe, they are closely linked to titles introducing rhetorical exercises of *ethopoiia*.[89] Both are variant forms of titles that we would find in such texts. For example, the title of the first poem would normally read Τίνας ἂν εἴπῃ λόγους (...) ὁ ἄχειρ νεκρὸς ἐκβρασθεὶς τῆς θαλάσσης. In both cases, the title suits the main text perfectly, since both poems are self-contained ethopoetic monologues.

However, it is not possible (nor, indeed, appropriate) to squeeze all the *Miscellaneous poems* into a single straitjacket in terms of genre. Various studies on 'genre' and 'mode' have paved the way for a more nuanced understanding of genre fluidity in Byzantium.[90] Modern scholars now see 'genre' as standing for a group of texts that share common characteristics, while 'mode' permeates various works that do not necessarily belong to the same group with regard to genre. Mode operates across genre boundaries, bringing heterogeneous texts closer together. This flexibility of the 'mode' results in interaction between the formal features of various genres and the emergence of the so-called genre hybridity (or *genus mixtum*). It is important to emphasize that, as in other literary traditions, be they pre-modern or modern, genre in Byzantium was not a static entity: it was based on an established tradition which formed the core of Byzantine rhetorical training, but, at the same time, it transformed to serve contemporary needs. Such transformations and adaptations reflect the preferences and strategies of an author and the communicative aspects of the genre in Byzantium, which aims to foster an exchange between the 'sender' and the 'receiver' of a text.[91] And in the twelfth century,

---

[89] On *ethopoiia*, see M. Hagen, Ἠθοποιΐα. *Zur Geschichte eines rhetorischen Begriffs* (Erlangen 1966); H. Hunger, *Die hochsprachliche profane Literatur der Byzantiner*, 2 vols. (Munich 1978), vol. 1, 108–16; and P. Roilos, *Amphoteroglossia: A Poetics of the Twelfth-Century Medieval Greek Novel* (Washington DC 2005). For ethopoetic monologues and dialogues in verse, see Lauxtermann, *Byzantine Poetry*, vol. 2, 77–87. For a case of *ethopoiia* in hymnography, see A. Zervoudaki, 'Hymnography in a Form of Rhetoric: An Interesting "Marriage" of Genres in a late Byzantine Hymnographic Ethopoiia', *REB* 69 (2011), 49–79.

[90] M. Mullett, 'The Madness of Genre', *DOP* 46 (1992), 233–43 remains a very influential study of this question. See also the highly interesting theoretical remarks in K. Kubina, 'Manuel Philes: A "Begging Poet"? Requests, Letters, and Problems of Genre Definition', in: A. Rhoby and N. Zagklas (eds), *Middle and Late Byzantine Poetry: Texts and Contexts* (Turnhout 2018), 147–81, at 150–56, and the discussion of the 'discursive mode' permeating various genres in Lauxtermann, *Byzantine Poetry*, vol. 2, 8.

[91] Ingela Nilsson, for instance, understands genre as 'typified rhetorical ways of acting in recurring situations—in that sense, as means of communication between writer, patron and audience'; see Nilsson, *Constantine Manasses*, 17.

many authors were very keen to invent new ways to communicate with their audience by combining characteristics of well-established genres with new ones, which resulted in the reshaping of old genres, mixing of genres, and even the creation of genres not to be found in old rhetorical books.[92] Prodromos' poems 73–74, 75, and 76 are texts with this kind of complex genre identity, which cannot be assigned to a single traditional group.

Poems 73–74 are a set of two hexametric poems containing many self-referential features. In terms of form and structure, they are partly modelled on Gregory Nazianzus' poem Ἀποτροπὴ τοῦ πονηροῦ καὶ τοῦ Χριστοῦ ἐπίκλησις (*Carm.* II.1.55), which is a prayer to Christ. In fact, the opening lines of both of these poems of Prodromos are strongly reminiscent of Gregory's poem.[93] Gregory opens his poem with an address to evil, admonishing it to vanish from his life, while he concludes with a plea to Christ for salvation in the hereafter. In Prodromos' poem, on the other hand, the I-person addresses his books, exhorting them to flee, for he receives no benefit from the erudition he has gained from them. He also expresses his strong desire to withdraw from public places, another idea evocative of Gregory of Nazianzus.[94] However, Prodromos, by mixing the mode of self-referentiality with features of religious and paraenetic poetry, all dressed in the garb of Homeric hexameters, shapes a text which, although it may bear some resemblance to various older genres or practices, at the same time is by no means an exact replica of any earlier text. Moreover, the two poems have adjusted to twelfth-century needs, since they are laced with lamentations by the poet for the degradation of true knowledge.

In the same vein, poem 75 is another good example of how a type of text with a long-established tradition can slightly shift its thematic focus to respond to contemporary conditions. The poem has a strongly moral, essayistic character, following the tradition of much of the poetry written before the twelfth century.[95] Most of these earlier poems—by renowned poets such as Georgios of Pisidia, Leo the Philosopher, and Christophoros Mitylenaios—revolve around issues of vanity and social inequality. Prodromos also focuses

---

[92] Good examples of these new genres are the (Ptocho)prodromic poems and the so-called *schedourgia* by Prodromos. For the former, see Kulhánková, '*Ptochoprodromika*'. For *schedourgia*, see Vassis, 'Theodoros Prodromos' and Agapitos, 'Schedourgia'.
[93] Compare the opening verse of Prodromos' poem (Ἔρρετ' ἐμοῦ βιότοιο ἀπόπροθεν, ἔρρετε, βίβλοι) with that by Gregory (*Poems*, II.1.55, 1: Φεῦγ' ἀπ' ἐμῆς κραδίης, δολομήχανε, φεῦγε τάχιστα· | φεῦγ' ἀπ' ἐμῶν μελέων, φεῦγ' ἀπ' ἐμοῦ βιότου; cf. also II.2.3 [1495] 211: Ἔρρετέ μοι, βίβλοι πολυηχέες ἔρρετε, Μοῦσαι).
[94] Lauxtermann, *Byzantine Poetry*, vol. 2, 156–57. See also N. Zagklas, 'Theodore Prodromos and the Use of the Poetic Work of Gregory of Nazianzus: Appropriation in the Service of Self-Representation', *BMGS* 40 (2016), 223–42, at 238–41.
[95] For this kind of poetry, see Lauxtermann, *Byzantine Poetry*, vol. 2, 148–57.

on social inequality, but he constructs a comparison between the good fortune of uneducated craftsmen and the bad fortune of highly educated people, making this another twelfth-century work lamenting the futility of letters.

It is worth noting that poems 73–74 and 75 even share the word σχετλιαστικοί ('disgruntled', 'indignant') in their rubrics, which before Prodromos occurs only in the title of a poem by Gregory of Nazianzus. Poem II.1.19, a self-referential work about Gregory's sufferings, is entitled σχετλιαστικὸν ὑπὲρ τοῦ αὐτοῦ παθῶν.[96] Poems 73–74 and 75 may be quite different from each other with regard to form and length—the first two are written in hexameters, the latter in dodecasyllables; the first two are short (both fourteen lines), the latter because of its essayistic nature extends to 167 lines—but the word σχετλιαστικοί allows us to draw a link between them: all of them include the element of complaint. Thus the articulation of complaints is a mode permeating all three poems, even if they do not seem to belong to the same category in terms of genre.

Poem 76 is a long narrative poem recounting the hardships of the personified Friendship.[97] The poem is rife with allegorical overtones and lengthy descriptions of the prowess of Friendship, ranging from the regulation of the divine order and erotic desire to that of friendship and civic order.[98] Most of the text is an ethopoetic monologue by Friendship, except for the first thirty-five and final thirty-seven verses, which assume the form of a dialogue between Friendship and a stranger. Herbert Hunger placed the work among those Byzantine poems which exhibit a dramatic form.[99] It is true that Prodromos' poem can be compared to many other twelfth-century works in the form of a dialogue, including the *Dioptra* by Philippos Monotropos or the poem by Michael Haploucheir. Because of its dramatic dialogue between the two protagonists, it even resembles another Prodromean work: the *Katomyomachia*. However, unlike the *Katomyomachia*, which owes a great deal to Euripides and Ps. Homer's *Batrachomyomachia*,[100] poem 76 follows other literary strands.

---

[96] The word occurs also in the titles of two poems by Ioannes Chortasmenos: see H. Hunger, 'Aus der letzten Lebensjahren des Johannes Chortasmenos: Das Synaxarion im Cod. Christ Church gr. 56 und der Metropolit Ignatios von Selybria', *JÖB* 45 (1995), 159–218, at 162 and 168.
[97] For previous discussions of the work, see E. Passamonti, 'Dell' Ἀπόδημος φιλία Di Teodoro Prodromo', *Rendiconti della Reale Accademia dei Lincei, Classe di scienze morali, storiche e filologiche* I (1892), 361–70, and Roilos, *Amphoteroglossia*, 187.
[98] For a brief summary of its rich content, see p. 332.
[99] See Hunger, *profane Literatur*, vol. 2, 145.
[100] Marciniak and Warcaba, '*Katomyomachia*'.

Prodromos was inspired in the main theme of his poem by Lucian's *The Runaways*.[101] In Lucian's work, the personified Philosophy recounts how she departed from the world because of the false philosophers: people who claim to be her followers, but act wickedly. In Prodromos, Friendship relates that she has decided to leave because of her husband, the personified World. Throughout the poem she complains that World abused her; he even replaced her with Animosity, forcing her to leave their house. In addition to the influence from Lucian, Prodromos' text was also influenced by the novelistic tradition. For example, vv. 127–136 include motifs which are typical of novel-writing practice: (i) the intertwining tree branches between the date palms; (ii) the eel which comes to the shore to mate with the viper; and (iii) the attraction between the magnet and iron. Moreover, in the opening lines of the poem Friendship summons the stranger to come and sit together with her next to a pine tree, a setting used in Plato and Achilles Tatius' novel.[102] Similarly, the concluding lines of the poem remind us of a novel. As with both ancient and Byzantine novels, it has a 'happy end', with the union of the two heroes (Friendship and a stranger) through marital ties.

Even the small corpus of *Miscellaneous poems* includes texts that reaffirm the common characterization of Prodromos as a genre-crossing author with a keen interest in breaking conventional barriers and pushing the boundaries of well-established genres. Just like 73–74, 75, and 76, many works by Prodromos are elastic texts when it comes to genre. This is hardly surprising if we keep in mind that Byzantine literature is an occasion-defined literature. Since most Byzantine texts were written and performed for a specific occasion, and since they often had a particular function within the social and intellectual environment of the author—such as self-representation, accrual of attention, support of pedagogical activity, and pursuit of social advancement—genre rules were easily modified and texts given new forms to elicit admiration. Thus genre should be understood as a medium which helped Prodromos and other authors to make their texts relevant to their audiences and convey a message on a particular occasion. However, this also carries an implication for our understanding of the genre: when the occasion is not clear (or there was no real-life occasion),

---

[101] The use of Lucian's *Runaways* as hypotext for Prodromos' poem has been noted in K. Praechter, 'Beziehungen zur Antike in Theodoros Prodromos' Rede auf Isaak Komnenos', *BZ* 19 (1910), 314–29, at 315.
[102] See *Miscellaneous poems*, 76.32–34.

many of its genre and functional aspects remain quite ambiguous—and this is very much the case for the five garden poems and some other *Miscellaneous poems*, as we will see in the next section.

1.2.3. Veiled Occasions: Poems 1–6 and the Orphanotropheion of St Paul

The first six poems of the corpus edited here form a cycle for Paul the Apostle, Gregory of Nazianzus, Basil of Caesarea, John Chrysostom, Gregory of Nyssa, and Saint Nicholas—all six of them prominent religious figures in Byzantium and dedicatees of innumerable poems written by well-known, less well-known, or even anonymous poets throughout the entire Byzantine period. These are not the only poems for these six figures in Prodromos' oeuvre: Paul is commemorated in the cycle of tetrastichs on the Old and New Testaments,[103] Gregory of Nazianzus, Basil of Caesarea, and John Chrysostom in the cycle of tetrastichs that describe various episodes of their lives, and Nicholas in a *schedos*.[104] What is more, all of them are celebrated in Prodromos' iambic calendar.[105] On other occasions, some of these six figures are even praised alongside one another in other Prodromean poems: historical poem 57 is an epigram about a representation of the Holy Virgin together with Christ, flanked by John Chrysostom, Gregory of Nazianzus, Basil of Caesarea, and St Nicholas; in historical poem 59, Prodromos himself appeals for help from Gregory of Nazianzus, Basil the Great, Gregory of Nyssa, and John Chrysostom in his struggle against a certain Barys who had accused Prodromos of heresy because of his keen interest in the classics; and in poem 24 of the present edition, St Nicholas and John Chrysostom are asked to intercede on behalf of an anonymous donor.

And yet, in none of these works by Prodromos are the six saints commemorated together; nor is there a similar group of six self-contained poems dedicated to them anywhere else in the Byzantine tradition.[106] Thus, this is thematically a unique cycle, raising a number of questions. Why did Prodromos decide to commemorate them together? What was the context

---

[103] Prodromos, *Tetrasticha*, 277–93.   [104] See Vassis, 'Theodoros Prodromos', 14–17.
[105] Acconcia Longo, *Calendario giambico*.
[106] The only comparable example is poems 13–18 by Ioannes Mauropous, ed. P. de Lagarde, *Iohannis Euchaitorum Metropolitae quae in Codice Vaticano Graeco 676 supersunt* (Göttingen 1882), commemorating Sts Paul and Chrysostom (13), Chysostom (14), Gregory of Nazianzus (15), Basil the Great (16), the three Hierarchs (17), and St Nicholas (18). As in the case of Prodromos' verses, the epigrams by Mauropous seem to belong together, constituting a kind of precursor to Prodromos' cycle.

for the composition of the cycle? Whatever the original occasion might have been, all six poems were intended to be performed together at the same time. Quite a few cross-references within the poems speak in favour of this hypothesis. The fourth poem on John Chrysostom, for example, opens in the following manner:

Χρυσολόγον μετὰ τοῖσι λιγαίνομαι Ἰωάννην

Among them I will sing in praise of John of the golden words

Here, the poet explicitly states that, among the other holy figures, he will also sing the praises of John Chrysostom. The final two poems, on Gregory of Nyssa and St Nicholas, open in a similar manner:

Γρηγόριον μετέπειτα κασίγνητον Βασιλείῳ

And then of Gregory, the brother of Basil,

Οἶκτον ἀτὰρ μετέπειτα λιγαίνομαι, οἶκτον ἀείδω

And then I sing the praises of compassion, I celebrate compassion

The words '*μετὰ τοῖσι*' and '*μετέπειτα*' tie these six poems tightly together. The text on St Paul, with which the cycle opens, contains some further hints about the identity of the donor and the occasion for which the entire cycle was composed. Before this present edition the poem on St Paul had been edited only once, in the so-called Basel edition,[107] which was later reprinted in volume 133 of *Patrologia Graeca*. In both of them, verses 22–23 read: Ἀλλὰ σύ, ὦ θεός, ἐν τούτοις δὴ Παύλου ἀρωγέ | μνώεο Θεοδώρου λάτριδος εὐσεβίας. However, in the two earliest manuscripts to transmit the text, Vat. gr. 305 and Paris. gr. 2831, we read:

ἀλλά με ὀξὺς ἔσωθι βιάσκεται ἰὸς ἐρώτων·
    μνώεο Θευδώρου λάτριδος εὐσεβέος

but the sharp dart of desire overpowers me inside.
Remember Theodoros, your devout servant

These two verses suggest two points: first, they speak for the dedicatory nature of the text; second, the person who dedicated this text to Paul was a certain

---

[107] See below, p. 156.

Theodoros. One could surmise that this Theodoros was the person who commissioned Prodromos to write these poems for an unknown occasion. If we take a look at the circle of Prodromos' patrons and clients, one candidate would be Theodoros Styppeiotes, who held a powerful position as imperial secretary to Manuel I Komnenos, before falling into disgrace and out of power sometime after 1158/1159.[108]

However, I would argue that the poem is not the result of a commission, but is, rather, linked with Prodromos himself and an occasion that took place in the church of the Orphanotropheion of St Paul. Prodromos' association with the school at the Orphanotropheion of St Paul was suggested a long time ago by Robert Browning, who argued for it on the basis of the epistolary correspondence between the author and his teacher and friend Michael Italikos.[109] Hörandner, in contrast, was rather more cautious regarding Prodromos' connection to the Orphanotropheion, maintaining that the poet simply took refuge in the alms-house attached to the Orphanotropheion, without obtaining an official teaching post.[110] Whether or not Prodromos held an official position at the school attached to the church of St Paul is difficult to say, although the words 'your devout servant' may suggest that Prodromos' status at the Orphanotropheion was higher than that of a mere resident of its alms-house.

It might come as a surprise that an epigram dedicated to St Peter is not included in this group. The Orphanotropheion, initially dedicated to Saint Zotikos, its fourth-century founder, was later rededicated by Emperor Justin II (r. 565–574) to Sts Peter and Paul.[111] However, in twelfth-century texts, Paul's role as patron of the Orphanotropheion seems to have superseded that of Peter.[112] For example, in Prodromos' monody for Stephanos Skylitzes, we are told that the deceased was appointed headmaster of the school attached to

---

[108] For Styppeiotes and his political downfall, see O. Kresten, 'Zum Sturz des Theodoros Styppeiotes', JÖB 27 (1978), 49–103; cf. also V. Koufopoulou, 'Δύο ἀνέκδοτα ποιήματα τοῦ Θεοδώρου Στυππειώτη', Βυζαντινά 15 (1989), 351–67.

[109] R. Browning, 'Unpublished Correspondence between Michael Italicus, Archbishop of Philippopolis, and Theodore Prodromos', Byzantinobulgarica 1 (1962), 279–97.

[110] Hörandner, Historische Gedichte, 27–28.

[111] On the Orphanotropheion, see S. Mergiali-Falangas, 'L'école Saint-Paul de l'orphelinat à Constantinople: bref aperçu sur son statut et son histoire', REB 49 (1991), 237–46; T. S. Miller, The Orphans of Byzantium: Child Welfare in the Christian Empire (Washington DC 2003), 176–246; cf. also Nesseris, Παιδεία, 41–46. For a study of the Orphanotropheion from an archaeological point of view, see K. Dark and A. Harris, 'The Orphanage of Byzantine Constantinople: An Archaeological Identification', BSl 66 (2008), 189–201.

[112] T. S. Miller, 'Two Teaching Texts from the Twelfth-Century Orphanotropheion', in: J. W. Nesbitt (ed.), Byzantine Authors: Literary Activities and Preoccupations, Texts and Translations Dedicated to the Memory of Nicolas Oikonomides (Leiden/Boston 2003), 9–22.

the Orphanotropheion of 'St Paul'.[113] In addition, in an oration written on the occasion of his entry into the Orphanotropheion, Prodromos names only Paul.[114] In light of this social and literary context, I believe that Prodromos' text on Paul—which precedes the other epigrams—is a dedicatory one, and it seems reasonable to suggest that Prodromos had in mind the patron saint of the Orphanotropheion and a very special occasion associated with the church. Prodromos' poem is not, after all, the only twelfth-century case related to the Orphanotropheion. Leo of Rhodes, who became metropolitan of Rhodes sometime before 1166, and who was a teacher at the Orphanotropheion, dedicated a verse *schedos* to the school's patron, St Paul.[115] In addition to Leo of Rhodes' poem, a twelfth-century nine-line verse composition preserved in the thirteenth-century ms. Marcianus gr. XI.31 requests St Paul to reward the victor of a grammar and *schedos* competition.[116] But it should be stressed that Prodromos' text is functionally and thematically different from these two examples, mainly because of its dedicatory nature.

If my hypothesis about the close relation between Prodromos' poem on St Paul and the Orphanotropheion of St Paul is correct, it should come as no surprise that the poems on the three holy Hierarchs (Chrysostom, Basil, and Gregory of Nazianzus) and Gregory of Nyssa are also included in this poetic cycle. In addition to the iconographic prominence these four enjoyed in Byzantine churches, they were also considered the greatest Christian teachers in the Byzantine tradition, and regarded as special patrons of learning. As a result, their works would have been read by the students of the Orphanotropheion, as the high number of surviving schedographical paraphrases of their works from the twelfth century indicates.[117] Moreover, for Prodromos, they were paradigmatic figures; as I mentioned, he even draws parallels between his intellectual pursuits and those of the church fathers in order to refute the accusations of Barys. The inclusion of the poem on St Nicholas in the cycle, in turn, strikes an even more personal chord in Prodromos' world, for we know that at some point Prodromos himself took the monastic habit under the name Nicholas;[118] hence, Nicholas was Prodromos'

---

[113] Prodromos, *Orations*, 38.267.82–84: ὁμοῦ δὲ ψήφῳ βασιλικῇ τὸν διδασκαλικὸν διέπειν ἔλαχε θρόνον τῆς τοῦ μεγίστου Παύλου διατριβῆς.

[114] Prodromos, *Orations*, 33.199.40: καὶ πάντα πᾶσι κατὰ τὸν ἐμὸν καὶ ἡμέτερον γενήσομαι Παῦλον.

[115] Miller, 'Two Teaching Texts', 12.

[116] R. Browning, 'Il codice Marciano Gr. XI 31 e la schedografia bizantina', in: *Miscellanea Marciana di Studi Bessarionei* (Padua 1976), 21–34, at 32; cf. also Miller, 'Two Teaching Texts', 18.

[117] Vassis, 'Φιλολόγων Παλαίσματα', 43–44.

[118] A. Papadopoulos-Kerameus, 'Εἷς καὶ μόνος Θεόδωρος Πρόδρομος', *Lětopis Istoriko-Filologičeskago Obščestva pri Imperatorskom Novorossijskom Universitetě, VII, Vizantijskij Otdelenie IV* (Odessa 1898), 385–402, here at 399. Also Hörandner, *Historische Gedichte*, 32.

personal patron and could not be absent from such a dedicatory cycle. Additionally, Nicholas' renowned compassion and generosity in assisting orphans are emphasized not only in the present poem but also in a Prodromean *schedos* dedicated to him.[119]

But what was the particular occasion connected with the Orphanotropheion that triggered the composition of these six poems? The answer is not at all clear, since the poems in their manuscript tradition have been deprived of their original context.[120] Some of them seem even to have been given an entirely new context. The poems on Gregory of Nazianzus and Basil of Caesarea were reused as laudatory book epigrams for the collections of these two church fathers.[121] The poem on Gregory of Nazianzus was added by a later scribe as a book epigram to the first folio of the thirteenth-century manuscript Paris. gr. 554, which is a rich collection of works by Gregory of Nazianzus. The same goes for the epigram on Basil of Caesarea, which is preserved in the fourteenth-century codex Athous Vatopedinus 56 and the fifteenth-century codices BAS gr. 12 and Athous Iberon 1418, all three manuscripts being rich anthologies of works by this church father. But since the six poems were written for the same occasion, it is very unlikely that these works were originally used as book epigrams by Prodromos. No written works are ascribed to St Nicholas, nor do we know of any book epigrams dedicated to him. However, the text concludes with a plea to the saint to grant Prodromos mercy, both in his earthly life and the hereafter. Similarly, in the final three verses of the first poem of the cycle, the poet asks St Paul to remember him on the Day of the Lord. As a result, both the first and the last poems of this group contain explicit features that can be found in dedicatory poems. But in marked contrast to the vast majority of dedicatory texts, the donor and author of this group of epigrams seems to be the same person, in light of the hint 'μνώεο Θευδώρου' in v. 22 of the first poem.

Another question regarding the practical use of these six texts is whether these poems were inscribed or performed. These possibilities were not mutually exclusive, while, as we have seen in the previous section, the lack of evidence concerning the original occasion for many of the *Miscellaneous poems* casts a veil of ambiguity over various aspects of their genre. However, these

---

[119] Prodromos, *Schede*, 16, 16-17: τίς ὀρφανὸς ἢ τίς ταπεινὸς οὐκ ἐπέτυχε τῆς τούτου ὅλης ἐπικουρίας.

[120] This is a fairly common phenomenon in Byzantine poetry; see Lauxtermann, *Byzantine Poetry*, vol. 1, 60.

[121] For an introduction to Byzantine book epigrams, see F. Bernard and K. Demoen, 'Byzantine Book Epigrams', in: W. Hörandner, A. Rhoby, and N. Zagklas (eds), *A Companion to Byzantine Poetry* (Leiden/Boston 2019), 404–29 (with previous bibliography).

six poems seem to have a strong performative nature. Unlike dodecasyllables, dactylic metres were not rhythmically appealing to the Byzantine ear, but they were still read and performed just like dodecasyllables. We might recall that Eugenianos praised Prodromos for his imperial panegyrics written in hexameters. Inspired by Homeric hymns, Prodromos furnishes the poems with praising epithets for these six holy figures and various episodes of their lives in hexametrical form.[122] The text of these six poems even contains some indications regarding their performance. All six poems have the heading 'Προσφωνητήριοι εἰς...',[123] which leaves no doubt that they are performative supplications addressed to these holy figures. The sense of performativity is increased yet further by the frequent use of the χαῖρε salutation (fourteen times)[124] and vocatives, as well as the opening verse of each poem, in which the poet proclaims he will sing the praise of the saints. More importantly, the form and the structure of these six texts are similar to those of Gregory of Nazianzus' poem ἀποτροπὴ τοῦ πονηροῦ καὶ τοῦ Χριστοῦ ἐπίκλησις' (*Carm.* 2.1.55).[125] It is no coincidence that Gregory's poem, like each poem of this cycle, consists of twelve elegiac couplets, while the title προσφωνητήριοι seems to be a modification of the word ἐπίκλησις. The epigrams are indeed prayers, as was Gregory's poem, with a Homeric hymnic character directed to these six saints.[126]

In light of the cross references, I would say that the poems were most probably delivered together by Prodromos himself in the church of the Orphanotropheion. Although the original occasion still remains quite ambiguous, as we cannot say if it involved only the presence of Prodromos or also the participation of other individuals associated with the Orphanotropheion (for example, the students), we may push the argument regarding the circumstances of its performance further by suggesting that each poem was read aloud by Prodromos in front of the depiction of each saint (probably in different places in the church).[127] The poet could have begun with St Paul, the

---

[122] Some of the historical poems by Prodromos resemble Homeric hymns: see A. Faulkner, 'Theodoros Prodromos' Historical Poems. A Hymnic Celebration of John II Komnenos', in: A. Faulkner, A. Vergados, and A. Schwab (eds), *The Reception of the Homeric Hymns* (Oxford 2016), 261–74.

[123] Cf. *LBG* s.v. ('Anrufungs-'). The word προσφωνητήριοι evokes the προσφωνητικός λόγος, which is described as a 'de facto encomium, but not a complete one' to a governor by Menander Rhetor (cf. *ODB* 3 1740), pointing to the firm rhetorical base of Prodromos' encomiastic poems.

[124] For the χαῖρε salutation, see L. M. Peltomaa, *The Image of the Virgin Mary in the Akathistos Hymn* (Leiden 2001), 36–39.

[125] This poem by Gregory was also used by Prodromos as a model for the structure of poems no. 75–76.

[126] For verse prayers and hymns, see Lauxtermann, *Byzantine Poetry*, vol. 2, 163–75.

[127] The first five poems do not include any evidence about the nature of the representations, but the final one most probably relates to a vita icon of St Nicholas.

patron of the church, whose representation would surely occupy a prominent place in the building, then continued with the poems on the four church fathers, which bridge the supplicatory hymns to Sts Paul and Nicholas. Because of the absence of such personal supplications in the four poems on the church fathers, some of these poems then 'floated from one context to another', and they were subsequently used as laudatory book epigrams in some late Byzantine manuscripts.

Unlike most Byzantine dedicatory texts, these six poems make no mention of an act of material dedication. There is no sign of an explicit or implicit indication of a donation made by Prodromos to the Church of St Paul. Prodromos offers 'gifts of words' instead of a material contribution, and expects spiritual salvation in return.[128] These poems should, therefore, be considered panegyrics, similar to those written by Prodromos for the emperor and other members of the Komnenian family. Prodromos does not pursue the acquisition of a material gift here, but a reward in the hereafter. They were composed, then, not on commission, unlike most of his poetry of praise, but for his own benefit, affording us a precious glimpse into a personal (or semi-personal) moment of Prodromos as poet-donor in the Orphanotropheion of St Paul.

---

[128] On this issue, see F. Bernard, 'Gifts of Words: The Discourse of Gift-Giving in Eleventh-Century Byzantine Poetry', in: F. Bernard and K. Demoen (eds), *Poetry and Its Contexts in Eleventh-century Byzantium* (Farnham/Burlington 2012), 37–51; cf. also Bernard, *Poetry*, 322–33.

2
A Writer on Command and His Strategies

In the introductory chapter, I have sketched the outlines of the corpus of Prodromos' poetry that forms the core of this book, and also briefly discussed some issues of authorship, genre, and occasion. However, if we want to develop a more rounded picture of the *Miscellaneous poems*, it is critical to view them in the context of Prodromos' oeuvre and Komnenian literary production more generally; otherwise many of their aspects and much of their value will be unnoticed by the reader. Composition on demand stood at the very heart of twelfth-century literary culture, pushing many authors to adapt to the challenging conventions of a socially very stratified system. Their success as authors was linked more often than not to their skill in attracting patrons who would further support their literary pursuits. We have come a long way in our understanding of twelfth-century literary patronage. Margaret Mullett's seminal study 'Aristocracy and Patronage in the Literary Circles of Comnenian Constantinople' paved the way in illustrating the close ties between patronage and literature during this period,[1] while Ingela Nilsson has taken our understanding a step further by investigating the poetics of Konstantinos Manasses' occasional writings.[2] However, there are still aspects of this social-literary phenomenon that are vague. What makes this investigation even more challenging is that patronage is an elusive concept,[3] quite often veiled by the language of friendship in Byzantine textual production, and by other subtle exchanges between the patrons and their clients. This chapter does not aim to offer a full picture of patronage in the twelfth century, nor examine examples of obvious patronage. Instead, it takes Prodromos and his work as a starting-point from which to explore the complex relationships between literary patronage and other aspects of intellectual activity. The lack of institutional patronage led the authors to devise various strategies and techniques to achieve renown and promote their personal interests. Many works switched function, demonstrating that the divisions between the

---

[1] M. Mullett, 'Aristocracy and Patronage in the Literary Circles of Comnenian Constantinople', in: M. Angold (ed.), *The Byzantine aristocracy IX to XIII Centuries* (Oxford 1984), 173–201.
[2] Nilsson, *Constantine Manasses*.   [3] Bernard, *Poetry*, 291.

different contexts of production and performance were permeable. The first section of this chapter seeks to emphasize Prodromos' polyvalent occupation as court orator and teacher, offering a more nuanced picture of his literary activity within the context of Constantinopolitan cultural life. The second section aims to demonstrate that the complaint about the futility of writing is a motif that permeated works written both for the court and the classroom. Complaints assumed the role of a literary mode, without detracting from their connection to a social reality. I argue that such complaints are part of a strategy on the part of Prodromos, to leverage his public persona as author and teacher in the intellectual market. Building upon Prodromos' multifaceted social and professional roles and the inclusion of his laments in a diverse array of compositions, the final part of the chapter takes a closer look at the multifunctionality of many of his works (including many of the *Miscellaneous poems*). Many of them circulated in different settings, and works originally intended for a specific occasion enjoyed another 'life' in new performative contexts. Again, Byzantine literature has often been divided into distinct categories for the sake of modern scholarship. In order to classify the abundance of themes and wide range of material, we tend to distinguish between religious and secular texts, teaching works and works without a teaching purpose, and so on. These kinds of classification, although very useful, have occasionally led us to impose a sense of inflexibility on many Byzantine authors. Thus, the model advanced in the closing section of this chapter aims at developing a more accurate understanding of the way Byzantine textual production operated.

2.1. Theodoros Prodromos and His Professions

Studies by many distinguished literary scholars and cultural historians frequently describe Theodoros Prodromos as the 'poet laureate' *par excellence* of the Komnenian court and a skilful professional writer at the service of the most powerful Constantinopolitan aristocrats.[4] To be sure, this is not merely a modern reconstruction of Prodromos' authorial activity. It owes much to Prodromos' self-fashioning. In many of his poems, he repeatedly markets his role as court poet and imperial herald.[5] A good example is his work *Verses of Farewell to Byzantium* (historical poem 79), where the author, completely

---

[4] See also above, pp. 1–2.
[5] See Bazzani, 'Theodore Prodromos', 214–18; cf. also E. Cullhed, 'Blind Bard', 50–58.

dejected, bids farewell to Constantinople, to follow his friend and teacher Stephanos Skylitzes, who has been appointed Metropolitan of Trebizond.[6] Prodromos briefly describes his own life in the capital, focusing on the image of his ruined shoes and clothes to emphasize the long distances he has covered from the city to the imperial palace—always, of course, as 'poet laureate' in the service of the court.[7]

Even though Prodromos was exceptionally savvy at projecting and promoting himself as learned and as court poet, this role was by no means simply a figment of his imagination. As has already been said, many of his poems were composed for a wide range of events and occasions at the Byzantine court. A significant number of these poems celebrate the expeditions and victories of Ioannes II Komnenos against the Turks and other barbarian enemies of the empire,[8] imperial weddings and births,[9] and the coronation ceremony of a co-emperor.[10] Others were written on the occasion of the death of members of the imperial family.[11] A number of ceremonial hymns are dedicated to the *demes*, reflecting the strong popularity of this type of ceremonial poetry in the second quarter of the twelfth century.[12] There are also quite a few dedicatory epigrams for various objects,[13] and prayers[14] commissioned by various well-to-do individuals. In his career, Prodromos enjoyed enormous and long-standing success at the imperial court. His surviving poems cover a timespan of approximately three decades, partly concurrent with the reigns of two emperors: Ioannes II Komnenos (r. 1118–1143) and his son, Manuel I Komnenos (r. 1143–1180).

Furthermore, many fellow-poets stress Prodromos' activity as imperial mouthpiece in their works. For example, in a poem written for the emperor Manuel I Komnenos we read:[15]

---

[6] For an analysis of this poem, see W. Hörandner, 'Theodore Prodromos and the City', in: P. Odorico and Ch. Messis (eds), *Villes de toute beauté: L'ekphrasis des cités dans les littératures byzantine et byzantino-slaves. Actes du colloque international, Prague, 25–26 novembre 2011* (Paris 2012), 49–62.
[7] Cf. Prodromos, *Historical poems*, 79.18–20: Χαῖρε, μέλαθρα μεγάλα πολυκτεάνων βασιλήων, | οἷς ἔπι πόλλ' ἐμόγησα καὶ ἄρβυλα πλεῖστα δάμαξα | πολλῆς ἠματίῃσι καὶ ἐννυχίοισι κελεύθοις.
[8] Historical poems 3, 4, 6, 8, 11, 15, 16, 18, 19, 30.
[9] Historical poems 13, 14, 20, 43, 44.   [10] Historical poem 1.
[11] Historical poems 2, 7, 23, 25, 26, 27, 29, 31–33, 39, 45, 49, 50, 60; they include various types of funerary discourse (monodies, epitaphs, consolatory speeches).
[12] Historical poems 4, 5, 9, 10, 11, 12, 13, 14; for their popularity in the twelfth century, see Hörandner, *Historische Gedichte*, 79–85, and Hörandner, 'Court Poetry: Questions of Motifs, Structure and Function', in: E. Jeffreys (ed.), *Rhetoric in Byzantium* (Aldershot, 2003), 75–85.
[13] Historical poems 21, 35–37, 41, 52.   [14] Historical poems 27, 34, 40, 47, 51, 55.
[15] Manganeios Prodromos, *Poems* (ed. Bernardinello), 10.21–32; trans. in M. Alexiou, 'Ploys of Performance: Games and Play in the Ptochoprodromic Poems', *DOP* 53 (1999), 91–109 (slightly modified).

Ναί, στόμα, στάξον Ὑμηττὸν ἐκ γλυκερῶν χειλέων,
εἰπὲ καὶ λόγον ζωτικὸν καὶ ζήσω καὶ σκιρτήσω,
εἰπὲ καὶ ζῶσάν σου φωνὴν ζωήν μοι χορηγοῦσαν.
ἰδοὺ τελέως ἤργησα, καὶ γὰρ ἐγγωνιάζω
25 καὶ κλῆρον ἔχω πατρικὸν τοῦτο τὸ νόσημά μου.
τρέμω καὶ τὴν ἐκμέτρησιν τοῦ κήρου τῆς ζωῆς μου·
πτοεῖ με γὰρ ὁ Πρόδρομος, ὁ προδραμὼν ἐκεῖνος,
ὁ ῥήτωρ ὁ περίφημος, ὁ προτεθρυλ[λ]ημένος,
ἡ χελιδὼν ἡ μουσουργός, ἡ λαλιστάτη γλῶττα,
30 μὴ τόπον ἑτοιμάζῃ μοι καὶ λίθον καὶ γωνίαν.

Yes, O mouth, drip Hymettus' honey from sweet lips,
speak a life-giving word and I will live and rejoice,
speak in your living voice, bestowing life upon me.
See, I've grown quite idle, and I hide myself away,
25 and I have this disease as my patrimony,
I tremble at the remaining measure of my life's candle.
For Prodromos, that one who ran before, frightens me,
the renowned rhetor, the far-famed one,
the musical swallow, the most loquacious tongue,
30 lest he prepare for me a place, a stone and a corner.

This passage has triggered fierce disagreements among modern scholars over the identity of 'Πρόδρομος' in line 27. In order to argue in favour of the poem's authorship by Theodoros Prodromos, some Byzantinists have even interpreted it as a reference to Prodromos' father or John the Forerunner.[16] Of course, here it is Manganeios Prodromos who refers to Theodoros Prodromos: the anonymous poet who describes himself as Prodromos' successor in the court acknowledges explicitly the latter's superiority as orator, comparing him to a music-making swallow and a well-versed tongue in order to convey Prodromos' matchless proficiency in the field of ceremonial oratory.

However, it should be emphasized that Prodromos' position as well-versed imperial orator and 'superstar author' at the emperor's court is just one side of the coin as regards his professional activity in twelfth-century Constantinople. A *schedos* by the little-known figure of the monk Ioannikios, a member of Prodromos' coterie of friends, for example, helps us to shed more light on the

---

[16] For a recent summary of this debate, see Kulhánková, 'Figuren und Wortspiele', 34–35.

picture of his activity as a teacher and the different levels of his intellectual undertakings:[17]

> καὶ τίς γὰρ οὐκ ἴσησι τοῦτον (sc. Πρόδρομον)—ὦ χάρις τῶν γραμματικῶν ἡ πολλὴ ἐπὶ γῆς!—ὡς ἱκανὸν ὄντα τῆς τέχνης αὐτῆς καὶ τῶν περὶ ταύτην διδάσκαλον· τίς οὐκ οἶδεν ἐμβοᾶ\<ν\> νέῳ παντὶ καὶ γηραιῷ ῥητόρων τοῦτον τὸν πρόκριτον; τίς οὐκ αἰνεῖ τῶν φιλοσόφων; ὅταν ἰαμβίζῃ ἡ δαψιλὴς τῶν τούτου λόγων βλύσις καὶ ἡρωΐζῃ τισίν, ἐμποιεῖ καινὸν θαυμασμόν. ὁμοίως δὲ καὶ λογογραφεῖ καὶ ἔτι σχεδοπλοκεῖ.

> Who does not praise him (sc. Prodromos)—O great grace of the grammarians on the earth—for being a qualified teacher of this craft and all the skills it involves. Who is not able to shout aloud to every young and old man that this man is the foremost of the rhetors? Who amongst the philosophers does not praise him? When he writes iambics an abundant stream flows from his works, and when he versifies in hexameters he causes a novel admiration to them. Similarly when he writes in prose and even when he composes *schede*.

Here, Ioannikios describes Prodromos as the most brilliant grammarian, rhetor, and philosopher, while making special reference to Prodromos' skills in the composition of iambs and hexameters. Ioannikios also mentions his talent as a prose writer and a schedographer. The significance of the reference to Prodromos' poetic skills is enhanced even more if we consider that Ioannikios seems to be the author of the Ps. Psellian poem 14,[18] a poem addressed to a fictional friend, containing instructions on how to write correct iambs. As a teacher of poetry, then, Ioannikios acknowledges Prodromos as the leading authority in the composition of iambics and hexameters, and connects this expertise with Prodromos' teaching activity.

But the person who presents Prodromos' career in the most balanced manner is Niketas Eugenianos, in his dodecasyllabic funerary poem for his teacher, to which I have already referred.[19] Eugenianos describes Prodromos

---

[17] The text cited here is the corrected version presented in Vassis, 'Theodoros Prodromos', 7, note 27.

[18] For the attribution of the work to the monk Ioannikios, see W. Hörandner, 'The Byzantine Didactic Poem—A Neglected Literary Genre? A Survey with Special Reference to the Eleventh Century', in: F. Bernard and K. Demoen (eds), *Poetry and Its Contexts in Eleventh-Century Byzantium* (Farnham/Burlington 2012), 55-67, at 62.

[19] It is worth noting that Eugenianos produced and delivered a set of three funerary works on the occasion of Prodromos' death: one in prose, and two in verse (of which one in hexameters and the other in dodecasyllables). For a discussion of Eugenianos' monodies for Prodromos, see Kyriakis,

as the panegyrist for the Komnenian family and the author of many epigrams for icons and tombs, as well as a gifted teacher, whose qualities are comparable to those of the authoritative philosophers of the past:[20]

135 ἐδυστύχησαν οἱ βασίλειοι πόνοι
 οἱ σὺν Θεῷ μέλλοντες εἰς φῶς ἡκέναι,
 τὸν Πρόδρομον φέροντες οὐκ ἐπαινέτην·
 ὑπερνεφῆ γὰρ ἆθλα καὶ στρατηγίας
 καὶ βαρβάρους πίπτοντας ἠναγκασμένους
140 τίς ὡς σὺ μουσόπνευστον ἐκφράσοι στόμα;
 [...]
150 καὶ κόσμον ἐκλέλοιπας σεπτῶν εἰκόνων·
 κοσμούμεναι γὰρ ἐκ λίθων καὶ μαργάρων
 ὡς κόσμον εἶχον ἐντελῆ σου τοὺς στίχους
 καὶ κόσμος ἦν ἄντικρυς ἡ στιχουργία
 τοῦ κοσμοποιοῦ μαργάρου τῶν εἰκόνων.
155 Ποῖον τὶ δυσθέατον ὑπὲρ τοὺς τάφους,
 ὧν ἐν πόνοις τίθησι καὶ κλῆσις[21] μόνη;
 Ἠγαλλόμην δὲ τοῖς τάφοις ὡς νυμφίοις
 χιτῶνα χρυσόστικτον ἠμφιεσμένοις
 τὴν χρυσεπῆ σου καὶ σοφὴν στιχουργίαν.
 [...]
 νῦν καὶ πόλιν Βύζαντος εὐθηνουμένην
 ἄλλοις τε χρηστοῖς ἀλλὰ δὴ καὶ τοῖς λόγοις·
 ὁ κόσμος ἐκλέλοιπε τῶν μαθημάτων,
 καὶ ταῖς Ἀθήναις ἔσχεν ἰσομοιρίαν·
255 κἀκεῖσε γὰρ παρῆλθεν Ἀκαδημία,
 Περίπατος[22] δὲ μέχρι καὶ σκιᾶς μόνης

'Professors and Disciples', 108–19. For the reasons behind the production of monodies for the same person in different forms, see Agapitos, 'Schedourgia', 18–22 and Zagklas, 'Prose and Verse', 229–48.

[20] Niketas Eugenianos, *Funerary poems*, 2. 35–140, 150–159, and 251–259 (with some alterations in the punctuation). Trans. of verses 150–159 in I. Drpić, 'Chrysepes Stichourgia: The Byzantine Epigram as Aesthetic Object', in: B. Bedos-Rezak and J. F. Hamburger (eds), *Sign & Design: Script as Image in a Cross-Cultural Perspective (300–1600 CE)* (Washington DC 2016), 51–69, at 55 (with some minor modifications). It is interesting that a similar description of Prodromos as panegyrist and teacher is included in Niketas Eugenianos, *Funerary oration on the death of Theodoros Prodromos*, at 452.1–12: ἄρτι πρώτως ὀλβίαν γλῶτταν παυσαμένην ὁρῶ πολλὰς ἑτέρας οὕτω παυσαμένας ὑπερφωνήσασαν, **γλῶτταν ἀσόφους σοφίζουσαν καὶ σοφοὺς κατατέρπουσαν**, ἀμαθεῖς συνετίζουσαν καὶ λόγῳ πενομένους ὀλβίζουσαν καὶ γνωστοὺς ἀφθόνητα οἱ προσανέχοντας θέλγουσαν, οἰχομένους πενθοῦσαν, λυπουμένους παιδαγωγοῦσαν, ἀστηρίκτους ἑδράζουσαν, **σκηπτούχων νίκας ὑμνοῦσαν**, εὐθυμοῦσι συγχαίρουσαν, ὀδυρομένοις συγκλαίουσαν καὶ πᾶσι πάντα γινομένην.

[21] The edition reads κλῆσις.   [22] The edition reads Περίπατα.

καὶ τοῦ Χρυσίππου τῆς Στοᾶς τὸ ποικίλον.
Μουσεῖον οὖν ἔμψυχον εἶχεν ἡ πόλις,
τὸν Πρόδρομον, σὲ τὴν τεραστίαν φύσιν.

135 The imperial labours that, God willing,
shall once see the light, have suffered misfortune,
for they won't have Prodromos as panegyrist.
For the sublime struggles and campaigns
and the future defeat of barbarians,
140 who will recount these things like you, mouth inspired by the Muses?
[…]
150 You have left behind the adornment of holy icons.
For, decorated with stones and pearls,
they also had your verses as a precious adornment;
surely the poetry was a form of adornment
for the decorated pearl of the icons.
155 What is more disagreeable to gaze upon than the tombs,
the very mention of which causes pain?
Yet I took great pleasure in the tombs, like bridegrooms
in a gold-threaded cloak, wrapped
in your golden words and learned poetry.
[…]
The city of Byzas, which [once] flourished
in many other fine things but above all in speeches,
has now been deprived of the adornment of your teachings.
It has suffered the same fate as Athens;
255 for there, too, the Academy fell into decline
and even the Peripatetic school
and the subtle Stoa of Chrysippos were but shadows.
The city had as living haunt of the Muses,
you, Prodromos, prodigious in nature.

Filled with the necessarily dramatic overtones of a funerary work, these passages recount the various intellectual activities of Prodromos, emphasizing the terrible misfortune that befell Constantinople upon his death. Future imperial conquests and victories will not receive the same praise and tributes as those lauded by Prodromos' panegyrics, while the intellectual life of Constantinople and its supreme educational system will decline, much as Athens did after the death of Plato, Aristotle, and Chrysippos. All the same, it is worth noting that Eugenianos' praise of Prodromos' teaching qualities conceals much behind the comparisons drawn with some celebrated teachers of the past. Eugenianos does not specify Prodromos' teaching post; he does not call his teacher a *grammatikos*, probably because a mention of this socially inferior profession would rob the monody of some of its rhetorical glitter. However, Prodromos himself takes pride in his multifaceted profession, as court poet and *grammatikos*, at a later stage of his career. In the fifth ptochoprodromic poem, Prodromos devotes the greatest part to his profession as court poet, by describing himself as a loyal servant of Eirene Doukaina, Ioannes II Komnenos, and now Manuel I Komnenos, while at the same time lauding himself as the 'father of the *grammatikoi*' (πατέρα τῶν γραμματικῶν).[23]

Although Prodromos' explicit references to his double profession are to be found at a later stage of his career, we may safely assume that the composition of oratorical works for the court and various aristocrats, as well as private tutorship, were integral to his career from its beginning to its end. For example, he clearly busied himself with the composition of schedographic texts over a long period of time, as evidenced by the approximate dates of two *schede*: the one a *schedos* in the form of consolation for Eirene Doukaina, composed on the occasion of the death of her son, the Sevastokrator Andronikos, as early as 1131;[24] the other a *schedos* on St Nicholas addressed to Theodoros Styppeiotes, at some point between 1155 and 1159.[25] Furthermore, Prodromos and monk Ioannikios formed a guild dedicated to the pursuit of schedographical practice from the 1130s through to the later years of Prodromos' life.[26] They were two of the most prolific schedographers of the second quarter of the twelfth century. Ioannikios' *schedos*, referenced above, is one of a group of such works that the two teachers exchanged in praise of each other.[27] Furthermore, Ioannikios, as an active scribe, put together a collection of his schedographical writings, while Prodromos even authored a book epigram for one of these manuscripts containing the schedographical collection of Ioannikios.[28] In one of the *schede* addressed to

[23] Prodromos, *Fifth Ptochoprodromic poem*, v. 47. For some remarks on the activity of Prodromos as teacher, see Nesseris, Παιδεία, 84–91.
[24] See K. Barzos, *Η Γενεαλογία των Κομνηνών*, 2 vols. (Thessaloniki 1984), vol. 1, 231, note 13. For a discussion of the date of Andronikos' death, see more recently M. Loukaki, 'Dating Issues: The Defection of Sebastokrator Isaakios Komnenos to the Danishmendid Turks, the Death of His Brother Andronikos Komnenos, and the Death of Their Mother Empress Irene Doukaina', *Symm* 32 (2022), 11–16, at 12.
[25] Vassis, 'Theodoros Prodromos', 12–13.
[26] For Ioannikios, see Papaioannou, *Michael Psellos*, 257–28 and Nesseris, Παιδεία, 139–57.
[27] Most of these *schede* remain unpublished; see above note 34.
[28] Prodromos, *Historical poems*, 63.

Ioannikios, Prodromos speaks about himself as '*καί με τὸν γέροντα*', and he refers to his poor health, probably alluding to his infection with smallpox some time at the beginning of 1140s.[29] In another unpublished *schedos* in Vat. Palat. gr. 92 (fols. 228ᵛ–229 ᵛ), we learn that when Prodromos had to withdraw from his teaching duties because of his bad health, Ioannikios probably served as his substitute during his absence.[30] These details suggest constant collaboration between Prodromos and Ioannikios, and continuous engagement of the former with teaching material.

Unfortunately, little is known about Prodromos' life; what survives is shrouded in ambiguity, making it difficult to describe and tie together the two main threads of his career as teacher and court poet. Wolfram Hörandner's study of Prodromos' life still remains the most authoritative one,[31] and most of the biographies written by later modern scholars are highly indebted to it.[32] Only Alexander Kazhdan, in his study, 'Theodore Prodromus: a Reappraisal' attempted to challenge some of Hörandner's views,[33] but some of his arguments are based on tenuous hypotheses and are occasionally the result of confusion, especially when it comes to the question of the 'three Prodromoi'.[34]

Despite the scarcity of evidence, however, Prodromos' career trajectory can be conventionally divided into three stages: (a) c. 1100–1122, (b) 1122–1143, and (c) 1143 to his death in 1156–58.[35] His commissions for the palace and aristocratic households help us to distinguish between these three stages.

We know almost nothing about Prodromos before the year 1122, when he composed a poem on the occasion of the coronation of the emperor Ioannes Komnenos' first son, Alexios Komnenos (historical poem 1). Whether this was his first commission from the Komnenian court is not certain. But in one of his later poems, he reminds Manuel I Komnenos that he entered the service of his grandmother Eirene Doukaina and her 'literary circle' from a very young age.[36]

---

[29] See Vat. Pal. gr. 92, fol. 177ʳ.
[30] Vassis, '*Φιλολόγων Παλαίσματα*', 62 (no. 199); cf. also Nesseris, *Παιδεία*, 49–50 and 374–76.
[31] Hörandner, *Historische Gedichte*, 21–35.
[32] See, among others, M. Bazzani, 'Historical Poems', 211–14; D'Ambrosi, *Gregorio Nazianzeno*, 20–29; T. Migliorini, *Gli scritti satirici in greco letterario di Teodoro Prodromo: introduzione, edizione, traduzione, comment*, PhD Thesis (Pisa 2010), XI–XVI; and Jeffreys, *Byzantine Novels*, 3–6.
[33] Kazhdan, 'Theodore Prodromus', 87–114.
[34] See W. Hörandner, 'Review of A. Kazhdan and S. Franklin (eds), *Studies on Byzantine Literature of the Eleventh and Twelfth Centuries* (Cambridge 1984)', *JÖB* 38 (1988), 468–73, at 469–70; see also Jeffreys, *Byzantine Novels*, 3, note 1.
[35] For this date of Prodromos' death, see Hörandner, *Historische Gedichte*, 32. Kazhdan, in contrast, argued that Prodromos lived until the 1170s; cf. Kazhdan, 'Theodore Prodromus', 92–93. However, Kazhdan fails to notice that Hörandner's date is based on the fact that, in a poem dating from not long after 1058, Manganeios explicitly says that his fellow poet is dead.
[36] Prodromos, *Fifth Ptochoprodromic poem*, vv. 21–23.

ἀλλ' ἀπ' αὐτῆς τῆς βρεφικῆς καὶ πρώτης ἡλικίας,
μίαν αὐλὴν ἐγνώρισα καὶ ἕναν αὐθέντην ἔσχον,
τὴν ἱερὰν βασίλισσαν, τοῦ κράτους σου τὴν μάμμην

But from infancy and early age,
I came to know one court and had a single mistress,
the holy empress, grandmother of your lordship.

Unfortunately, we cannot specify the exact circumstances under which Prodromos—despite his young age—entered the imperial court and started receiving such prestigious commissions. Perhaps Michael Italikos, one of Prodromos' teachers,[37] who was probably already a member of Eirene's close literary entourage and member of her rhetorical *theatron*,[38] had promoted his own student. Having noticed his talent in the composition of poetry, Italikos may have been the link between the young Prodromos and Eirene. But it is also possible that Eirene had seen the young Prodromos in a *schedos* contest or a poetic contest,[39] since members of the imperial family attended such school events. In one of the unpublished *schede* from the codex Vat. Pal. gr. 92, for example, the emperor himself is named as the judge of schedographical contests.[40]

Once again, in the fifth ptochoprodromic, addressed to Manuel I Komnenos, Prodromos specifically states that he switched patron only upon the death of Eirene Doukaina.[41] However, the only surviving poem written for Eirene was written together with the aforementioned *schedos* on the occasion of the death of the Sevastokrator Andronikos in 1131.[42] On the other hand, Elizabeth Jeffreys has argued that the first commissions for Ioannes II

---

[37] It is clear that Italikos was Prodromos' teacher from their letter correspondence. See, for example, Michael Italikos, *Letters*, 1.64.25-29: Πρώην μὲν γάρ, ὅτε σε ὁ Φοῖνιξ τὸν Ἀχιλλέα ἔτρεφον καὶ μύθων ῥητῆρα ἐτίθουν, αὐτὸς τῶν λόγων ἡγούμην· νῦν δὲ γεγηρακότος τοῦ σοῦ Φοίνικος, Ἀχιλλεῦ, ἄρχε λόγων αὐτός (= In the past, when I, Phoenix, was raising you, Achilles, and was rendering you a 'speaker of Words' [*Iliad* 9.443], I myself was leading the discourses; but now, as your Phoenix has grown old, you, Achilles, should take the lead in discoursing); trans. in S. Papaioannou, 'Language Games, Not the Soul's Beliefs: Michael Italikos to Theodoros Prodromos, on Friendship and Writing', in: M. Hinterberger and E. Schiffer (eds), *Byzantinische Sprachkunst: Studien zur byzantinischen Literatur gewidmet Wolfram Hörandner zum 65. Geburtstag* (Berlin/New York 2007), 218-33, at 224; this passage is also discussed in Hörandner, *Historische Gedichte*, 25.

[38] Michael Italikos, *Orations*, 15.146-147.1-4: Λόγον αὐτοματίσαι σοι ἐξ αὐτοσχεδίου γλώττης ἐν τῷδε τῷ λογιωτάτῳ θεάτρῳ προστέταχας, ὦ πασῶν βασιλίδων λογιωτέρα μοι δέσποινα καὶ πλέον ἢ πάντες τοὺς λόγους τιμήσασα.

[39] For these contests, see Bernard, *Poetry*, 254-66.

[40] See Vassis, 'Vaticanus Palatinus gr. 92', 54 (no. 114).

[41] Cf. Prodromos, *Fifth Ptochoprodromic poem*, vv. 21-27.

[42] For an alternative dating of this poem, see Hörandner, *Historische Gedichte*, 188.

Komnenos were produced after the recapture of Kastamon (c. 1134).[43] All this means that for many years Prodromos would have produced no commissions for Eirene or other members of the court, though it is possible these works simply have not survived. In my view, however, we should not take Prodromos' words in the poem to Manuel I at face value, nor should we date all Prodromos' poems for Ioannes Komnenos after 1134. For instance, historical poem 1, which celebrates the crowning of Alexios Komnenos, son of Ioannes, as co-emperor, was written in 1122. Some of the ceremonial hymns performed by the demes were likely written before 1134 as well. But even so, it cannot be denied that the number of commissions for ceremonial poetry in the first decade of his career as poet at the court does not seem to be large at all. Various reasons may lie behind this small number of commissions during this period. Prodromos was in an early stage of his career and was not yet particularly famous. But it is also possible that during these years Prodromos was occupied with the completion of some of his lengthy narrative works for the Constantinopolitan rhetorical *theatra*. For instance, although the writing of his novel *Rhodanthe and Dosikles* has been dated to the early 1130s,[44] it could also have been written much earlier for the rhetorical *theatron* of Eirene Doukaina.

Prodromos' career as poet of ceremonial poetry took off in the 1130s, with at least twenty-one commissions from Ioannes II Komnenos. But things changed once again in 1143, after the death of this emperor, as the number of imperial commissions declined. There may be two reasons for this: first, Prodromos may have fallen into disfavour with Ioannes' successor and son, Manuel I;[45] and second, Prodromos' gradually deteriorating health may have limited his literary activity at court. These two possibilities, combined with the steady rise of Manganeios Prodromos' popularity, may well have played a part in the diminishing number of imperial commissions Prodromos received. But I believe all these gaps in his activity as court poet and the small number of ceremonial works extant from certain stages of his career can easily be counterbalanced when we take account of his constant teaching activity.

As we have seen above, Prodromos' poem *Verses of Farewell to Byzantium*, written around 1140, discloses the poet's intention to follow his friend and teacher, Stephanos Skylitzes, who had been appointed to the bishopric of Trebizond. In it, Prodromos emphasizes the services he offered to the court as poet. However, Prodromos does not omit his scholarly and teaching

---

[43] Jeffreys, *Byzantine Novels*, 5.   [44] See Jeffreys, *Byzantine Novels*, 7–10.
[45] V. Stanković, 'A Generation Gap or Political Enmity? Emperor Manuel Komnenos, Byzantine Intellectuals and the Struggle for Domination in Twelfth Century Byzantium', *ZRVI* 44 (2007), 209–26.

pursuits.[46] This profession remained a cornerstone of his intellectual activity in Constantinople, and one that offered him a steady income to balance the inconstant stream of commissions. We may see Prodromos' roles as middle-class teacher and professional writer/orator as mutually complementary aspects of his intellectual identity. In fact, Prodromos was one of the few twelfth-century *literati* who switched between different levels and contexts of literary patronage in the Komnenian period. He produced not only ceremonial poetry for the Komnenian propaganda machine but also long narratives, such as his novel, and numerous satirical works. By way of comparison, we may note that other authors—such as Konstantinos Manasses and Ioannes Tzetzes—did not write ceremonial poems for the court, nor did authors of ceremonial poetry—such as Nikolaos Kallikles and Manganeios Prodromos—compose large-scale literary works. To be sure, Prodromos' literary versatility owes much to his social positions as courtly poet and teacher. His teaching activity and educational projects enabled him to consolidate his position in the intellectual and ceremonial life of the court, which in turn strengthened his teaching authority.[47]

Modern scholars have marginalized Prodromos' activity as teacher for the sake of his more dazzling activity as court poet, concentrating on his accomplishments as imperial mouthpiece and freelance writer. Take, for example, Robert Browning's words 'Prodromos, like several of his contemporaries, was a professional writer, and not an official or clergyman or teacher who happened to write'.[48] Although I agree with the essence of Browning's view, I think this assertion can be slightly misleading at the same time, for it downgrades, to a certain extent, the way many twelfth-century authors served as teachers. Prodromos took pride in his profession as teacher, being well aware that this was the main path for his social advancement within the highly competitive bureaucratic system of Komnenian Constantinople. Moreover, this profession became the genesis of many of his works. So, when approaching and exploring his works in terms of function and audience, we must always keep all Prodromos' identities before us: the celebrated court poet, the professional writer and rhetorician, and the inventive teacher.

---

[46] Prodromos, *Historical poems*, 79.40–41 and 45.
[47] As Floris Bernard has noted: 'Education is the cornerstone on which the meritocratic ideal of the intellectual elite is built. It transmits necessary competences and skills, forges ties of long-lasting friendship, and serves as a criterion on the basis of which careers are assigned.' Bernard, *Poetry*, 209.
[48] R. Browning, *The Byzantine Empire* (London 1980), 152. This idea is fully accepted in R. Beaton, 'Rhetoric of Poverty: The Lives and Opinions of Theodore Prodromos', *BMGS* 11 (1987), 1–28, at 4.

2.2. Complaints and the Futility of Letters: Tangled Mosaics of Reality and Fictionality

In light of the accounts by Ioannikios the monk, Niketas Eugenianos, and Theodoros Prodromos himself, it is clear that Prodromos was not a civil or ecclesiastical official, like Nikolaos Kallikles who served as an imperial physician at the same time as writing several poems for various members of the Byzantine court. Instead, Prodromos was a middle-class teacher, a *grammatikos*, whose rhetorical eloquence was highly appreciated by members of the Komnenian family and Constantinople's social elite. Unlike the earlier Byzantine period, when most poets were part of this upper class in Byzantine society,[49] many twelfth-century poets were members of the lower social stratum, scraping a livelihood together from writing and teaching. And Theodoros Prodromos, along with his peer Ioannes Tzetzes, seem, in this respect, to be the two best examples of this change in the social status of poets.[50] Both of them may count among the most renowned and prolific poets of the mid-twelfth century, but they never managed to fully turn their cultural capital into an improved social position by acquiring a high official post or an important teaching post.

The social insecurity inherent in the highly competitive intellectual environment of the capital shaped the prickly self-representation evident in Tzetzes' writings, compelling him to earn his living by serving as private secretary to various powerful individuals (such as Nikephoros Serblias and Ioannes Taronites)[51] and as grammarian through some prestigious imperial commissions of didactic poetry.[52] Prodromos, on the other hand, pursued a slightly different path. In building up a particularly wide network of clients,[53] he managed to become the most popular court orator and poet of the Komnenian family. But this was not an institutional position with a continuous flow of income;[54] as a consequence, his low social standing as a

---

[49] Lauxtermann, *Byzantine Poetry*, vol. 1, 39.   [50] Beaton, 'Rhetoric', 4–5.
[51] For Tzetzes' career, see M. J. Luzzatto, *Tzetzes lettore di Tucidide: note autografe sul codice Heidelberg Palatino greco 252* (Bari 1999), 141–42, and M. Grünbart, 'Prosopographische Beiträge zum Briefcorpus des Ioannes Tzetzes', *JÖB* 46 (1996), 175–226.
[52] For Tzetzes as author of didactic works, see A. Rhoby, 'Ioannes Tzetzes als Auftragsdichter', *Graeco-Latina Brunensia* 15/2 (2010), 167–83, and B. van den Berg, 'John Tzetzes as Didactic Poet and Learned Grammarian', *DOP* 74 (2020), 285–302. For a discussion of Tzetzes' teaching activity through his letter correspondence, see M. Grünbart, 'Byzantinisches Gelehrtenelend—oder wie meistert man seinen Alltag?', in: L. M. Hoffmann and A. Monchizadeh (eds), *Zwischen Polis, Provinz und Peripherie: Beiträge zur byzantinischen Geschichte und Kultur* (Wiesbaden 2005), 413–26.
[53] For Prodromos' network, see M. Grünbart, ''Tis Love That Has Warm'd Us: Reconstructing Networks in 12th-century Byzantium', *Revue Belge de Philologie et d'Histoire* 83/2 (2005), 301–13, at 311.
[54] Bernard, *Poetry*, 292.

grammatikos together with the fact that, in spite of his credentials, he never climbed the ladder of the Komnenian bureaucracy, have puzzled modern scholars and have led them to posit a 'crisis of literati'[55] and a shortage of administrative and ecclesiastical posts during this period. Other scholars have tried to explain this disjunction between his reputation and rewards on the basis of some self-referential details provided by Prodromos in his various writings. According to Elizabeth Jeffreys, this could be the result of a 'historical accident' and the bad health that Prodromos frequently references in many of his writings.[56] This hypothesis, although very attractive, does not fully explain why Prodromos did not manage to ascend, or even become part of, a pyramidal system that favoured men—like Prodromos—who knew how to use language to demonstrate their intellectual capacity. By the end of Ioannes II Komnenos' reign, Prodromos was approximately forty years of age and could reasonably have been given a promotion, after being an occasional imperial orator for more than two decades.[57] By way of comparison, Nikephoros Basilakes, who was roughly fifteen years younger than Prodromos, served as imperial notary and then as teacher of the Apostle at the Patriarchal school as early as 1140.[58]

Prodromos' failure to make his way within the complex social establishment has usually been discussed by scholars in conjunction with a particular group of his poems, namely the so-called 'begging poems', texts in which he bemoans all the sufferings he has had to endure as an intellectual in peril. He has been described as the father of 'begging poetry', or, as Roderick Beaton has put it, 'rhetoric of poverty'[59]—probably a more suitable term, lacking the pejorative connotations of 'begging'. But at the same time, the term 'rhetoric of poverty' raises questions regarding the veracity of the complaints these poets made, casting doubts on the reality of the circumstances they describe. Do these works describe real or fictitious situations? Self-reference and fiction intersect to such a degree, resulting in works with multilayered messages that are not always easy to decode. Being occasional works, it is certain that they are a means for the author to give expression to his voice and to advance, in a subtle way, his requests. Although it is very difficult to distinguish between truly self-referential and fictional elements, such poems usually have an extra-literary end and, arguably, are connected with reality.[60]

---

[55] See Bazzani, 'Theodoros Prodromos', 225. [56] Jeffreys, *Byzantine Novels*, 4.
[57] On Prodromos' date of birth, see Hörandner, *Historische Gedichte*, 22–23.
[58] A. Pignani, *Niceforo Basilace, Progimnasmi e monodie* (Naples 1983), 235–52; cf. *ODB* s.v.
[59] Beaton, 'Rhetoric', 1–28.
[60] For example, Kazhdan and Epstein have argued that these complaints mirror current socio-economic circumstances: A. P. Kazhdan and A. Wharton Epstein, *Change in Byzantine Culture in the*

Many of these works are directed to various powerful addressees, who belonged to the wider network of Prodromos' social environment, ranging from the emperor himself to various members of the imperial entourage and even a number of his students who have managed to find employment in the Constantinopolitan bureaucratic establishment. For example, in one of the poems addressed to Theodoros Styppeiotes, who had risen to become the imperial secretary of Manuel I Komnenos, Prodromos reports all the hardships he is currently facing, concluding with the following words:[61]

εἶτα φθαρείσης, ἄνθρωπε, τῆς γλώττης τοῦ Προδρόμου
ἑτέραν εὕροι τίς ἐν γῇ ταύτῃ παρισουμένην
καὶ σχετικῶς κηρύσσοντα τὸν αὐτοκράτορά μου;
οὐκ οἶμαι, κἂν παραφρονῶν τοῦτον λαλῶ τὸν λόγον.

If then, man, the tongue of Prodromos perishes,
who could find its equal on earth and <another Prodromos>
proclaiming the emperor in similar fashion?
No one I think; even if I am deranged I dare to utter such words.

Prodromos implores his former student to report his critical situation to the emperor; otherwise, he will be snatched away by Hades and no one will be able to write panegyrics for his beloved emperor. As we have noted, such highly self-assertive statements from Prodromos are a typical feature of his poetry, even when they are camouflaged behind expressions of self-disparagement. Moreover, it is obvious that in the concluding lines he is emphasizing his profession as courtly orator, and he employs one of the principal tactics of poetry with a petitionary purpose: to support the supplicant courtly orator is to support the emperor himself. A similar tactic is found in the well-known hexametric poem addressed to the emperor Ioannes II Komnenos' sister, Anna Komnene (herself a writer of considerable repute), sometime in the late 1130s:[62]

ἀγχοῦ γὰρ θανάτοιο κατήλυθον, αὐτὸν ἐς Ἄδην.
ἢ φάθι καί τι τέλεσσον ἐπάξιον οἷο λόγοιο
ἤ με κύνεσσιν ἔα καὶ γύπεσι κύρμα γενέσθαι

Eleventh and Twelfth Centuries (Berkeley 1985), 130–33 and 220–30. Most modern scholars follow this view; see, for instance, Lauxtermann, *Byzantine Poetry*, vol. 1, 36. For a more nuanced view about this issue, see the case of Manuel Philes in Kubina, *Manuel Philes*, 187–99.
[61] Prodromos, *Historical poems*, 71.96–99.
[62] Prodromos, *Historical poems*, 38.116–18, trans. in Cullhed, 'Blind Bard', 58.

For I am now close to death, to Hades itself.
Either grant and bestow upon me a gift that matches this speech
or let me become a prey to dogs and vultures.

Here Prodromos claims, once more, that he is close to death, and makes demands for an equal recompense to his dazzling speech. But while both poems to Theodoros Styppeiotes and Anna Komnene, as well as many other poems by Prodromos, are swarming with explicit requests for remuneration, it is almost never clear what kind of compensation he expects: is it a high-ranking post, a financial gift, or a payment in kind? He does not hesitate to plead vociferously for rewards, but he never specifies their preferred nature. Of course, in most of the poems, he is asking for financial support using veiled language, such as the words τροφή and πόσις.[63] In contrast with Michael Psellos, for example, who asked in the most obvious manner for the emperor Michael IV to grant him a bureaucratic post,[64] Prodromos does not voice any such explicit request for a similar reward in his writings. What are we to make of this? Did Prodromos not desire such an appointment or want the social advancement it promised? Most probably he did; but it seems that he is much more subtle when it comes to making such requests.

In the poem for Anna Komnene, for instance, we may deduce a tentative answer to the question of what kind of reward Prodromos expected in compensation for his speech by taking a closer look at vv. 49–55, in which Prodromos gives a detailed summary of his education:[65]

καὶ δὴ γραμματικῆς μὲν ἀπείριτον οἶδμα θαλάσσης
50 εὔπλοος ἐξεπέρησα, φορὸν δέ με πνεῦμα κατέπνει,
ῥητροσύνης μετέπειτα τὸν εὔριπον ἐξεπλοήθην,
εὔριπον ἀτρεκέως, τῇ γὰρ καὶ τῇ μεταπίπτει
ἀστατέων καὶ ἄνδιχ᾽ ἀείστροφον οἶμον ἐλαύνει·
ὠκεανὸς δέ μ᾽ ἔδεκτο μετήλυδα φιλοσοφίας,
55 μείζων ὠκεανοῖο μέρος μέγα τοῦ περὶ γαίην·

And the boundless sea, that of grammar,
I passed through, sailing fair; a favourable wind blew upon me,
I then traversed the straits of rhetoric,
truly unstable, for it changes this way and that

---

[63] See Prodromos, *Fifth Ptochoprodromic poem*, v. 33.
[64] Lauxtermann, *Byzantine Poetry*, vol. 1, 35; and Bernard, *Poetry*, 171–73.
[65] Prodromos, *Historical poems*, 38.49–55.

inconstantly, and carves an ever-changing path.
The ocean of philosophy received me, a traveller,
much larger than the ocean that encircles the earth.

Prodromos makes use of marine imagery to describe his training: grammar is a fair sea, rhetoric a narrow strait, and philosophy a boundless ocean. This passage has been read by scholars as simply referring to his education,[66] and in particular to the tripartite structure of the *trivium*, which includes the study of grammar, rhetoric, and philosophy. But we might go a step further in inferring the purpose of this poem, when these verses are seen in conjunction with Anna Komnene's words in book 15 of the *Alexiad* about the technique of schedography.[67] According to Anna, during her times, the study of schedography came to occupy a more important place than the study of classics. As scholars have frequently noted, Anna's view on schedography, or at least on the new type of schedography that emerged in the twelfth century,[68] is entirely negative. Prodromos, on the other hand, appears to have been among the leading proponents of schedography and its transformation into a separate literary genre or game in the twelfth century.[69] It is hardly likely that Prodromos' poem to Anna Komnene was sent after the production of the last book of the *Alexiad*, in which her denigration of *schede* appears. However, it is very possible that the poet was aware of Anna's stance towards schedography, and particularly the type of schedography which he, above all others, was

---

[66] See Hörandner, *Historische Gedichte*, 24.

[67] Anna Komnene, *Alexias*, XV.7.9, 18–32: τοῦ δὲ σχέδους ἡ τέχνη εὕρημα τῶν νεωτέρων ἐστὶ καὶ τῆς ἐφ᾽ ἡμῶν γενεᾶς. [...] ἀλλὰ νῦν οὐδ᾽ ἐν δευτέρῳ λόγῳ τὰ περὶ τούτων τῶν μετεώρων καὶ ποιητῶν καὶ αὐτῶν συγγραφέων καὶ τῆς ἀπὸ τούτων ἐμπειρίας· πεττεία δὲ τὸ σπούδασμα καὶ ἄλλα τὰ ἔργα ἀθέμιτα. ταῦτα δὲ λέγω ἀχθομένη διὰ τὴν παντελῆ τῆς ἐγκυκλίου παιδεύσεως ἀμέλειαν. τοῦτο γάρ μου τὴν ψυχὴν ἀναφλέγει, ὅτι πολὺ περὶ ταῦτα ἐνδιατέτριφα, κἄν, ἐπειδὰν ἀπήλλαγμαι τῆς παιδαριώδους τούτων σχολῆς καὶ εἰς ῥητορικὴν παρήγγειλα καὶ φιλοσοφίας ἡψάμην καὶ μεταξὺ τῶν ἐπιστημῶν πρὸς ποιητὰς τε καὶ ξυγγραφεῖς ᾖξα καὶ τῆς γλώττης τοὺς ὄχθους ἐκεῖθεν ἐξωμαλισάμην, εἶτα ῥητορικῆς ἐπαρηγούσης ἐμοὶ κατέγνων τῆς {τοῦ} πολυπλόκου τῆς σχεδογραφίας πλοκῆς. (=The technique of schedography is a discovery of the younger people and of our generation. [...] But now not even second place is allotted to those more exalted studies, the works of writers in poetry and prose and the knowledge that comes from them. This pursuit and other improper subjects are a game. I say this because I am distressed by the complete neglect of general education. This enrages my mind because I spent much time on these same diversions, and when I escaped from these puerile studies and took up rhetoric and applied myself to philosophy and as part of these studies I turned eagerly to the writers of poetry and prose, and from them I smoothed out the roughness of my speech; and then with the help of rhetoric I recognized the contortions of the tortuous construction of schedography.); trans. R. H. Robins, *The Byzantine Grammarians: Their Place in History* (Berlin/Boston 1993; reprint Berlin 2011), 129 (with modifications).

[68] See P. A. Agapitos, 'Grammar, Genre and Patronage in the Twelfth Century: Redefining a Scientific Paradigm in the History of Byzantine Literature', *JÖB* 64 (2014), 1–22, at 5–8; and P. A. Agapitos, 'Anna Komnene and the Politics of Schedographic Training and Colloquial Discourse', *Νέα Ῥώμη* 10 (2013 [2014]), 89–107.

[69] See the discussion on pp. 54–56.

known to have excelled in. If we assume that these verses were composed, at least in part, as a response to Anna's repudiation of this grammatical exercise, it is no coincidence that he makes no explicit mention of schedography; indeed, he consciously establishes a hierarchy, from grammar (which is an implicit reference to schedography), to rhetoric, and finally philosophy. Thus, Prodromos' verses should also be seen as an effort to advertise his versatile teaching skills, to represent himself as a universal teacher, and perhaps to become something more than a *grammatikos*.[70]

Although I do agree with other modern scholars who have tended to see these complaints as the result of his failure to gain an official post, it is also important to interpret them as a kind of medium used by Prodromos to further advance his intellectual activity in Constantinople. Prodromos was a real virtuoso in voicing concerns about the futility of letters, with quite a number of his works addressing the close connection between education, social failure, and poverty. Three of these works—all included in the *Miscellaneous poems*—have scarcely been discussed in this regard: that is, the diptych *Verses of protest at seeing the disregard of learning* (poems 73–74) and the long essayistic poem *Verses of protest regarding Providence* (poem 75). No one has examined the place of these texts within the corpus of what we have termed as 'begging poetry'.[71] First of all, it should be emphasized that these poems depart significantly from those of his poems which display the traditional features of what we call 'rhetoric of poverty'.[72] Unlike the poems addressed to Anna Komnene or Theodoros Styppeiotes, Prodromos does not address a lofty patron, beseeching him or her for financial support in order to be able to carry on his literary activity, whose ultimate and sole purpose is the singing of their praise.

Take, for example, poem 75, which is not directed to a powerful patron. Instead, the poet laments the economic inequality between two social groups: artisans devoid of any education, and intellectuals. The former are presented

---

[70] This hypothesis becomes even more plausible when we think that Prodromos seems to have been a member of the philosophical circle promoted by Anna Komnene and her husband Nikephoros Bryennios. In addition to the strong philosophical focus of the novel for Bryennios, Prodromos addressed to him the work *To the caesar or for the colour green*, a philosophical treatise revolving around ancient colour theories; for the text, see J. A. Cramer, *Anecdota græca e codd. manuscriptis bibliothecarum oxoniensium*, 4 vols. (Oxford 1835), vol. 3, 216–21; for an English translation and partial commentary, see E. Cullhed, 'To the Caesar or For the Color Green', in: F. Spingou (ed.), *The Visual Culture of Later Byzantium (c. 1081–c. 1350)*, 2 vols. (Cambridge 2022), vol. 1, 337–89.

[71] For example, Beaton, 'Rhetoric', 3–4 says only the following about poems 75–76: 'in the highly elaborate Homeric pastiche in hexameters, "Lament for the low prestige of learning" (MPG 33: 1419–22) the underpaid scholar furiously bids his books farewell, saying he'd be better off watching actors or streetshows. Since he refuses to debase himself so far, there is nothing for him but to sit alone.'

[72] The same goes for the poem *Verses of protest at seeing the disregard of learning*.

as boorish and rude, the latter as genteel and well-mannered. Although this is not explicitly mentioned, there is no doubt that Prodromos places himself in the second group, putting himself forward as the voice of his fellow have-nots. An effective method used here to bolster the image of the virtuous intellectual is the comparison of boorish artisans with the slanderers Meletus and Anytus, pilloried as Socrates' accusers in Plato's *Apology*, making gracious intellectuals like Prodromos analogues to Socrates (vv. 107-111). The latter is always viewed as the symbol *par excellence* of true virtue and wisdom.[73]

What is even more interesting about this poem is that it appears to be closely related to Prodromos' prose treatise entitled *On those who curse Providence on account of poverty* (Hörandner no. 151). As in the poem, the prose work employs similar motifs and phrasing,[74] but, more importantly, it also deals with inequality in terms of wealth between uneducated artisans and educated men, and the pivotal role of Providence and Fortune in the prosperity enjoyed by each of these two groups. An essential distinction should be made between these two texts, however: whereas the poem is a bold complaint against the inequality imposed on these two groups by Providence, the prose work refutes the argument that Providence is to be blamed for the inequality between them. Paul Magdalino has pointed out the close ties between the two works, noting: 'Prodromos did, however, balance this [the poem] with a more benign, prose treatise on Providence'.[75] On the other hand, Panagiotis Roilos has argued that the two works are examples of the fundamental rhetorical exercises of confirmation and refutation: the prose work is a sort of *anaskeuē*, rebutting the statement that Providence is to be blamed for this inequality, while the poem is a *kataskeuē*, offering confirmation of the statement that this inequality is directed by Providence.[76] I am not sure whether we have to do with a confirmation and a refutation, since the viewpoints adopted in the two works are not diametrically opposite. Rather, they offer slightly different perspectives on the same topic. Whatever the case, it is very possible that the two works were used for Prodromos' students. Practical reasons may have necessitated the employment of prose and metre, chiefly the teaching of verse and prose composition. Thus the poem and the prose work form a diptych used as an example of how one can write

---

[73] For Socrates in Byzantium, see M. Trizio, 'Socrates in Byzantium', in: C. Moore (ed.), *Brill's Companion to the Reception of Socrates* (Leiden/Boston 2019), 592-615.
[74] The text of the prose treatise is edited in *PG* 133, col. 1291-1312; all similarities between the two texts are noted in the apparatus fontium and the commentary of the poem.
[75] P. Magdalino, 'Cultural Change? The Context of Byzantine Poetry from Geometres to Prodromos', in: F. Bernard and K. Demoen (eds), *Poetry and Its Contexts*, 19-36, at 29.
[76] See Roilos, *Amphoteroglossia*, 297.

two works on the same topic in different forms and from slightly different points of view.

As noted above, in many of his works Prodromos refers to his education by establishing a hierarchical order which gives different statuses to grammar, rhetoric, and philosophy. As with the poem to Anna, he makes the prose treatise *On those who curse Providence on account of poverty* into a highly self-referential work:[77]

> Ἔγωγε, ὦ παρόντες (ἀλλ' ἀπείη Ἀδράστεια), γένους μὲν οὐ παντάπασι γέγονα χαμαιζήλου, ἀλλ' ἔστιν ἂν καὶ ζηλωτοῦ τοῖς πολλοῖς. Τὰ δέ μοι κατὰ τὸ σῶμα, κἂν εἰ μὴ τῆς ἄγαν ἀρίστης τετυχήκασι κράσεως, τέως γε μὴν οὐθὲν εἰλήχασιν[78] κολοβόν. Διδασκάλων προσεφοίτησα τοῖς ἀρίστοις· γραμματικὴν προὐτελέσθην· ῥητορείαν ἐξεμυήθην, οὐχ ἣν οἱ ψυχροὶ Σιμόκατοι καὶ οἱ κατ' αὐτούς, εἰπεῖν οἰκειότερον, ἀποπέρδουσιν, ἀλλ' ἣν Ἀριστεῖδαι καὶ Πλάτωνες ἀναπνέουσι. Τῆς Ἀριστοτέλους φιλοσοφίας, τῆς Πλάτωνος ὑψηλολογίας,[79] τῆς ἐν γραμμαῖς καὶ ἀριθμοῖς θεωρίας, ἔχω μὲν λέγειν ὡς οὐδὲν ἀφῆκα κατόπιν·

> But I, my fellows, and I say this without boasting, I hail from a family that is not entirely humble and may even seem envious to many. As far as my body goes, even though I don't happen to have an excellent constitution, at least I have not been maimed in any way. I trained with the most excellent teachers; I was first initiated in grammar; I was instructed in rhetoric, not the nonsense that ineffectual people like Simocates and their associates, to say it more appropriately, fart out, but the rhetoric that Aristides and Plato exhale. I can say that I have left behind nothing of Aristotle's philosophy, Plato's sublime ideas, geometry and algebra.

This passage involves an elaborate construction of a persona. The I-person takes pride in his education, ranging from grammar to the rhetoric of Aristides and Plato and Aristotle's philosophy. A few features should be noted here. First of all, the phrase 'ἔγωγε, ὦ παρόντες…' suggests an oral delivery, almost certainly before his students (or, alternatively, a group of literati). The prose work is further characterized by similar word combinations, e.g. 'ὦ φίλ' ἑταῖρε',[80] while v. 51 of the poem (Οὐκ ἀγνοῶ γοῦν, ὡς προείρηκα φθάσας)

---

[77] Prodromos, *On those who curse Providence on account of poverty*, 1297A–B.
[78] The ms. reads εἰλήχεσαν (sic).   [79] The edition reads ὑψολολογίας.
[80] Prodromos, *On those who curse Providence on account of poverty*, 1296B.

points in the same direction.[81] Furthermore, the passage from the prose work contains some evidence about Prodromos' education and life, and even a mention of his disease.

The insertion of self-referential information into a potentially didactic text is quite interesting.[82] Perhaps it was an effective medium to arouse the interest of his students or to enhance the teacher's authority in a school setting. In either case, it leads us back to the question of why twelfth-century poets included such complaints in their works. I do not question that social inequality may have led Prodromos and other poets to write poems full of complaints about their critical situation, but it is worth pointing out that the futility of literary pursuits was also an established literary *topos*.[83] A good example in this respect is the poem by Michael Haploucheir, in which the author expresses the same woes about the pointlessness of learning in the form of a dialogue.[84] That said, unlike Prodromos, Haploucheir was not a professional writer in pursuit of a high-ranking job. He was a member of the senate and an *orphanotrophos*, not an indigent teacher. This circumstance leads to the following question: why, then, did Haploucheir write a work filled with such woes? I am inclined to believe that the futility of letters had been established as a literary *topos* by the time Haploucheir picked up his pen to write his text. Moreover, as with Haploucheir's text, in which this motif does not serve an obvious extraliterary aim, some works by Prodromos lack this evident purpose as well. How else, then, should we interpret its integration into texts apparently intended for use in a school setting?

The definitive study of 'begging poetry' remains to be written: so far there has been no attempt to map this varied corpus and explore its history in the middle and late Byzantine periods. One thing is certain, though: 'begging poetry' emerged in a variety of genres and thematic settings.[85] We cannot

---

[81] Tzetzes makes use of similar phrases in his Homeric *Allegories*, dedicated to Bertha-Eirene of Sulzbach, the wife of Manuel I Komnenos; cf. Rhoby, 'Ioannes Tzetzes', at 162.

[82] The same has been argued for Tzetzes' letter correspondence and *Historiai* in Grünbart, 'Byzantinisches Gelehrtenelend', 414; cf. also A. Pizzone, 'The Historiai of John Tzetzes: A Byzantine "Book of Memory"?', *BMGS* 41.2 (2017), 182–207, at 204–05.

[83] As already noted in E. C. Bourbouhakis, ' "Political" Personae: The Poem from Prison of Michael Glykas: Byzantine Literature between Fact and Fiction', *BMGS* 31 (2007), 53–75, esp. 66: 'But rather than look to socio-economic circumstances, is it not just as likely that once in circulation within a genre, it became a topos, a literary motif at the disposal of writers quick to exploit a theme closely associated with certain forms?'.

[84] Ed. P. Leone, 'Michaelis Hapluchiris versus cum excerptis', *Byz* 39 (1969), 251–83.

[85] Krystina Kubina has argued that many poems of Manuel Philes which we would term as begging poems are in fact letters in verse; cf. Kubina, 'Begging Poet', 147–81; cf. also Kubina, *Manuel Philes*, 67–70. In the case of Prodromos, it is not always easy to classify many petitionary poems as letters: see N. Zagklas, 'Epistolarity in Twelfth-Century Byzantine Poetry: Singing Praises and Asking Favours *in Absentia*', in: K. Kubina and A. Riehle (eds), *Epistolary Poetry in Byzantium and Beyond: An Anthology with Critical Essays* (New York 2021), 64–77, at 67–68.

speak about a single genre of 'begging poetry', but we can say that it is a common theme that typifies many texts. I would argue that the lamentations of such authors used for social disparagement were turned into a kind of 'discursive mode'[86] employed across various types of poems, orations, letters, and even didactic works. As with other discursive forms or modes, such as *ekphrasis* or encomium, the 'rhetoric of poverty' spread through various types of twelfth-century poetry and prose, becoming integral to much of the literature written around this time.

This mode penetrated not only the works Prodromos directed to certain patrons but also works written for his students. Thus, these works of lament were used in different settings, and the embedded complaints acquired the form of a recurring thematic feature. Returning to the question of reality or fictionality of such works that has occupied many modern scholars,[87] in his study on Michael Glykas' *Prison Poem*, Bourbouhakis notes:[88]

> In effect, I am suggesting that we are sometimes too quick to look for social or other external factors which shaped the contents of Byzantine literature, without acknowledging the autonomy of the Byzantine imagination. A popular topos need not reflect genuine circumstances in order to achieve widespread currency; its origins and growth are more often a matter of the history of literature than the history of society. Of course, the former is an intrinsic part of the latter and can be read with a view to the sort of meaning Byzantine audiences found credible. Still, we should be wary about drawing direct correspondences between literature and actual circumstances. Literature depends, to a significant extent, on imaginative 'distortion'.

I am not sure I fully agree with Bourbouhakis' view; in my opinion, reality and imagination are not mutually exclusive, but rather interconnected. They coexist and overlap, making it difficult for us to distinguish between the 'model' and 'empiric' author.[89] In many twelfth-century works the first-person narrator and the poet converge to such a degree that they collapse into one; undoubtedly, in many cases they are identical. This should not be seen as a problem, but rather as a logical consequence of the process of writing. If we do not accept that this duality is present in Byzantine occasional literature, its

---

[86] See Lauxtermann, *Byzantine Poetry*, vol. 2, 19.
[87] See, for example, the response to Bourbouhakis' views about the fictionality of Michael Glykas' prison poem in M. D. Lauxtermann, 'Tomi, Mljet, Malta: Critical Notes on a Twelfth-Century Southern Italian Poem of Exile', *JÖB* 64 (2014), 155–76, at 159, note 23.
[88] Bourbouhakis, '"Political" Personae', 66.
[89] For these terms and their application to Manasses, see Nilsson, *Constantine Manasses*, 86–112.

very essence will be annulled. Even when a poet assumes an ethopoetic persona, the poems still contain some vestiges of truth about the author himself. For instance, irrespective of whether Prodromos assumes the persona of poor *pater familias* or wretched monk in his vernacular poems, or a Homeric mask in some of his hexametric poems, in such cases he nevertheless speaks about a dire poverty which is not entirely fictional. We should definitely be cautious in accepting these narrative strategies as conveying a completely truthful report of the writer's experience, but at the same time it would be wrong to argue that it is all literary fabrication. Because if we do so, we run the risk of deconstructing the sociocultural background of the author and thereby failing to determine the driving forces behind the composition of a specific text.

I would say that many twelfth-century poems resemble a magnifying glass which focuses on and thereby greatly amplifies one aspect of the life of a twelfth-century author. The fact that Prodromos styled himself as a poor intellectual is a form of self-fashioning, which may seem unwarranted or even a bit extravagant to the modern reader, but it helped Prodromos to amplify his authorial voice and the efficacy of his pleas. As has been said, Prodromos was fully aware that he was making his living both from his writings and from teaching. The number of his students could increase through an increase in commissions, while the mode of complaints would have an impact on the number of his commissions and thereby also students. At the same time, this was his style and his thematic palette in various works that are not necessarily the result of socio-economic causes. The mode of complaints became an integral part of his writing style: another distinctive feature of his personal literary brand which soon was imitated by his peers.

2.3. The Court, *Theatron*, and Classroom as 'Communicating Vessels'

Up to now, Prodromos' activity in three main performative settings—the court, the so-called 'rhetorical *theatron*', which stands for literary gatherings in Byzantium,[90] and the classroom—have been discussed. These three

---

[90] The term 'rhetorical *theatron*' is inclusive and elusive at the same time. In the twelfth century, it stands for the place where an author presented some of his works to potential literary patrons or even the setting in which he could defend his intellectual reputation in the presence of other peers. For some brief notes about the term in the eleventh century, see Bernard, *Poetry*, 98–101. For the element of intellectual antagonism in Prodromos' poetry, see N. Zagklas, 'Satire in the Komnenian Period: Poetry, Satirical Strands and Intellectual Antagonism', in: P. Marciniak and I. Nilsson (eds), *Satire in the Middle Byzantine Period: The Golden Age of Laughter?* (Leiden/Boston 2020), 279–303.

settings, which supported the cultural life of the capital, were very close, both physically and socially. Occasionally it is hard to distinguish between them since, for example, a rhetorical *theatron* could be held at court. In this section, I want to show the close connections between these three settings as venues for the consumption of Prodromos' textual production. In doing so, I want to challenge, to a certain degree, the idea that the original occasion for which a work was composed determined its function for good.[91] Though the occasion shaped the work upon its initial performance, works often enjoyed subsequent lives in new contexts.

Most poems and epigrams by Prodromos have come down to us only as 'literary' texts; consequently, the original occasion which triggered their composition is, in many cases, entirely unclear.[92] The existence of certain indications, such as rubrics, content, inscribed recipients, vocabulary, and so on, may occasionally allow us to reconstruct their initial function (as I have noted earlier),[93] but such reconstructions naturally do not convey a full picture of the original occasion and context. The pursuit of a text's original occasion becomes even more difficult when one considers that many twelfth-century authors, and particularly Theodoros Prodromos, did not adhere to specific conventions, rules, and forms. On the contrary, he broke barriers and crossed conventional boundaries. One of his most ground-breaking experiments was the conversion of the *schedos* from a mere grammatical exercise, exclusively designed for teaching purposes, into a self-standing literary genre suitable for performance at court[94]—or, as Garzya has put it, a kind of 'game', reaching its peak of popularity in the second quarter of the twelfth century.[95] Even Prodromos himself uses the word παίγνια ('game') to describe the composition and use of *schede*.[96]

Ioannis Vassis was the first modern scholar to demonstrate that Prodromos transformed schedography into a vehicle for the praise of Constantinopolitan imperial and upper-class patrons. In a seminal article,[97] he edited two such *schede* for the very first time, calling the attention of modern scholars to the elevation of schedography into a sort of new type of

---

[91] For the blurry line between use and function, see Kubina, *Manuel Philes*, 164–65.
[92] There is of course no strict distinction between 'functional' and 'purely literary' texts; see the discussion in Bernard, *Poetry*, 112–24.
[93] See pp. 16–20.
[94] Vassis, 'Theodoros Prodromos', 13; for a more recent study, see Agapitos, 'Schedourgia'.
[95] A. Garzya, 'Literarische und rhetorische Polemiken', 8; cf. also Mullett, 'Patronage', 182: 'and the new schedography, not so much a way of teaching grammar, more a tortuous game'.
[96] Cf. Prodromos, *Historical poems*, 79.45; for a different interpretation of this word, see Hörandner, 'Prodromos and the City', 61.
[97] Vassis, 'Theodoros Prodromos'.

court oratory. The first *schedos*, an encomium on St Nicholas, concludes with a verse epilogue prayer:[98]

Νικόλαε, φρούρει με συνήθως πάλιν·
οἶδας, πνέω σε, μαρτύρων οὐ προσδέῃ·
κανικλείου, ῥύου με συνήθως πάλιν·
οἶδας, φιλῶ σε, μαρτύρων οὐ προσδέῃ·
αὐτοκράτορ κράτιστε, βλαστὲ πορφύρας
(σὲ γὰρ ἐπισφράγισμα ποιῶ τοῦ λόγου),
νίκα τὸν ἐχθρόν, ὅστις ἀντάροιτό σοι,
μέμνησο τῆς σῆς προδρομικῆς ἑστίας
καὶ Νικολάου συμμαχοῦντος εὐτύχει.

Nicholas, protect me again as always;
you know that I inhale you, no proof is necessary.
Kanikleios,[99] save me again as always;
you know that I regard you with affection, no proof is necessary.
Most powerful emperor, offspring of purple
—for I make you the concluding seal of my work—
triumph over the enemy that may rise up against you,
remember the house of your Prodromos
and may you fare well with Nicholas as ally.

The *schedos*, then, has acquired a function comparable to other works written for performance in the court. Prodromos beseeches St Nicholas to protect the emperor in his struggle against the enemies of the empire, while the *epi tou Kanikleiou*—none other than Theodoros Styppeiotes—and the emperor are asked to rescue Prodromos once again from his oppressive poverty. And a triple plea for help directed to St Nicholas, Styppeiotes, and the emperor is not only part of the verse epilogue but also part of the prose text of the *schedos*. As Vassis has already pointed out, historical poem 72, a verse letter addressed to the *epi tou Kanikleiou*, Theodoros Styppeiotes, asks the high-ranking official to assist the poet, exhibiting some structural similarities to the *schedos*.[100] Just like the verse letter, the *schedos* was sent to Styppeiotes, perhaps even suggesting that they were sent together as a kind of diptych.[101]

---

[98] For the text of the *schedos*, see Vassis, 'Theodoros Prodromos', 16.
[99] The *epi tou kanikleiou* was a high-ranking title for one of the private imperial secretaries who kept the inkwell used by the emperor to sign official documents (cf. *ODB* 2 1101).
[100] Vassis, 'Theodoros Prodromos', 12.   [101] Zagklas, 'Prose and Verse', 239–40.

The second *schedos*, which Vassis included in his study to show the gradual development of schedography from a grammatical exercise into a fully fledged performative genre, is a text on the occasion of the death of Sevastokrator Andronikos, son of Alexios I Komnenos. This *schedos* is a consolatory text for Andronikos' mother Eirene Doukaina, and it should be read together with a prose monody as well as a hexametric poem of consolation (again for Eirene Doukaina).[102] We have, therefore, a triptych by Prodromos, of which each part fulfils a slightly different role in the multilayered process of mourning for a deceased person.[103] A further example demonstrating that schedography evolved into a separate literary genre is *historical poem* 56, in which Prodromos praises the Orphanotrophos Alexios Aristenos in four different metres. Unfortunately, the text of the *schedos* does not survive, but at the very beginning of the poem we are told that the Orphanotrophos had previously been celebrated by Prodromos in a prose discourse and a *schedos*.[104] In these three examples, we can see Prodromos' effort to achieve rhetorical variety by producing works in diverse forms for the same occasion, and a demonstration of the transformation of schedography from a school exercise into a fully fledged oratorical discourse.

In addition to the two *schede* edited by Vassis and the reference in the poem for the Orphanotrophos Alexios Aristenos, Ioannis Polemis has discovered and edited a *schedos* with many 'everyday words' which, he argues, corroborates the identification of Prodromos with (Ptocho)prodromos.[105] The verse epilogue of the *schedos* explicitly indicates that it was sent to a βασιλίς, which is probably to be identified with Eirene the Sevastokratorissa. More recently, Panagiotis Agapitos has discussed this *schedos* further by emphasizing its mixed language and the coexistence of playfulness and seriousness. He even argues that these features made such compositions appealing for many literary magnates. In another *schedos* Prodromos even describes his *schede* as oysters: they may have a rough shell, but they contain pearls. Prodromos took pride in his *schedourgia* and used it as a medium to compliment his patrons and ask for rewards, as he did in many of his poems.[106]

Given that schedography transcended the boundaries of the classroom and occasionally assumed the role of panegyric and petition, it is tempting to ask whether certain poems written for an occasion at court may in turn have

---

[102] Vassis, 'Theodoros Prodromos', 13 and 18–19.
[103] Agapitos, '*Schedourgia*', 18 and Zagklas, 'Prose and Verse', 241.
[104] Cf. Prodromos, *Historical Poems*, 56a.4: ὑμνησάμην σε πρῶτα πεζῷ τῷ λόγῳ and 9: ἐμελψάμην σε δεύτερον σχεδουργίᾳ; First, I praised you with prose discourse [...] then, I celebrated you with schedourgy; trans. In Agapitos, '*Schedourgia*', 19.
[105] See Polemis, 'Προβλήματα', 288–89.   [106] Agapitos, '*Schedourgia*', 9–12.

entered the classroom to be used by Prodromos as exemplary pieces for his own students. This study is not the place to discuss the Byzantine educational system in full, but we know that poetry was a part of grammatical instruction; as Floris Bernard has pointed out 'teaching in grammar includes exercises in the composition of poetry'.[107] As a grammarian, one of the subjects Prodromos would have taught was poetry, particularly ancient Greek poetry, including Homer, tragedy, and other forms. Even the personified 'grammar' in Prodromos' cycle on virtues and vices points to her close ties to poetry when talking about her qualities: 'I am the one who brings narratives together, I form words correctly, and attend to metre'. This illustrates how close the teaching of grammar and poetry in Byzantium were: grammar taught the composition of good poetry, including, of course, instruction in correct versification. And this close association of grammar with poetry in education was not just a theoretical statement, since many poems offering instructions for the correct composition of poetry were written by teachers. As mentioned above, Prodromos' fellow grammarian, the monk Ioannikios, was the author of Ps. Psellian poem 14, which is a short verse treatise aimed at training the student in the composition of correct iambs.

Training in poetry was sandwiched between the learning of grammar and rhetoric. Nicholas Mesarites (c. 1163–1217), in his epitaph on his brother Ioannes, tells us that Ioannes started writing poetry after acquiring a full command of the art of schedography.[108] But once the students had learned their grammar lessons and moved on to rhetoric, they did not forget the former.[109] The transition from one educational stage to the next had no definitive boundary. For example, the teaching of grammar could be combined with the use of progymnasmata (preparatory rhetorical exercises), and many twelfth-century *schede* acquired the form of progymnasmata. The ms. Vat. Pal. gr. 92, for example, includes many progymnasmata that are complex antistoichic *schede*,[110] corroborating that grammar and rhetoric as well as technical grammatical questions and issues of content coexist in many teaching exercises.

---

[107] Bernard, *Poetry*, 220.
[108] Nikolaos Mesarites, *Epitaphios for John Mesarites*, 28.15: Ἦν μὲν οὖν τὰ τῆς σχεδογραφίας ἐμμελετῶν τελεώτερα ἀκμαιότερόν τε καὶ συντονώτερον. ἔαρ κινοῦν εἰς ἰαμβεῖα ὡς εἰς τὰς ᾠδὰς τὰ στρουθία τοὺς τῶν παίδων μουσικωτέρους (=he therefore settled down to studying advanced schedography with greater enthusiasm and application. With spring inspiring the more musical of pupils to poetry as birds to song); trans. in M. Angold, *Nicholas Mesarites: His Life and Works (in Translation)* (Liverpool 2017), 153.
[109] For example, the progymnasmata stand for the transition between reading and writing; cf. R. Webb, *Ekphrasis, Imagination and Persuasion in Ancient Rhetorical Theory and Practice* (Farnham 2009), 17–19.
[110] Vassis, 'Φιλολόγων Παλαίσματα', 42.

Another development that emerges in twelfth-century teaching practice is the use of works with loose connections to everyday life. Robert Browning has pointed out that some school exercises are associated with a concrete historical event.[111] On this basis, Floris Bernard has argued that some eleventh-century poems were used as 'poetic exercises'; in particular, poems 8 and 52 by Christophoros Mitylenaios are such exercises, due to their attention to metrical and linguistic issues,[112] with the former referring to the death of Romanos, and the latter to the downfall of Michael V. It is true that the difficulty of various technical issues in writing and analysing poetry could be outweighed by the appealing content of these exemplary poems. Stimulating content could reduce the tedium of learning the rules of prosody and vocabulary and captivate the interest of the students. I would not go so far as to argue that some of the *Historical poems* by Prodromos are preparatory exercises intended to be used exclusively in a school setting, but it would be hardly surprising if a number of his ceremonial poems were 'recycled' and subsequently introduced into the classroom. Fortunately, we can extract an answer to this question from a poem addressed to Theodoros Styppeiotes:[113]

ἔτι τυγχάνων ἐν παισίν, ἔτι τὰ σχέδη γράφων
καὶ γραμματικευόμενος καὶ ποιηταῖς προσέχων
ἐξήρτησό μου τῶν σχεδῶν, ἐξήρτησο τῶν στίχων,
ἐκείνων δὲ καὶ μάλιστα τῶν ὑπὲρ βασιλέως·

still among children, still writing *schede*
and attending grammar school and preoccupied with poets
you were hanging on my *schede*, hanging on my verses,
particularly those praising the Emperor.

Two things should be noted here: first, in order to celebrate the victories of the emperor, Prodromos made use not only of poetry but also of schedography; second, and more importantly, both his *schede* and poems that praise the emperor were used both in the court and in the classroom. This seems to be the only instance in the entire Prodromean oeuvre where we find an explicit reference to the use of imperial panegyrics as a teaching tool (poetic exercise) for his students.

---

[111] R. Browning, 'schedografia', 22.
[112] Bernard, *Poetry*, 222–29; for a different view of the function of Mitylenaios' poem 8, see Lauxtermann, 'Byzantine Poetry', vol. 2, 81.
[113] Prodromos, *Historical poems*, 71.7–10.

But what reasons might have spurred Prodromos to introduce some of his ceremonial poetry in his teaching? Perhaps the lack of books, about which he constantly complains in many of his works, such as the encomium for the Patriarch Ioannes IX Agapetos and the poem *Verses of protest regarding Providence*, as well as in the satirical works *The Plato-lover, or the tanner* and *Sale of the political and poetical lives*.[114] But I believe the driving forces behind the practice of recycling the same work in various contexts are different. As I have already argued, Prodromos' fame as teacher and therefore the number of students he could attract were closely connected with his renown as one of the most celebrated rhetoricians and court poets of his time. As such, it would be surprising if he did not use some of his well-known poems as exemplary models in the training of his students, who were likely to become either grammarians themselves or staff members of the Komnenian bureaucracy, producing verses for their patrons and masters. Prodromos' peer Stephanos Meles, who served as *Logothetes tou Dromou*, was responsible for the composition of imperial panegyrics in verse.[115] Others even had to demonstrate their poetic skills to acquire a post. To enter the service of *Megas Hetairiarches* Georgios Palaiologos as a grammarian, Leo tou Megistou had to demonstrate his skills by improvising a poem on the spot about a stone relief depicting the muse Kalliope.[116]

Furthermore, Prodromos' use of some of his ceremonial poems in the classroom corroborates what Browning has noted about the developments in the thematic focus of teaching material.[117] It also corresponds with Prodromos' 'modernism' in the pedagogical method he developed in his approach to schedography—in sharp contrast with other intellectuals of his time, such as Anna Komnene, Eustathios of Thessaloniki and Ioannes Tzetzes.[118] However, it should be stressed that Prodromos was not alone in his progressive use of schedography; many well-known literati and successful teachers made extensive use of these compositions. Prodromos' teacher, Stephanos Skylitzes, as we learn from Prodromos' monody for him, was intensely preoccupied with the composition of *schede*.[119] Indeed, ms. Laurent.

---

[114] For these passages, see p. 330.

[115] Meles is praised for his poetic talent in the writing of imperial orations in verse in historical poem 69, vv. 1–17. Meles is, moreover, the author of two surviving poems: see O. Delouis, 'La Vie métrique de Théodore Stoudite par Stéphane Mélès (BHG1755m)', *AnBoll* 132 (2014), 21–54.

[116] O. Lampsidis, 'Die Entblößung der Muse Kalliope in einem byzantinischen Epigramm', *JÖB* 47 (1997), 107–10.

[117] Browning, 'schedografia', 22.   [118] See Agapitos, 'Grammar', 1–22.

[119] We are told that the burden of schedography ceased to trouble Stephanos Skylitzes when he was appointed teacher at the Orphanotropheion of St Paul; cf. Prodromos, *Orations*, 38.267.82–84: καὶ ὁμοῦ μὲν τῶν περὶ σχεδογραφίαν ἀπελύθη καμάτων, ὁμοῦ δὲ ψήφῳ βασιλικῇ τὸν διδασκαλικὸν διέπειν ἔλαχε θρόνου τῆς τοῦ μεγίστου Παύλου διατριβῆς.

Conv. Soppr. 2, fol. 204ᵛ, transmits an unpublished *schedos* in the form of letter in which the author speaks about his critical situation. The rubric of this particular *schedos* reads τοῦ κυροῦ Στεφάνου τοῦ Τραπεζοῦντος,[120] which leaves no doubt that it was written by Stephanos Skylitzes, who served as *maistor* in the Orphanotropheion of St Paul before becoming Metropolitan of Trebizond. On the other hand, the fact that Prodromos made use of some modern methods does not mean that he rejected 'tradition'. His commentary on Aristotle's *Posterior Analytics*, for example, clearly demonstrates that he remained faithful to the exegetical tradition that enjoyed immense popularity around this time.[121] I would, therefore, describe him as an easily adaptable intellectual and teacher operating both within and beyond the boundaries of established literary tradition and conventional educational techniques.[122]

These boundaries, often blurred, between classroom and other performative settings seem to have further implications for the circulation and consumption of texts. Let us go back to the relationship between patronage and composition in the works of Prodromos. A great deal of his work was the outcome of a patronage system, from which both he and his patrons benefitted. But literary patronage was a complex phenomenon that took various forms and incentivized different types of texts, ranging from gifts and dedications to commissions and works in which the author sought assistance to carry on his literary activity.[123] In some cases, Prodromos even combined these forms of patronage. For example, in some ceremonial poems for the emperor, he complains about his grim situation and the neglect of learned men by the emperor, while articulating another plea for help, thus combining the tropes of imperial encomium with that of lament and supplication. At the same time, not all his works were the outcome of direct patronage; for example, the two poems about his illness (*Historical poems* 77 and 78) appear to indicate a personal moment of literary genesis. Both poems are personal prayers based on the structure of Gregory of Nazianzus' *Carm.* II, 1, 55.[124] On another occasion—as we have seen in Chapter 1—Prodromos acted as donor of six

---

[120] Polemis, 'Προβλήματα', 281; see also Nesseris, Παιδεία, vol. 1, 120.

[121] See, for example, P. A. Agapitos, 'The Politics and Practices of Commentary in Komnenian Byzantium', in B. van den Berg, D. Manolova, and P. Marciniak (eds), *Byzantine Commentaries on Ancient Greek Texts, 12th–15th Centuries* (Cambridge 2022), 41–60.

[122] There is a single exception, however: unlike many contemporary writers, who produced didactic poetry in political verse, Prodromos did not make use of this type of teaching exercise. Instead he seems to have preferred dodecasyllables and hexameters for his poetic exercises: see N. Zagklas. '"How Many Verses Shall I Write and Say?": Writing Poetry in the Komnenian Period', in: W. Hörandner, A. Rhoby, and N. Zagklas (eds), *A Companion to Byzantine Poetry* (Leiden/Boston 2019), 237–63, at 255.

[123] See Bernard, *Poetry*, 291–333.

[124] Zagklas, 'Appropriation in the Service of Self-Representation', 239–40.

hymnical prayers addressed to St Paul, Gregory of Nazianzus, Basil the Great, John Chrysostom, Gregory of Nyssa, and St Nicholas (*Miscellaneous poems* 1–6). All six are closely connected to pictorial representations in the Church of the Orphanotropheion of St Paul.[125] These texts do not appear to solicit a material gift for their composition, but rather express longing for spiritual salvation. Although it is possible that at some point they were performed in a literary *theatron* or the classroom—both venues that would help him attract more attention from his peers—it cannot be denied that their original purpose was not directly related to mundane patronage. For this reason, it is critical to distinguish, when possible, between responding to the patronage of wealthy individuals and the composition of works to express personal piety, or, to put it even more clearly, between 'transactional' and 'devotional' composition.

But for many other works by Prodromos the exact circumstances of their textual genesis are not clear. We do not have any internal or external evidence to the texts to indicate whether they are result of literary patronage, personal piety, or pedagogical necessity. For example, some of Prodromos' major works do not record a recipient in their manuscript tradition. This is the case for the poetic cycles of tetrastichs on the Old and New Testaments, the three Hierarchs, the great martyrs Theodoros, Georgios, and Demetrios, and the two verse calendars. How should we interpret the lack of any evidence in the rubrics? One might argue that this situation results simply from the precarious process by which works were disseminated or that they were written for an alternative setting of textual consumption (such as an ecclesiastical context) that would not indicate a recipient. Such explanations may be correct, but I would like to suggest another possibility. As we have remarked in the previous chapter, poems 62–66 may have simply been literary reflections without necessarily serving a pragmatic need at the time of their composition. But it is possible that these literary reflections later acquired a fixed place in a real-life occasion. As Floris Bernard has pointed out, literature as *Selbstzweck* and *Sitz im Leben* are not always diametrical opposites.[126] Many works by Prodromos may have initially been composed within his self-contained literary world and only later used on a specific occasion. Prodromos could have held a collection of such works in reserve, whose genesis may not be obviously connected to an occasion. However, this does not mean that he did not draw from this reserve—when necessary—to retrieve whichever composition would fit a real-life occasion. I would argue that some of the

---

[125] See above pp. 24–30.   [126] Bernard, *Poetry*, 336.

Miscellaneous poems could be part of this repository, and could subsequently have been applied in different settings: the court, the *theatron*, the classroom, and other sites suitable for textual consumption.

It is not a coincidence that the function of many of these works is elusive. Some of them could have been used on various real-life occasions. The poetic cycle on virtues and vices (poems 29–54) is a case in point. It is possible that some of the twenty-six epigrams were used as inscriptions for depictions of virtues and vices on various kinds of objects, but we cannot exclude the possibility that they were presented to his students. Indeed, the strongly moralizing tone of most of them points in this direction.[127] Additionally, they could have also been used as riddles for the students, especially if Prodromos presented them in the class without their rubrics. A good example of a poem that could potentially have had a dual function is the first epigram on the *Dodekaorton* (poem 22), the festal cycle of the church:

Εὐαγγελισμός, γέννα, κλήσεως θέσις,
χεὶρ Συμεών, βάπτισμα, φῶς Θαβωρίου,
Λάζαρος ἐκ γῆς, βαΐα, σταυροῦ ξύλον,
ἔγερσις, ἄρσις, Πνεύματος παρουσία.

Annunciation, Nativity, the name-giving,
the hand of Simeon, Baptism, the light of Tabor,
Lazarus from the depths, Palm Sunday, the wood of the Cross,
Resurrection, Ascension, the appearance of the Holy Spirit.

Here the rhetorical technique of the so-called 'verse-filling asyndeton' is used,[128] squeezing all twelve Christological feasts together in just four lines. The poem could not only be read in one breath, but it also potentially acquires a double function. First, it could have been used to inscribe an object with a small surface area; and second, as a mnemonic text to help the students to memorize all the twelve Christological feasts of the *Dodekaorton*.[129] And this is not the only work from the corpus of *Miscellaneous poems* to build upon

---

[127] See W. Hörandner, 'Teaching with Verse in Byzantium', in: W. Hörandner, A. Rhoby, and N. Zagklas (eds), in *A Companion to Byzantine Poetry* (Leiden/Boston 2019), 459–86, at 471–72.

[128] For the Latin tradition, see E. R. Curtius, *Europäische Literatur und lateinisches Mittelalter* (Bern 1948), 287; for the Byzantine tradition, see the brief remarks in W. Hörandner, 'Epigrams on Icons and Sacred Objects: The Collection of Cod. Marc. gr. 524 Once Again', in: M. Salvadore (ed.), *La poesia tardoantica e medievale: Atti del I Convegno Internazionale di Studi, Macerata, 4-5 maggio 1998* (Alessandria 2001), 117–24, at 120, and Drpić, *Epigram*, 201.

[129] It is also worth noting that the poem survives on fol. 142^r of ms. Vind. Hist. 106, immediately following a mnemonic poem by Pediasimos on the twelve labours by Hercules.

the technique of 'verse-filling asyndeton'. A three-line epigram on the hospitality of Abraham (poem 8) reads:

Ἀβραάμ, Σάρρα, μόσχος, Ἰσμαήλ, Ἄγαρ,
ἄρτοι, τράπεζα, δρῦς, τὸ δῶμα, καὶ τέλος
Τριὰς Κύριος—τὸ ξένον!—ξενίζεται.

Abraham, Sarah, calf, Ishmael, Hagar,
loaves, table, oak, house, and finally
the Triune Lord—oh wonder—is the guest.

Since it recapitulates all the features necessary for the reconstruction of both the story and its iconographical representation, it indicates usage as both an inscription and a mnemonic exercise in a school context.

Poems 11–20 and 57–61 are poetic cycles of ten epigrams on St Barbara and five epigrams on a ring, respectively. As with other poems by Prodromos, they claim a potential double function. Since both poetic cycles are 'shuffling around the same words and conceits',[130] it is possible that they were written for a donor in order for him/her to choose the one most suited to the occasion.[131] But in the absence of a donor, a second possibility is that they were read in the classroom as a kind of rhetorical exercise or as exemplary poems, in order for Prodromos to show his students how stylistic and rhetorical variation on the same subject matter could be achieved. In fact, we know that one of the poems was used as a school exercise. The final epigram from the poetic cycle on St Barbara is transmitted in the Cypriot codex Vat. Reg. gr. PP Pii II 54, on fol. 409[r–v], among a collection of *schede*. The short epigram has indeed been turned into a *schedos* with interlinear glosses and various grammatical remarks (see Figure 2.1). Even if its performative context changed at later point, it is possible that it was used in a school setting in the twelfth century.

This is not the only text with an epigrammatic structure and nature to be used as an exercise. A verse *schedos* by a certain Christodoulos Hagioeuplites commemorating, once again, St Barbara, has come down to us, together with other *schede*, in Marc. gr. XI.31.[132] This non-antistoichic metrical *schedos*

---

[130] H. Maguire, *Image and imagination: The Byzantine Epigram as Evidence for Viewer Response* (Toronto 1996), 8–9.
[131] See Maguire, *Image*, 8–9; Lauxtermann, *Byzantine Poetry*, vol. 1, 42–43; Bernard, *Poetry*, 306–07; Drpić, *Epigram*, 37–39.
[132] Ὁρῶν σε, καλλίμαρτυ σεμνὴ Βαρβάρα, | ὁρῶν σε, καλλίνικε σεπτὴ παρθένε, | ὡς ἐξ ἀκάνθης ἀνατείλασαν ῥόδον | ἄρτι προκύψον τῆς κάλυκος ἡδύπνουν, | 5 εὐωδίας σοβοῦσαν ἀθέου πλάνης, | ἀγάμενος τέθηπα, πῶς ἔφυς ῥόδον | ἐκ τῆς ἀκάνθης τοῦ πατρὸς Διοσκόρου. | Φυεῖσα δ' ὡς εὔοσμον ἁπαλὸν ῥόδον | ἄκανθα γίνῃ τῷ πατρὶ τραχυτάτῳ, | 10 κεντοῦσα καὶ κνίζουσα τούτου τὰς

64 A WRITER ON COMMAND AND HIS STRATEGIES

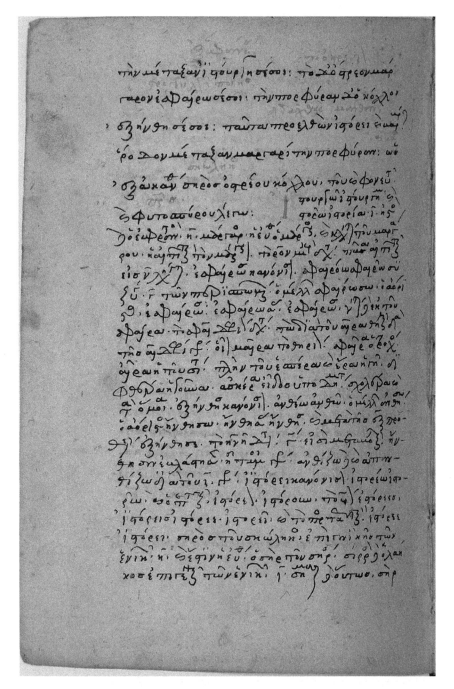

Figure 2.1 Vat. Reg. gr. PP Pii II 54, fol. 409[r-v]

2.3. THE COURT, *THEATRON*, AND CLASSROOM 65

resembles the cycle of poems on St Barbara in its wording. We can infer from its manuscript that Hagioeuplites penned this verse *schedos* as an exemplary poem for his own students, but if it had not been transmitted in a collection of schedographic material, we would not have guessed that it was used as such.[133] If anything, it appears as a conventional religious epigram; it opens with the formula Ὁρῶν σε[134] and continues with an extremely vivid description of Barbara's martyrdom, perhaps corresponding to a relevant depiction. Thus, Prodromos' and Hagioeuplites' epigrams on Barbara were probably used in their teaching. As noted earlier, poetry and schedography often intersect; they seem to be two overlapping circles, for both were taught at the very beginning of the *enkyklios paideia*. At the same time, one may rightly wonder whether many surviving poems, assumed to be literary epigrams, could in fact be verse *schede*.

That said, I think it is also imperative to distinguish—whenever possible—between texts designed to be used primarily in the classroom and those meant to be performed in other settings. It is clear that for some of the *Miscellaneous poems* the original circumstances of their textual genesis was a teaching environment. Such is probably the case for the four *ethopoiiai* (poems 69 and 70–72), but this does not mean that they were not reused in different settings later: presented, for instance, to a literary gathering. For other poems (e.g. poems 1–6, 9, 10, 26), we may posit an inscriptional or performative function in various imperial, ecclesiastical, or literary settings, but again this does not mean that they were not used at a later stage as models by Prodromos' students.

In addition to the potential double function of many of the *Miscellaneous poems*, as epigrams with both inscriptional and teaching value, some other texts by Prodromos may also have served a double function. As noted, the cycle of tetrastichs on the Old and New Testaments has no recipient; in fact,

---

φρένας | καὶ κατατιτρώσκουσα καρδίαν μέσην. | ἢ καὶ γὰρ οὐκ ἔνυξας αὐτοῦ τὰς φρένας; | ἢ καὶ γὰρ οὐκ ἤμυξας αὐτοῦ καιρίως, | οὐχὶ τὸ κῆρ ἔτρωσας αὐτοῦ τὰς φρένας; | 15 ἡνίκα τοῦτον ᾔσχυνας κατακράτος | καὶ Μαρκιανοῦ κατέβαλες τὸ θράσος, | οὔκουν θεοῖς πεισθεῖσα δοῦναι θυσίαν | κωφοῖς ξοάνοις καὶ ματαίοις καὶ πλάνοις; | κἂν φεῦ ὁ δύσνους, ὁ τρισάθλιος πλέον, | 20 τὴν σὴν κεφαλὴν ἐκθερίζει τῷ ξίφει | **καὶ παρθενικῶν αἱμάτων σου τοῖς λύθροις** | καταμολύνῃ τὰς μιαιφόνους χέρας. | **ἀλλὰ φθάνει τάχιον ἡ θεία δίκη**, | καὶ τμητικὸν δρέπανον ἐκτείνασά μοι | 25 **ἄωρον ἐξέκοψεν αὐτὸν ὡς στάχυν**, | καὶ τὴν ἄκανθαν τὸν Διόσκορον φλέγει, | τοῦτον κεραυνόβλητον ἐργασαμένη. | Θάλλεις δὲ σύ, Βαρβάρα, πάλιν ὡς ῥόδον | ῥοδωνιαῖς ἀνθοῦσα ταῖς οὐρανίαις. The text is edited in C. Gallavotti, 'Nota sulla schedografia di Moscopulo e suoi precedenti fino a Teodoro Prodromo', *Bolletino dei Classici* III.4 (1983), 3–35, at 30–32. What is more, the text also survives in other schedographical collections: Vat. Pal. gr. 92, fol. 171ʳ⁻ᵛ and Vat. Reg. gr. PP Pii II 54, fol. 333ᵛ; see Nesseris, Παιδεία, vol. 2, 30–31.

[133] Unfortunately, there is no comprehensive study of the didactic function of epigrammatic poetry. For some brief notes, see Hörandner, 'Teaching', 463–64.

[134] This formula is very common in epigrams; cf. I. Vassis, *Initia Carminum Byzantinorum* (Berlin/New York 2005), 548.

very little is known about the production and use of this major poetic cycle.[135] The poems obviously could have been used as inscriptions on various works of art, and in particular as book epigrams for illustrated manuscripts.[136] The double redaction, in both dodecasyllable and hexameter, was perhaps an effort on the part of Prodromos to suit the differing tastes of potential patrons and donors.[137] At the same time, however, it would hardly be a surprise if Prodromos used these tetrastichs, of which he was so proud,[138] in his teaching. They are excellent models, covering the greater part of the Old and New Testaments. Some can be considered as 'mnemonic poems',[139] while the double redaction makes them suitable for the classroom as well, useful for teaching students the two different metres, dodecasyllable and hexameter. In the same vein, the double redaction of the tetrastichs on the three holy Hierarchs might have been meant both to accompany depictions of the three holy Hierarchs and as a type of school exercise.[140] Even though Niketas Eugenianos, in his dodecasyllabic funerary poem for Prodromos, specifically asserts that the purpose of much of his poetry was to laud the imperial family or to adorn icons and tombs,[141] I do not believe that all of them were intended to serve only one of the functions identified by Eugenianos. Both the ceremonial and epigrammatic poetry of Prodromos could be used in the class, and much teaching material could be used in the court.[142]

In light of these observations, similar questions emerge regarding other Prodromean writings, such as his grammar, his novel, and his numerous satirical writings in the style of Lucian. Were these works commissioned by literary patrons? Were they presented in a literary *theatron*, or were they used in a school setting?

---

[135] Though Grigorios Papagiannis has produced a very sound edition, he did not address such questions in his introduction; cf. M. D. Lauxtermann, 'Book Review of Gr. Papagiannis, Theodoros Prodromos: Jambische und hexametrische Tetrasticha auf die Haupterzälungen des Alten und des Neuen Testaments', *JÖB* 49 (1999), 367-70, vol. 1, at 367.

[136] Lauxtermann, 'Papagiannis', 368-69; and Lauxtermann, *Byzantine Poetry*, vol. 1, 79.

[137] A comparable example is the double redaction of historical poem 26, a tomb epigram for Ioannes II Komnenos. On these two epigrams, see I. Vassis, 'Das Pantokratorkloster von Konstantinopel in der byzantinischen Dichtung', in: S. Kotzabassi (ed.), *The Pantokrator Monastery in Constantinople* (Boston 2013), 203-49, at 234-36.

[138] Prodromos, *Historical Poems*, 59.168-82.

[139] Prodromos, *Tetrasticha on the Old and New Testaments*, 9a, 97a, 206a.

[140] M. D'Ambrosi, 'The Icon of the Three Holy Hierarchs at the Pantokrator Monastery and the Epigrams of Theodore Prodromos on Them', in: S. Kotzabassi (ed.), *The Pantokrator Monastery in Constantinople* (Boston/Berlin 2013), 143-51, argues that the epigrammatic cycle was probably meant to be inscribed next to depictions in the Pantokrator Monastery. However tempting this hypothesis might be, D'Ambrosi unfortunately does not provide any convincing evidence.

[141] See the discussion on pp. 35-37.

[142] A further indication for the use of Prodromos' poetry in a school setting is his elevation to the status of model poet in the thirteenth century; see Ps. Gregorios Korinthios, *On the Four Parts of the Perfect Speech*, 108, 162-65.

Let us begin with his grammar, a work dedicated to Eirene the Sevastokratorissa,[143] probably intended to introduce this princess of foreign origin to the complexities of Atticizing Greek.[144] The presentation copy for Eirene has even survived: Panaghiou Taphou 52, a splendid illustrated manuscript written when Prodromos was still alive.[145] But after the grammar in Panaghiou Taphou 52 was presented to Eirene, Prodromos would not have placed his personal copy of the work in his library without using it again for any other purpose or on other occasions. He could have easily adapted the work for his classroom by simply leaving out the various acclamations to the princess, such as φιλολογωτάτη μοι βασιλίδων, φιλολογωτάτη καὶ βασιλικωτάτη ψυχή, ἀρίστη μοι βασιλίδων, μεγαλεπηβολωτάτη μοι βασιλίδων, σεβασμία μοι κεφαλή. Such adaptation was a common practice in Byzantium. For example, Michael Psellos' poem *De inscriptionibus Psalmorum*, a work initially written for the emperor Konstantinos IX Monomachos, was used later in Psellos' career when he became the tutor for young Michael Doukas (later Michael VII), and even for other groups of students. This is evident from the adaptations found in the various witnesses to the text, in which the vocatives are replaced by other words and all the imperial addressees excised.[146]

Unlike the grammar, which contains numerous indications of its dedication to Eirene throughout the text, the exact circumstances of the textual genesis of Prodromos' novel, *Rhodanthe* and *Dosikles*, would remain obscure were it not for the manuscript Heidel. Pal. gr. 43. Since this codex transmits the novel with a dedicatory poem for the then-Caesar Nikephoros Bryennios, we know that a copy of the novel was presented to this renowned literary patron.[147] Nikephoros Bryennios was not only the inscribed recipient but also present in the actual audience—together with other literary patrons and

---

[143] For Eirene the Sevastokratorissa, see E. Jeffreys, 'The Sebastokratorissa Irene as Patron', in: L. Theis, M. Mullett, and M. Grünbart (eds), *Female Founders in Byzantium and Beyond* (Vienna 2014), 177–94; cf. also Rhoby, 'Sebastokratorissa Eirene', 305–36.

[144] Zagklas, 'Byzantine Grammar', 84–85. It is, therefore, possible that the grammar dates before the works written by other writers for Eirene.

[145] P. L. Vokotopoulos, *Byzantine Illuminated Manuscripts of the Patriarchate of Jerusalem* [Μικρογραφίες τῶν βυζαντινῶν χειρογράφων τοῦ Πατριαρχείου Ἱεροσολύμων], translated from the Greek by D. M. Whitehouse (Athens 2002), 186–88.

[146] See Hörandner, 'Didactic Poem', 58–59; cf. also Bernard, *Poetry*, 127–28.

[147] For the dedicatory poem, see P. A. Agapitos, 'Poets and Painters: Theodoros Prodromos' Dedicatory Verses of His Novel to an Anonymous Caesar', *JÖB* 50 (2000), 173–85; cf. also Jeffreys, *Byzantine Novels*, 7–10 (with previous literature). For other works commissioned by Bryennios see ibid. 7, note 32. It has gone rather unnoticed that Prodromos' prose work *To the caesar or for the colour green*, no. 145 from Hörandner's list, is another work addressed to Bryennios. Moreover, it is worth noting that the dedicatory poem compares the novel to a painting—this is a well-known *topos*—while the prose work is a philosophical treatise about ancient colour theories.

literati—for its performance in the *theatron*, probably of Eirene Doukaina.[148] Does this mean it was only used twice? No, of course not: other members of the Komnenian family, aristocrats, and intellectuals would certainly have read it or heard its reading in aristocratic households as the work was gradually disseminated.

What is particularly interesting is that the genesis of this work is, to a certain extent, linked to the classroom. Based on *Rhodanthe and Dosikles* 8.52 ('never whet my blade on my teachers'), Elizabeth Jeffreys has argued, 'There are some hints of classroom humour, suggesting that some of the set-pieces may have begun life as "fair copies" of school exercises'.[149] In addition, the composition of *Rhodanthe* and *Dosikles* is based to a great extent on the use of *ethopoiiai*.[150] Indeed, poem 71 of the present edition, which is an *ethopoiia* with a strong resemblance to a passage-*ethopoiia* of Prodromos' novel, seems to confirm Jeffreys' hypothesis that some parts of the novel were actually composed as school exercises.[151] But what happened after the completion of the novel? Was *Rhodanthe* and *Dosikles* among the texts which Prodromos used in his class? The monk Ioannikios, in a partially published *schedos*, praises Prodromos for his novel:[152] τίς ἐπὶ τῷ παρ' αὐτοῦ συγγραφέντι βιβλίῳ οὐ δίδωσι κλέος (spelled οὐ δὴ Δοσικλέος to test the schedographic skills of his pupils). Aside from the popularity that the novel seems to have enjoyed among contemporary literati, two further details can be adduced from this passage. First, being a *schedos*, the text by Ioannikios was used in the classroom. Second, the students, who were expected to solve Ioannikios' schedographic riddle/puzzle, must then have known Prodromos' novel. Does this mean that they had read parts or all of the novel in the classroom? It is not easy to say, but we should emphasize that, in writing such a work, Prodromos was principally seeking glory and social advancement. Hence, his students, who were pursuing similar careers, would presumably also be trained to compose similar rhetorical works. Some of them indeed followed his lead, such as Niketas Eugenianos, who authored the verse novel *Drosilla & Charikles*, which drew upon Prodromos' in both structure and motifs. Thus, it is highly likely that Prodromos had presented his novel to Eugenianos and some of his other students as a recent example of novel composition. We also know that the ancient novels were read and used in class, most likely in the

---

[148] Jeffreys, *Byzantine Novels*, 9–10. [149] Jeffreys, *Byzantine Novels*, 15.
[150] Roilos, *Amphoteroglossia*, 61–65.
[151] The recycling of material is quite common in the twelfth century; take, for example, the case of Konstantinos Manasses: Nilsson, *Constantine Manasses*, 171–84.
[152] Text in Vassis, 'Theodoros Prodromos', 7, note 27.

form of excerpts. Ms. Vat. Pal. gr. 92, for example, transmits two *schede* that are paraphrases of excerpts of Achilles Tatius' novel.[153]

Even more complicated and ambiguous are the numerous instances of his satirical works in the Lucianic style, since the absence in them of any inscribed recipients, in contrast to his novel and grammar, leaves much more room for speculation. There is a tendency on the part of contemporary scholars to place them within a school context,[154] but it is equally possible that these Lucianic works were also circulated in rhetorical *theatra* and were part of twelfth-century literary culture. The *theatron* should be considered as a place of rhetorical *epideixis* where the writer could exhibit and promote his literary works and thereby his reputation, even if the writings were produced for didactic purposes. Intellectuals who took part in these *theatra* could scrutinize the work and influence its circulation. In addition, a didactic origin does not diminish the highly aesthetic value of these texts, nor does it preclude a readership outside the class. In other words, sophisticated literary and rhetorical works, didactic or not, could have been used both in and beyond the classroom.

Taken together, many Prodromean texts seem to have been designed to potentially serve more than one purpose and fit more than one context. Theodoros Prodromos, on account of his threefold position as court poet, professional writer and intellectual, and teacher, 'channelled' compositions for three settings—court, *theatron*, and classroom—which can be compared to a system of communicating vessels in which fluid can move easily from one to another. Whatever the primary purpose of his works, the texts could thereafter be channelled to other 'vessels', since Prodromos moved in all of these seemingly unconnected settings. To return to the *Miscellaneous poems*, we should emphasize once more that the absence of a recipient by definition facilitates their circulation and multifunctionality. However, the existence of a recipient or a donor does not prevent the subsequent circulation of Prodromos' works in different environments. Even the so-called *Historical poems* of Prodromos offer only a glimpse into their performative contexts, which nevertheless could rapidly change in the oral or written dissemination of his works. We may be reminded of the case of the priest Michael, the

---

[153] I. Nilsson and N. Zagklas, '"Hurry Up, Reap Every Flower of the *Logoi!*": The Use of Greek Novels in Byzantium', *GRBS* 57 (2017), 1120–48.

[154] See P. Marciniak, 'Theodore Prodromos' Bion Prasis: A Reappraisal', *GRBS* 53 (2013), 219–39, 225 ff. Moreover, some twelfth-century *schede* for students are paraphrases of Lucian's works; for an example, see P. Marciniak, 'Teaching Lucian in Middle Byzantium', *Antiquitas Perennis* 14 (2019), 267–79. For a recent study of *Bion Prasis*, see K. Chryssogelos, 'Theodore Prodromos' Βίων πρᾶσις as a Satire', *MEG* 21 (2021), 303–12.

enthusiastic reader of Prodromos, who recited some of his works in Philippopolis, causing a delightful aesthetic pleasure to Michael Italikos.[155] Although we may never discover the exact context, it is quite likely to have been different from the purpose which Prodromos had in mind when he produced these works. Thus, as modern readers we should bear this in mind when we read Byzantine poetry—indeed, Byzantine literature more generally—as many of these texts had multilayered contexts, as texts travelled back and forth, from court to *theatron* or classroom; from *theatron* to court or classroom; from classroom to court or *theatron*.

---

[155] Michael Italikos, *Letters*, 1.64.1-6: Ὁ γοῦν παρὼν οὑτοσὶ παπᾶς Μιχαὴλ πλέον ἀέρος ἀναπνεῖ τοὺς λόγους τοὺς σούς, πάντα πεζὸν λόγον, πᾶν ἰαμβεῖον ἐπὶ στόματος ἔχων. Καὶ ἐπειδάν ποτε τῶν πραγμάτων ἀνέκυψα, προσέταττόν τι κρουμάτιον ἀπὸ τῆς σῆς κιθάρας ἐπᾷσαί μοι, καὶ ᾖδεν εὐθὺς καὶ ἐπέρρει κατατείνων τὸ μέλος ἀκάθεκτον καὶ ἐλάλει ἔμμετρά τε καὶ ἄμετρα καὶ ἀμέτρως ἀμφότερα. Προσετίθει γάρ τι καὶ ἀφ' ἑαυτοῦ ταῖς σαῖς χάρισι· (=This present priest Michael breathes your discourses more than air, holding every bit of prose, every iamb upon his tongue. As soon as I emerged from my work, I ordered him to soothe me with a little musical phrase from your *kithara*, and immediately he sang and straining poured forth his unruly song, speaking both metrical and prosaic discourses without rhythm. For he added a bit of his own to your charms.); trans. in S. Papaioannou, 'Language Games', 223-24 (with minor modifications); for this passage, see also W. Hörandner, 'Zur kommunikativen Funktion byzantinischer Gedichte', in: I. Ševčenko and G. G. Litavrin (eds), *Acts, XVIIIth International Congress of Byzantine Studies, Selected Papers* (Shepherdstown 2000), IV, 104-18.

3
Formal Features
Metre and Prosody

As we have seen, Theodoros Prodromos earned respect and admiration among his peers for his poetry. In a *schedos*, Ioannikios the monk, a fellow learned teacher and poet, praised Prodromos for the abundant stream gushing forth from his iambic works,[1] most probably alluding to their rhythmical qualities. In the same text, Ioannikios continues his praise by saying that Prodromos also elicited the admiration of his contemporaries for the composition of hexametric poetry. For our better understanding of Prodromos' stature as one of the most talented poets of his time, it is important to look at the metrical characteristics of the *Miscellaneous poems* written in both dactylic and accentual metres. Thus, this chapter takes us away from questions of context and function by exploring more technical aspects of the selected corpus: namely, the poems' rhythmical and prosodic features.

The designation *Miscellaneous poems* is borne out in their metrical diversity. They include works in various kinds of metres, ranging from dodecasyllables and political verse to hexameters and pentameters. The first part of this chapter examines various aspects of the poems in dodecasyllable and political verse, placing an emphasis on stress regulation at the caesura and the line ending. The second part shifts our attention to the reappearance of dactylic metres in the twelfth century, offering some observations about Prodromos' role in this development. It provides a brief discussion of the dactylic pentameters of the *Miscellaneous poems*, along with some quantitative statistical evidence regarding the metrical features of his entire surviving corpus of hexameters. The last two parts focus on prosody and the phenomenon of hiatus of the *Miscellaneous poems*.

---

[1] See the discussion of this passage on p. 35.

Theodoros Prodromos: Miscellaneous Poems: An Edition and Literary Study. Nikos Zagklas, Oxford University Press.
© Nikolaos Zagklas 2023. DOI: 10.1093/oso/9780192886927.003.0003

3.1. Accentual Metres

Unlike dactylic pentameters and hexameters, which have a long tradition in the history of Greek poetry, going back to antiquity, political verse and the dodecasyllable are metres that came into existence during Byzantine times. Both of them are accentual metres, rhythmically appreciated by the Byzantine ear because they comply with the rules of isosyllaby, stress regulation, and isometry.[2] Political verse always counts fifteen syllables. It has a caesura after the eighth syllable, and from the eleventh century onwards a stress is placed on the sixth or eighth syllable.[3] It was used widely in religious and secular hymns, as well as in didactic poetry, and eventually became the main metrical medium of vernacular poetry.[4] The Byzantine dodecasyllable has a more hybrid nature than political verse. Just like political verse, it pays heed to accentual rhythm, but it is also aware of the rules of prosody because of its close ties to its ancient ancestor, the iambic trimeter.[5] The main rules of the Byzantine dodecasyllable are the following: (i) each dodecasyllable consists of twelve syllables; (ii) there is a caesura after either the fifth or seventh syllable; and (iii) its line ending is paroxytone (in other words, the stress falls on the eleventh syllable).

3.1.1. Dodecasyllables

The majority of Prodromos' surviving work consists of dodecasyllables: approximately 11,000 dodecasyllabic verses survive under his name, ranging from epigrams, letters, and ceremonial poems to a novel (*Rhodanthe and Dosikles*) and a dialogue in dramatic form (*Katomyomachia*). Similarly, the lion's share of the *Miscellaneous poems* are written in this metre: 751 out of 1,002 lines. The results of the examination of these 751 dodecasyllables are in

---

[2] For an excellent study of all these three characteristics of Byzantine accentual poetry, see the section *Appendix metrica* in Lauxtermann, *Byzantine Poetry*, vol. 2.

[3] Until the end of the tenth century the stress falls on the sixth syllable; see Lauxtermann, *Byzantine Poetry*, vol. 2, 329.

[4] The most influential studies on this metre still remain M. Jeffreys, 'The Nature and Origin of the Political Verse', *DOP* 28 (1974), 141–95, and M. D. Lauxtermann, *The Spring of Rhythm: An Essay on the Political Verse and Other Byzantine Metres* (Vienna 1999); cf. also Lauxtermann, *Byzantine Poetry*, vol. 2, 329–30, 336–38, 362–63.

[5] On the Byzantine dodecasyllable, see the fundamental study of P. Maas, 'Der byzantinische Zwölfsilber', *BZ* 12 (1903), 278–323, and the extremely illuminating remarks in the *Appendix Metrica* in Lauxtermann, *Byzantine Poetry*, vol. 2; cf. also A. Rhoby, 'Vom jambischen Trimeter zum byzantinischen Zwölfsilber: Beobachtung zur Metrik des spätantiken und byzantinischen Epigramms', *WSt* 124 (2011), 117–42; F. Bernard, 'Rhythm in the Byzantine Dodecasyllable: Practices and Perceptions', in: A. Rhoby and N. Zagklas (eds), *Middle and Late Byzantine Poetry: Texts and Contexts* (Turnhout 2018), 13–41.

3.1. ACCENTUAL METRES

line with surveys which have been part of editions of his poetry produced in the last few decades.[6] Moreover, they concur with the main rules of the Byzantine dodecasyllable described above:

(i) Prodromos firmly sticks to the principle of isosyllaby. All 751 lines count twelve syllables, without any hypermetric or hypometric lines.

(ii) All verses have a caesura after either the fifth or seventh syllable, but Prodromos favours the use of the former. Of the 751 dodecasyllabic verses, the caesura after the fifth syllable (=C5) is found in 64.5% of the lines (498 vv.). The caesura after the seventh syllable (=C7), on the other hand, is found in 35.2% (265 vv.). However, it is not always easy to determine whether a dodecasyllable has a C5 or C7 since a two-syllable word is occasionally placed between the two caesuras:[7]

1. **8.1**: Ἀβραάμ, Σάρρα,/μόσχος,/Ἰσμαήλ, Ἅγαρ,
2. **14.6**: ἆρ' ἀετός σε,/μάρτυς,/οὐ κόραξ κύει. C7
3. **24.10**: αἰτουμένους μὲν/ὧδε/κἀμοὶ καὶ τέκνοις C7
4. **25.2**: ὁ πανδαμάτωρ/οὗτος/ᾐδέσθη χρόνος C7
5. **25.12**: ἀνθ' ὧν με δοῦλον/ὄντα/τῆς ἁμαρτίας C5
6. **26.6**: ἀντιστρόφον πως/εἶχον/οἱ πόδες θέσιν· C5
7. **26.7**: εἰς οὐρανοὺς γὰρ/εἷλκεν/αὐτὸν ὁ δρόμος. C5
8. **75.121**: καὶ τῆς Προνοίας/χρῆμα/τῆς σοφωτάτης. C5
9. **75.131**: Ἀλλ' ἐν κενοῖς μοι/ταῦτα/πρὸς τὸ χρυσίον· C5
10. **76.72**: κιχρᾶν ἐκείνῳ/τοῦτον/εἰς νυκτῶν σέλας. C5
11. **76.137**: Οὐδέν τι πάντως/ἄλλο/Φιλίας δίχα. C7
12. **76.190**: ἄσεμνος ὕβρις,/ἅλμα,/κραυγή, θροῦς ὅσος.

In most of these cases, one must decide for a C5 or C7 on the basis of questions related to syntax or semantics.[8] For example, cases 5–6 and 8–11 are C5, while cases 2–4 and 7 are C7. By contrast, cases 1 and 12 are even more challenging, since the insertion of a two-syllable noun between C5 and C7 does not allow us to give a definitive answer: because of the asyndeton both types of caesura are valid in these two cases without changing the meaning of the text.

---

[6] See Hunger, *Katz-Mäuse-Krieg*, 30–39; Hörandner, *Historische Gedichte*, 125–28; Acconcia Longo, *calendario giambico*, 71–73; Papagiannis, *Tetrasticha*, vol. 1, 183–87; D'Ambrosi, *Gregorio Nazianzeno*, 56–60. Some of the few works that have not been the subject of an extensive metrical examination include his novel and the tetrastichs on the lives of Basil the Great and John Chrysostom.

[7] On this issue, see also Hörandner, *Historische Gedichte*, 126, note 278, and Papagiannis, *Tetrasticha*, vol. 1, 183–84.

[8] See Lauxtermann, *Byzantine Poetry*, vol. 2, 357–58.

In general, the rhythm does not seem to change significantly across different clusters of Prodromos' poetry: *Miscellaneous poems* (C5: 64.5% and C7: 35.2%), *Historical poems* (C5: 66.8% and C7: 33.2%),[9] *Tetrasticha on the Old and New Testaments* (C5: 68.8% and C7: 31.2%).[10] That said, when we look at some individual poems, the frequency of C5 and C7 is not the same between them, possibly because of their different genre features and performative function. Take, for example, poems 11–20 (an epigrammatic cycle on St Barbara) and poem 76 (a narrative work in the form of a dialogue). The latter poem has a C7 in 95 lines (31.9%), the former possesses a lower number of C7, namely 16 verses (25.5%). On the other hand, the rhythm of poem 76 is closer to that of *Katomyomachia* (C7, 32%), which is another narrative poem in the form of dialogue.

Prodromos makes use of the following stress patterns at the caesura:

Caesura	Oxytone	Paroxytone	Proparoxytone
C5	55.42% (264 vv.)	38.35% (186 vv.)	6.22% (31 vv.)
C7	1.47% (four verses)	29.04% (78 vv.)	69.48% (183 vv.)

What we can see in this table is that the oxytone stress before C7 is an exception, occurring only in four lines (76.8, 38, 287, and 288). The proparoxytone stress before C5 is not particularly exceptional, but it can still be characterized as infrequent in his poetry: *Miscellaneous poems* (6.22%), *Historical poems* (7.3%),[11] *Tetrasticha on the Old and New Testaments* (7%).[12] Its frequency in Prodromos is lower than in the work of some of his contemporaries. For example, the use of this type of metrical stress pattern in an anonymous poem from southern Italy is 13%.[13] But it is still much higher than that of Nikolaos Kallikles, who goes to extremes, making use of a proparoxytone stress before C5 only twice in his entire corpus.[14]

(iii) Prodromos usually follows the well-established Byzantine rule of a paroxytone line ending. There are 743 lines with such an ending, but there are eight lines which deviate from this rule:[15] five have a proparoxytone ending (a), and another three have an oxytone ending (b).

---

[9] Hörandner, *Historische Gedichte*, 127.
[10] Papagiannis, *Tetrasticha*, vol. 1, 185–86; cf. also Lauxtermann, *Byzantine Poetry*, vol. 2, 359.
[11] Hörandner, *Historische Gedichte*, 127.   [12] Papagiannis, *Tetrasticha*, vol. 1, 185.
[13] I. Vassis and I. Polemis, Ἕνας Ἕλληνας ἐξόριστος στὴν Μάλτα τοῦ δωδέκατου αἰώνα (Athens 2016), 30.
[14] R. Romano, *Nicola Callicle, Carmi* (Naples 1980), 39.
[15] For a recent discussion of this issue and the tendencies throughout the Byzantine period, see Lauxtermann, *Byzantine Poetry*, vol. 2, 320–23.

a)
7.3: *Τριὰς κύριος – τὸ ξένον – ξενίζεται*
59.1: *Ἐρᾷ τὰ δένδρα καὶ φιλεῖ καὶ **μίγνυται***
59.2: *ἐρῶμεν, οὐ φιλοῦμεν, οὐ **μιγνύμεθα**.*
76.285: *τὰ ποῖα; λέξον ὡς ἐγὼ **παράσχομαι**.*
76.296: *ἔργῳ δ' ἀπαρνήσαιο. Καὶ μὴν **ὤμοσα***
b)
76.19: *θύραθεν; ὥστε καὶ νομισθῆναι θανεῖν.*
76.248: *Ἀλλ' οὐχ ὁ Βίος ταῦτα, τὴν δ' Ἔχθραν λαβών*
76.293: *Ναὶ καὶ θανατᾶν. Φ. Καὶ φθονοῦσι μὴ φθονεῖν*

Two of the proparoxytone endings occur in poem 59, a two-line epigram which is part of a poetic cycle (poems 57–61). Since these two proparoxytone endings are to be found immediately after each other and result from the use of the same word (μίγνυμι), one can tentatively argue that they reflect a conscious rhythmical choice of the poet. Whatever the case, Prodromos seems to be more flexible in the use of stress pattern at the end of lines in these dodecasyllabic poems than many of his fellow poets.[16] Statistically speaking, in this corpus, the proparoxytone and oxytone endings comprise approximately 1% of the total number of dodecasyllabic lines, which is slightly higher than is the case in other groups of poems: 0.26% in the *Tetrasticha on the Old and New Testaments*,[17] 0.8% in the *Historical poems*,[18] and 0.9% in *Rhodanthe and Dosikles*.[19]

3.1.2. Political Verse

Political verse is the dominant metre in the *Historical poems*, mostly used for ceremonial hymns performed by the *demes*.[20] In the present corpus, only poems 55 and 56 are written in political verse, making it the least represented metre. What is interesting is that both poems were probably used as inscriptions, even though political verse is not a very common metrical medium in epigrammatic poetry. No other epigram by Prodromos survives in this metre. Even the evidence from surviving metrical inscriptions bears witness to its infrequency for the composition of epigrams in Byzantium.[21]

---

[16] Lauxtermann, *Byzantine Poetry*, vol. 2, 322.
[17] See also Papagiannis, *Tetrasticha*, vol. 1, 183.
[18] Hörandner, *Historische Gedichte*, 126.   [19] Lauxtermann, *Byzantine Poetry*, vol. 2, 322.
[20] The *Historical poems* include no fewer than 3,373 lines in political verse; see Hörandner, *Historische Gedichte*, 123.
[21] Rhoby, *Byzantinische Epigramme*, vol. 1, 63–65; vol. 2, 40–41; vol. 3, 89–90; and vol. 4, 69.

76 FORMAL FEATURES: METRE AND PROSODY

As noted above, political verse is divided into two hemistichs, of eight and seven syllables, respectively. Following Byzantine metrical practices that emerged after the year 1000, the stress before the caesura falls on either the sixth or the eighth syllable. Twelve verses (63.2%) of poems 55 and 56 have an oxytone stress before the caesura, while seven verses (36.8%) have a proparoxytone stress. It is worth noting that the difference in frequency between an oxytone and a proparoxytone stress at the caesura is similar to that of Prodromos' ceremonial hymns in political verse (oxytone: ca 60% and proparoxytone: ca 40%).[22]

The stress patterns in the first hemistich of poems 55 and 56 are quite diverse. Most of them have three stresses just on the even syllables:

(i) 2, 4, and 6 ⇨ x ´ x ´ x ´ x x[23]
(ii) 2, 4, and 8 ⇨ x ´ x ´ x x x ´[24]

Another four verses have a stress on the first syllable followed by one or more stresses on even syllables: (i) ´ x x ´ x ´ x x;[25] (ii) ´ x x ´ x ´ x ´;[26] and (iii) ´ x x x x ´ x x.[27]

As for the second hemistich, most of the verses have only two stresses on the even syllables:

(i) 10 and 14 ⇨ x ´ x x x ´ x[28]
(ii) 12 and 14 ⇨ x x x ´ x ´ x[29]

But there is also one hemistich with three stresses: 10, 12, and 14 ⇨ x ´ x ´ x ´ x.[30] Some hemistichs have a stress on the ninth syllable and the penultimate syllable: ´ x x x x ´ x;[31] another two verses have a stress on the ninth, the tenth, and the penultimate syllable: ´ x x ´ x ´ x.[32] When we compare the stress patterns of these two poems with the ones of the *Historical poems*, we notice that in the first hemistich the most popular stress patterns are the same: (i) x ´ x ´ x ´ x x; and (ii) x ´ x ´ x x x ´.[33] As for the second hemistich, Prodromos prefers x ´ x ´ x ´ x for the composition of his ceremonial hymns,[34] but in poems 55–56 this stress pattern is used only three times.

---

[22] Hörandner, *Historische Gedichte*, 131.   [23] 55.1, 5; 56.1, 2, 8.
[24] 55.3, 4, 6, 7, 8; 56.4, 6, 7.   [25] 55.2.   [26] 55.9, 10.   [27] 56.5.
[28] 55.2, 3, 4, 5, 6, 8; 56.2, 3, 5, 8.   [29] 56.4 and 9.   [30] 55.9.
[31] 55.1, 6, 7; 56.1, 6; the hemistichs in the opening verses of poems 55 and 56 include exactly the same wording: δέξαι σου παραινέτην; on the other hand, in v. 6 the wording is very similar: φρίττε μὴ κυλισθῶσι (poem 55) and τάχα σοι κυλισθῶσι (poem 56).
[32] 55.10; 56.7.   [33] Hörandner, *Historische Gedichte*, 131.
[34] Hörandner, *Historische Gedichte*, 133.

In addition to the caesura after the eighth syllable, four verses have a secondary pause, the so-called diaeresis after the fourth syllable (D4):[35]

55.9   τί με κρατεῖς; \ σκιὰν κρατεῖς· / πνοὴν κρατεῖς ἀνέμου
55.10 τί με κρατεῖς; \ καπνὸν κρατεῖς, / ὄνειρον, ἴχνος πλοίου
56.1   οὐκ ἔτυχες, \ οὐκ ἔλαβες, / οὐκ ἔσχες μου τὰς τρίχας
56.4   γυμνὸς εἰμί \ καὶ τῶν χειρῶν / ἐξολισθήσας τούτων

In the first two verses the bipartite structure of the hemistich forms a question and a reply of the poetic voice. In the third verse the two parts are part of an asyndeton.

3.2. Dactylic Metres: A Strong Revival in the Twelfth Century

After the time of Ioannes Geometres and throughout the eleventh century, dactylic metres can claim no more than a role of limited importance in the history of Byzantine poetry, with most poets preferring the use of rhythmically more appealing metres, such as the Byzantine dodecasyllable or political verse. The *Various Verses* of Christophoros Mitylenaios, for example, consist of 2,596 verses, of which only 197 are written in dactylic hexameter and 23 in dactylic pentameter. By contrast, the surviving oeuvre of the other two most important eleventh-century poets, Ioannes Mauropous and Michael Psellos, does not include any poems in dactylics.

If it were not for Prodromos, the production of dactylic poetry would have fared no better in the twelfth century. The oeuvre of two well-known Komnenian poets suffices to demonstrate this: Nikolaos Kallikles, a generation older than Prodromos, is the author of 821 verses, all of which were written in dodecasyllables; similarly, the vast corpus of approximately 17,000 verses by Manganeios Prodromos, the successor to Prodromos in the role of courtly poet, includes only dodecasyllable and political verse. Thus, Prodromos should be credited for the twelfth-century revival of the hexameter and its extensive use on various occasions.[36] He is the most prolific poet of dactylic

---

[35] Lauxtermann, *Byzantine Poetry*, vol. 2, 380–81.

[36] Of course he does not stand alone; quite a few twelfth-century authors followed his lead. For example, Ioannes Tzetzes used hexameters in his *Carmina Iliaca* and in the prefatory and concluding parts of his didactic poem *On Meters* for his brother Isaak Tzetzes; Niketas Eugenianos' novel includes three passages in dactylic metre (*Drosilla and Charikles* 3.263–288, 297–320 and 6.205–235), as do two of his monodies for Theodoros Prodromos; Peter the monk wrote an hexametric epitaph for Prodromos; and Michael Choniates authored 538 hexameters (poems 1–5). In addition, there are many anonymous poems in hexameters, such as a *Poem on the Reconquest of Dorylaion* (ed. Spingou).

poetry in the mid-twelfth century, and one of the most prolific in the middle and late Byzantine periods more generally, with a surviving corpus of approximately 2,863 hexameters and 116 pentameters.[37] This includes the following poems: sixteen *Historical poems* (1224 vv.),[38] fifteen *Miscellaneous poems* (140 vv.),[39] the hexametric tetrastichs on the Old and New Testaments (1172 vv.), the hexametric tetrastichs on the lives of Gregory of Nazianzus, Basil of Caesarea, and John Chrysostom (228 vv.),[40] the hexametric tetrastichs on the great martyrs Theodoros, Georgios, and Demetrios (68 vv.), the hexametric preface to his novel (24 vv.), and the hexametric oracle embedded in the narrative of his novel (Book 9.196–204).

The reasons behind the wide use of this archaic metre remain quite ambiguous.[41] Why did Prodromos produce a wide array of types of texts, including teaching exercises, religious hymns, imperial encomia, letters, petitions, funerary works, and epigrams in a metre that, as Marc Lauxtermann has pointed out, 'lacks substance: it is prosodic prose without any rhythmical rules, it is merely semi-poetry with Homeric gibberish'?[42] This is not the place to go into detail, but I believe that all these poems were initially 'poetic experiments' by Prodromos, probably another development intimately connected with the Byzantine class, which he decided to transfer to the public sphere, lending a Homeric flourish to his court poetry.

As a 'Homer-venerating society',[43] the twelfth-century cultural elite seems to have welcomed Prodromos' metrical experiments with the hexameter with enthusiasm, turning it into a popular metre at court, at least for a while. The popularity of the Homeric epics in the twelfth century went beyond their use for pedagogical purposes by some well-known intellectuals,

[37] For some studies of the hexameters by Prodromos, see C. Giannelli, 'Epigrammi di Teodoro Prodromo in onore dei senti megalomartiri Teodoro, Giorgio e Demetrio', in: *Studi in onore di Luigi Castiglioni* (Florence 1960), 333–71 = *SBN* 10 (1963), 349–78, at 360–67; Hörandner, *Historische Gedichte*, 124–25; Papagiannis, Tetrasticha, vol. 1, 164–83; Lauxtermann, 'Papagiannis', 367–68; D'Ambrosi, *Gregorio Nazianzeno*, 60–79.

[38] Historical poems 2, 3, 6, 8, 26a, 27, 38, 42, 56b, 61, 62, 68, 69, 77, 78, and 79.

[39] Poems 1–6, 21, 27–28, 68, 69, 70–72, and 73–74.

[40] For the tetrastichs on the latter two church fathers, I consulted the outdated Basel edition.

[41] For some brief remarks on the place of hexameters in twelfth-century poetry, see E. Jeffreys, 'Why Produce Verse in Twelfth-Century Constantinople?', in: P. Odorico, P. A. Agapitos, and M. Hinterberger (eds), *'Doux remède…': Poésie et poétique à Byzance. Actes du IVe colloque international philologique, Paris, 23–24–25 février 2006* (Paris 2009), 219–28, at 223–24.

[42] Lauxtermann, *Spring*, 71.

[43] L. Neville, 'Lamentation, History, and Female Authorship in Anna Komnene's Alexiad', *GRBS* 53 (2013), 192–218, at 194. For the twelfth century as the 'golden age' of Homeric studies in Byzantium, see A. Basilikopoulou-Ioannidou, Ἡ ἀναγέννησις τῶν γραμμάτων κατὰ τὸν ΙΒ΄ αἰῶνα εἰς τὸ Βυζάντιον καὶ ὁ Ὅμηρος (Athens 1971); R. Browning, 'Homer in Byzantium', *Viator* 8 (1978), 15–33 (repr. in R. Browning, *Studies on Byzantine History, Literature and Education* (London 1977), no. XVII); F. Pontani, *Sguardi su Ulisse* (Rome 2005); F. Pontani, V. Sarris, and V. Katsaros (eds), *Reading Eustathios of Thessalonike* (Berlin/Boston 2017).

such as Ioannes Tzetzes and Eustathios of Thessaloniki. Even members of the Komnenian family were fervent upholders of the epics and therefore recipients of hexametric poems by Prodromos. Anna Komnene, whose *Alexiad* owes a great deal to the Homeric epics, was the addressee of the historical poem 38, a petitionary poem of 119 hexameters. Anna's brother, Isaak Komnenos, who is the addressee of poem 42, an encomium of 61 hexameters, was the author not only of a number of hexametric poems (now lost)[44] but also of an as yet unedited Byzantine commentary on the *Iliad*.[45] The strong revival of dactylic metre in the twelfth century goes hand in hand with the huge popularity of the Homeric epics in the contemporary literary culture of the upper class.

3.2.1. Pentameters

Unlike the *Historical poems*, which include only 24 pentameters (historical poem 56c), the *Miscellaneous poems* have no fewer than 92 pentameters. The reason for the large number of pentameters is that quite a few of the *Miscellaneous poems* are in elegiac distichs (poems 1–6 and 68–72). Most of the pentameters have a paroxytone line ending (80.44%). However, there are 18 lines (19.56%) with other kinds of line ending: 13 with a proparoxytone and another 5 with an oxytone one. The poem with the largest number of non-paroxytone endings (25%) among the corpus is no. 69: four of its nine pentameters deviate from this rule (vv. 4, 8, 12, and 16).

It is true that the pentameters usually consist of two symmetrical hemistichs with identical stressing at the caesura and the line ending.[46] Occasionally, Prodromos even places similarly sounding words (5.2: ποιμένι Καισαρέων, ποιμένα Νυσσαέων) or even exactly the same word (2.6: τῆς νέον ἡμετέρης καὶ ποτὲ ἡμετέρης) at the end of the two hemistichs. It should be noted that only 10.86% of the verses have different stress at the end of the two hemistichs. For example, in seven cases there is an oxytone caesura combined with a paroxytone ending, all of which occur within a single poetic cycle (1.6, 8, 10, 20; 2.4; 3.20; 5.10).

---

[44] Isaak Komnenos, *Kosmosoteira Typikon*, 106.5-8: πρὸς ταύταις δὲ καὶ ἑτέραν βίβλον κατέλιπον, ἣν πόνῳ μακρῷ στιχιδίοις ἡρωικοῖς (…) συντέταχα.
[45] See F. Pontani, 'The First Byzantine Commentary on the *Iliad*: Isaac Porphyrogenitus and His Scholia in Par. gr. 2682', *BZ* 99 (2006), 559–604.
[46] Lauxtermann, *Byzantine Poetry*, vol. 2, 332.

3.2.2. Hexameters: A Quantitative Survey

As already noted, the poetic work of Prodromos includes a grand total of 2,863 dactylic hexameters, allowing us to draw some clear conclusions about so-called verse patterns, caesura, and stress regulation:

i. Verse patterns
Prodromos makes use of no fewer than twenty-five patterns (d stands for dactyl and s for spondaic):

ddddd(s) (1,440 cases=50.21%)	sddds(s) (5 cases=0.17%)
sdddd(s) (338 cases=11.77%)	ddsds(s) (5 cases=0.17%)
ddsdd(s) (316 cases=11.07%)	dsdds(s) (4 cases=0.14%)
dsddd(s) (263 cases=9.21%)	sssdd(s) (4 cases=0.14%)
dddsd(s) (226 cases=7.91%)	dsssd(s) (3 cases=0.1%)
sdsdd(s) (48 cases=1.68%)	ssdsd(s) (2 cases=0.07%)
dsdsd(s) (43 cases=1.5%)	dsdss(s) (2 cases=0.07%)
sddsd(s) (42 cases=1.47%)	sdsds(s) (2 cases=0.07%)
dssdd(s) (37 cases=1.29%)	sdssd(s) (1 case=0.03%)
ddssd(s) (29 cases=1.01%)	ssdds(s) (1 case=0.03%)
dddds(s) (26 cases=0.91%)	ssdds(s) (1 case=0.03%)
ssddd(s) (20 cases=0.70%)	ssssd(s) (1 case=0.03%)
dddss(s) (6 cases=0.21%)	

Although quite a few of these combinations are rare in his poetry (for example, the last four occur just once in his corpus), the final total (25) is much higher than that of the late antique poets (e.g. Nonnus 9, Paul the Silentiary 6, Georgios Pisides 6), confirming Giannelli's observation that the construction of Prodromos' hexameters is closer to Homeric hexameters than the Nonnian ones.[47] Another conclusion we can draw from the above table is that long holodactylic verses are extremely common in Prodromos. Half of his surviving corpus consists of this type of hexameter (1,440 verses). It is difficult to say whether this is a coincidence or whether it hints at an experimental task undertaken by Prodromos to achieve isosyllaby and impose certain rhythmical qualities on his hexameters. Whatever the case, Prodromos' hexameters mirror a clear holodactylic tendency when compared with the work of ancient and Byzantine poets.

---

[47] Giannelli, 'Epigrammi', 367.

Spondaics per verse	Prodromos	Homer	Gregory	Nonnus	Geometres[48]
0 s	50%	19%	32%	38%	36%
1 s	40%	42%	49%	48%	42%
2 s	8%	30%	17%	13%	18%
3 s	<1%	8%	2%	–	<4%
4 s	0.03% (1 case)	<1%	?	–	–

It is worth noting that, in contrast with other poets who favoured the pattern dsddd(s) (Homer and Nonnus) and ddsdd(s) (Ioannes Geometres), Prodromos frequently starts his hexameters with a spondaic followed by four dactyls: namely, sdddd(s), which represents c. 12% of his entire corpus. Another Byzantine poet who is fond of this particular pattern is Gregory of Nazianzus:[49]

Verse pattern	Prodromos	Gregory	Homer	Nonnus	Geometres[50]
ddddd(s)	50%	32%	19%	38%	36%
sdddd(s)	12%	19%	13%	9%	8%
ddsdd(s)	11%	6%	4%	2%	13%
dsddd(s)	9%	15%	15%	23%	12%
dddsd(s)	8%	9%	8%	14%	8%
sdsdd(s)	<3%	3%	3%	<1%	3%
dsdsd(s)	<2%	4%	6%	9%	2%
sddsd(s)	<2%	4%	6%	4%	2%
dssdd(s)	<2%	<2%	3%	<1%	2%
ddssd(s)	1%	<1%	1%	–	3%
dddds(s)	<1%	<1%	<1%	–	1%
ssddd(s)	<1%	<4%	8%	–	3%

---

[48] For the figures for Nonnus (Dionysiaca), Gregory of Nazianzus and Homer, see G. Agosti and F. Gonnelli, 'Materiali per la storia dell' esametro nei poeti cristiani greci', in: M. Fantuzzi and R. Pretagostini (eds), *Struttura e storia dell' esametro Greco*, 2 vols. (Rome 1995), vol. 1, 289–434, at 373; for Ioannes Geometres, see E. M. van Opstall, *Jean Géomètre: Poèmes en hexamètres et en distiques élégiaques. Edition, traduction, commentaire* (Leiden/Boston 2008), 83.

[49] Another Byzantine poet who favours this pattern is Christophoros Mitylenaios: see M. De Groote, 'The Metre in the Poems of Christopher Mitylenaios', *BZ* 103 (2011), 571–94, at 573.

[50] For the figures for Nonnus (Dionysiaca), Gregory of Nazianzus and Homer, see Agosti and Gonnelli, 'Materiali', vol. 1, 373. For Homer, see also M. van Raalte, *Rhythm and Metre: Towards a Systematic Description of Greek Stichic Verse* (Leiden 1986), 56, and A. Ludwich, *Aristarchs homerische Textkritik nach den Fragmenten des Didymos dargestellt und beurteilt, nebst Beilagen* (Leipzig 1885), Zweiter Teil, § 37, Spondeen und Daktylen, 301–26. For Ioannes Geometres, see van Opstall, *Jean Géomètre*, 84.

I am not suggesting a direct dependence of Prodromos' hexameters on those of Gregory of Nazianzus, but the popularity of the church father as model *par excellence* of hexametric poetry in Byzantium makes some kind of metrical influence possible.

ii. Caesura

The masculine caesura (3a) represents 31.99% of all lines, the feminine caesura (3b) 62.75%, and the so-called *medial caesura* (3c), which came into existence in late antiquity, 3.29%.[51] On the other hand, the *hephtimemeres* (4a), a caesura after the princeps of the fourth foot, is quite rare, occurring only in 1.57% of Prodromos' dactylic hexameters. Similarly, the coexistence of two caesuras (2c+4c) after the second (2c) and the fourth biceps (4c), which emerged in the middle Byzantine period,[52] represents less than 2% of the entire corpus. It must also be noted that a considerable portion of Prodromos' hexameters (62.98%) have a 'bucolic diaeresis' after a 3a (33.41%) or a 3b (66.58%) caesura.[53]

What we can conclude from the following table is that the primacy of the feminine caesura over the masculine in Prodromos' hexameters brings him closer to Homer and some late antique poets (e.g. Gregory of Nazianzus and Nonnus) than many other Byzantine poets, such as Ioannes Geometres or Christophoros Mitylenaios, whose hexameters show a clear preference for masculine over feminine caesuras.[54]

Caesuras	Prodromos	Nonnus	Gregory	Homer	Geometres	Mitylenaios[55]
2c+4c	<2%	–	–	–	4%	1.67
3a	31.99%	19%	21%	42%	45%	47.78%
3b	62.75%	81%	79%	57%	28%	37.78%
3c	3.29%	–	–	–	20%	8.89%
4a	1.57%	–	–	1%	3%	3.88

---

[51] See Agosti and Gonnelli, 'Materiali', vol. 1, 322 and 380–81.

[52] On this particular caesura, see F. Scheidweiler, 'Studien zu Johannes Geometres', *BZ* 45 (1952), 277–319, at 292–94; cf. also van Opstall, *Jean Géomètre*, 81. For examples of this type of caesura in Prodromos, see Giannelli, 'Epigrammi', 360 ff; Papagiannis, *Tetrasticha*, vol. 1, 180; and D'Ambrosi, *Gregorio Nazianzeno*, 72.

[53] This is another characteristic shared by Prodromos and Gregory of Nazianzus; cf. C. Simelidis, *Selected Poems of Gregory of Nazianzus: I.2.17; II.1.10, 19, 32: A Critical Edition with Introduction and Commentary* (Göttingen 2009), 56: 'A masculine or feminine caesura will be coupled with a bucolic diaeresis in 72.3% and 63.75% of cases, respectively.'

[54] Niketas Eugenianos is another twelfth-century poet who favours the feminine caesura—it represents 88% of his hexameters; cf. Lauxtermann, *Byzantine Poetry*, vol. 2, 360–61.

[55] De Groote, 'Metre', 574–76.

iii. Stress patterns at the caesura and the line ending

Caesura	Oxytone	Paroxytone	Proparoxytone
3a	14.01%	80.08%	5.91%
3b	2.58%	9.93%	87.49%
3c	23.31%	33.82%	43.61%

What we can see in this table is that Prodromos shows a clear tendency to regulate the stress at both the masculine and feminine caesuras: whereas the stress at the masculine caesura falls on the penultimate syllable (80.08%), in the feminine caesura it falls on the antepenultimate syllable (87.49%).[56] This stress regulation before the caesura may hint at a revival of the Nonnian and Pisidian rules.[57] It is very tempting to think that Prodromos consciously follows the metrical rules of late antique poets. For example, we know that he was well-acquainted with the poetic work of Nonnus.[58] Whatever the case, Prodromos is not the only twelfth-century poet who regulates the position of the stress; an anonymous author of a poem about the reconquest of Dorylaion in 1175 regulates the stress before the feminine caesura,[59] while Niketas Eugenianos does so before both the feminine and masculine caesuras.[60]

As far as the position of the stress at the end of the hexameters is concerned, Hörandner has claimed that there is no clear tendency: 'für die Betonung am Versschluß ist bei Prodromos weder im Hexameter noch im Pentameter irgendeine Regelung erkennbar'.[61] However, this does not seem to be the case. In 65.97% of the lines there is a stress on the penultimate, 21.19% on the last syllable, and 12.43% on the antepenultimate.[62]

The above quantitative survey may show that hexameter was nothing more than a mummified ancient metre. Unlike the dodecasyllable and political verse, it does not comply with the fundamental Byzantine metrical rule of isosyllaby. But at the same time this survey helps us to understand that its ideological connotations due to its ties to the Homeric epics were strong enough for the Byzantines to overlook the fact that it was a 'failed metrical experiment' with no rhythmical qualities.[63] The composition of

---

[56] This has already been noted in Lauxtermann, 'Papagiannis', 367–68; cf. Lauxtermann, *Byzantine Poetry*, vol. 2, 331.
[57] Lauxtermann, 'Papagiannis', 367–68.
[58] K. Spanoudakis, 'Nonnus and Theodorus Prodromus', *MEG* 13 (2013), 241–50.
[59] See F. Spingou, 'A Poem on the Refortification of Dorylaion in 1175', *Symm* 21 (2011), 137–68, at 160; cf. also Lauxtermann, *Byzantine Poetry*, vol. 2, 331.
[60] Lauxtermann, *Byzantine Poetry*, vol. 2, 331–32.
[61] Hörandner, *Historische Gedichte*, 125.   [62] Lauxtermann, *Spring*, 70.
[63] Lauxtermann, *Byzantine Poetry*, vol. 2, 285.

hexameters had become a kind of internal process for the Byzantine poets, involving the painstaking counting of long and short syllables. One could compare Prodromos' hexameters to his art of schedography. As we saw in Chapter 2, Prodromos compares his *schede* to oysters: they may have a rough shell, but they contain pearls. Similarly, the hexameters may have been rhythmically rough, but they contain prosodic pearls. The writing of hexameters had been transformed into an esoteric pursuit, possibly understood by only a small number of people with a specialized knowledge or interest. But it is certain that this small intellectual circle was enthusiastic about Prodromos' skill in writing Homeric hexameters.

3.3. Prosody

Despite the fact that Prodromos is one of the most prolific and skilled Byzantine poets, he does not escape prosodic lapses. It was on these grounds that the nineteenth-century classicist Isidor Hilberg described him as 'epigone' (as he did all well-known middle and late Byzantine poets).[64] However, a number of scholars have pointed out the challenges all Byzantine poets faced in the terrain of prosody:[65] they did their best to follow the classical rules of prosody, without being able to notice the differences with their ear. In the corpus under consideration, Prodromos adheres by and large to classical rules of prosody regarding the short vowels ε and ο and long η and ω. On the other hand, the so-called dichrona (α, ι, and υ) are scanned freely.[66]

Some prosodic errors are associated with the use of proper names: for example, Μακεδονίου (2.14) and Σοδόμων (12.2);[67] in both cases the short vowels ε and ο are measured as long. Prodromos also commits prosodic errors which are not concerned with proper names. Take, for example, 9.10 ἐπαγρυπνοῦντες: υ is measured as short though it is before two consonants; and 74.6 ἀποσκεδάζευ: -σκε- is counted as long.

---

[64] See the well-known article I. Hilberg, 'Kann Theodoros der Verfasser des Χριστὸς πάσχων sein?', *WSt* 8 (1886), 282–314, where Hilberg gave the following classification: (a) 'Klassiker', (b) 'Epigonen', and (c) 'Stümper'. For a refutation, see Maas, 'Zwölfsilber', 279, note 1; cf. also Lauxtermann, *Byzantine Poetry*, vol. 2, 325.

[65] This is even more clear in the case of the Byzantine dodecasyllable, where some tensions between theory and practice are to be noticed: see W. Hörandner, 'Beobachtungen zur Literarästhetik der Byzantiner: einige byzantinische Zeugnisse zu Metrik und Rhythmik', *BSl* 11 (1995), 279–90; Lauxtermann, 'Velocity', 9–33; and Bernard, 'Rhythm', 13–41.

[66] For examples in other works by Prodromos, see Hörandner, *Historische Gedichte*, 124, and Papagiannis, *Tetrasticha*, vol. 1, 164–65.

[67] Cf. also Papagiannis, *Tetrasticha*, vol. 1, 177.

Although diphthongs are normally measured as long, there are four exceptions: the proper name Ἡρακλείτου (75.141), and another three words in poem 10: δραμοῦμαι (v. 5), τούτου (v. 7), and στερήσει (v. 16). Interestingly enough, all three prosodic errors in poem 10 occur at the caesura:

10.5 Διψῶν πιεῖν **δραμοῦμαι** καὶ λαβεῖν κόρον
10.7 φλοῖσβος πολὺς ἐκ **τούτου**, τοῦτό μοι φόβος
10.16 αὐχμῶσαν ἐν **στερήσει** τῶν θείων λόγων

The same poem has another prosodic mistake immediately preceding the caesura in line 4. This time the prosodic mistake concerns a vowel which should be long by position:

10.4 Ἀτλαντικὸν πέλαγος, Βοσπόρου πλάτος.

But the list of the prosodic errors in poem 10 does not finish here. In line 20 (καί σοι **θαρρῶν** εἴσειμι τόνδε τὸν πόνον) the first syllable of θαρρῶν is short though the vowel is followed by two consonants. So many mistakes within a single poem are rather uncommon for Prodromos, casting doubts on the authorship of this poem. That said, I decided to include it in the corpus, since it shares some word similarities with other poems by Prodromos and survives together with other works by Prodromos in the manuscripts. What is more, some serious prosodic violations are to be found elsewhere in his work.[68]

Unlike its ancient ancestor, the Byzantine pentameter allows the use of a short syllable instead of a long one before the caesura (the so-called *brevis in longo*).[69] Similarly, Prodromos' pentameters contain quite a few instances of such *brevis in longo*: for example, 2.10 (πλέον), 2.14 (Σαβελλιάο), 2.16 (τάμε), 3.2 (εὐπαγέα), 3.12 (παγκρατέι), 3.18 (ἀέρα), and 71.10 (δαιτυμόνες).

Three further important aspects of prosody include (a) Attic correption, (b) epic correption, and (c) the use of double consonants.

3.3.1. Attic Correption

In ancient Greek, a syllable followed by a plosive and a liquid or a nasal may be measured short. The reason is that these consonant clusters do not 'close' the preceding syllable. This phenomenon is called Attic correption. Just like

---

[68] For example, in historical poem 2, v. 62, the eta in the word σιδηροῦν is measured short.
[69] Lauxtermann, *Byzantine Poetry*, vol. 2, 269.

other Byzantine poets, Prodromos does not make a consistent use of Attic correption.[70] Take, for example, the consonant cluster -βρ-, which frequently allows for correption (e.g. 3.19, 3.23, 5.19), but in other cases it does not (12.1 or 13.6). Another good example is the cluster -θλ-: in some poems Prodromos measures the preceding syllable short (e.g. 4.13; 4.24) and in some others long (3.19 and 5.19). Similarly, there are metrical correptions before the consonant cluster -τλ- (1.10; 1.14; 4.16; 13.4), but this is again not a consistent practice, since there are also examples without correption (e.g. 21.9 and 73.12). The same goes for -σμ- (correption in 1.2, 3.24, 4.13; no correption in 1.13 and 3.8). Finally, the correption before the cluster -δν- (76.283) is very interesting. On the other hand, the correption in 9.10 (νύκτα) is probably an error.

3.3.2. Epic Correption

When a word begins with a vowel, the long end vowel or diphthong of the word that precedes it is shortened. This phenomenon is called epic correption. It is not to be found in the accentual metres of the corpus, but it is very common in its dactylic metres, occurring no fewer than 40 times. The most frequent cases of epic correption concern the diphthong -αι-: 1.3, 6, 21; 2.1, 9; 3.1, 20; 4.1, 11; 5.3; 6.1, 3, 13, and 23; 6.7, 9; 27.1, 4; 28.1, 2; 68.3, 4, 7; 69.9 (twice), 12; 72.3; 73.6, 7, and 14; 74.5, 10. Out of these 31 cases, 14 are related to the conjunction καί. Epic correption also occurs immediately before the caesura: five times at a feminine caesura (1.3; 4.13; 21.8; 73.14; 5.19), two at a masculine caesura (4.11; 70.7), and nine at a *bucolic diaeresis* (2.1; 3.1; 4.1; 4.1; 27.1, 4; 28. 1; 68.4; 74.24).

3.3.3. Duplication of Consonants

The use of double consonants to lengthen the preceding short vowel or dichronon is common in Prodromos' dactylic poetry.[71] Here, short vowels and dichrona are lengthened before the double consonants -μμ- and -σσ- in the following cases:

---

[70] Lauxtermann, *Byzantine Poetry*, vol. 2, 290–91.
[71] See also Papagiannis, *Tetrasticha*, vol. 1, 168–75.

3.14: δείξας ἑοῖο λόγου ἀρραγέεσσι (.....) λίνοις.
68.1: Υἱέος ἡμετέρου με φιτύσσατο (....) δῖα θυγάτηρ
69.1: Ξεῖνε, τί νῦν με δέδορκας, ἑὸν περὶ ὄμμα πετάσσας (...)
73.13: ὔμμεσιν (...) ἐμμογέων· τό δ' ἐτώσιος ἔπλετ' ὀιζύς
74.24: Εἰ δ' ἄρα μὴ θυμέλῃσι παρέμμεναι (...) ἔσχες ἐέλδωρ,

On the other hand, duplication of the consonants -σ- in the word ἁπάντε(σ)σι in 2.19 and -ν- in the word ἀναδαίν(ν)υμαι, which occurs three times in poem 69 (once ἀναδαίν(ν)υμαι, twice δαίν(ν)υμαι), is not necessary.

3.4. Hiatus

Let us conclude this chapter with some brief remarks about the hiatus, which occurs when two vowels clash at the boundary of two successive words because of the lack of an intervening consonant. In following the Byzantine practice, Prodromos avoids hiatus in the dodecasyllabic poems. The 751 dodecasyllables do not have a single example of hiatus. To avoid hiatus, Prodromos frequently drops the final vowel before a word that begins with a vowel. Take, for example, 9.10 παρ' ὅλην; 9.24 ἀλλ' οὐδέ; 14.4 καθ' Ἡσαΐαν; 14.6 ἆρ' ἀετός; 19.8 ἀφ' ὕψους, etc.

Again following Byzantine practice, Prodromos allows hiatus in the dactylic metres. Even though he makes extensive use of elision in the dactylic poems,[72] the 232 dactylic verses (23.15% of the entire corpus) have no fewer than 73 instances of hiatus.[73] In the 92 dactylic pentameters (9.18% of the total), 22 instances of hiatus are found. Out of the 22 instances, 12 occur at the caesura (1.20; 2.22; 3.6, 14; 4.18; 6.2; 70.4, 8; 71.2). In the 140 dactylic hexameters (13.97% of the total), 51 instances of hiatus occur, of which 10 (1.9; 2.15; 4.9; 75.1, 9; 76.15, 20, and 28; 70.9; 74.3) at a masculine or feminine caesura (3a or 3b) and 15 at a *bucolic diaeresis* (2.1; 3.1; 4.1, 11, and 19; 5.9; 6.1; 27.1; 28.4; 68.3; 69.1, 5; 71.5; 73.9, 14). As for the hiatus after καί, it occurs 8 times (4.11; 6.11, 13; 21.7, 9; 68.7, 12; 75.19).

---

[72] Approximately eighty cases of elision are to be found in the dactylic poems. Some of these elisions are not common in classical poetry, such as 1.8 γράμμαθ' and 3.11 κακοφρονέοντ' (elisions of ι); and 71.12 λίσσομ'.

[73] We encounter a similar picture in the tetrastichs on the Old and New Testaments; see Papagiannis, *Tetrasticha*, vol. 1, 181–82 and 187.

4
Manuscript Transmission

The first systematic survey of the vast manuscript transmission of the entire work of Theodoros Prodromos was carried out by Wolfram Hörandner in his doctoral thesis 'Studien zur Überlieferung der Werke des Theodoros Prodromos', submitted in 1966 at the University of Vienna. This thesis was never published as a separate study; instead, it was included as an introductory chapter to his edition of the *historische Gedichte*.[1] Hörandner's list of the manuscript tradition of Prodromos' work remains an extremely useful research tool, but since the focus there is on the *Historical poems*, it occasionally pays less attention to other works (including the *Miscellaneous poems*). For example, the folios of the manuscripts with the *Miscellaneous poems* are quite frequently not indicated. Moreover, some manuscript descriptions are outdated, since his edition appeared approximately five decades ago. The first section of this chapter comprises brief descriptions of all the manuscripts which transmit the poems. The second section then discusses Vaticanus gr. 305, the main textual witness to Prodromos' work. Building upon these two sections, the third section looks at the reception of the *Miscellaneous poems* in the late Byzantine and post-Byzantine periods. The final section briefly discusses the relationships between the manuscripts.

4.1. Description of the Manuscripts

Eighty-seven manuscripts dating from the thirteenth to the nineteenth centuries contain one or more poems of the present corpus. None of the manuscripts transmits all the *Miscellaneous poems* together. Twenty-seven of the manuscripts were unknown to Hörandner (they are indicated with *), while his list is not always accurate, since some of the poems do not survive in all the manuscripts he included in his survey. Poem 70 is not transmitted in Lond. Harl. 5624,[2] nor are poems 62–66 and 76 preserved in Esc. Y-III-9 and

---

[1] Hörandner, *Historische Gedichte*, 135–48.   [2] Hörandner, *Historische Gedichte*, 55.

Theodoros Prodromos: Miscellaneous Poems: An Edition and Literary Study. Nikos Zagklas, Oxford University Press.
© Nikolaos Zagklas 2023. DOI: 10.1093/oso/9780192886927.003.0004

Vat. gr. 1126, respectively.[3] The manuscript descriptions, based mainly on inspections *in situ* and secondary literature, are kept short. They aim to provide basic information about various aspects of the manuscripts, including dating, codicological details, contents, and select bibliography. Manuscripts dating later than the sixteenth century do not bear a siglum, and their descriptions are normally shorter. If a manuscript is not used for the construction of the critical text (irrespective of whether it dates before or after the sixteenth century), the exact title of a poem is given in its description. Whenever a folio number is not accompanied by (r) or (v), it refers to both its sides.

AUSTRIA

Vienna, Österreichische Nationalbibliothek

1. (*Vz*) *Vindobonensis Historicus gr. 106*

14th cent.; paper; 210 × 145/150 mm.; IV + 187 folios (I–IV, 186 and 187 flyleaves); 22–25 lines per page; written by Γεώργιος ὁ θύτης.

Contents: e.g. Konstantinos Manasses, Michael Louloudes, Ioannes Pediasimos, Ioannes Tzetzes, Iakovos of Bulgaria, Ioannes of Damascus, and some unedited verses.

Miscellaneous poems: fol. 142^r (22).

Bibliography: H. Hunger, *Katalog der griechischen Handschriften der Österreichischen Nationalbibliothek, Teil 1. Codices historici, Codices philosophici et philologici* (Vienna 1961), 112–13.

2. (*Vu*) *Vindobonensis Philologicus gr. 110*

16th cent. (middle, before 1562); paper; 260 × 185 mm; II + 553 (+2a, 65a 249a–γ, 518a) folios (I, II, 249a–γ, 546, 547 flyleaves); 23 lines per page; a two-volume manuscript (1^r–249^v and 250^r–553^v) written by Mathousalas Kabbades (cf. the subscriptions on fols. 11^v, 243^v, 246^r, 368^v). According to a note on fols. II^r and 518a^v, the manuscript was collected by Augier Ghislain de Busbecq (1522–1592), during his service as ambassador of Ferdinand I of Austria in Constantinople.

Contents: mainly philosophical works, e.g. Georgios Pachymeres, Simplikios, Themistios, Alexander of Aphrodisias, Michael Psellos, Maximos the Confessor, Gregory of Nyssa, Nemesios of Emesa, Georgios Gemistos Plethon, Nikephoros

---

[3] Hörandner, *Historische Gedichte*, 53.

Blemmydes, the astrological poem of Konstantinos Manasses (attributed wrongly to Prodromos), Theodoret of Cyrrhus, etc.

Miscellaneous poems: fol. 532ᵛ (62–66: 'ἐπὶ κήπῳ').

Bibliography: Hunger, *Codices historici, Codices philosophici et philologici*, 218–22 (with bibliography); M. Vogel and V. Gardthausen, *Die griechischen Schreiber des Mittelalters und der Renaissance* (Leipzig 1909; repr. Hildesheim 1996), 270; Hörandner, *Historische Gedichte*, 147; C. N. Constantinides and R. Browning, *Dated Greek Manuscripts from Cyprus to the Year 1570* (Washington DC/Nicosia 1993), 308–11, esp. note 6; L. S. B. MacCoull, 'Mathousala Macheir and the Melkite Connection', *Script* 50 (1996), 114–16; R. S. Stefec, 'Zu einigen zypriotischen Handschriften der Österreichischen Nationalbibliothek', *RBNS* 49 (2012), 53–78, at 65, note 43.

3. (Vi) *Vindobonensis Philologicus gr. 149*

14th cent.; paper; 230/235 × 140/150 mm.; VII + 358 folios with 21–30 lines per page; as with the previous manuscript, it was acquired by Augier Ghislain de Busbecq (1522–1592), who was Ferdinand's ambassador in Constantinople (cf. fols. Vʳ and 354ᵛ).

Contents: e.g. Georgios Pisides, Michael Psellos, Symeon the New Theologian, Konstantinos Manasses, Christophoros Mitylenaios, Libanius, Gregory of Nazianzus, anonymous works, Symeon (the son of Seth), Ioannes of Damascus, Ps-Dionysios Areopagites, Basil of Caesarea, Ioannes (metropolitan of Kiev), Diadochos, Neilos, Sozomenos of Bethelia, Splenios, Nikephoros I (patriarch of Constantinople), excerpts from various authors (John Chrysostom, Theodoret of Cyrrhus, Makarios of Alexandreia, Isidoros of Pelousion, Anastasios Sinaites, Barsanouphios, Ioannes Klimax, and Dorotheos), Michael Glykas, Nikephoros Blemmydes, Perdikas of Ephesos, Gregorios of Cyprus, and Andronikos Komnenos (Doukas) Palaiologos.

Miscellaneous poems: fols. 173ᵛ (7), 173ᵛ (8), 173ᵛ (25).

Bibliography: Hunger, *Codices historici, Codices philosophici et philologici*, 250–55 (with bibliography); F. Gonnelli, *Giorgio di Pisidia, Esamerone* (Pisa 1998), 35; M. de Groote, *Christophori Mitylenaii, Versvvm variorvm, collectio crypte* (Turnhout 2012), L.

4. (Vt) *Vindobonensis Theologicus gr. 249*

16th cent. (middle); paper; 208/212 × 145/150 mm.; XII + 101 (+54α–γ, 54α–η) folios (I–X, 87–90 flyleaves); 26 lines.

Contents: various theological works, including Athanasios of Alexandreia, anonymous epigrams (unedited), Theophylaktos Simokattes, anonymous paraphrase of the psalms, Gregory of Nazianzus, Metrophanes of Smyrna,

Basil of Caesarea. Also, on fols. 79ᵛ–80ʳ: a list of titles of some poems of Prodromos and Kallikles, as well as of the *Synopsis Sacrae Scripturae* of Nikephoros Kallistou Xanthopoulos (perhaps a preliminary table of contents for a planned edition).

Miscellaneous poems: fols. 51ᵛ–52ᵛ (29–54: 'τοῦ σοφωτάτου Ψελλοῦ ἴαμβοι εἰς ἀρετὰς καὶ κακίας').

Bibliography: H. Hunger (with the collaboration of W. Lackner and Ch. Hannick), *Katalog der griechischen Handschriften der Österreichischen Nationalbibliothek, Teil 3/2. Codices historici, Codices Theologici 201-337* (Vienna 1992), 170–73 (with bibliography).

5. (Z) *Vindobonensis Suppl. gr. 125*

13th cent. (second half); paper (oriental); 210/215 × 150 mm; II + 14 folios (I + 14 flyleaves); partly 2 cols; 33–35 lines. The manuscript is in poor condition due to an unsuccessful restoration.

Contents: anonymous verses (inc. Φαρισαΐζων, ἱεροῦ μακρὰν γίνου), Gregory of Nazianzos, Michael Hagiotheodorites, anonymous works, Niketas Seides, Maximos Monachos, Poems from the Palatine Anthology.

Miscellaneous poems: fol. 4 (62–66), 4ᵛ (55–56), 4ᵛ (58).

Bibliography: H. Hunger (with the collaboration of C. Hannick), *Katalog der griechischen Handschriften der Österreichischen Nationalbibliothek, Teil 4. Codices Supplementum Graecum* (Vienna 1994), 212–14 (with bibliography); Hörandner, *Historische Gedichte*, 164–65.

BULGARIA

Sofia, The Scientific Archives of the Bulgarian Academy of Sciences

6. (Y) *Sofiensis Centri 'Ivan Dujčev' gr. 12**

15th cent. (1st quarter); paper; 290/210 × 200/60 mm.; 168 folios; written by an unknown scribe (the same scribe added the poem on Basil of Caesarea in the fourteenth-century manuscript Ax).

Contents: a rich collection of Homilies by Basil of Caesarea, anonymous verses on Gregory of Nyssa, Gregory of Nyssa, Ps. Justinus Martyr (Theodoret of Cyrrhus?).

Miscellaneous poems: fol. 4ᵛ (3).

Bibliography: D. Getov, *A Catalogue of Greek Manuscripts in the Scientific Archives of the Bulgarian Academy of Sciences* (Sofia 2010), 28–32 (with bibliography).

FRANCE

Lyon, Bibliothèque municipale

7. (Ly) *Lugdunensis 122 (52)* *

16th–17th cent.; paper; 134 × 92 mm.; 215 folios.

Contents: e.g. Θεοτοκία ἀπολυτικὰ ψαλλόμενα ἐν ὅλῳ ἐνιαυτῷ, Isaak Monachos, Dionysios Stoudites, Basil of Caesarea, Maximos the Confessor, Epiphanios of Salamis, Dionysios of Alexandreia, Theodoretos of Cyrrhus, Nemesios of Emesa, etc.

Miscellaneous poems: fols. 15–17ʳ (29–54: 'τοῦ σοφωτάτου Μιχαὴλ τοῦ Ψελλοῦ, ἴαμβοι εἰς τὰς ἀρετὰς καὶ κακίας').

Bibliography: H. Omont, *Inventaire sommaire des manuscrits grecs de la Bibliothèque nationale et des autres bibliothèques de Paris et des Départements*, 4 vols. (Paris 1886–98; repr. 4 vols., Hildesheim/Zurich/New York 2000), vol. 3, 371.

Paris, Bibliothèque Nationale de France

8. (Py) *Parisinus gr. 554*

13th cent.; parchment; 242 folios; fols. 1–3 were written by a later hand (in the 15th cent.); it belonged to the cardinal Niccolò Ridolfi.

Contents: a praise poem on Gregory of Nazianzus by Ioannes Eugenikos, followed by a rich collection of works by Gregory of Nazianzus.

Miscellaneous poems: fols. 1ᵛ–2ʳ (2).

Bibliography: Omont, *Inventaire sommaire*, vol. I, 85–86.

9. (R) *Parisinus gr. 854*

13th cent.; paper (oriental); 260 × 170 mm. (260 × 150 Markesinis); II + 422 folios; a collection of four originally separate codices: (a) 1–120, (b) 121–244, (c) 245–327, and (d) 328–422, of which the second contains works of Prodromos; at least two scribes (a) 1–34, 48–350, 361–366, 377–378, 382–405, 420–422 (b) 35–47, 360, 367–376, 379–381, 406–419ʳ, or one scribe with two different handwritings (cf. Markesinis). According to a monogram on fol. Aʳ, the manuscript belonged to the private library of the Abramius family from the island of Corfu, but sometime after 1533 it was sold together with other books to various book collectors.

Contents: e.g. Nilus of Sinai, Ioannes of Damascus, Gregorios Thaumatourgos, Germanos I (patriarch of Constantinople), Germanos II (patriarch of Constantinople), Athanasios of Alexandreia, Palaephatus, Epiphanios of Constantinople, Anastasios Sinaites, an anonymous work, Konstantinos VII Porphyrogennetos, Clement of Alexandria, Maximos the Confessor, Sophronios of Jerusalem, Georgios Choiroboskos, Georgios Pisides, Gregory of Nyssa, Geoponica, Libanius, Chorikios of Gaza, various anonymous works, Geometres' poem on St Panteleemon, etc.

Miscellaneous poems: fols. 228^v–229^r (29–54), 229^r (7), 229^v–230^r (9), 230^r (62–66), 232 (11–20).

Bibliography: Omont, *Inventaire sommaire*, vol. 1, 159–60; L. Sternbach, 'Spicilegium Prodromeum', *Rozprawy Akademii Umiejętności, Wydział filologiczny*, ser. II, 24 (1904). 336–68 (also published separately: Krakow 1904) 1–12; Hörandner, *Historische Gedichte*, 143 and 156–57; Gonnelli, *Giorgio di Pisidia*, 25 (with bibliography); B. Markesinis, 'Les extraits de S. Maxime le Confesseur transmis par le Parisinus gr. 854 (13e s.)', *Orientalia Lovaniensia Periodica* 31 (2000–05), 109–17 (with bibliography); B. Markesinis, 'Janos Lascaris, la bibliothèque d'Avramis à Corfou et le Paris. Gr. 854', *Script* 54 (2000), 302–06; D. F. Jackson, 'Janus Lascaris on the Island of Corfu in A.D. 1491', *Script* 57 (2003), 137–39.

10. (Pi) *Parisinus gr. 997*

a. 1231; parchment; 160 × 108 mm.; 321 folios; a palimpsest codex written by the monk Germanos Lignos in Nicaea.

Contents: Niketas of Herakleia (commentary on the homilies of Gregory of Nazianzus).

Miscellaneous poems: fols. 320^r (27–28), 320^r–321^v (21).

Bibliography: Omont, *Inventaire sommaire*, vol. 1, 199; *RGK* 2.68; Vogel and Gardthausen, *Schreiber*, 68; G. Prato, 'La produzione libraria in area Greco-Orientale nel periodo del regno Latino di Constantinopoli (1204–1261)', in: G. Prato (ed.), *Studi di Paleografia Greca* (Spoleto 1994), 38.

11. (Pc) *Parisinus gr. 1277*

13th cent.; paper (oriental) without watermarks (fols. 9–16, 308–309, Parchment); VI + 309 + III' folios; 1–8 225 × 145 mm. (240 × 160 mm. Gonnelli), the fol. from parchment 240 × 150 mm., 17ff. 245 × 150 mm. (240 × 160 Gonnelli); written by ten different scribes (cf. Papagiannis), the ms. was owned by a certain Eustathios [cf. fol. 307^v: τοῦτο τὸ βιβλίον ἐστὶν Εὐσταθίου τοῦ σαλων(οῦ)?].

Contents: mainly theological texts such as works by Basil of Caesarea, Gregory of Nyssa, Michael Psellos, Gregory of Nazianzus, Georgios Pisides, Nikolaos (metropolitan of Corfu), Sententiae of Aesop, Nikolaos Mouzalon, Symeon Logothetes, Maximos the Confessor, etc.

Miscellaneous poems: fol. 200^v (22–23).

Bibliography: Omont, *Inventaire sommaire*, vol. 1, 284–85; Hörandner, *Historische Gedichte*, 143; Papagiannis, *Tetrasticha*, vol. 1, 38–39 (with bibliography); Gonnelli, *Giorgio di Pisidia*, 26 (with bibliography); B. Janssens, *Maximi Confessoris ambigua ad Thomam una cum epistula secunda ad eundem* (Turnhout 2002), LXXIII and LXXVI–LXXX (with comprehensive bibliography).

12. (Pz) *Parisinus gr. 1630*

14th cent.; paper (oriental); 159 × 112 mm.; XIX + 278 (+217a, 221a, 261a, –171–180) folios; written by Chariton from the Hodegon Monastery between 1319 and 1346; it belonged to Antonios Eparchos (fol. B8ᵛ Κτῆμα Ἀντωνίου τοῦ Ἐπάρχου, ὃ δέδωκε τῷ κραταιῷ βασιλεῖ Κελτῶν ἐμπεριέχεται δέ, ὅσα ἐν τῷ ἑξῆς πίνακι γράφεται).

Contents: Nikephoros Kallistou Xanthopoulos, Galen, Theophilos Protospatharios, Theophanes Chrysobalantes, Michael Psellos, Manuel Philes, Apollinarios, Ioannes Geometres, Epiphanios of Salamis, Anastasios Sinaites, Gregorios Thaumatourgos, Andreas of Crete, Gregory of Nyssa, Herodian, Christophoros Mitylenaios, Basileios Megalomites, Leon Bardales, Georgios Pisides, Proklos, Alexandros of Aphrodisias, St Maximos, Hippocrates, Ioannes of Antiocheia, Lucian, Moiris, γνῶμαι and various anonymous treatises.

Miscellaneous poems: fols. 138ʳ (69), 138ʳ (68), 170ʳ (57–61).

Bibliography: Omont, *Inventaire sommaire*, vol. 2, 109–12; RGK 1.23, 2.32, 3.36; Lauxtermann, *Byzantine Poetry*, vol. 1, 290–93; de Groote, *Christophori Mitylenaii*, XLII; I. Pérez Martín, 'Les Kephalaia de Chariton des Hodèges (Paris, BNF Gr. 1630)', in: P. Van Deun and C. Macé (eds), *Encyclopedic Trends in Byzantium?* (Leuven/Paris/Walpole, MA 2011), 361–81 (with detailed bibliography).

13. (P) *Parisinus gr. 2831*

13th cent.; paper (oriental); 140 × 225 mm; I + 164 + II' folios; the ms. was written by several hands (Papagiannis has argued for five or even seven hands).

Contents: Lexical fragments, Theocritus, Georgios Pisides.

Miscellaneous poems: fols. 122ʳ (22–23), 122ʳ (57–61), 122 (73–74), 146 (62–66), 151ᵛ (1).

Bibliography: Omont, *Inventaire sommaire*, vol. 3, 46–47; Hörandner, *Historische Gedichte*, 157–59; Papagiannis, *Tetrasticha*, vol. 1, 39–41; D'Ambrosi, *Gregorio Nazianzeno*, 108.

14. (Pt) *Parisinus gr. 2870*

16th cent. (second half); paper; 224 × 152 mm.; I + 48 folios; written by Ἄγγελος Βεργίκιος.

Contents: Georgios Pisides.

Miscellaneous poems: fols. 39ʳ–42ʳ (75: 'Στίχοι τινὲς σχετλιαστικοὶ εἰς τὴν πρόνοιαν τοῦ σοφοῦ Θεοδώρου τοῦ Προδρόμου'), 42ᵛ–48ʳ (76: 'Τοῦ αὐτοῦ, ἐπὶ ἀποδήμῳ φιλίᾳ, στίχοι, κατὰ διάλογον').

Bibliography: Omont, *Inventaire sommaire*, vol. 3, 52; *RGK* 1.3, 2.3; Vogel and Gardthausen, *Schreiber*, 2–6; Gonnelli, *Giorgio di Pisidia*, 28.

15. (Pf) *Parisinus gr. 3019*
15th cent.; paper; 248 folios.
Contents: Libanius, several epigrams, Philostratus.
Miscellaneous poems: fol. 206ʳ (62).
Bibliography: Omont, *Inventaire sommaire*, vol. 3, 93.

16. (Pa) *Parisinus gr. 3058*
16th cent. (terminus ante quem 1519); paper; 374 folios; written by Arsenios of Monembasia for Pope Leo X.

Contents: Συναγωγὴ παροιμιῶν (Violarium) by Michael Apostoles supplemented with gnomic and moral texts of various ancient Greek and Byzantine authors, ranging from Simonides and Menander to Isidoros of Pelousion, Michael Psellos, and Ioannes Tzetzes.

Miscellaneous poems: fols. 35 (55), 36ʳ–37ᵛ (29–54).

Bibliography: Omont, *Inventaire sommaire*, vol. 3, 101; *RGK* 1.27, 2.38, III no. 46; Vogel and Gardthausen, *Schreiber*, 42–44; N. Agiotis, 'Tzetzes on Psellos revisited', *BZ* 106 (2013), 1–8, at 3.

17. (Su) *Parisinus Suppl. gr. 501*
15th cent.; paper; 19 folios; the handwriting is very similar to that of Michael Kritoboulos (cf. *RGK* 2.384).
Contents: Konstantinos Manasses (the astrological poem).
Prodromos: fol. 18ᵛ (62–64).
Bibliography: Omont, *Inventaire sommaire*, vol. 3, 270; Hörandner, *Historische Gedichte*, 159.

GERMANY

Heidelberg, Ruprecht-Karls-Universität

18. (H) *Heidelbergensis Palatinus gr. 43*
13th cent. (15th cent. Stevenson, 12th cent. Agapitos); paper (oriental); VI + 93 + VI' folios (38ʳ is blank); one scribe with two handwritings: style A: fols. 1ʳ–34ʳ, 34ᵛ–38ᵛ, 83ʳ–93ʳ and style B: fols. 34ʳ–83ʳ (cf. Agapitos).
Contents: Proklos, Ps. Phocylides, Musaeus Grammatikos.

Miscellaneous poems: fols. 36ᵛ (62–66), 90 (55–56), 90ᵛ (57–61), 90ᵛ (68).

Bibliography: H. M. Stevenson, *Codices manuscripti Palatini Graeci Bibliothecae Vaticanae* (Rome 1885), 23; Hörandner, *Historische Gedichte*, 151; P. A. Agapitos, 'Poets and Painters: Theodoros Prodromos' Dedicatory Verses of His Novel to an Anonymous Caesar', *JÖB* 50 (2000), 173–85, at 173–74.

19. (He) *Heidelbergensis Palatinus gr. 356*

13th cent. (15th cent. Stevenson); paper (oriental); IV + 196 + III' folios (196ᵛ is blank); mutilated at the beginning; among the owners of the ms. were Arsenios Apostoles (fol. IIIᵛ: τὸ παρὸν βιβλίον κτῆμά ἐστιν Ἀρσενίου τοῦ Μονεμβασίας) and George, Count of Corinth (fol. IIIᵛ: one reads τὸ νῦν δὲ Γεωργίου Κόμητος τοῦ Κορινθίου).

Contents: e.g. Libanius, Michael Psellos, Severos, Phalaris, Gregory of Nazianzus, Basil of Caesarea, Apollonius of Tyana, Synesios of Cyrene, Theophylaktos Simokattes, John Chrysostom, Isocrates, Agapetos Diakonos, Ioannes Tzetzes, Konstantinos Stilbes, Eustathios Kanikles, Sententiae, Georgios Choiroboskos, Konstantinos Manasses, some riddles (unedited), Epiphanios, etc.

Miscellaneous poems: fols. 167ʳ (7), 167ʳ (8), 167ᵛ (62–66), 168ʳ (55–56).[4]

Bibliography: Stevenson, *Palatini Graeci*, 203–07; Hörandner, *Historische Gedichte*, 140; J. Diethart and W. Hörandner, *Constantinus Stilbes, Poemata* (Munich 2005), XX; http://digi.ub.uni-heidelberg.de/diglit/cpgraec356.

Göttingen, Niedersächsische Staats- und Universitätsbibliothek

20. *Philologigus gr. 4*

18th cent.; paper; 200 × 140 mm.; 189 pages.

Contents: poems from the Anthologia Graeca, along with the notes of Claudius Salmasius.

Miscellaneous poems: p. 171 (62–66), 171 (68).

Bibliography: W. Meyer, *Die Handschriften in Göttingen*, vol. 1 (Berlin 1893) 3–4.

21. (Go) *Philologicus gr. 29*

13th cent. (fols. 1–11, 127–136, 138, 165–167, 174–176, 183 from the 16th cent.); paper; 183 folios.

Contents: Pindar, Nikolaos Kallikles, Christophoros, Mitylenaios, Nicander (Theriaka and Alexipharmaka).

Miscellaneous poems: fol. 137ʳ (26).

---

[4] Hörandner did not notice that fol. 167ᵛ–168ʳ preserve the historical poem 7.

Bibliography: Meyer, *Göttingen*, 9–10; A. Crugnola, *Scholia in Nicandri Theriaca cum glossis* (Milan–Varese 1971), 3–6.

Munich, Bayerische Staatsbibliothek

22. (*Mo*) *Monacensis gr. 306**

16th cent. (second half); paper; IV + 63 (+2a, 18a, 18β, 21a, 38a, 49a) folios (I^r, II, IV^v, 2a, 3, 18^v, 18a, 18β, 21a, 38β, 49a, 63 are blank); written by Andreas Darmarios.

Contents: Proklos, Andronicus of Rhode, Hippolytus of Rome, Dexippus, Michael Psellos, an anonymous post-Byzantine dodecasyllabic epigram (εἰς τὸν μέλλοντα βίον), and various other treatises.

Miscellaneous poems: fol. 61 (55–56).

Bibliography: I. Hardt, *Catalogus codicum manuscriptorum graecorum bibliothecae Regiae Bavariae*, 5 vols. (Munich 1806–12), vol. 3, 241–44; *RGK* 1.13, 2. 21.

GREAT BRITAIN (UNITED KINGDOM)

London, British Library

23. (l) *Londiniensis Add. 10014*

15th–16th cent.; paper; 190 × 140 mm.; 294 folios; written by at least nine different scribes: (a) 3–47; (b) 48–67; (c) 68–113; (d) 114–142^v; (e) 143–148^v; (f) 149–152; (g) 153–264; (h) 265–279, 287–294(?); (i) 280–286; the codex changed many hands before entering the British Library in January 1836.

Contents: e.g. Makarios of Alexandreia, Ephraem the Syrian, a vita of Adam et Eve, Damaskenos the Studite, Eusebius of Caesarea, Acts of the Quinisext Council, John Chrysostom, Philippos Monotropos, Basil of Caesarea, Gregory of Nazianzus, Michael Psellos, a treatise on the twelve months, Jokes of Hierokles, Manuel Philes, Georgios Pisides, Michael Glykas, and various other treatises, etc.

Miscellaneous poems: fols. 221^r (57–61: 'εἰς δακτύλιον ἔχοντα σφραγῖδα ἐρῶντας δύο, καὶ ἀπὸ τῶν στέρνων αὐτῶν δύο δένδρα ἐκπεφυκότα, καὶ εἰς ἕνα συγκορυφούμενον κόρυμβον'), 224^v (7: 'εἰς τὸν Ἀβρὰμ ξενίζοντα τὴν ἁγίαν Τριάδα').

Bibliography: Hörandner, *Historische Gedichte*, 142 and 154; O. Lampsides, '῎Ενα ἀνδριακὸ χειρόγραφο στὴ Βιβλιοθήκη τοῦ Λονδίνου', *Θεολογία* 60 (1989), 167–75; https://www.bl.uk/manuscripts/FullDisplay.aspx?ref=Add_MS_10014 (with bibliography); K. Kubina, 'Manuel Philes and the Asan

Family: Two Inedited Poems and Their Context in Philes' Œuvre (Including Editio Princeps)", *JÖB* 63 (2013), 177–98, at 179.

24. (Lh) *Londiniensis Harl. 5624*

14th (2nd half) – 15th cent.; paper; 211/150 × 137/90 mm.; 423 folios; two main scribes: the first was responsible for fols. 15–196 and the second for fols. 290–392; fols. 206ᵛ–209 were written by Michael Kalophrenas.

Contents: Letters, theological, and astrological works, e.g. Theophylaktos Simokattes, Hexameters on the Acts of the Apostles (unedited?), Fragment on the Apostle Peter, Ps. Phocylides, Michael Synkellos, Ἐπιτομὴ νέα γραμματικὴ (a grammar book), Φιλοσοφίας ὅροι περὶ οὐσίας καὶ συμβεβηκότος, Ὅροι φιλοσοφίας κατὰ στοιχεῖον, Formulary for ecclesiastical letters, Lord's Prayer, Τύπος καὶ ὑπογραμμὸς βεβαίωσις τῆς πίστης, Michael Kalophrenas, sacro-profane Sententiae, Τεχνολογία περὶ ἀντιστοίχων, Περὶ μέτρων, Philosophical diagrams, Agapetus diaconus, Horoscope of 12 Loci, Ioannes of of Damascus, Michael Psellos, Theodoros Laskaris, Riddles, Manuel Mazaris, Pisides, *Hexaemeron* (lines 1151 ff.), Ps. Dionysios Areopagites, Basil of Caesarea, Περὶ μουσικῆς, Περὶ ἀστρονομίας, Notes about the Procession of the Holy Spirit from the Father and not from the Son, Περὶ γραμματικῆς, Σύνοψις τῶν πέντε φωνῶν, Death-bed advice to a son, Symeon Metaphrastes, Περὶ τῆς γενέσεως τοῦ δυσσεβοῦς Μωάμεθ, Ὅρκος τῶν Μουσουλμάνων πρὸς Χριστιανούς, Table of lunar zodiacal motion.

Miscellaneous poems: fols. 12ʳ–13ᵛ (75); the first 22 verses of the poem were also copied by the same hand on fol. 14ʳ.

Bibliography: R. Nares, *A Catalogue of the Harleian Manuscripts in the British Museum*, 3 vols. (London 1808–12), vol. 3, 282; *RGK* 2.382; Vogel and Gardthausen, *Schreiber*, 312–13; Hörandner, *Historische Gedichte*, 142; http://www.bl.uk/manuscripts/FullDisplay.aspx?ref=Harley_MS_5624 (with bibliography).

Oxford, Bodleian Library

25. (Ba) *Bodleianus Barocci 197*

a. 1343 or early in 1344; paper; 315 × 205 mm.; folios 673, 32 lines to a page; written by the hieromonk Galaktion Madarakis.

Contents: dozens of works of theological and hagiographical interest.

Miscellaneous poems: fols. 209ᵛ–210ᵛ (11–20).

Bibliography: H. O. Coxe, *Bodleian Library Quarto Catalogues, I. Greek Manuscripts* (Oxford 1969; repr. with corrections from the edition of 1853), 341–51; *RGK* 1.44; *PLP* 7 no. 16102; Vogel and Gardthausen, *Schreiber*, 63; A. Turyn, *Dated Greek Manuscripts of the Thirteenth and Fourteenth*

Centuries in the Libraries of Great Britain (Washington DC 1980), 108–12; S. Kotzabassi, *Die handschriftliche Überlieferung der rhetorischen und hagiographischen Werke des Gregor von Zypern* (Wiesbaden 1998), 152–55; A. Giannouli, 'Eine Rede auf das Akathistos-Fest und Theodoros II. Dukas Laskaris (BHG3 1140, CPG 8197)', *JÖB* 51 (2001), 259–83, at 270–71; T. Antonopoulou, 'Ἀνώνυμο ποίημα για την αγία Βαρβάρα από τον κώδικα Barocci 197', in: Th. Korres, P. Katsoni, I. Leontiadis, and A. Goutzioukostas (eds), *Φιλοτιμία: Τιμητικὸς τόμος για την ομότιμη καθηγήτρια Ἀλκμήνη Σταυρίδου-Ζαφράκα* (Thessaloniki 2011, 69–74; repr. in *Βυζαντινή Ομιλητική, Συγγραφείς και κείμενα* (Athens 2013), 480–85); E. Kiapidou, 'Critical Remarks on Theophylact of Ohrid's Martyrdom of the Fifteen Martyrs of Tiberiopolis: The Editorial Adventure of a Text from the Middle Ages', *Parekbolai* 2 (2012), 27–47 (with bibliography).

26. (B) *Bodleianus Roe 18 (olim ecclesiae S. Trinitatis apud insulam Chalcen)*

a. 1349 (on fol. 476ᵛ: ἐτελειώθη ἡ βίβλος αὕτη διὰ χειρὸς ἐμοῦ Κω(νσταντίνου) τοῦ σοφοῦ κ(α)τὰ μῆνα σεπτ(έμβ)ριον τῆς β΄ ἰν(δικτιῶνος) τοῦ ͵ςωνζ΄ ἔτους); paper; 300 × 205 mm; 475 folios; written by Konstantinos Sophos.

Contents: a miscellaneous codex, e.g. Manuel Philes, a number of legal treatises, Photios, Theodoros Stoudites, Theodoros Balsamon, Petros Chartophylax, Basil of Caesarea, Nikephoros I (patriarch of Constantinople), Sisinnios II (patriarch of Constantinople), Elias of Crete, Niketas of Herakleia, Nikephoros Chartophylax, Ioannes of Karpathos, Konstantinos Manasses, Gregory of Nazianzus, Georgios Pisides, Ioannes Tzetzes, etc.

Miscellaneous poems: fols. 446ʳ (22–23), 449ʳ (7), 450ᵛ (57–61).

Bibliography: Coxe, *Bodleian*, 471–79; *RGK* 1.232, 2.374; *PLP* 26431; Hörandner, *Historische Gedichte*, 139 and 150–51; Gonnelli, *Giorgio di Pisidia*, 23 (with bibliography); Kubina, 'Asan Family', 178–79.

GREECE

Athens, Βιβλιοθήκη τῆς Βουλῆς τῶν Ἑλλήνων

27. *Atheniensis Greek Parliament 57*

17th–18th cent.; paper; 220 × 150 mm.; 363 folios (1ʳ–3ᵛ, 72ᵛ, 76, 96ᵛ, 111ᵛ, 112, 181ʳ, 224ᵛ, 231ᵛ, 269ᵛ, 324, 353ᵛ, 354, 362ᵛ, 363ʳ are blank); written by various hands.

Contents: works of Lucian, Basileios of Seleukia, Theodoros Doukas Laskaris and various post-Byzantine works such as Theodosios Zygomalas, Konstantinos Ioannou Zacharopoulos, and Athanasios Parios.

Miscellaneous poems: fols. 182ʳ–187ᵛ (76: 'Κυροῦ Θεοδώρου τοῦ Πτωχοπροδρόμου ἐπὶ ἀποδήμου τῇ φιλίᾳ'); on fols. 188ʳ–195ʳ there follows a prose exegesis of the poem.

Bibliography: S. Lambros, 'Κατάλογος κωδίκων τῆς βιβλιοθήκης τῆς Βουλῆς', *NE* 3 (1906), 113–21, at 119–21.

Ἐθνικὴ Βιβλιοθήκη τῆς Ἑλλάδος

28. Atheniensis EBE 1183*

18th cent.; paper; 170 × 220 mm.; 190 folios.

Contents: poems from the Greek Anthology, Konstantinos Manasses (excerpts from Χρονικὴ Σύνοψις); various riddles, etc.

Miscellaneous poems: fols. 39ʳ–41ᵛ (29–54: 'τοῦ σοφωτάτου Ψελλοῦ ἴαμβοι εἰς ἀρετὰς καὶ κακίας'), 46ʳ–54ʳ (76: 'κυροῦ Θεοδώρου τοῦ Προδρόμου ἐπὶ ἀποδήμῳ τῇ φιλίᾳ').

Bibliography: I. A. Sakkelion, Κατάλογος τῶν χειρογράφων τῆς Ἐθνικῆς Βιβλιοθήκης τῆς Ἑλλάδος (Athens 1892), 218; O. Lampsidis, 'Les "Gnomologia" tirés de la Chronique de K. Manassès', *Byz* 55 (1985), 118–45.

29. Atheniensis EBE 1264*

17th cent.; paper; 150 × 110 mm.; 177 folios.

Contents: Chrysoloras (Αἱ τοῦ Χρυσολωρᾶ μονόστιχοι Γνῶμαι κατὰ στοιχεῖον ἐκ διαφόρων ποιητῶν), various theological and hagiographical texts, Gregory of Nazianzus, anonymous verse encomium on Gregory of Nazianzus, Leo VI.

Prodromos: fols. 174ʳ–176ʳ (29–54: 'τοῦ σοφωτάτου Ψελλοῦ ἴαμβοι εἰς τὴν ἀρετὴν καὶ τὴν κακίαν').

Bibliography: Sakkelion, Κατάλογος, 229–30.

30. (An) Atheniensis EBE 3104*

16th cent. (middle); 175 × 120 mm. (174 × 110 Politis); 342 folios (Politis counted 331 fol.); written by Mathousalas Macheir; according to fol. 340ᵛ, the book was owned at some point by a certain Gerasimos (τὸ παρῶν (sic) ὑπάρχει Γερασίμου Ἱερομονάχου).

Contents: a theological miscellany mainly with works by Basil of Caesarea (homilies on the Hexaemeron and *Adversus Eunomium*).

Miscellaneous poems: fols. 10ʳ–12ᵛ (29–54: 'Τοῦ σοφωτάτου Ψελλοῦ ἴαμβοι εἰς ἀρετὰς καὶ κακίας').

Bibliography: L. Politis, 'Δύο χειρόγραφα ἀπὸ τὴν Καστοριά', *Hell* 20 (1967), 29–41, at 30, note 2; Vogel and Gardthausen, *Schreiber*, 270; Hörandner,

Historische Gedichte, 147; Constantinides and Browning, *Cyprus*, 308-11, note 6; MacCoull, 'Mathousala Macheir', 114-16.

31. (Mt) *Metochii S. Sepulchri 797*

15th-16th cent.; 140 × 95 mm. (138 × 94 mm. Papadopoulos-Kerameus); 120 folios; written by Isaac the monk (cf. fol. 77ʳ).

Contents: an anonymous poem on the holy Apostles, Ioannes of Damascus, John Chrysostom, Theodoros Abu Qurra, Ps. Makarios, Isaiah of Gaza, Ephraem the Syrian, Ps. Dionysios Areopagites, Loukas Chrysoberges, Symeon of Thessaloniki, Anastasios Sinaites, Neilos of Ankyra, Georgios Scholarios, Niketas of Herakleia, Gregory of Nazianzus, Niketas David Paphlagon, Aristotle, Theodoros Stoudites, Dionysios the monk, Leo VI, Manuel Moschopoulos, Agapetos Diakonos, Symeon the New Theologian.

Miscellaneous poems: fols. 80ᵛ-81ʳ (62-66).

Bibliography: A. Papadopoulos-Kerameus, Ἱεροσολυμιτικὴ Βιβλιοθήκη ἤτοι κατάλογος τῶν ἐν ταῖς βιβλιοθήκαις τοῦ ἁγιωτάτου ἀποστολικοῦ τε καὶ καθολικοῦ ὀρθοδόξου πατριαρχικοῦ θρόνου τῶν Ἱεροσολύμων καὶ πάσης Παλαιστίνης ἀποκειμένων ἑλληνικῶν κωδίκων, 5 vols. (St Petersburg 1894-1915), vol. 5, 286-91; Hörandner, *Historische Gedichte*, 140.

Ἱστορικὴ καὶ Ἐθνολογικὴ Ἑταιρεία

32. *Athen. Hist. - Ethn. Het. 66*

18th cent.; paper; 220 × 150 mm.; 213 folios (8, 17, 42, 65, and 82 are blank); written by three scribes.

Contents: various canons, John Chrysostom, and some treatises on metres.

Miscellaneous poems: fols. 67ʳ-81ᵛ (76: 'Κυροῦ Θεοδώρου ἐπὶ ἀποδήμῳ τῇ φιλίᾳ').

Bibliography: S. Lambros, 'Κατάλογος τῶν κωδίκων τῆς Ἱστορικῆς καὶ Ἐθνολογικῆς Ἑταιρείας', *NE* 7 (1910), 83-84.

Lesbos, Ἱερὰ Μονὴ Λειμῶνος

33. *Lesbiacus monasterii Leimonos 219*

17th cent.; paper; 153 × 105 mm.; 120 folios; written by Akakios the hieromonachos.

Contents: Gregory of Nazianzus, Theodoros Stoudites, Maximos Planoudes, Ioannes Komnenos Sozopolites, Sophronios of Jerusalem, and other anonymous verse works.

Miscellaneous poems: fols. 42ʳ-45ᵛ (29-54: 'Τοῦ σοφωτάτου Ψελλοῦ ἴαμβοι εἰς ἀρετὰς καὶ κακίας καὶ τὰς μὲν ἀρετὰς ποίει τὰς δὲ κακίας φεῦγε').

Bibliography: A. Papadopoulos-Kerameus, Κατάλογος τῶν ἐν ταῖς βιβλιοθήκαις τῆς νήσου Λέσβου ἑλληνικῶν χειρογράφων (Μαυρογορδάτειος Βιβλιοθήκη I/2 = Ὁ ἐν Κωνσταντινουπόλει Ἑλληνικὸς Φιλολογικὸς Σύλλογος 15, Παράρτημα) (Istanbul 1884), 110.

Elassona, Μονὴ τῆς Ὀλυμπιωτίσσης

34. *Elassona Olympiotisses 80*

18th cent.; paper; 215 × 150 mm.; 227 folios with 28 lines.

Contents: Ioannes Tzetzes and various post-Byzantine works.

Prodromos: fols. 223ᵛ-224ʳ (29-54: 'Τοῦ σοφωτάτου Ψελλοῦ ἴαμβοι εἰς ἀρετὰς καὶ κακίας').

Bibliography: E. Skouvaras, Ὀλυμπιώτισσα: Περιγραφὴ καὶ ἱστορία τῆς Μονῆς. Κατάλογος τῶν χειρογράφων-Χρονικὰ Σημειώματα. Ἀκολουθία Παναγίας τῆς Ὀλυμπιωτίσσης. Ἔγγραφα ἐκ τοῦ Ἀρχείου τῆς Μονῆς (1336-1900), 2 vols. (Athens 1967), 297-98.

35. *Elassona Olympiotisses 83**

18th cent.; paper; 220 × 176 mm.; I fol. + 81 pp + 48 pp. + I fol. + 20 pp. + VII fol. with a varying number of lines.

Contents: only works by Prodromos.

Miscellaneous poems: pp. 1-13 (76: 'Τοῦ αὐτοῦ Θεοδώρου ἐπὶ ἀποδήμῳ τῇ φιλίᾳ'), 13-? (75: 'Τοῦ αὐτοῦ εἰς τὴν θείαν πρόνοιαν').

Bibliography: Skouvaras, Ὀλυμπιώτισσα, 299.

Mount Athos

36. *Athous, Dionysiou 594*

17th cent.; paper; 200 × 140 mm.; pp. 278 (138 is blank); written by a single scribe; on p. 238 there is an illustration, while later notes are to be found on p. 278.

Contents: a *mathematarion* including Γνῶμαι μονόστιχοι κατὰ στοιχεῖον ἐκ διαφόρων ποιητῶν (pp. 1-77), Sententiae of Aesop (pp. 78-137), Gregory of Nazianzus 'περὶ τῶν τοῦ βίου ὁδῶν' (pp. 139-170), Τοῦ αὐτοῦ τετράστιχα (pp. 171-200), Agapetos Diakonos, 'Ἔκθεσις κεφαλαίων παραινετικῶν' (pp. 239-277).

Miscellaneous poems: pp. 201-237 (76: 'Κυροῦ Θεοδώρου Προδρόμου ἐπὶ ἀποδήμῳ τῇ φιλίᾳ').

Bibliography: E. Dionysatis, 'Συμπληρωματικὸς κατάλογος ἑλληνικῶν χειρογράφων Ἱερᾶς Μονῆς Διονυσίου Ἁγίου Ὄρους', ΕΕΒΣ 27 (1957), 233-71, at 235-36.

37. (Ac) *Athous, Docheiariou 108 (2782)**

15th cent.; paper; 205 × 145 mm.; folios 262 (−1−11, 16−20, 29, 154· + 248ᵃ; the fol. 21 has been misplaced after fol. 34, while 62ᵛ is blank); mutilated at the beginning and end; written by four different hands: (a) fols. 12−134, 137−186, 203−228, 262; (b) fols. 187−199, 229−254; (c) fols. 200−202, 255−261; and (d) fols. 135−136ᵛ.

Contents: e.g. Anastasios Sinaites, Ephraem the Syrian, Sophronios of Jerusalem, Andreas of Crete, John Chrysostom, Georgios of Nikomedeia, Gregorios Palamas, Basil of Caesarea, Ioannes of Damascus, Isaac the Syrian, works of Gennadios Scholarios, Athanasios of Alexandreia, Libanius, Gregorios of Cyprus, Theodoros Stoudites, Abbas Kassianos, etc.

Miscellaneous poems: fol. 258ᵛ (62−63).

Bibliography: S. Lambros, *Catalogue of the Greek Manuscripts on Mount Athos*, 2 vols. (Cambridge 1895−1900), vol. 1, 247−48.

38. *Athous, Hagiou Paulou 9*

a. 1783; paper; 225 × 170 mm.; pages α−δ + 350 (+15α, 93α, 147α −25, 99, 148); the pp. β−δ, 233−240, 328, and 340−346 are blank; written by three scribes: (a) pp. 1−232 (one column), (b) pp. 241−327, 347−350 (Ἰωάννης ὁ Κρη(τη)ς (sic)—two columns), and (c) pp. 329−339 (two columns).

Contents: e.g. Petros Damaskenos, Michael Psellos, Manuel Philes, Nikolaos Kallikles, Nikephoros Kallistou Xanthopoulos.

Miscellaneous poems: fols. 276ʳ−278ᵛ (75: 'τοῦ αὐτοῦ σχετλιαστικοὶ εἰς τὴν Πρόνοιαν'), 279ʳ (55−56: 'τοῦ αὐτοῦ εἰς εἰκονισμένον τῷ βίῳ (sic)'), 279−280 (62−66: 'ἀνεπίγραφα').

Bibliography: Lambros, *Mount Athos*, vol. 1, 20−21; L. Politis and M. L. Politi, *Βιβλιογράφοι 17ου−18ου αἰῶνα: Συνοπτικὴ Καταγραφή* (Athens 1994), 482; Hörandner, *Historische Gedichte*, 163; D'Ambrosi, *Gregorio Nazianzeno*, 104−05; R. S. Stefec, 'Die Synaxarverse des Nikephoros Xanthopoulos', *JÖB* 62 (2012), 145−61, at 147.

39. *Athous, Iberon 509 (olim 4629)**

17th cent. (towards the end); paper; 220 × 170 mm.; 562 (+ 8α, 9α, 23α, 79α, 80α, 97α, 108α, 111α, 132α, 171α, 200α, 203α, 302α, 313α, 322α, 366α, 379α, 441α, 477α, 478α, 478β, 499α, 501α, 507α, 543α) folios (8α, 12ᵛ, 23α, 34ᵛ, 35ᵛ, 43ᵛ, 50ᵛ, 54ᵛ, 79α, 97α, 105ᵛ, 108α, 111α, 121, 132α, 147ᵛ, 162ᵛ, 171α, 187ʳ, 188ᵛ, 192ᵛ, 200α, 203α, 206ᵛ, 213ᵛ, 238ᵛ, 262ᵛ, 283ᵛ, 302α, 313α, 322α, 351ᵛ, 353ᵛ, 360ᵛ, 366α, 379α, 403ᵛ, 404ᵛ, 408ᵛ−409, 441α, 460ᵛ, 477α, 478β,

489ᵛ, 499a, 501a, 507a, 511ᵛ, 543a and 560ᵛ–561 are blank); various scribes worked together on the execution of the manuscript.

Contents: mainly texts of theological interest, e.g. homilies for the period of the Great Lent, homilies on the Gospels of Matthew and Luke, homilies on the feasts of the Lord and the Virgin Mary, an exegesis of Liturgy, a text by Fragkiskos Skoufos of the year 1670, and an oration in praise of Patriarch Athanasios III penned by Antonios Lesbios.

Miscellaneous poems: fols. 544ʳ–545ʳ (29–54: 'Τοῦ σοφωτάτου Ψελοῦ (sic) ἴαμβοι εἰς ἀρετὰς καὶ κακίας').

Bibliography: Lambros, *Mount Athos*, vol. 2, 160.

40. (Ae) *Athous, Iberon 765**

16th cent.; paper; 116 folios.

Contents: e.g. John Chrysostom, Theodoret of Cyrrhus, Theodoros Stoudites, Ioannes of Damascus, Gregory of Nazianzus, Ioannes Geometres, Michael Psellos, Basil of Caesarea, various theological works, etc.

Miscellaneous poems: fols. 102ʳ–104ʳ (29–54).

Bibliography: Lambros, *Mount Athos*, vol. 2, 223.

Inaccessible to me.

41. (Bi) *Athous, Iberon 1418**

15th cent. (first half); paper; 295 × 220 mm.; 196 folios; a book epigram on fol. 173 informs us that it was written by a certain Ioannes (not the same person as Ioannes Eugenikos).

Contents: mainly works of Basil of Caesarea.

Miscellaneous poems: fols. 172ᵛ–173ʳ (3).

Bibliography: P. Sotiroudis, Ἱερὰ Μονὴ Ἰβήρων. Κατάλογος ἑλληνικῶν χειρογράφων. ΙΑ΄ (1387–1568) (Mount Athos 2007), 77–80.

42. *Athous, Karakallou Chart. 79**

17th cent.; paper; 205 × 140 mm.; pp. 616 (84, 85, 105–111, 236–241, 330–337, 381, 483, 509, and 617 are blank). The manuscript was written by at least three different hands: (a) pp. 2–104, 242–329, 510–557; (b) pp. 112–241, 338–508; and (c) pp. 558–616.

Contents: Theodoros Stoudites, Ioannes Zonaras, and various post-Byzantine texts (a life of St Onouphrios penned by Agapios Landos and an oration by Theodoros Palladas on the ten holy martyrs).

Miscellaneous poems: fols. 80ʳ–83ᵛ (29–54: 'Τοῦ σοφωτάτου Ψελοῦ· (sic) ἴαμβοι στίχοι εἰς ἀρετὰς καὶ κακίας').

Bibliography: Lambros, *Mount Athos*, vol. 1, 139.

43. Athous, Laura Λ 62 (1552)*

18th cent.; paper; 220 × 160 mm.; *II* + 298 + *I'* folios (64ᵛ, 138ᵛ, 152ᵛ-154ᵛ, 188, 235ᵛ-236ʳ, and 242ᵛ are blank).

Contents: a *mathematarion* with works of Basil of Caesarea, Plutarch, and Michael Psellos.

Miscellaneous poems: 1: 'τοῦ αὐτοῦ προσφωνητήριοι εἰς τὸν μέγαν ἀπόστολον Παῦλον' (fols. 231-237), 76: 'Κυριοῦ (sic) Θεοδώρου τοῦ Προδρόμου ἐπὶ ἀποδήμῳ τῇ φιλίᾳ' (fols. 139ʳ-152ʳ).

Bibliography: S. Eustratiades, *Catalogue of the Greek Manuscripts in the Library of the Laura on Mount Athos, with Notices from other Libraries* (Cambridge, MA 1925), 274-75; A. Skarveli-Nikolopoulou, Τὰ μαθηματάρια των ελληνικων σχολείων της Τουρκοκρατίας: Διδασκόμενα κείμενα, σχολικά προγράμματα, διδακτικές μέθοδοι· συμβολή στην ιστορία της νεοελληνικής παιδείας (Athens 1993), 569.

44. Athous, Laura Ω 34 (1844)

18th cent.; paper; 210 × 160 mm.; 229 (+ fols. 12a, 36a, 160a, 161a, 174a, 194; –fols. 133, 144), folios (12ᵛ-12ᵃᵛ, 36ᵃᵛ, 41ᵛ, 92, 98ᵛ, 106ᵛ, 118, and 162ᵛ are blank); many scribes; one of them notes at the bottom of fol. 98ʳ: τέλος τῶν κανόνων διὰ χειρὸς ἐμοῦ Πέτρου Σαμπέλη).

Contents: a *mathematarion* containing, e.g. works of Agapetos, Thalassios, Gregory of Nazianzus, Niketas David Paphlagon, Michael Psellos, Basil of Caesarea, as well as various canons.

Prodromos: fols. 192ʳ-193ᵛ (1-6), 198ʳ-204ᵛ (76: 'Θεοδώρου τοῦ Προδρόμου τῇ φιλίᾳ').

Bibliography: Eustratiades, *Laura*, 331-32.

45. Athous, Panteleemonis 683*

18th cent. (last quarter); paper; 240 × 170 mm.; 821 pages (32-40, 201, 202, 440, 503, 504, 528, 696, 724, 775, and 776 are blank); after a work of Gerasimos Vlachos a note reads: χεὶρ Σεβαστοῦ Πατμίου 1785 Ἰουνίου 18 (p. 563). Many scribes worked together for the production of this manuscript. One of them notes on p. 155: τέλος σχολίων τοῦ ἐν ἁγίοις πατρὸς ἡμῶν Γρηγορίου τοῦ Θεολόγου 1785 Ἰουναρίου 30 εὔχεσθαι ὑπὲρ ἐμοῦ Ἀντωνίου παπᾶ Λιγίζου υἱὸς Κολατζήζογλος. On p. 563 we read χεὶρ Σεβαστοῦ Πατμίου 1785 Ἰουνίου 18, and the same hand adds notes on pp. 695 (τῷ συντελεστῇ τῶν καλῶν Θεῷ δόξα/αχπε Ἰουλίου ιη΄/τέλος τῆς ἐξηγήσεως Γρηγορίου τοῦ Θεολόγου), 774 (χρηστῶν ἀπάντων Χριστὸς ἀρχὴ καὶ τέλος/1785 Ἰουνίου 10), and 821 (τέλος τῆς ἐξηγήσεως του πρεσβευτικοῦ λόγου·/τῷ συντελεστῇ τῶν καλῶν Θεῷ δόξα).

Contents: e.g. scholia on the orations and poems of Gregory of Nazianzus (among others, those of Niketas of Herakleia on the gnomic tetrastichs of Gregory of Nazianzus), scholia on Hesiod ("Ἔργα καὶ ἡμέραι) and Homer (Ὀδύσσεια), Libanius, Gregory of Nazianzus, etc.

Miscellaneous poems: fol. 564ᵛ (29-54: 'Τοῦ σοφωτάτου Ψελλοῦ ἴαμβοι εἰς ἀρετὰς καὶ κακίας').

Bibliography: Lambros, *Mount Athos*, vol. 2, 413-14.

46. (Ax) *Athous Vatopedinus 56**

a. 1330 (421ᵛ); paper; 268/271 × 205/212 mm.; 424 (+136a, 163a, 202a) folios (1-3 flyleaves); 2 cols with 27 lines per page; though the ms. was written by Kallistos of Vatopedi, the poem of Prodromos was added by a fifteenth-century hand to be identified with Y.

Contents: a collection of works of Basil of Caesarea (letters and homilies); there are also two works of Cyril of Jerusalem.

Miscellaneous poems: fol. 3ᵛ (3).

Bibliography: E. Lamberz, *Katalog der griechischen Handschriften des Athosklosters Vatopedi, Codices 1-102*, 1 vol. (Thessaloniki 2006), vol. 1, 243-48 (with bibliography); *PLP* no. 10466.

47. *Athous Vatopedinus 95**

a. 1611 (fols. 109-140) and first half of 17th cent. (fols. 1-107, 141-217); paper; 143/145 × 100/102 mm; 217 folios; written by four different scribes: (a) 1-107; (b) fols. 109-155ʳ. 156-179ʳ; (c) fols. 180-211, and (d) 212-217.

Contents: e.g. Anastasios Sinaites, Paul (bishop of Monemvasia), Theophilos of Alexandreia, various Vitae, Marcus Eremita, Theophanes Eleabulkos, Zosimas Monachos, Leo VI, Neilos of Ankyra, Menander, etc.

Miscellaneous poems: fols. 183, 208, 205-206 (29-54: 'Τοῦ σοφωτάτου Ψελλοῦ, Ἴαμβοι εἰς ἀρετὰς καὶ κακίας').

Bibliography: Lamberz, *Vatopedi*, vol. 1, 393-400 (with bibliography).

Patmos, Μονὴ τοῦ Ἁγίου Ἰωάννου τοῦ Θεολόγου

48. *Patmiensis 407*

19th cent.; paper; 469 pages (according to Sakkelion).

Contents: Nikephoros Kallistou Xanthopoulos and works of various post-Byzantine authors.

Miscellaneous poems: pp. 853-857 (29-54: 'Τοῦ σοφωτάτου Μιχαὴλ τοῦ Ψελλοῦ στίχοι ἰαμβικοὶ εἰς ἀρετὰς καὶ τὰς κακίας').

Bibliography: I. A. Sakkelion, Πατμιακὴ Βιβλιοθήκη, ἤτοι ἀναγραφὴ τῶν ἐν τῇ βιβλιοθήκῃ τῆς κατὰ τὴν νῆσον Πάτμον γεραρᾶς καὶ βασιλικῆς μονῆς τοῦ Ἁγίου Ἀποστόλου καὶ Εὐαγγελιστοῦ Ἰωάννου του Θεολόγου τεθησαυρισμένων χειρογράφων τευχῶν (Athens 1890), 181-82.

HUNGARY

Budapest, private collection of Philippos Tialos

49. *Budapestensis Tialos 3*
18th cent.; paper; pages not counted; the current location of the manuscript is unknown.
Miscellaneous poems: fols. 190ᵛ–191ʳ (55–56).
Bibliography: S. Lambros, "Ἡ βιβλιοθήκη τῆς Ἑλληνικῆς κοινότητος Βουδαπέστης καὶ οἱ ἐν τῇ πόλει ταύτῃ σωζόμενοι ἑλληνικοὶ κώδικες", NE 8 (1911), 70–79, at 78–79.
Inaccessible to me.

ISRAEL

Jerusalem, Πατριαρχικὴ Βιβλιοθήκη

50. *Hierosolymitanus Sabaiticus gr. 462**
18th cent.; paper; 422 folios.
Contents: a *mathematarion* containing works by Plutarch, Demosthenes, Synesios, Basil of Caesarea, Gregory of Nazianzus, Euripides, Aristophanes, etc.
Miscellaneous poems: fols. 32ʳ–37ʳ (29–54: 'Τοῦ σοφωτάτου Ψελλοῦ ἴαμβοι εἰς ἀρετὰς καὶ κακίας').
Bibliography: Papadopoulos-Kerameus, Ἱεροσολυμιτικὴ Βιβλιοθήκη, vol. 2, 557–58.

51. *Hierosolymitanus Nikod. 14*
18th cent.; paper; 93 folios.
Contents: Ioannes Zonaras, Maximos the Confessor.
Miscellaneous poems: fols. 1–9 (76).
Bibliography: Papadopoulos-Kerameus, Ἱεροσολυμιτικὴ Βιβλιοθήκη, vol. 3, 192.

ITALY

Florence, Biblioteca Medica Laurenziana

52. (Lc) *Laurentianus Conv. Soppres. 48*
14th cent.; parchment; 258 × 171 mm.; V + 299 + V′ folios; Filippomaria Pontani has argued that the ms. was executed in Constantinople around the

time of Planoudes. It once belonged to the book collector Antonio Corbinelli, and passed to the library of the *Badia Fiorentina* Monastery after his death. Note also that at some point it was in the hands of Giorgio Antonio Vespucci (cf. Pontani).

Contents: *Iliad* (accompanied by *scholia*), some anonymous poems (cf. Pontani), Ioannes Tzetzes, etc.

Miscellaneous poems: fols. 292^r–292^v (29–54).

Bibliography: A. M. Bandini, *Catalogus codicum manuscriptorum Bibliothecae Mediceae Laurentianae*, 3 vols. (Florence 1764–70), vol. 3 I, 13*; F. Pontani, 'Dodecasillabi anonimi su Michele VIII nel Conv. Soppr. 48', in: *Filologia, papirologia, storia dei testi. Giornate di Studio in Onore di Antonio Carlini, Udine, 9–10 dicembre 2005* (Pisa/Rome 2008), 63–82.

53. (Fc) *Laurentianus Conv. Soppres. 121 (C. 558)*

14th cent.; parchment; 276 × 188 mm.; 357 folios (357^r is blank); Fc was copied by a certain Leon (cf. fol. 3^r Ἰησοῦ, βοήθ<ει> τῷ σῷ δούλῳ Λέοντι).

Contents: e.g. various orations by Gregory of Nazianzus accompanied by a commentary of Niketas of Herakleia and Basileios Minimos, Basil of Caesarea, Gregory of Nyssa, anonymous poems on the Crucifixion and the Theotokos (the latter is unedited), and a riddle.

Miscellaneous poems: fol. 357^v (11–20).

Bibliography: Bandini, *Catalogus*, vol. 3, 20*; F. Halkin, 'Les manuscrits grecs de la Bibliothèque Laurentienne à Florence: Inventaire hagiographique', *AnBoll* 96 (1978), 5–50, at 36.

54. (C) *Laurentianus Plut. V 10*

The ms. was completed on 30 August 1282 (on fol. 180^v: Μην(ὶ) αὐγούστω εἰς τ(ὰς) λ τῷ ͵ϛψϟʹ τ(ῆς) ἰνδ(ικτιῶνος) ι̑ (14th cent. Bandini, 1st half of the 14th cent. Arnesano); paper/parchment (fols. 150–177); 185 × 135 mm.; II + 247 + I' folios (fols. I–II are blank); of southern Italian provenance (either from Otranto or more likely from the region of Maglie); written by various copyists (five according to Arnesano).[5]

Contents: Ioannes Tzetzes, Ioannes Geometres, Georgios Pisides, Rogerios of Otranto, Nikolaos (Nicola) of Otranto, Anna Komnene, Georgios (chartophylax of Gallipoli), Ioannes Grassos, Niketas the Philosopher, Germanos (patriarch of Constantinople), Christophoros Mitylenaios, Nikolaos (metropolitan of Corfu), Babrian Tetrastichs of Ignatios the Deacon, Gregory of Nazianzus,

---

[5] De Groote has argued, on the basis of a note to be found on fol. 179^v, that one of the copyists is a certain Leon; cf. de Groote, *Christophori Mitylenaii*, XXXI.

Leon the Philosopher, Methodios (patriarch of Constantinople), and Andreas of Crete.

Miscellaneous poems: 20 (fol. 196ʳ).

Bibliography: Bandini, *Catalogus*, vol. 1, 23–30; Hörandner, *Historische Gedichte*, 140 and 151; Gonnelli, *Giorgio di Pisidia*, 19 (with bibliography); D. Arnesano, *La minuscula 'barocca': Scritture e libri in Terra d'Otranto nei secoli XIII e XIV* (Galatina/Congedo 2008), 87 (with bibliography); de Groote, *Christophori Mitylenaii*, XXXI–XXXII.

55. (L) *Laurentianus Acq. e Doni 341*

Beginning of the 16th cent.; paper; 155 × 110 mm.; fol. 271 + αω (239ᵛ–240ʳ are blank); written by a single unidentified scribe, but on fol. 237ʳ a note by a second scribe refers to the fall of Constantinople (‚στ⟩ξα′ μαίω κθ′ ὥρ(α) γ′); the ms. changed many hands, including a certain Ioannes (fol. 1ʳ: κ(αὶ) τόδε πρὸ(s) τοῖς ἄλλοις, Ἰωάννου, υἱοῦ συμεών), Μανουὴλ Ζαριφόγλου (fol. aʳ Ἥδε ἡ πικτὶς ὑπάρχει Μανουήλου τ[οῦ] | υἱὸς <---> Ζαριφόγλου καὶ <--->), and E. Miller (in year 1885); it entered the Laurenziana in 1927.

Contents: Niketas Eugenianos, Philostratus, Gregorios Grammatikos, Konstantinos of Syros, Nonnus, Niketas of Herakleia, Niketas David Paphlagon, Apollonius of Tyana, Libanius, Phalaris, Nikephoros Kallistou Xanthopoulos, Loukas Chrysoberges, Gregory of Nazianzos, Eustathios Makrembolites, Theophylaktos Simokates, various anonymous epigrams, etc.

Miscellaneous poems: fols. 100ᵛ (70–72), 100ᵛ–101ʳ (69), 102ᵛ (26), 108ᵛ–109ʳ (62–66), 110 (55–56), 120ᵛ–121ᵛ (11–20), 121ᵛ (21), 123ᵛ–124ʳ (24).

Bibliography: Gallavotti, 'Novi Laurentiani Codicis Analecta', *SB* 4 (1935), 203–36, at 220–23; Giannelli, 'Epigrammi', 351; Hörandner, *Historische Gedichte*, 141 and 152–53; F. Conca, *Nicetas Eugenianus, De Drosillae et Chariclis amoribus* (Amsterdam 1990), 10–11; M. Marcovich, *Theodori Prodromi Rhodanthes et Dosiclis amorum libri IX* (Stuttgart/Leipzig 1991), V; Tziatzi-Papagianni, 'Theodoros Prodromos Historisches Gedicht LXXVIII', *BZ* 86–87 (1993–94), 363–82, at 364 (with bibliography); Stefec, 'Synaxarverse', 148–49 (with bibliography).

56. (Ls) *Laurentianus San Marco 318*

13th–14th cent. (14th cent. Bandini); oriental paper; 190/155 × 130/100 mm.; 79 folios; of southern Italian provenance (region of Otranto); was once owned by Niccolò Niccoli; following Niccoli's death (22 January 1437) the ms., along with his entire collection, entered the Laurenziana.

Contents: Georgios Kabasilas, Barsanouphios, Antonios III Stoudites, Maximos the Confessor, Michael Synkellos, Ps. Kyrillos, various anonymous homiletical, lexicographical, and grammatical works.

Miscellaneous poems: fol. 1ʳ (29–54).

Bibliography: Bandini, *Catalogus*, vol. 3, 35*; T. Migliorini, 'Un epigramma inedito di Giorgio Cabasila nel Laur. S. Marco 318', *MEG* 8 (2008), 1–29, at 4–14.

Milan, Biblioteca Ambrosiana

57. (As) *Ambrosianus H 22 sup. (426)**

16th cent. (15th cent. Martini/Bassi); paper; 213 × 153 mm. (212 × 148 mm. Martini/Bassi); I + 370 folios (21, 33ᵛ, 58, 59, 226, 278, 289–291, 320–322, 343, 365–370ʳ are blank); once in the possession of a certain Νικόλαος and the humanist Gian Vincenzo Pinelli, it entered the Ambrosiana in 1609.

Contents: e.g. Manuel Philes, New Testament apocrypha, Rufus of Ephesus, Maximos the Confessor, Poems from the Palatine Anthology, Hesiod (ἔργα καὶ ἡμέραι) followed by a lexicon, Libanius, Konstantinos Laskaris, Eusebius of Caesarea, Clement of Alexandreia, Holobolos, Theocritus, Pythagoras, Ps. Phocylides, Hesiod (Ἀσπίς), Ioannes Tzetzes, Markos Mousouros, Apollonius of Rhode, Homer, Manuel Moschopoulos, Plutarch, Demetrios of Phaleron, Maximos Planoudes, Tryphon, Gennadios Scholarios, Nikephoros Kallistou Xanthopoulos, Michael Psellos, Nikephoros Blemmydes, some hagiographical texts, etc.

Miscellaneous poems: fols. 93ᵛ–94ʳ (29–54: 'τοῦ σοφωτάτου Ψελλοῦ ἴαμβοι, εἰς ἀρετὰς καὶ κακίας').

Bibliography: A. Martini and D. Bassi, *Catalogus codicum graecorum Bibliothecae Ambrosianae*, 2 vols. (Milan 1906; repr. Hildesheim/New York 1978), 505–15; C. Pasini, *Inventario agiografico dei manoscritti greci dell'Ambrosiana* (Brussels 2003), 115–16.

Venice, Biblioteca Nazionale Marciana

58. (I) *Marcianus gr. Z 436 (coll. 314; olim Bessarionis 296)*

13th cent.; paper; 260/200 × 180/120; 161 folios (75, 84ᵛ, 106ᵛ are blank); written by a single southern Italian scribe; the first three folios of the manuscript are badly damaged.

Contents: various anonymous poems, a couple of anonymous letters, Ps. Pythagoras, Konstantinos Stilbes, Ioannes Euchaites, Lucian, Kallistratos, Synesios, Themistios, Leo VI.

Miscellaneous poems: fols. 2ᵛ (55–56), 2ᵛ–3ᵛ (75).

Bibliography: E. Mioni, *Bibliothecae divi Marci Venetiarum codices graeci manuscripti*, 2 vols. (Rome 1981–85), vol. 2, 205–07 (with bibliography); Hörandner, *Historische Gedichte*, 154–55; Diethart and Hörandner, *Constantinus Stilbes*, XVIII.

59. (m) *Marcianus gr. Z 512 (coll. 678; olim Bessarionis 308)*
13th cent.; paper; 210 × 140 mm. II + 269 folios with a varying number of lines (22–29).

Contents: e.g. Maximos of Tyre, Alexander Numenios, Gregorios of Corinth, a grammatical work, Aelios Herodian, Georgios Choiroboskos, Zenobios, Romanos Philoponos, Herennius Philon, Michael Psellos, Diogenes Laertios, Theon of Smyrna, Proklos, Kleomedes, Basileios Megalomytes, various anonymous riddles (unedited), a poem on St Panteleemon attributed wrongly to Ioannes Geometres, etc.

Miscellaneous poems: fols. 260^r (7: 'Εἰς τὸν Ἀβραὰμ ξενίζοντα τὴν ἁγίαν Τριάδα'); 260^r (9: "Ἐπὶ ἀναγνώσει'), 260^v (62–66: "Ἐπὶ κήπῳ').

Bibliography: Mioni, *Bibliothecae*, vol. 2, 369–74 (with bibliography); Hörandner, *Historische Gedichte*, 155.

60. (M) *Marcianus gr. Z 524*
Late 13th cent.; paper (oriental); 250 × 160 mm; II + 292 folios; earlier it was argued that it was the outcome of five or seven scribes, but more recently Foteini Spingou has argued that most of it was written by a single scribe.

Contents: a rich collection of eleventh- and twelfth-century poetry, including works by Michael Psellos, Theophylaktos of Ohrid, Andronikos the Protekdikos, Ioannes Tzetzes, Manganeios Prodromos, Konstantinos Manasses, Nikolaos Kallikles, Konstantinos Stilbes, Theodoros Balsamon; also works by Georgios Choiroboskos, Ignatios, Arethas of Kaisareia, and Cassianus Bassus.

Miscellaneous poems: fol. 97^v (26).

Bibliography: Mioni, *Bibliothecae*, vol. 2, 399–407; Hörandner, 'Marc. gr. 524', 117–24; Paolo Odorico and Charis Messis, 'L'anthologie Comnène du cod. Marc. gr. 524: Problèmes d'évaluation', in: W. Hörandner and M. Grünbart (eds), *L'épistolographie et la poésie épigrammatique: projets actuels et questions de méthodologie* (Paris 2003), 191–213; A. Rhoby, 'Zur Identifizierung von bekannten Autoren im Codex Marcianus Graecus 524', *MEG* 10 (2010), 167–204; de Groote, *Christophori Mitylenaii*, XLVIII–XLIX; F. Spingou, *Words and Artworks in the Twelfth Century and Beyond. Twelfth-Century Poetry on Art from MS. Marcianus Gr. 524* (Tolworth, Surrey 2021), 13–22.

Naples, Biblioteca Nazionale

61. (N) *Neapolitanus II D 4 (olim monasterii Ioannis ad Carbonariam)*
13th cent. (second half/14th cent. Gelzer and Orsini); paper (oriental); 235 × 165 mm; 242 (+239a, −150–159, 212) folios; a collection of three initially separate manuscripts, within which twelve different hands can be identified;

fols. 77ᵛ–112ʳ (where Prodromos' poems are to be found) were written by Eugenianos Ioannas.

Contents: e.g. Lykophron of Chalkis, Ioannes Tzetzes, Hesiod, Dionysios Periegetes, Palaephatus, Germanos II (patriarch of Constantinople), Ps. Phocylides, Musaeus, Christophoros Mitylenaios, Nikephoros (patriarch of Constantinople), Oppian, some treatises on grammar and prosody, etc.

Miscellaneous poems: fols. 91ʳ (55–56), 91 (62–66), 91ᵛ (68), 97ᵛ (7), 97ᵛ (8), 97ᵛ–98ʳ (10), 98ʳ (25), 98ᵛ (73–74), 98ᵛ–99ʳ (76).

Bibliography: M. R. Formentin, *Catalogus codicum Graecorum Bibliothecae nationalis Neapolitanae*, 2 vols. (Rome 1995), vol. 2, 5–10 (with bibliography); Hörandner, *Historische Gedichte*, 143 and 156; T. Gelzer, 'Bemerkungen zu Sprache und Text des Epikers Musaios', *Museum Helveticum* 24 (1967), 129–48, at 132; P. Orsini, *Musée, Héro et Léandre* (Paris 1968), XXXIV; de Groote, *Christophori Mitylenaii*, XXXIX; T. Migliorini and S. Tessari, "Ῥεῖτε δακρύων, ὀφθαλμοί, κρουνοὺς ἡματωμένους: Il carme penitenziale di Germano II patriarca di Constantinopoli', *MEG* 12 (2012), 155–80, at 157.

62. (Nd) *Neapolitanus II D 22 (olim Farnesianae Bibliothecae)*

14th cent. (first half); paper; 160 × 115 mm.; *III* + 315 (+185a, 231a, 309a) folios; mutilated at the beginning.

Contents: Gnomologion, Ioannes Tzetzes, Agapetos Diakonos, Sententiae of Aesop, and an anonymous riddle.

Miscellaneous poems: fol. 315ʳ (62 and 65).

Bibliography: Formentin, *Catalogus*, vol. 2, 25–27 (with bibliography); Hörandner, *Historische Gedichte*, 143.

63. (Ne) *Neapolitanus III AA 6 (olim III A 6)**

14th cent., paper; 174 × 121 mm; V + 214 + IV'folios; the texts were written by at least ten copyists, of whom one is a certain Nikandros Rhakendytes (cf. fol. 58ᵛ).

Contents: e.g. Sententiae, letters, riddles, Ioannes Kinnamos (*ethopoiia*), Gregory of Nazianzus, Basil of Caesarea, Ἠθοποιία Σεβήρου σοφιστοῦ, Thomas Gorianites, Germanos II (patriarch of Constantinople), anonymous verses, Nikephoros Basilakes, Isaak Tzetzes, Photios, Maximos the Confessor.

Miscellaneous poems: fols. 106ᵛ–107ʳ (11–20).

Bibliography: S. Cyrillus, *Codices Graeci mss. Regiae Bibliothecae Borbonicae descripti*, 2 vols. (Naples 1832), vol. 2, 199–202; M. M. Colonna, 'Il ms. Neapolitanus gr. III AA 6', *Nicolaus* 5 (1977), 325–64; Papagiannis, *Tetrasticha*, vol. 2, 55–56; Op de Coul, *Théodore Prodrome*, vol. 1, 48 (with bibliography).

Rovereto, Biblioteca Civica

64. (Ro) *Roveretinus 28**

13th–14th cent.; parchment; 160 × 115 mm.; 150 folios; written by Meletios the hieromonachos (on fol. 68ᵛ ἐτελειώθη τὸ παρὸν τουτὶ βιβλιδάριον παρ' ἐμοῦ | Μελετίου ἱερομονάχου· καὶ οἱ μετερχόμενοι αὐτὸ εὔχεσθέ μοι).

Contents: e.g. mainly lexicographical material, some anonymous iambic poems, Michael Psellos, etc.

Miscellaneous poems: fol. 119ᵛ (55–56).

Bibliography: C. M. Mazzucchi, 'Uno sconosciuto codice greco di lessicografia', *Aevum* 83 (2009), 411–23.

NETHERLANDS

Leiden, Universiteitsbibliotheek

65. *Leidensis B.P.G.* (*Bibliothecae Publicae Graeci*) *88*

18th cent. (first half); paper; 210 × 260 mm.; written by Johannes Daniel van Lennep.

Contents: poems from the *Anthologia Graeca*, along with the notes of Claudius Salmasius.

Miscellaneous poems: fol. 156ʳ (70: 'Αἴνιγμα εἰς τὴν νεφέλην'), 156ʳ–157ʳ (62–66: 'Epig. in hortum'), 157ʳ (57–61: 'Εἰς τὸν δακτύλιον ἔχοντα σφραγίδα ἐρῶντας δύο καὶ ἀπὸ τῶν στέρνων αὐτῶν δύο δένδρα ἐκπεφυκότα εἰς ἕνα συγκορυφούμενα κόρυμβον').

Bibliography: K. A. de Meyier (with the assistance of E. Hulshoff Pol), *Codices bibliothecae publicae graeci: Codices manuscripti/Bibliotheca Universitatis Leidensis*, VIII (Leiden 1965), 179–81 (with bibliography).

66. (Lq) *Leidensis Vossianus gr. Q 26*

a. 1568; Paper; 225/150 × 157/85 mm.; 47 folios with 24 lines; written by Ἄγγελος Βεργίκιος.

Contents: Georgios Pisides.

Miscellaneous poems: fols. 41ʳ–44ᵛ (75: 'Στίχοι σχετλιαστικοὶ εἰς τὴν πρόνοιαν').

Bibliography: K. A. de Meyier, *Bibliotheca Universitatis Leidensis. Codices manuscripti VI. Codices Vossiani graeci et miscellanei* (Leiden 1955), 130; *RGK* 1.3, 2. 3; Vogel and Gardthausen, *Schreiber*, 2–6; Gonnelli, *Giorgio di Pisidia*, 20.

67. (Vo) *Leidensis Vossianus gr. Q. 42**

15th cent. (second half); paper; 212/165 × 145/110 mm.; III + 201 + III' folios (1, 99, 116ᵛ, 154ᵛ are blank); 23 lines; written by Δημήτριος Ἄγγελος; fols. 1–3 may have been written by a different scribe from the rest manuscript.

Contents: works of Aristotle (*De animalium generatione* II.V and *De animalium partibus* II.IV).
Miscellaneous poems: fols. 2ᵛ-3ʳ (29-54).
Bibliography: de Meyier, *Codices manuscripti VI*, 150-51.

ROMANIA

Bucharest, Biblioteca Academiei Române

68. (Bu) *Bucurestensis Academiei Române gr. 601 (214)*
15th-16th cent.; paper; 300 × 200 mm.; 415 folios (1-2 blank); once in the possession of Ioannes Likinios (fol. 3ʳ: Οἰκονόμου Μονεμβασίας Ἰωάννου ἱερέως τοῦ Λικινίου).
Contents: e.g. Didache, anonymous verses, Gennadios Scholarios, and numerous anonymous treatises on various subjects.
Miscellaneous poems: 55-56 (fol. 352ᵛ), 62-66 (fols. 352ᵛ-353ʳ).
Bibliography: C. Litzica, *Catalogul manuscriptelor grecești* (Bucharest 1909), 285-89.

69. *Bucurestensis Academiei Române gr. 646**
18th cent. [1774]; paper; 240 × 170 mm.; 1282 pages.
Contents: Basil of Caesarea, Gregory of Nazianzus, Plutarch, Antonios Byzantios, Lucian, Isocrates, Konstantinos Dapontes, etc.
Miscellaneous poems: pp. 1071-1078 (29-54: 'Τοῦ σοφωτάτου Ψελλοῦ εἰς ἀρετὰς καὶ κακίας μεταφρασθέντα παρὰ Κωνσταντίνου Δαπόντε').
Bibliography: Litzica, *Catalogul*, 358-61; Skarveli-Nikolopoulou, Μαθηματάρια, 781-82.

RUSSIA

St Petersburg, Rossijskaja Akademija Nauk, Biblioteka (BAN)

70. *Petropolitanus AN RAIK 181 (B 28)*
18th cent. (second half); paper; 211/173 × 161/82 mm.; 174 folios.
Contents: Nikolaos Kallikles, Nikephoros Kallistou Xanthopoulos, Theophilos Korydalleus.
Miscellaneous poems: fols. 4ᵛ-7 (1-4 and 6), 78-82 (75), 89ʳ-89ᵛ (55-56), 90-91 (62-66).

Bibliography: I. N. Lebedeva, *Opisanie rukopisnogo otdela biblioteki Akademii Nauk SSSR* (St Petersburg 1973), 156–58; D'Ambrosi, *Gregorio Nazianzeno*, 103.

SPAIN

El Escorial, Biblioteca Real

71. (E) *Escorialensis y-III-9 (gr. 332)*
14th cent. (fols. 1–7, 136–151, and 214–218 date to the 15th cent.); paper; 213 × 142 mm.; 20–22 lines; written by six different copyists; at some point in the possession of Antonios Eparchos.
Contents: Nikephoros Kallistou Xanthopoulos, Ioannes Mauropous, Gregory of Nazianzus, Synesios of Cyrene, Basil of Caesarea, Libanius, Matthaios Kantakouzenos, Ioannes Zonaras.
Miscellaneous poems: 197ᵛ (22–23), 197ᵛ (7), 198ʳ–199ʳ (75).
Bibliography: G. de Andrés, *Catálogo de los códices griegos de la Real Biblioteca de El Escorial*, 3 vols. (Escorial 1968), vol. 2, 227–29; Papagiannis, *Tetrasticha*, vol. 1, 51–52 (with bibliography).

SWITZERLAND

Bern, Burgerbibliothek

72. (Be) *Bern 48 B*
14th–15th cent.; paper; 192 × 140 mm.; 145 folios; written by a certain Alexios (on fol. 141ʳ Εἴληφε τέλος, σὺν Θεῷ παντεργάτῃ· | βίβλος Μανασσῆ, παρ' ἐμοῦ Ἀλεξίου· | Οἱ δ' ἀναγιγνώσκοντες ταύτην ἐκ πόθου, | δέησιν θ(ε)ῷ ὑπὲρ ἐμοῦ ποιεῖτε· | ὅπως εὕρω ἵλεον αὐτ(ὸν) ἐν κρίσει—DBBE 5739); the codex once belonged to Arsenios Apostoles (fol. 1ʳ Τὸ παρὸν βιβλίον κτῆμα ἐστὶν τοῦ Ἀρσενίου τοῦ Μονεμβασίας), and later to his nephew Georgios Korinthios (fol. 1ʳ Τὸ νῦν δ' εἶναι Γεωργίου κόμητος τοῦ Κορινθίου τοῦ ἀνεψίου αὐτου).
Contents: Konstantinos Manasses (Σύνοψις Χρονική).
Miscellaneous poems: fols. 141ᵛ–144ᵛ (55–56), 142ᵛ–143ᵛ (62–66).
Bibliography: H. Omont, 'Catalogue des manuscrits grecs des Bibliothèques Suisse: Bâle, Berne, Einsiedeln, Genève, St. Gall, Schaffhouse et Zürich', *Centralblatt für Bibliothekswesen* 3 (1886), 385–452, at 420–21; *RGK* 1.232,

3.374; O. Lampsidis, *Constantini Manassis Breviarium Chronicum*, 2 vols. (Athens 1996), vol. 1, LXXX–LXXXI (with bibliography); P. Augustin, 'À propos d'un catalogue récent: Remarques philologiques et historiques sur quelques manuscrits grecs conservés à la Bibliothèque de la Bourgeoisie de Berne ou ayant appartenus à Jacques Bongars', *Script* 63 (2009), 121–41, at 133.

TURKEY

Istanbul (Constantinople), Πατριαρχικὴ Βιβλιοθήκη

73. *Constantinopolitanus monasterii Panagiae Camariotissae in Chalce insula 165**

a. 1 January 1642 – 26 July 1644; paper; 150 × 100 mm.; 77 folios (1–15 flyleaves); written by Galaktion the hieromonachos (on fol. 45^v Τέλος τῆς θείας λειτουργί(ας) τῶν προηγιασμέν(ων)· | καὶ ἐτελειώθησαν ἐκ χειρὸς ἁμαρτωλοῦ κ(αὶ) ἀναξίου δού | λου τοῦ φιλαν(θρώπ)ου θ(εο)ῦ ἡμῶν, καὶ κ(υρίο)υ Ἰ(ησο)ῦ Χ(ριστο)ῦ. | Γαλακτίωνος ἱερομονάχου τοῦ ἁγιορείτου. | Ἐπὶ ἔτους αχμβ (ἰνδικτιῶνος) τ(ης)· | ἐν μηνὶ Ἰανουαρίῳ α΄. | τῷ δὲ θ(ε)ῷ ἡμῶν δόξα ἀμήν).

Contents: liturgical texts, exapostilarion on the Theotokos, an anonymous poem on the monastic habit, Gregory of Nazianzus, a treatise on prosody, etc.

Miscellaneous poems: fols. 61^r–63^r (29–54: 'Τοῦ σοφωτάτου Ψελλοῦ ἴαμβοι εἰς ἀρετὰς καὶ κακίας').

Bibliography: M. Rizou-Kouroupou and P. Gehin, *Catalogue des manuscrits conservés dans la Bibliothèque du Patriarcat Oecuménique, Les manuscrits du monastère de la Panaghia de Chalki*, 2 vols. (Turnhout 2008), vol. 1, 401–03 (with bibliography).

Γραφεῖα τῆς ἐκκλησίας Παναγίας (τῶν Εἰσοδίων)

74. *Constantinopolitanus Γραφεῖα τῆς Ἐκκλησίας Παναγίας τῶν Εἰσοδίων 27**

18th cent. (first half); paper; 206 × 154 mm.; 157 folios (70–72, 98–100, 121–124 are blank).

Contents: a *mathematarion* containing works of Synesios, Basil of Caesarea, Lucian, Plutarch, Themistios, and Gregory of Nazianzus.

Miscellaneous poems: fols. 141–152 (76: 'Τοῦ κυρίου Θεοδώρου Προδρόμου ἐπὶ ἀποδήμῳ τῇ φιλίᾳ' μεθ' ἑρμηνείας καὶ σχολίων').

Bibliography: A. Papadopoulos-Kerameus, 'Δύο κατάλογοι ἑλληνικῶν κωδίκων ἐν Κωνσταντινουπόλει, τῆς Μεγάλης τοῦ Γένους Σχολῆς καὶ τοῦ Ζωγραφείου', IRAIK 14 (1909), 33–85, at 72.

75. *Constantinopolitanus Γραφεῖα τῆς Ἐκκλησίας Παναγίας τῶν Εἰσοδίων 32**
18th cent. (second half); paper; 202 × 152 mm.; 376 pages; written by Konstantinos Dapontes.
Contents: Manuel Philes, Ioannes Zonaras, Meletios Galesiotes, Michael Psellos, Joseph Bryennios, Konstantinos Manasses, Stephanos of Byzantium, Leo VI, various works of Konstantinos Dapontes and other post-Byzantine texts.
Miscellaneous poems: p. 24 (55–56: 'Εἰς τὸν βίον εἰκονισμένον'), pp. 101–104 (29–54: 'Τοῦ σοφωτάτου Ψελλοῦ ἴαμβοι εἰς ἀρετὰς καὶ κακίας').
Bibliography: Papadopoulos-Kerameus, 'Δύο κατάλογοι', 74–79.

VATICAN CITY

Biblioteca Apostolica Vaticana

76. (Vr) *Vaticanus gr. 207 (olim 1100)*
13th cent. (1267–1269 Nikitas); paper; 290 × 223 mm. (290 × 221 Mercati and de' Cavalieri); VII + 373 folios (II^v, III, VI, 164^v, 263^v are blank); on fol. V^r there is an index written by Allatius; fols. 1–3, where the poems by Prodromos were copied, were added later (different quality of paper).
Contents: e.g. Sopater (διαίρεσις ζητημάτων), Germanos II (patriarch of Constantinople), Ps. Dionysios Areopagites, A poem of a certain Arsenios (Verses on Holy Sunday), two poems of Bartholomaios Malomytes (unedited), Nikolaos of Corfu (poem), Gregorios of Corinth (poem), Michael Italikos, some anonymous poems, and various prose works of astrological and philosophical nature.
Miscellaneous poems: fol.1^v (55–56), 1^v (62–66).[6]
Bibliography: I. Mercati and P. F. de' Cavalieri, *Vaticani Graeci: Codices 1–329* (Vatican City 1923), 249–54; P. Canart, 'À propos du Vaticanus graecus 207: Le recueil scientifique d'un érudit constantinopolitain du XIIIe siècle et l'emploi du papier "à zig-zag" dans la capitale byzantine', in *Illinois Classical Studies* 7 (1982) [= *Studies in Memory of Alexander Turyn (1900–1981)*, part Four], 271–98; D. Z. Nikitas, *Eine byzantinische Übersetzung von Boethius' 'De hypotheticis syllogismis'* (Göttingen 1982), 9–14; Migliorini and Tessari, 'Germano', 157–58.

77. (V) *Vaticanus gr. 305 (olim 218)*
For a detailed discussion of this manuscript, see the next section, pp. 122–30.

---

[6] The left column of the folio under consideration is heavily damaged.

Miscellaneous poems: fols. 30ʳ (27-28), 94ᵛ-97ᵛ (76), 97ᵛ-99ʳ (75), 103ᵛ (70-72), 103ᵛ-104ʳ (69), 104ʳ (68), 109ʳ-109ᵛ (55-56), 117 (22-23), 117ᵛ (7), 117ᵛ (57-61), 117ᵛ-118ʳ (73-74), 121ᵛ (62-66), 126ᵛ-128ʳ (1-6), 128ᵛ (26).

78. (W) *Vaticanus gr. 306 (olim 989)*

13th-14th cent.; paper (oriental); 276 × 182 mm.; II + 237 (+170a) folios with approximately 28 lines; two initially separate manuscripts bound together [(a) fol 1-128 with 16 quires[7] and (b) 129-237 with 14 quires, of which the last is a *trinion*]; both parts seem to have been written by the same scribe; the folio under consideration is written in two columns with 31 lines.

Contents: Menander, Christophoros Mitylenaios, a collection of Sententiae, Nikephoros Basilakes, Proklos, Michael Psellos (letters), Niketas Magistros, Prokopios, Elias (commentary on Aristotle's Categories).

Miscellaneous poems: fols. 54ᵛ (7), 54ᵛ (8), 54ᵛ (10), 55ᵛ (22-23).

Bibliography: Mercati and de' Cavalieri, *Codices*, 450-54; Hörandner, *Historische Gedichte*, 146 and 161-62; Op de Coul, *Théodore Prodrome*, vol. 1, 51-52 (with bibliography); de Groote, *Christophori Mitylenaii*, XLV; S. Papaioannou, *Michael Psellus, Epistulae*, 2 vols. (Berlin/Boston 2019), vol. 1, CX-CXI.

79. (X) *Vaticanus gr. 307 (olim 668)*

13th cent.; paper (fol. III + 228 from parchment); 175 × 120 mm.; VII + 228 (+35a) folios (I, IIᵛ, 35, 227ᵛ are blank); the ms. consists of 31 quires: 1 × 4 (VII), 1 × 6 (6), 1 × 8 (14), 7 (8-1: 21), 3 × 8 (45), 6 (8-2: 51), 3 × 8 (75), 7 (8-1: 81), 5 × 8 (121), 1 × 6 (127), 12 × 8 (223), 1 × 4 (228); written by an unidentified hand; Allatius supplemented the manuscript with a pinax (fol. IIʳ), on fol. 5ᵛ a fifteenth-century hand wrote *Phisica Aristotelis in Greco*, while various notes are to be found on fol. 228.

Contents: Aristotle (*physicorum*) with Themistios' paraphrase, Michael Psellos, excerpts from medical treatises, a poem of Konstantinos Akropolites, some anonymous poems.

Miscellaneous poems: fols. I (29-54), IIʳ (62-66), IIʳ (57-61).

Bibliography: Mercati and de' Cavalieri, *Codices*, 454-56; Hörandner, *Historische Gedichte*, 146 and 162.

80. (Σ) *Vaticanus gr. 1126 (olim 887*)*

14th cent.; parchment (the flyleaves from paper); 112 × 90 mm. (105-110 × 83 mm. Gonnelli); folios II + 296 + I (7ᵛ, 8ʳ, 219ʳ-220ᵛ, 224ᵛ, 293ʳ-295ʳ are blank);

---

[7] Not 17 quires as noted in de Groote, *Christophori Mitylenaii*, XLV.

a pocket-size manuscript of 36 quires (36 × 8);[8] many scribes worked together on its execution; it belonged to Nicola Bartholomeo de Columnis (cf. fol. II^r).

Contents: e.g. a treatise on metre, Georgios Pisides, Prosouch, Manuel Melissenos, Manuel Philes, Evangelistarion.

Miscellaneous poems: fols. 148 (57–61: 'Εἰς δακτύλιον ἔχοντα σφραγῖδα ἐρῶντας δύο, καὶ ἀπὸ τῶν στέρνων αὐτῶν δύο δένδρα ἐκπεφυέντα καὶ εἰς ἕνα συγκορυφούμενον κόρυμβον'), 151^v (7: 'εἰς τὸν Ἀβρὰμ ξενίζοντα τὴν ἁγίαν Τριάδα'), 273^r (22–23: 'εἰς τοὺς ιβ' ἑορτὰς').

Bibliography: Giannelli, *Teodoro Prodromo*, 351; Hörandner, *Historische Gedichte*, 146 and 163; Papagiannis, *Tetrasticha*, vol. 1, 61 (with bibliography); Gonnelli, *Giorgio di Pisidia*, 33 (with bibliography); G. Stickler, *Manuel Philes und seine Psalmenmetaphrase* (Vienna 1992), 237; Migliorini, *Teodoro Prodromo*, L; W. Hörandner, 'Weitere Beobachtungen zu byzantinischen Figurengedichten und Tetragrammen', *Nea Rhome* 6 (2009), 291–304, at 294 (with bibliography); Kubina, 'Asan Family', 180.

81. (Vg) *Vaticanus gr. 1702*

13th–16th cent.; paper; II + 207 + I folios (I^v, II^r, 15^v–21^v, 27^v–28^v, 36^v–38^v, and 41^v–44^v are blank); according to Giannelli and Canart, the ms. is composed of six codicological units, but there seem rather to be three: (i) 1–38 (243 × 172 mm., XVI), (ii) 39–44 (250 × 170 mm., XIV), and (iii) fols. 45–207 (263 × 177 mm., XIII). The last part of the manuscript was written by two scribes (scribe A, fols. 45–92^r; scribe B fols. 92–207).

Contents: e.g. Hermes Trismegistus, Ps. Galen, Nikolaos Kabasilas, Alexander of Aphrodisias, various progymnasmata, Sententiae of Aesop, Anastasios Sinaites, Athanasios of Alexandreia, Gregory of Nazianzus, Ps. Dionysios Areopagites, Nikolaos Kallikles, Michael Psellos, Aratus, Cleomedes, etc.

Miscellaneous poems: fols. 89^v–90^r (11–20).

Bibliography: C. Giannelli and P. Canart, *Codices Vaticani graeci 1684-1744* (Rome 1961), 45–51; Giannelli, 'Teodoro Prodromo', 350–51.

82. *Vaticanus gr. 2363*

17th cent.; paper; 260 × 186 mm.; I + 93 folios.

Contents: exclusively works by Prodromos.

Miscellaneous poems: fol. 5^v (27–28: 'τοῦ κυρίου Θεοδώρου τοῦ φιλοσόφου καὶ Προδρόμου στίχοι ἡρωικοὶ εἰς τὴν σταύρωσιν').

---

[8] The beginning of a quire is usually indicated with a Greek number on the upper right side of the folio.

Bibliography: Hörandner, *Historische Gedichte*, 146; Op de Coul, *Théodore Prodrome*, vol. 1, 53-54 (with bibliography).

83. (Ha) *Vaticanus Palatinus gr. 367*

a. 1317-20 (13th cent. Stevenson); paper (oriental); 255 × 185 mm.; IV + 195 folios (39^v, 98^v, 100^v are blank); fols. 1^r-179^v were written in Cyprus by Konstantinos Anagnostes (but the handwriting style on fols. 148-158^r and 162-163^r is slightly different); in addition to Anagnostes, there exist a scribe B (fols. 181^r-195^v) and a scribe C (fol. 180).

Contents: e.g. Sophronios of Jerusalem, Sententiae, detailed account of the liturgy, 'text for stage performance of the Passion Cycle of Jesus Christ', Germanos I (patriarch of Constantinople), Ioannes of Damascus, Andreas of Crete, Anastasios Sinaites, Excerpt from the Physiologos, Epiphanios of Constantinople, Euthymios Zigabenos, Makarios Kaloreitis, On the dates of Easter and other festivals, Spaneas, a treatise on geometry, Symeon Metaphrastes, Konstantinos Anagnostes, Ioannes Geometres, anonymous poems, Michael Grammatikos, Palladas, Gregorios II of Cyprus, Neilos of Ankyra, Germanos I (patriarch of Constantinople), Theophilos Antecessor, etc.

Miscellaneous poems: fols. 146^v (7), 146^v (8).

Bibliography: Stevenson, *Palatini Graeci*, 229-35; A. Turyn, *Codices graeci Vaticani saeculis XIII et XIV scripti annorumque notis instructi* (Vatican City 1964), 117-24; Constantinides and Browning, *Cyprus*, 153-59; A. Beihammer, *Griechische Briefe und Urkunden aus dem Zypern der Kreuzfahrerzeit: Die Formularsammlung eines königlichen Sekretärs im Vaticanus Palatinus Graecus 367* (Nicosia 2007) (with bibliography).

84. (Re) *Vaticanus Reg. Gr. Pii II 54**

c. 1320; paper (oriental); 183 × 130; I + 470 folios; written by Romanos Anagnostes.

Contents: a collection of grammatical and schedographical works.

Miscellaneous poems: fol. 409 (20).

Bibliography: H. Stevenson, *Codices Manuscripti Graeci Reginae Svecorum et Pii PP. II Bibliothecae Vaticanae* (Rome 1888), 170-71; Constantinides and Browning, *Cyprus*, 171-73 (with bibliography).

85. (Vc) *Vaticanus Chisianus gr. R.IV.11**

13th (2nd half) - 14th (1st half) cent. [13th cent. De Cavalieri]; parchment; 160 × 115 mm.; II + 112 + II folios (the flyleaves of paper); of 14 quires: 6 × 8 (48), 8-1 (55), 4 × 8 (87), 1 × 10 (97), 8-1 (104), 1 × 8 (112); a palimpsest written in the Otranto region (most probably in the same scriptorium and by the same hand as Ls). The text beneath is an evangelium written in the ninth or tenth century.

Contents: Ioannes of Damascus, Michael Psellos, Andreas of Kaisareia, Ioannes Botaneiates, Clement of Alexandria, Physiologos, Gnomologion.

Miscellaneous poems: fol. 79^v (29–54).

Bibliography: P. F. de Cavalieri, *Bibliotecae Apostolicae Vaticanae codices manu scripti recensiti: Codices Graeci Chisiani et Borgiani* (Rome 1927), 12–15; Arnesano, *La minuscula 'barocca'*, 76 (with bibliography); P. Canart, 'Les palimpsestes en écriture majuscule des fonds grecs de la Bibliothèque Vaticane', in: S. Lucà (ed.), *Libri palinsesti greci: conservazione, restauro digitale, studio. Atti del Convegno internazionale, Villa Mondragone—Monte Porzio Catone—Università di Roma 'Tor Vergata'—Biblioteca del Monumento Nazionale di Grottaferrata, 21–24 apr. 2004* (Rome 2008), 71–84, at 81; S. J Voicu, *Note sui palinsesti conservati nella Biblioteca Apostolica Vaticana*, in: *Miscellanea Bibliothecae Apostolicae Vaticanae XVI* (Vatican City 2009), 445–54.

86. (O) *Vaticanus Ottobonianus gr. 324*

15th cent. (14th–15th cent. Gonnelli); paper; 195 × 132 mm. (191 × 125 mm. Feron and *B*attaglini); 323 fol.[9] (292^v is blank); written by an unidentified hand.

Contents: Georgios Pisides, Theophylaktos of Ohrid, Konstantinos Manasses, Gregory of Nazianzus, Christophoros Mitylenaios, παραινέσεις ἠθικαὶ σύντομοι (194^v unedited), and Ioannes Tzetzes.

Miscellaneous poems: fol. 14^r (25).

Bibliography: E. Feron and F. Battaglini, *Codices manuscripti Graeci Ottoboniani Bibliothecae Vaticanae* (Rome 1893), 170–71; Hörandner, *Historische Gedichte*, 163–64; Lampsidis, *Constantini Manassis*, vol. 1, CXXV–CXXVII; Gonnelli, *Giorgio di Pisidia*, 33; de Groote, *Christophori Mitylenaii*, XLVIII.

87. (Vb) *Vaticanus Urbinas gr. 134*

15th cent. (first half); paper; 230/221 × 142/143 mm. (211 × 149 mm. Stornajolo); IV + 258 + I fol. (26^v, 42, 78, 123, 133, 145^v, 159–163, 165^v, 214–216, 222, 248^v–249 are blank); written by different hands: the first being responsible for fols. 1–26, 223–236^v, 237^v–247, and 250–258^v; the second for fols. 27–41; the third for fol. 237^r; the fourth for fols. 220–221; the fifth for fol. 132 (identified as Ἰωάννης Ἀργυρόπουλος); and the sixth for fols. 43–131 and 134–219. The poem was written by the sixth hand, which is to be identified

---

[9] 333 according to the catalogue.

with Kreionerites Frangopoulos (cf. fol. 96ʳ: Κρειονερίτου τοῦ Φραγγοπούλου τὰ γράμματα ταῦτα); the ms. was most probably written in the Petra Monastery in Constantinople (cf. Palau).

Contents: Nikephoros Gregoras, Theophylaktos Simokattes, Phalaris, Aristotle, Plato, Dion (letters), Niketas Eugenianos, Michael Psellos, Konstantinos Manasses, Mazaris, Ioasaph the hieromonachos.

Miscellaneous poems: fol. 122ᵛ (62–64).

Bibliography: C. Stornajolo, *Codices Urbinates Graeci Bibliothecae Vaticanae descripti* (Rome 1895), 248–55; *RGK* 3.356; Vogel and Gardthausen, *Schreiber*, 237; Marcovich, *Rhodanthes et Dosiclis*, V; C. Palau, *Mazaris, Giorgio Baiophoros e il monastero di Prodromo Petra, Nea Rhome* 7 (2010), 367–97.

4.2. *Vaticanus Graecus* 305 and Its Prodromean Collection

Vaticanus gr. 305 is one of the most important manuscripts for Prodromos' output, containing one of the richest collections of his works, both in prose and verse. In the catalogue of the codices 1–329 of *Biblioteca Apostolica Vaticana*, Giovanni Mercati and Pio Franchi de' Cavalieri have provided a very comprehensive description of the manuscript,[10] while their description has been further supplemented by Wolfram Hörandner,[11] Grigorios Papagiannis,[12] and more recently by Michiel Op de Coul[13] and Mario D'Ambrosi.[14] But despite all these studies, some questions regarding the circumstances of its production remain insufficiently addressed. In this section, I will consider various aspects of the manuscript and the place of the collection of Prodromean works within it.

The manuscript has lost its original binding: it was rebound in 1484 ('ligatus de novo'), and for a second time sometime between 1846 and 1878, as we can infer from the Papal coat of arms of Pius IX still visible today on the leather spine. However, the original arrangement of the quires has been preserved, as shown by the Byzantine quire signatures as well as the *pinax*—written by the main scribe—which corresponds to the sequence of the works in the main part of the manuscript. The original book block consists of VI–IX + 209 folios of oriental paper (29 quires in total), while the front flyleaves (fol. I–V) were added later, probably after its first rebinding in 1484.[15] But what is particularly interesting is that we can distinguish four

---

[10] Mercati and de' Cavalieri, *Codices*, 443–50.
[11] Hörandner, *Historische Gedichte*, 159–61.
[12] Papagiannis, *Tetrasticha*, vol. 1, 56–58.
[13] Op de Coul, *Théodore Prodrome*, vol. 1, 49–50.
[14] D'Ambrosi, *Gregorio Nazianzeno*, 107–10.
[15] For a detailed description of the content of the flyleaves, see Mercati and de' Cavalieri, *Codices*, 450.

separate codicological units, probably produced at different stages:[16] 1st unit, fols. VI–IX (Meligalas and table of contents); 2nd unit, fols. 1–138 (Prodromos); 3rd unit, fols. 139–170 (Nicander); and 4th unit, fols. 171–209 (Porphyry, Heraclitus, Libanius, etc.).

The first codicological unit (fols. VI–IX) consists of a binion.[17] However, this unit must be divided into two parts: part 1, fols. VI–VII (Meligalas); part 2, fols. VIII–IX (the *pinax* of V). This is an 'enriched unit', to use a term coined by Johan Peter Gumbert,[18] as fols. VI–VII were not written at the same time or by the same scribe as fols. VIII–IX. The first part (fols. V–VII), initially used as protection for the first codicological unit, was written much later, at some point in the mid-fourteenth century, by Manuel Meligalas.[19] Meligalas added five of his letters, some anonymous poems, fragments of Libanius, and other texts.[20] The second part (fols. VIII–IX), on the other hand, was written by the codex's main scribe and contains the *pinax* (table of contents) of the entire manuscript. Thus, this unit was expanded by Meligalas when he came into possession of the codex.

The *pinax* shows that the following codicological unit, which contains dozens of works by Prodromos, was written at a different stage from the remaining two units (units 3 and 4). The title: πίναξ ἀκριβὴς τῆς παρούσης πυξίδος τοῦ σοφοῦ Προδρόμου (accurate table of contents of the present book by the wise Prodromos) on fol. VIII^r (see Figure 4.1) indicates that the *pinax* in its original form was not meant to describe the contents of the entire codex as it survives today, but only the part with the works by Prodromos.[21] This part was therefore initially a book on its own. There is more evidence to support this claim: after having listed all the works by Prodromos, as well as a work of Konstantinos Stilbes, added due to the availability of blank space, the scribe notes on fol. IX^v that another section begins with another work—the *Theriaka* of Nicander of Colophon.[22] In addition, the titles of the works by Prodromos listed in the *pinax* are written in black ink, while their numbers are in red. The entry relating to the *Theriaka* and the entries corresponding to the works of

---

[16] Eva Nyström has established a number of useful criteria for the distinction between the different codicological units; see E. Nyström, *Containing Multitudes: Codex Upsaliensis Graecus 8 in Perspective* (Uppsala 2009), 59–62; cf. also J. P. Gumbert, 'Codicological Units: Towards a Terminology for the Stratigraphy of the Non-Homogeneous Codex', *Segno e Testo* 2 (2004), 17–42.
[17] Mercati and de' Cavalieri, *Codices*, 450.
[18] See Gumbert, 'Codicological Units', 30–33.
[19] Ch. Gastgeber, 'Manuel Meligalas: Eine biographische Studie', in: Ch. Gastgeber (ed.), *Miscellanea codicum Graecorum Vindobonensium 1, Studien zu griechischen Handschriften der Österreichischen Nationalbibliothek* (Vienna 2009), 51–84, at 62–63.
[20] For a detailed description, Gastgeber, 'Meligalas', 62–63.
[21] See also Mercati and de' Cavalieri, *Codices*, 443.
[22] Fol. IX^v: ἕτερον βιβλίον τὰ Θηριακὰ τοῦ Νικάνδρου (a cross is placed directly before the title).

124 MANUSCRIPT TRANSMISSION

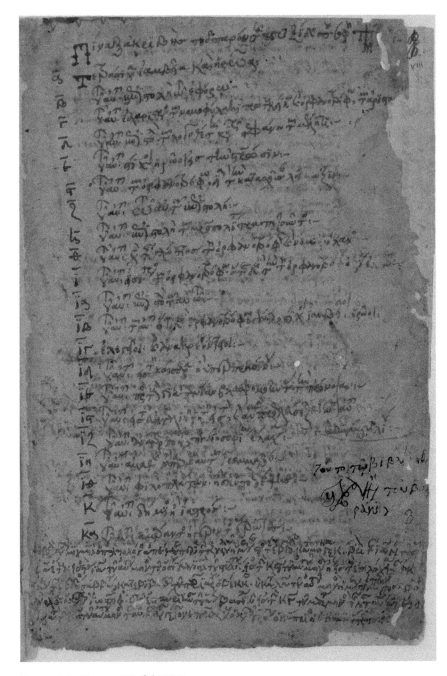

Figure 4.1 Vat. gr. 305, fol. VIII[r]

the last codicological unit, however, are executed in red ink, indicating that they were later insertions by the same hand.

The second codicological unit is the longest one in the manuscript, since it consists of 16 quaternions, a ternion, and a binion (fols. 1–138 = 5 × 8: 40, 1 × 6: 46, 11 × 8: 134, 1 × 4: 138). The rubrication on fol. 1^r indicates the beginning of a new unit. Towards the end of the manuscript, however, some space was left for the scribe to copy a work of Konstantinos Stilbes, while a later scribe (probably in the fourteenth century) added a poem on the Archangel Michael.[23] Fols. 139–170, made up of four quaternions, constitute the third unit of the codex. At the rubric of the first folio of the unit (fol. 139) there is a decoration, as in the case of the first folio of the previous unit (fol. 1). Moreover, a new text starts on fol. 139^r: that is, Nicander's *Theriaka*, along with a very detailed commentary in the margins. On the last folio a colophon of the scribe fills some blank space. The final codicological unit (fols. 171–209), made up of 4 quaternions, a ternion, and binion (2 × 8: 184, 1 × 6: 190, 2 × 8: 206, 1 × 3: 209), contains works of Porphyry, Heraclitus, Libanius, Ps. Herodotus, Menander, Theodoros Balsamon, and Nikephoros Saponopoulos. The scribe, as in the case of the two previous units, adds a rubrication on the first folio of the unit (fol. 171). The last binion was added since there was not enough space left for the text of Ps. Herodotus.[24] It appears that the scribe copied the rest of the texts of this unit (from the bottom of 207^v) slightly after he had finished copying the text of Ps. Herodotus and probably at different times. The decoration normally signifying the start of a new unit is placed next to the title of Menander's paraenesis, while the ink and the writing style vary somewhat in the last two folios.

Although Vat. gr. 305 consists of various codicological units, it was written by a single thirteenth-century scribe. The only exceptions are the flyleaves (I–V), the first part of the first codicological unit (fols. VI–VII) written by Manuel Meligalas, a note describing some events of 1282 at the bottom of the fol. VIII^r, a poem in the margin of fol. 94^v (probably by the same scribe who added the note on fol. VIII^r), a poem on Archangel Michael on fol. 138^v, and several post-Byzantine notes scattered throughout the manuscript.[25] The name of the main scribe is known to us thanks to the colophon on fol. 170^v:

---

[23] Inc. Πρώτου φάους ὢν δεύτερον θεῖον σέλας. For its editions cf. I. Vassis, *Initia Carminum Byzantinorum* (Berlin/New York 2005), 653.
[24] In fact, the scribe did the same in the second unit, since the last quire of that unit is a binion. In doing so, he managed to complete the copying of Prodromos' works.
[25] Mercati and de' Cavalieri, *Codices*, 450.

Ἐτελειώθη τὸ παρὸν βιβλίον τῶν θηριακῶν τοῦ Νικάνδρου κατὰ τὴν κγ' ἀπριλλ. τῆς ιβ' (ἰ)νδικτ(ιῶνος), γραφὲν διὰ χειρὸς Θεοφυλάκτου τοῦ Σαπωνοπούλου.

The present book of the Theriaka by Nicander was completed on 13 April of the twelfth indiction, written by the hand of Theophylaktos Saponopoulos.

However, this subscription raises some puzzling questions. To begin with, little is known about the scribe Theophylaktos Saponopoulos.[26] According to the *Repertorium der griechischen Kopisten*, Saponopoulos has not been identified as the scribe of any other Byzantine manuscript,[27] but Christian Gastgeber has noticed that the *pinax* on fol. VII[r-v] of codex Vindob. suppl. gr. 39 was also written by him in the beginning of the fourteenth century.[28]

Some scholars have argued that Theophylaktos Saponopoulos should be identified with Theodosios Saponopoulos.[29] The latter was *protonotarios* in Constantinople until roughly 1283;[30] sometime between 1283 and 1289 he became a monk on Mount Auxentios and thereafter in the Lavra Monastery on Mount Athos. He was also known to be a fierce adversary of Gregorios II Kyprios and Church union. The problem concerning the different names of the two individuals—the scribe is called Theophylaktos, the *protonotarios* and later monk is named Theodosios—could easily be resolved if we suppose that Theodosios was the name Theophylaktos assumed after he took the monastic habit. Moreover, Vat. gr. 305 has been dated much earlier, either before 1268/69 or even 1253/54, when Saponopoulos would have still been called Theophylaktos.[31] This dating has been suggested due to the aforementioned subscription, which documents that the codex was completed on '13 April of the twelfth indiction' and a note on fol. VIII[r] reporting the events of 1282.[32] However, this particular note was added, as Schreiner has already noted, by a fourteenth-century scribe;[33] the year 1282 cannot, therefore, be used as a safe indication to determine the *terminus ante quem* for the completion of the codex.

If the identification of Theophylaktos' hand in the early fourteenth-century codex Vindob. suppl. gr. 39 by Gastgeber is correct,[34] then the scribe of Vat. gr. 305 was active around c. 1300. Moreover, since the note on fol. VIII[r] of the manuscript reporting the events of 1282 is probably a later addition, it

---

[26] *PLP* 24845.　　[27] *RGK* 3.233.
[28] Gastgeber, 'Meligalas', 59.　　[29] *PLP* 24844.
[30] Hörandner, *Historische Gedichte*, 161, and C. N. Constantinides, *Higher Education in Byzantium in the Thirteenth and Early Fourteenth Centuries* (Nicosia 1982), 67.
[31] See Hörandner, *Historische Gedichte*, 161.　　[32] Hörandner, *Historische Gedichte*, 161.
[33] P. Schreiner, *Die byzantinischen Kleinchroniken*, 3 vols. (Vienna 1975–79), vol. 1, 600.
[34] Hunger, *Katalog*, vol. 4, 70; cf. also Gastgeber, 'Meligalas', 51–84.

becomes clear that Theophylaktos could hardly have been the same person as Theodosios, who had left Mount Auxentios (located in the Asiatic suburbs of Constantinople) for Mount Athos in the early 1290s, when Theophylaktos was still active as a scribe.[35]

What was the purpose of this book? Both Vat. gr. 305 and Vindob. suppl. gr. 39 seem to have been part of Theophylaktos Saponopoulos' personal library.[36] Vat. gr. 305 is not a deluxe manuscript commissioned by, for example, a member of the Palaeologan aristocracy. Many quires were formed from folios whose outer edges were severely cropped during production, rather than during a later restoration.[37] In addition to its appearance, the contents of the manuscript, too, show that Saponopoulos wrote it for his own use. His great interest in the works of one the most celebrated twelfth-century authors must be viewed in the context of the early Palaeologan interest in works written before 1204. Saponopoulos' case is highly intriguing, as his realm of interest surpasses the chronological boundaries of the twelfth century and extends to classical poetry, demonstrated by the fact that he copied the *Theriaka*, a 958-line hexametric poem of the second century BC. Saponopoulos' interest in poetry and his literary background is further illustrated on fol. 171ʳ, where Porphyry's work on the Homeric question is to be found. In the margin of this folio, next to the rubricated title, Theophylaktos added an epigram of the ninth-century poet Leo the Philosopher on Porphyry, from the *Greek Anthology* (IX.214):[38]

Τῇ τῶν λόγων σου κογχύλῃ, Πορφύριε,
Βάπτεις τὰ χείλη, καὶ στολίζεις τὰς φρένας.

Porphyry, with the purple of your discourses
you dye the lips and clothe the mind in splendour.

Saponopoulos' acquaintance with the *Greek Anthology* is an indication of his keen interest in poetry. This should come as no surprise, however, since it fits into the literary context of the late thirteenth century, when the *Planudean Anthology* was put together.

---

[35] It is interesting to note that Mario D'Ambrosi—with the help of Giuseppe De Gregorio—claimed on palaeographical grounds that the manuscript was produced in the third quarter of the thirteenth century. See D'Ambrosi, *Gregorio Nazianzeno*, 107–09, esp. note 360.
[36] Gastgeber, 'Meligalas', 66.
[37] The most severely cropped quires are the following: 3, 4, 5, 7, 11, 17.
[38] Trans. W. R. Paton, *The Greek Anthology*, 5 vols. (Cambridge, MA/London 1918; 6th reprint 1979), vol. 3, 111 (slightly modified).

But there is a further hint suggesting that Vat. gr. 305 was created for the scribe's own needs. On fol. 209ᵛ, Theophylaktos Saponopoulos copied four dodecasyllabic poems written by a certain Nikephoros Saponopoulos.[39] Scholars have already argued that this individual must be a member of Theophylaktos' family entourage.[40] If so, Theophylaktos may have wanted to have a copy of the poetic work of his kinsman and even to save these obscure compositions from oblivion. In one of these four poems, we are told that Nikephoros Saponopoulos is the brother of a Saponopoulos who served as Προκαθήμενος τοῦ κοιτῶνος in Nicaea between 1254 and 1260.[41] Thus, the Saponopouloi appear to have been holders of imperial offices under the Laskarids in Nicaea before the recapture of Constantinople in 1261. This suggests that Nicaea could also be the birthplace of Theophylaktos Saponopoulos, who later moved to Constantinople.[42]

In any case, such details suggest that the content of the manuscript represents, to a large extent, a selection made by Theophylaktos Saponopoulos. But what about the part of the codex with Prodromos' work, which constitutes approximately two-thirds of the entire manuscript (137 out of 209 folios)? Are there any patterns concerning the arrangement of this codicological unit that initially stood as a book on its own? The textual arrangement does not seem to follow a clear-cut generic or thematic classification, but there are a number of interesting points to be noted. Most of Prodromos' poetry was copied on fols. 1–27 and 88ᵛ–129ʳ. Folios 1–27 contain the poetic cycle of tetrastichs on the Old and New Testaments as well as that on the lives of Gregory of Nazianzus, Basil of Caesarea, and John Chrysostom, while fols. 88ᵛ–129ʳ contain a miscellaneous *sylloge* of Prodromos' poetry, ranging from court and satirical poems to self-referential and epigrammatic texts.[43] On the other hand, the prose works of Prodromos are placed on fols. 27ᵛ–88ᵛ and 129ʳ–137ᵛ. But there are two exceptions: the hexametric poems on the crucifixion (27–28) and historical poem 56 are placed on fol. 30ʳ and fols. 39ʳ–40ᵛ,

---

[39] See *PLP* 24848. For the text of the poems, see F. J. G. La Porte du Theil, 'Notice d'un manuscrit de la bibliothèque du Vatican, coté CCCV, parmi les manuscrits Grecs', *Notices et extraits des manuscrits de la Bibliothèque Nationale et d'autres bibliothèques* 8/2 (1810), 249ff. The first three poems have a religious subject matter (the first is dedicated to the holy martyrs Gourias, Samonas, and Habidos of Edessa, the second to Gregory of Nyssa, and the third to John Chrysostom), while the final one is self-referential.

[40] Hörandner, *Historische Gedichte*, 161.

[41] Γνήσιος αὐθόμαιμος ἀνδρὸς κοσμίου | Βασιλικὴν ἀξίαν ἀνεζωσμένου, |[...] κοιτῶνι προκαθημένου; cf. La Porte du Theil, 'Notice d'un manuscrit', 252.

[42] It is interesting to note that Manuel Philes appears to be close to the family as well: Philes composed an epitaph for a certain Saponopoulos, Domestikos of the Themes (*PLP* 24842), and his children, see M. Gedeon, 'Μανουὴλ τοῦ Φιλῆ ἱστορικὰ ποιήματα', *Ekklesiastike Aletheia* 3 (1882/83), 215–20, 246–50, 655–59, at 248–49.

[43] For the exact place of the *Miscellaneous Poems* in this manuscript, see p. 118.

respectively, together with several prose letters. While there is no obvious explanation for placing a religious epigram together with the letters, the second work is an encomiastic poem for Alexios Aristenos copied after some letters addressed to the same person. Moreover, the division between prose and poetry is not always careful, since no blank space is left between Prodromos' works. For example, once Saponopoulos finished with Prodromos' cycle on fol. 27^v, he continued on the same folio and within the same quire, copying letters of Prodromos. It is not easy to determine whether he copied it from one single manuscript or by selecting them from different manuscripts. Mario D'Ambrosi has argued the former, suggesting that it goes back to a now-lost master copy.[44] I am not sure whether the manuscript represents a collection put together by Prodromos himself, but I believe there are good reasons for saying that Vat. gr. 305 with its rich selection of Prodromos' works is a copy of a manuscript written in the twelfth century, which may even have originated in the circle of one of his peers.

Theophylaktos Saponopoulos played a role of paramount importance in the *Nachleben* of Prodromos' work. The part of the manuscript that contains Prodromos' works was initially an individual codex: a single-author book—a 'Prodromean book'—that subsequently became part of a miscellaneous book. But Saponopoulos was not the only one interested in Prodromos' work. Manuel Meligalas, as noted above, came into possession of the manuscript some time during the fourteenth century, before its acquisition by the Vatican Library in the fifteenth century.[45] Another possessor of the manuscript was a certain Michael Barakis.[46] Barakis added a poem at the bottom of fol. 138^v, on the Archangel Michael, and most probably a 17-line poem in the margin of fol. 94^v. The latter poem has been neglected since its *editio princeps*.[47] Its numerous prosodic errors allow us to conjecture that it was probably authored by Barakis himself. The poem is to be found on fol. 94^v, next to the historical poem 58, an epitaph which asks the passer-by to abstain from violating the tomb of a certain monk named Athanasios. It is worth noting that while the last verse of the poem by Prodromos reads ἀφεὶς ἄφυρτον τὴν κόνιν τοῦ κειμένου, the anonymously transmitted poem opens Ἐκλικμήσω σου καὶ τὴν κόνιν, εἰ δέοι,[48] indicating a strong connection between the two poems. One may even argue that the latter poem was added in the margins of Vat. gr.

---

[44] D'Ambrosi, *Gregorio Nazianzeno*, 110.
[45] Gastgeber, 'Meligalas', 51–84; cf. also B. Mondrain, 'Les écritures dans les manuscrits byzantins du XIVe siècle, quelques problématiques', *RSBN* 44 (2007), 157–96, at 174–76.
[46] See fol. VIII^r: Τοῦτο τῷ βιβλί(ον) ἐστὶ Μιχαὴλ τοῦ Βαράκιν.
[47] La Porte du Theil, 'Notice d'un manuscrit', 177 (repr. in: *PG* 133, col. 1072).
[48] Cf. historical poem 58, v. 17.

305 during the reading of Prodromos' text in this very manuscript, making it a kind of gloss which engages in interaction with its Prodromean hypotext. In any case, the author of the poem seems to have been well-acquainted with the work of Prodromos; for example, in the very same poem he employs the rare word χρυσολάτρης, attested in Prodromos' poems 6 and 75.[49]

4.3. Dissemination in the Twelfth Century and Beyond

The twelfth century has often been seen as the 'golden age' of Byzantine poetry, due to a remarkable amount of verse production.[50] The exponential growth of poetry during this period overlaps with another fascinating development: the burgeoning self-assertion of many authors, which grew steadily after the year 1000, reaching its peak in the twelfth century.[51] To shape their self-representation and foster their authorial and literary distinctiveness, many of them put together collections of their works that follow certain patterns and evince self-conscious choices. The poetry book of Ioannes Mauropous is the best-known example,[52] but this practice continued even in the twelfth century. For instance, we know that Isaak Komnenos, the younger brother of Ioannes II Komnenos, bequeathed to the Kosmoteira Monastery a book containing his own letters, *ekphraseis*, and even poems in heroic, iambic, and political metres.[53]

Unfortunately, neither Isaak Komnenos' book nor any other anthologies or collections of contemporary poets actually produced in the twelfth century survive. No autographs of twelfth-century poets such as Theodoros Prodromos, Nikolaos Kallikles, Konstantinos Manasses, or Manganeios Prodromos have come down to us. However, after the recapture of Constantinople in 1261—an event that triggered a remarkable revival of rhetoric and prompted the Byzantines to shape their cultural memory by looking to the past and striving to establish strong connections with the rhetorical and ceremonial tradition of the twelfth century—a substantial number of anthologies and collections

---

[49] V. 9: εἰ πού τι χρυσοῦ, τὸ χρυσόλατρες γένος.
[50] See Jeffreys, 'Verse', 219–28 and Zagklas, 'Poetry in the Komnenian Period', 237–63.
[51] See Lauxtermann, *Byzantine Poetry*, vol. 1, 36–37 and vol. 2, 192–97; see also the various studies in A. Pizzone (ed.), *The Author in Middle Byzantine Literature: Modes, Functions, and Identities* (Berlin/Boston 2014).
[52] Bianconi, 'Piccolo assaggio', 89–103; cf. Bernard, *Poetry*, 128–48.
[53] Isaak Komnenos, *Kosmosoteira Typikon*, 106.5–8, transl. N. Patterson Ševčenko, 'Kosmosoteira: *Typikon* of the sebastokrator Isaac Komnenos for the monastery of the Mother of God *Kosmosoteira* near Bera', in *Byzantine Monastic Foundation Documents A Complete Translation of the Surviving Founders' Typika and Testaments edited by John Thomas and Angela Constantinides Hero with the assistance of Giles Constable* (Washington DC 2000), no. 29, 787–858, at 844, par. 106.

was produced.[54] This section summarizes and expands the results presented in the previous two. It aims to discuss the continuous use of the texts edited in *Miscellaneous poems* and Prodromos' works more broadly from the Komnenian period down to the nineteenth century, their dissemination across Byzantium and beyond, and their reuse and adaptation in new contexts.

But let us begin with the dissemination of Prodromos' works in the twelfth century. Unlike Prodromos' poetry, which has not come down to us in a manuscript copied during his lifetime, his grammatical treatise for Eirene the Sevastokratorissa still survives in a twelfth-century manuscript, *Panaghiou Taphou* 52, a deluxe illuminated codex produced some time in the mid twelfth century, when Prodromos was still alive.[55] We may not have contemporary witnesses to his poetic works, but a *sylloge* of the cycle of tetrastichs on the Old and New Testaments preserved in *Laura B* 43 is dated by some scholars to the twelfth century.[56] There is yet more evidence for the circulation of Prodromos' poetry in the twelfth century. Some of his poems were circulated orally. As noted earlier, a certain priest Michael in Philippopolis recited poems by Prodromos from memory.[57] In addition, many of his peers were well-read in his corpus, including Manganeios Prodromos, Niketas Eugenianos, and the lesser-known poets Ioannikios the monk and Peter the monk. All of them borrowed verses from Prodromos' works and composed poems with similar characteristics in terms of literary features and genre. But while these four authors were contemporary to Prodromos—some even belonged to Prodromos' inner intellectual circle—and thus could have attended the literary *theatra* in which Prodromos presented some of his works, there are other authors who could only have known Prodromos' poems from manuscripts or pamphlets that circulated both in and outside the capital. For example, in the second half of the twelfth century, Michael Haploucheir used, in his single surviving poem, a substantial number of verses from two of Prodromos' works: the poems *Against a lustful woman*[58] and *Verses of protest regarding Providence* (poem 75), of which the latter is

---

[54] For a study of poetry collections and anthologies in Byzantium, see F. Spingou, 'Byzantine Collections and Anthologies of Poetry', in: W. Hörandner, A. Rhoby, and N. Zagklas (eds), *A Companion to Byzantine Poetry* (Leiden/Boston 2019), 381–403.

[55] P. L. Vokotopoulos, *Byzantine illuminated manuscripts of the Patriarchate of Jerusalem* [Μικρογραφίες τῶν βυζαντινῶν χειρογράφων τοῦ Πατριαρχείου Ἱεροσολύμων], translated from the Greek by D. M. Whitehouse (Athens 2002), 186–88.

[56] The dating of the manuscript has been placed by other scholars in the thirteenth century; on this issue, see Lauxtermann, 'Papagiannis', 369.

[57] See pp. 69–70.

[58] In his history of Byzantine literature, Karl Krumbacher noted that the opening verse of Haploucheir's work is identical to that of Prodromos' poem; see K. Krumbacher, *Geschichte der byzantinischen Litteratur von Justinian bis zum Ende des Oströmischen Reiches (527–1453)* (Munich ²1897), 767.

part of the present edition. Hörandner pointed out that Haploucheir's poem borrowed thirteen verses almost verbatim from Prodromos' poem.[59] In addition to these thirteen verses, there are two other verses whose composition seems to have been inspired by Prodromos' poem. But Haploucheir's imitation is not limited to the borrowing of these fifteen verses. As with Prodromos' poem, Haploucheir's text thematizes the futility of letters by building upon the popular twelfth-century *topos* of the wealthy boor and the poor sage. Furthermore, the personification of Fortune, who appears very briefly in Prodromos (vv. 117-127), is transformed in Haploucheir into an almighty goddess who controls the laws of nature, thereby resembling Divine Providence. On the basis of these lexical and thematic affinities, we might imagine that Haploucheir had on his desk a manuscript with some works by Prodromos, and took a special interest in one of them.

Although the exact dating of Laura B 43 with its *sylloge* of the tetrastichs on the Old and New Testaments cannot be ascertained, we are sure that Parisinus gr. 997 is one of the earliest manuscripts containing works of Prodromos. It was copied as early as 1231 by a certain monk named Germanos Lignos, in the region of Nicaea. Towards the end of the manuscript, Germanos included poems 55-56 and 27-28, together with Hörandner nos. 126, 157, and 208. The transmission of Prodromos' poetry before 1261 and the revival of the Komnenian rhetorical tradition in Palaeologan book culture is significant, since it suggests that the poems of Prodromos were read and copied during the years of exile in Nicaea. But Parisinus gr. 997 may not have been the only manuscript containing Prodromos' works in Nicaea. Poems 1-6, invocatory hymns for six saints, include in their rubric the extremely rare word προσφωνητήριος, while a number of unedited prose hymns by Theodoros II Laskaris in Vind. Philol. gr. 321 are grouped under the heading ὕμνοι διάφοροι προσφωνητήριοι.[60] Thus it may well have been the case that Prodromos invocatory hymns were known to Laskaris.

The second half of the thirteenth century marked a turning point in the circulation of Prodromos' work. As already noted, numerous books containing Komnenian rhetorical works, both in prose and verse, were produced from the second half of the thirteenth century onwards. We should see,

---

[59] W. Hörandner, 'Prodromos-Reminiszenzen bei Dichtern der Nikänischen Zeit', *BF* 4 (1972), 88-104, at 101-03 and W. Hörandner, 'Musterautoren und ihre Nachahmer: Indizien für Elemente einer byzantinischen Poetik', in: P. Odorico, P. A. Agapitos, and M. Hinterberger (eds), *'Doux remède...' Poésie et poétique à Byzance: Actes du IVe colloque international philologique, Paris, 23-24-25 février 2006* (Paris 2009), 201-17, at 211.

[60] P. Agapitos and D. Angelov, 'Six Essays by Theodore II Laskaris in Vindobonensis Phil. Gr. 321: Edition, Translation', *JÖB* 68 (2018), 39-75, 50.

therefore, the copying of approximately twenty-seven manuscripts, dated to the second half of the thirteenth and fourteenth centuries, all of which include several of the poems under consideration, in the context of this cultural revival. The most important of these manuscripts is undoubtedly Vat. gr. 305, a treasure trove of Prodromean works, which, as I illustrated in the previous section, was a book copied in Constantinople in the last quarter of the thirteenth century. Vat. gr. 305 may have Constantinopolitan provenance, but Prodromos' works transcended the boundaries of the capital and circulated in various other regions, both in the provinces and even outside Byzantium. Vaticanus Pal. gr. 367, for example, is a Cypriot codex containing the first poem on Abraham (poem 7) and the poetic cycle on the *Dodekaorton* (poems 22–23). However, by far the most manuscripts without Constantinopolitan provenance were written in southern Italy. There are at least four such codices: Laur. Plut. V 10, containing the poetic cycle on St Barbara (poems 11–21); Laur. San Marco 318 and Vat. Chisianus gr. R.IV.11, containing the cycle on virtues and vices (poems 29–54); and Marc. gr. 436, containing the two poems on Life (poems 55–56) and the long poem *Verses of protest regarding Providence* (poem 75). Indeed, Laur. Plut. V 10 is one of the two manuscripts— the other is Vat. gr. 1276—which are deemed the most important testimonies for the circulation of Greek poetry in southern Italy.[61] Whereas no poem from the group in question is preserved in Vat. gr. 1276, it is well known that it contains a number of Prodromos' tetrastichs on the Old and New Testaments, suggesting that his poems were read along with the works of southern Italian poets.[62] What is more, southern Italian poets took a special interest in Prodromos' poetry, and did not hesitate even to write compositions in his style. For example, in Vat. gr. 1276 (fol. 31ʳ) we are told that Nicholas of Otranto supplemented tetrastichs on the Old and New Testaments with his own verses on the lance of Longinus and on the descent from the Cross, since they were missing from the exemplar he had at his disposal.[63] We can also see that the wide reception of Prodromos' work within the Greek literary circles of

---

[61] For the manuscript, see A. Acconcia Longo and A. Jacob, 'Une anthologie salentine du XIVᵉ siecle: le Vaticanus Gr. 1276', *RSBN* 17–19 (1980-1982), 149-228; cf. de Groote, *Christophori Mitylenaii*, XLV–XLVI.

[62] See Papagiannis, *Tetrasticha*, vol. 1, 60–61.

[63] Nikolaos of Otranto, ed. Longo and Jacob, 193: Οὗτοι δὲ ἔλιπον ἀπὸ τοῦ ἀντιγράφου, ἤτοι τοῦ λογχεύματος καὶ τῆς ἀποκαθηλώσεως, οὓς ἀνεπλήρωσε Νικόλαος Ὑδροῦντος. Οὗτοι δὲ ἔλιπον ἀπὸ τοῦ ἀντιγράφου, ἤτοι τοῦ λογχεύματος καὶ τῆς ἀποκαθηλώσεως, οὓς ἀνεπλήρωσε Νικόλαος Ὑδροῦντος. = 'These [verses] were missing from the exemplar, namely those on the thrust of the lance [of Longinus] and on the descent from the Cross, which Nikolaos of Otranto filled in'; see also K. Kubina and N. Zagklas, 'Greek Poetry in a Multicultural Society: Sicily and Salento in the 12th and 13th Centuries', in: K. Kubina and N. Zagklas (eds), *Why Write Poetry? Transcultural Perspectives from the Later Medieval Period*, *Medieval Encounters* 2024 (forthcoming).

southern Italy is not limited to his poetic work, if we take into consideration that Vat. Pal. gr. 92 (13th cent.), which transmits the richest twelfth-century schedographical collection, was executed in a southern Italy scriptorium.[64]

The number of manuscripts copied in the late Palaeologan period and slightly after the fall of Constantinople is also high. Approximately ten manuscripts are datable to the fifteenth century. In many of these manuscripts the poems have acquired a completely new function. As noted earlier, the poems on Gregory of Nazianzus and Basil of Caesarea were turned into book epigrams that preface collections of their works in Paris. gr. 554 and Sof. Centri 'Ivan Dujčev' gr. 12 and its copy (Athous Vatop. 56), respectively.[65] Vat. Ottobonianus gr. 324 is of great interest because it includes Prodromos' epigram about an icon of the Theotokos (poem 15), along with a significant portion of his ceremonial poetry and other twelfth-century works by authors such as Manasses and Tzetzes. At the bottom of fol. 174^v, immediately after some works by Prodromos, there are two brief texts of didactic nature. In fact, the second poem[66] is reminiscent of a poem by the monk Ioannikios preserved in Vat. Pal. gr. 92, since many verses are lexically identical.[67] In both poems—that of Ioannikios and of the unidentified scribe—the teachers advise their students to be eager for learning and eschew idleness. More important for our purposes is that the book seems to have been the exemplar of a teacher using the poems, including Prodromos' epigram on the Theotokos, as teaching material.

The widespread circulation of Prodromos' poetry in manuscripts during the late Byzantine era, both within Constantinople and elsewhere, coincides once again with the appropriation of his work by some late Palaeologan authors. Ioannes Chortasmenos was undoubtedly the author best acquainted with Prodromos' works during this period. Chortasmenos wrote, among other works, a funerary work upon the death of Andreas Asan and his son Manuel Asan. Hörandner has already noted that a substantial number of

---

[64] Arnesano, *La minuscula 'barocca'*, 78. On the other hand, Polemis has suggested that the manuscript might have been produced in Epirus: see I. D. Polemis, 'Μία ὑπόθεση γιὰ τὴν προέλευση τῆς σχεδογραφικῆς συλλογῆς τοῦ κώδικα Vaticanus Palatinus graecus 92', in: E. Karamalengou and E. D. Makrygianni (eds), Ἀντιφίλησις: *Studies on Classical, Byzantine and Modern Greek Literature and Culture. In Honour of John-Theophanes A. Papadimitriou* (Stuttgart 2009), 558–65.

[65] For the relation of the two manuscripts, see p. 146.

[66] Φιλεῖτε, παῖδες, τοῦ γράφειν καθ' ἡμέραν | καὶ μυσταγωγοῦ τοὺς λόγους ποθεῖτέ μοι, | γράφοντες αὐτοὺς ἔνδοθεν τῆς καρδίας, | τὴν δ' ἀργίαν μισεῖτε καὶ ῥαθυμίαν | 5 καὶ τὴν κακίστην πάμπαν ἀπροσεξίαν | ὠθεῖτε μακρὰν ἐξ ὑμῶν ὡς φευκτέαν· | οὕτω φρονοῦντες καὶ φιλοῦντες τοὺς πόνους | καὶ μυσταγωγῶν τοὺς λόγους πεπεισμένοι, | βραχεῖ χρόνῳ λάβητε δόξαν καὶ κλέος. The poem is also transmitted in the seventeenth-century manuscript *Iberon* 751 (olim 4871); cf. Lambros, *Mount Athos*, vol. 2, 219.

[67] Verses 4, 7, and 9 are strongly reminiscent of verses 9, 8, and 1 from Ioannikios' poem; for the text of Ioannikios, see Vassis, 'Φιλολόγων Παλαίσματα', 45.

verses (78 out of 131) of this work are borrowed from a funerary poem for Eirene Sevastokratorissa's husband Andronikos Komnenos and from various books of Prodromos' novel Rhodanthe and Dosikles.[68] What is more, Chortasmenos' work is a mixture of prose and verse, a common practice in Prodromos' works.[69] But some of the *Miscellaneous poems*, too, were read by late Palaeologan authors. Joseph Bryennios, a priest and writer in the same intellectual circle as Chortasmenos, is the author of *"Ἔκφρασις παραδείσου Νάξου*', a poem of 106 lines which describes the garden in the residence of the Latin governor of the island of Naxos.[70] It is certain that Bryennios had read and used Prodromos' cycle of epigrams 'To a Garden' (poems 62–66), since his wording often closely imitates Prodromos' poems.[71] Similarly, another fifteenth-century author, not so well known, Andronikos Doukas Sgouros, was also inspired by Prodromos' works. Sgouros composed two hexametric poems, both of which are preserved in the sixteenth-century Mone Platuteras 2 (pp. 670–671) in Corfu. The first is dedicated to the Holy Trinity, the second to Gregory of Nazianzus. The final verse of the poem on Gregory is actually borrowed from Prodromos' poem for Nicholas (poem 6).[72]

Scribal transmission of the *Miscellaneous poems* does not diminish after the fifteenth century. Print eventually became the primary means of distribution for many of Prodromos' poems, but it did not put an end to the production of manuscripts with his works. Printed editions of his poems started emerging as early as the first half of the sixteenth century,[73] but manuscripts copies continued to be produced well into the eighteenth century and beyond. Approximately forty manuscripts are datable to the sixteenth century onwards. Some of them were written by Western scholars (e.g. Leid. B.P.G. 88 and Vat. gr. 2363), while others were copied in various Greek and Greek-speaking communities throughout the Ottoman period, especially in the region of Mount Athos, at the Patriarchal Academy in Istanbul, and in the Greek Academies in Romania. One of the reasons behind the constant scribal transmission is that it allowed much more space for annotations and interlinear glosses. Take, for example, some *mathemataria* (textbooks) for Greek-speaking students dating to the Ottoman period (Athen. Hist.—Ethn. Het. 66,

---

[68] Hörandner, 'Musterautoren und ihre Nachahmer', 201–17, at 212.
[69] See Zagklas, 'Prose and Verse', 246.
[70] Text in N. Tomadakis, 'Ἰωσὴφ μοναχοῦ τοῦ Βρυεννίου ἐπιστολαὶ λ'', *ΕΕΒΣ* 46 (1983–86), 279–360, at 337–40.
[71] For the parallels, see the *apparatus fontium* of the first poem (no. 62) of the cycle.
[72] I was able to find this similarity with the help of the catalogue. A future edition of these poems will reveal more similarities between the poems. Until then, see P. Tzivara and S. Karydis, Ἡ βιβλιοθήκη τῆς μονῆς Πλατυτέρας Κέρκυρας, Χειρόγραφα—Ἔντυπα—Ἀρχεῖο (Athens 2010), 94.
[73] For a list of the editions, see pp. 157–59.

Athous Docheiariou 108, Athous Laura Λ 62 etc.),[74] which mainly include poems 1-6, 29-54, and 76. The last of these poems is also transmitted in some manuscripts along with a prose *exegesis* of it, as in Athen. Greek Parliament 57.

But the reuse of some of the poems in the post-Byzantine period goes beyond their transformation into teaching exercises. They were used in new contexts, occasionally even in a reworked form. There are three such examples: the first epigram on the hospitality of Abraham, the epigrammatic cycle on virtues and vices, and the first poem of the cycle on Life.

The first epigram, on the hospitality of Abraham, ended up as a book inscription in the sixteenth-century illuminated manuscript Vatop. 1161.[75] On folio 323ᵛ there is a miniature of the three angels seated next to a banquet along with Abraham and Sarah. On the left side of the depiction, Prodromos' modified epigram reads as follows:[76]

Ἡ ἁγ(ία) Τριάς,
Βουθυτεῖς Ἀβραὰμ γέρον;
«ἀλλὰ δεῖπνον καὶ τράπεζαν ἀρτύω.»
«(καὶ) δὲ τῖς, ᾧ τὸ δεῖπνον ἀρτύεις;
καὶ αὐτὴ καὶ Θεὸς βοῦν ἐσθίουσι;»[77]

The holy Trinity
'Are you sacrificing an ox, aged Abraham?'
'No, but I am preparing dinner and a table.'
'And who is the guest for whom you prepare dinner?
And will the holy Trinity and God eat beef?'

Although the two works share both wording and theme, the text in Vatop. 1161 recasts Prodromos' poem in prose form.

The cycle on virtues and vices also underwent some modifications. This had already begun during its dissemination in the Byzantine era. Various scribes added or excised verses, sometimes even entire epigrams. For instance, two of the oldest manuscripts (Parisinus gr. 854 and Vaticanus gr. 307) transmit an extra verse after the epigram on 'Ψεῦδος': τελῶ δ' ὀλέθρου τοῖς ἐρασταῖς μου βόθρος. In Vossianus gr. Q. 42 many epigrams are omitted—such as the

---

[74] On *mathemataria*, see Skarveli-Nikolopoulou, Μαθηματάρια.
[75] S. M. Pelekanides, Οἱ θησαυροὶ τοῦ ἁγίου Ὄρους (Εἰκονογραφημένα χειρόγραφα. Παραστάσεις–ἐπίτιτλα–ἀρχικὰ γράμματα), 4 vols. (Athens 1991), vol. 4, 322.
[76] I have normalized the spelling of the manuscript. For example, it reads βουθητής instead of βουθυτεῖς and γέρων instead of γέρον.
[77] The ms. reads εἰσείσει instead of ἐσθίουσι.

4.3. DISSEMINATION IN THE TWELFTH CENTURY AND BEYOND 137

poems on the virtues ἐλεημοσύνη, λύπη, φιλοσοφία, ῥητορική—while a new vice, φθόνος, is introduced. A prominent case is the sixteenth-century manuscript Paris. gr. 3058, written, as noted earlier, by Arsenios of Monemvasia, who wrongly ascribes the epigrams to Michael Psellos. In addition to the twenty-six epigrams, Arsenios included four new texts on fol. 37ᵛ of the manuscript. As with the other twenty-six epigrams, these four poems constitute personifications: of geometry, astronomy, medicine, and architecture.⁷⁸ However, the authorship of these four texts by Prodromos must be discarded, mainly on prosodic grounds. The most conspicuous deviation from the standard metrical rules is that in five out of the eight verses the seventh syllable is measured as long instead of short, a mistake that Prodromos would hardly make.⁷⁹ Though there is no clear evidence for their authorship, I would say that they were composed by Arsenios himself, since Paris. gr. 3058 is the first textual witness to these four texts.

The circulation of Prodromos' works in the post-Byzantine period goes beyond their inclusion in manuscripts and printed editions. In 1734, the first poem on the personification of Life (poem 55) was painted next to an image in the Byzantine church of Panagia Krina on Chios.⁸⁰ Both the inscription and image were painted by the artist Michael Anagnostou Chomatzas (see Figure 4.2). The text of the poem is placed above the image of two figures: on

---

⁷⁸ The text of the four iambic couplets from Paris. gr. 3058 reads as follows:

Γεωμετρία
Ἐγὼ πολλοὺς ἀγνώστους, γνωστὰς δεικνύω,
διὰ μετρικῶν σημείων σχοινισμάτων.
Ἀστρονομία
Ἐγὼ τὸν νοῦν λεπτύνω τῶν μυουμένων,
τοῦ προθεωρεῖν τὸ συμφέρον τοῦ χρόνου.
Ἰατρική
Ἐν ὑγιείᾳ ὄντας αὐξάνω τάχος,
εἰ δὲ πρὸς τέλος, θάττον πέμπω τῷ τάφῳ.
Τεκτονική
Ὕλην τὴν ἀνείδεον εἰς εἶδος φέρω,
καὶ εἰδοποιῶ τοῖς ὁποσοῦν χρωμένοις.

⁷⁹ The only exception is poem 10, whose authorship by Prodromos is not certain.

⁸⁰ The reuse of Byzantine verses as inscriptions in the post-Byzantine period is quite a common practice. A very good example is an inscription in the church of Hagios Ioannes Theologos (a. 1552) in Kastoria, which derives from the metrical calendar of Christophoros Mitylenaios. As rightly observed by Rhoby, the artist did not copy the texts from the collection of Mitylenaios' works but from the *Menaia*: see A. Rhoby, 'On the Inscriptional Versions of the Epigrams of Christophoros Mitylenaios', in: F. Bernard and K. Demoen (eds), *Poetry and Its Contexts in Eleventh-Century Byzantium* (Farnham/Burlington 2012), 147–54, at 148. In addition to Mitylenaios' texts, many other Byzantine poems by Ioannes Damaskenos, Symeon the Metaphrast, and Ioannes Geometres were used as post-Byzantine inscriptions: see A. Paul, 'Dichtung auf Objekten: Inschriftlich erhaltene griechische Epigramme vom 9. bis zum 16. Jahrhundert: Suche nach bekannten Autorennamen', in: M. Hinterberger and E. Schiffer (eds), *Byzantinische Sprachkunst: Studien zur byzantinischen Literatur gewidmet Wolfram Hörandner zum 65. Geburtstag* (Berlin/Leipzig 2007), 234–65, at 237–38, 241–42, and 244.

Figure 4.2 Chios, church of Panagia Krina, 18th c., inscription (Prodromos' poem 55)

the right stands Bios, represented naked, with wings, on wheels, holding a scale in his right hand; on the left is Kosmos, in a sumptuous dress, holding Bios aloft by his hair.[81] Compared with the text preserved in the manuscripts, the post-Byzantine inscription at Chios teems with errors and variants.[82] These mistakes perhaps suggest that the artist inscribed Prodromos' text from memory without a manuscript before him. Wolfram Hörandner, for example, has identified an 'inscriptional and partly oral tradition' for the poem, while he suggested that the eighteenth-century artist could have copied the depiction along with the inscription from an earlier monument.[83]

We conclude this section with a comparison of the number of manuscripts preserving parts of the *Miscellaneous poems* with that of the *Historical poems*. This comparison demonstrates the enormous popularity of the former group compared with the latter. Eighty-seven manuscripts preserve one or more poems from the first group, as opposed to the roughly thirty-five manuscripts containing at least one poem of the second group.[84] It might seem to be a somewhat arbitrary and simplistic comparison, but it demonstrates that the texts of this much smaller corpus (just 1,002 verses) survive in many more manuscripts than those of the *Historical poems*, which contains 6,912 verses (more than a third of the surviving verses by Prodromos). The *Miscellaneous poems* were probably more popular because it was much easier for many of them to have a second life. Many *Historical poems* evoke a socially ephemeral occasion, ranging from a ceremonial celebration to epistolary communication. By contrast, many of the *Miscellaneous poems* are more ambiguous, enabling them to maintain social and cultural relevance for years to come.[85]

---

[81] For a similar case, see the description by Kaisarios Dapontes of a similar image, followed by the text of poem 55; K. Dapontes, Καθρέπτης Γυναικῶν, 2 vols. (Leipzig 1766), vol. 2, 410–11.

[82] For the text of the inscription, see C. Bouras, ʾἈλληγορικὴ παράστασις τοῦ βίου-καιροῦ σε μια μεταβυζαντινὴ τοιχογραφία στὴ Χίο', Ἀρχαιολογικὸν Δελτίον 21, Aʹ, 1966 (1967), 26–34.

[83] Hörandner, 'Occasional Poetry', 238. Bouras maintained that the nine last verses were not inscribed, since the second part of the epigram is not in accord with the conceit of the image in Panagia Krina (cf. Bouras, ʾἈλληγορικὴ παράστασις', 31) That is likely, but it is worth noting that we are dealing with two self-contained poems that form a cycle; see below, p. 161.

[84] See Hörandner, *Historische Gedichte*, 149–65.

[85] A good example is the epigrammatic cycle of epigrams on virtues and vices: because of the strong gnomic nature of all these epigrams, the cycle was included in twenty-five late Byzantine and post-Byzantine manuscripts. For instance, when Arsenios Apostoles copied the manuscript Paris. gr. 3058 for Pope Leo X with the title Ἰωνιά at the beginning of the sixteenth century, he included the epigrammatic cycle in a rich collection of sayings, which begins on fol. 31ʳ under the heading 'Γνῶμαι συλλεγεῖσαι ἐκ διαφόρων ποιητῶν φιλοσόφων καὶ ῥητόρων ἐπὶ διαφόροις ὑποθέσεσι'.

4.4. The Relationships between the Manuscripts

'Eine Überlieferungsgeschichte der Gesamtheit der historischen Gedichte läßt sich nicht schreiben'

Such was Wolfram Hörandner's judgement of the relationships between the manuscripts transmitting the *Historical poems* in the *prolegomena* to his edition,[86] and the same goes for the 'Überlieferungsgeschichte' of the *Miscellaneous poems*. Twenty-six manuscripts written from the seventeenth century onwards are not taken into consideration here, since they do not offer any new or superior readings and thus do not contribute to the establishment of a more reliable text.[87] Even so, it is not possible to subdivide the sixty-one remaining manuscripts into families and construct a proper *stemma codicum*, for two reasons: first, because no single manuscript transmits all seventy-six poems together; and second, because of the lack of material for comparison between the manuscripts. Most of the poems consist of a very small number of verses (with very few 'Bindefehler' (binding errors) and 'Trennfehler' (separating errors)), which means that any effort to establish the exact relationship between them would be impossible. Thus, what follows here is a brief discussion of the relationships between some of the manuscripts which evidence clear links, with the ultimate aim of eliminating direct apographs in order to avoid an overburdened *apparatus criticus*.

4.4.1. Manuscript V

V contains most of the poems (773 out of 1,002 verses of the present edition), while its importance for the reconstruction of the text has been demonstrated in all the previous editions of Prodromos' works.[88] The following survey simply confirms its importance by taking into consideration only the earliest witnesses or the manuscripts which transmit more than two poems:

---

[86] Hörandner, *Historische Gedichte*, 166.
[87] It is worth noting that many of them do not derive from an earlier manuscript but an early printed edition. For example, codd. nos. 27, 28, 32, 35, 38, 43, and 44 derive from the Basel edition.
[88] E.g. Hörandner, *Historische Gedichte*, 166–74; Papagiannnis, *Tetrasticha*, vol. 1, 94; Op de Coul, *Théodore Prodromos*, vol. 1, 56–59; D'Ambrosi, *Gregorio Nazianzeno*, 126.

1. Manuscripts V and P: poems 1, 57, 61, 62, 64, 73, and 74

Poem 1   v. 15 ἔκγονε] ἔκγονα P
v. 21 βιάσκεται] βιάσκετεν P
v. 23 θοώκῳ] θωόκῳ P
Poem 57   v. 1 ἐκ] om. P
Poem 61   v. 1 ἐν] μὲν P
Poem 62   v. 11 χαρᾶς] χαρὰ P
Poem 64   v. 2 φάγῃς] φάγεις P
Poem 73   v. 4 δήνεα] μήχεα P
v. 8 ἐρίζοι] ἐρίαν P
v. 12 ἀνέτλην] ἔτλην P
Poem 74   v. 2 ἀπέγρεο] ἀπείργεο P
v. 4 ἐναυομένη] ἐναγόμενη P
v. 6 γελωτοπόνοισι] γελωτωπόνοισι P
μίμοισι] μίμοισιν P
v. 7 παικτοῖσι] om. P

2. Manuscripts V and E: poems 7, 22–23, and 75

Poem 23   v. 6 λύσις] φύσις E
v. 9 τὸ σταυροῦ ξύλον] τὸ τοῦ σταυροῦ ξύλον E
Poem 75   v. 2 ἀχανὴς] ἀφανὴς E
v. 3 Ἀμβακοὺμ] Ἀββακοὺμ E
v. 6 ὤ] ὦ E
v. 14 ἐμμέσους] ἀμέσους E
v. 19 αὔξῃ] αὔξει E
v. 25 ὑπενθεὶς] ἐπενθεὶς E
v. 27 κάχληκα] κάχλυκα E
v. 28 κοῦφος] om. E
v. 28 πλέων] πλέον E
v. 34 τὴν] om. E
v. 45 φθορὰν] φθορὰς E
v. 70 αἴσχιστον] ἔχθιστον E
v. 71 τε post καλῶν add. E
v. 79 ὅλας] ὅλους E
v. 105 ὀρθὰ] ὀρθοὺς E
v. 110 ἕνδεκα] ἐνδία E
v. 112 Ἄνυτος] Ἄννυτος E
v. 115 Ἐπάγχομαι] ὑπεύχομαι E

v. 116 θέλω θανεῖν] θέλων βλέπῃ E
v. 121 καὶ] τὸ E
v. 126 ὠνόμασε] ὠνόμασεν E
v. 133 ἀπόλοιτο] ἀπόλοιο E
τῶν βροτῶν] τῆς βροτῆς E
v. 142 γέλως δέ] δὲ γέλου E
v. 143 τὸ] ὁ E
v. 161 τε] om. E
v. 164 ἔλεξας] ἔδοξας E

3. Manuscripts V and R: poems 7 and 63–66

Poem 7	v. 5 ἀπορρήτους] θεοπνεύστους R
	v. 7–8 ὡς ... θύεις] om. R
Poem 63	v. 3 ἐκδιώξας] ἐκδιώξον R
	v. 5 λαμβάνου] λάμβανε R
Poem 65	v. 6 ψόφῳ] ζόφῳ R
Poem 66	v. 3 ἔννοιαν] εἴδησιν R
	v. 5 αἱματοῖ] αἱματεῖν R

4. Manuscripts V and Pi: poems 27–28

Although Pi was written earlier than V, it possesses a number of inferior readings:

Poem 27	v. 2 πικρὸν] πίκρον Pi
Poem 28	v. 2 νέκυν] νέκυν om. Pi
	υἷα] ὑέα Pi
	v. 3 ἑτέρωθε] ἑτέροσε Pi

What is more, in contrast with V, Pi transmits poem no. 6. It is therefore certain that they belong to different branches.

5. Manuscripts V and Z: poems 55–56 and 62–66

| Poem 55 | v. 7 παρίπταμαί] περίπταμαί Z |
| | κνήμας] κνίμας Z |

6. Manuscript V and edition Gu.: poems 1–6, 55–56, 62–66, 75, and 76

As shown in the survey below, V always offers betters readings than Gu.[89]

---

[89] For this edition and its important role in establishing a critical text, see below, pp. 157–59.

4.4. THE RELATIONSHIPS BETWEEN THE MANUSCRIPTS

Poem 1
    v. 15 πολιῆς] πόλιος Gu.
    v. 18 δεινὲ] δεινὰ Gu.
    v. 21 ἀλλά με ὀξὺς ἔσωθι βιάσκεται ἰὸς ἐρώτων] Ἀλλὰ σύ, ὦ θεός, ἐν τούτοις δὴ Παύλου ἀρωγὲ Gu.
    v. 22 εὐσεβέος] εὐσεβίας Gu.
    v. 23 προπροήμενος] τε προήμενος Gu.

Poem 2
    v. 3 ῥητροσύνης] ῥηθροσύνης Gu.
    κῦδος (metri gratia)] κῦδος Gu.
    ἠδὲ] ἠΰ Gu.
    v. 8 νόοις] νόσοις Gu.
    v. 9 ἐπιμίγνυται] ἐπὶ μίγνυται Gu.
    v. 13 ἀδινάων] ἀδεινάων Gu.
    v. 16 τάμεν] τάμε Gu.
    ἀπέτμαγε] ἀπέτεμνε Gu.
    v. 21 Τριάδι] Τριάδα Gu.

Poem 3
    v. 10 θ' ἅμα] δ' ἅμα Gu.
    v. 12 ἐγειραμένου] ἀειράμενον Gu.
    v. 23 εὔπορον] εὔπορων Gu.
    ἰθύντος] ἰθύντορ Gu.

Poem 4
    v. 1 λιγαίνομαι] λιγαίνομεν Gu.
    v. 4 ἐμμελέα] εὐμελέα Gu.
    v. 6 σειρὴν ἡμετέρη σύν τε δέουσ' ἀνέρας] σειρὰ δὲ θ' ἡμετέρη συντεδέους ἀνέρας Gu.
    v. 7 καί τε] καί συ Gu.
    ὀπαζομένη] ὀπαζόμενος Gu.
    v. 8 ἄγγελε] ἄγγελος Gu.
    v. 10 θεηγορίης] θεηγορίας Gu.
    v. 14 ἐσθλῆς] ἐσθλὰ Gu.
    δικοσύνης] δικαιοσύνης Gu.
    v. 15 χήρης] χήρους Gu.
    v. 18 ἄρχου] ἀρχὸν Gu.
    v. 20 πτολίων] πολίων Gu.
    v. 22 ἐς] εὖ Gu.
    v. 24 κε] καὶ Gu.
    ἔστ' ἀέθλια] ἐστὶν ἄεθλα Gu.

Poem 5
    v. 2 ποιμένι] ποιμένα Gu.
    Νυσσαέων] Νυσσεέων Gu.
    v. 5 κοσμογενείης] κοσμογονείης Gu.

                 v. 14 γενέτης] γενέτην Gu.
                 v. 24 σταλάει] σταλάεις Gu.
Poem 6   v. 2 οἶκτος] οἶκτον Gu.
                 v. 3 ἤ] ἦ Gu.
                 v. 8 θηλυτέρων] θυγατέρων Gu.
                 v. 11 τέμνοντα] τέμνων τε Gu.
                 Βελίαν] Βελίου Gu.
                 v. 14 ὅσ τ'] ὥς τ' Gu.
                 v. 15 τ'] δ' Gu.
                 v. 17 ὅσ τ'] ὥστ' Gu.
                 ναύτην] ταύτην Gu.
                 v. 18 λυγρῆσι] λυγρὸν ᾖσι Gu.
                 v. 21 οἰκτοσύνης πάτερ ἐσθλῆς] οἰκτοσύνῃ πάτερ ἐσθλὲ Gu.
                 τεῷ] Θεὸς Gu.
                 ὀπάζων] ὀπάζῃ Gu.
Poem 55   v. 2 τρίχας] τρίβους Gu.
                 v. 7 παρίπταμαί] περίπταμαί Gu.
Poem 56   v. 2 τρίχας] τρίβους Gu.
Poem 64   v. 5 μύρτον] μίλτον Gu.
Poem 75   v. 2 κριμάτων] χρημάτων Gu.
                 v. 28 ἀνάρρουν] ἀνὰ ῥοῦν Gu.
                 v. 29 φεύξεταί] φθέγξεταί Gu.
                 v. 36 λευκότητος] γλαυκότητος Gu.
                 v. 43 Ἐπικούρειο] Ἐπικούριον Gu.
                 v. 49 εἴποιμεν] εἴποι μὴ Gu.
                 v. 51 γοῦν] γοῦν Gu.
                 v. 55 κυλίνδρους] κυλίνδους Gu.
                 v. 69 προσήκων] προσῆκον Gu.
                 v. 75 μαθήσεως...θύραν] om. Gu.
                 v. 76 ὀδοῦσι...πλέον] om. Gu.
                 v. 81 γαύρων] γαυρῶν Gu.
                 v. 98 κακοῖς] καινοῖς Gu.
                 v. 102 λωποδυτεῖ] λωποδυτοῖ Gu.
                 v. 107 Μέλητος] Μέλιτος Gu.
                 v. 108 Μέλητος] Μέλιτος Gu.
                 v. 118 Τὸ δ'] τόδ' Gu.
                 v. 122 ξύμφυλος] ξύμφιλος Gu.
                 v. 125 ἀσυμφύλους] ἀσυμφίλους Gu.

v. 133 ἀπόλοιτο] ἀπόλοιο Gu.
v. 145 Ὄντων γὰρ τούτων] ὄντως γὰρ ὄντως Gu.
v. 159 χλοάζοντες] χνοάζοντες Gu.

Poem 76 v. 5 χιτώνιον] χυτώνιον Gu.
v. 21 ἄντικρυς] ἀντικρὺς Gu.
vv. 25–26 ὕβρεις … γνάθοιν] om. Gu.
v. 30 μὴ] μὰ Gu.
v. 38 ἀσωμάτοις] ἀσωμάτως Gu.
δευτέρως] δευτέροις Gu.
v. 40 οἷον] οἶον Gu.
Θρόνοις] θρόνις Gu.
v. 41 αὔλοις] αὔλαις Gu.
v. 42 γὰρ] μὲν Gu.
v. 47 κἀκ τῶν] κακτῶν Gu.
v. 56 καίει φύσει] φύσει καίει Gu.
v. 60 εἰ χρὴ] ἀρχῇ Gu.
v. 61 εἰ μὴ] εἰμὴ Gu.
v. 75 διίστηται] διίσταται Gu.
v. 79 κοινὸν] καινὸν Gu.
v. 82 ἡ μεσιτεύουσα] ὑμέσι τένουσα Gu.
ὑγρότης] ὑγρότην Gu.
v. 94 τὲ] τι Gu.
v. 96 συνεμπλεκουσῶν] τῶν συμπλεκουσῶν Gu.
v. 112 γὰρ] γοῦν Gu.
v. 124 –] διδοὺς γὰρ ἄρτον, ἰχθὺν ἀντιλαμβάνει add. Gu.
v. 125 πᾶσαι πόλεις] πόλεις πᾶσαι Gu.
v. 129 Τίς γὰρ] Τί γὰρ Gu.
v. 130 τὸ] καὶ Gu.
vv. 133–134 ὡς … <θηρίῳ>] om. Gu.
v. 137 τι] τοὶ Gu.
v. 138 κρατεῖται] καρατεῖται Gu.
v. 150 μείγνυται] μίγνυται Gu.
v. 165 ἡμᾶς δὲ τύπτων ἐξάγει. Νόμοι, νόμοι] ἡμᾶς τύπτων ἐξάγει. Ὦ νόμοι, νόμοι Gu.
v. 168 ἀγνοῶ νὴ τὴν θέμιν] ἀγνοῶν καὶ τὴν θέμιν Gu.
v. 182 τῶν] τὸν Gu.
v. 183 πάσχω δὲ πρὸς φαῦλον τε ἀμβλυωπίαν] πάσχω δὲ πρὸς φαῦλον τε ἀμβλυωπίαν Gu.

v. 187 ὄμμα] αἷμα Gu.
v. 190 κραυγὴ] κραγὴ Gu.
v. 194 ἀλλ' ὁ τρισανόητος ἄθλιος Βίος] ἀλλ' ὁ τρισάνοικτος καὶ ἄθλιος βίος Gu.
v. 213 κοινώνημα] κοινόνημα Gu.
v. 231 σπάθην] σπάτην Gu.
v. 241 μίτραν] μήτραν Gu.
ἐν ποδοῖν] ἐκ ποδοῖν Gu.
v. 256 αὐτοῖς τοῖς τέκνοις] αὐτῆς τοῖς τέκνοις Gu.
v. 268 ἀπαθῶς πρὸ] ἀπαθῶν πρὸς Gu.
v. 272 πιτυρίου] ποτηρίου Gu.
v. 273 τῆς ἴδης] τοῦ ἤδους Gu.
v. 274 μὴ] μοῖ Gu.
v. 284 εἴ] εἴσι Gu.
v. 289 λαλεῖν] λαχεῖν Gu.

I have tracked down a limited number of cases where other witnesses offer better readings than V:

Poem 1	v. 11 χαλκομελής P Gu.] χαλκειμελὴς V
Poem 64	v. 2 τρυγήσεις Be H L He Mt N P R Vb Vr X Z Gu.] τρυγήσῃς V
Poem 75	v. 94 E I] post v. 94 iterum v. 90 add. V
	v. 107 Μέλητος E I] Μέλιτος V
	v. 108 Μέλητος E I] Μέλιτος V
Poem 76	v. 70 δίσκον Gu.] δύσκον
	v. 124 καὶ παντὸς ἅπας ἐνδεὴς ὁ τεχνίτης Gu.] om. V
	v. 180 ἅλες Gu.] ἅλυς V
	v. 203 μῖσος Gu.] μύσος V

4.4.2. The Remaining Manuscripts

7. Manuscripts Ax and Y: Poem 3

Both manuscripts contain only the poem on Basil the Great; both of them were written by the same unidentified fifteenth-century scribe and share a number of binding errors against V:

Poem 3	v. 3 εἴδεϊ V] εἴδει Ax Y
	v. 4 σιγόωντα V] σιγέοντα Ax Y
	v. 16 φάναι V] φαεῖναι Ax Y
	v. 24 εὐκοσμίη V] εὐκοσμία Ax Y

What is more, Ax contains errors of its own, which means that it is a copy of Y and will not be taken into consideration.

Poem 3   v. 16 μερόπεσι Ax] μερόπεσσι V Y
         v. 19 μῖραν Ax] μοῖραν V Y

8. Manuscripts B and l: poem 7

As Hörandner has already noted, l is a direct copy of B.[90] The validity of his argument is further corroborated by my investigation, since the two mss share a unique reading:

poem 7   v. 8 Θύεις B l : φέρει V : φύεις (cet. codd.).

Moreover, l displays a minor individual error:

v. 2 Οὔκ] Οὔ l

9. Manuscripts R and m: poems 7, 9, and 62–66

Both Sternbach and Hörandner have pointed out that m is a direct apograph of R.[91] This is also confirmed by the following survey:

Poem 7   v. 5 ἀπορρήτους] θεοπνεύστους R m
           vv. 7–8 ὡς…θύεις] om. R m
Poem 64   v. 3 ἐκδιώξας] ἐκδιώξον R m
           v. 5 λαμβάνου] λάμβανε R m
Poem 65   v. 6 ψόφῳ] ζόφῳ R m

Moreover, it is worth noting that in one instance the scribe of m corrects his exemplar R by writing ἐκλάπη (v. 15) instead of ἐκλάμπῃ.

10. Manuscripts B and Σ: poems 6, 22–23, and 57–61

Whereas Hörandner maintained that Σ and B derive from the same exemplar,[92] Papagiannis has convincingly shown that Σ is actually a copy of B.[93] That is also corroborated by the following survey:

Poem 6   v. 8 φέρει V : φύεις cet. codd.] θύεις B Σ
Poems 57–61 tit. ἐκπεφυκότα V : ἐκπεφυκότα cet. codd.] ἐκπεφυέντα B Σ
             tit. Συγκορυφούμενον V : συγκορυφούμενον cet. codd.]
             Συγκορυφούμενα B Σ

It will therefore not be included in the *apparatus criticus* of the edition.

---

[90] Hörandner, *Historische Gedichte*, 154.   [91] Cf. Hörandner, *Historische Gedichte*, 155.
[92] Ibid. 170.   [93] Papagiannis, *Tetrasticha*, vol. 1, 94–95.

11. Manuscripts Vg and Ne: poems 11–20

Vg and Ne share a striking variant that allow us to place them within a separate group from the rest of the manuscripts:

Poem 12	v. 1 οὐρανόβρυτοι] οὐρανόβλητοι Vg : οὐρανόβλυτοι Ne
Poem 17	v. 1 ἡδύκρεων] ἡδύκρεως Vg Ne
Poem 20	v. 4 καὶ κόχλος ἐξήνεγκεν αὖθις πορφύραν] τὴν πορφύραν δ' ὁ κόχλος ἐξήνθησέ σοι Vg Ne

However, Vg possesses quite a few errors of its own:

Poem 12	v. 2 παιδοφθόρον] παιδοφθόρων Vg
	v. 3 κεραύνιοι] κεραύνιος Vg
	v. 5 ἐφ'] ἀφ' Vg
Poem 13	2 ἀνελεῖς] ἀνέλης Vg
Poem 16	v. 4. ἐμπεσὸν] ἐκπεσὸν Vg
Poem 17	v. 1 ἀλλὰ τέλματος τόκος] ἀνὰ τέλματος τόπον Vg
	v. 2 καὶ Βαρβάρα γοῦν βορβόρου κἂν ἐξέφυ] καὶ βορβόρου γοῦν Βαρβάρα κἂν ἐξέφυ Vg
	v. 4 πᾶν] πᾶς Vg
Poem 19	v. 4 ἠκόνησας] ἠκονήσω Vg

The same goes for Ne:

Poem 14	v. 5 ἐξάγεις] ἐξάγῃς Ne
Poem 16	v. 5 βρύει] βρέχει Ne
Poem 17	v. 3 ὅμως] ὅπως Ne

In addition, Ne does not transmit poem 18. Thus it is reasonable to assume that Vg and Ne derive from a common, now lost, exemplar, but they seem to be independent of each other.

12. Manuscript C: poem 20

C belongs to a separate branch from the rest of the manuscripts transmitting the cycle on St Barbara (11–20), for two reasons: (a) it transmits only the last poem of the cycle; and (b) it contains a number of peculiar variants and errors:

Poem 20	v. 4 ἐξήνθησέ] ἐθρέψατό C
	v. 5 προσελθὼν ἱστόρει καὶ Βαρβάραν] πρόσελθε Βαρβάραν καθιστόρει C
	vv. 5–6] ordo versuum diversus est C
	v. 6 μαργαρίτην] μάργαρον καὶ C
	τοῦ καὶ φονευτοῦ καὶ φυτοσπόρου λέγω] om. C

4.4. THE RELATIONSHIPS BETWEEN THE MANUSCRIPTS

13. Manuscripts Pi and L: poem 21

Poem 21 v. 1 φύσι] φύσει L
v. 2 σειρὴ] σειρὰν L
v. 5 ἀνάρσιον] ἀνόσιον L
v. 6 φύτις] φύτης L
ἑὴν] τεὴν L

On the basis of these variations, it is hard to determine whether L is a direct copy of Pi or whether they are copies of a now-lost exemplar.

14. Manuscripts N and O: poem 25

Unlike Vi, N and O omit v. 7, which mean that they are not its direct copies. At the same time, they have some striking errors of their own.

Poem 25 vv. 5–6 ἐντεῦθεν … πρατηρίου] om. N
v. 8 ὀφθῆναι] ὠφθῆναι N
v. 11 κρείττω] νέαν N

Poem 25 v. 8 φθορᾶς … μέρος] om. O
v. 11 ἤνεγκα] ἤνεικα O
καὶ πρὸς νέαν ἄγαγε καὶ κρείττω πλάσιν post v. 14 add. O

Both manuscripts were copied around the same time, but they do not contain the same works by Prodromos. However, it is reasonable to assume that they go back to the same exemplar regarding the text of poem 25.

15. Manuscripts V, E, I, and edition Gu.: poem 75

E, I, and Gu. seem to stand closer to each other in comparison with V:

Poem 75 v. 76 om.] E I Gu.
v. 104 ἰδὼν σοφοὺς μὲν E I Gu.] ἰδὼν μὲν σοφοὺς V
v. 133 ἀπόλοιτο] ἀπόλοιο E I Gu.

Nonetheless, in one case of minor importance Gu. stands closer to V than to E and I:

Poem 75 v. 3 Ἀμβακοὺμ V Gu.] Ἀββακοὺμ E

16. Edition Gu. and manuscripts Pt and Lq: poem 75

The closely related codices Pt and Lq were written by the same scribe (i.e. Ἄγγελος Βεργίκιος) in the second half of the sixteenth century. They should be considered as direct apographs of Gu. because they share all its errors:

Poem 75	v. 2 κριμάτων] χρημάτων Gu. Pt Lq
	v. 28 ἀνάρρουν] ἀνὰ ῥοῦν Gu. Pt Lq
	v. 29 φεύξεταί] φθέγξεταί Gu. Pt Lq
	v. 36 λευκότητος] γλαυκότητος Gu. Pt Lq
	v. 43 Ἐπικούρειον] Ἐπικούριον Gu. Pt Lq
	v. 49 εἴποιμεν] εἴποι μὴ Gu. Pt Lq
	v. 51 γοῦν] γοῦν Gu. Pt Lq
	v. 55 κυλίνδρους] κυλίνδους Gu. Pt Lq
	v. 69 προσῆκων] προσῆκον Gu. Pt Lq
	v. 75] om. Gu. Pt Lq
	v. 76] om. Gu. Pt Lq
	v. 81 γαύρων] γαυρῶν Gu. Pt Lq
	v. 98 κακοῖς] καινοῖς Gu. Pt Lq
	v. 102 λωποδυτεῖ] λωποδυτοῖ Gu. Pt Lq
	v. 107 Μέλητος] Μέλιτος Gu. Pt Lq
	v. 108 Μέλητος] Μέλιτος Gu. Pt Lq
	v. 118 Τὸ δ'] τόδ' Gu. Pt Lq
	v. 122 ξύμφυλος] ξύμφιλος Gu. Pt Lq
	v. 125 ἀσυμφύλους] ἀσυμφίλους Gu. Pt Lq
	v. 133 ἀπόλοιτο] ἀπόλοιο Gu. Pt Lq
	v. 145 Ὄντων γὰρ τούτων] ὄντως γὰρ ὄντως Gu. Pt Lq
	v. 159 χλοάζοντες] χνοάζοντες Gu. Pt Lq

Moreover, Lq and Pt have some shared errors of their own:

Poem 75	v. 23 ἐπεισκυκλητέον] ἐπεισκυλητέων Lq Pt
	v. 83 δέ] om. Lq Pt
	v. 84 δέ] μέν Lq Pt

The same applies to poem 76, preserved only in Pt (not in Lq).

Poem 76	v. 5 χιτώνιον] Χυτώνιον Gu. Pt
	v. 21 ἄντικρυς] ἀντικρὺς Gu. Pt
	vv. 25–26 ὕβρεις … γνάθοιν] om. Gu. Pt
	v. 30 μὴ] μὰ Gu. Pt
	v. 38 ἀσωμάτοις] ἀσωμάτως Gu. Pt
	δευτέρως] Δευτέροις Gu. Pt
	v. 40 οἷον] οἶον Gu. Pt
	Θρόνοις] θρόνις Gu. Pt

v. 41 ἀΰλοις] ἀΰλαις Gu. Pt
v. 42 γὰρ] μὲν Gu. Pt
v. 47 κἀκ τῶν] κακτῶν Gu. Pt
v. 56 καίει φύσει] φύσει καίει Gu. Pt
v. 60 εἰ χρὴ] ἀρχῇ Gu. Pt
v. 61 εἰ μὴ] εἰμὴ Gu. Pt
v. 75 διίστηται] διίσταται Gu. Pt
v. 79 κοινὸν] καινὸν
v. 82 ἡ μεσιτεύουσα] ὑμέσι τένουσα Gu. Pt
ὑγρότης] ὑγρότην Gu. Pt
v. 94 τὲ] τι Gu. Pt
v. 96 συνεμπλεκουσῶν] τῶν συμπλεκουσῶν Gu. Pt
v. 112 γὰρ] γοῦν Gu. Pt
v. 124 –] διδοὺς γὰρ ἄρτον, ἰχθὺν ἀντιλαμβάνει add. Gu. Pt
v. 125 πᾶσαι πόλεις] πόλεις πᾶσαι Gu. Pt
v. 129 Τίς γὰρ] Τί γὰρ Gu. Pt
v. 130 τὸ] καὶ Gu. Pt
vv. 133–134 ὡς...<θηρίῳ>] om. Gu. Pt
v. 137 τι] τοὶ Gu. Pt
v. 138 κρατεῖται] καρατεῖται Gu. Pt
v. 150 μείγνυται] μίγνυται Gu. Pt
v. 165 ἡμᾶς δὲ τύπτων ἐξάγει. Νόμοι, νόμοι] ἡμᾶς τύπτων ἐξάγει. Ὦ νόμοι, νόμοι Gu. Pt
v. 168 ἀγνοῶ νὴ τὴν θέμιν] ἀγνοῶν καὶ τὴν θέμιν Gu. Pt
v. 182 τῶν] τὸν Gu. Pt
v. 183 πάσχω δὲ πρὸς φαῦλον τε ἀμβλυωπίαν] πάσχω δὲ πρὸς φαῦλον τε ἀμβλυωπίαν Gu. Pt
v. 187 ὄμμα] αἷμα Gu. Pt
v. 190 κραυγὴ] κραγή Gu. Pt
v. 194 ἀλλ' ὁ τρισανόητος ἄθλιος Βίος] ἀλλ' ὁ τρισάνοικτος καὶ ἄθλιος βίος
v. 213 κοινώνημα] κοινόνημα
v. 231 σπάθην] σπάτην Gu. Pt
v. 241 μίτραν] μήτραν Gu. Pt
ἐν ποδοῖν] ἐκ ποδοῖν Gu. Pt
v. 256 αὐτοῖς τοῖς τέκνοις] αὐτῆς τοῖς τέκνοις Gu. Pt
v. 268 ἀπαθῶς πρὸ] ἀπαθῶν πρὸς Gu. Pt

v. 272 πιτυρίου] ποτηρίου Gu. Pt
v. 273 τῆς ἴδης] τοῦ ἤδους Gu. Pt
v. 274 μή] μοῖ Gu. Pt
v. 284 εἴ σοι] εἴσι Gu. Pt
v. 289 λαλεῖν] λαχεῖν Gu. Pt

Consequently, Pt and Lq will not be included in the *apparatus criticus* of the present edition.

17. Manuscripts Pa, An, Ae, As, Ly, and Vt: poems 29–54

Manuscripts An, Ae, As, Ly, and Vt are direct copies of Pa: (i) in all of them the cycle of epigrams is attributed to Michael Psellos; (ii) as with Pa, they transmit four extra iambic couplets not found in earlier manuscripts;[94] and (iii) they contain almost all its individual readings.

Poem 31	v. 1 χαλκοῦν ὅπλον] χοῦς ἐν βίῳ Pa An Ae As Ly Vt
	v. 2 χωρὶς] ἄτερ Pa An Ae As Ly Vt
Poem 32	v. 2 κτησαμένους] κεκτημένους Pa An Ae As Ly Vt
Poem 35	v. 2 κριῷ] ψεύδει Pa An Ae As Ly Vt
Poem 37	v. 2 ἑρκίων] οἰκίσκων Pa An Ae As Ly Vt
Poem 40	v. 2 τελοῦσα] πέλουσα Pa An Ae As Ly Vt
Poem 41	v. 2 ἀδυνατοῦν] ἀδυνατῶν Pa An Ae As Ly Vt
Poem 42	v. 1 Ἄναρθρον ἀρθρῶ καὶ παραλελυμένον] Τὰ νεῦρ' ἀνορθῶ, τὰ παραλελυμένα Pa An Ae As Ly Vt
Poem 43	v. 2 ὅσοι φρονοῦντες ἀφελῶς] ὅσοι ῥάθυμοι ἀφελῶς Pa An Ae As Ly Vt
Poem 44	v. 2 καταμόνας] κατὰ μόνας Pa An Ae As Ly Vt
Poem 45	v. 2 ῥέγχειν μέγα] χάσμη μόνην Pa An Ae As Ly Vt
Poem 49	v. 1 Ὅσων] ὅσον Pa An Ae As Ly Vt
	σκνιφὸς τρόπος] σκιφὸς βίος Pa An Ae As Ly Vt
	v. 2 μαρτυρίαν] ἁμαρτίαν Pa An Ae As Ly Vt
Poem 50	v. 2 δὲ πιμπλῶ] δ' ἐμπιπλῶ Pa Ae As Ly
Poem 51	v. 1 καί¹] τὰ Pa An Ae As Ly Vt
Poem 53	ἀντιθέτων] ἀντιπάλων Pa An Ae As Ly Vt
	v. 2 ξυρόν] ψυχρῷ Pa An Ae As Ly Vt

[94] See 136–37.

Moreover, most of these manuscripts contain a number of individual errors:

Poem 30	v. 1 φθόνον]	φθόνου An
Poem 31	v. 1 Ὑπηρετεῖ]	ἐπηρετεῖ An
Poem 39	v. 1 Αἰσχρῶν]	ἰσχρῶν An
Poem 30	v. 1 δόλου]	δόλον As
Poem 39	v. 1 κάρος]	κόρος As
Poem 51	v. 2 ἐργάζομαί δε]	ἐργάζομε δϊ As
Poem 52	v. 1 Ἴσον]	ἴσον As
Poem 33	v. 1 ἐμβρύοις]	ἐμβρίοις Ly
Poem 35	v. 2 τεῖχος]	τύχος Ly
Poem 40	v. 1 χρωμένοις]	χρομένοις Ly
Poem 42	v. 2 ἐξεγείρω]	ἀνεγείρω Ly
Poem 48	v. 2 θεοῦ]	θεῷ Ly
Poem 40	v. 2 τῶν]	τοῦ Vt
Poem 47	v. 2 σκότος]	σκόπος Vt
Poem 50	v. 2 πιμπλῶ]	ἐμπλῶ Vt
Poem 53	v. 2 στομῶ δὲ γλῶσσαν, ὡς ξυρόν, τῇ διπλόῃ] στομῶ γλῶσσαν δὲ ψυχρὴ τῇ διπλόῃ Vt	

As a result, they will not be used for the reconstruction of the text.

18. Manuscripts Vc and Pa: poems 29–54

Manuscripts Vc and Pa share two errors, but it remains uncertain whether this is enough to claim a direct link between them.

Poem 30	v. 2 συλλαβὸν] συλλαβὼν Pa Vc
Poem 32	v. 2 κτησαμένους] κεκτημένους Pa Vc

19. Manuscripts Z, Su, and Vu: poems 62–66

Su and Vu are direct copies of Z, since all three share two striking binding errors:

Poem 62	v. 8 θάλλεις … χλόης] θάλλῃ, μαραίνῃ·τοῦτο καὶ τῶν ὑδάτων Z Vu / θάλεις, μαραίνῃ τοῦτο δὴ καὶ τῶν ὑδάτων Su
	v. 9] om. Z Vu Su

In addition, Su displays some errors of its own:

Poem 62	v. 3 κρίνον] κρῖνον Su
Poem 63	v. 2 ἀγάλλομαι] ἀγάλομαι Su

Poem 64 v. 2 τρυγήσεις] τρυγήσης Su
v. 3 λίχνον] λύχνον Su
vv. 7–8] om. Su

On the basis of the above investigation, fourteen manuscripts—An, As, Ae, Ax, l, La, Lq, Ly, m, Pt, Σ, Su, Vt, Vu—dating up to the sixteenth century will not be taken into consideration, since they do not contribute to the construction of a critical text of the *Miscellaneous poems*.

5
Previous Editions and Prolegomena

5.1. From Hieronymus Guntius to the Present Edition

'Κύρου Θεοδώρου τοῦ Προδρόμου ἐπιγράμματα ὡς παλαιότατα, οὕτω καὶ εὐσεβέστατα, ἐν οἷς πάντα τῆς ἑκατέρας διαθήκης κεφάλαια, ὡς ὀλβιώτατα συλλαμβάνονται, καὶ τ' ἄλλα τινά, ἃ πίναξ τῇ ἑπομένῃ σελίδι ἰδίᾳ δηλοῖ.'

'Cyri Theodori Prodromi epigrammata ut uetustissima, ita pijssima, quibus utriusque testamenti capita felicissime comprehenduntur: cum alijs nonnullis, quae Index uersa pagella singillatim explicat.'

This double title, in Greek and Latin, prefaces the so-called Basel edition of Hieronymus Guntius (c. 1511–1552), published in 1536.[1] Originally from the southern German town of Biberach, Guntius was enrolled as a student at the University of Basel when his edition appeared.[2] At some point during the same year he was appointed headmaster of the school of the former Dominican convent in Basel. Three years later, in 1539, he began his career as a Protestant pastor, first in the Swiss municipality of Oberwil, then in Münchenstein, and finally in Rümlingen.[3] Guntius' interest in Byzantine texts developed in the context of a general positive attitude towards Greek Antiquity and Byzantium which developed among many humanists and Protestant reformers during the sixteenth century.[4] From the title of the edition ('πάντα τῆς ἑκατέρας διαθήκης κεφάλαια'), it is clear Guntius wanted to emphasize Prodromos' cycle of tetrastichs on the Old and New Testaments, a work which would have attracted the interest of any sixteenth-century Protestant theologian with a solid knowledge of Greek. In contrast, all the

---

[1] H. Guntius, *Cyri Theodori Prodromi epigrammata ut uetustissima, ita pijssima, quibus omnia utriusq(ue) testamenti capita felicissime comprehenduntur: cum alijs nonnullis, quae Index uersa pagella singillatim explicat* (Basel 1536).
[2] According to the matriculation list of the University; cf. H. G. Wackernagel, *Die Matrikel der Universität Basel 1460–1818*, 5 vols. (Basel 1951–80), vol. 2, 9.
[3] Cf. F. Hieronymus, *Ἐν Βασιλείᾳ πόλει τῆς Γερμανίας. Griechischer Geist aus Basler Pressen. Ausstellungskatalog Universitätsbibliothek Basel 4. Juli bis 22. August 1992* (Basel 1992), 754 (458).
[4] See, for example, A. Ben-Tov, *Lutheran Humanists and Greek Antiquity: Melanchthonian Scholarship between Universal History and Pedagogy* (Leiden/Boston 2009).

other works included in the book are grouped together under the generic title 'καὶ τ' ἄλλα τινά'/'cum alijs nonnullis'. The Basel edition contains a number of the *Miscellaneous poems*: that is, poems 1-6 (λ 4ᵛ-7ᵛ), 55-56 (ξ 2ʳ), 62-66 (ξ 3), 75 (ν1ʳ-4ʳ), 76 (μ3ʳ-7ᵛ). In addition to the rich Prodromean collection, it also includes works by Ioannes Mauropous,[5] Michael Psellos, Nikolaos Kallikles, and Nikephoros Kallistou Xanthopoulos.

A dedicatory letter affords us some insights into Guntius' background and the genesis of his edition. The letter is addressed to his former teacher, Ludwig Lopadius from Constance, who was the author of a Greek textbook.[6] Guntius emphasizes the didactic value of these poems, telling Lopadius that they could facilitate the teaching of grammar and metre. In the concluding lines of the letter, Guntius asks Lopadius to pass on his greetings to Jakob Zwingli and his brothers, the sons of Ulrich Zwingli, leader of the Reformation in Switzerland at the time.[7]

The letter goes into some detail regarding various aspects of the texts included in the book and how Guntius had come across them, but by far the most important part of the letter is on fol. a3ᵛ,[8] where we are told that the edition is based on a manuscript, now lost, brought by the German humanist and reformer Simon Grynaeus[9] from England two years before the publication of the Basel edition. Ioannes Honter, another well-known sixteenth-century humanist, is credited for deciphering many places which were difficult to read because of the poor condition of the manuscript. It is not clear where exactly Grynaeus discovered this manuscript during his expedition to England, but we know that he spent most of the time in Oxford, and particularly in the newly founded Corpus Christi library, so it may well be that the manuscript was part of this collection.[10] Whatever the case, after his return to Basel and Guntius' production of the edition, the manuscript was

---

[5] It includes Mauropous' poems 13-17. It is worth noting that in the rubric they are attributed to 'Ioannes Psellos', which is a mistake of course.

[6] P. Stotz, 'Heinrich Bullinger (1504-1575) and the Ancient Languages', in: E. Campi, S. De Angelis, A.-S. Goeing, and A. Grafton (eds), *Textbooks in Early Modern Europe* (Geneva 2008), 113-38, at 128.

[7] Guntius was in the service of Zwingli between 1526 and 1529; see Wackernagel, *Die Matrikel*, vol. 2, 9.

[8] Guntius, *Cyri Theodori Prodromi*, fol. a3ᵛ: ... ἐκεῖνο δὲ πρὸ ἐτῶν δύο ἀνὴρ ἄριστος ἐκ Βρεταννίας ἐκόμισεν ὁ Σίμων Γρυνεῖος δόξῃ καὶ δόγμασι καλοῖς πολυφέρτατος ἁπάντων Γερμανῶν. Καί τις ἄλλος τότε λίαν ἐκπρεπὴς ἀνὴρ παιδείας, καὶ ποικίλας γλώττας εὖ εἰδὼς ὁ Ἰωάννης τοὐπίκλην Ὀντηρός δὲ Κορωνεὺς εἰς φιλομαθούντων κοινωφελίαν μετεγράψατο δυσανάγνωστα ὄντα διὰ τὴν ἀρχαιότητα ἐν τῷδε πάμπολλα, μικρόν θ' ὅσον αὐχμῷ δὴ πεφθαρμένα, ὁμοῦ τ' εὐρῶτι πεπαλυμένα. Τοιγαροῦν ἔγωγε πάλιν ἤδη, ἐφ' ᾧ τ' ἐμμελῆ καὶ εὐκοσμητὰ πάντα προεκδιδῶνται, ναὶ μὰ παρὰ μυῶν κεκαρμένα περ ἐπανωρθωσάμην πλεῖστα συντεθείς.

[9] For more details on this issue, see P. Ş. Năsturel, 'Prodromica', *Βυζαντινά* 13(2) (1985), 761-70, esp. 766-70.

[10] M. E. Welti, 'Der Gräzist Simon Grynaeus und England', *Archiv für Kulturgeschichte* 45 (1963), 232-42, at. 234.

lost, meaning we cannot compare the edition to the exemplar. The edition's importance in the manuscript tradition of Prodromos' works has been frequently noted by many other editors of various works by Prodromos.[11]

However, the Basel edition was not the first printed book to contain poems from the present corpus. Around 1519, Arsenios Apostoles published an edition of a part of the material from Paris. gr. 3058, including Prodromos' poems 29–55.[12] The same Apostoles had also produced the very first printed edition of a work by Theodoros Prodromos: his *Katomyomachia*, published under the name *Galeomyomachia* sometime around 1495. The editions by Arsenios Apostoles and Hieronymus Guntius, two scholars from very different backgrounds—the former Greek Orthodox, the latter a German Protestant—may be the earliest ones, but they only anticipate the future keen editorial interest in Prodromos' *Miscellaneous poems*. Many of these poems continued to appear in subsequent editions in the centuries to come. What follows is a chronological list of the editions (with an indication of the ms(s). or earlier edition used for each of them):

- C. Gesner, *Heraclidis Pontici qui Aristotelis aetate vixit allegoriae in Homeri fabulas de diis, nunc primum è Graeco sermone in Latinum translatae* (Basel 1544), poems 29–54 (pp. 622–628): probably using the Basel edition.
- F. Morellus, *Prosopopoeia virtutum et vitiorum* (Paris 1611), poems 7 (p. 16) and 29–54 (pp. 4–11): ms. R.
- F. Morellus, 'Carmen gr. iambographi in divam Barbaram virginem et martyrem', in: *Trimetros è Bibliotheca regia eruit, recensuit & senariis latinis expressit. His accesserunt M. Ant. Mureti Hymni, et senatoris tolosani epigramma in eandem Divam, cum graeca eiusdem F. Morelli metaphrasi* (Paris 1614), poems 11–20 (4–11): ms. R.
- K. Dapontes, Καθρέπτης Γυναικῶν, 2 vols. (Leipzig 1766), vol. 2, poem 55 (p. 411).
- Ἱερογραφικὴ Ἁρμονία ἐκ διαφόρων ἐμμέτρων Ποιημάτων Θεοδώρου τοῦ Πτωχοπροδρόμου, Γεωργίου τοῦ Πισίδου καὶ Νικηφόρου τοῦ Ξανθοπούλου εἰς ἕν συντεθεῖσα καὶ διορθωθεῖσα, ἀξιοχρέως προσεφωνήθη τῷ παναγιωτάτῳ καὶ θειοτάτῳ Οἰκουμενικῷ Πατριάρχῃ κυρίῳ κυρίῳ (sic) Καλλινίκῳ παρὰ τοῦ ἐξ Ἀνδρουπόλεως Ἐλλογιμωτάτου μεγάλου

---

[11] Papagiannis, *Tetrasticha*, vol. 1, 84–86 and D'Ambrosi, *Gregorio Nazianzeno*, 115.
[12] A. Apostoles, Γέρας εἴ μ' ὀνομάσειας σπάνιον τῶν σπουδαίων, οὐκ ἂν ἁμάρτοις δηλαδή, τῆς ἀληθείας φίλε (Rome c. 1519), fols. 127ʳ–129ᵛ. Another section of the material from Paris. gr. 3058 was published in Apostoles, Ἀποφθέγματα.

Ἀρχιδιακόνου τῆς Ἁγίας τοῦ Χριστοῦ μεγάλης Ἐκκλησίας κυρίου Κυρίλλου οὗ καὶ τοῖς ἀναλώμασι διὰ κοινὴν τοῦ γένους ὠφέλειαν ἤδη τύποις ἐξεδόθη. Ἐν τῷ τοῦ Πατριαρχείου τῆς Κωνσταντινουπόλεως τυπογραφείῳ. Ἱερογραφικὴ Ἁρμονία. (Istanbul 1802), poems 62-66 (the number of the page is not indicated in the edition, but it precedes the table of contents), 75 (pp. 108-110), 76 (pp. 103-107): using the Basel edition.

- F. J. G. La Porte du Theil, 'Notice d'un manuscrit de la bibliothèque du Vatican, coté CCCV, parmi les manuscrits Grecs', *Notices et extraits des manuscrits de la Bibliothèque Nationale et d'autres bibliothèques* 8 (1810) 2, poems 7 (p. 193), 8 (p. 193), 27-28 (p. 531), 55-56 (p. 191), 57-61 (p. 194), 68 (p. 185), 69 (p. 184), 70-72 (pp. 183-184), 75 (p. 195), 26 (p. 210): ms. V.
- J. F. Boissonade, *Marini Vita Procli* (Leipzig 1814; repr. Amsterdam 1966), 62-66 (pp. 70-71): ms. Pf.
- J. F. Boissonade, *Anecdota Graeca e codicibus regiis*, 4 vols (Paris 1829-1833; repr. Hildesheim 1962) vol. 3, poem 7 (p. 8): using the edition by La Porte du Theil.
- F. Dübner, *Fragmenta Euripidis iterum edidit, perditorum tragicorum omnium nunc primum collegit Fr. Guil. Wagner... accedunt indices locupletissimi. Christus patiens, Ezechieli et Christianorum poetarum reliquiæ dramaticæ. Ex codicibus emendavit et annotatione critica instruxit Fr. Dübner. Theodori Prodromi Amicitia exsulans*, in: Euripidis perdit. Fabul. Fragmenta ed. G. Wagner (Paris 1846), poem 76 (pp. 83-90): using the edition by Gesner with a number of emendations.
- N. Piccolos, *Supplément à l'anthologie grecque, contenant des épigrammes et autres poésies légères inédites* (Paris 1853), 29-54 (pp. 220-224): ms. Lc.
- E. Miller, *Manuelis Philae carmina*, 2 vols. (Paris 1855-57; repr. Amsterdam 1967), vol. 2, poems 4 (pp. 355-356: mss R and m), 22-23 (p. 389: ms. Σ), 57-61 (p. 269: ms. Σ).
- J. P. Migne, *Patrologia cursus completus. Series graeca*, 161 vols. (Paris 1857-66), vol. 133, poems 1-6 (pp. 1224A-1230A: using the Basel edition), 7 (1223B-C: using the edition by La Porte du Theil), 22-23 (pp. 1223A-B: using the edition by Miller), 76 (pp. 1419C-1422A: using the edition by La Porte du Theil), 55-56 (pp. 1419A-1420°: using the Basel edition), 68 (1418B: using the edition by La Porte du Theil), 69 (1416C-1517B: using the edition by La Porte du Theil), 70-72 (1415C: using the edition by La Porte du Theil), 75 (pp. 1333A-1340A: using the Basel edition).

5.1. FROM HIERONYMUS GUNTIUS TO THE PRESENT EDITION 159

- J. P. Migne, Patrologia cursus completus. Series graeca, 161 vols. (Paris 1857–66), vol. 120, poems 22–23 (pp. 1197 A–B): using the edition by Miller.
- L. Sternbach, Nicolai Calliclis Carmina (Krakow 1903), poem 26 (pp. 15–16): ms. M.
- L. Sternbach, 'Spicilegium Prodromeum', *Rozprawy Akademii Umiejętności, Wydział filologiczny*, ser. II, 24 (1904). 336–368 (also published separately: Krakow 1904), poem 11–20 (pp. 1–12)): mss Ba, C, Ne, and R, as well as using the edition by Morellus.
- S. Papadimitriou, *Feodor Prodrom* (Odessa 1905), poem 10 (pp. 178–179)—ms N; poem 67: ms. Z.
- N. Festa, 'Nota sui versiculi in vitia et virtutes', in: *Miscellanea Ceriani. Raccolta di scritti originali* (Milan 1910), poems 29–54 (pp. 569–576): mss Lc and Ls, as well as using the editions by Arsenios and Gesner.
- C. Welz, *Analecta Byzantina. Carmina inedita Theodori Prodromi et Stephani Physopalamitae* (Diss. Straßburg) (Leipzig 1910), poems 62–66 (p. 61–62): mss H and N.
- I. Sajdak, *Historia critica scholiastarum et commentatorum Gregorii Nazianzeni* (Krakow 1914), poem 2 (pp. 258–259): ms. Py.
- S. Lambros, 'Σύμμικτα• Βυζαντιακὰ Ἐπιγράμματα', *NE* 8 (1911), poems 62–66 (pp. 100–101): ms. Vu.
- S. Eustratiades, 'Ἁγιορειτικῶν κωδίκων σημειώματα τῆς βιβλιοθήκης τοῦ Βατοπεδίου', *Γρηγόριος ὁ Παλαμᾶς* 3 (1919), 552–563, poem 3 (p. 557): ms. Ax.
- I. Mercati and P. F. de' Cavalieri, *Vaticani Graeci: Codices 1–329* (Vatican City 1923), poem 8 (p. 451): ms. W.
- S. Follet, 'Deux épigrammes peu connues attribuées à Philostrate', *Revue de Philologie* 38 (1964), 242–52, poems 62–66: ms. Pf.
- S. G. Mercati, *Collectanea Byzantina*, 2 vols. (Bari 1970), vol. 2, poem 20 (p. 355): ms. C.
- W. Hörandner, *Theodoros Prodromos. Historische Gedichte* (Vienna 1974), poem 67 (p. 57): ms. Z.
- R. Romano, *Nicola Callicle, Carmi* (Naples 1980), poem 26 (p. 120): mss Go M L V.
- P. Cavallero, *La tragedia después de la tragedia. La evolución del género dramático desde el s. IV a.C. hasta Bizancio* (Granada 2018), poem 76 (pp. 280–88): a simple collation of previous editions.

It is clear that previous to this present edition, most of the poems were scattered here and there in outdated editions. These editions were usually based either on a single manuscript or, in the best cases, on a very small number of manuscripts selected by chance. What is more, some of them are merely reprints of earlier editions. Take, for example, poem 7, edited by Gabriel de La Porte du Theil in 1810, and reprinted by Boissonade in his *Anecdota Graeca e codicibus regiis* some twenty years later; or poem 76, first edited by Guntius, and then included in the editions of Gesner, Dübner, and Kyrillos, with none of its editors aware of Vat. gr. 305. Even Prodromos' authorship was contested, as some of the poems were printed in the corpora of other Byzantine authors. Emmanuel Miller included poems 4, 22–23, and 57–61 in his nineteenth-century edition of Manuel Philes, while more recently Roberto Romano inserted poem 26 in his edition of the poems of Nikolaos Kallikles.

5.2. The Present Edition

This edition includes seventy-six poems, ranging from short epigrams of two lines to longer poems, with poem 76 being the longest (297 iambics). One of the most distinctive features of the *Miscellaneous poems* is that many of them are cycles of poems on the same subject or written for the same occasion. Poems 1–6 form a cycle on six holy figures; 11–20 a cycle on St Barbara; 22–23 a set of epigrams on the twelve dominical feasts; 27–28 a set of epigrams on the crucifixion; 29–54 a group of twenty-six epigrams on virtues and vices; 55–56 a set of poems on the personification of Life (*Bios*); 57–61 a group of five couplets on a ring; 62–66 another group of five poems under the title 'To a Garden'; 70–72 an ethopoetic cycle of varying lines (four, six, and four verses, respectively); and finally, 73–74 are a diptych of poems about the degradation of learning.

All the poems in each cycle are both mutually dependent and independent. They revolve around the same subject and are equally important textual witnesses to the original occasion. A wide array of evidence allows us to specify their interconnections: their manuscript tradition, the way they are presented in the manuscripts (ink colour), their rubrics, and even the number of verses. A good example is the first cycle (poems 1–6). Some of these poems survive alone in many manuscripts: the poem on Basil the Great is preserved in Athous Vatopedinus 56 and Athous Iberon 161; the one on Gregory of Nazianzus in Paris. gr. 554; the one on St Paul in Paris. gr. 2831. All six are grouped together in Vat. gr. 305 (on fols. 126^r–127^v). What is more, each poem consists of 24 verses (or 12 elegiac couplets), and there are many textual cross-references among them.[13] Similarly, the ten texts of the cycle on St Barbara (poems 11–20) do not have a homogeneous manuscript tradition. Unlike the other nine poems, poem 18 is not preserved in Neapolitanus III A 6, while others are transmitted separately: poem 16 is preserved alone in Laurent. Conv. Soppres. 121, and poem 20 only in Laurent. Plut. V 10 and Vat. Reg. gr. PP Pii II 54.

Some other poems pose even more challenges when it comes to the issue of transmission, problems that have led previous scholars to edit them as single poems. Take, for example, the set of two poems on the personification of Life. In all previous editions these have been presented as single textual unit of nineteen verses. However, in reality this is a cycle of two poems, the first of which has ten verses, the second nine. The confusion derives from the fact that the two poems are almost always transmitted together, except for in the later manuscript Paris. gr. 3058, which includes only the first poem. In the sixteenth-century manuscript Laurent. Acq. e Doni 341, the second poem has in the margins the heading εἰς τὸ αὐτὸ, a clear indication that the second part is a separate poem on the same subject matter. In some earlier manuscripts, such as the thirteenth-century Heidelbergensis Palatinus gr. 43 and the late fourteenth-century Bern 48 B, the first letter of each poem is marked with red ink, and the opening verse in each is identical—'Ἐμέ, τὸν βίον, ἄνθρωπε, δέξαι σου παραινέτην—in both cases forming an address to the viewer from the personified Life. In a similar vein, poems 73–74 are two poems of fourteen and thirteen lines respectively, in which the opening verse of each poem is the same: Ἔρρετ' ἐμοῦ βιότοιο ἀπόπροθεν, ἔρρετε βίβλοι, while in Vat. gr. 305 the first letter of both opening verses is indicated with red ink.

How to document these peculiarities of the corpus was one of the main editorial dilemmas, since it is important to show both that they are part of a broader group, but also that they are self-contained texts with a distinctive manuscript tradition and other distinguishing traits. As a result, each poem is provided with its own apparatus, irrespective of whether it is part of a cycle or not. The apparatus has three parts: (I) An *apparatus codicum et editionum* with all the manuscript(s) and edition(s) that have been consulted for the poem in question; (II) an *apparatus fontium et locorum parallelorum*; and (III) an *apparatus criticus*.

The *apparatus fontium et locorum parallelorum* indicates a range of textual references, ranging from direct quotations ('sources') and parallels with other authors—earlier, contemporary and later—to cross-references within the

---

[13] See above p. 25.

corpus of Prodromos' writings. The aim of such an expansive apparatus is to indicate the place of these texts in the history of Greek literature by recording the intertextual links with earlier works, the impact of the poems on later works, and Prodromos' practice of recycling his own verses across his works. Whenever the links between Prodromos' text and that of other authors are loose, the abbreviation cf. is placed before the citation.

The text of the present edition reproduces mainly that of Vat. gr. 305, with the exception of the poems which are not included in this manuscript. The *apparatus criticus* is normally negative, but occasionally it switches to positive for the sake of clarity. Typical orthographical errors attributable to the phenomenon of *iotacism* and confusion between ϵ/αι, ο/ω, β/υ, σθ/στ are normally not indicated in the apparatus.[14] The same goes for the movable ν, while any change of the breathing and accentuation is noted only when the meaning of the word or verse is altered. The order of the *sigla codicum* in both apparatuses is alphabetical. Whereas the present edition does not aim to overburden the *apparatus criticus*, it would not do justice to previous editions to leave out some interesting variants or even some emendations, especially since some of these editions are difficult to consult.[15] Conversely, if the reading of a previous edition derives from a manuscript that has been taken into consideration for the present edition, that edition is excluded from the *apparatus criticus*. Of course, all the readings peculiar to the Basel edition are meticulously recorded, for, as I noted in the previous section, its manuscript exemplar is now lost.

As for the main text of the poems, following the practice of the most reliable manuscripts, I have opted for μὴ δέ and γοῦν instead of μηδέ and γ'οῦν, respectively. Similarly, in most of the manuscripts the negation οὐχ' is written with an apostrophe.[16] On the other hand, iota subscripts have been restored according to the rules of traditional spelling and grammar, whether the manuscripts indicate them or not; in the same way, the coronis has been restored to mark crasis.[17] The names of the persons of the Holy Trinity (Πατήρ/Νοῦς, Υἱός/Λόγος, Πνεῦμα, as well as Θεός, Τριάς, Κύριος) as well as that of personified ideas (e.g. Φιλία and Ξένος) are consistently written with capital letters.

---

[14] For example, verses 5 and 10 of poem 10 read ποιεῖν instead of πιεῖν in ms. N.

[15] For a similar editorial approach, see T. Antonopoulou, *Leonis VI Sapientis Imperatoris Byzantini Homiliae* (Turnhout 2008), CCXX–CCXXII.

[16] The elided form οὐχ' seems to be in fashion in the work of Michael Psellos and twelfth-century texts; see also E. Kaltsogianni, *Το αγιολογικό και ομιλητικό έργο του Ιωάννη Ζωναρά: εισαγωγική μελέτη, κριτική έκδοση* (Thessaloniki 2013), 498.

[17] For example, the scribe V writes καντεῦθεν instead of κἀντεῦθεν.

5.2.1. Accentuation of the Clitics

It was almost 120 years ago that Paul Maas, in his monumental study of the Byzantine dodecasyllable, advised modern editors not to remain silent about how manuscripts present the accentuation of the clitics:[18] namely, monosyllabic and some disyllabic words which do not bear their own accent, attaching themselves in pronunciation to the preceding word to form a single word cluster (for example, ἄνθρωπός τις istead of ἄνθρωπος τίς). However, only recently have some editors taken this issue more seriously.[19] Recent theoretical studies have contributed to a better understanding of this highly technical and complex issue, pointing to the tension between the grammatical tradition and Byzantine practice, or between stress and visual accent.[20] To make things more difficult for the modern editor, Byzantine scribes do not treat the clitics consistently.[21] But for all these challenges, this edition mostly reproduces the situation in the most reliable witnesses of the poems. In what follows, the disparities and variations that arise among some manuscripts are briefly discussed.[22]

The personal pronouns *Μου/μοι/με* and *σου/σοι/σε* are always clitic. In following the classical rule of clitics after a paroxytone word, they are treated as such even when they are used at the caesura, which may result in the formation of a less desired proparoxytone C5 such as 24.15: ὅ δ' ἐκπόνει μοι/τῆς δεήσεως λύσιν L or 25.10 ἐπριάμην σε/τὴν ἁπάντων δεσπότιν ViNO. By contrast, some manuscripts are characterized by a degree of inconsistency in their use of some other 'typical enclitics'. For instance, though the indefinite pronoun τις is clitic in most of the manuscripts, there are some exceptions:

18.2 *Μή* τις BaRL: μὴ τις Vg
75.4 ἴδοι τι VI: ἴδοί τι E: ἴδοι τί Gu.
75.64 *Καί* τις VEsILh Gu.: καὶ τίς Lh
76.206 ταῦτά τις V: ταῦτα τίς Gu.

Similarly, the conjunction τε is normally treated as enclitic by the scribes, but in two instances the manuscripts do not agree:

---

[18] Maas, 'Zwölfsilber', 320; cf. also Lauxtermann, *Spring of Rhythm*, 98.
[19] Papagiannis, *Tetrasticha*, vol. 1, 211-20 and de Groote, *Christophori Mitylenaii*, LXXIII-XCIV.
[20] J. Noret, 'L'accentuation byzantine: en quoi et pourquoi elle diffère de l'accentuation savante actuelle, parfois absurde', in: M. Hinterberger, *The Language of Learned Byzantine Literature* (Turnhout 2014), 96-146; Lauxtermann, *Byzantine Poetry*, vol. 2, 305-19; and Bernard, 'Rhythm', 30-34.
[21] As noted in Lauxtermann, *Byzantine Poetry*, vol. 2, 307.
[22] The examination of the enclitics is based on all manuscripts dating up to the sixteenth century and the Basel edition.

2.24 σούς τε V Gu.: σοὺς τὲ Py.
75.161 ὀπτῶν τε E Gu.: ὀπτῶν τὲ VI.

In both cases the metre is of no help, while even the scribe of Vat. gr. 305 treats it in one case as clitic (poem 2) and in another case as non-clitic (poem 75). In the edition, however, I chose to write both cases without accents. On another occasion it is interesting to observe that τε is non-clitic before a C5, which may indicate the scribe's practice of avoiding a proparoxytone C5 with the enclitic acquiring the role of a secondary *metrical* stress:[23]

76.94 ἀλλ' εἰς μέσον τὲ/τῶν ὀπωρῶν τὴν φθίσιν V (μέσον τὶ Gu.)

In contrast to classical grammatical rules, the first person singular of the verb εἰμί does not behave as clitic in the following three cases:

56.4 γυμνὸς εἰμὶ VBeHHeILMoNVrZ Gu.
68.3 φορευμένη εἰμὶ VHPz
76.174 μὲν εἰμὶ V Gu.

It is worth noting that in the last of these cases both scribes (V and Gu.) placed an accent on εἰμί right after μὲν at C5 (Ἐγὼ μὲν εἰμὶ/χαροπός, χρηστὰ βλέπω). It should be emphasized that the accent on μὲν is purely graphematic; the verb εἰμί is the one which bears the stress.

The third person singular ἐστί(ν) is accentuated in the following cases:

68.5 δυσαλθέος ἔστιν VHNPz
76.16 ἔρημος οὖν ὁ Κόσμος/ἐστὶ φιλίας VN Gu.
76.154 εἰ τῶν μελῶν δ' εὔρυθμος/ἐστὶν ἡ σχέσις V: εὔρυθμός ἐστιν Gu.
76.202 ἢ τίς ποτ' ἐστίν V Gu.

In 76.16 and 154, the accent is kept because ἐστιν follows right after a C7. Thus, both verses adhere to a fundamental Byzantine rule: no enclisis across the caesura.[24] The Basel edition does not have an accent on the word ἐστιν in verse 154, even though this would mean that it forms a single unit with a word before the caesura. But in this case, it is not clear whether the lost manuscript exemplar of the Basel edition originally had an enclisis across the caesura. It is more likely that, being less aware of the Byzantine practice, Guntius

---

[23] On this issue, see Lauxtermann, *Byzantine Poetry*, vol. 2, 312–13.
[24] Lauxtermann, *Byzantine Poetry*, vol. 2, 315–16.

removed the stress from the verb ἐστι(ν) to follow the classical rules of grammatical theory.

Let us now turn to the so-called 'new enclitics'—words that do not behave as such in classical Greek—to note some interesting features. The particles μέν and μήν never appear as clitics in the manuscripts which preserve the *Miscellaneous poems*. Both Papagiannis and De Groote have argued that the few exceptions to this rule are most likely only scribal errors,[25] but Lauxtermann has offered quite a few examples of clitic μέν.[26] As for the particle δέ, it normally bears accent, with a few exceptions:

12.3 κεραύνιοι καὶ νῦν δε/πυρὸς λαμπάδες BaRNeVg (νῦν δὲ L)
76.38 ἐν τοῖς ἀσωμάτοις δε/δευτέρως νόοις V (ἀσωμάτως δὲ Gu)
76.76 Ξηρὸν τὸ πῦρ, ὑγρόν δε/χύσις ἀέρος V (ὑγρὸν δὲ Gu.)

Once again the scribes do not all follow the same lead. Whereas L and Gu. put an accent on the word, V and other manuscripts do not. To complicate things further, in other cases the word carries an accent in V:

76.118 τῷ χαλινεργάτῃ δε/τὸν στρατηλάτην V Gu.
76.287 Ἔξεστιν. Ἐν λύπαις δε/λυπεῖσθαι νόθοις; V Gu.
76.288 Μάλιστα. Τὰς στρεβλὰς δε/φεύγειν διπλόας V

In all the above examples δέ is before a caesura at the seventh syllable. Even if it bears an accent, it should be emphasized that this does not result in the formation of an oxytone C7. As we have seen, Prodromos systematically avoids stress on the 7th position before the C7. The stress one should take into account is the one in the preceding word. For example, 76.118 needs to be read τωχαλινεργάτῃ δε/τονοστρατηλάτην.

Similarly to the particle δέ, the elided particle δ' is mostly orthotonic (39 examples), but in the following cases it is clitic:

5.23 ἐρατόν δ' V Gu.
9.12 εὐθύς δ' R the scribe replaced the grave with an acute: εὐθὺς δ' m;
9.25 σύ δ' Rm
10.21 σύ δ' WN Pa.
18.3 σκοπός δ' BaRLVg
19.7 σύ δ' BaRLVg: σύ δ' Ne.

---

[25] Papagiannis, *Tetrasticha*, vol. 1, 215 and de Groote, *Christophori Mitylenaii*, XCI.
[26] Lauxtermann, *Byzantine Poetry*, vol. 2, 307–09.

28.3 ἁγνός δ' VPi
69.11 σύ δ' VLPz
75.13 τό δ' VP
76.204 σύ δ' V Gu.
76.237 Ἐπάν δ' V Gu.
76.248 τήν δ' V Gu.
76.266 σέ δ' V Gu.

It is difficult to say why the particle δ' is clitic in all these cases, but perhaps it derives from the fact that it follows an oxytone word.[27] Moreover, in many of the above examples δ' is clitic after monosyllabic words (mostly the pronoun σύ),[28] but again it is difficult to conclude with absolute certainty whether this explains why it throws its accent onto the preceding word.

Although this complete lack of scribal consistency may be irritating and seem nonsensical to the modern editor, and although on some occasions it may be the result of scribal errors, tracking such variations does tell us something about Byzantine scribal practice. In a way it is similar to the case of Byzantine prosody: it relies upon an established tradition—although one that was indistinguishable to the Byzantine ear—but it also gave rise to some particular Byzantine conventions. To a certain degree the use of clitics in Byzantium indicates the gap between theory and practice, so it is important to pay heed to the manuscripts.

5.2.2. Punctuation

As with enclitics, numerous studies of punctuation in Byzantine manuscripts have appeared in recent years.[29] As a result, the movement in modern editorial practice to record manuscript punctuation faithfully—after a certain degree of normalization—is gaining more and more momentum,[30] notwithstanding some

---

[27] Papagiannis, *Tetrasticha*, vol. 1, 217.
[28] De Groote, *Christophori Mitylenaii*, XC–XCI.
[29] On this issue, see the papers in A. Giannouli and E. Schiffer, *From Manuscripts to Books: Vom Codex zur Edition: Proceedings of the International Workshop on Textual Criticism and Editorial Practice for Byzantine Texts (Vienna, 10–11 December 2009)* (Vienna 2011). For some further interesting remarks, see E. C. Bourbouhakis, *Not Composed in a Chance Manner: The Epitaphios for Manuel I Komnenos by Eustathios of Thessalonike* (Uppsala 2017), 195–209.
[30] See, for example: D. R. Reinsch, *Michaelis Pselli Chronographia*, 2 vols. (Berlin/Boston 2014), vol. 1, xxxii–xxxvi and Bourbouhakis, *Epitaphios*, 195–209.

who still oppose the practice.[31] That said, scholarly attention to punctuation has almost entirely been focused on prose texts, without any comprehensive studies of texts written in verse.[32] In the case of Vat. gr. 305, Theophylaktos Saponopoulos places a kind of (punctuation) sign at the end of almost every single verse, even when there seems to be no need. It is, therefore, clear that these marks have a visual function indicating to the reader the pauses to be taken into consideration when reading aloud.[33] This function becomes all more obvious when we compare the presentation of poetry to that of prose within Vat. gr. 305, since the latter texts do not have a sign at the end of every single line.

Although Vat. gr. 305 is not an autograph, the present edition occasionally reproduces its punctuation. A good example is verses 7–9 from the first text of the epigrammatic cycle (poems 62–66), especially when they are compared with the punctuation of previous editions (see Figure 5.1):

Vaticanus gr. 305, fol. 121ᵛ, To a Garden

New edition	Previous edition (Welz 1910)
Ὁρᾷς, θεατά, τοῦ φυτῶνος τὴν χάριν,	Ὁρᾷς θεατὰ τοῦ φυτῶνος τὴν χάριν,
πρόκυψον, ἄψαι τῶν φυτῶν, οὐδεὶς φθόνος.	πρόκυψον, ἄψαι τῶν φυτῶν· οὐδεὶς φθόνος.
ἰδοὺ κρίνον τρύγησον, ἀλλὰ σωφρόνως·	Ἰδοὺ κρίνον τρύγησον, ἀλλὰ σωφρόνως.
ἰδοὺ χλόη τρύφησον, ἀλλὰ μετρίως·	Ἰδοὺ χλόη τρύφησον, ἀλλὰ μετρίως.
ὕδωρ ἰδοὺ ῥόφησον, ἀλλ' οὐκ εἰς κόρον·	Ὕδωρ ἰδοὺ ῥόφησον, ἀλλ' οὐκ εἰς κόρον·
ὡς ἐν τύποις δὲ καὶ σεαυτόν μοι βλέπε.	ὡς ἐν τύποις δὲ καὶ σεαυτόν μοι βλέπε.
ἀνθεῖς, ἀπανθεῖς, τοῦτο δὴ καὶ τοῦ κρίνου·	Ἀνθεῖς ἀπανθεῖς, τοῦτο δὴ καὶ τοῦ κρίνου,
θάλλεις, μαραίνῃ, τοῦτο δὴ καὶ τῆς χλόης·	θάλλεις μαραίνῃ, τοῦτο δὴ καὶ τῆς χλόης,
ῥέεις, παρέρχῃ, τοῦτο καὶ τῶν ὑδάτων.	ῥέεις παρέρχῃ, τοῦτο καὶ τῶν ὑδάτων.
ἄν, ὡς ἔφην, ἄνθρωπε, τὸν κῆπον βλέπῃς,	Ἄν, ὡς ἔφην, ἄνθρωπε, τὸν κῆπον βλέπεις,
πλήσεις μέν, οἶδα, καὶ χαρᾶς τὴν καρδίαν,	πλήσεις μέν, οἶδα, καὶ χαρᾶς τὴν καρδίαν,
καὶ ψυχικὴν δὲ κερδανεῖς σωτηρίαν.	καὶ ψυχικὴν δὲ κερδανεῖς σωτηρίαν.

---

[31] B. Bydén, 'Imprimatur? Unconventional Punctuation and Diacritics in Manuscripts of Medieval Greek Philosophical Works', in: A. Bucossi and E. Kihlman (eds), *Ars Edendi Lecture Series* 2 vols. (Stockholm 2012), vol. 2, 155–72, and E. Cullhed, 'Editing Byzantine Scholarly Texts in Authorized Manuscripts', in: E. Göransson, G. Iversen, and B. Crostini (eds), *The Arts of Editing Medieval Greek and Latin: A Casebook*, Toronto 2016, 72–95; cf. also M. D. Lauxtermann, 'His, and Not His: The Poems of the Late Gregory the Monk', in: A. Pizzone (ed.), *The Author in Middle Byzantine Literature: Modes, Functions, and Identities* (Berlin/Boston 2014), 77–86, at 85, n. 22.

[32] For a significant exception, see Bernard, 'Rhythm', 25–30.

[33] In the case of the dodecasyllables, it is also a further indication that each line is free-standing in terms of rhythm and content; see also Bernard, 'Rhythm', 26–27.

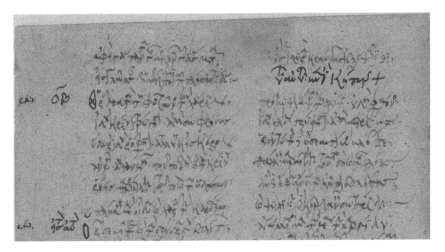

Figure 5.1 Vat. gr. 305, fol. 121ᵛ

I should note, however, that it has not always been possible to adopt the punctuation of the manuscript. For example, in v. 2 a comma has been inserted in this edition to separate the two imperative forms 'πρόκυψον' and 'ἄψαι'. Thus, I have chosen a middle path for the presentation of the punctuation, which reflects the situation in the manuscript as much as possible, but also departs from it, especially when there is a risk of causing confusion to the modern reader. As result, a comma has been added before the vocatives, although in the manuscripts a punctuation mark (either a ἄνω στιγμή or a ὑποστιγμή) can only be found after them. Likewise, parenthetical sentences are usually indicated with em dashes, while no exclamation marks are used in the Greek text. Finally, all texts are accompanied by English translations, intended to make them easily comprehensible to the modern reader.[34]

---

[34] For most texts it is the very first time that they have been translated into a modern language. There are only a few exceptions: Poem 28 has been translated in Maguire, *Image*, 20; poems 62–66 in Nilsson, 'Literary Garden', 14–29; and poems 73–74 in M. J. Kyriakis, Theodoros Prodromos and his Adversities', Δίπτυχα Ἑταιρείας Βυζαντινῶν καὶ Μεταβυζαντινῶν Μελετῶν 4 (1986/1987), 58–93. In the first two cases I have used Maguire's and Nilsson's translations (with some modifications), while in the third case my interpretation of the text is quite different from that of Kyriakis.

Greek Text and Translation

TABULA SIGLORUM ET ABBREVIATIONUM IN APPARATIBUS ADHIBITORUM

CODICES

Ac	*Athous Docheiariou 108 (s. XV)*
B	*Bodleianus Roe 18 (s. XIV)*
Ba	*Bodleianus Barocci 197 (s. XIV)*
Be	*Bern 48 B (s. XIV–XV)*
Bi	*Athous Iberon 1418 (s. XV)*
Bu	*Bucurestensis Academiei Române gr. 601 (s. XV–XVI)*
C	*Laurentianus Plut. V 10 (s. XIII)*
E	*Escorialensis Y-III-9 (s. XIV)*
Fc	*Laurentianus Conv. Soppres. 121 (s. XIV)*
Go	*Göttingen, phil. gr. 29 (s. XIII)*
H	*Heidelbergensis Palatinus gr. 43 (s. XIII)*
Ha	*Vaticanus Palatinus gr. 367 (s. XIV)*
He	*Heidelbergensis Palatinus gr. 356 (s. XIII)*
I	*Marcianus gr. Z 436 (s. XIII)*
L	*Laurentianus Acq. e Doni 341 (s. XVI)*
Lc	*Laurentianus Conv. Soppres. 48 (s. XIV)*
Lh	*Londiensis Harl. 5624 (s. XIV–XV)*
Ls	*Laurentianus San Marco 318 (s. XIV)*
M	*Marcianus gr. Z 524 (s. XIII)*
Mo	*Monacensis gr. 306 (s. XVI)*
Mt	*Metochii S. Sepulchri 797 (s. XV–XVI)*
N	*Neapolitanus II D 4 (s. XIII)*
Nd	*Neapolitanus II D 22 (s. XIV)*
Ne	*Neapolitanus III A 6 (s. XIV)*
O	*Vaticanus Ottobonianus gr. 324 (s. XV)*
P	*Parisinus gr. 2831 (s. XIII)*
Pa	*Parisinus gr. 3058 (s. XVI)*
Pc	*Parisinus gr. 1277 (s. XIII)*
Pf	*Parisinus gr. 3019 (s. XV)*
Pi	*Parisinus gr. 997 (s. XIII)*

Py   Parisinus gr. 554 (s. XV)
Pz   Parisinus gr. 1630 (s. XIV)
R   Parisinus gr. 854 (s. XIII)
Re   Vaticanus Reg. gr. Pii II 54 (s. XIV)
Ro   Roveretinus 28 (s. XIII–XIV)
V   Vaticanus gr. 305 (s. XIII)
Vb   Vaticanus Urbinatus gr. 134 (s. XV)
Vc   Vaticanus Chisianus gr. R.IV.11 (s. XIII)
Vg   Vaticanus gr. 1702 (s. XIII)
Vi   Vindobonensis Phil. gr. 149 (s. XIV)
Vo   Vossianus Gr. Q. 42 (s. XV)
Vr   Vaticanus Gr. 207 (s. XIII)
Vz   Vindobonensis Hist. gr. 106 (s. XIV)
W   Vaticanus Gr. 306 (s. XIII–XIV)
X   Vaticanus Gr. 307 (s. XIII)
Y   Sofiensis Centri 'Ivan Dujčev' Gr. 12 (s. XV)
Z   Vindobonensis suppl. gr. 125 (s. XIII)

EDITORES

Ar.	Arsenios	Bo.	Boissonade
Dü.	Dübner	Fe.	Festa
Ge.	Gesner	Gu.	Guntius
Ky.	Kyrillos	La.	Lambros
Merc.	Mercati	Mi.	Migne
Mil.	Miller	Mo.	Morellus (1611)
Mor.	Morellus (1614)	Pa.	Papadimitriou
Pi.	Piccolos	Sa.	Sajdak
Th.	La Porte du Theil	We.	Welz

CETERA

<>	addenda
add.	addidit, addiderunt
app. cr.	apparatus criticus
cf.	confer
corr.	correxit/correxerunt

i.e.	id est
in marg.	in margine
om.	omisit/omiserunt
text.	textus
tit.	titulus
vers.	Versus

1 (H 120)
Προσφωνητήριοι εἰς τὸν μέγαν ἀπόστολον Παῦλον

Παῦλον ἀειδώμεσθα Θεοῦ στόμα αἰὲν ἐόντος,
ἐκλογίης σκεῦος, κήρυκα παγκόσμιον.
χαῖρ' ἐμὸν ἦτορ, Παῦλε, καὶ εἰς θρασὺ τοῦτο μυθεῦμαι
φίλτρῳ ὑπ' ἀμβροσίῳ θυμὸν ἁλισκόμενος.
5 χαῖρ' ὀπαδῶν Χριστοῖο μέγα κλέος· ὃς ῥα Θεοῖο
βαστάσας οὔνομ' ἐθνῶν ἄντα καὶ ἡγεμόνων,
ὃς πρὸ μὲν ἂρ κυκέεσκες ὑπέρθυμα πίστιν ἀγαυὸν
γράμμαθ' ὑπὸ σκιερῷ ἥμενος ἀφραδέως,
αὐτὰρ ἔπειτ' ἀνέπαυσας ἑοῖς ἀτρύτοις καμάτοισιν,
10 οὓς ἐφ' ὑγρῆς κρατερῶς καὶ στερεῆς ἀνέτλης·
πτηνέ τε πεζέ τε χαλκομελής, ἀκάματος, ἀτειρής,
ὃς χθόνα πᾶσαν ἔβης καὶ φρίκα ποντογόνον
ἠέλιον κατ' ἄνακτα κυκλῶν τετρακίονα κόσμον,
πουλυπαθές, πολύτλα, ναυαγέ, μαστιγία.
15 νῦν πολιῆς Ῥώμης, νῦν Ταρσίδος ἔκγονε γαίης,
ἠματίην κακίην ἐξαγοραζόμενος,
πάντα πρόπασιν ἐών, ὄφρα πάντας κάρτα σαώσῃς,
δεινὲ μυθησέμεναι στάθμη ἐπιστολάων,
ῥητήρ τε πρηκτήρ τε παναίολος οἷος ἀπ' ἄλλων.
20 Παῦλε, φίλη κεφαλή, οἶδα θρασυστομέων,
ἀλλά με ὀξὺς ἔσωθι βιάσκεται ἰὸς ἐρώτων·
μνώεο Θευδώρου λάτριδος εὐσεβέος,
ἡνίκα θεσπεσίῳ προπροήμενος ἀμφὶ θοώκῳ
ἀνδρομέου βιότου μέτρα δικασπολέεις.

V P | Gu. Mi.

---

1 Θεοῦ...ἐόντος] Hom., Il. 1, 290; Od. 1, 263 **2** ἐκλογίης σκεῦος] Act. 9, 15 **6** Act. 15, 2
7 πίστιν ἀγαυὸν] cf. Hom., Il. 17, 557 **10** cf. Apoll. Rhod., Arg. 4, 1359–1360 **13** Ἥέλιον κατ' ἄνακτα] cf. Prodr., Carm.hist. 56b, 14; τετρακίονα κόσμον] cf. Orph. Hymni 39
16 Eph. 5, 16 **17** I Cor. 9, 22 **19** ῥητήρ τε πρηκτήρ] cf. e.g. Hom., Il. 9, 443; Strab., Geograph. IX 5, 5, p. 608, 8; Plutarch., An seni respublica gerenda sit 795E, 8; Himer., Fragmenta ex incertis orationibus 1, 20–21; Phot., Biblioth. Cod. 243, 369a 39, p. 103 Henry VI

9 καμάτοις ἀτρύτοισιν P **11** χαλκειμελής V **15** πόλιος Gu. | ἔκγονα P **18** δεινὰ Gu. | στάθμῃ] χρὴ δι' Gu. **19** οἷος Gu. **20** φιλῆ Gu. **21** βιάσκετεν P | ἰὸς scripsi : ἰὸς V P Gu. | Ἀλλὰ σύ, ὦ θεός, ἐν τούτοις δὴ Παύλου ἀρωγὲ Gu. **22** Θεοδώρου Gu. | εὐσεβίας Gu. **23** τε προήμενος Gu.

Invocatory verses to Paul the great Apostle

Let me praise Paul, mouth of the eternal God,
chosen vessel, herald to all the world.
Hail my desire, Paul, and I say this with boldness,
for I have been seized in my heart by a divine charm.
5   Hail, great glory of the companions of Christ;
you glorified the name of God against pagans and rulers,
you who at first dared to perturb the good faith
because you foolishly remained in the shadow of the Law,
but then soothed it through the ceaseless toils
10 that you stoutly endured by sea and land.
On wing and foot and limbs of bronze, untiring, unyielding,
you passed through every land and sea-born terror,
encircling the four pillars of the world like the Sun god,
suffering much, enduring much, shipwrecked, scourged.
15 At one moment you are the son of Rome, at another the child of Tarsus,
redeeming daily wickedness,
being all things to all men, so that you might truly save all;
forceful in speech through the measure of your letters,
a speaker of words and doer of deeds shining more than all others.
20 Beloved Paul, I know that I speak with bold words,
but the sharp dart of desire overpowers me inside.
Remember Theodoros, your devout servant,
when, sitting before all others upon your divine throne,
you judge the measures of human life.

2
Ὅμοιοι εἰς τὸν Θεολόγον Γρηγόριον

Θευλογίης μέγα κάρτος ἀείσομαι, ἁγνὸν ἰρῆα
Γρηγόριον, Ῥώμης ποιμένα κουροτέρης,
ῥητροσύνης κῦδος ἠδὲ πυρὸς μένος ἀττικοῖο,
πνείοντα κρατερῆς εὖχος ἐπογραφίης
5 παντοδαπῆς σοφίης ἐπ' ἀπείρονα κύκλα κιόντα,
τῆς νέον ἡμετέρης καὶ ποτὲ ἡμετέρης.
παρθενίης μέγα χαῖρ' ἐπιήρατε νυμφίε νύμφης,
ἣ πρὸ μὲν ἐν Τριάδι καί τ' ἀΰλοισι νόοις
καὶ καθαρῇσι τρίτον ψυχαῖς ἐπιμίγνυται ἀνδρῶν,
10 σόν δε γέγηθε πλέον ἀμφιέπουσα λέχος.
χριστιανῶν λάχεος χαῖρε πρόμε, πίστιος ἕρμα,
ὑψηχὲς Τριάδος Στέντορ ὑπερμενέος,
πῆμ' ὀλοὸν μανίης ἀδινάων αἱρεσιάων,
πῆμα Σαβελλιάο, πῆμα Μακεδονίου,
15 πῆμα τμηξιθέου ὀλοόφρονος ἀνδρὸς Ἀρείου·
ὃς θεότητα τάμε, σοῖς δ' ἀπέτμαγε λόγοις.
χαῖρε λόγων μελέδημα, λαλοῦν ἀφίδρυμα σοφίης,
ζωὸν ἄγαλμ' ἐπέων καί τε λογογραφίης,
σκιρτητά, πενθῆτορ, ἀπάντεσι παντὸς ἀνάσσων,
20 Τριάδα μὲν πνείων, Τριάδα δ' ἐκλαλέων,
Τριάδι δὲ ζώων, Τριάδος δ' ὑπὲρ ἦτορ ὀλέσκων,
ἧς σὺ μὲν ἀμφὶ πόλῳ ἄρτι πάρεδρος ἔης,
ἡμῖν δ', ὥς τε μέλισσα, καλὸν μέλι κάλλιπες ὧδε,
σούς τε λόγους ἑτέρους καὶ τὸ «ἔμελλεν ἄρα».

V Py | Gu. Mi. Sa.

1-2 cf. Prodr., Tetrast.Greg.Naz.14b, 4   2 Ῥώμης...κουροτέρης] cf. Prodr., Carm.hist. 8, 2
3 Greg.Naz., Or. 43, 23, 15, p. 174; Anthol. Gr. 8 91, 4   3-4 cf. Prodr., Tetrast.Greg.Naz.
2a, 1 et 8b, 1   8-11 Greg.Naz., Carm. II.1, 34 [515] 8-10   10 cf. Anthol. Gr. 5 272,
4   11 Greg.Naz., Carm. II.2, 1 [1460] 115-117   13 ἀδινάων αἱρεσιάων] cf. Prodr., Tetrast.
Basil. 1b, 1   19 ἀπάντεσι...ἀνάσσων] cf. e.g. Hom., Il. 12, 242; Od. 9, 552; Eud., Homeroc. 1,
1198   24 ἔμελλεν ἄρα] Greg.Naz., Or. 43, 1, 1, p. 116

tit.: ἕτεροι εἰς τὸν μέγαν Γρηγόριον τὸν Θεολόγον ἡρωελεγεῖοι Py   1 θεολογίης Py (θευλογίης
corr. Sa.) | ἱρῆα] ἱερῆα Py   3 ῥηθροσύνης Gu. | κῦδος Gu. | ἠδὲ] ἠΰ Py Gu.   6 ἡμετέρης²] ὑμετέρης
Mi.   7 ἐπιήρανε Mi.   8 νόοις Gu.   9 ἐπὶ μίγνυται Gu.   12 ὑψηλὲ Py | ὑπηρμένος Mi.
13 ἀδεινάων Gu.   14 Σαβελλείας Py (Σαβελλιάο corr. Sa.) | Μακηδονίου Py   16 ἀπέτεμνε Gu.
20 Τριάδα²] Τριάδι Py (Τριάδα corr. Sa.)   21 Τριάδι] Τριάδα Gu.   22 ἧς] ἦ Py | ἀμφιπόλῳ Mi.

Similar verses to Gregory the Theologian

I will praise the great force of theology, the pure priest,
Gregory, shepherd of the younger Rome,
glory of eloquence and force of Attic fire,
breathing out the pride of vigorous epic poetry,
5 moving through infinite circles of every kind of wisdom,
ours newly, and ours forever.
Hail, most beloved groom of the bride Chastity;
she who before had lain with the Trinity and the incorporeal angels
and, thirdly, with the pure souls of men,
10 but who took even greater pleasure in honouring your bed.
Hail, leading warrior of the Christians' lot, bulwark of the faith,
resounding Stentor of the almighty Trinity,
deadly scourge of the frenzy of clamorous heresies,
bane of Sabellios, blight to Makedonios,
15 ruin of baleful Arius who separated God from God.
He who divided the divine nature, he was cut off through your orations.
Hail, pride and joy of Eloquence, speaking image of Wisdom,
living statue of Epic and Prose,
a writer both exuberant and mournful, surpassing all in all respects,
20 breathing the Trinity, disclosing the Trinity to us,
living for the Trinity, surrendering life itself for the Trinity,
whose companion you now are in the vault of heaven,
while, like a bee, you left for us here such fine honey,
the '$\xi\mu\epsilon\lambda\lambda\epsilon\nu\ \mathring{a}\rho a$' and your other orations.

3
Ὅμοιοι εἰς τὸν Μέγαν Βασίλειον

Καππαδοκῶν Βασίλειον ἀείσομαι ἀρχιερῆα,
ἤθεσιν εὐπαγέα καὶ σταθερὸν ξυνέσει,
εἴδεϊ καὶ βιότητι διδάσκαλον ἀγνοσυνάων
καὶ σιγόωντα μέγαν κήρυκα σωφροσύνης·
5 βένθος ἅπαν λογικοῖο δαήμενον ὠκεανοῖο
νηῒ ὑπ' εὐσκάρθμῳ ὀξυπόροιο νόου.
χαῖρε μάκαρ Βασίλειε, βίου μερόπων παιδευτά,
ἁρμονίη κόσμου νῦν πλέον ἐκμελέος,
θειογόνου σοφίης μέγ' ἀμύμονος ἐσθλὲ σαφητά,
10 τῆς θ' ἅμα ὀψιτέρης καί τε παλαιοτέρης,
Εὐνομίου μέγα πῆμα κακοφρονέοντ' ἐνὶ θυμῷ,
πνεύματι παγκρατέι λύσσαν ἐγειραμένου·
τοῦ ῥὰ σαθρᾶς σοφίης κενοκόμπου τὰς λαβυρίνθους
δείξας ἑοῖο λόγου ἀρραγέεσσι λίνοις.
15 κτίσιος ὃς δεδάηκας ἀφ' ὑψόθεν αἴτια πάσης,
οὐδὲ δαεὶς φθόνεσας ἐκ μερόπεσσι φάναι.
γαίην δ' εὐρυτάτην καὶ αἰθέρος ἄτρυτον οἶμον,
πνοιοδότην τ' ἀέρα καὶ σέλας αἰθόμενον
καὶ ζώων τὰ γένεθλα βροτοῖς κατὰ μοῖραν ἔειπες,
20 χθὼν ὅσα καὶ ὅσ' ἀὴρ καί τε θάλασσα φέρει,
καὶ χλοερῆς βοτάνης ἰδιώματα πάντα μυθήσω.
χαῖρε μονοτροπίης στάθμιον ἀζυγέος·
χαῖρε βροτῶν βιότητος ἐπ' εὔπορον οἶμον ἰθύντορ,
γήραος εὐκοσμίη, χαλινὲ κουροσύνης.

V Y Bi | Gu. Mi. Eu.

1 cf. Anthol. Gr. 8 6, 1   **4** Anthol. Gr. 8 4, 3   **5** Anthol. Gr. 8 10, 1–2   **18** σέλας αἰθόμενον] cf. e.g. Hom., Il. 8, 563; Hes., Theog. 867; Scutum 59; Pind., Fragm. 52f, 97; Prodr., Carm.hist. 38, 3   **19** κατὰ…ἔειπες] cf. e.g. Hom., Il. 1, 286; Od. 2, 251; Eud., Homeroc. 1, 895; Prodr., Carm.hist. 8, 6

tit. στίχοι ἡρωελέγειοι εἰς τὸν Μέγαν Βασίλειον Υ   **2** vers. om. Eu.   **3** εἴδει Υ   **4** σιγέοντα Υ   **5** λογικοῖς Mi. | δαήμερον Bi   **8** ἐκ μελέος Bi Mi.   **10** θ'] δ' Gu. Bi   **12** ἀειράμενον Gu.   **13** τὰς] τοὺς Mi.   **14** ἀρραγέεσσι Eu.   **16** ἐν Bi Mi. | φαεῖναι Υ   **20** φέρει] φύει Eu   **23** εὔπορων Gu. | ἰθύντος Gu.

Similar verses to Basil the Great

I will praise Basil, the archbishop of Cappadocia,
firm in character and steadfast in sagacity,
teacher of chastity in both appearance and habit,
and great herald of temperance even when silent;
5   you understood every depth in the ocean of intellect
through the nimble vessel of your keen mind.
Hail, blessed Basil, instructor for the life of mortals,
harmony in a world now more dissonant than ever,
great interpreter of the perfectly immaculate wisdom born of God,
10 both the recent and the older one,
great bane to the soul of the malignant Eunomius,
who incited raging madness against the almighty Spirit;
the mazes of that vainglorious boaster's flawed wisdom
you exposed with the unbroken threads of your learning.
15 You learned from on high the cause of all Creation,
and you did not refuse to disclose it to mortals.
You rightly spoke to mortals of the wide earth and the unending path of
    the ether,
the breath-giving air and the burning light,
and of the origin of the animals
20 all those borne upon land, air and sea,
and you spoke of all that pertains to the green pasture.
Hail, measure of the unwedded solitude;
hail, guide of human life towards an easy path,
adornment of age, bridle of youth.

4
Ὅμοιοι εἰς τὸν ἅγιον Ἰωάννην τὸν Χρυσόστομον

Χρυσολόγον μετὰ τοῖσι λιγαίνομαι Ἰωάννην,
Ῥώμης ὀψιτέρης ἀρχιερῆα μέγαν,
εὐκέλαδον μεγάλοιο χελιδόνα πνεύματος ἁγνοῦ,
δόγματος εὐαγόρου κίθαριν ἐμμελέα.
5 χαῖρ' ἀγαθὴ κραδίη, χρυσοῦν στόμα, γλῶσσα λιγεῖα,
σειρὴν ἡμετέρη σύν τε δέουσ' ἀνέρας
καί τε φίλης βιότητος ὀπαζομένη μακρὰ κύκλα,
ἄγγελε οἰκτοσύνης, ἐλπὶς ἀλιτροβίων,
ἦτορ ἐὸν μερόπων ὑπὲρ ἐκπνείων ταλαεργῶν,
10 θειοφραδὲς μεγάλης μύστα θεηγορίης,
σὰρξ ἀποχῆς ὁσίη καὶ ἀϋλίη ἔνδοθεν ὕλης,
πτηνὲ νόον, γενέτωρ βίβλου ἀπειρεσίης,
Ἀντιοχεῦ γενέθλην, κόσμου δέ τε παντὸς ὄνειαρ,
ἐσθλῆς δικοσύνης κλισμὸν ἐὸν προνέμων,
15 οὕνεκα γὰρ χήρης πολυπήμονος ἀμπελεῶνος
ἔκ τε θοώκου ἔβης ἐξορίην τ' ἀνέτλης.
ἐν Κομάνοις δέ σ' ἔδω Βυζαντιάς, οὐ κατὰ κόσμον,
ἐσθλὸν ἐὸν θεμένη ἀρχοῦ ἀτασθαλίῃ
ἀλλοτρίῃ ἐνὶ χώρῃ· ἀτὰρ σύ γ' οὐ λίπες ἔμπης
20 ὃν θρόνον, ἥν τε πόλιν βασιλίδα πτολίων,
ἀλλὰ μετὰ τριάκοντα λυκαβάντων ὅλα κύκλα
ἐς πυμάτην Ῥώμην ἀνακομιζόμενος.
νεκρὸς ἐὼν περ ἔειπες «ἅπάντεσσιν ἀμφ' εἰρήνην»·
τοῖα κε φιλαρέτων ἔστ' ἀέθλια βίου.

V | Gu. Mi.

---

3 cf. Ioh. Geom., Carm. hex. et el. 300, 57   4 κίθαριν ἐμμελέα] cf. e.g. Ioh. Chrys., Expos. in Ps., PG 55, 497; Mich. Italic., Or. 41 236, 6; Eust.Thessal., Sermones 2, p. 38, 13–14   5 ἀγαθὴ κραδίη] cf. e.g. Orph., Lithica 5; Theoph. Ochr., Carm. 14, 70 χρυσοῦν στόμα] cf. Prodr., Tetrast.Chrysost. κ7r, 1a, 4; λv, 12a, 1   12 πτηνὲ νόον] cf. Anthol. Gr. 8 91, 4; Georg. Pisid., De vita humana 50   17 οὐ κατὰ κόσμον] cf. e.g. Hom., Il. 2, 214; Od. 3, 138; Theocr., Id. 15, 41; Apollon. Rhod., Arg. 4, 360; Opp., Hal. 2, 282

---

1 λιγαίνομεν Gu.   3 ἐγκέλαδον Mi.   4 εὐμελέα Gu.   6 σειρὰ δὲ θ' ἡμετέρη συντεδέους ἀνέρας Gu.   7 καί τε] καί σὺ Gu. | ὀπαζόμενος Gu.   8 ἄγγελος Gu.   10 θεηγορίας Gu.   14 ἐσθλὰ δικαιοσύνης Gu.   15 χήρους Gu. : κλήρους Mi.   16 τ' om. Mi.   7 Κομάνοις] καμάτοις Mi.   18 ἀρχὸν Gu.   20 πολίων Gu. | πτολήων cum ι supra η V   22 ἐς] εὖ Gu.   24 κε] καὶ Gu. | ἐστὶν ἄεθλα Gu.

Similar verses to Saint John Chrysostom

    Among them I will sing in praise of Ioannes of the golden words,
    great archbishop of the later Rome,
    sweet-singing swallow of great and pure spirit,
    harmonious lyre of praiseworthy doctrine.
5   Hail, noble heart, golden mouth, clarion tongue,
    our siren binding men together
    and granting them long years of pleasant life,
    angel of compassion, hope of those who live in wickedness,
    breathing your last for the sake of humans burdened by toil,
10 divine initiate in great theology,
    flesh of abstention, holy and incorporeal within a material world,
    winged mind, author of books without number,
    offspring of Antioch, yet profit to the entire world,
    giving up your seat of divine justice:
15 for it was because of the vineyard of the much-suffering widow
    that you left your see and endured exile,
    and Byzantium shamefully gave you to Komana,
    banishing her brave patriarch because of her ruler's wickedness
    to a foreign land; but you did not leave for always
20 your see and your city, the queen of cities,
    for after the passing of thirty years
    you were finally brought back to Rome.
    Though dead, you said 'peace be to you all';
    such are the rewards for lovers of virtue.

5
Ὅμοιοι εἰς τὸν Νυσσαέα Γρηγόριον

Γρηγόριον μετέπειτα κασίγνητον Βασιλείῳ,
   ποιμένι Καισαρέων, ποιμένα Νυσσαέων
μέλψομαι οὐχ᾽ ὑπὲρ αἶσαν ἀγάφρονα ἄνδρα καὶ ἐσθλόν,
   δεύτερον Εὐνομίου πῆμα θεοπτολέμου,
5 δεύτερον ἀρχεγόνοιο σαφήτορα κοσμογενείης,
   πλάσιος ἀνδρομέης ἵστορ᾽ ἐριφραδέα.
χαῖρε φύσις πτερόεσσα, ταχὺς νόος, ἡδὺ μύθημα,
   ἡδυμελὴς χαρίτων κῆπος ἐριπλοκάμων,
γλῶσσα μέλι σταλάουσα Ὑμηττίου ἥδιον οἷον,
10   φρὴν σταθερή, καθαρῆς ἄνθεμα σωφροσύνης,
δυσσεβέοντος ὄλεθρε, θεμείλιον εὐσεβεόντων,
   ὀρθοτόμε Τριάδος λάτρι μεγασθενέος,
ἀτραπὸν ὃς σκιόεσσαν ἀείσματος ὑψηλοῖο,
   κρυψινόου μεγάλου, τοῦ Σαλομὼν γενέτης,
15 εὔπορον ἄμμιν ἔφηνας ἑῆς φαέεσσι σοφίης
   σκῶλον ἅπαν βαλέων οἴμου ἀπ᾽ ἐκ μεσάτης·
ὃς μὲν Νυσσαέεσσιν ἐπίσκοπος οἷον ἐτύχθης,
   οὐδ᾽ ἄρα Νυσσαέας οἷον ἐπεσκόπεες,
πάντα βροτῶν δὲ γένεθλα τὸ σὸν πέλεν, ἠδ᾽ ἔτι καὶ νῦν
20   πάντα τεοῖσι λόγοις κόσμον ἐπισκοπέεις.
ὑμνητὰ μακάρων, περιώσιον εὖχος ἰρήων,
   ὃς λόγον ἀμφὶ βίῳ καὶ βίον ἀμφὶ λόγῳ
ἤρμοσας ἐμμελέως· ἐρατόν δ᾽ ὑπὸ λίνον ἀείσας
   οὔασιν ὃς κραδίης χάρμα μέγα σταλάει.

V | Gu. Mi.

3 οὐχ᾽ ὑπὲρ αἶσαν] cf. e.g. Hom., Il. 3, 59; Prodr., Carm.hist. 8, 213   **6** πλάσιος ἀνδρομέης] cf. Prodr., R&D 1, 67   **12** cf. Prodr., Tetrast.Greg.Naz. 11b, 1   **13–16** cf. Mich. Psell., Theol. I 7, p. 28, 15–18   **19** πάντα…γένεθλα] cf. Sophoc., OT 1424–1425   **23** ἐρατόν…ἀείσας] Hom., Il. 18, 570

2 ποιμένι] ποιμένα Gu. | Νυσσεέων Gu.   **5** κοσμογονείης Gu.   **14** γενέτην Gu.   **18** ἐπισκοπέεις Mi.   **24** σταλάεις Gu.

Similar verses to Gregory of Nyssa

And then of Gregory, the brother of Basil,
shepherd of Caesarea, shepherd of the people of Nyssa,
a right-minded and dauntless man, I will duly sing,
second bane of Eunomius, the enemy of God,
5 second interpreter of the primordial origin of the world,
eloquent narrator of human creation.
Hail, winged nature, swift mind, sweet expression,
mellifluous garden of the fair Graces,
whose tongue drips with honey sweeter than that of Mount Hymettus,
10 steadfast in mind, offering of spotless temperance,
destroyer of the impious, foundation of the pious,
undeviating servant of the omnipotent Trinity.
You made accessible to us the shadowy path of the lofty Song,
the highly enigmatic one, of which Solomon is the author,
15 through the rays of your wisdom
by casting aside every obstacle from the midst of the path;
you were an excellent bishop for the people of Nyssa,
for you tended not only to them,
but all the offspring of mankind became yours, and even now
20 you watch over the entire world through your writings.
Encomiast of blessed men, unsurpassed pride of priests,
you suitably matched your word to your life
and your life to your word. Singing the lovely song of Linos,
you drip immense joy into the ears of the heart.

6
Ὅμοιοι εἰς τὸν ἅγιον Νικόλαον

Οἶκτον ἀτὰρ μετέπειτα λιγαίνομαι, οἶκτον ἀείδω,
οἶκτον ἐπικροτέω, οἶκτος ἐμῇ κιθάρῃ
μέλπεται—ἢ μερόπεσσι τί λώϊον οἰκτοσυνάων;—,
Νικόλεων Λυκίης ἀρχιθόωκον ἁγνόν.
5 χαῖρ' ἐλέοιο θάλασσα, γλυκύρροε, σωσιάνειρα,
οὔατα καὶ κραδίῃ γοργὰ λιταζομένοις·
ὃς πολιὸν πενίης βαρυνούσου λύσαο ἄνδρα,
τρισσῶν θηλυτέρων δυστυχέων γενέτην
νύκτα δι' ὀρφναίην χρυσοῦ βαλέων ἀποδέσμους
10 τρισσοὺς λαθριδίῃ, κἄμπαλιν ἴχνι' ἄγων·
ὃς προτόνους τέμνοντα καὶ ἱστία πάντα Βελίαν
νηὸς ὑγροσκελέος, νηὸς ἀελλομάχου
πόντισας ἔς τε βέρεθρα καὶ ἠερόεντ' ἐς Ἀΐδην·
ὅς τ' ἐν ὕπνοις μολέων κοίρανον ἀμφὶ μέγαν
15 χρυσολάτρην τ' ἐφ' ὕπαρχον ἐλύσαο ἀνέρας οἴτου
δεινὸν ὁμοκλήσας καὶ δέος ἀμφιχέας·
ὅς τ' ἀπ' ἄκρης ποτὶ ναῦν ναύτην πεσέοντα κεραίης
καὶ λυγρῇσι κόρης ἀμφιδέοντα μόρον
ζωὸν ἑοῖς ἑτάροισι θαλασσοπόνοισιν ὄπασσας,
20 χεῖρά τε καί τε νόον εἰς πόλον ἀμπετάσας.
χαῖρε Θεοῦ κραδίη, χαῖρ' οἰκτοσύνης πάτερ ἐσθλῆς,
σπλάγχνα Θεοῦ μερόπων οὕνεκα πιμπράμενα.
χαῖρε, καὶ ὑμνητῆρι τεῷ χάριν ἀμφὶς ὀπάζων
ἔς τε ῥέοντα κάτω καί τε μένοντα βίον.

V | Gu. Mi.

---

5 Andron. Duc. Sgouros., Carm. 9 (p. 94): [...] θάλασσα γλυκόρροε σωσιάνειρα **9–10** cf. Vitae et Miracula Nicolai Myrensis, Vita compilata. I 222, 21–27 **9** νύκτα δι' ὀρφναίην] cf. e.g. Hom., Il. 10, 83; Od. 9, 143; Apoll., Metaphrasis psalmorum 2, 118, 101; Eud., Homeroc. 1, 1638; Anthol. Gr. 9 361, 3; Prodr., Tetrast. 113b, 2 et 219b, 3 **11** cf. Nic.Basilac., Progymn. 26, 123 **12** cf. Prodr., Carm.misc. 69, 6 **13** ἠερόεντ' ἐς Ἀΐδην] cf. e.g. Hom., Il. 8, 13; Eud., Homeroc. 3, 55 **16** δεινὸν ὁμοκλήσας] cf. e.g. Hom., Il. 5, 439; Eud., Homeroc. 1, 1791; Orph., Argon. 819 **17** ποτὶ ναῦν] cf. e.g. Hom., Il. 12, 273; Od. 3, 298; Quint. Smyrn., Posthom. 1, 824 **20** cf. Anthol. Gr. App. 6 268, 2; cf. etiam Marinus, Vita Procli 697; Prodr., Tetrast.Greg.Naz. 10b, 1–2 **22** σπλάγχνα/πιμπράμενα] cf. Prodr., R&D 2, 300 **23–24** cf. Anthol. Gr. 1 26, 2

---

2 οἶκτος] οἶκτον Gu. **3** ἢ Gu. **4** Νικόλαον Mi. | Λυκίης] Νικίης Mi. **7** λύσαιο Mi. **8** θυγατέρων Gu. **9** βαλέων ἀποδέσμους] βασιλέων ἀπὸ δεσμοῦ Mi. **10** λατριδίῃ Mi. | ἴχνε Mi. **11** τέμνων τε Gu. | Βελίου Gu. **14** ὅσ τ'] ὥς τ' Gu. **15** τ'] δ' Gu. **17** ὅσ τ'] ὥστ' Gu. | ναύτην] ταύτην Gu. **18** λυγρὸν ᾖσι Gu. | ἀμφιθέοντα Mi. **19** ὄπασσας scripsi : ὄπασας V Gu. **21** οἰκτοσύνη πάτερ ἐσθλὲ Gu. **23** τεῷ] Θεὸς Gu. | ὀπάζῃ Gu.

Similar verses to Saint Nicholas

And then I sing the praises of compassion, I celebrate compassion,
I applaud compassion, with my lyre compassion is lauded
—what is better for humans than compassion?—,
Nicholas the chaste archbishop of Lycia.
5   Hail, ocean of mercy, sweet-streaming, man-saving,
attentive ears and heart for those praying.
You freed the grizzled man from burdensome poverty,
father of three unfortunate maidens,
covertly placing three sacks of gold
10 during the dark of night and then retracing your steps again.
The Devil, who cut off the forestays and all the sails
of the ship drenched and fighting the storm,
you plunged into the pits of hell and murky Hades.
By appearing in the dreams of the great lord
15 and gold-worshipping governor, you freed the men from their horrible fate,
threatening a terrible thing and spreading fear around.
The sailor who fell from the yard arm to the ship's deck
and gazed upon imminent death with mournful eyes
you returned alive to his sea-tossed comrades
20 by stretching out your hand and mind to the sky.
Hail, heart of God; hail, father of noble compassion,
God's innermost burning affection for mankind.
Hail, and grant twofold grace to the one who sings your praise,
in both the fleeting life below and the life that endures.

7 (H 121)
Εἰς τὸν Ἀβραὰμ ξενίζοντα τὴν ἁγίαν Τριάδα

«Τί ταῦτα ποιεῖς; βουθυτεῖς, Ἄβραμ γέρον;»
«οὔκ, ἀλλὰ δεῖπνον καὶ τράπεζαν ἀρτύω.»
«ὁ δαιτυμὼν τίς, ᾧ τὸ δεῖπνον ἀρτύεις;»
«ἡ Τριὰς αὐτή.» «καὶ Θεὸς βοῦν ἐσθίει;»
5 «οὐ γὰρ ἐρευνῶ τοὺς ἀπορρήτους λόγους.»
«ὡς ὑπέρευγε πίστεως τῆς σῆς, γέρον·
ὡς ὑπέρευγε τοῦ φιλοξένου βίου·
καρπὸν γὰρ ἀμφοῖν, καρπὸν ὀσφύος φέρει.»

B V E Ha He N R Vi W | Mo. Mi. Mil.

Carm. Gen. 18, 1–16
1 cf. Prodr., Carm.hist. 74, 80   **8** καρπὸν ὀσφύος] cf. Prodr., Carm.hist. 63, 15; R&D 6, 370

tit.: om. E : στίχοι τοῦ Προδρόμου κύρου Θεοδώρου εἰς τὸν πατριάρχην Ἀβραὰμ ξενίζοντα τὴν ἁγίαν Τριάδα He : εἰς τὸν Ἀβραὰμ καὶ τὴν ἁγίαν τριάδα, κατ' ἐρώτησιν καὶ ἀπόκρισιν Mo.
1 Ἀβραὰμ E R   **4** καὶ] ὁ E | ἐρῶ supra καὶ add. R   **5** ἀπορρήτους] θεοπνεύστους R : θεοπλάστους Mo.   **6** om. Mi. Mil.   **7** ab ὡς ὑπέρευγε text. om. R   **8** φέρει] φύεις E Ha He N Vi W : θύεις B

8 (H 122)
εἰς τὸ αὐτὸ

Ἀβραάμ, Σάρρα, μόσχος, Ἰσμαήλ, Ἄγαρ,
ἄρτοι, τράπεζα, δρῦς, τὸ δῶμα, καὶ τέλος
Τριὰς Κύριος—τὸ ξένον!—ξενίζεται.

He N Vi W

Gen. 18, 1–16

tit. om. He

On Abraham entertaining the Holy Trinity

'What are you doing here? Are you sacrificing an ox, aged Abraham?'
'No, but I am preparing dinner and a table'
'Who is the guest for whom you prepare dinner?'
'The Holy Trinity itself!' 'And does God eat beef?'
5   'I do not enquire into secret doctrines.'
'Hurrah, for your faith, old man!
Hurrah, for your hospitality,
for it brings a fruit to you both—a fruit from your loins.'

On the same

Abraham, Sarah, calf, Ishmael, Hagar,
loaves, table, oak, house, and finally
the Triune Lord—oh wonder—is the guest.

9 (H 123)
Ἐπὶ ἀναγνώσει

Ὁ παμβασιλεὺς ἐξανέστη τοῦ τάφου·
ἡ συναγωγὴ τῶν Ἰουδαίων, μάθε
πῶς ἐξανέστη τοῦ τάφου κεκλεισμένου
καὶ κειμένου δ' ἄνωθεν αὐτοῦ τοῦ λίθου,
5 καθὼς προῆλθεν ἐκ πύλης κεκλεισμένης,
τῆς παρθενικῆς ἐσφραγισμένης πάλιν.
«ψευδὲς τὸ ῥητόν· τίς γὰρ ἂν πίστιν λάβῃ;
τὸ γὰρ ἀληθὲς τοῖς μαθηταῖς ἐκλάπη.»
ποῖ δ' οἱ φύλακες ἦσαν; οὐκ ἐν τῷ τάφῳ
10 ἐπαγρυπνοῦντες παρ' ὅλην γε τὴν νύκτα;
«ὀλίγον ἀφύπνωσαν ἐκ ῥᾳθυμίας,
εὐθύς δ' ὁ νεκρὸς τοῖς μαθηταῖς ἐκλάπη.»
ἀσυλλόγιστον εἶπας· αἱ γὰρ σφραγίδες
σῶαι μένουσιν, ὡς λέγεις, ἐν τῷ τάφῳ·
15 εἰ γὰρ ὁ Χριστὸς τοῖς μαθηταῖς ἐκλάπη,
οὐκ ἦν ὁ τάφος ἐσφραγισμένος πάλιν.
πίστευε λοιπόν, τὴν ἀνάστασιν λέγε·
τοῖς στρατιώταις μηδαμῶς χρυσοῦν δίδου
Χριστὸν κλαπέντα μαρτυρεῖν πανταχόσε,
20 ἐπείπερ οὐ δόξουσιν ἀληθῶς λέγειν.
ὁ γὰρ ἀληθὴς ἀμετάβλητος Λόγος
ἀρκεῖ τοσαῦτα τοῖς Ἰουδαίοις λέγειν·
τυφλοὶ γὰρ ὄντες, οὐ δύνανταί τι βλέπειν,
ἀλλ' οὐδὲ κωφεύοντες ἀκούειν ὅλως.
25 σὺ δ' ἐξαναστάς, ὦ Θεοῦ θυηπόλε,
τὸν εὐλογητὸν τοῖς προκειμένοις δίδου.

R | Mil.

Carm. Matth. 28, 11–15
3–6 cf. Procl., Hom. Thom. 33 VII, 20; Christus Patiens 2500–2503; Prodr., Tetrast. 263a, 1–4
9–10 cf. Rom.Melod., Cant. 42, 16, 5, IV p. 474

7 λάβοι in app. cr. Mil.   **15** ἐκλάπῃ in app. cr. Mil. : ἐκλάμπῃ R

For a Reading

The King of all has risen from the tomb.
Hear, O gathering of the Jews,
how he arose from the sealed tomb,
even though a stone lay upon it,
5 just as he came forth from the closed gate,
the virginal gate, which was sealed again.
'This is a lie. Who would believe such a thing?
The truth is that he was stolen by his disciples.'
But where were the guards? Were they not at the tomb
10 keeping watch all night long?
'When they fell asleep for a while due to fatigue,
the corpse was immediately stolen by the disciples.'
You talk nonsense, for the seals
remained unbroken, as you said, upon the tomb.
15 For if Christ were stolen by the disciples,
the tomb would not have been sealed up again.
So have faith, proclaim the resurrection;
do not give the soldiers gold
to bear witness everywhere that Christ was stolen,
20 for it will become clear that they do not tell the truth.
The true immutable Word of God
suffices to say these things to the Jews,
for since they are blind, they can see nothing;
and neither do they hear, for they are completely deaf.
25 So arise, O priest of God,
give the blessing to these present words.

10 (H 133)

Ἡδὺς ποταμὸς ὁ προκείμενος λόγος·
ἡδὺς ποταμός, ἀλλὰ δύσβατος λίαν·
ῥεῖθρον γὰρ ἐκχεῖ καρδίας καθηδῦνον,
Ἀτλαντικὸν πέλαγος, Βοσπόρου πλάτος,
5   διψῶν πιεῖν δραμοῦμαι καὶ λαβεῖν κόρον·
τὸ ῥεῦμα φρικτόν, πομφόλυγες ἐκ βάθους,
φλοῖσβος πολὺς ἐκ τούτου· τοῦτό μοι φόβος.
διπλῇ μερίμνῃ τήκομαι· καὶ τί πάθω;
ἕλκει μὲν ἔνθα δίψα συντήκουσά με
10 θέλοντα πιεῖν· ἐκ δὲ θατέρου μέρους
ὁ τοῦ βυθοῦ με πάλιν ἀνθέλκει φόβος.
τί γοῦν δράσω; λαλεῖτε πρὸς τοῦ κυρίου,
ἄθροισμα σεπτὸν καὶ φίλη ξυναυλία.
οὐ πρὸς κόρον πίοιμι καὶ καθυγράνω
15 ψυχὴν ἐμὴν τακεῖσαν ἐξ ἁμαρτίας,
αὐχμῶσαν ἐν στερήσει τῶν θείων λόγων;
οὐκ ἂν θέλουσι συμμετασχεῖν πλησμίως
ἡμῖν παρέξω καὶ καθηδύνω φρένας;
ναί, σαῖς γὰρ εὐχαῖς προστιθῶ τὴν ἐλπίδα,
20 καί σοι θαρρῶν εἴσειμι τόνδε τὸν πόνον.
σύ δ' ἀλλ' ἀναστὰς εὐλόγει μοι τὸν λόγον.

W N | Pa.

---

1 cf. Man. Philes, Carm. App. 43, 1 (II p. 349)   **4** cf. Prodr., Carm. contra anum adulteram 9   **8** διπλῇ μερίμνῃ] cf. Aesch., Pers. 165; Eurip., Orest. 633   **13** φίλη ξυναυλία] cf. Niceph. Ouran. Carm. 34, p. 131   **15** cf. Canones Maii, can. 6, od. 8, trop. 5, 179–180, p. 56

1 om. N   **4** ἀτλαντικοῦ Pa.   **5** διψῶ W | δραμοῦμαι] αἱροῦμαι W   **6** πομφόλυγγες W   **7** τοῦτό μοι] τὶς ἐμοὶ N   **8** διπλῇ μερίδι N : ἐν πλημμυρίδι Pa.   **9** ἔνθεν Pa.   **12** τοῦ κυρίου] τοὺς οὐρανούς Pa.   **13** συναυλία N   **17** πλησμίαν N : πλησμίας Pa.   **18** ὑμῖν Pa. : ἡμῖν W N   **21** μου Pa.

The present sermon is a sweet river;
a sweet river, yet nigh impassable;
for it gushes forth, sweetening the heart,
an Atlantic Ocean, the breadth of the Bosporus;
5   thirsting, I will run to drink and to satisfy myself.
Its flood is fearful, bubbling from the depths,
a great roar comes from it; this causes me fear.
I waste away in double anguish; and what will happen to me?
Thirst is consuming me and drags me there
10 because I want to drink from it; but for the other part,
the fear of its depths pulls me in the opposite direction again.
What shall I do? Speak in the name of God,
O holy assembly and dear congregation.
Shall I not drink to satiety and
15 water my soul, shrivelled from sin,
parched by the lack of the divine words?
Shall I not offer it to you, who indeed desire greatly
to partake of it and gratify your hearts?
Certainly yes, for I will add hope to your prayers,
20 and having gained courage from you I will take on this task.
But you [priest], stand up and give your blessing to the sermon.

11(H 124)
Εἰς τὴν ἁγίαν Βαρβάραν

Λαμπρῶν ὁ πατὴρ ἀξιοῖ σε τῶν γάμων,
τῶν γὰρ θεϊκῶν, χριστομάρτυς Βαρβάρα,
καὶ βασιλικὴν ἐνδύει σε πορφύραν
χρωννύς σε τῶν σῶν αἱμάτων τῇ κογχύλῃ.
5 λαμπὰς δὲ γαμήλιος αὐτὸς ἐστί σοι
ὅλος κεραυνόβλητος ὀφθεὶς ὑψόθεν.

R Ba L Ne Vg | Mor. St.

1-2 Ioh. Damasc., Laud. S. Barb. 12, 23-25   3-4 cf. Ioh. Damasc., Laud. S. Barb. 16, 36; Ioh. Maurop., Canon. III, 96-102 (p. 126)   4 cf. Ioh. Damasc., Laud. S. Barb. 11, 4-5

tit. ἀνωνύμουστίχοιτρίμετροιπερὶτῆςἁγίας ΒαρβάραςMo.   1 ἀξιοῖ] σὸςMo.   2 χριστόμαρτυν L: χριστόμαρτυ Ba : χριστομάρτυ R   3 ἐνδύει σε] ἐνέδυσε L   4 χωννύς Ba : χρωννύ R | αἱμάτων] ὀμμάτων L   5 λαμπρά γε γαμίλιος αὐτὸς λαμπάς σοι Ne : Λαμπὰς δὲ γ᾽ αὐτός ἐστί σοι γαμήλιος Mor.

12

Πρηστήριοι πρὶν οὐρανόβρυτοι φλόγες
παιδοφθόρον φθείρουσι Σοδόμων πόλιν,
κεραύνιοι καὶ νῦν δὲ πυρὸς λαμπάδες
παιδοκτόνον φλέγουσιν αἰσχρὸν πατέρα.
5 ὁ γὰρ ἐφ᾽ ὕψους ἐκδικεῖ πατὴρ φθάνων
τὴν εἰς σέ, μάρτυς, πατρικὴν ἀστοργίαν.

R Ba L Ne Vg | Mor. St.

1-2 cf. Ioh.Damasc., Laud. S. Barb. 18, 20-22; Petr.Argiv., Barbar. p. 206, 384-85   1 Πρηστήριοι/φλόγες] cf. Prodr., Carm.hist. 64a, 17; 74, 29; Nic. Eugen., D&C 6, 398   3 κεραύνιοι/λαμπάδες] cf. Eurip., Suppl. 1011; Eurip., Bacch. 244 et 594

tit. εἰς τὴν αὐτὴν L   1 οὐρανόβλυτοι Ne   2 παιδοφθόρων Vg | πτόλιν L St.   3 κεραύνιος Vg   5 ὁ] σὸς L | ἀφ᾽ Ba Vg | πατὴρ φθάνων] πῦρ φθάνον Ba | γ᾽ post γὰρ add. Mor.

On St Barbara

    Your father deems you worthy of splendid marriages,
    indeed of divine ones, martyr of Christ, Barbara,
    and dresses you in imperial purple,
    colouring you with the purple dye of your blood.
5   He himself is your wedding torch,
    set all afire by lightning from on high.

    Once flashes of fire bursting out from heaven
    destroyed the child-corrupting city of Sodom,
    while now thunderstruck torches of fire
    burn the wicked child-slaying father.
5   The Father coming from on high punishes
    the paternal heartlessness towards you, martyr.

13

Ὁ τεκνοφόντης, ἴσχε μαργῶσαν χέρα,
μὴ κατενεγκὼν ἀνέλῃς τὴν παρθένον.
οὐ σὸν τὸ τέκνον οὐδὲ σῆς ἐξ ὀσφύος·
εἰ τοῦτο γὰρ ἦν, οὐκ ἀποσφάττειν ἔτλης
5 τὴν παῖδα τὴν εὔπαιδα, δύσπατερ πάτερ.
πλὴν οὐ βραδύπους ἡ Δίκη· τὸ πῦρ φθάνει.

R Ba L Ne Vg | Mor. St.

1 μαργῶσαν χέρα] cf. e.g. Eurip., Hecub. 1128; Hesych., Lexic. μ 275; Phot., Lexic. μ 109, 1; Suda μ 186, 1 6 Anthol. Gr. 8 246, 2 et 8 247, 1; cf. etiam Christ. Hagioeupl., Carm. p. 31, 24

tit. εἰς τὴν αὐτὴν L   1 ὦ τεκνοφόντης Mo. | ἔσχε L   2 ἀνέλῃς] ἀνέλεις R : ἀνεθεὶς Ba : ἀνέλε L : ἀνελεῖς Ne

14

Καλὸν κακοῦ κόρακος ὠὸν εὑρέθης
καὶ τὴν παλαιὰν ᾔσχυνας παροιμίαν·
οὐκοῦν ἐπῳάσαντος ἐν σοὶ τοῦ Λόγου,
συλλαμβάνεις μὲν πνεῦμα καθ' Ἡσαΐαν,
5 νεόττιον δὲ μαρτυρικὸν ἐξάγεις·
ἆρ' ἀετός σε, μάρτυς, οὐ κόραξ κύει.

R Ba L Ne Vg | Mor. St.

1-2 cf. Aesop., Prov. 51, 1   **3-5** cf. Is. 26, 18

tit. εἰς τὴν αὐτὴν L   5 ἐξάγῃς Ne   6 ἆρ' L

O child-murderer, restrain your raging hand,
do not strike the maiden down and slay her.
She is not your child nor of your loins;
for if this were so, you would not dare to kill
5   the finest child, most unrighteous father.
But justice is not slow-footed—the fire arrives forthwith.

You turned out to be a good egg from a bad crow,
putting the old saying to shame.
So, once the Word of God broods over you,
you conceive the Spirit according to Isaiah,
5   and you bring forth a newly-hatched martyr;
hence, martyr, an eagle sired you, not a crow.

15

Προέρχεται μὲν ἐκ καλάμης ὁ στάχυς·
πλὴν ἀλλὰ τὸν μὲν ἀποθήκη λαμβάνει,
τὴν δὲ φλέγει πῦρ· ἄρα γοῦν καὶ Βαρβάρα
καλαμίνης προῆλθε πατρὸς ὀσφύος.
5 οὐκοῦν Θεοῦ μὲν ἀποθήκη Βαρβάραν,
πῦρ δὲ φλογίζον τὴν καλάμην λαμβάνει.

R Ba L Ne Vg | Mor. St.

Carm. Ioel 3, 13; Matth. 13, 24–30; Apc. 14, 15–16
2 cf. Prodr., Carm.hist. 16, 196; 33b, 9   6 cf. Prodr., Carm.hist. 16, 102; 17, 229

tit. εἰς τὴν αὐτὴν L   1 προσέρχεται Mo.   2 τὸ μὲν R (τὸν μὲν corr. Mor. St.)   3 τηνδὲ R (τὴν δὲ corr. Mor. St.) | ἄρα Ba Mor.   4 πατὴρ Ba

16

Τὸν Θεσβίτην κτείναντα τοὺς Βάαλ θύτας
οὐράνιον πῦρ ἀναδιφρεύει φθάνον·
τὸν σὸν δέ, μάρτυς, πατέρα κτείναντά σε
ὀλέθριον πῦρ ἐκπεσὸν καταφλέγει·
5 διπλοῦν γὰρ ἴσως οὐρανὸς τὸ πῦρ βρύει,
ἓν μὲν κολάζον, ἓν δὲ πῦρ σωτηρίου.

R Ba Fc L Ne Vg | Mor. St.

1–2 III Regn. 18, 17–40

tit. εἰς τὴν αὐτὴν L   1 Θεσβύτην R (Θεσβίτην corr. St.) | Βαὰλ St.   4 ἐμπεσὸν Ba L Vg
5 βρύει] βρέχει Ne   6 σωτήριον Mor.

The ear of corn comes forth from a stalk of straw;
but while a storehouse receives the former,
flames consume the latter. Barbara, too,
sprang from a father with straw-like loins.
5   Thus the storehouse of God admits Barbara,
while burning flames receive the straw.

After the Tishbite killed the priests of Baal,
heavenly fire came to lift him up;
on your own father, martyr, who murdered you,
a deadly fire rains down, and burns him up;
5   for heaven pours forth two sorts of fire,
one that punishes and the other of salvation.

17

Ἡδύκρεων σῦς, ἀλλὰ τέλματος τόκος·
καὶ Βαρβάρα γοῦν βορβόρου κἂν ἐξέφυ,
ὅμως πρόκειται τῷ Θεῷ τροφὴ ξένη
καὶ πᾶν τὸ συσσίτιον αὐτοῦ λαμπρύνει·
5 χαίρει Θεὸς γὰρ ἀπὸ σαπρῶν βολβίτων
ἄρτους ἑαυτῷ καθαροὺς παριστάνων.

R Ba L Ne Vg | Mor. St.

3 τροφὴ ξένη] cf. Prodr., Carm.hist. 45, 47; 74, 59   5 σαπρῶν βολβίτων] cf. Prodr., Carm.hist. 17, 180

tit. εἰς τὴν αὐτήν L   1 ἡδὺ κρεῶν Ba : ἡδύκρεως Ne Vg | ἀνὰ τέλματος τόπον Vg   2 καὶ βορβόρου γοῦν Βαρβάρα κἂν ἐξέφυ Vg   3 ὅμως] ὅπως Ne   4 πᾶς Vg   5 γὰρ θεὸς L   6 παριστάναι Mor.

18

Πατὴρ ὁ θυτήρ, παῖς τὸ θῦμα παρθένος·
τί τοῦτο; μή τις καὶ πάλιν Ἰεφθάε
θυγατροθυτεῖ τῷ Θεῷ; μὴ σύ, ξένε.
τοὔργον μὲν ἴσον, ὁ σκοπὸς δ' ἐναντίος·
5 πλὴν ἀλλ' ἰδού, πῦρ ὑετίζεται ξένον
τὸν ἱερευτήν, οὐ τὸ θῦμα συμφλέγον.

R Ba L Vg | Mor. St.

tit. εἰς τὴν αὐτήν L   2 ὁ ante Ἰεφθάε add. Mo.   3 θύγατρα θυτεῖ Mor.

Pork is tender meat, but it comes out of mud.
And Barbara, even though born of filth,
is presented to God as an exotic repast
bringing glory to his entire banquet,
5 for God rejoices in offering
pure loaves of bread to himself from putrid cow-dung.

Father the sacrificer, virgin child the sacrifice;
What is this? Is this another Jephthah
sacrificing his own daughter to God? Don't even think it, stranger!
The deed might have been the same, but the aim was the opposite.
5 Above all, behold, wondrous fire rains upon
the butcher, while the offering is unburnt.

19

Τὸν Ἰσαὰκ μὲν Ἀβραὰμ θύων πάλαι
μάχαιραν ηὐτρέπιζε καὶ πῦρ καὶ ξύλα,
ὁ βάρβαρος δὲ Βαρβάραν πατὴρ θύων
τῆς μὲν μαχαίρας ἠκόνησας τὸ στόμα,
5 τὸ πῦρ δ' ἀφῆκας, ἀλλὰ δὴ καὶ τὰ ξύλα·
πλὴν καὶ τὸ πῦρ ἄνωθεν οὐρανὸς βρέχει,
καὶ σύ δ' ὁ θυτὴρ ἀρκέσεις ἀντὶ ξύλων
πάρεργον ὀφθεὶς τῶν ἀφ' ὕψους ἀνθράκων.

R Ba L Ne Vg | Mor. St.

1-2 Gen. 22, 1-13   **2** cf. Prodr., Tetrast. 24a, 4   **4** μαχαίρας/στόμα] cf. e.g. Prodr., Carm.hist. 4, 106 et 287; 59, 76; R&D 1, 19

tit. εἰς τὴν αὐτὴν L   **1** μὲν] om. Ne   **4** ἠκονήσω Vg L : ἠκόνησεν in marg. coni. Mo.   **5** ἀφῆκας cum -εν supra -ας R : ἀφῆκεν Mor.   **6** ἄνωθεν οὐρανὸς βρέχει] ἄνωθε καὶ τὸ πῦρ φλέγει R St.   **7** ἀρκέσας Ba   **8** ὄφθης Ba | [α]φ' ὕψους ἀνθράκων in marg. Vg

20

Ἄν ἐξ ἀκάνθης εὐγενὲς τρυγᾷς ῥόδον,
ὁ σὴρ δὲ τὴν μέταξαν ἱστούργησέ σοι,
τὸ δ' ὄστρεον μάργαρον ἐσφαίρωσέ σοι,
τὴν πορφύραν δ' ὁ κόχλος ἐξήνθησέ σοι,
5 δεῦρο προσελθὼν ἱστόρει καὶ Βαρβάραν,
ῥόδον, μέταξαν, μαργαρίτην, πορφύραν,
ὡς ἐξ ἀκάνθης, σηρός, ὀστρέου, κόχλου,
τοῦ καὶ φονευτοῦ καὶ φυτοσπόρου λέγω.

R Ba C Fc L Ne Re Vg Z | Mor. St.

1 cf. e.g. Ioh. Damasc., Laud. S. Barb. 9, 21-22; Christ. Hagioeupl., Carm. p. 31, 3   **1-4** Nic. Eugen., Mon. in Theod. Prodr. p. 456, 17; Nic. Basilac., Progymn. 5, 11-12; Rog. Hydr., Carm. p. 174, 4-9   **2-4** cf. Ioh. Damasc., Laud. S. Barb. 19, 20-21

tit. εἰς τὴν αὐτὴν L   **1** εὐγενὲς] εὐφυὲς C : ἀγενὲς Mor.   **2** σῆς L | μετάξιν R   **4** τὴν] καὶ C | δ'] om. C | ὁ] ἡ R ἐξήνθησέ] ἐθρέψατο C : ἐξύφανέ L : ἐξήρπασέ Mor. | καὶ κόχλος ἐξήνεγκεν αὖθις πορφύραν Vg Ne   **5** δεῦρο προσελθὲ Βαρβάραν καθιστόρει C | δεῦρο] ταῦτα Re | προελθὼν Ba L Vg | **6-7** ordo versuum diversus est C   **6** μαργαρίτην] μάργαρον καὶ C   **8** om. C

In the old days Abraham prepared dagger,
fire and wood to sacrifice Isaac.
You, barbarian father, whetted
the dagger's blade to sacrifice Barbara,
5   leaving aside the fire, but also the wood;
but heaven rains fire from on high,
and you, sacrificer, will suffice in place of wood,
and fall victim to coals of fire pouring down from on high.

If you pluck a noble rose from thorns,
if the worm weaves silk for you,
if the oyster rounds the pearl for you,
if the shellfish produces purple dye for you,
5   come here and recount the life of Barbara,
the rose, silk, pearl, purple
from the thorn, silkworm, oyster, shellfish,
I mean the murderer and begetter.

21 (H 125)
Εἰς τὴν ἁγίαν Βαρβάραν

Φύσι παγγενέτειρα, βιόσπορε, πότνα, μεγαλκές,
σειρὴ κοσμοδέτειρα, διδάσκαλε συμφροσυνάων·
ἦ ῥὰ τοκεῦσι τόκοις τε πόθου ἐφύτευσας ἀνάγκην,
τὴν θῆρες μὲν ἔτισαν ἀτὰρ βροτὸς ᾔσχυνεν ἀνήρ·
5 οὐχ᾽ ὁράᾳς τόδε ἔργον ἀνάρσιον οὐδὲ θεμιτόν;
φεῦ, τίς ἐκεῖ κατὰ παιδὸς ἑὴν ἀνατείνατο χεῖρα,
ὄφρα μὲν ἔκ τε τάμῃσι καὶ αἵματι δάκτυλα βάψῃ;
οὐδέ τε χεὶρ νάρκησεν, ἄορ δ᾽ οὐκ ἔκπεσε χειρός,
ἀλλ᾽ ἔτλη καὶ ἔρεξε τόσον, γίγαν ἤλιε, μύσος
10 ἡλίκον οὔποτ᾽ ἔρεξε λέων μέγας οὔποτε φωλάς.

Pi L

1 φύσι παγγενέτειρα] cf. Anthol. Gr. 12 97, 4   **8** cf. Hom., Il. 8, 328; Ioh. Damasc., Laud. S. Barb. 18, 16–17

tit. τοῦ αὐτοῦ (i. e. Θεοδώρου Προδρόμου) εἰς τὴν ἁγίαν Βαρβάραν ὅμοιοι (i. e. ἡρωικοὶ στίχοι) Pi : εἰς τὴν αὐτὴν ἡρωικοὶ L   **1** φύσει L   **2** σειρὰν L   **5** ἀνάρσιον] ἀνόσιον L   **6** φύτις Pi : φύτης L | ἑὴν] τεὴν L

On St Barbara

Nature, mother to all, seed of life, gracious lady, almighty,
cord that binds the world, teacher of conciliation;
you who implanted the need for affection between parents and children,
which the beasts honoured, but a mortal man dishonoured;
5   do you not see that this deed is unnatural and against all law?
Oh horror, who stretched out his hand there
against his own child to behead [her] and stain his fingers with blood?
Neither did his hand grow numb, nor did the sword fall from it,
but, great Sun, he dared to perform a vile murder
10 such as the great lion lurking in his lair never wrought.

22 (H 127)
Εἰς τὰς ιβ΄ ἑορτὰς τοῦ Κυρίου ἡμῶν Ἰησοῦ Χριστοῦ

Εὐαγγελισμός, γέννα, κλήσεως θέσις,
χεὶρ Συμεών, βάπτισμα, φῶς Θαβωρίου,
Λάζαρος ἐκ γῆς, βαΐα, σταυροῦ ξύλον,
ἔγερσις, ἄρσις, Πνεύματος παρουσία.

V B E Ha P Pc Vz W

tit. τοῦ αὐτοῦ (i.e. Μανουὴλ Φιλῆ sed τοῦ Πτωχοπροδρόμου in marg.) εἰς τὰς δώδεκα ἑορτάς B : om. E : εἰς τὰς Δεσποτικὰς ιβ΄ ἑορτὰς Ha : εἰς τὰς Δεσποτικὰς ἑορτὰς Pc : στίχοι τοῦ μακαριοτάτου κυρίου Θεοδώρου τοῦ Προδρόμου περὶ τῶν δεσποτικῶν ἑορτῶν Vz : τοῦ αὐτοῦ εἰς τὰς ιβ΄ ἑορτὰς W
1 εὐαγγελισμός legi non potest in P   **3** βάϊα V

23

Τὸ χαῖρε, παῦλα τῆς παλαιγόνου λύπης.
ἡ γέννα, ῥίζα πλάσεως τῆς δευτέρας.
ἡ κλῆσις, εἰκόνισμα τῆς σωτηρίας.
ἡ Συμεὼν χείρ, δεῖγμα τοῦ γραπτοῦ νόμου.
5 ἡ βάπτισις, κάθαρσις ἀνθρώπων ῥύπου.
τὸ τοῦ Θαβὼρ φῶς, τῆς ἐμῆς νυκτὸς λύσις.
ὁ Λάζαρος, φροίμιον αἴσχους θανάτου.
ψυχῶν ἔαρος σύμβολον, τὰ βαΐα.
ἁμαρτίας σταύρωμα, τὸ σταυροῦ ξύλον.
10 θανῇ θανῇς, ἔγερσις ἡ τοῦ Κυρίου.
ἄρσις πεσόντων, ἄρσις ἡ τοῦ Δεσπότου.
τὸ Πνεῦμα, τέρμα τῆς ἐμῆς σωτηρίας.

V B E Ha P Pc W | Mig. Mil.

tit. ἐφερμηνευτικοὶ τῶν αὐτῶν Pc   **1** παῦλα] λύτρον W   **2** ῥίζα] τύπος Mil.   **6** λύσις] φύσις E   **8** ψυχῆς Mig.   **9** τὸ σταυροῦ ξύλον] τὸ τοῦ σταυροῦ ξύλον E : τοῦ σταυροῦ ξύλον X

On the twelve Feasts of our Lord Jesus Christ

Annunciation, Nativity, the name-giving,
the hand of Simeon, Baptism, the light of Tabor,
Lazarus from the earth, Palm Sunday, the wood of the Cross,
Resurrection, Ascension, the appearance of the Holy Spirit.

The salutation, end of the ancient sorrow.
The birth, rootstock of the second creation.
The name, image of salvation.
The hand of Simeon, pattern of the written law.
5 The Baptism, purgation of human filth.
The Tabor light, deliverance from my darkness.
Lazarus, prelude to the shaming of death.
Symbol of souls' spring, Palm Sunday.
Crucifixion of sin, the wood of the cross.
10 Demise of death, the Resurrection of the Lord.
Elevation of the fallen, the ascent of the Lord.
The Holy Spirit, fulfilment of my salvation.

24 (H 129)
Εἰς τὴν ὑπεραγίαν Θεοτόκον

Πολλοῖς τὸν ἐκ σοῦ πικράνας, ἁγνή, τρόποις,
σχεῖν μέν σε θερμὴν ἱλεωτέραν θέλω,
γυμνὸς δὲ πάσης τυγχάνω παρρησίας,
αἰσθάνομαι γὰρ τῶν ἐμαυτῶν σφαλμάτων.
5 οὐκοῦν μεσίτας πρῶτον εἰς σὲ λαμβάνω
τὸν χρύσεον ῥοῦν δογμάτων Ἰωάννην
καὶ Νικόλαον ἄλλο ῥεῦμα θαυμάτων·
ὧν καὶ λαβοῦσα τὰς παρακλήσεις, κόρη,
τὴν πρὸς θεὸν σὴν ἀντίδος δυσωπίαν
10 αἰτουμένοις μὲν ὧδε κἀμοὶ καὶ τέκνοις
τὴν εὐμάρειαν εὐτυχεῖν τὴν ἐν βίῳ,
ἐν τῇ κρίσει δὲ δεξιὰν λαχεῖν στάσιν.
ὑμῶν δ' ὁ μὲν σύμπραττε καὶ συνευδόκει,
θερμουργέ, γοργέ, πρὶν δεηθῇ τις φθάνων·
15 ὁ δ' ἐκπόνει μοι τῆς δεήσεως λύσιν,
τῶν γὰρ θεϊκῶν σὺ γραφεὺς λυτηρίων.

L
---
3 cf. Hymn. Acath. 13, 16 (p. 35)   **6-7** cf. Prodr., Carm.hist. 57, 9–10   **10-11** cf. Prodr., Carm. hist. 75, 112–113

---
2 ἱλεωτέραν scripsi : ἱλεώταιραν L   **10** αἰτουμένοις scripsi : αἰτουμένους L

On the Most Holy Mother of God

Since I have angered your son in many ways, Virgin,
I want to have you as my ardent and merciful intercessor,
but I am void of any freedom to speak,
for I am aware of my own sins.
5 So I claim first as mediators to you
John, he of the golden stream of teachings,
and Nicholas, from whom flows the other stream of miracles.
And having received their supplications, Maiden,
pass on in turn your entreaty to God
10 for me and my children who are asking here
that we may attain good fortune in life
and obtain a place on the right on the Day of Judgement.
The first of the two of you, assist and comfort me,
fervent and swift, on hand even before a person prays.
15 The other, redeem my petition,
for you underwrite divine deliverance.

25 (H 130)
Εἰς εἰκόνα τῆς ὑπεραγίας Θεοτόκου

Ἀλλ' οὐδὲ τὸν σόν, ὦ Θεοῦ μῆτερ, τύπον
ὁ πανδαμάτωρ οὗτος ᾐδέσθη χρόνος·
φθερεῖν δὲ τὴν μόρφωσιν ἠπείλησέ σου,
πατὴρ ἁπάντων καὶ φθορεὺς δεδειγμένος·
5 ἐντεῦθεν ἡ σώσασα τὴν δούλην φύσιν
ἀπημπολήθης—ὢ ξένου πρατηρίου·
ἐντεῦθεν ἡ τέξασα τὴν ἀφθαρσίαν
φθορᾶς κεκινδύνευκας ὀφθῆναι μέρος.
ἀλλ' αὐτὸς εὔνου θερμότητι καρδίας
10 ἐπριάμην σε τὴν ἁπάντων δεσπότιν
καὶ πρὸς νέαν ἤνεγκα καὶ κρείττω πλάσιν·
ἀνθ' ὧν με δοῦλον ὄντα τῆς ἁμαρτίας
καὶ ψυχικὸν παθόντα παντελῆ φθόρον,
ἀνταγόρασον σαῖς λιταῖς πρὸς τὸν Λόγον.

N Vi O

2 πανδαμάτωρ/χρόνος] cf. e.g. Simon., Fragm. 26, 5; Bacchyl., Epinicia 13, 168; Anthol. Gr. 16 275, 2 et App. 3 133, 4; Const. Manass. Vit. Opp. p. 38, 28   7 cf. Man. Philes, Carm., cod. Florent., 66, 4 (I p. 241)   9 εὔνου/καρδίας] cf. Prodr., Carm.hist. 73, 6   14 cf. Prodr., Carm.misc. 67, 4

tit. τοῦ αὐτοῦ (i.e. Θεοδώρου Προδρόμου) εἰς εἰκόνα τῆς Θεοτόκου ἀνακαινισθεῖσαν, ἐξωνησθεῖσαν παρ' αὐτοῦ Vi : Θεοδώρου τοῦ Προδρόμου O   5-7 om. N   6 πρατορίου Vi   7-8 om. O   8 ὠφθῆναι N   9 θερμοτάτης Vi   11 ἤνεικα O | κρείττω] νέαν N Vi | καὶ πρὸς νέαν ἄγαγε καὶ κρείττω πλάσιν post v. 14 add. O

On an icon of the most holy Mother of God

But not even your image, O Mother of God,
did this all-subduing Time respect;
it threatened to ruin your form,
as it is both father and destroyer of all.
5   And thus you, who saved enslaved nature,
were sold—what a strange bargain!
And thus you, who gave birth to immortality,
risked becoming part of this world of decay.
But I myself, because of the fervour of my grateful heart,
10 have purchased you, the queen of all things,
and brought you to a new and better condition;
in return, ransom me, a slave of sin,
who has completely defiled his soul,
through your prayers to the Divine Word.

26 (H 131)
Εἰς τὸν ἅγιον Πέτρον σταυρούμενον

Τῷ Δεσπότῃ μὲν ἦσαν οἱ πόδες κάτω
σταυρουμένῳ σταύρωσιν ὀρθίαν πάλαι·
ἐξ οὐρανοῦ γὰρ ἦλθεν εἰς ἡμᾶς κάτω,
ὡς ὄμβρος εἰς γῆν, ὡς ἐπὶ χλόην δρόσος·
5 ἀντιστρόφως δὲ τῷ Πέτρῳ σταυρουμένῳ
ἀντίστροφον πως εἶχον οἱ πόδες θέσιν·
εἰς οὐρανοὺς γὰρ εἷλκεν αὐτὸν ὁ δρόμος.

V Go Ma L

1-2 Matth. 27, 35; Marc. 15, 24   **3-4** cf. Prodr., Tetrast. 97b, 2-3   **4** cf. Nic.Callic., Carm. 9, 21; Prodr., R&D 4, 281

tit. τοῦ Μιτυληναίου εἰς τὸν ἅγιον Πέτρον Go : τοῦ κυρίου ἡμῶν Ἰησου Χριστοῦ καὶ τοῦ ἁγίου Πέτρου Ma : εἰς τὸν ἅγιον Πέτρον L   **7** οὐρανὸν L | εἷλκεν...δρόμος] εἶχον ἐκ γῆς τὸν δρόμον Go Ma

On St Peter crucified

    Long ago, the feet of the Lord faced down,
    when he was crucified on an upright standing cross;
    for he came from heaven down to us,
    as heavy rain upon the earth, as dew on the grass;
5   conversely, for the crucified Peter
    his feet were placed in the opposite direction;
    for his path of faith drew him up to heaven.

27 (H 132)
Εἰς τὴν σταύρωσιν ἡρῶοι στίχοι

Μὴ σύ γε, ἀγριόθυμε, τετρήνεαι ἁγνὰ θεοῖο
δάκτυλα, μὴ σὺ χολῆς πικρὸν ἐντύνεαι κρητῆρα
χείλεσι παμμεδέοντος, μὴ δὲ σὺ δουρὸς ἀκωκῇ
πλευρὰν ἀκηράτην οὐτάσεαι. ἢ σὺ μὲν οὖτα
5 καὶ σὺ δὲ χεῖρα τέτραινε, χολὴν δὲ σὺ αὖτε κέραιρε,
ὡς γὰρ ἐγὼν Ἀΐδαο φύγω γένυν, ἢ πρό με μάρψεν.

V Pi | Th.

Carm Ioh. 19, 29/34; Prodr., Tetrast. 229a, 3

2-3 cf. Mich. Psell., Orat. Hagiogr. 3b, 155-156   3 δουρὸς ἀκωκῇ] cf. e.g. Hom., Il. 10, 373; Opp., Hal. 4, 551; Eud., Homeroc. 1, 1962; Prodr., Carm.hist. 2, 53   4 cf. Ioh. Maurop., Canones III, 236-7 (p. 134); Anthol. Gr. App. 1 370, 2 Inscr.metr. Me83, 2 (ed. Rhoby, Byzantinische Epigramme auf Ikonen und Objekten der Kleinkunst, II, p. 258)   6 cf. Trag. Adesp., Fragm 208; Hesych., Lex. ε 2425

tit.   τοῦ κυρίου Θεοδώρου τοῦ φιλοσόφου καὶ Προδρόμου στίχοι ἡρωικοὶ εἰς τὴν σταύρωσιν Pi

28
Εἰς τὸ αὐτὸ ὅμοιοι

Πνοιὴν πνοιοδότης μὲν ἐρεύγεται ἐνθάδ' Ἰησοῦς·
μήτηρ δ' ἁγνοτόκεια νέκυν στοναχίζεται υἷα,
ἁγνός δ' αὖθ' ἑτέρωθε δάκρυ σταλάῃσι μυητής,
δεξιτερῇ βαλέων φίλον κάρα· θαῦμα ἰδέσθαι.

V Pi

Carm. Ioh. 19, 26

2 μήτηρ δ' ἁγνοτόκεια] cf. Prodr., Tetrast. 238b, 1; Carm. hist. 8, 46   4 θαῦμα ἰδέσθαι] cf. e.g. Hom., Il. 5, 725; Od. 6, 306; Hes., Theog. 575; Eud., Homeroc. 3, 97; Prodr., Carm.hist. 6, 87; 8, 121; Tetrast. 127b, 3

2 νέκυν om. Pi | υἷα Pi

Hexameters on the Crucifixion

Do not pierce, you wild one, the pure hand of God!
Do not prepare the bitter bowl of gall
for the lips of the Ruler of all! And do not wound his unblemished side
with the point of the lance! Or rather, do wound it
and do pierce His hand and do mix the gall again,
that I may thus flee from the jaws of Hades which have already seized me.

Similar verses on the same subject

Here Jesus, the giver of breath, yields his last breath;
his mother, who gave immaculate birth, bewails her dead son,
while, on the other side, the chaste disciple lets tears fall,
as he rests his head in his right hand; a marvel to behold!

29 (H 154)
Εἰς τὰς ἀρετὰς καὶ τὰς κακίας

Ἀγάπη

Ἔγωγε πηγὴ καὶ περιρρέω κύκλῳ,
τὰς γὰρ ἁπάσας ἀρετὰς σφίγγω κύκλῳ.

R X Lc Ls Pa Vc Vo | Mo.

1 περιρρέω κύκλῳ] cf. Nic.Eugen., D&C 3, 78

tit. τοῦ Προδρόμου Lc : τοῦ Πανιώτου εἰς τὰς ἀρετὰς καὶ εἰς τὰς ἀντιθέτους αὐταῖς κακίας Ls : τοῦ αὐτοῦ σοφωτάτου Ψελλοῦ ἴαμβοι εἰς ἀρετὰς καὶ κακίας Pa : τοῦ Πανιώτου Vc : om. Vo : ἀνωνύμου ἔπος ἰαμβικόν, εἰς τὰς ἀρετὰς καὶ τὰς κακίας Mo.   1 πηγὴ] τὴν γῆν Vo | περιρέω Lc   2 γ' post ἁπάσας add. Mo. | σφίγγω κύκλῳ] ὁμοῦ φέρω Vo

30
Μῖσος

Μηνιθμόν, ὀργήν, συμπλοκὴν δόλου, φθόνον,
καὶ χαλεπὸν πᾶν συλλαβὼν φέρω πάθος.

R X Lc Ls Pa Vc Vo | Fe. Mo.

1 θεσμοὺς διαιρῶ καὶ φύσιν τοὺς νόμους Vo | δόλον Ls Fe. Mo. | φθόνον] φόνον Ls   2 καὶ τοὺς ἀδριφοὺς ἐγείρω καταλλήλους Vo | συλλαβὸν R X Ls Vc

31
Ἐξουσία

Ὑπηρετεῖ μου τῷ κράτει χαλκοῦν ὅπλον
καὶ κυριεύω τοῦ λόγου χωρὶς λόγου.

R X Lc Ls Pa Vc Vo

1 χαλκοῦν ὅπλον] cf. Prodr., Carm.hist. 17, 124

1 κράτει] κάλλει Vc | χαλκοῦν ὅπλον] χοῦς ἐν βίῳ Pa   2 χωρὶς] ἄτερ Pa | Φθόνος οὐδὲν λυπῶ ἢ τοὺς ἔχοντας μόνους καὶ κατεσθίω τούτων τὴν ψυχ(...) post 3b add. Vo

On Virtues and Vices

Love

I am a spring and flow from all sides,
for I enclose all graces in a circle.

Hatred

Wrath, anger, a web of deceit, envy,
and every cruel feeling, gathering them up I carry them.

Power

The brazen weapon serves my power
and I lord over reason without reason.

32
Φρόνησις

Συνάγομαι μὲν ἐκ μακρᾶς ἐμπειρίας,
τιθῶ δὲ σεπτοὺς τοὺς ἐμὲ κτησαμένους.

R X Lc Ls Pa Vc Vo | Mo.

---

1 συνάπτομαι Vo : συνηγόμην Mo.   2 κεκτημένους Pa Vc | κεκτημένους ἐμὲ Mo.

33
Ἀφροσύνη

Ἔοικα τυφλοῖς ἢ διύγροις ἐμβρύοις
ἐκ σπαργάνων στέρξασα τὴν ἀγνωσίαν.

R X Lc Ls Pa Vc Vo

---

2 cf. Inscr. metr. IT, 1 (ed. Rhoby, Byzantinische Epigramme auf Stein, III, p. 406)

---

2 στέρξασα] δ' ἔστερξα Ls : στέργουσα Vo

34
Δικαιοσύνη

Ἐγὼ συνιστῶ τῷ ζυγῷ μου τὰς πόλεις
καὶ πύργος αὐταῖς χρηματίζω καὶ τάφρος.

R X Lc Ls Pa Vc Vo

---

2 αὐτοῖς R | τάφρος] τεῖχος Vo

Prudence

I am acquired from long experience,
and I make those who have obtained me illustrious.

Foolishness

I look like the blind or feeble newborns,
for I have loved ignorance from infancy.

Justice

I strengthen cities with my yoke,
and I serve as rampart and ditch for them.

35
Ἀδικία

Ἀρχὴ μάχης ἔγωγε καὶ μήτηρ φόνου,
καὶ τεῖχος εὐρὺ τῷ κριῷ καταστρέφω.

R X Lc Ls Pa Vc Vo

1 μήτηρ φόνου] cf. Rhet. Anon., Problemata rhetorica in status 8 403, 17; Ioh. Chrys. In Io. PG 59, 211

1 φόνου] φθόνου Lc R   2 τεῖχος ἐρύττω καὶ καταστρέφω πόλεις Vo | κριῷ] κρημνῷ Lc : ψεύδει Pa

36
Ἀνδρεία

Ἐγὼ διδάσκω τοὺς ἀρηϊμανίους
πότε, πρὸς οὕς, πῶς, καὶ δι' οὓς μαχητέον.

R X Lc Ls Pa Vc Vo | Mo.

tit. ἀνδρεία] Ἀφοβία Lc   1 ἀρηϊμανίας R : ἀρειομανίτας Vo : ἀρηϊμανέας Mo. | ἐχθροὺς ἀναιρῶ καὶ κατασφάττω ξίφει in marg. Ls   2 πῶς, καὶ δι' οὓς μαχητέον] τε καὶ διαμαχητέον Vo | πλούτου τε βάρος καὶ στεφάνους πα[ρέ]χω in marg. Ls

37
Δειλία

Στερῶ στεφάνων καὶ σκύλων καὶ λαφύρων,
ὅσοι μένειν στέργουσιν ἐντὸς ἑρκίων.

R X Lc Ls Pa Vc Vo | Fe.

2 στέρουσιν Lc | ἑρκύων R Vc : ἑρκέων Ls Fe. : οἰκίσκων Pa

Injustice

I am the origin of battle and mother of murder,
and I destroy the broad city-wall with the battering ram.

Fortitude

I instruct the bellicose
when, against whom, how, and for whom they must fight.

Cowardice

I deprive of their crowns and booty and spoils
all those who desire to stay within the walls.

38
Σωφροσύνη

Τὸν σώφρονα ζῆν ᾑρετισάμην βίον,
φεύγουσα τὴν ἄθεσμον ἀκολασίαν.

Ls Pa R Vc Vo X

39
Ἀκολασία

Αἰσχρῶν γυναικῶν συμπλοκαί, μέθης κάρος
ἐμοὶ προεκρίθησαν ἐκ βρεφουργίας.

R X Lc Ls Pa Vc Vo

40
Ἀλήθεια

Φῶς χρηματίζω καὶ λύχνος τοῖς χρωμένοις,
πρώτη τελοῦσα τῶν Θεοῦ θυγατέρων.

R X Lc Ls Pa Vc Vo | Fe.

1 λύχνον Fe.   **2** τελοῦσα] πέλουσα Pa Fe. : τέ εἰμι Vo | τῶν θεοῦ legi non potest in Ls

Chastity

I chose to lead a chaste life,
avoiding unlawful intemperance.

Intemperance

Intercourse with shameful women, drunken torpor;
these have been preferred by me from infancy.

Truth

I am a light and a lantern to those who avail themselves of me;
I am the first of the daughters of God.

41
Ψεῦδος

Ὑπόστασιν σχεῖν ἀδυνατοῦν ἰδίαν,
καὶ τὴν ἐνυπόστατον ἡττῶ πολλάκις.

R X Lc Ls Pa Vc Vo

1 ἀδυνατῶν Pa : ἀδυνάτων Lc   2 ἡττῶ] νικῶ Vo | τελῶ δ' ὀλέθρου τοῖς ἐρασταῖς μου βόθρος post vers. 2 add. R X

42
Ἐλπίς

Ἄναρθρον ἀρθρῶ καὶ παραλελυμένον
καὶ τοὺς ῥαθύμους ἐξεγείρω πρὸς πόνους.

R X Lc Ls Pa Vc Vo

1 cf. Prodr., R&D 8, 525

1 Τὰ νεῦρ' ἀνορθῶ, τὰ παραλελυμένα Pa   2 καὶ ῥαθύμους δὲ διεγείρω πρὸς πόνους Vo

43
Ἀνελπιστία

Ἔκλεισα πολλοῖς τὰς παραδείσου πύλας,
ὅσοι φρονοῦντες ἀφελῶς εἵλοντό με.

R X Lc Ls Pa Vc Vo | Mo. Pi.

1 παραδείσου πύλας] cf. e.g. Ps. Epiph., Hom. in divini corporis sepulturam PG 43, 452B; Ps. Ioh. Chrys. In illud: Memor fui dei PG 61, 698; Theod. Bals., Carm. 29, 35; Mich. Chon., Carm. 7, 15 (p. 395)

1 πολλοὶ Vo | τὰς] τοῦ Ls   2 ὅσοι φρονοῦντες ἀφελῶς] ὅσοι ῥάθυμοι ἀφελῶς Pa : ὅσοι φρονοῦσιν ἀφελῶς Lc : ὅσοι φρονοῦντες τοὺς ἐν κρίσει Vo : ὅσοι φρονοῦντες γ' ἀφελῶς Mo. : οἳ σαθρὰν οὖσαν corr. Pi.

Falsehood

Unable to possess my own substance,
I often destroy the substance of others.

Hope

I give strength to the powerless and weak,
and rouse the idle to labour.

Hopelessness

I closed the gates of Paradise to many,
especially those who naively chose me.

44
Προσευχή

Ἐγὼ μόνη δίδωμι τοῖς στέργουσί με
τῷ δημιουργῷ προσλαλεῖν καταμόνας.

R X Lc Ls Pa Vc Vo | Mo.

2 cf. Man. Philes, Carm., cod. Florent., 211, 114 (I p. 387)

1 μόνη δίδωμι] βεβαιῶ μόνη Vo | με] μοι Lc   2 καὶ ante τῷ add. Vo | καταμόνας] κατὰ μόνας Pa Vo : κ(α)τ(ὰ) μόνου Mo.

45
Ῥᾳθυμία

Οὐπώποτε τρόπαιον ἀνεστησάμην,
ἀεὶ γὰρ ὑπνῶ καὶ φιλῶ ῥέγχειν μέγα.

R X Lc Ls Pa Vc Vo

2 ῥέγχειν] χάσμη Pa : ῥέγκειν Lc | φιλῶ ῥέγχειν] ῥέγχειν φιλῶ Vo | μέγα] μόνην Pa

46
Ταπεινοφροσύνη

Εἰς οἷον ὕψος τοὺς ἐμοὺς ἄγω φίλους,
τρανῶς τελώνης μαρτυρεῖ μου τὸ κράτος.

R X Lc Ls Pa Vc Vo

tit. ταπίνωσις Vo   1 φίλους ἄγω R : φέρω φίλους X   2 μου τὸ κράτος legi non potest in Ls

Prayer

I alone allow those who love me
to speak with God in private.

Idleness

I have never yet raised a trophy,
for I am always asleep and love to snore loudly.

Modesty

To what heights I elevate my friends,
the power that I have, is clearly shown by the tax-collector.

47
Ὑψηλοφροσύνη

Ἀεὶ κατασπῶ καὶ κάτω ποιῶ ῥέπειν,
καὶ μαρτυρεῖ νοῦς ὁ σκότος χρηματίσας.

R X Lc Ls Pa Vc Vo | Ar. Ge. Fe.

2 σκότος] σκότῳ Pa (σκότος corr. Ar. Fe. Ge.) | δὴ post σκότος add. Vo

48
Ἐλεημοσύνη

Ὁ σχών με πιστὴν τῷ βίῳ τούτῳ φίλην,
ἑαυτὸν ἰσοῖ τῷ Θεοῦ θείῳ λόγῳ.

R X Lc Ls Pa Vc | Mo.

1 πιστὸν X | τῷ βίῳ τούτῳ] τοῦ βίου τούτου Lc Pi | φίλον X   2 ἑαυτὸν] εὖ αὐτὸν Mo. | θεῷ R Lc

49
Ὠμότης

Ὅσων κακῶν αἴτιος ὁ σκνιφὸς τρόπος,
ὁ πλούσιος πρόχειρος εἰς μαρτυρίαν.

R X Lc Ls Pa Vc Vo | Mo.

1 ὅσον Pa | κακὸν Pa | σκιφὸς Pa : σκνηφὸς Lc : κρυφὸς Vo : σκνιπὸς Mo. | τρόπος] βίος Pa   2 μαρτυρίαν] ἁμαρτίαν Pa

Arrogance

I always drag people down and make them incline downward,
and the Angel that is darkness, bears witness to this.

Mercy

He who has me as a loyal friend in this life
will make himself equal to the divine Word of God.

Cruelty

That parsimony is responsible for many vices,
the rich man is at hand to bear witness.

50
Χαρὰ

Τείνω τὰ νεῦρα καὶ κρατύνω τὸν τόνον,
ὁρμῆς δὲ πιμπλῶ τοὺς παραλελυμένους.

R X Lc Ls Pa Vc Vo

1 τείνω] τέγγω X   **2** ἐργάζομαί δε καὶ λογισμῶν ἐκστάσεις Vo | δὲ πιμπλῶ] δ' ἐμπιπλῶ Pa : ἐπιμπλῶ Lc

51
Λύπη

Καὶ νεῦρα συνθλῶ καὶ παραλύω τόνον,
ἐργάζομαι δὲ καὶ λογισμῶν ἐκστάσεις.

R X Lc Ls Pa Vc | Mo.

1 καὶ¹] τὰ Pa | συθλῶ R | τόνον] μέλη R.   **2** ἐκσταθεὶς Mo.

52
Φιλοσοφία

Ἴσον Θεῷ τίθημι τὸν στέργοντά με
τὴν γνῶσιν αὐτῷ τῶν ὅλων δωρουμένη.

R X Lc Ls Pa Vc

Joy

I stretch nerves to the uttermost and strengthen the sinews,
and I fill the exhausted with the urge to act.

Grief

I break the nerve and enfeeble the sinews,
and I am the cause of distracted thoughts.

Philosophy

I make the one yearning for me equal to God,
as I grant him the knowledge of all things.

53
Ῥητορικὴ

Ἐγὼ πνέω πῦρ κατὰ τῶν ἀντιθέτων,
στομῶ δὲ γλῶσσαν ὡς ξυρὸν τῇ διπλόῃ.

R X Lc Ls Pa Vc | Mo.

1 cf. Prodr., Carm.misc. 76, 205

1 ἀντιπάλων Pa : ἀντιδίκων Mo.   2 ξυρόν] ψυχρῷ X Pa : ξηρῷ Lc : ψυχὴν Ls : ξυρῷ R | ὡς ξυρόν] καὶ ξυρῷ Mo.

54
Γραμματικὴ

Τῶν ἱστοριῶν συναγωγὸς τυγχάνω
καὶ λέξιν ὀρθῶ καὶ μέτροις ἐφιστάνω.

R X Lc Ls Pa Vc | Mo.

1 συναγωγὸς] ἀγωγὴ Ls : συναγωγὰς Mo.   2 μέτροις] λόγοις R | ἐφιστάνω] μετανιστάνω Ls

Rhetoric

I exhale fire against opponents,
and I hone the tongue, like a sword, with a double-edged razor.

Grammar

I am the one who brings narratives together,
I form words correctly, and attend to metre.

55 (H 155)
Εἰς εἰκονισμένον τὸν βίον

Ἐμὲ τὸν βίον, ἄνθρωπε, δέξαι σου παραινέτην·
ἔτυχες, εὗρες, ἔλαβες, κατέσχες μου τὰς τρίχας;
Μὴ πρὸς ῥαστώνην ἐκδοθῇς, μὴ πρὸς τρυφὴν χωρήσῃς,
μὴ δὲ φρονήσῃς ὑψηλὰ καὶ πέρα τοῦ μετρίου.
5 γυμνόν με βλέπεις· νόησον γυμνόν μου καὶ τὸ τέλος.
ὑπὸ τοὺς πόδας μου τροχοί· φρίττε μὴ κυλισθῶσι.
περὶ τὰς κνήμας μου πτερά· φεύγω, παρίπταμαί σε,
ζυγὰ κατέχω τῇ χειρί· φοβοῦ τὰς μετακλίσεις.
τί με κρατεῖς; σκιὰν κρατεῖς· πνοὴν κρατεῖς ἀνέμου.
10 τί με κρατεῖς; καπνὸν κρατεῖς, ὄνειρον, ἴχνος πλοίου.

V Be Bu H He I L Mo N Pa Ro Vr Z | Gu.

1 Ἐμέ, τὸν βίον, ἄνθρωπε/μὴ δὲ φρονήσῃς ὑψηλὰ] cf. Man. Philes, Carm., cod. Paris., 168, 6 (II p. 192)   2 cf. Prodr., Carm.hist. 1, 59   4 Rom. 11, 20   5 γυμνόν...τέλος] cf. Eccl. 5, 14; Iob 1, 21   9–10 cf. Const.Manas., A&K 9 160, 1–2   10 ἴχνος πλοίου] cf. Ioh. Damasc., Sacra Parallela PG 95, 1124D

tit. εἰς εἰκονισμένον βίον πολιτικοὶ Be : εἰς τὸν βίον L : περὶ τοῦ χρόνου Mo : εἰς τὸν βίον εἰκονισμένον Pa : om. He Z : εἰς εἰκονισμένον τῷ βίῳ Gu.   2 τρίχας] τρίβους Gu.   3 ἐκδοθεὶς He Mo | χωρήσῃς om. Vr   4 om. I   5 μου] σου Be   6 τροχὸς Mo | φρίττε] βλέπε N Bu   7 περὶ τὰς κνήμας] ὑπὸ τοὺς πόδας μου Mo | κνίμας He | μου πτερά] πτέρυγας I | φεύγε N : φεύγων Ro | περίπταμαί Bu H Mo N Vr Z Gu. | φεύγων Ro | σε] σου Pa   8 μετακλήσεις Bu   9–10 Τί με κρατεῖς; Σκιὰν κρατεῖς· Καπνὸν κρατεῖς, ὄνειρον, ἴχνος πλοίου L

On the Image of Life

O Man, receive me, Life, as your advisor.
Did you chance upon, discover, take, seize my locks?
Do not give way to idleness, do not yield to self-indulgence,
do not exult beyond measure!
5   You see me naked; consider that my end is naked too.
Wheels beneath my feet, fear lest they begin to roll!
Wings around my calves. I flee, I fly past you.
I hold the balance in my hand. Fear their precarious movements!
Why do you hold on to me? You hold a shadow; you hold a breath of wind.
10 Why do you hold on to me? You hold smoke, a dream, the wake of a ship.

56

Ἐμὲ τὸν βίον, ἄνθρωπε, δέξαι σου παραινέτην.
οὐκ ἔτυχες, οὐκ ἔλαβες, οὐκ ἔσχες μου τὰς τρίχας;
μὴ σκυθρωπάσῃς τοῦ λοιποῦ, μὴ δὲ δυσελπιστήσῃς.
γυμνὸς εἰμὶ καὶ τῶν χειρῶν ἐξολισθήσας τούτων,
5 ἴσως μεταρρυήσομαι πρὸς σὲ καὶ μεταπέσω·
ὑπὸ τοὺς πόδας μου τροχοί· τάχα σοι κυλισθῶσι.
περὶ τὰς κνήμας μου πτερά· τρέχω, προσίπταμαί σοι.
ζυγὰ κατέχω· τάχα σοι τὴν πλάστιγγα χαλάσω.
μὴ τοίνυν ἀποπροσποιοῦ τὰς ἀγαθὰς ἐλπίδας.

V Be H He I L Mo N Ro Vr Z | Gu.

2 cf. Prodr., Carm.hist. 1, 59   **9** ἀγαθὰς ἐλπίδας] cf. e.g. II. Thess. 2, 16

tit. εἰς τὸ αὐτὸ L : ἄλλως Mo   **2** τρίχας] τρίβους Gu.   **3** δυσελπισθήσῃς N : δυσελπιστήσας Mo   **4** κιλυσθώσι N   **5** μετωρρυήσομαι Mo | σὲ] δὲ Gu.   **6** versus bis in Vr   **7** πρὸς ἵπταμαί Bu   **9** Ἐμὲ, τὸν βίον, ἄνθρωπε, δέξαι σου παραινέτην post vers. **9** add. Be

O Man, receive me, Life, as your advisor.
Did you not chance upon, discover, seize my locks?
Do not look downcast for the remainder of life, do not lose your hope!
I am naked, and having escaped from these hands,
5   perhaps I will flow towards you and change in your favour.
Wheels beneath my feet, perhaps they will turn for you.
Wings around my calves; I run, I fly towards you.
I hold the balance; perhaps I will tip the scales in your favour.
So, do not now discard your good hopes!

57 (H 156)
Εἰς δακτύλιον ἔχοντα σφραγῖδα ἐρῶντας δύο καὶ ἀπὸ τῶν στέρνων αὐτῶν δύο δένδρα ἐκπεφυκότα καὶ εἰς ἕνα συγκορυφούμενα κόρυμβον

Ἐκ τῶν ποθούντων δένδρα τοῖς δένδροις γάμος,
αὐτοῖς δὲ τοῖς ποθοῦσιν οὐδαμοῦ γάμος.

V B H P Po Pz X

tit. εἰς δακτύλιον ἔχοντα σφραγῖδα ἐρῶντας δύο, καὶ ἀπὸ τῶν στέρνων αὐτῶν δύο δένδρα ἐκπεφυένta καὶ εἰς ἕνα συγκορυφούμενον κόρυμβον V : εἰς δακτύλιον ἔχοντα σφραγῖδα ἐρῶντας δύο, καὶ ἀπὸ τῶν στέρνων αὐτῶν δύο δένδρα ἐκπεφυκότα καὶ εἰς ἕνα συγκορυφούμενα κόρυμβον H Po : legi non potest in P : τοῦ αὐτοῦ (i.e. Θεοδώρου Προδρόμου) εἰς δακτυλίδιν ἔχον σφραγίδας ἐρῶντας δύο, καὶ ἀπὸ τῶν στέρνων αὐτῶν δύο δένδρα ἐκπεφυκότα καὶ εἰς ἕνα συγκορυφούμενα κόρυμβον X

58
Εἰς τὸ αὐτὸ

Ἐκ καρδιῶν τὰ δένδρα καὶ ξυνεπλάκη·
ἔρως, ἔρως, σύναπτε καὶ τὰς καρδίας.

V B H P Po Pz X | Th.

tit. om. Po X   **1** ἐκ om. P | συνεπλάκη Th.

59
Εἰς τὸ αὐτὸ

Ἐρᾷ τὰ δένδρα καὶ φιλεῖ καὶ μίγνυται·
ἐρῶμεν, οὐ φιλοῦμεν, οὐ μιγνύμεθα.

V B H P Po Pz X

tit. om. Po X

On a ring that has a seal engraving of two lovers and two trees that grow out of their breasts and come together into one canopy

From those who desire trees, a union for the trees,
but for lovers themselves nowhere is there a wedding.

On the same

From hearts trees grow and intertwine;
Eros, Eros, unite also their hearts.

On the same

The trees love one another and kiss and intertwine;
we love each other, but we neither kiss nor intertwine.

60
Εἰς τὸ αὐτὸ

Ἔρως, τὰ δένδρα καὶ φύεις καὶ μιγνύεις,
τὰ στέρνα δ' ἐξέρρηξας, οὐχὶ μιγνύεις.

V B H P Po Pz X | Th.

___

tit. om. Po X   2 ἐξέρραξας X : ἐξέρηξας Th.

61
Εἰς τὸ αὐτὸ

Εἰς δένδρον ἓν τὰ δένδρα συμπεφυκότα
δοίητε καρπὸν τῶν ἐρώντων τὸν γάμον.

V B H P Po Pz X

___

tit. om. Po X   1 ἕν] μὲν P

On the same

Eros, you make trees grow and intertwine,
but you broke their hearts, you do not intertwine them.

On the same

You trees that have grown into one,
may you bear the marriage of the lovers as your fruit.

62 (H 158)
Ἐπὶ κήπῳ

Ὁρᾷς, θεατά, τοῦ φυτῶνος τὴν χάριν,
πρόκυψον, ἅψαι τῶν φυτῶν, οὐδεὶς φθόνος.
ἰδοὺ κρίνον τρύγησον, ἀλλὰ σωφρόνως·
ἰδοὺ χλόη τρύφησον, ἀλλὰ μετρίως·
5 ὕδωρ ἰδοὺ ῥόφησον, ἀλλ' οὐκ εἰς κόρον·
ὡς ἐν τύποις δὲ καὶ σεαυτόν μοι βλέπε.
ἀνθεῖς, ἀπανθεῖς, τοῦτο δὴ καὶ τοῦ κρίνου·
θάλλεις, μαραίνῃ, τοῦτο δὴ καὶ τῆς χλόης·
ῥέεις, παρέρχῃ, τοῦτο καὶ τῶν ὑδάτων.
10 ἄν, ὡς ἔφην, ἄνθρωπε, τὸν κῆπον βλέπῃς,
πλήσεις μέν, οἶδα, καὶ χαρᾶς τὴν καρδίαν
καὶ ψυχικὴν δὲ κερδανεῖς σωτηρίαν.

V Ac Be Bu H He L Mt N Nd P Pf R Vb Vr X Z | Gu. Ky. We.

1-5 cf. Greg. Nyss., in cant. cant., Hom. 5, p. 154, 1–3   **2** cf. Ios. Bryennius, Epist. 20, 62   **7-8** cf. Greg.Naz., Carm. II.1, 89 [1442] 3; Ios.Bryennius, Epist. 20, 98–99   **12** ψυχικὴ/σωτηρίαν] cf. Prodr., Carm.hist. 21, 21

tit. Θεοδώρου τοῦ Προδρόμου, εἰς κῆπον Ac Mt : om. He : στίχοι τοῦ Φιλοστράτου Pf : εἰς κῆπον Vb : σοφωτάτου κύρου Θεοδώρου τοῦ Προδρόμου X : ἀνεπίγραφα Gu.   **1** φυτῶντος Mt | τοῦ φυτῶνος τὴν χάριν] ἁρμονίαν φυτῶνος Ky.   **2** ἅψε Pf | τοῦ φυτοῦ Nd | φόνος Mt   **3** κρῖνον Mt | τρύγησον] τρύφησον Pf | σωφρόνης Bu   **5** ῥόφησον, ἀλλ' οὐκ εἰς κόρον] ῥόφυσιν ἀλλ' οὐκ εἶχεν Bu   **7** Ἀνθεῖς Mt | ἀπανθεὶς Mt   **8** θάλλεις, μαραίνῃ τοῦτο καὶ τὸ τῆς χλόης Ac Mt : θάλλῃς, μαραίνῃ· τοῦτο καὶ τῶν ὑδάτων Z   **9** om. Z | παρέρχει Bu   **10** βλέπεις Ac Mt Vb We.   **11** χαρᾶς τὴν καρδίαν] χαράς τε καὶ δόξης Bu | χαρὰ P   **12** σωτηρίας Mt

To a Garden

You see, beholder, the beauty of this garden;
look around, touch the fruits—there is no envy!
Behold the lily, gather it, but with restraint!
Behold the grass, enjoy it, but with moderation!
5 Behold the water, gulp it down, but not to satiety!
And behold yourself as an exact replica of me:
you flourish and wither—so does the lily,
you thrive and die—so does the grass,
you flood and recede—so do the waters.
10 If you, man, behold the garden as I said,
you will, I am sure, fill your heart with joy
and earn spiritual salvation.

63
Εἰς αὐτὸ

Ὁρῶν σε, κῆπε, καὶ τὰ δένδρα σου βλέπων,
ἀγάλλομαι μὲν τῇ θέᾳ τὴν καρδίαν,
φαντάζομαι δὲ τῆς Ἐδὲμ τὸ χωρίον
καὶ βούλομαι μὲν τοῖς φυτοῖς προσεγγίσαι.
5 πλὴν τοῦ φυτοῦ τὴν γεῦσιν εἰς νοῦν λαμβάνω,
ἐξ οὗ φαγὼν ὤλισθον εἰς ἁμαρτίαν·
θέλω τρυγῆσαι καὶ φαγεῖν, ἀλλὰ τρέμω,
μὴ γνώσεως τὸ ξύλον ἐκφαγὼν θάνω.

V Ac Be Bu He L Mt N P R Vb Vr X Z | La.

2 Gen. 2, 8   8 γνώσεως ... ξύλον] Gen. 2, 9

tit. εἰς τὸν αὐτὸν V Bu L Vr : εἰς αὐτὸ Ac H Vb X Z : om. Be He P Gu. : εἰς τὸ αὐτὸ N R : ἕτερον Mt   1 καὶ] τὶ Ac   2 ἀγάλλομαι] ἐκπλήττομαι N R Z : ἐκπλήττομαι supra [ἀ]γάλλομαι scrib. H | μὲν τῇ θέᾳ τὴν καρδίαν] τῇ θείᾳ καρδίᾳ Bu   4 τοῖς] τῖς Mt | καὶ βούλομαι μὲν legi non potest in Vr | προσεγγίσω Bu   5 τὴν om. Bu | λαμβάνων corr. La.   6 ὄλισθα Mt : ὄλισθον Vr

64
Εἰς αὐτὸ

Ἄνθρωπε, δεῦρο καὶ τρύγησον καὶ φάγε·
ἀκινδύνως γὰρ καὶ τρυγήσεις καὶ φάγῃς,
μόνον τὸ λίχνον ἐκδιώξας μακρόθεν,
τὸν ὑάκινθον κεῖρε, τοῦ κρίνου δρέπου,
5 τρύγα τὸ μύρτον, λαμβάνου τοῦ βαλσάμου,
οὐχ ὡς δι' αὐτῶν θηλυνεῖς τὴν καρδίαν,
ἀλλ' ὡς τρυγήσῃς μυστικὴν εὐωδίαν,
τοῖς κτίσμασι γνοὺς τὸν κτίσαντα δεσπότην.

V Be Bu H L He Mt N P R Vb Vr X Z | Gu. We.

tit. εἰς τὸν αὐτὸν V L Vr : εἰς τὸ αὐτὸ N R : ἕτερον Mt : om. Be Bu He P Gu.   1 τρύγησε Bu   2 om. Bu | τρυγήσῃς S V | φάγοις L : φάγεις N P Vb Z   3 τὸν Bu | ἐκδιώξον R   4 δρέπῃ L Vb   5 μύρτον] μίλτον Gu. : μύλτον Mt | λάμβανε R X : λαμβάνεις Bu   7 ἄλλως Bu | τρυγήσεις We. | μυστικῶς Bu   8 τοῖς κτίσῃσι H (ταῖς κτίσεσιν corr. We.)

On the same

Beholding you, garden, and looking at your trees
I am overwhelmed in my heart at the sight,
I imagine you to be the place of Eden,
and I wish to approach your plants.
5 But the tasting of the fruit comes to my mind,
the fruit from which I ate and fell into sin;
I wish to gather and eat, but I tremble in fear
lest I die eating from the Tree of Knowledge.

On the same

Come here, man, gather the fruits and eat!
For without danger you may gather and eat,
once you have driven gluttony far away,
cut down the hyacinth, pluck the lily,
5 harvest the myrtle, partake of the balsamon,
not that your heart thereby should become effeminate,
but to gather their mystical fragrance,
recognizing the Lord Creator in what he has created.

65
Εἰς αὐτὸ

Βαβαί, πόσαις ὁ κῆπος ἡδοναῖς βρίθεις·
κρινωνιὰς ἐκεῖθεν εὐθαλεῖς φύεις,
ῥοδωνιὰς ἐντεῦθεν ἀνθούσας φέρεις,
ἰωνιαῖς τέθηλας, ἄνθεσι βρύεις,
5 ὕδωρ ἀναρρεῖς ἐκ φλεβὸς τεραστίας,
ἀνατρέχον μὲν ὑπὸ λεπτῷ τῷ ψόφῳ,
ἰδεῖν δὲ λαμπρὸν καὶ πιεῖν ὑπὲρ μέλι,
καὶ τοὺς ὁρῶντας ἡδύνεις πολυτρόπως.

V Be Bu H He L Mt N Nd P R Vr X Z | Gu. Ky. La. We.

tit. εἰς τὸν αὐτὸν V L Vr : εἰς τὸ αὐτὸ N R : om. Be Bu He Gu.   **1** πόσον He | ἡδονὸν He | βρίθει Bu   **2** φύεις] φύσεις La. : φέρεις Mt   **3** φέρεις] φύεις Mt   **4** ἰωνιῶς Mt | τέθηλλας Vb   **5** ἀναρρυεῖς Bu | ἐκφλεβὸν We.   **6** ἀνατρέχων Bu He Nd | ψόφῳ] ζόφῳ R : λόφῳ Ky.   **7** πιεῖν] ποιεῖν N

66
Εἰς αὐτὸ

Τὴν καλλονήν, ἄνθρωπε, τοῦ ῥόδου βλέπων
καὶ τὰς ἀκάνθας εὐφυῶς περισκόπει,
κἀντεῦθεν εἰς ἔννοιαν ἐλθὲ τοῦ βίου.
ὡς ὁ τρυγῶν γὰρ τὸ γλυκύπνοον ῥόδον,
5 ἐκ τῶν ἀκανθῶν αἱματοῖ τοὺς δακτύλους,
οὕτως ἁπάντων ἀγαθῶν κοινωνία
ἁλίσκεται μέν, ἀλλὰ μυρίοις πόνοις·
οὐκ ἔστι γὰρ ἄμοχθον οὐδὲν ἐν βίῳ.

V Be Bu H He L Mt N P R Vr X Z | Gu. La. We.

tit. εἰς τὸν αὐτὸν V L Vr : εἰς τὸ αὐτὸ N R : ἕτερον Mt : om. Be Bu He Gu.   **1** καλλωνὴν N   **2** ἐμφυῶς L : εὐφυεῖς in app. cr. We.   **3** ἔννοιαν] εἴδησιν R X   **5** αἱματεῖν R Vr   **6** κοινωνίας Bu   **7** ἁλίσκεται] εὑρίσκεται La.   **8** βίῳ] κήπῳ Bu

On the same

Oh my! With how many pleasures do you teem, garden!
You bloom with lilies over there,
you flourish with roses over here,
you blossom with violets, you burst with flowers,
5   you pour forth water from marvellous springs,
it surges up with a gentle murmur,
splendid to behold and sweeter than honey to drink,
and you delight your spectators in many ways.

On the same

Beholding, man, the beauty of the rose,
examine shrewdly also its thorns,
and let this lead you to reflect on life.
Just as he who picks the sweet-smelling rose
5   will make his fingers bleed from the thorns,
so is the union with all good things:
it is achieved, but with innumerable pains;
for nothing in life is free from hardship.

67 (H 164)
εἰς εἰκόνα τῆς ὑπεραγίας θεοτόκου

Ὁ μὲν σὸς υἱὸς καὶ Θεὸς, Λόγος, κόρη,
λύθροις ἑαυτοῦ τὸ πρὶν ἠγόρασέ σε·
σὺ δὲ πραθέντα ταῖς ἁμαρτίαις πάλιν
ἐξαγόρασον ταῖς λιταῖς σου, παρθένε,
5 Γεώργιον σὸν λάτριν Ἀντιοχέα
τῆς εὐτυχοῦς προὔχοντα Σικελαρχίας.

Z | Ho. Pa.
___
4 cf. Prodr., Carm.misc. 25, 14
___
1 θεοῦ corr. Pa.   6 προὔχοντα Ho. : προὔχοντο Z

On an icon of the most holy Mother of God

    Your son and God, the Word, maiden,
    ransomed you before with his own blood.
    But you, Virgin, redeem with your prayers
    the one who was in turn sold because of his sins,
5   your servant Georgios of Antioch,
    head of the prosperous state of Sicily.

68 (H 160)
Αἴνιγμα εἰς τὴν νεφέλην

Υἱέος ἡμετέρου με φιτύσσατο δῖα θυγάτηρ·
ἠέρι δ' ἐμπελάω τῷ περιγειοτέρῳ.
υἷιν ἐμὸν λαγόνεσσι φορευμένη εἰμὶ καὶ αὐτή,
τὸν δέ τε γειναμένη, ὄλλυμαι· ὃς δὲ βροτοῖς
5 λιμοῦ ἀργαλέοιο δυσαλθέος ἔστιν ἀκέστωρ·
τὸν γενεὴ μερόπων ἡ δυσαρεστοτάτη
καί τε μάλιστα φιλεῖ καὶ ἀπεχθαίρῃσι μάλιστα.
γνῶθι με· τίς τελέθω, ὃν τέκον, ὅς με τέκεν.

V H N Pz | Th.

---

1 cf. Greg.Naz., Carm. II.1 [559] 490 3 cf. Anthol. Gr. 1 44, 2 4–5 ὃς ... ἀργαλέοιο] cf. Hymn. Hom., In Cererem 310–311 5 cf. Prodr., Carm.hist. 46, 45

tit. ἕτεροι εἰς τὸ αὐτὸ τοῦ Προδρόμου Pz 1 ἡμετέρου] ὑμετέρου H N | θυγάτηρ] νεφέλην N 2 ἠέρι] ἔριδ Pz | ἀμπελάω V N Pz 4 γειναμένην V N | βροτοῖσι Pz 5 λοιμοῦ Pz (λιμοῦ corr. in marg.) 6 δυσσαρεστοτάτη H : δυσσαρεστοτάτην N 7 ἀπεχθαίρουσι N 8 τεκεῖν Th.

Riddle on the cloud

The heavenly daughter of my own son gave birth to me;
I am near the air that surrounds the earth.
I am also the one who carries my son in my womb,
but once I bring him forth, I perish; he is for mortals
5   the healer of troublesome and deadly famine.
The most peevish race of mortals
both loves and loathes him intensely.
Know me: who I am, whom I brought forth, who gave birth to me.

69 (H 161)
Ὑποθετικοὶ ἐπί τινι ἐκβρασθέντι τῆς θαλάσσης ἄχειρι νεκρῷ

Ξεῖνε, τί νῦν με δέδορκας ἐὸν περὶ ὄμμα πετάσσας;
οὐ πτολέμοιο βίη, οὐ φονόεσσα μάχη,
οὐδέ τ' Ἄρης βροτολοιγὸς ἐμὰς ἀπενόσφισε χεῖρας,
οἶδμα δέ μ' ἀτρυγέτου πέφνεν ἁλὸς μέλεον·
5 κύμασι γὰρ μαχόμην ἐϋσέλμου ἔνδοθι νηός,
νηὸς ὑγροσκελέος, νηὸς ἀελλομάχου·
ὑγρόβιον δὲ γένος καὶ εἰναλινήχυτος ἰχθὺς
ἀμετέρων χεράων ζεῦγος ἐθοινίσατο.
ἰχθὺς δαίνυται ἄνδρα, ἀνὴρ δ' ἀναδαίνυται ἰχθύν·
10 ἄμφω δαιτυμόνες, ὢ πόποι, ἀμφοτέρων.
ξεῖνε, σύ δ' ἄρ γενέταισιν ἐμοῖς ἐμὰ ῥήματ' ἔνισπε·
γουνοῦμαι καὶ ἄχειρ· λίσσομ' ἄναυδος ἐών.
δυστυχεῖς, παύσασθε τραπέζης ἰχθυοέσσης,
λείψαθ' ἁλιτρεφέα ζῷα θαλασσοπόρα,
15 μή ποτ' ἐμοὺς ἀπροόπτως θοινίζησθε φονῆας
καί με λάθητε τόκον δαινύμενοι σφέτερον·
μήτηρ θ', ἥ μ' ἐλόχευσας, ἕλοις πάλιν ἔνδοθι γαστρός,
ζωὸν γειναμένη, δεχνυμένη δὲ νέκυν.

V L Pz | Mi.

1 ὄμμα πετάσσας] cf. e.g. Roman. Mel. Cant. 40, 11, 8, IV p. 398; Canones Augusti, can. 5 (2), od. 9, trop. 2, 250, p. 70; Prodr., Carm.hist. 6, 53; 61, 12   4 cf. e.g. Hes., Theog. 131; Quint. Smyrn., Posthom. 7, 181; Nonn., Dion. 1, 112;   6 cf. Prodr., Carm.misc. 6, 12   15 cf. Nonn., Dion. 5, 443   17 Iob 1, 21; μήτηρ... ἐλόχευσας] cf. Anthol. Gr. App. 2 522, 1

3 τ'] π' L   4 μέλεον] βέλει Pz   5 ἐϋσέλμου] εὐσήμου Pz   8 ἐθοινήσατο L   9 δαίνυται scripsi : δαίννυται V L Pz | δαίννυν τ' post δαίννυται add. L | ἀναδαίνυται scripsi : ἀναδαίννυται V L Pz   11 γενέτησιν Pz   12 λίσομ' Pz   14 λείψασθ' Pz   15 θοινίζησθε scripsi : θοινίζεσθε V : θοινίζοισθε L : θοινίξοισθε Pz   16 δαινύμενοι V L (δαινύμενοι corr. Mi.) : δαινύμιοι Pz

Hypothetical verses about a dead body without hands washed up by the sea

Stranger, why are you now staring at me with your wide-eyed gaze?
Neither the violence of the war nor murderous battle,
nor Ares, the destroyer of men, snatched away my hands,
but a wave of the restlessly swirling sea struck me, the wretched one,
5   for I was battling the waves inside a well-benched ship,
a ship drenched to the gunwales, a ship fighting the storm;
the ocean-born race, the fish swimming in the salty brine
devoured both of my hands.
Fish feasts on man, man in turn feasts on fish.
10 Both of them, alas, eat the flesh of both.
But stranger, convey my words unto my parents;
I implore you, even without hands; I beseech you, although speechless.
Poor parents, refrain from the banquet full of fish,
forsake the creatures raised by the sea, swimming in the salty brine,
15 lest you eat my own murderers by mistake
and feast unaware on your own offspring:
because then, mother, you who bore me, you would take me again in your belly,
having brought me forth alive, you would receive me dead.

70 (H 162)
Στίχοι ὑποθετικοὶ εἰς Παυσανίαν ἀπολιθωθέντα διὰ τὸν θάνατον τοῦ υἱοῦ αὐτοῦ Πέτρου

Πέτρος ἔχω Πέτρον. Ἤρετο τίς· «τίνα;» οὐκ ἐπικεύσω.
 υἱέα Παυσανίου, ξεῖν᾽, ἑκατοντάλιθος,
Παυσανίας δὲ πατήρ, τρίτος πέτρος, οὕνεκα Πέτρου,
 οὐ γὰρ ἔπαυσ᾽ ἀνίην υἷιν ὑποστενάχων.

V L | Mi. Th.

1 οὐκ ἐπικεύσω] cf. Hom., Il. 5, 816; Od. 4, 350; Prodr., Carm.hist. 6, 149; 38, 23

3 οὕνεκα V L   4 ἀνίαν L | υἷιν] υἱὸν Mi. | ὑποστοναχέων L

71
Εἰς τὸ αὐτὸ

Ὅς Νιόβην πολύδακρυν, ἀμειψαμένην ἐπὶ πέτρην
 φύσιος ἐκ μερόπων, λάινον οὐ δέχεαι,
πέτρην τὰν δακρυχεύμονα τὰν μέγας αἰθέριος Ζεύς
 ἀθανάτῳ γλυφίδι στήσατο γλυψάμενος,
5 δέρκεο Παυσανίην πολυπενθέα οὕνεκα παιδὸς
 πέτρον· ἀτὰρ πετρίνην δέχνυσο καὶ Νιόβην.

V L | Mi. Th.

1 Νιόβην πολύδακρυν] Eust. Macremb., H&H 10, 10, 2.3   3 αἰθέριος Ζεύς] cf. Nonn., Dion. 18, 263; Mus. Grammat., Hero et Leander 8   5 παυσανίην πολυπενθέα] cf. Prodr., Carm.hist. 2, 70

1 ὅς] ὡς L 2 λώινον L   3 πέτρην, τάνον, δακρυχεύμονα τάνον μέγας αἰθέριος Ζεύς V Mi. Th.   5 πολυπονθέα L | οὕνεκα V L

Hypothetical verses about Pausanias petrified by the death of his son Peter

I, the burial stone, hold Peter. Someone asked: (Peter) whom? I won't hide it from you.
I, stranger, the tomb of one hundred stones, contain Pausanias' son,
while Pausanias the father becomes a third stone because of Peter,
for he did not put an end to his grief but utters a low moan for his son.

On the same

You who do not believe that the tearful Niobe
turned from a human into hard stone
—the weeping rock that the great heavenly Zeus erected,
having carved it with his immortal chisel—,
5 see here the mournful Pausanias who was turned into stone
for his son, and then accept that Niobe, too, was transformed into stone.

72
Εἰς τὸ αὐτὸ

Παυσανίην ἡ λύπη ἀπ' ἀνέρος ἔκφανε πέτρον
ἐς τόδε ἀνδρομέην φύσιν ἀμειψαμένη.
ἦ καὶ γηθοσύνη ἀπὸ πέτρου τέξεται ἄνδρα;
Οὒ ξένε· ῥᾳοτέρη φύσις ἔγεντο κακοῦ.

V L | Mi. Th.

2 ἀνδρομέαν L   **4** ἐγένετο L | κακοῦ] κεροῦ L

On the same

Grief turned Pausanias from man to stone
altering his human nature to this stone before you.
Or can joy bring forth man from stone?
No stranger! Harm transforms nature more easily.

73 (H 142)
Σχετλιαστικοὶ ἐπὶ τῇ ἀτιμίᾳ τοῦ λόγου

Ἔρρετ' ἐμοῦ βιότοιο ἀπόπροθεν, ἔρρετε βίβλοι.
ἔρρε πρόπαν μελέδημα παλαιγενέων ἀνθρώπων·
μηκέτ' ἐμοὶ πελάοις, ἄλλους δέ τε δίζεο φῶτας.
ἔρρετ' Ἀριστοτέλους πολυμήχανα δήνεα τέχνης,
5 θευλογίη τε Πλάτωνος, ἅπασά τε φιλοσοφίη,
Ἐμπεδοκλῆος ἄριστα μελήματα, Μοῦσαι Ὁμήρου,
Μοῦσαι Δημοκρίτοιο καὶ Ὀρφέος, ὃν τέκε πατὴρ
Ὕαγρος, οὐδ' ἄρα οἱ περὶ ᾄσμασιν ἄλλος ἐρίζοι.
οἴχεο ῥητροσύνη, ἐξοίχεο ὀρθογραφίη·
10 ἄλλα θ' ὅσα χθονίοισι λόγῳ ἐπὶ κῦδος ὀπάζει
ἔρρετε· ἄλλῳ ἔοιτε μεληδόνος ἄξια πολλῆς,
οὐκ ἐμοί. ἦ γὰρ ἐγὼ κενεὸν περὶ μόχθον ἀνέτλην,
ὕμμεσιν ἐμμογέων· τὸ δ' ἐτώσιος ἔπλετ' ὀϊζύς,
μαψίδιόν τε μέλημα καὶ ἀπάτη ἀφρονεόντων.

V P N | Th.

1 cf. Greg.Naz. Carm. II, 2.3 [1495] 211; Anthol. Gr. App. 3 255, 1 ; Prodr., Carm.hist. 77, 12–13; Tetrast. 165b, 1–2   2 παλαιγενέων ἀνθρώπων] cf. Hymn. Hom., In Cererem 113; Melet. Galesiot., Alphabetalphabeton 131, 24   4 πολυμήχανα δήνεα τέχνης] cf. Hom., Od. 10, 289; Oppian., Hal. 3, 1; Anthol. Gr. 1 10, 68; Prodr., Tetrast. 6b, 3; Prodr., Carm.hist. 42, 38; Euth. Torn., Carm 1 (ed. Papadopoulos-Kerameus) 53, (p. 190)   10 κῦδος ὀπάζει] cf. e.g. Hom., Il. 8, 141; Od. 3, 57; Greg.Naz., Carm. I, 1.26 [503] 61; I, 2.2 [609] 388; Anthol. Gr. App. 1 131, 4   13–14 cf. Prodr., Carm.hist. 38, 84

2 Ἔρρε, πρόπαν μελέδημα] ἔρρετε πάμπαν μελῴδημα N   4 δήνεα] μήχεα P   7 δημοκράτοιο N 8 ὕγρος N | ἐρίαν P : ἐρίσει N   11 πολλεῖς P   12 ἀνέτλην] ἔτλην P   13 ὕμμεσιν] om. N | τὸ] om. N

Verses of protest at seeing the disregard of learning

Begone from my life; away, my books!
Depart, all efforts of men born long ago!
Approach me no longer, but seek out other men.
Begone versatile wiles of Aristotle's craft,
5 Plato's theology, and all philosophy,
all those excellent things for which Empedocles cared, Muses of Homer,
Muses of Democritus and Orpheus, whom his father Oeagrus
begot, and whom no one can rival in singing.
Flee, rhetoric! Leave, orthography!
10 Together with all arts which, through speech, bring glory to mortals,
begone! May you be worthy of attention from another,
but not me. For, truly, I have suffered in vain
when working hard for you; it has become worthless woe,
futile concern, and a trick played on the foolish.

74

Ἔρρετ' ἐμοῦ βιότοιο ἀπόπροθεν, ἔρρετε βίβλοι.
θυμέ, σύ δ' ἐκ σοφίης μὲν ἀπέγρεο, οὐκ ἐθέλων περ·
μηδ' ἄρ' ἕκητι λόγοιο μέγ' ἄχνυσο· μὴ δέ σε λύπη
θυμοβόρος κρατείτω ἐναυομένη φίλα γυῖα.
5 ἀλλὰ βίβλων τε λόγων τε καὶ ἀτελέος μελεδῶνος
τηλοῦ ἀποσκεδάζευ· ἀτὰρ θυμέλῃσι μεθίζευ
καί τε γελωτοπόνοισι παρέζεο καί τε μίμοισι,
παῖζε δ' ἐν οὐ παικτοῖσι· τὰ γὰρ βροτοὶ ἴσασιν ἄρτι
τιμᾶν ἀφρονέοντες, ἄπιστα δὲ θεσμὰ λόγοιο.
10 εἰ δ' ἄρα μὴ θυμέλῃσι παρέμμεναι ἔσχες ἐέλδωρ,
ἧσο σιγῇ ἀκέων, πάτον ἀνθρώπων ἀλεείνων,
μηδ' ἀγορῇ μερόπων πωλέσκεο κυδιανείρῃ
καὶ τάχα δυσβόρους κόσμου προφύγῃς μελεδῶνας.
ἔρρετ' ἐμοῦ βιότοιο ἀπόπροθεν, ἔρρετε βίβλοι.

V P N | Th.

4-5 μὴ δέ...κρατείτω] cf. Sophoc., Oedip. Colon. 1207   4 ἐναυομένη...γυῖα] cf. e.g. Hom., Il. 13, 85; Od. 8, 233   7 παῖζε δ' ἐν οὐ παικτοῖσι] cf. e.g. Ioh. Chrys., Contra eos qui subintroductas habent virgine 7, 17 (p. 67); in ep. ad Rom. PG 60, 674; Theod. Stud., Epist. 477, 12; Mich.Psell., Theol. I 17, p. 69, 13; Mich. Glyc., Quaestiones in sacram scripturam II 59, 10, p. 133; Const.Manass., Breviar. Chron. 5008; Eust.Thessal., Comm. In Hom. Il. 16, 14 (III p. 797, 30-31)   9 ἄπιστα...λόγοιο] cf. Prodr., R&D 7, 333   10 ἔσχες ἐέλδωρ] cf. Prodr., Carm.hist. 3, 88; Tetrast. 162b, 4   11 πάτον...ἀλεείνων] cf. e.g. Hom., Il. 6, 202; Ioh.Tzetz., Epist. 19 p. 37, 2; Chil. 7, 868; Anacharsis 1325; Nic.Choniat., Histor. p. 645, 71   12 Hom., Il. 1, 490

---

2 ἀπέγρεο] ἀπείργεο P 3-7 om. N   4 ἐναγόμενη P   7 μίμοισιν P   8 παικτοῖσι] om. P | βροτὸν N   9 θερμὰ λογοίο N : θέσαν τὰ λόγοιο Th.   10 θυμέλῃσι in marg. P | παρέμμεναι ἔσχες] ἐνί ξεμεν ἔσχεν N   11 ἐλεείνων N   12 προφύγῃς μελεδῶνας] προσφύγῃσθα μερίμνας N

Begone from my life; away, my books!
My soul, rouse yourself from wisdom, even against your will.
Do not grieve much for the sake of learning! Nor let soul-consuming sorrow,
setting fire to your beloved limbs, gain control of you.
5   Instead, retreat far from books and discourses,
and never-ending suffering. Take a seat instead beside the stage,
and sit close to jesters and mimes,
amuse yourself with things that are not funny! For men have now learned
to honour such things, the fools, and the rules of learning have no say anymore.
10 But if you have no desire to be next to the stage,
then say nothing, and shun the path of men,
do not frequent the assemblies, where men win glory,
and perhaps you will avoid the exhausting sufferings of the world.
Begone from my life; away, my books!

75 (H 143)
Σχετλιαστικοὶ εἰς τὴν Πρόνοιαν

Οὐκ ἀγνοῶ μέν, δημιουργέ μου Λόγε,
ὡς ἀχανὴς ἄβυσσος ἐν σοὶ κριμάτων·
οὐ τὴν φυλακὴν Ἀμβακοὺμ παρατρέχω
σκοποῦντος ὡς ἴδοι τι καὶ πύθοιτό τι·
5 οὐ Παῦλον αὐτὸν ἀγνοῶ, τὸ σὸν στόμα,
«ὦ γνώσεως» λέγοντα «καὶ πλούτου βάθος».
πείθει με τιμᾶν τὴν Πρόνοιαν μυρία·
τοῦ παντὸς ἡ κίνησις ἡ τεταγμένη·
ἥλιος αὐτὸς τοῖς ἀνωτάτω δρόμοις
10 ἀντιτρέχων μέν, ἀλλὰ δὴ καὶ συντρέχων,
βρύων δὲ φῶς, μετρῶν δὲ τὸν πάντα χρόνον,
ὥρας δὲ τὰς τέτταρας εὐρύθμως τρέπων,
γεννῶν δὲ καὶ χειμῶνα καὶ τίκτων θέρος
καὶ τὰς ἐν ἀμφοῖν ἐμμέσους ποιῶν κράσεις,
15 λάμπων, ἀνίσχων ὡς γίγας ἐκ τῆς ἕω,
μεσουρανῶν ἔπειτα, τὴν δύσιν φθάνων,
δύνων, τρέχων, κάτωθεν ἀνίσχων πάλιν,
καὶ νύκτα τίκτων καὶ κύων τὴν ἡμέραν·
αὔξη σελήνης καὶ πολύτροπος φθίσις
20 τοῦ νυκτερινοῦ γλαυκοφεγγοῦς ἡλίου.
οἶδα Προνοίας ἔργα καὶ τὰ τῶν κάτω.
τοὺς γὰρ πρὸς αὐτῷ τῷ σεληναίῳ κύκλῳ
ἱστῶντας αὐτὴν μὴ δ' ἐπεισκυκλητέον.

V E I Lh | Gu. Ky. Mi.

1 cf. Christ.Mityl., Carm. 13, 1   2 Ps. 35, 7; Ps. Prodr., Carm.hist., Epitaphius in Alexium. 22
3-4 Hab. 2, 1   6 cf. Rom. 11, 33; Prodr., In Illud PG 133, 1301C–1302B

tit. τοῦ κυροῦ Θεοδώρου τοῦ Προδρόμου, στίχοι ἰαμβικοί, εἰς τὴν θείαν πρόνοιαν Lh   **2** ἀχανὴς] ἀφανὴς E | χρημάτων Gu.   **3** οὐ τὴν Lh] αὐτὴν V E I Gu. | Ἀββακοὺμ E I : Ἀβακοὺμ Lh   **4** ἴδοι τι] ἴδοιτο Lh | πείθοιτό Lh   **6** ὦ E   **7** πείθει με τιμᾶν] πείθη τι μὲν τὲ Lh   **8** ἡ κίνησις] συγκίνησις Lh   **9** αὐτοῖς Lh | ἀνωτάτης Lh   **10** om. Lh   **11** δὲ²] μὲν Lh | φάος Ky. | μετρῶν δὲ] καὶ μετρῶν I : μετρὸν τὸν Lh   **12** εὐρύθμως] εὐθύμως Lh | τρεπτῶν I : τρέχων Lh   **13** γενῶν Lh | καὶ] om. Lh   **14** ἐμμέσους] ἀμέσους E : ἐν μέσῳ I : ἀμέσους Lh   **15** εὐνίσχων Lh   **16** δ' post μεσουρανῶν add. Lh | δύσιν] φύσιν Lh   **19** αὔξει E : αὔξις Lh   **20** γλαυκοφαγγοῦς Lh   **22** πρὸς αὐτῷ] ἐπ' αὐτῷ Lh   **23** ἐπισκυκλητέων Lh : ἐπισκυλητέον Ky.

Verses of protest regarding Providence

    I am not unaware, my Creator, Word [of God],
    that the depth of your judgements is vast;
    nor do I neglect this guard-post of Habakkuk,
    who keeps watch to see and hear something;
5 nor am I unaware of Paul, your own mouth,
    who says 'O the depth of the riches and knowledge'.
    Numerous things persuade me to honour Providence:
    the orderly motion of the universe;
    the sun itself on its paths through the heavens,
10 sometimes running contrary to them, sometimes with them,
    pouring forth light and marking all of time,
    shifting the four seasons regularly,
    both begetting winter and bringing forth summer,
    and creating temperate conditions in both intermediate seasons,
15 shining, rising like a giant from the east,
    then reaching its peak and arriving in the west,
    setting, running, and rising again from below,
    both bringing forth night and conceiving day;
    the waxing of the moon and the manifold waning
20 of the night's sun gleaming white.
    I know that the works below the heavens are also those of Providence.
    For I won't bring in the discussion the viewpoints
    of those who attribute this foresight to the lunar cycle.

ἢ τίς γὰρ ἐστήριξε τὴν γῆν ἐν μέσῳ
25 ὕδωρ ὑπενθεὶς βάθρον ἀπείρῳ βάρει,
εἰ μὴ Προνοίας τῆς σοφῆς σοφὸς λόγος;
ἄγε βραχὺν κάχληκα ῥίψον εἰς ὕδωρ·
μὴ νήξεταί σοι κοῦφος ἀνάρρουν πλέων,
μὴ φεύξεταί σοι τοῦ βυθοῦ τὸν πυθμένα;
30 εἰ γοῦν ὁ κάχληξ ταῦτα, πῶς τὴν γῆν ὅλην
ὁρῶν ἐφ' ὑγρῶν ἀρρεπῶς ἱσταμένην
οὐκ ἐνθυμηθῶ τὴν Πρόνοιαν εὐθέως;
τίς πηγνύει μὲν εἰς νέφος τὴν ἀτμίδα
καὶ τοῦ νέφους τὴν πῆξιν εἰς ὄμβρον λύει;
35 τίς χιόνος δὲ τὰ πρόσωπα σεμνύνει
ἐκ λευκότητος ἐμφύτου ψιμμυθίου;
σφαιροῖ δὲ τὴν χάλαζαν ἐν τόρνῳ ξένῳ;
τρέφει δὲ τὴν ἄγρωστιν ὀρθρίᾳ δρόσῳ;
τίς ἀνέμους ἔταξε τοὺς εὐθυπνόους,
40 οἷς ἀντέταξε τοὺς ἀνακαμψιπνόους;
καὶ συνελών, τίς τὴν καθ' ἡμᾶς οὐσίαν
σοφῶς κυβερνᾷ τὴν πολυτροπωτάτην;
κἂν τὴν Ἐπικούρειον ἀδολεσχίαν
λέληθε ταῦτα, καίπερ οὐ λαθεῖν δέον.
45 εἰ γὰρ μία ναῦς, ἵππος εἷς φθορὰν πάθοι
χωρὶς χαλινῶν καὶ κυβερνήτου δίχα,
καὶ τὴν μὲν εἰσδέξαιτο πόντιος δράκων,
τὸν δὲ σφαλέντα θὴρ χαραδραῖος φάγοι·
πῶς ἂν ἀκυβέρνητον εἴποιμεν μένειν
50 τὸ κοσμικὸν πλήρωμα, τὴν πᾶσαν κτίσιν;
οὐκ ἀγνοῶ γοῦν, ὡς προείρηκα φθάσας,
ὡς κριμάτων ἄβυσσος ἐν σοί, Χριστέ μου·
πλὴν εἰς τὸ βάθος οὐ δυνάμενος βλέπειν
καὶ τοὺς ἑκάστου συννοεῖν κρυπτοὺς τρόπους

24-25 Gen. 1, 6 **27** cf. Prodr., Carm.hist. 6, 33 **38** cf. Nic.Eugen., D&C 5, 19 **39-40** cf. Ps. Arist., De Mundo 394b 35-36; Posidon., Fragm. 337a, 24; Ioh. Stob., Anthol. 1.40.1.227; Prodr., R&D 6, 208

---

25 ἐπενθεὶς E : ἐπιθεῖς Lh | βάθρον] βάρον Lh **28** κοῦφος om. E | ἀνάρουν Lh : ἀνὰ ῥοῦν Gu. | πλέον E **29** φεύξεταί] φθέγξεταί Gu. **30** γοῦν] γὰρ Lh **31** ἀρεπῶς Lh **32** εὐθυμηθῶ Μι. **34** τῶν νέφων Lh | τὴν] om. E **35** τὸ πρόσωπον Lh | σεμνύνει] μηνύει I **36** λευκότητος] γλαυκότητος Gu. **38** τρέφει] στρέφει Lh | ὀρθρίᾳ] ἐνθεία I **39** ἔταξεν Lh **40** ἀντέταξεν Lh **42** τὴν bis Lh **43** Ἐπικούριαν Lh : Ἐπικούριον Gu. | ἀδοσχίαν Lh **45** ναῦς] om. Μι. | φθορᾶς E | πάθῃ Lh **46** χαλινοῦ Lh **48** φάγει Lh **49** εἴποι μὴ Gu. **51** γοῦν] οὖν Gu. : μὲν Lh | προείρηκας Lh **52** κριμάτων] ἀφ[…] E **53** τό] στὸ Lh

For who supported the earth in the middle,
25 putting down water of boundless weight as a foundation beneath it,
if not the wise word of ingenious Providence?
Take a small pebble, throw it into the water:
shall it not swim for you, lightly floating on the tide,
shall it not escape sinking to the bottom of the deep water?
30 If these things happen to a pebble,
how would I not instantly think of Providence
when I see the entire earth standing unshakeably upon the waters?
Who freezes vapour into a cloud
and melts the solidity of the cloud into rain?
35 Who glorifies the countenance of snow
with the natural whiteness of its pigment?
Who rounds the hail with a wondrous lathe?
Who nurtures the grass with the morning dew?
Who marshals the straight-blowing winds
40 and sets against them the gyrating winds?
In summary, who governs with wisdom
our most variable nature?
Even if these things escaped the notice of
the Epicurean prattler, it should not have been so.
45 A ship would be lost without a pilot,
a horse would be ruined without its reins,
the one would be swallowed by a monster of the sea,
while the beast of the cliff would devour the stumbling horse.
How then could we say that the fullness of the universe,
50 all of creation, remains without a helmsman?
As I said earlier, I am not unaware
that there is an abyss of judgements within you, my Christ.
But since I am not able to peer into its depths
and understand the hidden ways of each event,

55 πρὸς τοὺς κυλίνδρους ἄχθομαι τῶν πραγμάτων
καὶ δυσχεραίνω τὰς νεμήσεις τῶν βίων.
ἢ πῶς ὁ τέκτων, ὁ κναφεύς, ὁ λατόμος,
ὁ βυρσοδέψης, ὁ σκυτεύς, ὁ γηπόνος,
ὁ λοιπὸς ὄχλος τῆς βαναυσίδος τύχης,
60 σοφῶν μὲν ἀνδρῶν, τοῖν γενοῖν δὲ κοσμίων,
ὡς δεσπότης ἄρξειεν οἰκετιδίων,
καὶ νῦν μὲν ἐντρίψειεν αὐτοῖς κονδύλους,
νῦν δ' ἐξ ἁμάξης ὑβριοῖ, τὸ τοῦ λόγου;
καί τις μὲν ὀψόπωλιν αὐχῶν μητέρα
65 ἢ γοῦν ὀπωρόπωλιν ἢ καπηλίδα
καὶ πατρὸς υἱὸς τυγχάνων ἀνωνύμου
τυχὸν ξύλων ἄρχοντος ἢ ξύλων πράτου
ἢ τῶν ὅσα πρίαιο καὶ τριωβόλου·
ἀγροῖκος ἀνὴρ καὶ προσήκων βλαυτίῳ,
70 σκαπανέως πρόσωπον αἴσχιστον φέρων,
ἄιδρις εἰς πᾶν τῶν καλῶν καὶ τιμίων,
καὶ μὴ δ' ὅπως κνήσαιτο γινώσκειν ἔχων,
πιεῖν διδαχθεὶς καὶ μεθυσθῆναι μόνον
ἢ καὶ φαγέσθαι τῶν σελευκίδων πλέον,
75 μαθήσεως δὲ μὴ δὲ κρούσας τὴν θύραν
ὀδοῦσι κείρων τῆς ὑπήνης τὸ πλέον,
ἐν τῷ λαλεῖν δὲ σιέλων χέων πίθους·
ἐκεῖνος οὗτος εὐπορεῖ μὲν ἀργύρου,
ὅλας δὲ πλίνθους ἐνδέδυται χρυσίου,
80 κτίζει δὲ λαμπρὰς οἰκίας χρυσοστέγους,
ἵππων δὲ γαύρων ἀγέλας ὅλας τρέφει
ἐκ θετταλῆς γῆς καὶ πέδων Ἀρραβίας,
χρυσοῖς δὲ τούτους ἐνστολίζει φαλάροις,

---

55 cf. Anacharsis 707–709   57–59 cf. Haplouch., Dram. 67–69   64 cf. Haplouch., Dram. 69   75 cf. Prodrom., in eos qui ob paupertatem providentiae conviciantur PG 133, 1294A   77 cf. Haplouch., Dram. 71   80 cf. Prodr., Carm.hist. 30, 395

---

55 κυλίνδους Gu. | ἔχθομαι Lh   57 κναφὲς Lh   59 βαναύσιος Lh | τύχης] τέχνης Lh   60 τῶν γενῶν Gu. | κοσμίων] τιμίων Lh   61 οἰκέτει δίων Lh   62 αὐτῷ | κονδύλοις Lh   66 τυγχάνων] ὑπάρχων Lh   67 τυχῶν Lh | ξύλων¹] ξύλον Lh | ἄρχοντος I | ξύλων πράτου] ξυλοπράτου Lh   68 τριοβόλου I   69 προσῆκον Gu. | βλατίων Lh   70 σκαμπανέως Lh | αἴσχιστον] ἔχθιστον E Lh | 71 καλλῶν Lh | τε post καλῶν add. E   74 Σελευκίων Lh   75–76 om. Gu.   75 τὴν θύραν om. I | δὲ²] om. I   77 χέων] λαλεῖν I : χρεῶν Lh   78 εὐπορεῖν Lh | ἀργύρους Lh   79 ὅλους E   80 οἰκείας Lh   81 γαυρῶν Gu. Mi. | τρέφῃ Lh   82 Ἀραβίας Lh   83 ἐνστολίζει] ἔχει ἐνστολίζει Lh

55 I grieve for the turn of affairs
and am furious at the distribution of lives.
How can the carpenter, the fuller, the stonecutter,
the tanner, the cobbler, the farmer,
the remaining throng of vulgar craftsmen
60 rule over wise men, noble in their lineage,
just as a master commands his servants,
now giving them thrashings,
now insulting them coarsely, to use the common phrase?
And someone boasts that his mother is a grocer
65 or a fruitmonger or a tavern-keeper,
and that he is the son of an anonymous father,
perhaps of a 'prince of logs' or a timber-merchant,
or of such lumber as you would buy for a three-obol piece;
an utter bumpkin in his shoes,
70 bearing the most shameful visage of a digger,
ignorant in every way of anything good and honourable,
he does not even know how to scratch himself,
he only has learned to guzzle drink and become inebriated,
or to devour even more food than the Seleucids.
75 He never knocked on the door of learning,
he cuts his abundant beard with his teeth,
when he talks, he spews out jars of saliva;
such a man has plenty of silver,
he dons entire ingots of gold,
80 builds splendid houses with roofs out of gold,
nurtures entire flocks of splendid horses
from the region of Thessaly and the land of Arabia;
he adorns them with golden ornaments,

προέρχεται δὲ τῆς λεωφόρου μέσον
85 ὑπὸ προπομποῖς ἀρχικῶς ἐσταλμένος
καὶ προσκυνεῖται καὶ θεοῦ τιμὴν ἔχει.
ἄλλος δὲ σεμνός, εὐγενὴς τῶν ἐξ ἔω,
καλὸς μὲν εἶδος, καλλίων δὲ τὸν βίον,
λόγων μαθητὴς καὶ διδάσκαλος λόγων
90 πανημέριος ἐνσχολάζων ταῖς βίβλοις
παίδευσιν ἀσκῶν καὶ τρυφῶν τὸ μανθάνειν,
ἀνέστιος πρόεισιν, ἄθλιος, πένης,
μὴ δὲ τρύφους γοῦν εὐπορῶν πιτυρίου·
τῆς ἀρετῆς δὲ φίλος ὢν καὶ τῶν λόγων,
95 οὐδὲ βραχείας εὐτυχεῖ τιμῆς μέρος,
τωθάζεται δὲ καὶ διώκεται πλέον·
τί μὴ τὸ πάντων δυσθεώτερον λέγω;
οὐ γὰρ ἀποχρῶν τοῖς κακοῖς πλουτεῖν μόνον
ἐν πᾶσιν ἄλλοις τοῖς δοκοῦσι τιμίοις,
100 ἀλλὰ προαρπάζουσι καὶ τὰ βιβλία,
ὡς κτῆσιν ἀργήν, ὢ μεγίστης ζημίας·
καὶ λωποδυτεῖ τοὺς λόγους τὸ χρυσίον.
ὤ μοι, πόσους ἔρρευσα δακρύων πίθους
ἰδὼν σοφοὺς μὲν ἐν μέσῳ συνεδρίῳ
105 λαλοῦντας ὀρθὰ καὶ περιφρονουμένους,
παράφρονας δὲ πλουσίους τιμωμένους.
ληρεῖ Μέλητος, καὶ διδάσκει Σωκράτης·
καὶ ζῇ Μέλητος, καὶ τελευτᾷ Σωκράτης.
ὁ συκοφάντης ἐκδιδράσκει τὰς δίκας,
110 οἱ δ' ἕνδεκα κρίνουσι τοὺς ἐλευθέρους·
καὶ τρίβεται μὲν φάρμακον τῷ γεννάδᾳ,
ὁ δ' Ἄνυτος πέφευγε τὴν τιμωρίαν.
Χριστὸν πένης ἔλεξε, δυσσεβῶς λέγει·
πλούσιος Ἀντίχριστον, εὐσεβῶς λέγει.

84-85 cf. Haplouch., Dram. 73-74; Ptochoprodr. 4, 305; Ioh. Tzetz., Epist. 14 p. 26, 21-22 et 67 p. 97, 16-17   **87** cf. Haplouch., Dram. 76: εὐγενὴς … ἔω] Iob 1, 3   **92** cf. Haplouch., Dram. 77   **93** cf. Prodr., Carm.misc. 76, 272; Prodr., R&D 3, 422   **100** Euth. Torn., Carm. 4 (ed. Hörandner) 42; cf. Haplouch., Dram. 78-79   **108-112** cf. Nic.Eugen., Mon. in Theod. Prodr. p. 456, 13-14

85 προπομπῶν Lh : προπομπῆς Ky.   **86** ἔχει] φέρει Lh   **87** ἐξέω Lh | λόγου μαθητὴς post ἐξ ἔω add. Lh   **88** ab καλὸς μὲν εἶδος text om. Lh   **91** τὸ] τῷ I   **94** τοῦ λόγου I | v. 90 post v. 94 iterum add. V   **97** τὸ] τῶν Ls   **98** κακοῖς] καινοῖς Gu. : κοινοῖς Mi.   **101** κτίσιν I   **102** λωποδυτοῖ Gu.   **104** ἰδὼν μὲν σοφοὺς V   **105** ὀρθοὺς E   **107** Μέλιτος V Gu. | διδάσκει] τελευτᾷ Σωκράτης I   **108** om. I | Μέλιτος V Gu.   **110** Οἱ δ'] οἰδ' Gu. | ἕνδεκα] ἐνδία E   **112** Ἄννυτος E   **114** legi non potest in I

and proceeds down the middle of the thoroughfare,
85 escorted by attendants like a prince,
and he receives obeisance, and is honoured like a god.
But another one, however, is modest, of noble eastern stock,
honourable in appearance, but much more honourable in his mode of living,
both student of orations and teacher of orations,
90 spending all his time with books,
labouring at his education and revelling in learning;
he is homeless, wretched, poor,
and does not even have a hunk of bran bread;
for though he is fond both of virtue and learning,
95 he does not even obtain a share of meagre honour,
and he is mostly mocked and persecuted.
Why should I not speak about the most hateful thing?
It is not enough for the wicked alone to grow rich
among all others who are honourable,
100 but they even snatch the books away,
like worthless possessions—O greatest loss!
Gold even plunders learning.
Alas, how many jars of tears I wept
when I saw wise men in the midst of the council
105 scorned for speaking rightly,
while wealthy madmen were honoured.
Meletus blathers and Socrates enlightens,
but Meletus continues to live, while Socrates loses his life.
The accuser escapes the punishment,
110 while the eleven sentence free citizens.
The venomous hemlock is ground for Socrates, the noble one,
while Anytus escapes punishment.
The poor speaks of Christ—he talks impiously;
The rich of the Antichrist—he talks piously.

115 ἐπάγχομαι πρὸς ταῦτα· μισῶν τὸν βίον,
θέλω θανεῖν, ἥλιον οὐ θέλω βλέπειν.
ἐντεῦθεν εἰσήγαγεν ἄλλος τὴν τύχην,
τὸ δ' αὐτόματον ἄλλος, Ἑλλήνων δύο·
ἄμφω δὲ κοινῶς τὴν ἀκυβερνησίαν.
120 ἐντεῦθεν ἠγνόησαν οἱ τότε χρόνοι
καὶ τῆς Προνοίας χρῆμα τῆς σοφωτάτης.
ἐντεῦθεν ἡ ξύμφυλος ἀνθρώπων φύσις
ἔγνω διασπασθεῖσα πρὸς μέρη δύο
καὶ κλήσεων ἄδικος ἐγράφη νόμος
125 τὸ πλάσμα τέμνων εἰς τομὰς ἀσυμφύλους·
καὶ τὸν μὲν ὠνόμασε δοῦλον ἡ τύχη,
τὸν δὲ προσεκλήρωσε τοῖς ἐλευθέροις.
ἀρχηγὲ κακῶν, χρυσέ, γῆς τυφλὸν τέκνον,
ὡς ἀπόλοιο καὶ παρέλθοις ἐκ μέσου,
130 τὸ στασιῶδες χρῆμα καὶ κοσμοφθόρον.
ἀλλ' ἐν κενοῖς μοι ταῦτα πρὸς τὸ χρυσίον·
τί γὰρ πεπαρῴνηκεν ἄψυχος φύσις;
ὡς ἀπόλοιτο τῶν βροτῶν ἡ φαυλότης,
οἳ τοὺς καλοὺς κρίνουσιν ἐξ εὐτυχίας
135 καὶ τοὺς κακοὺς τοὔμπαλιν ἐξ ἀτυχίας.
ὦ τάλανες πένητες, ἄθλιον γένος,
πλούτου μετ' αὐτοῦ καὶ σὺν αὐτῷ χρυσίῳ
τῆς ἀρετῆς τὴν δόξαν ἀφῃρημένοι·
ὅμως ὁ κόσμος ἀγαθὸν πῶς ἂν δράσῃ
140 «ἐν τῷ πονηρῷ κείμενος»; λέγει Λόγος.
ὦ μοι πόσον δάκρυον ἐξ Ἡρακλείτου,
πόσος γέλως δὲ πάλιν ἐκ Δημοκρίτου·
ὁ μὲν κατοικτίσαιτο τὸν μωρὸν βίον,
οὗτος δὲ μωκήσαιτο τοὺς ἀβελτέρους.
145 ὄντων γὰρ τούτων ἐξ ἑκατέρου τρόπου
χρὴ σφᾶς ἑαυτοὺς καὶ γελᾶν καὶ δακρύειν.

115-116 cf. Nic.Eugen., D&C 6, 105 **122** cf. Prodr., Carm.hist. 40, 19 **128** cf. Ps. Phoc., Sententiae 44; Etymol. Magnum 321, 45 s.v. ἕκητι; Ps. Zonar., Lexicon χ 1842, 2; Prodr., Tetrast. 23b, 4; Haplouch., Dram.110 **140** cf. Ioh. 5, 19

115 Ἐπάγχομαι] ὑπεύχομαι E **116** θέλων βλέπῃ E **118** Τὸ δ'] τόδ' Gu. **121** καὶ] τὸ E | τῆς σοφωτάτης legi non potest in I **122** ξύμφιλος Gu. **125** ἀσυμφίλους Gu. **127** τὸν δὲ in lacuna E **130** τὸ in lacuna E **133** ἀπόλοιο E I Gu. | τῆς βροτῆς E **142** γέλως δὲ] δὲ γέλου E **143** ὁ] τὸ E Gu. **145** ὄντων γὰρ τούτων] ὄντως γὰρ ὄντως I Gu.

115 I struggle with these things, I scorn life,
I want to die, I no longer wish to look upon the sun.
That is why one man introduced fortune,
and another one coincidence, both of them Hellenes;
both alike assert there is no governance.
120 Those times were unaware
of the existence of Providence, supreme in wisdom.
That is why human nature, from the same stock,
understood itself to be split into two parts,
and the unjust custom of name-calling was introduced,
125 which divides mankind into two incompatible parts,
with Fortune calling the one 'slave',
and categorizing the other as 'free man'.
Gold, first cause of evil, blind child of earth,
may you perish and pass from our midst,
130 seditious and world-destroying wealth.
But these imprecations against gold are in vain for me.
How could inanimate nature be so abusive?
The evil of those humans should be destroyed,
who judge men good because of their good fortune
135 and bad, conversely, because of their misfortune.
O wretched poor, miserable race,
together with this wealth and gold,
you are deprived of virtue's glory;
but how could the world act well
140 'if it lies in evil', to quote the Word.
Alas, what tears from Heraclitus,
but also what laughter from Democritus!
The former would lament the foolish life,
the latter would mock the stupid men.
145 Since there are both types of people,
they should laugh and weep about themselves.

ἐμοὶ δὲ τίς χρήσειε σαλπίζον στόμα,
ἀγχίστροφον δὲ γλῶσσαν εἰς λόγου πλάτος
καὶ πρὸς κορυφὴν Παρνασοῦ στήσας ἄκραν,
150 ὡς ἐξ ἀπόπτου τὴν βοὴν διευρύνω,
εἰπεῖν παράσχοι ταῦτα πρὸς τοὺς πλουσίους;
οἱ χρυσολάτραι ποῖ πλανᾶσθε πλούσιοι;
οἵαν δὲ καὶ στέλλεσθε, δείλαιοι, τρίβον;
ὁ πλοῦτος ὕλη γῆς ῥέουσα συντόμως,
155 ἧς οἱ κακοὶ φέρουσι πάντως τὸ πλέον.
τί κακίους γίνεσθε πλουτοῦντες πλέον;
εὕρημα κυνὸς ἡ σεβαστὴ πορφύρα·
ὁ μάργαρος κύημα φαῦλον ὀστρέου·
λίθοι τὸ σύμπαν, οἱ χλοάζοντες λίθοι·
160 ὁ λαμπρὸς οἶκος ἐκ τιτάνου καὶ ξύλων,
ὀπτῶν τε πλίνθων καὶ λίθων ἐξεσμένων,
γῆς τίτανος, γῆς ξύλα, γῆς πάντες λίθοι·
τὴν γῆν δὲ τιμῶν καὶ σέβων οὐκ αἰσχύνῃ;
εἶεν· τί ταῦτ' ἔλεξας, ἄγριον στόμα;
165 σίγα, σίγα, δείλαιον· οὐκ ὀρθῶς λέγεις.
τῶν κριμάτων γὰρ τοῦ Θεοῦ τὸν πυθμένα
ἐξιχνιάζειν οὐδὲ Παῦλος ἰσχύει.

147 cf. Ex. 19, 16/19; Anacharsis 754   161 cf. Prodr., Melet. 41

159 χνοάζοντες Gu.   161 τε] om. E   162 τῆς τίτανος γῆς, ξύλα γῆς, πάντες λίθοι Mi.   164 ἔλεξας] ἔδοξας E

Who would furnish me with a mouth like a trumpet,
a quick tongue capable of profound speech,
and putting me on the highest peak of Parnassus,
150 so that I might unleash my cry from a distant vantage point,
allow me to speak these things to the wealthy?
Why are you, rich men, worshippers of gold, deceived?
Why do you, wretched fellows, set out on such a path?
Wealth is an earthly material vanishing in an instant,
155 which the wicked certainly possess all the more.
Why do you become even more villainous the richer you get?
The venerable purple is a dog's discovery,
the pearl is a shameful offspring of the oyster,
all are stones, pale stones.
160 The splendid house of gypsum and wood,
of baked bricks and carved stones;
gypsum is from the earth, wood is from the earth, all stones are from the earth.
Are you not ashamed to honour and revere the earth?
So be it; why did you say these things, savage mouth?
165 Hush, hush, wretched one! You are not speaking properly,
for not even Paul is able to search out
the depth of God's judgements.

76 (H 153)
Ἐπὶ ἀποδήμῳ τῇ Φιλίᾳ

Ξένος. Ὦ Φιλία δέσποινα, πάντιμον κάρα,
ποῦ καὶ πόθεν; καὶ ταῦτα μεστὴ δακρύων,
στυγνή, κατηφής, τὴν κόμην ἐσκυλμένη,
κύπτουσα πρὸς γῆν, ὠχριῶσα τὴν χρόαν,
5 χιτώνιον πενθῆρες ἠμφιεσμένη,
ἀτημελὴς τὸ ζῶσμα καὶ τὸ βλαυτίον,
καὶ τὴν κακίστην ἀλλαγὴν ἠλλαγμένη·
ὁ δὲ στολισμὸς ὁ πρίν, ἡ δὲ πορφύρα,
ἡ δ' εὐπρέπεια καὶ τὸ τοῦ χείλους ῥόδον,
10 ὁ δὲ πλόκαμος, ἡ δὲ τῆς ζώνης χάρις,
αἱ δ' ἀρβυλίδες, ἡ δὲ λοιπὴ σεμνότης,
ᾤχοντο πάντα πρὸς τὸ μηδὲν ἀθρόα.
καὶ νῦν γυναιξὶν ἐμφερὴς θρηνητρίαις,
στυγνὴ βαδίζεις· ἀλλὰ ποῦ δὴ καὶ πόθεν;
15 **Φιλία.** γῆθεν πρὸς αὐτὸν τὸν Θεὸν καὶ Πατέρα.
Ξ. ἔρημος οὖν ὁ Κόσμος ἐστὶ φιλίας;
Φ. ἔρημος, ὃς τοσοῦτον ἐξύβριζέ με.
Ξ. ὕβριζε; **Φ.** καὶ θύραθεν ἐξέρριπτέ με.
Ξ. θύραθεν; **Φ.** ὥστε καὶ νομισθῆναι θανεῖν.
20 **Ξ.** εἶτ' ἐξέκεισο; **Φ.** καὶ μεμαστιγωμένη.
Ξ. μελαγχολᾶν τὸν Κόσμον ἄντικρυς λέγεις,
οὕτω μανικῶς ἐμπαροινήσαντά σοι;
Φ. τί δ' ἂν τὰ λοιπὰ τῶν ἐμῶν παθῶν μάθῃς;

V N | Gu. Dü. Ge. Ky. Mi.

2 ποῦ καὶ πόθεν] Plat., Phaedr. 227a; Prodr., R&D 2, 156; Catomyom. 327   2–3 μεστὴ...κατηφής] Lucian., Fugit. 3, 2–3   3 τὴν...ἐσκυλμένη] cf. Anthol. Gr. 5 259, 3   4 κύπτουσα...γῆν] cf. Prodr., R&D 7, 340; ὠχριῶσα...χρόαν] cf. Anthol. Gr. 5 259, 4;   5 χιτώνιον πενθῆρες] cf. e.g. Greg. Nyss., De sancto Theodoro p. 68, 21; Ioh. Chrys., De sancto Melet. PG 50, 519; Roman. Mel., Cant. 17, 12, 1, 11 p. 284 Grosdidier; Ioh. Zonar., Epitome Histor. II 445, 1   7 cf. Nic. Eugen., Epit. in Theod. Prodr. p. 222, 1   9 τὸ...ῥόδον] cf. Prodr., R&D 6, 293   13 cf. e.g. Ioh. Chrys., Fr. in Jer. PG 64, 856D; Const.Manass., Breviar. Chron. 5259; Man. Philes, Carm. [ed. Martini] 92, 87

tit. τοῦ κύρου Θεοδώρου Προδρόμου ἐπὶ ἀποδήμῳ τῇ φιλίᾳ. Ξένος καὶ Φιλία Gu.   2 ποῦ] ποῖ Dü. Ge. : ποῦ καὶ legi non potest in N   5 χυτώνιον Gu. (χιτώνιον corr. Ky.)   14 ποῦ] ποῖ Dü. Ge.   21 ἄντικρυς Gu. Dü.   23 ab Τί δ' ἂν text. om. N

On Friendship's departure

Stranger. O Friendship, most honourable lady,
where are you going and whence? And, moreover, filled with tears,
sullen, dejected, with dishevelled hair,
bent earthward, with pale skin,
5   clad in a mourning garment,
with shabby girdle and slippers,
and with form most terribly altered.
The former clothing, the purple,
the beauty and the blush of your lips,
10 the locks, the grace of the girdle,
the boots, all the other majesty of your appearance,
all of them have suddenly come to naught.
And now you resemble women in mourning,
you walk glumly along; but where are you going and whence?
15 **Friendship.** I am departing the earth, to God the Father.
Str. Then is the World bereft of Friendship?
Fr. Indeed abandoned, for he insulted me so much.
Str. Did he insult you? **Fr.** He even threw me out the door!
Str. Out the door? **Fr.** So that people even think I am dead.
20 **Str.** And then you were left outside? **Fr.** And indeed scourged!
Str. Are you saying that the World has gone totally mad,
treating you so abusively like a drunk?
Fr. What if you hear my other sufferings?

ὅσους παρ' αὐτοῦ κονδύλους ἐνετρίβην,
25 ὕβρεις ὅσας ὑπεῖχον <...> ὅσας.
νῦν μὲν κατ' ἀμφοῖν πυγμαχοῦντος ταῖν γνάθοιν,
νῦν δ' ἐνθοροῦντος λὰξ κατ' αὐτῆς γαστέρος.
ἐῶ τὰ λοιπὰ καὶ τὰ μείζονα, Ξένε·
ἦ γὰρ μαθὼν ἤλγησας ἂν τὴν καρδίαν.
30 **Ξ.** μὴ μὴ πρὸς αὐτοῦ τοῦ πατρός σου, Φιλία,
μηδὲν σιγήσῃς, ἀλλά μοι τὸ πᾶν φάθι.
Φ. οὐκοῦν καθιζήσαντες ἀμφὶ τὴν πίτυν,
—ὁρᾷς τὸ δένδρον ὡς καλόν τε καὶ μέγα;—
τὸ πᾶν ἐπεξέλθωμεν ἤδη τοῦ λόγου.
35 **Ξ.** ἰδοὺ καθιζήκαμεν· ἄρξαι τοῦ λέγειν.
Φ. ἐγὼ τὰ πρῶτα τῷ Θεῷ, τῇ Τριάδι
ἀεὶ σύνειμι καθαρῶς ἡνωμένη·
ἐν τοῖς ἀσωμάτοις δὲ δευτέρως νόοις
καὶ ταῖς τρισὶ τριάσι ταῖς ἄνω μένω,
40 οἷον Χερουβὶμ καὶ Σεραφὶμ καὶ Θρόνοις
καὶ ταῖς προλοίποις ἀΰλοις στραταρχίαις.
ἐγὼ γὰρ αὐταῖς καὶ πρὸς αὐτὰς τὴν σχέσιν
καὶ πρὸς τὸ θεῖον καὶ πρὸς ἀλλήλας νέμω·
καὶ τὰς τοσαύτας τῶν ἄνω μυριάδας
45 εἰς ἓν συνάπτω καὶ μίαν σειρὰν πλέκω.
ἑωσφόρος μόνος με πρὶν ἀπεστράφη,
κἀκ τῶν ἀφ' ὕψους ἀντύγων κατεστράφη.
οὕτως μέν, οὕτως ἡ νοουμένη κτίσις
ἐμοὶ κρατεῖται καὶ μένει φρουρουμένη.
50 τὴν γὰρ θεατὴν καὶ κατ' αἴσθησιν φύσιν,
τὸ κοσμικὸν πλήρωμα, τὴν κάτω κτίσιν,
τίς ἀμφιβάλλει μὴ κρατεῖσθαι Φιλίᾳ;
ὁ φλήναφος γὰρ Ἐμπεδοκλῆς ἐρρέτω
τὸ νεῖκος εἰπὼν δημιουργὸν τῶν κάτω.

24 cf. e.g. Plutarch., Alc. 8.1, 3; Brut. 9.3, 1; Diog. Laert., Vitae philosophorum 6, 41, 251; Lucian., Prom. 10, 9; Phot.Lexic.ε 1049, p. 105; Prodr., Amarantus 71, 13; Gregor. Antioch., Or. 3, 234–35 (p. 642)   **27** ἐνθοροῦντος λάξ] cf. Hom., Od. 17, 233   **29** cf. Prodr., Catomyom. 364   **33** cf. Plat., Phaedr. 229a 8; Achil.Tat., L&C 1, 16, 2.1   **34** Aesch., Prometh. 870   **40** cf. Prodr., Carm. hist. 19, 74   **45** καὶ...πλέκω] Hom., Il. 8, 19; 23, 115   **47** Prodr., R&D 1, 279; Carm.hist. 74, 92   **51** cf. Prodr., Carm.misc. 75, 50

24-25] om. Gu. Dü. Ge. Ky.   **25** ὑπεῖχον scripsi : ὑπῆχον V   **29** ᾗ Dü.   **30** Μὴ] μὰ Gu. Ge. (μὴ corr. Dü.) Ky   **38** ἀσωμάτως Gu. | δευτέροις Gu.   **40** οἷον Gu. | θρόνις Gu. (θρόνοις corr. Ky.)   **41** ἀΰλαις Gu.   **42** γὰρ] μὲν Gu. Ge.   **47** κακτῶν Gu. (κἀκ τῶν corr. Ky.)

All the beatings I endured at his hands,
25 all the insults, all the <…> I suffered.
One moment he is striking both my jaws,
the next he kicks me in the belly.
I will pass over the rest, and the even graver things, Stranger;
for if you learned of it, you would grieve in your heart.
30 **Str.** No, no, Friendship, in the name of your father,
do not keep silent, but tell me everything.
Fr. Well, if we sit by this pine tree
—do you see how beautiful and tall it is?—
I will rehearse the entire story.
35 **Str.** Here, we're settled! Begin your tale!
Fr. First, I always exist with God,
purely united with the Holy Trinity.
Second, I dwell among the incorporeal intelligences
and the three heavenly Triads:
40 these are the Cherubim and Seraphim and the Thrones,
and all the other immaterial orders of intelligences;
For I give them their relationship to those orders
and to the divine nature and to one another
and I join the innumerable myriads of celestial beings
45 into one, and I weave them into a single chain.
In days past only Lucifer rejected me,
and he was cast down from the vault of heaven.
In this way, the immaterial creation
is maintained and guarded by me.
50 The visible and perceptible nature,
the universal perfection, the earthly creation,
who questions that it is maintained by Friendship?
Away with the windbag Empedocles,
who says that strife is the creator of the world.

274 TEXT AND TRANSLATION

55 τί γὰρ νοήσει καὶ συναίσθεται τίνος
ἄνθρωπος οὐ γνοὺς ὡς τὸ πῦρ καίει φύσει,
ἀλλ' εἰς πυρὸς κρατῆρας ἐμπεσὼν μέσους;
ἢ τίς τὸν εὐρὺν οὐρανὸν καὶ τὸν μέγαν,
ἄκαμπτον ὄντα τὸ πρὶν εὐθυωρίαν,
60 εἰ χρὴ πιθέσθαι τοῖς λόγοις τοῦ φαμένου,
ἔκαμψεν εἰς τὴν σφαῖραν, εἰ μὴ Φιλία;
οἷον γὰρ εἰπεῖν ὡς καλοῦ καὶ κοσμίου
ἐρῶν ἑαυτοῦ πρὸς κύκλον συνεστράφη
ἑαυτὸν αὐτῷ φιλιῶν πανταχόθεν
65 καὶ πάντα πᾶσι συμπερισφίγγων μέρη.
ἐγὼ τὰ κύκλα τῶν ἀπείρων ἀστέρων,
ἁπλῶς ἁπάντων, ἁπλανῶν, πλανωμένων
ἔταξα δεσμῷ καὶ συναφῇ πανσόφῳ.
ἐγὼ φιλιῶ τῷ σεληναίῳ κύκλῳ
70 τὸν ἡλιακὸν δίσκον, ὃς τὸ φῶς βρύει,
καὶ φιλιῶ τοσοῦτον ὡς καὶ λαμπάδας
κιχρᾶν ἐκείνῳ τοῦτον εἰς νυκτῶν σέλας.
ἐγὼ τὸ πᾶν πλήρωμα τοῦ παντὸς βίου
πλοκῇ ξυνεστὼς φύσεων ἐναντίων
75 καινῶς ἑνίζω, κἂν διίστηται φύσει.
ξηρὸν τὸ πῦρ, ὑγρόν δε χύσις ἀέρος
καὶ γειτονοῦσι ταῦτα καὶ μέσον μάχη·
ἀλλ' ἐμβαλοῦσα τοῖν δυοῖν ἐναντίοιν
κοινὸν τὸ θερμόν, τὴν μάχην ἀνατρέπω.
80 θερμὸν μὲν ἀήρ, ἀλλ' ὕδωρ ψυχρὸν φύσει,
ἀγχιθυρεῖ δὲ καὶ κατ' ἀλλήλων πνέει,
ἀλλ' ἡ μεσιτεύουσα τούτοις ὑγρότης
ἄμφω ξυνάπτει καὶ πρὸς εἰρήνην φέρει.
ὕδωρ μὲν ὑγρόν, ἡ δὲ γῆ τοὐναντίον,

---

69 τῷ...κύκλῳ] cf. Prodr., Carm.misc. 75, 22   **70** τὸν...δίσκον] cf. Prodr., Tetrast. 5a, 2

55 συναίσθηται Dü.   **56** φύσει καίει Gu.   **59** εὐθυωρίᾳ Dü.   **60** εἰ χρή] ἀρχῇ Gu. : χρὴ γὰρ Dü.   **61** εἰμὴ Gu.   **70** δύσκον V   **74** ξυνεστὸς Ge. (ξυνεστὼς corr. Dü.)   **75** καινῶς] κοινῶς Dü. Ge. | διίσταται Gu.   **79** κοινὸν] καινὸν Gu. : καινῶς Ky.   **82** ἡ μεσιτεύουσα] ὑμέσι τένουσα Gu. (ἡ μεσιτεύουσα corr. Ky.) Ge. (ὑμέσι ἐνοῦσα corr. Dü.) | ὑγρότην Gu. (ὑγρότης corr. Ky.) Ge. (ὑγρότης corr. Dü.)   **83** ξυνάπτου Ge. (ξυνάπτει corr. Dü.)

55 Because what could he understand, what could he grasp,
   this man who did not know that fire burns by nature,
   but fell into the centre of a fiery crater?
   And the wide and vast sky,
   which was before an unbending straight course,
60 —if we should believe the person who spoke these words—
   who formed it into a sphere, if not Friendship?
   As if, so to say, [the sky] desired beauty and order
   and was therefore bent into a sphere
   reconciling with itself on all sides,
65 squeezing all its parts together at the same time.
   I ordered the cycles of the stars,
   of all of them, both the fixed and the wandering ones,
   according to a most wise bond and union.
   I reconcile the solar disc, which pours forth light,
70 with the lunar circle,
   and I reconcile them to such a degree
   that the sun lends the moon its light to shine at night.
   The full complement of all life
   brought together in an intertwining of opposite natures,
75 I unite marvellously though it stands apart by nature.
   The fire is dry, the stream of air moist;
   although they are close neighbours yet there is contest between them.
   However, by putting heat, common to both,
   between the two opposing elements, I put an end to the battle.
80 Air is hot, but water is cold by nature;
   they stand close at hand and blow against each other,
   but the moisture between these two elements
   unites them both and brings them to peace.
   Water is moist, but the earth exactly the opposite;

85 μέση δ' ἐν ἀμφοῖν ἐμπεσοῦσα ψυχρότης
φίλιον αὐτοῖς ἐμβραβεύει τὸν βίον.
τοιαῦτα τὰ στοιχεῖα τοῦ παντὸς βίου.
τὰς τέτταρας δὲ τοῦ γίγαντος ἡλίου
τροπὰς τίνος φαίημεν; οὐχὶ Φιλίας;
90 χειμὼν γὰρ εὐθὺς οὐ τέτραπται πρὸς θέρος
τῶν ποιοτήτων σφῶν ἐναντιουμένων,
ἀλλ' εἰς ἔαρ μετῆλθεν, εἶτα πρὸς θέρος·
καὶ τοῦ θέρους ἡ κρᾶσις, οὐκ εἰς τὸ κρύος,
ἀλλ' εἰς μέσον τὲ τῶν ὀπωρῶν τὴν φθίσιν.
95 κἀντεῦθεν ὥσπερ ἐξ ἁπαλῶν παρθένων
συνεμπλεκουσῶν τὰς κρόκας καὶ τοὺς μίτους,
—ὥρας δὲ ταύτας γνῶθί μοι τὰς παρθένους—
καλὴ τελεῖται τῶν ἐτῶν ἱστουργία.
ἐγὼ συνιστῶ τὸν βροτήσιον βίον·
100 εὐρωστία καὶ κάλλος ἄμφω Φιλίας,
ἄμφω Φιλίας ἔργα· πῶς ζητεῖς; μάθε·
ἂν ἡ τετρακτὺς τῶν χυμῶν σχῇ φιλίαν,
καλῶς ἔχει τὸ σῶμα, καὶ μακρὰν νόσοι.
εἰ τῶν μελῶν δ' εὔρυθμος ἐστὶν ἡ σχέσις,
105 ἔχει δὲ καὶ σύστοιχον ἀλληλουχίαν,
ἐνδύεται δὲ καὶ χρόαν εὐχρουστέραν·
κάλλος καλεῖται τοῦτο τοῖς παλαιτέροις.
ἡ γοῦν ὑγεία καὶ τὸ κάλλος Φιλίας.
ἐγὼ πολίζω τὰς πόλεις, ἡ Φιλία,
110 κἂν εἰ πόλεις λέγοι τις αὐτὰς τὰς πόλεις,
κἂν αὐτὸ μᾶλλον τῶν πολιτῶν τὸ στῖφος.
πλίνθοι γὰρ ὀπταὶ καὶ λίθων ξεστῶν βάρη
ἐμοὶ ξυνῆλθον εἰς ἑνὸς τοίχου κτίσιν·
δυὰς δὲ τοίχων ἀμφὶ γωνίαν μίαν
115 καὶ γωνίαι τέσσαρες εἰς πλήρη δόμον.
ἐγὼ συνιστῶ τὰς παρ' ἀνθρώποις τέχνας
καὶ τῷ σκυτεῖ μὲν φιλιῶ τὸν κναφέα
τῷ χαλινεργάτῃ δὲ τὸν στρατηλάτην
καὶ τῷ γεωργῷ τὸν βάναυσον συνδέω

104-105 cf. Prodr., R&D 1, 43   112 cf. Prodr., Oper. (Cramer III) p. 217, 25

94 τὲ] τὶ Gu.   96 συνεμπλεκουσῶν scripsi : συνπλοκουσῶν V : τῶν συμπλεκουσῶν Gu.
112 γὰρ] γοῦν Gu. Ge. (γὰρ corr. Dü.)

85 the moderate chill falling on them both
endows them with an intimate coexistence.
Such are the elements of all life.
Whose should we say are the four seasons
of the giant sun? Do they not belong to Friendship?
90 Winter is not turned immediately into summer
because of their opposite qualities,
but it turns into spring, then into summer.
The climate of summer does not turn immediately into icy cold,
but into the in-between season and the withering of fruits.
95 In this way, as if made by tender maidens
interweaving the warp and the theft
—know that for me these are the chaste seasons—,
the texture of time is well accomplished.
I bring human life into being;
100 both strength and beauty derive from Friendship,
both are works of Friendship. Do you ask how? Learn this:
if all four humours are in friendly harmony,
the body will be healthy and diseases kept at bay.
If the arrangement of the limbs is well-proportioned
105 and has balanced consistency,
it endows the skin with a healthy complexion.
This is called beauty by the ancients.
So well-being and beauty come from Friendship.
I, Friendship, build cities,
110 whether one calls 'cities' the cities themselves
or rather the citizens assembled therein.
For the fire-baked bricks and the loads of hewn stones
were assembled by me for the construction of a single wall.
A pair of walls forms a single corner,
115 and four corners a complete house.
I bring together human crafts,
and I make the fuller a friend of the cobbler,
the commander of the bridle-maker,
and I unite the artisan with the farmer

120 καὶ τεχνίτην ἅπαντα παντὶ τεχνίτῃ·
χρῄζει γὰρ ὄντως ἁλιεὺς πᾶς γηπόνου,
διδοὺς γὰρ ἰχθὺν ἄρτον ἀντιλαμβάνει·
καὶ γηπόνος πᾶς αὖθις ἀσπαλιέως
καὶ παντὸς ἅπας ἐνδεὴς ὁ τεχνίτης·
125 κἀντεῦθεν εὖ πάσχουσιν αἱ πᾶσαι πόλεις.
ἐγὼ γάμου σύμπαντος ἡ νυμφοστόλος.
ἐγὼ τὸ θῆλυ πρὸς τὸν ἄρρενα τρέπω.
ἐγὼ τὸν ἄνδρα πρὸς τὸ θῆλυ συντρέπω.
τίς γὰρ μύραιναν, τὴν θαλασσίαν ὄφιν,
130 τὸ πόντιον πέπεικεν ἐκλιπεῖν βάθος,
ἀναδραμεῖν δὲ τῆς θαλάσσης τὴν ῥάχιν,
ἐπιδραμεῖν δὲ καὶ τὸ χερσαῖον πέδον,
ὡς ἂν συναφθῇ καὶ συνέλθῃ πρὸς γάμον·
ἡ ποντικὴ θὴρ τῷ γεηρῷ <θη>ρίῳ;
135 τίς τοῦ σιδήρου τὴν ἅπασαν οὐσίαν
δούλην καθιστᾷ τῆς μαγνήτιδος λίθου;
οὐδέν τι πάντως ἄλλο Φιλίας δίχα.
ἐμοὶ τὸ πᾶν ζῇ καὶ κρατεῖται καὶ μένει.
εἴπω τὸ μεῖζον καὶ σιγάτω πᾶς λόγος.
140 ἐγὼ Θεὸν τὸν ὄντα τὸν παντεργάτην,
τὸ Πατρὸς ἐκσφράγισμα, τὸν μέγαν Λόγον,
τὸ παμφαὲς φῶς, τὴν ὑπέρθεον φύσιν,
τὸν ἄχρονον νοῦν, τὴν χρονουργὸν οὐσίαν,
ἐλθεῖν ἔπεισα μέχρι γῆς καὶ τῶν κάτω
145 καὶ τὴν παθητὴν προσλαβεῖν ὅλην φύσιν
καὶ σωματικὴν ἐνδυθῆναι πορφύραν
ἐκ παρθενικῶν αἱμάτων ὑφασμένην,
παθεῖν, θανεῖν, φεῦ, τῆς τοσαύτης ἀγάπης,
δι' ἧς τοσοῦτον ἔργον —ὦ φίλτρου ξένου.

120-125 Arist., Pol. 1291a1 **127-128** cf. etiam Prodr., Carm.hist. 43c, 16; Eust. Macremb., H&H 10, 3, 2.10-14; Const. Manass., A&K 1, 21a; Nic. Eugen., D&C 4, 139-142; Libistrus & Rhodamne 173-175 **129-134** Achil.Tat., L&C 1, 18, 3-5; Const.Manas., A&K 21a; Libistrus & Rhodamne 179-181 **131** cf. Prodr., R&D 5, 450 **135-136** Achil.Tat. L&C 1, 17, 2; cf. etiam Prodr., Carm. hist. 43c, 17; Nic.Eugen., D&C 4, 137-138; Const.Manas., A&K M 21a **141** πατρὸς ἐκσφράγισμα] cf. Prodr., Carm.hist. 50, 19 **142** τὸ παμφαὲς φῶς] cf. Prodr., Carm.hist. 63, 1 **146-147** cf. Man. Philes, Carm. (Braounou-Pietsch) 23, 15-16

124] om. V | post 124 διδοὺς γὰρ ἄρτον, ἰχθὺν ἀντιλαμβάνει add. Gu. **125** πόλεις πᾶσαι Gu. **129** τί γὰρ Gu. **130** τὸ] καὶ Gu. **133-134**] om Gu. **134** <θη>ρίῳ supplevi **137** τι] τοὶ Gu. **138** κρατεῖται] καρατεῖται Gu. (κρατεῖται corr. Ky.)

120 and every craftsman with every craftsman.
For every fisherman truly needs the farmer,
for he gives fish and receives bread in return;
and every farmer in turn needs the angler,
and every craftsman depends on all craftsmen;
125 and hence, all cities fare well.
I escort the bride at every wedding.
I turn the female to the male.
I also turn the man to the woman.
For who persuaded the eel, snake of the sea,
130 to abandon the marine depths,
traverse the sea surface
and run over the dry land
in order to be united and joined in marriage;
the creature of the sea with the creature of earth?
135 Who makes the very nature of iron
a slave to the magnet?
None other than Friendship.
Everything lives, is maintained and endures through me.
I will say what is the greatest thing, and then let all speech cease.
140 The true God, creator of all,
image of the Father, the great Word,
brightest of lights, supremely divine nature,
timeless mind, essence which creates time:
I persuaded him to come down to earth and the creation below
145 and to take on all passible nature
and to don the fleshly purple
woven from virginal blood,
to suffer, to die, alas, for so much love,
such a great deed because of this love—O what extraordinary affection!

150 δι' ὃ χρονικῶς μείγνυται τῷ σαρκίῳ,
ὁ κυριεύων καὶ χρόνου καὶ σαρκίου,
καὶ συνανιστᾷ τὴν πεσοῦσαν εἰκόνα
ἐν τῷ καθ' αὑτὸν ἀναχωνεύσας πάθει.
τοιαῦτα τἀμὰ πρὸς βροτοὺς ἔργα, Ξένε·
155 τοιαῦτά μου τὰ δῶρα τὰ πρὸς τὸν Βίον·
ἀλλ' εἰς νεκροὺς τὰ μῦρα τῆς παροιμίας,
ἀλλ' εἰς ὄνους ἡ λύρα τοὺς κανθηλίους.
ἐλάνθανον γὰρ ἀχαρίστῳ δραπέτῃ,
ὅλην ἐμαυτὴν ἐκδιδοῦσα τῷ Βίῳ,
160 ὃς τὴν ἐμὴν μὲν ἀθετεῖ συνουσίαν·
δείλαιος ἀνδρῶν εἰς δ' ἀγεννῆ μαχλάδα,
Ἔχθραν καλοῦσι, τὴν ἀτάσθαλον ῥέπει.
τῆς δουλίδος γὰρ Μωρίας ξυνεργίᾳ
αὐτὴν μὲν ἐντὸς εἰσάγει τῆς οἰκίας,
165 ἡμᾶς δὲ τύπτων ἐξάγει. νόμοι, νόμοι·
καὶ τοὺς ἀθέσμους οὐδὲ κἂν κλέπτῃ γάμους,
ἀλλ' ἀναφανδὸν ἐκτελεῖ τὴν αἰσχύνην,
καίτοι πρὸ πάντων ἀγνοῶ, νὴ τὴν Θέμιν.
τί φλαῦρον ἡμῖν, ὥστε λῦσαι τὸν γάμον;
170 τί δ' ἀγαθὸν πρόσεστι τῇ μοιχαλίδι,
ὥστε πρὸς αὐτὴν ἀντενέγκαι τὸν πόθον;
εἰ γάρ με ταύτῃ συγκρίνειν βούλοιτό τις,
ὀκνῶ τὰ κομψὰ μέμψιν εὐλαβουμένη.
ἐγὼ μὲν εἰμὶ χαροπός, χρηστὰ βλέπω
175 καὶ μειδιῶ τὰ πλεῖστα καὶ χάριν πνέω·
κἂν δεῖ λαλεῖν, ἐνταῦθα γλυκύτης ὅση·
κἂν δεῖ γελᾶν, ἐνταῦθα σεμνότης ὅση.
ἐν συμπλοκαῖς σὺ μανθάνεις τοὺς δακτύλους,
ἐν τοῖς βαδισμοῖς τοὺς πόδας δ' οὐκ ἂν μάθῃς;

---

152 cf. Canones Iulii, can. 35, od. 8, trop. 4, 243–244, p. 468; Canones Decembris, can. 5, od. 8, trop. 7, 368, p. 73   153 Gen. 1, 26   158–159 Anth. Gr. 10 87, 1   161 εἰς δ' ἀγεννῆ μαχλάδα] cf. Prodr., Carm. contra anum adulteram 89   168 νὴ τὴν Θέμιν] cf. Prodr., R&D 8, 94

150 μίγνυται V Gu.   156 παροιμίας in marg. scrib. V   158 δραπέτην Mi.   161 δ'] om. Gu.   165 ἡμᾶς τύπτων ἐξάγει. Ὢ νόμοι, νόμοι Gu. (ἡμᾶς δὲ τύπτων ἐξάγει. Νόμοι, νόμοι corr. Dü.)   168 ἀγνοῶν καὶ τὴν θέμιν Gu.   178 σὺ] οὐ Dü.   179 μάθοις Dü.

150 For this He mingled with flesh in time,
He who is Lord both of time and of the flesh,
and makes the fallen image rise,
recasting it through his suffering in his own image.
Such are my deeds for mortals, Stranger;
155 such are my gifts to the world;
but they are as perfumes for the dead, as the maxim goes,
as the lyre to the witless ass.
For I did not realize that I devoted myself
to that ungrateful runaway, the World,
160 who rejects my company.
The wretched man prefers a low-born whore,
whom men call Animosity, the wicked one.
With the help of the slave-girl Folly
he brings her into the house
165 and throws me out with blows. O laws, laws!
He does not even conceal the unlawful unions,
but consummates this shame before the eyes of all,
though I don't know anything, I swear it.
What did I do wrong, for him to dissolve our union?
170 Which virtue does the adulteress have,
that he transferred his desire to her?
For if someone wants to compare me with her,
I hesitate to name my merits because I fear reproach.
I have flashing eyes, I look propitious
175 and I mostly smile, and I exhale grace;
and if I have to speak, then with so much sweetness;
and if I have to laugh, then with so much dignity.
In weaving, do you not come to know your fingers?
By walking, do you not learn to know your feet?

180 κἂν νῦν πλακοῦντες, νῦν δ' ἅλες τρέφωσί με,
οὐ τοὺς πλακοῦντας προκρίνω τῶν ἀλάτων.
ἐν τοῖς ἀγαθοῖς τῶν πέλας γοργὸν βλέπω,
πάσχω δὲ πρὸς τὸ φαῦλον ἀμβλυωπίαν.
ἐναντίας πέφευγα κακίας δύο,
185 τὴν ὑπόκρισιν, τόν τε πέρπερον τρόπον.
ἐμοῦ μὲν οὖν τοσαῦτα, τῆς δ' Ἔχθρας τίνα;
φόνιον ὄμμα, χεῖρες ἡματωμέναι,
ὕπωχρος ὄψις, ἐκτετηγμέναι γνάθοι,
φωνὴ τραχεῖα, βάρβαρος δὲ τὸ πλέον,
190 ἄσεμνος ὕβρις, ἅλμα, κραυγή, θροῦς ὅσος.
τίς οὖν φρονῶν ἄνθρωπος, εἰπέ μοι, Ξένε,
τοιάνδ' ἀφεὶς ἕλοιτο τοιάνδε βλέπειν
Βάκχην ἀτεχνῶς ἀγρίαν καὶ μαχλάδα;
ἀλλ' ὁ τρισανόητος ἄθλιος Βίος
195 τοιαῦτα τολμᾷ καὶ τόσην ἀδικίαν.
ἐγὼ δὲ καὶ τοσαῦτα παθοῦσα, Ξένε,
ὅμως φιλῶ μου τὸν ξυνευνέτην πάλιν.
πῶς γὰρ δυναίμην μὴ φιλεῖν ἡ Φιλία;
ἀλλ' «ἐν κενοῖς» εἴποι τις ἴσως «ὦ γύναι,
200 κακηγορεῖς τὸν ἄνδρα καὶ πόρρω λόγου.
δέον κακῶς γὰρ τὴν θεράπαιναν λέγειν,
ἥ τίς ποτ' ἐστίν, ἣν ἔφης σὺ Μωρίαν,
αὕτη γὰρ αὐτὸν εἰς τὸ μύσος ἕλκύει·
σύ δ' ἀλλ' ἐκείνην ἐξάγεις τῆς εὐθύνης,
205 πνέεις δὲ πῦρ ἄντικρυς ἀμφὶ τὸν Βίον.»
εἰ ταῦτά τις πρόθοιτο πιθανῶς τάχα,
ἀντιπροθοίμην ταῦτα πιθανωτέρως·
ἐφ' ᾧ γὰρ ἡμῶν μὴ κλύων τῶν γνησίων
ὅλας παρέσχεν ἀκοὰς τῇ δουλίδι,

---

193 cf. Nonn., Dion. 46, 124   205 πνέεις δὲ πῦρ] cf. Prodr., Carm.misc. 53, 1

180 ἅλες] ἅλυς V   182 τῶν] τὸν Gu.   183 πάσχω δὲ πρὸς φαῦλον τε ἀμβλυωπίαν Gu. Ge. (πάσχω δὲ πρὸς φαῦλον τιν' ἀμβλυωπίαν φαῦλον corr. Dü.)   184 ἐναρτίας Ge.   187 ὄμμα] αἷμα Gu.   190 κραυγὴ] κραγὴ Gu. (κραυγὴ corr. Ky.)   194 ὁ τρισανόητος] ὁ τρισάνοικτος καὶ Gu. (ὁ τρισανόητος corr. Ky.) Ge. (οὖν ὁ τρισάνοικτος corr. Dü.)   202 ἥτις Dü.   203 μῖσος Gu.

180 And if have sometimes cakes and sometimes savouries to eat,
I do not value cakes above savouries.
I notice at once the good which is close,
but I am dim-sighted towards what is bad.
I have fled from two hostile evils:
185 hypocrisy and an arrogance.
Such are my merits; but what are those of Animosity?
A murderous eye, blood-stained hands,
sallow visage, wasted cheeks,
a rough voice, the most barbarous one,
190 indecent insolence, jumping around, screaming, so much noise.
So what sensible man, Stranger, tell me,
passing over all these things would truly prefer to look upon
such a savage Bacchante and whore?
And yet the thrice-mad and wretched World
195 dares such things and such great injustice.
Having suffered such torments, Stranger,
nevertheless I will always love my spouse.
For how could I, Friendship, not love?
But perhaps someone will say: 'Oh woman,
200 you slander your spouse in vain and for no good reason.
For you should blame the slave-girl
—or whoever this is—whom you call Folly,
for she drags him towards that filth.
However, you absolve her of any accusation
205 and instead you breathe fire against the World.'
If someone were to say such words in a persuasive manner,
I would oppose them more persuasively with these:
Instead of listening to me, his true companion,
he was all ears for the slave-girl,

210 καίτοι μαθὼν τὸ δοῦλον ἐχθρὸν δεσπόταις.
πλὴν ἀλλὰ καὶ πῶς τῆς λυσιγάμου γάμος;
ἢ πῶς Φιλίας μὴ παρούσης τῷ γάμῳ
ἔσται τὸ κοινώνημα τῆς συνουσίας;
βλέπεις φρενῖτιν ἣν νοσεῖ, βλέπεις μέθην,
215 ὁρᾷς μανικὴν ἐκτροπήν, ὁρᾷς νόσον;
οὐδ' αὐτὸ γοῦν ἔγνωκεν ὡς Ἔχθρας φύσις
οὐκ οἶδε δεσμεῖν, ἀλλὰ τοὺς δεσμοὺς λύειν.
ὅπως δὲ σαφῶς τοῖς καθ' ἡμᾶς ἐντύχῃς,
κἀκ τῶν θύραθεν τὸν λόγον πιστωτέον.
220 ἡ μὲν γὰρ ἐμπίπτουσα καὶ πρὸς τὴν φύσιν,
αὐτὴν ἑαυτῇ φιλονεικεῖν κορθύει.
τὸν Ἐτεοκλῆ καὶ Πολυνείκη βλέπε·
Ἔχθρας γὰρ ἀμφοῖν ἐγχορευσάσης μέσον,
ἑκάτερος τέθνηκεν ἐξ ἑκατέρου.
225 ἐγὼ δὲ συνδέουσα τοὺς ἀλλοτρίους,
κρείττους καθιστῶ συγγενῶν ὁμογνίων.
ὁ γὰρ Ὀρέστης καὶ Πυλάδης οἱ φίλοι
ἐμοὶ κατεπράξαντο τοὺς τόσους ἄθλους.
ἀκήκοας, βέλτιστε, τῆς τραγῳδίας,
230 ἐντεῦθεν ἀντάκουε τῆς ῥαψῳδίας.
ἕως μὲν Ἔχθρα τὴν σπάθην Ἀχιλλέως
θήγει κατ' αὐτοῦ τοῦ Μυκηναίου ξίφους,
ὁ Πριάμου παῖς πυρφόρος πρὸς τὸν στόλον
τῆς θετταλικῆς ἠρεμούσης ἀσπίδος·
235 κόλον δὲ τὸ πρὶν μακρὸν εἰς χεῖρας δόρυ
Αἴαντι τῷ γίγαντι τῷ πελωρίῳ.
ἐπὰν δ' ἐγὼ λάβοιμι τὸν τοῦ Πηλέως,
ἄλλως ῥιφέντος τοῦ κύβου τοῦ τῆς μάχης,
ὁ χθὲς διώκων εἰς φυγὴν νῶτα κλίνει,
240 καὶ νεκρὸς Ἕκτωρ ὁ στροβῶν τὴν Ἑλλάδα
τὴν μίτραν οἰκτρῶς ἐν ποδοῖν ἐζωσμένος,
ἱππηλατῶν δείλαιον ἱππηλασίαν,
χαίτας ἐκείνας τὰς καλὰς καὶ κοσμίας

---

210 cf. Hermog., Corpus Rhetor. III, 4, 11–12 (p. 21)   **214** cf. Nic.Eugen., D&C 4, 217 et 5, 97   **234** Hom., Il. 18, 478–608   **235-236** Hom., Il. 16, 116–117

213 κοινόνημα Gu. (κοινώνημα corr. Ky.)   **231** σπάτην Gu. (σπάθην corr. Ky.)   **241** μήτραν Ge. (μίτραν corr. Dü.) Gu. (μίτραν corr. Ky.) | ἐκ ποδοῖν Gu.

210 though he should know that 'servants are hostile to their masters'.
But how is marriage possible with the one who dissolves the union?
Or how is the communion of union possible
without Friendship being present in the marriage?
Do you see the madness which afflicts him? Do you see the drunkenness?
215 Do you see the raving perversion? Do you see the disease?
He does not even realize that the nature of Animosity
does not know how to create bonds but only to dissolve them.
As you may encounter in our own tradition,
can be proved true from pagan texts as well.
220 For she, by attacking nature,
stirs nature up to contend with herself.
Behold Eteocles and Polyneices!
When Animosity danced in their midst,
each fell at the other's hand.
225 But I, uniting those who are strangers,
form a stronger bond between them than members of the same family.
For the friends Orestes and Pylades
performed such labours for me.
My dear friend, you heard the tragedy;
230 now then pay heed to the epic in turn.
While Animosity whets the blade of Achilles
against the very same Mycenaean sword,
the son of Priam sets the fleet on fire,
while the Thessalian shield remained at rest;
235 and the once-long spear is blunt
in the hands of the great giant Ajax.
But when I received the son of Peleus,
the dice of battle rolled in another way.
He who, the day before, was in pursuit, turned his back and fled,
240 and Hector who tormented Greece was dead,
girded pitilessly with a belt around his feet,
a charioteer in a terrible chariot race,
dragging that beautiful and lovely hair of his,

καὶ τὸν καλὸν βόστρυχον εἰς κόνιν σύρων
245 καὶ τὸ τρόπαιον τοῖς Ἀχαιοῖς ὡς μέγα.
οὕτω διεστήκαμεν ἀλλήλων, Ξένε,
καὶ βελτίων τίς; σοὶ δίδωμι τὴν κρίσιν.
ἀλλ' οὐχ' ὁ Βίος ταῦτα, τὴν δ' Ἔχθραν λαβών,
ἐμὲ ξένην ἔδειξε καὶ τῆς ἑστίας.
250 ἐγὼ μὲν οὖν ἄνειμι πρὸς τὸν Πατέρα,
ἡ δ' Ἔχθρα λοιπὸν ἐγχορευέτω κάτω
καὶ παιζέτω τὰ τέκνα ταύτης εἰς μέσον.
βούλῃ μαθεῖν τὰ τέκνα τῆς Ἔχθρας τίνα;
υἱοὶ Φθόνος, Λόχος τε καὶ τρίτος Φόνος,
255 θυγατέρες δὲ Κακία, Μῆνις, Μάχη.
αὕτη μὲν οὖν, ὡς εἶπον, αὐτοῖς τοῖς τέκνοις
παρρησιαζέσθωσαν ἀμφὶ τὸν Βίον.
ἐγὼ δὲ λοιπὸν πρὸς τὸν αἰθέρα τρέχω·
οἶκτος δὲ πᾶς καὶ πᾶσα φιλανθρωπία
260 καὶ ζῆλος ἔμφρων καὶ καλῶν πάντων ἔρως·
ὁρᾷς ὅπως ἅπαντα συμφεύγουσί μοι;
Ξ. καὶ ταῦτα μέν, δέσποινα Φιλία, βλέπω·
συνεννοῶ δὲ καὶ τὸ μέλλον οὗ δράμῃ
καὶ δακρύω μὲν τῆς ἀβουλίας χάριν
265 τὸν οἰκτρὸν ὄντως καὶ ταλαίπωρον Βίον,
σὲ δ' ἄξια δρᾶν, ὧνπερ ἀνέτλης, κρίνω.
πλὴν ἀλλ' ἰδού σε ποτνιῶμαι δακρύων,
πρὸς τοῦ τεκόντος ἀπαθῶς πρὸ τῶν χρόνων,
πρὸς τῶν ἀΰλων οὐσιῶν σύνελθέ μοι,
270 τὴν καλύβην εἴσελθε, τὴν στέγην μάθε,
ἀπορρόφησον φιάλης νηφαλίου
καὶ τοῦ τρύφους γεύθητι τοῦ πιτυρίου
καὶ τῆς ἴδης μέτασχε καὶ τῶν ἁλάτων.
Φ. μὴ τοῦτο μή, μὴ τοῦτο, μὴ τοῦτο, Ξένε.

244 Nonn., Dion. 46, 276 **258** πρὸς...τρέχω] cf. Anthol. Gr.16 380, 2; Man. Philes., Carm., cod. Florent., 107, 3 (I p. 295) **272** cf. Prodr., Carm.misc. 75, 93 **273** cf. R&D 2, 51; 2, 92; 9, 62

256 αὐτῆς τοῖς τέκνοις Gu. (αὐτοῖς τοῖς τέκνοις corr. Ky. et Dü.) **266** ἀνέτλης] ἂν ἔτλης Ge. (ἀνέτλης corr. Dü.) **268** ἀπαθῶν πρὸς Gu. : ἀπαιτῶν, πρὸς Dü. Ge.|χρόνων] θρόνων Dü. **272** πιτυρίου] ποτηρίου Gu. **273** τῆς ἴδης] τοῦ ἤδους Gu. Ge. (τοῦ γ' ἔδους corr. Dü.) Ky. **274** μὴ] μοῖ Gu.

those fine curls, through the dust
245 like a great trophy for the Achaeans.
Such is the difference between us, Stranger,
and who is better? I let you judge!
But the World cared not for these things; seizing Animosity
he made me a stranger and threw me from the house.
250 Therefore while I ascend to the father,
let Animosity dance around below
and her children frolic in the middle.
Do you want to learn who are the children of Animosity?
Her sons are Envy, Ambush, and the third, Murder;
255 her daughters are Vice, Wrath, Battle.
Let her, as I said, together with her children,
speak and act boldly around the World.
So I fly high to heaven;
all pity, all kindness,
260 just ambition, and love for all that is good:
do you see how all these things flee along with me?
Str. Of course I see these things, lady Friendship!
I understand the future before him,
and I mourn his lack of wisdom,
265 the truly miserable and wretched World,
while I think that you acted properly given the sufferings you endured.
But here I beseech you loudly with tears
by the One who fathered you without suffering before all time,
by the immaterial beings, please come with me
270 enter my hut, become familiar with my chamber,
drink from the sober goblet,
taste of the hunk of coarse bread,
and share salt and firewood with me.
Fr. No, no, not this, Stranger!

275 ἅλις γὰρ ὧν πέπονθα τῷ πρόσθεν χρόνῳ.
τί πλειόνων δεῖ; τῶν παρελθόντων ἅλις.
Ξ. δίκαια φῇς, δέσποινα, καὶ καλῶς λέγεις·
οἷς γὰρ πέπονθας καὶ τὰ μέλλοντα κρίνεις.
ὅρκῳ δ' ἐγώ σοι πιστοποιῶ τὸν λόγον.
280 οὐδὲν γὰρ ἂν δράσω σε τῶν ἐναντίων,
οὐκ αἰσχυνῶ τὸ φίλτρον, οὐ τὴν ἀγάπην,
οὐχί, πρὸς αὐτῶν, ὧν ἔφης, φρικτῶν λόγων.
Φ. δύναιο δ' ἄν μοι ταῦτα προσφέρειν ἔδνα,
εἴ σοι παράσχω τοῦ γάμου τὰς ἐγγύας;
285 Ξ. τὰ ποῖα; λέξον ὡς ἐγὼ παράσχομαι.
Φ. χαίρειν ἐπ' ἄλλων ἀγαθοῖς ἔξεστί σοι;
Ξ. ἔξεστιν. Φ. ἐν λύπαις δὲ λυπεῖσθαι νόθοις;
Ξ. μάλιστα. Φ. τὰς στρεβλὰς δὲ φεύγειν διπλόας;
λαλεῖν δὲ ταῦτα καὶ φρονεῖν ἐν καρδίᾳ;
290 Ξ. καὶ τοῦτο πάντως. ἄλλο λοιπὸν πυνθάνου.
Φ. ἔχειν τὰ σαυτοῦ τῶν φίλων ἐν δευτέρῳ;
Ξ. ἔχειν. Φ. Δι' αὐτοὺς καὶ θανατᾶν πολλάκις;
Ξ. ναὶ καὶ θανατᾶν. Φ. καὶ φθονοῦσι μὴ φθονεῖν;
Ξ. ναί. Φ. τοὺς δὲ βασκαίνοντας ἀγαπᾶν; Ξ. πάνυ.
295 Φ. δέδοικα ταῦτα μὴ λόγῳ μὲν προσδέχῃ,
ἔργῳ δ' ἀπαρνήσαιο. Ξ. καὶ μὴν ὤμοσα.
Φ. ἄθρει τὸν ὅρκον ὡς ἐμὲ ξυλλαμβάνεις.

284 εἴ σοι] εἴσι Gu. (εἴ σοι corr. Ky.) **289** λαλεῖν] λαχεῖν Gu. (λαλεῖν corr. Ky.)

275 What I have already suffered is enough.
What need have I of further sufferings? Enough of those that are past!
Str. You speak justly and well, lady,
for you judge the future on the basis of what happened.
I swear, I give you my word.
280 I would do nothing against you,
neither would I dishonour affection, nor love,
never, because of the terrible tales you have told.
Fr. Are you able to offer me these wedding gifts,
if I grant you the pledges of marriage?
285 **Str.** Which gifts are these? Tell me, so that I may offer them.
Fr. Can you rejoice over another's blessings?
Str. Certainly! **Fr.** Can you feel sorrow at the distress even of the lowly?
Str. Absolutely yes! **Fr.** Can you avoid twisted and ambiguous words?
Can you say these things and mean them wholeheartedly?
290 **Str.** In every way. Ask something else.
Fr. Can you put yourself second to your friends?
Str. I can put myself second. **Fr.** And you would die for them repeatedly?
Str. Yes, I would even die. **Fr.** And not begrudge those who envy you?
Str. Yes! **Fr.** Can you love those who malign you? **Str.** By all means!
295 **Fr.** I fear that you accept these things in what you say,
but deny them in what you do. **Str.** Truly I have sworn an oath.
Fr. Observe your oath as you receive me.

Commentary

Poems 1–6

A cycle of six hymns for Sts Paul, Gregory of Nazianzus, Basil the Great, John Chrysostom, Gregory of Nyssa and Nicholas (for a detailed discussion of their structure and their association with the Orphanotropheion of St Paul, see section 1.2.3).

1. Invocatory verses to Paul the great Apostle

1. Paul's representation as God's mouth is very common in Prodromos: see, for example, *Tetrasticha on the Old and New Testaments*, 284b.1: Παῦλος ἔφα, στόμα Χριστοῦ ἔφα; *Historical poems*, 56a.34: τί δ' οὐχ ὁ Παῦλος, τοῦ θεοῦ μου τὸ στόμα; and *Miscellaneous poems*, 75.5: οὐ Παῦλον αὐτὸν ἀγνοῶ, τὸ σὸν στόμα.

4. The text assumes a personal tone here. The word φίλτρον is often used in Byzantine epigrams to express the donor's devotion and affection.

7–8. This is a reference to the earlier stage of Paul's life when, as a Pharisee, he was committed to the Law (the Torah) to the extent of persecuting Christians.—κυκέεσκες: a *hapax legomenon* (see *LBG s.v.*). Note that *PG* prints κυκεύεκες, which is a mistake.

9–14. These verses refer to Paul's missionary tasks. Prodromos uses a wide range of rare epithets to stress the laborious nature of these missions. Take, for example, the *hapax legomenon* χαλκομελής (see *LBG*, s.v.) or the Homeric ἀτειρής (e.g. *Iliad* 3.60 and 5.292).

11. πτηνέ τε πεζέ: Paul is described with the same set of epithets in Prodromos, *Tetrasticha on the Old and New Testaments*, 278a.4: ὦ πτηνὲ πεζέ, ποῦ σέ τις δραμὼν φθάσει.

13. Paul resembles the Sun, King of Heaven and symbol of supreme power. The motif is usually reserved for praise of the emperor in Prodromos and contemporary imperial oratory: see Hörandner, *Historische Gedichte*, 103–06.

14. Paul's shipwrecks are reported in *2 Corinthians* 11.25 and *Acts* 27.39–44. The use of πολύτλα, the most common epithet for Odysseus (e.g. *Iliad* 8.97

and *Odyssey* 5.171), creates a comparison between Paul's hardships and those of the Homeric hero.

15-16. Rome and Tarsus are juxtaposed here. Paul was from Tarsus (*Acts* 21.39), acquiring his Roman citizenship upon his birth. Paul made tactical use of his Roman citizenship when he came close to being flogged, in how he negotiated his case (e.g. *Acts* 22.22-29). Prodromos, *Tetrasticha on the Old and New Testaments*, 292a, titled Εἰς τὰς ἐν Ἰεροσολύμοις πληγὰς Παύλῳ, ὅτε καὶ Ῥωμαῖον ἑαυτὸν ἐκάλει, builds on the same idea:

–Ταρσὸς πατρίς σοι, Παῦλε, τῆς Κιλικίας·
καὶ πῶς σὺ σαυτὸν παῖδα τῆς Ῥώμης λέγεις;
–Τὸν καιρὸν οὕτως ἐξεώνημαι, ξένε·
τῶν ἡμερῶν γὰρ οἶδα τὴν πονηρίαν.

–Tarsus of Cilicia is your ancestral land, Paul.
How could you call yourself a child of Rome?
–O stranger, I redeem the time in this way,
for I am aware of the wickedness of our days.

19. Achilles was instructed by Phoenix to become a good 'speaker of words' and 'doer of deeds' (*Iliad* 9.443); here Prodromos describes Paul as a matchless orator and doer, further contributing to the comparison of Paul with Homeric heroes.

20. φίλη κεφαλή stands for the personal and dedicatory character of the text. Moreover, it is one of the most common forms of address in Byzantine letter-writing practice (cf. M. Grünbart, *Formen der Anrede im byzantinischen Brief vom 6. bis zum 12. Jahrhundert* (Vienna 2005), 280-85).

22-24. Prodromos is not only the author but also the one addressing this poem to Paul on an unknown occasion at the Orphanotropheion (see pp. 26-27). The two concluding verses of the poem include another two *hapax legomena*: προπρόειμι (line 23) and δικασπολέω (line 24). The former word is not recorded in the *lexica*; it means 'sit before all others' and it should be viewed as an analogue to 'προπρόκειμαι', another *hapax legomenon* by Prodromos (see *Tetrasticha on the Old and New Testaments*, 71b.1).

2. Similar verses to Gregory the Theologian

1. Gregory was credited with the honorary title 'theologian' at the Council of Chalcedon in 451. Byzantine poets invented various motifs to emphasize his

292   COMMENTARY

theological dexterity. For example, Theodoros Stoudites and Ioannes Geometres compared it to thundering. For a detailed discussion of motifs used by the Byzantine poets for the praise of Gregory, see K. Demoen and E. M. van Opstall, 'One for the Road: John Geometres, Reader and Imitator of Gregory Nazianzen's Poems', in: A. Schmidt (ed.), *Studia Nazianzenica II* (Turnhout 2010), 223-48, at 227.

2. Gregory was consecrated Bishop of Constantinople in May 381.

3. Here Prodromos focuses on Gregory's rhetorical efficacy by using the standard imagery of a fiery mouth. Gregory is usually compared to the great Attic orators of the past, while the Byzantines even claimed that his rhetorical potency outshone that of Demosthenes; cf. A. Rhoby, 'Aspekte des *Fortlebens des Gregor von Nazianz in byzantinischer und postbyzantinischer Zeit*', in: M. Grünbart (ed.), *Theatron: Rhetorische Kultur in Spätantike und Mittelalter/ Rhetorical Culture in Late Antiquity and the Middle Ages* (Berlin/New York 2007), 409-17, at 412-13.—'Ρητροσύνης: a variant for ῥητορική coined by Prodromos (*Historical poems*, 38.52; 42.38; 56c.12; also *Miscellaneous poems*, 75.9). This rare form recurs in Euthymios Tornikes, *Poems* (ed. Papadopoulos-Kerameus), 1b.49, an author who was well-read in Prodromos' poetry.

4. A reference to Gregory's rich production of hexameter verses. Gregory's surviving poetic corpus runs to approximately 17,000 verses; cf. C. Simelidis, *Selected Poems of Gregory of Nazianzus: I.2.17; II.1.10, 19, 32: A Critical Edition with Introduction and Commentary* (Göttingen 2009), 21. His poetry was considered the model *par excellence* for many Byzantine authors; cf. e.g. Simelidis, *Gregory of Nazianzus*, 57-74. For his influence on Prodromos, see Zagklas, 'Appropriation in the Service of Self-Representation', 223-42.

5-6. This is a reference to Hellenic wisdom. Byzantines usually called it 'θύραθεν σοφία', considering it alien to Christianity, but Prodromos refers to it as 'ours' to praise Gregory because he recognized that Hellenic wisdom belonged to the Christians in the first place.

7-10. Gregory proclaimed the negation of bodily pleasures in many of his works. For a list of Gregory's encomia of virginal life, see J. A. McGuckin, 'Gregory: The Rhetorician as Poet', in: J. Børtnes and T. Hägg (eds), *Gregory of Nazianzus: Images and Reflections* (Copenhagen 2006), 193-212, at 203, note 42. In verse 7, Prodromos calls Gregory 'groom of personified Chastity'. Prodromos, *Tetrasticha for Gregory of Nazianzus*, 5, entitled 'Εἰς Γρηγόριον ὄναρ τῇ παρθενίᾳ ὡς γυναικὶ ὁμιλοῦντα', revolves around Gregory's vision of chastity described in Gregory of Nazianzus, *Poems*, II.1.45 [1369-72] 229-270. The hexametric tetrastich has the form of a dialogue between Gregory and Chastity:

–Γρηγόριε, προτιόσσευ ἐμὸν πολυήρατον εἶδος·
ἤν με λάβῃσθα βίοιο συνέμπορον, αἰθέρα δ' ἔλθῃς.
–Τίς δὲ σύ, παρθενίη; περὶ χείλεσι χείλεα βάψα,
σὸν λέχος ἀμφιέποιμι, γάμος δ' ἀποτῆλε μολείτω.

–O Gregory, behold my lovely figure!
If you take me as your companion for life, you will enter heaven.
–Who are you, Virginity? I touch my lips to your lips,
may I tend your bed and may marriage come to me from afar.

Verse 10 claims an interesting intertextual link to σὸν λέχος ἀμφιέποιμι. In the tetrastich, Gregory expresses his fervent feelings towards Chastity by saying that he is willing to 'protect her bed' and take her as his wife, while here we are told that Chastity rejoices in protecting Gregory's bed and uniting with him.

11. πίστιος ἕρμα is modelled on the Homeric 'ἕρμα πόληος' (e.g. *Iliad* 16.549, *Odyssey* 23.121). Moreover, Gregory of Nazianzus uses variants of this formula: 'ἕρμα λόγοιο' (e.g. Gregory of Nazianzus, *Poems*, II.1.13 [1228] 5) and 'ἕρμα γυναικῶν' (*AP* VIII.28.6).

12. This *synkrisis* is designed to emphasize Gregory's passionate defence of Trinitarian doctrine. Stentor was a Greek hero of the Iliad particularly known for his voice (cf. *Iliad* 5.785-786), which was as loud as that of fifty men. The Homeric passage gave rise to the proverbial 'Stentorian voice' (Aristotle, *Politica*, 1326b.6-7), which recurs elsewhere in Prodromos. For instance, in the satirical poem *Against a lustful old woman* (ed. Migliorini, v. 93: τὰ στίγματα κράζουσιν ἀντὶ Στεντόρων), the marks of her aged body are shouting in the place of Stentor. For the use of the maxim throughout the Byzantine period, see D. K. Karathanasis, *Sprichwörter und sprichwörtliche Redensarten des Alterturms in den rhetorischen Schriften des Michael Psellos, des Eustathios und des Michael Choniates sowie in anderen rhetorischen Quellen des XII. Jahrhunderts*, unpublished PhD thesis (Munich 1936), 30.

13-15. Prodromos juxtaposes three well-known Christological heresies—Sabellianism, Macedonianism, and Arianism—to highlight Gregory's instrumental role in the defence of Trinitarian doctrine against various Trinitarian heresies. Note that τμηξίθεος is a *hapax legomenon* (see *LBG* s.v.).

16. ὃς θεότητα τάμε: Arianism contested the equality of the three Persons of the Trinity.—σοῖς δ' ἀπέτμαγες λόγοις: the importance of Gregory's orations during the Trinitarian disputes of the fourth century is another typical motif in Byzantine poems. For example, Theodoros Stoudites, *Poems*, 67.3–4:[1]

καὶ πάσας ἀπρὶξ μωράνας τὰς αἱρέσεις
τὸν κόσμον ἐστήριξας ἐν τοῖς σοῖς λόγοις

and by making all heresies at once look foolish, you fastened the world to the anchor of your words.

18. Gregory is praised for both his poetry and orations. For the wide reception of the orations in Byzantium, see J. Sajdak, *Historia critica scholiastarum et commentatorum Gregorii Nazianzeni, Pars I* (Krakow 1914), and V. Somers, *Histoire des collections complètes des Discours de Grégoire de Nazianze* (Louvain-la-Neuve 1997). For the sixteen orations that became part of the liturgical repertoire during the tenth century (the so-called 'Liturgical Homilies'), see V. Somers-Auwers, 'Les collections byzantines de xvi discours de Grégoire de Nazianze', *BZ* 95 (2002), 102–35.

19. A puzzling verse, particularly the contrast between Σκιρτητά and πενθῆτορ. The latter is a *hapax legomenon* (see *LBG* s.v.), which one could interpret as an allusion to Gregory's gloomy character, reflected very frequently in his own writings: see P. L. Gilbert, *On God and Man: The Theological Poetry of St. Gregory of Nazianzus* (Crestwood NY 2001), 2–3. The former word is often used to describe the leaping up and down of deities associated with the Dionysian Mysteries, namely Dionysus (cf. *Orphic Hymns* 45.7: ἐλθέ, μάκαρ, σκιρτητά, φέρων πολὺ γῆθος ἅπασι and *AP* IX.524.19: σκιρτητήν, Σάτυρον, Σεμεληγενέτην, Σεμελῆα,) and Satyr (*Orphic Hymns* 11.4–5: ἐλθέ, μάκαρ, σκιρτητά, περίδρομε, σύνθρονε Ὥραις). However, it is more probable that the two words refer to Gregory's rhetorical achievements, and in particular his panegyrical and funerary orations. The word πενθητήριος is used in this sense in Manasses, *Funerary oration on the death of Nikephoros Komnenos*, 60–62: τοῦ λόγου τῷ πορφυρέῳ μόνῳ καὶ τῷ λευκῷ τῶν ἐπαίνων ἐξυφανθήσεται ἢ καὶ τοῦ μέλανος συγκράματος τῶν πενθητηρίων προσδεηθήσεται.

23. Gregory's orations are compared to the sweetness of honey, an ancient *topos* also used by Prodromos in *Tetrasticha for Gregory of Nazianzus* 3a.2: μέλιττα μούσης· κηροπλαστεῖς γὰρ λόγους. The analogy between Gregory and bees has a multilayered meaning: first, it emphasizes Gregory's rhetorical qualities, because bees had been considered as birds of the Muses since

---

[1] Transl. in Lauxtermann, *Byzantine Poetry*, vol. 1, 17.

antiquity (cf. e.g. Sophocles, *Fragments*, 155, and Aristophanes, *Ecclesiazusae*, 974); and second, it references Gregory's selective attitude towards classical wisdom, for Prodromos has in mind the words of Basil of Caesarea that it must be plucked out of its pagan context 'as a bee gathers honey' (Basil of Caesarea, *Oratio ad adolescentes*, IV.35–52).

24. 'τὸ ἔμελλεν ἄρα' is the opening of Gregory's oration 43, a funerary oration for Basil the Great. It is common practice among Byzantine authors to refer to this particular oration with this set of words: Psellos, *Theologica*, 61, is entitled: Ἐκ τοῦ "Ἔμελλεν ἄρα", εἰς τὸ 'καὶ εἰ τὸ πάντα ἐν πᾶσι κεῖσθαι', while a poem by an anonymous twelfth-century poet bears the rubric: Ἐπὶ ἀναγνώσει τοῦ Ἔμελλεν ἄρα (at the recitation of Ἔμελλεν ἄρα), which means that the poem was performed before the reading of Gregory's oration.[2] Another good example is Ps. Gregorios Korinthios, *On the Four Parts of the Perfect Speech*, 102: "Ἔμελλεν ἄρα πολλὰς ἡμῖν ὑποθέσεις τῶν λόγων ἀεὶ προτιθεὶς ὁ μέγας Βασίλειος.

3. Similar verses to Basil the Great

1. Basil acquired the bishopric of Caesarea in 370.

4. The motif of silence is very common in Byzantine epigrammatic poetry written for depictions of saints—it already occurs in Nazianzus' epigram on Basil (*AP* VIII.4.3–5).

6. εὐσκάρθμῳ: though an epithet of horses in Homer (*Iliad* 13.31), here it defines 'νηΐ' (before Prodromos only found in Quintus of Smyrna, *Posthomerica*, 14.10). Prodromos is fond of such alterations: the word 'ὑγροσκελὴς'—normally combined with 'ἵππος'—is used of 'ναῦς' in *Miscellaneous poems*, 6.12 and 71.5.

8. A contrast between the harmony of Basil's mode of life and the lack of harmony in the earthly world.

9–10. Basil is praised here not for his excellence in sacred and secular learning, but for his exegetical works on various books of the Old and New Testaments. Note that verse 9 includes two *hapax legomena*: (i) θειογόνος (see *LBG* s.v.), coined *metri gratia* instead of the common form θεογόνος; and

---

[2] *Seven Anonymous Byzantine Epigrams*, ed. G. Tserevelakis, 'Ἑπτά ανέκδοτα βυζαντινά επιγράμματα από τον κώδικα Marcianus Graecus 524', *Βυζαντινός Δόμος* 17–18 (2009–10), 265–92, at 280.

(ii) σαφητής (see *LBG* s.v.). In poem 4, Gregory of Nyssa is also called 'interpreter', but with the use of the variant form σαφήτωρ.

11-12. Eunomius was the leader of the neo-Arians and one of the most rigorous opponents of Basil. Basil wrote three books to rebut his Trinitarian heresy (*Adversus Eunomium*).

15-16. A reference to Basil's homilies of the *Hexaemeron*, a set of nine sermons dealing with the six days of creation. Their value is emphasized in two ways: first, Basil is divinely inspired (ἀφ' ὑψόθεν), making his work comparable to the Old and New Testaments; and second, he is praised for making known to all men the origin and the structure of the universe. For the place of Basil's work in the Hexaemeral literary tradition, see P. M. Blowers, *Drama of the Divine Economy: Creator and Creation in Early Christian Theology and Piety* (Oxford 2012), 126–29.—ἐκ μερόπεσσι φάναι: tmesis (ἐκφάναι).

17-21. The content of the *Hexaemeron* is here condensed: the creation of heaven and earth, light, plants, and animals.—πνοιοδότης is a *hapax legomenon* (see *LBG* s.v.) occurring three times in Prodromos: in the present poem and in *Tetrasticha on the Old and New Testaments*, 264b.3, it is used as an epithet of air; in the hexametric poem on the Crucifixion (*Miscellaneous poems*, 28.1) as an epithet of Christ.

22-23. Basil is praised for setting out rules for monastic life (see also line 3).

4. Similar verses to Saint John Chrysostom

1. μετὰ τοῖσι: Prodromos' praise of John Chrysostom immediately follows that of Gregory of Nazianzus and Basil of Caesarea, because the three together are the three Holy Hierarchs. A feast dedicated to them was instituted by Ioannes Mauropous in the eleventh century.

2. John Chrysostom was appointed Patriarch of Constantinople in the autumn of 397.

3. Prodromos also calls Chrysostom 'swallow of Christ' in *Tetrasticha for John Chrysostom*, 22a.3 (λ4ʳ) τὸν ἡδὺν εἰπεῖν τὴν Χριστοῦ χελιδόνα. This imagery is interesting, since the swallow heralds the arrival of spring (first in *Sappho, Fragments*, 135–136), a *topos* in many Byzantine *ekphraseis* of spring. For this type of text in Byzantium, see M. Loukaki, 'Ekphrasis Earos: Le topos de la venue du printemps chez des auteurs byzantins', *Parekbolai* 3 (2013), 77–106.

5. γλῶσσα λιγεῖα: the word λιγύς (fem. λίγεια in classical Greek, λιγεῖα or λιγεία in post-classical Greek) is used as an epithet of the Sirens in many authors, e.g. Alcman, *Fragments*, 30.1: ἁ Μῶσα κέκλαγ' ἁ λίγηα Σηρήν or Apollonius of Rhodes, *Argonautica*, 4.892: λίγειαι Σειρῆνες. What is more, one of the Sirens was called Λίγεια, e.g. Herodianus, *De prosodia catholica*, 3.1, page 258, 22: εἰς ἣν ἐξεβράσθη Λίγεια ἡ Σειρήν or Tzetzes, *Histories*, VI.709: Τρεῖς ἦσαν αἱ Σειρῆνες μὲν ᾠδῇ κηλοῦσαι πάντας,/ἡ Λευκωσία, Λίγεια μετὰ τῆς Παρθενόπης. In addition to Prodromos, other twelfth-century authors praise their addressees with the same set of words. Take, for example, the praise of Alexios Aristenos in Basilakes, *Orations*, 1.24.21-22: ὦ γλῶττα <u>Σειρὴν</u> τῷ ὄντι <u>λιγεία</u>, ὦ νοῦς καὶ γλώττης ῥεούσης ὀξύτερος.

6. Chrysostom's voice is as alluring as that of the Sirens, but unlike the Homeric Sirens, who divide men with their deceptive songs (cf. *Odyssey* 12.39-54), Chrysostom unites them. This motif is used extensively in Prodromos' work to describe holy figures with matchless rhetorical talent; in addition to Chrysostom, Sts Peter and Paul are called Sirens in *Tetrasticha on the Old and New Testaments*, 208b.3 and 289b.4. It is even used fairly frequently for the praise of learned high-ranking officials, such as Gregorios Kamateros (*Orations*, 36.239.24) or Stephen Meles (*Historical poems*, 69.5).— σύν τε δέουσ' is the result of *tmesis* (συνδέουσ').

10. θειοφραδὲς is a *hapax legomenon* (see *LBG* s.v.).

11. As in the poems for Gregory and Basil, Prodromos emphasizes Ioannes' celibacy.

12. πτηνὲ νόον: a common oratorical device used to praise the intellectual and rhetorical capabilities of an addressee: see, among many examples, the following poem, in which Gregory of Nyssa is described as 'φύσις πτερόεσσα' (v. 7).—γενέτωρ βίβλου ἀπειρεσίης: many epigrams extol Chrysostom's prolificity; for example, Philes (ed. Braounou-Pietsch) 102.2 reads: ἀεὶ δὲ λαλεῖς ἀπὸ τῶν βίβλων.

15. The story has it that a poor widow asked the help of Chrysostom when the Empress Eudoxia coveted and took her vineyard by force. Chrysostom supported the widow and attacked Eudoxia by making use of the biblical parallel of Naboth's vineyard (1 *Kings* 21.1-16). For the story, see C. Baur, *Der heilige Johannes Chrysostomus und seine Zeit*, 2 vols. (Munich 1929-30), 2, 142-45. The story is part of many Chrysostom vitae, including the ones by Theodoros of Trimithous, Georgios of Alexandreia, and Symeon Metaphrastes; for a list of the Vitae including the story, see Baur, *Der heilige Johannes Chrysostomus*, 1, XX-XXI. In addition to this poem, Prodromos also refers to the story in *Tetrasticha for John Chrysostom*, 16 (λ2ᵛ-λ3ʳ): εἰς Εὐδοξίαν τὸν τῆς χήρας ἀμπελῶνα λαμβάνουσαν.

16-19. We are told that Chrysostom was unjustly deposed from his see and was exiled to Komana. This event is also recorded in *Tetrasticha for John Chrysostom*, 18 (λ3ʳ): εἰς τὴν ἐξορίαν Ἰωάννου.

17. ἔδω is a very rare post-classical third-person aorist used instead of the usual form ἔδωκε. It is also found in Prodromos, *Rhodanthe and Dosikles*, 4.377.

21-22. The translation of the relics of Chrysostom from Komana back to Constantinople was conducted in 438, thirty years after his death, by his disciple St Proklos, Patriarch of Constantinople.

23. A reference to this miracle is also included in Prodromos, *Iambic calendar*, 27 January (p. 111): Ἡ ἀνακομιδὴ τοῦ Χρυσοστόμου, ὅτε καὶ νεκρὸς εἶπε τὸ «Εἰρήνη πᾶσιν»

Θανὸν τὸ χρυσοῦν καὶ πάλιν λαλεῖ στόμα.

5. Similar verses to Gregory of Nyssa

1. μετέπειτα: a further piece of lexical evidence supporting the strong connection between the six poems (see p. 25).

2. ποιμένα Νυσσαέων: Gregory was consecrated bishop of Nyssa in 372. He was dethroned in 376 due to his opposition to Valens' support of the Homoians, but he regained his see in 378.

4. Gregory wrote three books which complemented the polemical writings of his brother, Basil of Caesarea, against Eunomius.

5-6. These lines highlight Gregory's contribution to a complete Christian creation narrative: his treatise 'On the Making of Man' (*De opificio hominis*) supplements the *Hexaemeron*, a work by Basil of Caesarea dealing with cosmogony up to the creation of the animals.

7. φύσις πτερόεσσα stands for Gregory's rhetorical competence, since a number of words in this section of the poem (ἐριφραδέα, ἡδὺ μύθημα, ἡδυμελής) denote the art of effective speaking. Moreover, Prodromos employs the Homeric phrase 'ἔπεα πτερόεντα' in *Historical poems*, 6.101 to speak of orators and wise men praising the emperor both in prose and verse.

8. Prodromos compares Gregory to a mellifluous garden full of Graces with lovely hair, most probably inspired by the imagery of the *Song of Songs*, where the chaste woman is compared to a locked garden, while in *Song of Songs* 7.6.2 there is a reference to the flowing locks of her hair. Since many novel authors draw heavily on the *Song of Songs*, there are certain analogies between Prodromos' verse and other contemporary or later Byzantine novels: take, for example, Makrembolites, *Hysmine and Hysminias* 1.4.1: τὸν κῆπον…'Ο δὲ μεστὸς ἦν χαρίτων καὶ ἡδονῆς; Andronikos Palaiologos, *Kallimachos and Chrysorroe*, 810–11: τὰς χάριτας ὑπὲρ αὐτὴν τὴν τῶν χαρίτων φύσιν·/βοστρύχους εἶχεν ποταμούς, ἐρωτικοὺς πλοκάμους; *Achilleid* 767: τὰς χάριτας τὰς τοῦ περιβολίου. Taken together, the verse hints at Gregory's commitment to a chaste life and his exegesis of the *Songs of Songs* (see also lines 13–16).

9. Gregory's honey-dripping tongue is sweeter than the honey of Mount Hymettus. Hymettian honey was renowned in antiquity and became a *topos* to denote rhetorical skill. It is a recurrent motif in Prodromos' work for various addressees—including saints, contemporary intellectuals, and learned high-ranking officials—but also in many other twelfth-century texts. For example, in Eugenianos, *Funerary Oration on the Death of Theodoros Prodromos*, 456.8–9, we are told that Prodromos' orations were more beautiful than Adonis and sweeter than the honey of Hymettus; and in Basilakes, *Orations*, 1.18.26–27, the sweetness of Alexios Aristenos' mouth is paralleled to the honey of Hymettus. For the representation of Mount Hymettus in Byzantine literature, see A. Rhoby, *Reminiszenzen an antike Stätten in der mittel- und spätbyzantinischen Literatur: Eine Untersuchung zur Antikenrezeption in Byzanz* (Göttingen 2003), 219–20. For the popularity of Hymettus' honey in Byzantine texts, see also Hörandner, *Historische Gedichte*, 493.

11. While Gregory causes destruction to those who abandon God's way, he is a stronghold for those who lead a pious life. The juxtaposition of the singular 'δυσσεβέοντος' and the plural 'εὐσεβεόντων' is interesting. Though metrical reasons may lie behind the choice of 'δυσσεβέοντος' over 'δυσσεβεόντων', the use of the singular may also hint at Eunomius, the most fierce adversary of orthodox Trinitarian theology. Note also that θεμείλιον in the singular is a later form attested, for example, in Nicander, *Theriaka* 608, and Nonnus, *Dionysiaca* 26.86.

13–16. A reference to Gregory's homilies on the *Song of Songs*. Although many early Christian authors—such as Origen, Athanasios of Alexandreia, Eusebius of Caesarea, and Neilos of Ankyra—composed treatises on the text, Gregory was considered by the Byzantines the most authoritative exegete. His allegorical interpretation enjoyed enormous popularity, as is witnessed by its reception history. In the eleventh century, poem 2 by Michael Psellos is a didactic poem paraphrasing Gregory's homilies: see L. Bossina, 'Psello distratto: Questioni irrisolte nei versi In Canticum', in: V. Panagl (ed.), *Dulce Melos: La poesia tardoantica e medievale. Atti del III Convegno internazionale di Studi, Vienna, 15–18 novembre 2004* (Alessandria 2007), 337-60. In the twelfth century, the letters of Iakovos Monachos addressed to Eirene the Sevastokratorissa rely extensively on Gregory's commentary: see E. and M. Jeffreys, *Iacobi Monachi Epistulae* (Turnhout 2009), XXI/XXXVIII-XXXIX; cf. also E. M. Jeffreys, 'The Song of Songs and Twelfth-Century Byzantium', *Prudentia* 23 (1991), 36–54.

14. κρυψινόου...γενέτης: Gregory succeeded in deciphering Solomon's hidden thoughts in the *Song of Songs*; hence, his wisdom matches that of Solomon.—κρυψινόου: the same word is used in Psellos' exegetical poem on the Song of Songs (cf. Psellos, *Poems*, 2.291: ἄλλο δὲ τοῦτο πέφυκε τοῦ λόγου τὸ κρυψίνουν).—τοῦ is here the Homeric relative pronoun (in Attic οὗ).

19-20. The idea of the perpetual nature of Gregory's writings is repeated in the *Iambic calendar*, 10 January (p. 110): ζῆς καὶ θανὼν ζῆς, Νυσσαεῦ, τοῖς βιβλίοις and *Calendar in tetrasticha*, 50.199-200: ἀλλὰ τῇ Νυσσαέων ἀφῆκεν αὐτὸν ἐμπνέοντα ταῖς βίβλοις.

21. Ὑμνητὰ μακάρων refers to the collection of Gregory's funerary orations, but also to the numerous *vitae* or *encomia* for various saints.

23. Linus was a mythical minstrel who invented rhythm and melody. His name first appears in *Iliad* 18.569-572, where a lyre-playing young boy sings the Linus-song. In Hesiod and the tragic poets, Linus is considered the father of threnody. Λῖνος (with long iota) is a later form instead of Λίνος (with short iota) used in Homer, Hesiod, and other classical authors.

6. Similar verses to Saint Nicholas

1-3. Here Prodromos calls Nicholas 'οἶκτος' five times, making him a paradigm of compassion.—μετέπειτα: a further lexical link between the six poems.—οἶκτος ἐμῇ κιθάρῃ μέλπεται: the lyre stands for Prodromos' poetry. Prodromos usually summons David to extol the emperor and other addressees of his poems with his lyre (e.g. *Historical poems*, 17.60).

4. Prodromos coined the *hapax legomenon* 'ἀρχιθόωκος' (see *LBG* s.v.), possibly having in mind the rare words 'ἀμφιθόωκος' or 'ὑψιθόωκος', both of which occur in works by Gregory of Nazianzus (cf. *PGL* s.v.).

5. Χαῖρ' ἐλέοιο θάλασσα has a double meaning: first, Nicholas' compassion is as boundless as the sea; second, it refers to Nicholas' close relationship to the sea, as the patron saint of sailors.

7-20. Four miracles attributed to St Nicholas are juxtaposed in this part of the poem. It is possible that Prodromos relied on various hagiographical vitae of Nicholas or even oral tradition to describe these miracles. Moreover, it is possible that the poem was performed in front of a vita icon of Nicholas, since the first vita icon of the saint dates from as early as the eleventh century: see N. P. Ševčenko, *The Life of Saint Nicholas in Byzantine Art* (Turin 1983), 29, and Ševčenko, 'The Vita Icon and the Painter as Hagiographer', *DOP* 53 (1999), 149-65.

7-10. The first story is that of the three maidens who were in danger of engaging in prostitution because their father could not afford to pay dowries for their marriages; they were finally saved thanks to St Nicholas, who left three bags of gold in front of their house during the night. For Byzantine texts and vita icons, including this story, see Ševčenko, *The Life of Saint Nicholas*, 86-87. The story is also included in a *schedos* by Prodromos on Nicholas: see Vassis, 'Theodoros Prodromos', 16 (lines 12-13).

11-13. The second story is a well-known sea miracle: St Nicholas defeated the devil, who caused a violent storm with the intention of sinking a ship heading to the Holy Land. For texts preserving this story, see Ševčenko, *The Life of Saint Nicholas*, 98 (for icons with this story, see 98-99).—Βελίαν: a rare form in place of the common 'Βελίαρ'. The TLG shows three occurrences (among them Gregory of Nazianzus, *Poems*, II.1.44 [1359] 76), while it is reused in Prodromos, *Tetrasticha for Basil of Caesarea*, 15b.2 (κ6ʳ).— νηὸς ὑγροσκελέος: ὑγροσκελής is first attested in Libanius, *Letters*, 672.1.4, as an epithet of horses (cf. *LSJ* s.v.). In the twelfth century, it is used only as an epithet of ships; cf. also Prodromos, *Historical poems*, 15.48 and Komnene, *Alexias*, IV.7.2, 7.

14-16. The third story is that of the three generals: the city eparch Ablabius, who had been bribed, accused three guiltless generals of treachery. Nicholas responded to the pleas of the three men, appearing in the dreams of Constantine the Great and the eparch and commanding them to release the three generals. For the sources of this story, see G. Anrich, *Hagios Nikolaos*, 2 vols. (Leipzig 1913-17), at 1, 67-96 (under the title *Praxis de Stratelatis*) and Ševčenko, *The Life of Saint Nicholas*, 115. This story is the exclusive subject matter of an anonymous poem of 630 verses written around 1300: see S. G. Mercati, 'Vita giambica di S. Nicola di Mira secondo il codice Messinese greco 30', in: *Collectanea Byzantina*, 2 vols. (Rome 1970), vol. 1, 44-65. The story is also attested in a *schedos* by Prodromos for St Nicholas: see Vassis, 'Theodoros Prodromos', 16 (lines 10-11).

17-20. The final story is a resurrection miracle: St Nicholas resurrected a mariner who was compelled by the devil to plunge to the deck, leading to his death.—πεσέοντα (v. 17) and ἀμφιδέοντα (v. 18) (instead of πεσόντα and ἀμφιδόντα, respectively) are artificial aorist participles, for which there is no parallel. Prodromos will have opted for these forms *metri causa*.

7-8. On Abraham entertaining the Holy Trinity

The subject of these two epigrams is the Hospitality of Abraham (*Genesis* 18.1-16).[3] The epigrams are quite different to each other: the first assumes the form of a dialogue between the beholder and Abraham, the second describes the episode in the form of a list. Yet both poems express a feeling of confusion and lack of understanding regarding the consumption of food by the Holy Trinity. This sense of puzzlement is probably intended to express a sense of awe at the miracles of faith, a device frequently used in Byzantine epigrams. But it is also possible that it echoes views expressed in early Byzantine biblical exegesis, such as the writings of Theodoret of Cyrrhus.[4] The poems could have been written for an icon. Prodromos certainly did write such material: the historical poem 63 is an epigram commissioned by Konstantinos Alopos for an icon depicting this same scene.[5]

Poem 7

8. This refers to the birth of Isaac to Abraham and Sarah in their old age, as prophesied by the Holy Trinity.

Poem 8

1. Sarah was the first wife of Abraham, Hagar her Egyptian slave girl, and Ishmael the first son of Abraham, born to Abraham by Hagar.

---

[3] For the *philoxenia* of Abraham in Byzantium, see *ODB* 3 1664.
[4] See *PG* 80, col. 177C.   [5] Hörandner, *Historische Gedichte*, 495-96.

9. For a Reading

The poem is based on *Matthew* 28.11–15, which describes how the Jews attempted to distort the story of Christ's Resurrection by saying that his disciples secretly stole his body from the sealed and guarded tomb.[6] Throughout the poem, the Jews are castigated for their reluctance to accept Christ's resurrection. The poem has the form of a debate including propositions in support of and against Christ's resurrection. It was intended to introduce the reading of homily on this subject, but it is not possible to identify the precise text, since both manuscripts transmit it detached from the homily. Moreover, a large number of Byzantine homilies expound this particular gospel passage.[7]

Rubric: Hörandner suggested that the title of the poem should be emendated into 'ἐπὶ ἀναστάσει' to suit its content (cf. Hörandner, *Historische Gedichte*, 47), but this is not necessary, since the title refers to its function: the poem was read before a homily; see Antonopoulou, 'Recited Metrical Prefaces', 62.

1. This line is a metrical heading indicating the main theme of the poem; the main text of the poem begins from line two.

4–5. Christ's rising from a sealed tomb is paralleled to his birth from the virgin womb of the Holy Virgin (*Ezekiel* 44.2). The imagery of the Virgin as sealed gate is popular throughout the Byzantine period, particularly in hymnographical texts; S. Eustratiades, Ἡ Θεοτόκος ἐν τῇ ὑμνογραφίᾳ (Paris 1930), 67–68. The imagery is also used in *Tetrasticha on the Old and New Testaments*, 185a.2 and 263a.4.

24–25. A request to the celebrating priest to bless the reading of the homily that follows; for some remarks on this topos, see Antonopoulou, 'Recited Metrical Prefaces', 58 and 75.

10.

As we have seen, this poem contains five serious prosodic errors (in lines 4, 5, 7, 16, and 20), bringing into question its authorship by Prodromos.[8] But if the poem was indeed written by Prodromos, it is the second work from his oeuvre

---

[6] The same story is included in *Acta Pilati*; see K. von Tischendorf, *Apocalypses Apocryphae* (Leipzig 1866; repr. Hildesheim 1966), 315–16.

[7] See T. Antonopoulou, 'On the Reception of Homilies and Hagiography in Byzantium: The Recited Metrical Prefaces', in: A. Rhoby and E. Schiffer (eds), *Imitatio—Aemulatio—Variatio: Akten des internationalen wissenschaftlichen Symposions zur byzantinischen Sprache und Literatur* (Vienna 2010), 57–79, at 62, no. 35.

[8] See the discussion on p. 85.

intended as an introduction to the reading of a homily. The poem does not contain any direct indication as to the identity of the homily. It has come down to us without a title and its main text lacks any concrete reference. As with the previous poem, its manuscript tradition is also of no help. Both manuscripts containing the poem transmit it separately from the homily. The I-person repeatedly states that the homily is like a river full of sweetness but all the while inaccessible. The text teems with words of exhortation for moderation in the consumption of 'water', which have the purpose of emphasizing the challenging theme of the homily.

The comparison of the homily to a river seems to be a commonplace in this type of text. A good example of this comparison is Manganeios Prodromos' 'On a reading of St Gregory the Theologian', which was intended as an introduction to Gregory's homily no. 19 (*ad Iulianum exaequatorem*).[9] In verses 6–15, Manganeios likens Gregory's homily to the Euphrates. Another text building upon this imagery is a two-line poem attributed to Theodoros Prodromos. It is preserved in the manuscript Marc. gr. 498, fol. 379^r, under the title Στίχοι εἰς τὴν ἱστορίαν τοῦ ἁγίου Βασιλείου:[10]

Γλυκὺς ποταμὸς, ἀλλὰ δύσβατος λίαν,
ῥαθυμίας τὸ ῥῆμα σὺν πόνῳ πίνε.

Sweet river, yet nigh impassable;
drink the word of idleness with labour.

It is not easy to say whether this short poem was written by Theodoros Prodromos, but it may suggest that the present untitled work was intended to introduce a sermon by Basil of Caesarea.

5. Prodromos contemplates the concept of surfeit at length in *Rhodanthe and Dosikles* 5.144-162. For a similar use of the concept, compare *Miscellaneous poems* 62 and 64.

12-13. Here the church congregation is explicitly addressed. It has been suggested that the poem was delivered by Prodromos in the church attached to the Orphanotropheion of St Paul: see Antonopoulou, 'Recited Metrical Prefaces', 63.

---

[9] See Antonopoulou, 'Recited Metrical Prefaces', 63-64. For the text of the poem, see E. Miller, 'Poésies inédites de Théodore Prodrome', *Annuaire de l'Association pour l'encouragement des études greques en France* 17 (1883), 18-64, at 45.

[10] For the text of the poem, see Papadimitriou, *Prodrom*, 178-79.

21. This is an address to the officiating priest to bless the oration which will be delivered after the poem; this address is typical for this type of text, see Antonopoulou, 'Recited Metrical Prefaces', 58 and 75.

11–21. On St Barbara

The subject of these poems is St Barbara, a popular female martyr tortured and eventually beheaded by her own father, the pagan King Dioscorus. Legend has it that Dioscorus was struck by lightning as a divine punishment for his gruesome deed. Poems 11 to 20 are in iambics forming a single poetic cycle, while poem 21 is written in hexameters. The ten poems of the cycle do not consist of the same number of verses: the first eight poems are sestets, the last two octets. The poems are not verse renditions of the life of St Barbara. Instead, all of them revolve around the concept of the virtuous daughter and wicked father. In making use of various biblical episodes, proverbial expressions, and similes, Prodromos praises Barbara and castigates Dioscorus.

A large number of Byzantine works are preoccupied with Barbara's *passio*, including a good deal of poetry.[11] In particular, two other twelfth-century works share many common characteristics with Prodromos' poems: a poem in the fourteenth-century manuscript Vat. gr. 743,[12] and a group of twelve iambic epigrams in the thirteenth-century manuscript Marc. gr. 524.[13] Just like the hexametric poem by Prodromos, the anonymous hexametric poem in Vat. gr. 743 opens with the following imagery: whereas the animals honour the law of nature and do not consume their offspring, the wretched father slaughtered his own daughter. Prodromos' iambic cycle and the cycle in Marc. gr. 524 bear even closer resemblance to each other: they make copious use of stock motifs and standard similes to emphasize the antithesis between the

---

[11] For a detailed list and bibliography, see T. Antonopoulou, 'Ἀνώνυμο ποίημα για την αγία Βαρβάρα από τον κώδικα Barocci 197', in: T. Korres, P. Katsoni, I. Leontiadis, and A. Goutzioukostas (eds), Φιλοτιμία. Τιμητικός τόμος για την ομότιμη καθηγήτρια Αλκμήνη Σταυρίδου-Ζαφράκα (Thessaloniki 2011), 69–74, at 69; cf. also N. Zagklas, 'Astrology, Piety and Poverty: Seven Anonymous Poems in Vaticanus gr. 743', *BZ* 109.2 (2016), 895–918, at 90.

[12] Zagklas, 'Seven Anonymous Poems', 908–09.

[13] The work is partially edited in S. Lambros, "Ὁ Μαρκιανὸς κῶδιξ 524', *NE* 8 (1911), 3–59, 123–92, at 32–33.

righteous daughter and unrighteous father;[14] some of their verses are similar in terms of structure and content,[15] and they employ a similar vocabulary.[16]

Poem 12

1-2. As noted in the apparatus, the comparison of the lightning which burnt Barbara's father to the fire that consumed the city of Sodom is commonplace in Byzantine works on St Barbara, such as those by Ioannes of Damascus and Peter of Argos.

Poem 13

5. Prodromos puns on παῖς/εὔπαις and πατήρ/δυσπατήρ to emphasize the contrast between the good daughter and the wicked father. The word combination πάτερ δύσπατερ is created by analogy to *Odyssey* 23.97 μῆτερ ἐμὴ δύσμητερ, imitated by many, e.g. Lycophron, *Alexandra* 1174 ὦ μῆτερ ὦ δύσμητερ. Note that δυσπατήρ is a *hapax legomenon* (see *LBG* s.v.). Its nominative form is not attested, but one would expect δυσπάτηρ (cf. *LSJ* δυσμήτηρ).

6. Πλὴν οὐ βραδύπους ἡ Δίκη: as indicated in the apparatus, this is borrowed from the poetic corpus of Gregory of Nazianzus. Yet, with the insertion of the particle 'οὐ', the verse has assumed exactly the opposite meaning.

Poem 14

1-2. A twist on the Aesopian proverb 'κακοῦ κόρακος κακὸν ᾠόν' to answer the requirements of the comparison between the bad father and the good

---

[14] Compare Prodromos' poem 14, v. 1 Καλὸν κακοῦ κόρακος ᾠὸν εὑρέθης, poem 15, v. 1 Προέρχεται μὲν ἐκ καλάμης ὁ στάχυς, and poem 17, vv. 1-2 Ἡδύκρεων σῦς, ἀλλὰ τέλματος τόκος/καὶ Βαρβάρα γοῦν βορβόρου κἂν ἐξέφυ with the anonymous poems in Marcianus: poem 66⁵, v.1 Ἄργυρος ἡ παῖς ἐκ πατρὸς μολιβδίνου and poem 180, vv. 1-2 οὐχ' ὡς μελίσσης, ὡς δὲ κηφῆνος γόνος,/πικρὸν πρὸ προῆλθε γλυκερόν.
[15] Compare Prodromos' poem 11, v. 1 Πρηστήριοι πρὶν οὐρανόβρυτοι φλόγες and poem 14, v. 5 διπλοῦν γὰρ ἴσως οὐρανὸς τὸ πῦρ βρύει with the anonymous poems in Marcianus: poem 66⁵, v. 6 πρηστὴρ δὲ τὸν μόλιβδον ἐξ ὕψους φλέγει and poem 181, v. 6 Τί καὶ πάλιν πῦρ οὐρανὸς κάτω βρέχει.
[16] For example, both cycles use the word 'τεκνοφόντης', which does not occur elsewhere; cf. *LBG* (s.v. τεκνοφόντης).

daughter. For the proverb, see E. L. von Leutsch and F. G. Schneidewin, *Corpus Paroemiographorum Graecorum*, 2 vols. (Göttingen 1839-51), 1, 107 (IV no. 82) and Karathanasis, *Sprichwörter*, 115.

'Ησαΐαν: Isaiah is the first 'great prophet' of the Old Testament. The biblical book of Isaiah enjoyed immense popularity in Byzantine times (see *ODB* 2 1013-14). He appears twice elsewhere in Prodromos: in *Historical poems*, 17.291-300, where Prodromos borrows words from Isaiah and other Old Testament prophets to address groups of decastichs to the emperor Ioannes Komnenos on the occasion of the campaign against the Persians; and in *Historical poems*, 72.8-9, an epistolary poem for Theodoros Styppeiotes, which includes a reference to the coal placed in the mouth of Isaiah.

Poem 16

1-2. A reference to Elijah and the confrontation with the priests of Baal (cf. *3 Kings* 18.17-40). The story appears twice in other works of Prodromos: *Historical poems*, 59.80-81 and *Tetrasticha on the Old and New Testaments*, 171a-b.—Θεσβίτην: a common designation of Elijah (cf. *3 Kings* 17.1: Καὶ εἶπεν Ἡλιού ὁ προφήτης ὁ Θεσβίτης ἐκ Θεσβῶν τῆς Γαλααδ).

6. The reading πῦρ σωτηρίου can be defended: see the lexical collocation θυσία σωτηρίου in the Septuagint, e.g. *Leviticus* 9.4; cf. also *PGL*, s.v., σωτήριος, §5.

Poem 17

2. Ἡδύκρεως is rare: it occurs five times in Aristotle (cf. *TLG*), once in Michael Psellos, *Letters*, 107.4, and another time in Michael Italikos, *Letters*, 7.9 (ἡδύκρεων ἄλλως τὸ ζῷον). Italikos' letter is addressed to Prodromos. In it, Italikos wonders why Prodromos prefers tender meat over cheese. It is likely that Prodromos borrowed the word from Italikos' letter, or the other way round.

2. There is a pun here on the words 'Βαρβάρα' and 'βορβόρου', which is designed to emphasize the contrast between the moral maiden and the immoral father. Puns on the name of saints are typical in verse *synaxaria*; see H. Hunger, 'Byzantinische Namensdeutungen in iambischen Synaxarversen', Βυζαντινά 13 (1983), 1-16.

308 COMMENTARY

3. τροφή is used extensively in hymnographical texts for the Holy Virgin: Eustratiades, Ἡ Θεοτόκος s.v. τροφή; see also M. Cunningham, 'Divine Banquet: The Theotokos as a Source of Spiritual Nourishment', in: L. Brubaker and K. Linardou (eds), *Eat, Drink, and Be Merry (Luke 12:19): Food and wine in Byzantium* (London 2007), 236-44.

6. ἄρτους is another word of Marian typology in Byzantine hymnography: Eustratiades, Ἡ Θεοτόκος s.v. ἄρτος.

Poem 18

2-3. Jephthah was a judge in the Old Testament. He is best known for sacrificing his own daughter as a result of a rash vow he took before defeating the Ammonites (*Judges* 11.30-40). This story is also the main subject of Prodromos, *Tetrasticha on the Old and New Testaments*, 100.

Poem 19

1-2. In *Genesis* 22.1-13, God asked Abraham to sacrifice his son Isaac to test his faith. This story also appears in *Tetrasticha on the Old and New Testaments*, 24.

3. The same wordplay—between Βαρβάρα and βάρβαρος—occurs in an anonymous tenth-century poem for Barbara (ἡ Βαρβάρα δὲ Βαρβάρου μισεῖ τρόπους). For the text, see Lauxtermann, *Byzantine Poetry*, vol. 1, 316.

Poem 20

5. In Greek the word ἱστορέω is ambiguous, since it can mean 'recount/narrate' or 'depict/paint'. However, the former seems to fit the meaning of the verse better; hence, the poem could have been used as a preface to a hagiographical vita of St Barbara.

Poem 21

1-2. The opening address to personified Nature includes an accumulation of expressive nouns, word combinations, and rare epithets.—βιόσπορε: before

Prodromos, this occurs only in the fragmentarily preserved work of Dioskoros of Aphrodito (cf. *LBG* s.v.).—**Πότνα**: in Homeric epics, an honorary title mostly of 'θεά' (cf. *LSJ* s.v.).—**κοσμοδέτειρα συμφροσυνάων**: an otherwise unattested word combination: the word 'κοσμοδέτειρα' is a *hapax legomenon* (cf. *LBG* s.v.), while 'συμφροσύνη' is very rare (*LSJ* and *LBG* s.v.). The form συμφροσυνάων is modelled on the Homeric ἀφροσυνάων (cf. *Odyssey* 16.178 and 24.458).

22–23. On the twelve Feasts of our Lord Jesus Christ

These two epigrams reflect the same version of the so-called *Dodekaorton*,[17] including the following twelve Christological feasts in chronological order: Annunciation, Nativity, Circumcision, Hypapante (Presentation in the Temple), Epiphany, Transfiguration, Raising of Lazarus, Palm Sunday, Crucifixion, Resurrection, Ascension, and Pentecost. The first epigram is a list of the twelve feasts, with each verse including three feasts; the second epigram is a twelve-line text, with each line briefly describing a single Christological feast.[18]

The developments of complex iconographic programmes depicting the dominical feasts also gave rise to the production of epigrammatic cycles, including those of Georgios of Pisidia, Ignatios Magistor, the so-called Anonymous Patrician,[19] Ioannes Mauropous,[20] and the two anonymous collections known as *DOP* 46 and *DOP* 48.[21] In the twelfth century, Gregorios of Corinth authored a cycle of twelve epigrams—all between nine and eleven verses long—on the *Dodekaorton*, including the following Christological feasts: Nativity, Epiphany, Hypapante (Presentation in the Temple), Annunciation, Palm Sunday, Crucifixion, Deposition, Pentecost, Resurrection, Antipascha (St Thomas), Ascension, and Transfiguration.[22]

Unlike most of these Byzantine cycles, which consist of self-contained poems, Prodromos' two epigrams are single textual entities. The form and structure of these two Prodromean epigrams resembles some works by late Byzantine

---

[17] For the *Dodekaorton*, see *ODB* 2 868–69 and *RbK* I s.v. Dodekaorton.
[18] It resembles his iambic calendar, which was also written in the form of monostichs.
[19] For a detailed discussion of the cycles by Georgios of Pisidia, Ignatios Magistor, and the Anonymous Patrician, see Lauxtermann, *Byzantine Poetry*, 1, 180–87.
[20] Bernard, *Poetry*, 138–39.
[21] W. Hörandner, 'Ein Zyklus von Epigrammen zu Darstellungen von Herrenfesten und Wunderszenen', *DOP* 46 (1992), 107–15 and Hörandner, 'A Cycle of Epigrams on the Lord's Feasts in Cod. Marc. gr. 524', *DOP* 48 (1994), 117–33.
[22] H. Hunger, 'Gregorios von Korinth, Epigramme auf die Feste des Dodekaorton', *AnBoll* 100 (1982), 637–51.

authors. The first epigram is similar to three poems by Nikephoros Kallistou Xanthopoulos, of six, four, and three verses, respectively.[23] The only difference is that Nikephoros replaced the Circumcision of Christ with the Dormition of the Virgin. The second text, in turn, is comparable to a poem by Manuel Philes, entitled Ἕτεροι στίχοι ὅμοιοι εἰς τὰς δεσποτικὰς ἑορτάς.[24]

Poem 22

1. κλήσεως θέσις: this is the feast of Circumcision, commemorated on 1 January. According to *Luke* 2.21, eight days after his birth, Christ was circumcised and was named Jesus; this name was given to him by Gabriel at the Annunciation. This feast is not included in any other Byzantine poem on the *Dodekaorton*, but Prodromos refers to it elsewhere, in *Calendar in tetrasticha* 35.

24. On the Most Holy Mother of God

A large number of dedicatory epigrams addressed to the Holy Virgin ask her to intercede with God in the hereafter for the remission of a donor's sins. However, this epigram builds upon a double plea for intercession: first, John Chrysostom and St Nicholas are asked to intercede with the Virgin in favour of the donor (vv. 5-7); then, the Virgin is asked to intercede with God on behalf of John Chrysostom and St Nicholas (vv. 8-9). Even though the rubric of the epigram only refers to the Virgin, this double request for intercession suggests that the poem was written for a depiction of the Virgin Mary along with John Chrysostom and St Nicholas. Verses 10-11 constitute a plea on behalf of an unknown donor to grant him and his children good fortune both on earth and in heaven. It is possible that both the unknown donor and his children were represented in the picture, next to the Virgin Mary, John Chrysostom, and St Nicholas.

2. The ms. reads ἰλεώταιραν, but I have opted for the emendation ἰλεωτέραν: see, for example, Nikolaos Mesarites, *Narrative of the coup of John the fat*,

---

[23] For the text of the poems, see H. Guntius, *Cyri Theodori Prodromi epigrammata ut uetustissima, ita pijssima, quibus omnia utriusq(ue) testamenti capita felicissime comprehenduntur: cum alijs nonnullis, quae Index uersa pagella singillatim explicat* (Basel 1536), fol. 4.
[24] For the text, see Miller, *Manuelis Philae*, vol. 2, 420-21, poem 61.

48.4: ἱλεωτέρᾳ φωνῇ. Another possible emendation would be ἱλεώτειραν, as an analogue to κοσμοδέτειρα in *Miscellaneous poems*, 21.2.

6-7. Chrysostom is praised for writing several orations, and Nicholas for working many miracles. These two verses are to be found in a slightly altered form in *Historical poems*, 57.9-10, which shows that Prodromos is very fond of reusing the same wording or even copying verses verbatim in different poems. Historical poem 57 is an epigram commissioned by Andronikos Kamateros for a depiction of the Virgin, flanked by John Chrysostom and St Nicholas on the one side and Gregory of Nazianzus and Basil of Caesarea on the other.[25] As in poem 57, John Chrysostom and St Nicholas are depicted next to each other in the picture.

25. On an icon of the Most Holy Mother of God

This dedicatory epigram commemorates the restoration of an icon of the Holy Virgin.[26] The central theme of the epigram is based on imagery associated with the slave trade.[27] The all-subjugating power of time has not respected the Virgin's *typos*—her image on the icon. Though the Virgin Mary set enslaved mankind free by giving birth to the Word of God, she is now sold in a market like a slave. But the unknown donor, who is described as a slave of his sins, bought and renovated the icon out of his fervent love for the Virgin Mary. In the concluding verse, the renovation is compared to the payment of a ransom, which will release the donor from his moral captivity.

Rubric: according to Vind. Phil. gr. 149, Prodromos not only wrote the epigram but also purchased the icon on which it was meant to be inscribed. However, it is more likely that this is an example of intentional fallacy on the part of the scribe of Vind. Phil. gr. 149.

1-4. πανδαμάτωρ χρόνος: 'time subdues all'. As noted in the apparatus, this is a proverbial phrase first used in lyric poetry (Simonides and Bacchylides). The image of time as destroyer is common in epigrams commemorating the

---

[25] See Hörandner, *Historische Gedichte*, 469.
[26] The restoration of icons became quite popular in the twelfth century; see M. Chatzidakes, 'Χρονολογημένη βυζαντινή εικόνα στη Μονή Μεγίστης Λαύρας', in: N. A. Stratou (ed.), *Byzantium: Tribute to Andreas N. Stratos*, 2 vols. (Athens 1986), 225-40; cf. also Drpić, *Epigram*, 156-57; for twelfth-century epigrams associated with this practice, see note 115 in Drpić.
[27] As already noted in Drpić, *Epigram*, 281.

restoration of Byzantine icons; for example, an epigram from the *Anthologia Marciana* (Lambros no. 43, vv. 3-4) reads: τύπου δὲ σεπτοῦ σοῦ κατίσχυσε χρόνος | καὶ πρὸς φθορὰν ἤνεγκεν ἀστάτως ῥέων.

26. On St Peter crucified

A short poem on the martyrdom of St Peter, who was crucified during the reign of the emperor Nero, as reported in the apocryphal *Acts of Peter* (chapter 37). The imagery of the epigram is based on the crucifixion of Christ and the upside-down crucifixion of Peter. The upright crucifixion of Christ symbolises his descent to earth, while the reverse crucifixion of St Peter symbolises his ascension to heaven. In Byzantine iconography, the martyrdom of Peter is depicted in cycles relating to the deaths of the Apostles.[28]

Rubric: the poem is attributed to Christophoros Mitylenaios and Nikolaos Kallikles in some manuscripts. For its authorship by Prodromos, see pp. 14-15.

7. The mss Go and Ma read εἰς οὐρανοὺς γὰρ εἶχον ἐκ γῆς τὸν δρόμον, which is printed in the edition by Romano. However, I have opted for the reading of V and L, since it fits better to the meaning of the line: St Peter's faith in God paved his way to heaven.

27-28. Hexameters on the Crucifixion

Even though the Crucifixion of Christ is the subject of both epigrams, the focus is not the same. The first epigram concentrates on the vinegar offered to Christ and the role of the soldier who pierced Christ's side to confirm his death (*John* 19.29 and 34). The second epigram focuses on the scene of the crucified Christ, flanked by the Virgin Mary and St John (*John* 19.26). The episode of the Crucifixion appears again in Prodromos' tetrastichs on the Old and New Testaments.[29] Although there are dozens and dozens of Byzantine

---

[28] cf. *ODB* 2 1637.
[29] Cf. Prodromos, *Tetrasticha*, 229a-b. It is worth noting that the iambic tetrastich was later inscribed on a fifteenth-century icon of the Crucifixion, now to be found in Moscow; see A. Rhoby, *Byzantinische Epigramme auf Ikonen und Objekten der Kleinkunst* (Vienna 2010), vol. 2, 124-26 (with bibliography). There are more tetrastichs used as inscriptions in late Byzantine period. For example, tetrastich 186a was inscribed in the church of the Panagia at Merona in Crete (1380-1400);

epigrams on the Crucifixion, only a small number of them are in hexameter. Other than these two poems and the hexametric poem from the tetrastichs on the Old and New Testaments, there is also a poem ascribed to Anastasios Quaestor, also known as 'Stammer' (AP, XV.28).[30]

Poem 27

1. ἀγριόθυμε is always negatively connotated. Here it is used as an epithet for a soldier, in *Historical poems* 8.51 and 228 for a barbarian, while in the poetic works of Gregory of Nazianzus and Ioannes Geometres it relates to demons; see also van Opstall, *Jean Géomètre*, 194.

3. παμμεδέοντος is a common epithet of Christ in poems composed before and after Prodromos (e.g. *AP*, XV.40.40: Χριστὸν παμμεδέοντα κασίγνηταί τε ἔται τε and Theodoros Metochites, *Poems*, 18.364: ἡμετέρῳ νύ τ' ἄνακτι παμμεδέοντι Χριστῷ).

Poem 28

1. πνοιοδότης: see above p. 296.

2–3. The sorrow of the Holy Virgin and St John is a typical image in Byzantine iconography of the Crucifixion. For some rare depictions of tears in Byzantine art, see H. Maguire, 'The Depiction of Sorrow in Middle Byzantine Art', *DOP* 31 (1977), 123–74.—σταλάῃσι: note the use of a pseudo-Homeric subjunctive instead of the indicative; cf. also 70.7: ἀπεχθαίρῃσι is another example of the subjunctive used instead of the indicative.—μυητής recurs in *Historical poems*, 79.44. Kambylis translated the word as *Lehrer* ('teacher'): A. Kambylis, *Prodromea* (Vienna 1984), 121–22. However, Hörandner has convincingly argued that it means 'disciple': Hörandner, 'Prodromos and the City', 61.

---

see M. Patedakis, 'Μια επιγραφή με ηγεμονική διάσταση. Επίγραμμα του Θεοδώρου Προδρόμου στο Βίβλος γενέσεως (ευαγγ. Ματθαίου 1.1) από την Παναγία στον Μέρωνα', in: M. S. Patedakis and K. D. Giapitsoglou (eds), *Μαργαρίται. Μελέτες στη Μνήμη του Μανόλη Μπορμπουδάκη* (Sitia 2016), 328–59. Moreover, Dora Konstantellou is working on tetrastich 262a (on the Deposition of Christ) which was inscribed on a fresco in a small private church on the island of Naxos in the early fourteenth century.

[30] For some annotations on the poem, see Lauxtermann, *Byzantine Poetry*, vol. 1, 110–11.

29–54. On Virtues and Vices

These twenty-six epigrams form a single cycle usually transmitted in the manuscripts under the generic title, 'On Virtues and Vices'. Their arrangement in the cycle usually shows symmetry, with a side-by-side juxtaposition of a virtue with its opposite vice.[31] There is one exception, however: the cycle opens with the epigram of the personified 'Ἀγάπη' and is followed by two vices (i.e. 'Μῖσος' and the negatively connotated 'Ἐξουσία'). What is more, the cycle does not conclude with virtues and vices, but with the subjects of 'Φιλοσοφία', 'Ῥητορική', and 'Γραμματική', which form the lower division of Byzantine education (the so-called *trivium* in the West). All epigrams have a strong paraenetic tone and the same narrative design: in each epigram a virtue or a vice assumes the I-person describing various qualities or faults.

Representations of personifications of virtues and vices were popular in the visual culture of the Byzantines. This popularity gave rise to epigrammatic poetry for various kinds of objects, such as illuminated manuscripts[32] and even drinking cups.[33] This synergy of written word and image is even recorded in Byzantine novels. For example, Book 2 of Eustathios Makrembolites' *Hysmine and Hysminias* includes a description of paintings of the personified cardinal virtues along with Eros and the personified twelve months upon the walls of the garden of Sosthenes in Aulikomis; the author inserted iambic epigrams into the narrative which relate to the images of the virtues.[34]

---

[31] However, the cycle was modified and expanded during its manuscript dissemination; see pp. 136–37.

[32] For example, two Gospel manuscripts (Marc. gr. Z 540 and *Felton* 710/5), dating to the first half of the twelfth century, contain canon tables decorated with personified Months and Virtues. See Roilos, *Amphoteroglossia*, 166 and E. Jeffreys, 'The Labours of the Twelve Months', in: E. Stafford and J. Herrin (eds), *Personification in the Greek World: From Antiquity to Byzantium* (Aldershot 2005), 309–23, at 318–19.

[33] For example, four anonymous epigrams were used as verse inscriptions on a drinking cup with depictions of the virtues (Lambros 153 No. 236). On these epigrams, see F. Spingou, *Words and Artworks in the Twelfth Century and Beyond: Twelfth-Century Poetry on Art from MS. Marcianus Gr. 524* (Tolworth, Surrey 2021), 122.

[34] See Roilos, *Amphoteroglossia*, 45–68; cf. also C. Cupane, 'Das erfundene Epigramm: Schrift und Bild im Roman', in: W. Hörandner and A. Rhoby (eds), *Die kulturhistorische Bedeutung byzantinischer Epigramme: Akten des internationalen Workshop (Wien, 1.–2. Dezember 2006)* (Vienna 2008), 19–28.

31. Power

2. τοῦ λόγου χωρὶς λόγου: here Prodromos plays with the ambiguity of the word *logos* and its multiple meanings in Greek ('words', 'reason', etc.). Although I have opted for the translation 'and I lord over reason without reason', an alternative interpretation could be 'and I lord over reason without words'.

34. Justice

1. τῷ ζυγῷ μου: for the image of justice with scales (*zygos*) in Byzantine literature, see Roilos, *Amphoteroglossia*, 153–54. Prodromos, however, offers various other images of justice in his novel, e.g. *Rhodanthe and Dosikles* 4.69: 'τὸ τῆς Δίκης γὰρ ὄμμα τῆς πανοπτρίας' and 5.228 '[...] ἡ μάχαιρα τῆς Δίκης'. Just as 'Justice' here establishes cities, so too does the personified *Friendship* in *Miscellaneous poems*, 76.109-110.

36. Fortitude

8. Ἀνδρεία: *Anthologia Marciana* (Lambros no. 60) also contains a couplet on 'Fortitude':

Ἐπὶ τῇ εἰκόνι τῆς ἀρετῆς ἀνδρείας
Ψυχὴν ἔγωγε κρατύνω καὶ σαρκίον
πρὸς τὰς ὁρατὰς καὶ νοουμένας μάχας.

On the image of the virtue Fortitude
I strengthen soul and body
for visible and invisible battles.

Unlike the epigram from the *Anthologia Marciana*, which describes fortitude in a broader sense, in Prodromos' text fortitude is closely connected with military undertakings. Note that the word ἀρηϊμάνιος (bellicose) is a *hapax legomenon* (see *LBG* s.v.) instead of the usual word ἀρειμάνιος. Nikolaos Mesarites, *Epitaphios for John Mesarites*, 46.8 has ἀρεϊμάνιος.

40. Truth

2. Personified Truth is described as daughter of Zeus in Pindar, *Olympia*, 10.4 and *Fragments*, 204.

46. Modesty

2. Prodromos may have in mind the parable of the Pharisee and the tax collector (cf. *Luke* 18.9–14), the evangelist Matthew, who was a former tax collector (cf. *Matthew* 9.9–13; *Mark* 2.14 and *Luke* 5.27), or even the meeting of Jesus and Zacchaeus (*Luke* 19.1–10). All three stories were included in his cycle of tetrastichs on the Old and New Testaments (see *Tetrasticha on the Old and New Testaments*, 248, 197, and 249, respectively). However, the parable of the Pharisee and the tax collector seems the most relevant: the tax collector there is modestly personified.

47. Arrogance

2. This is a reference to the fall of Lucifer described in *Isaiah* 14.12.

49. Mercilessness

2. An allusion to *Luke* 16.19–31, which recounts the story of the rich man and Lazarus.

53. Rhetoric

2. διπλόη stands for the duplicitous nature of prowess in rhetoric (for further remarks, see Roilos, *Amphoteroglossia*, 30).

55–56. On the Image of Life

These two epigrams revolve around the theme of earthly and heavenly life, based on the personification of *Bios* (Life) and its representation, which derives from the well-known Lysippean statue of *Kairos*.³⁵ Like *Kairos*, Prodromos' *Bios* (Life) has winged feet, stands on wheels, holds scales in his hand, and has a bald head, except for a short cluster of hair on his forehead. This representation of *Kairos* was intended to emphasize the brevity of life and the importance of taking full advantage of its opportunities: you have to grasp his hair when he is in front of you, because once he moves past you, your opportunity is lost. However, the meaning of the personified *Bios* (Life) in Prodromos is slightly different from that of *Kairos*, adapting to the Christian ethos. In the first poem, *Bios* addresses the beholder, who has managed to seize him by the tuft of his hair, thereby living and experiencing life in full. But then *Bios* showers him with various admonitions and advice. He incites him not to give in to pleasure-seeking and immoderate habits, because earthly life is ephemeral. In the second poem, *Bios* addresses a person who has failed to seize him, advising him not to give up hope, because things may change.

The iconography of *Kairos* and its relation to *Bios* and *Chronos* seems to have been a subject of debate among twelfth-century authors. For example, Ioannes Tzetzes, both in his letters[36] and his *Histories*,[37] claims that people who behave as if they know everything and talk nonsense identify Lysippos' *Kairos* with *Bios* and not with *Chronos*.[38] Unlike Prodromos' representation of *Bios*, Tzetzes' *Chronos* stands on a globe, is deaf, and holds a razor. This debate may even mirror a direct intellectual dispute between Prodromos and Tzetzes. Whatever the case, the popularity of personified Bios triggered the genesis of a large number of epigrams in the late Byzantine period. But the representation of *Bios* in these texts is not always the same as the one offered by Prodromos: in a hexametric poem by Euthymios Tornikes, *Bios* is described with wheels but without wings;[39] in the epigram 'On a naked lad representing the image of *Bios*' by Manuel Philes,[40] *Bios*

---

[35] For Kairos, see A. Muñoz, 'Le rappresentazioni allegoriche della vita nell'arte bizantina', *L'Arte* 7 (1904), 130–45; A. B. Cook, *Zeus: A Study in Ancient Religion*, 2 vols. (Cambridge 1926), vol. 2, part 2: the appendix on Kairos is on pp. 859–68; V. Grecu, 'Die Darstellung des Καιρός bei den Byzantinern', *SBN* 6 (1940), 147–54; C. Bouras, 'Ἀλληγορικὴ παράσταση τοῦ βίου-καιροῦ σε μια μεταβυζαντινὴ τοιχογραφία στὴ Χίο', *Ἀρχαιολογικὸν Δελτίον* 21, Αʹ, 1966 (1967), 26–34.

[36] Tzetzes, *Letters*, 70.

[37] Tzetzes, *Histories*, VIII.200 (Περὶ Λυσίππου); X.322 (Περὶ Ἀλεξάνδρου παραδραμόντος καιρὸν καὶ τῆς τοῦ χρόνου παρὰ Λυσίππου ἀναστηλώσεως), and X.323 (Περὶ τῶν παραληρούντων τὴν τοῦ χρόνου ἀναστήλωσιν βίου εἶναι ἀναστήλωσιν καὶ οὐ χρόνου).

[38] See Cook, *Zeus*, vol. 2, part 2, 864; cf. Roilos, *Amphoteroglossia*, 164, note 201.

[39] Tornikes, *Poems* (ed. Papadopoulos-Kerameus), 3.9: ἄκουον σε, Βίε, τροχὸν ἔμμεναι καὶ ἑτέρους περ.

[40] Philes, ed. Miller, vol. 1, 32, poem 67. On this poem, see S. Klementa, 'Vom bequemen Luxusdasein zur vergänglichen Lebenszeit. Die Personifikation des Bios', in: G. Brands and H. Gabelmann (eds), *Rom und die Provinzen: Gedenkschrift für Hanns Gabelmann* (Mainz 2001), 209–14.

does not have wheels under his feet; and the sixteenth-century Monacensis gr. 306 transmits on fol. 62^(r-v), immediately following Prodromos' poem on *Bios*, a yet unpublished anonymous poem on the same subject ('Ἐπίγραμμα εἰς τὸν μέλλοντα βίον'), with *Bios* holding a balance in his left hand and a razor in his right one.

Poem 55

2. An allusion to one of the main visual characteristics of *Kairos*: he was bald on the back of his head with only a tuft of hair on his forehead.

5. On nudity in Byzantium, see *ODB* 3 1500-1501 and B. Zeitler, 'Ostentatio Genitalium: Displays of Nudity in Byzantium', in: L. James (ed.), *Desire and Denial in Byzantium* (Aldershot 1999), 185-91. On nudity in Byzantine art, see H. Maguire, 'The Profane Aesthetic in Byzantine Art and Literature', *DOP* 53 (1999), 189-205, at 200-203. Nudity seems to be closely linked to death in Prodromos' work, cf. *Rhodanthe and Dosikles*, 6.494, where Dosikles envisages Rhodanthe naked after her presumed death in a storm at sea.

9-10. Earthly life is paralleled to a shadow of smoke in Sophocles, *Antigone*, 1170, and *Philoktetes*, 94. The same idea appears in Manasses, *Aristandros and Kallithea*, 160: see Jeffreys, *Byzantine Novels*, 330.

57-61. On a ring that has a seal engraving of two lovers and two trees that grow out of their breasts and come together into one canopy

These five epigrams refer to the seal engraving of a ring bearing the image of two trees growing from the breasts of two lovers.[41] They are based on the association of intertwining tree branches with erotic desire, a well-known novelistic *topos* which first occurs in Achilles Tatius' novel *Leucippe and Clitophon*. Book 1.17, 3-5, includes a reference to the love story of the male and female palm trees. Book 1.15, 2, describes the motif in a subtler manner, including the image of intertwined trees in a garden.[42] But this motif, as a symbol expressing desire, permeated various texts singing the praises of love,

---

[41] For Byzantine rings, see J. Spier, *Late Byzantine Rings, 1204-1453* (Wiesbaden 2013).
[42] ἔθαλλον οἱ κλάδοι, συνέπιπτον ἀλλήλοις ἄλλος ἐπ' ἄλλῳ, αἱ γείτονες τῶν πετάλων περιπλοκαί, τῶν φύλλων περιβολαί, τῶν καρπῶν συμπλοκαί. The wording of the novel is very close to that of the five epigrams.

becoming particularly popular in wedding songs. For example, Ps. Menander' discussion of the epithalamium contains the following:[43]

Περὶ δὲ δένδρων ἐρεῖς, ὅτι κἀκεῖνα οὐκ ἄμοιρα γάμων· οἱ γὰρ ἐπὶ ταῖς κόμαις σύνδεσμοι φιλοτεχνήματα γαμούντων δένδρων εἰσί, καὶ τοῦ θεοῦ ταῦτά ἐστιν εὑρήματα.

As to trees, you should point out that they too are not without their part in marriage, for the tendrils on leaves are devices of mating trees, and these too are inventions of God.

The same motif appears again in the discussion of the 'bedroom speech', the so-called *kateunastikos*:[44]

... καὶ δένδρα δένδρεσιν ἐπιμίγνυται, ἵνα τοῦτο γένηται τελετὴ καὶ γάμος.

... Trees mingle with trees, so that this becomes their initiation and marriage

However, it is worth noting that Prodromos slightly modifies the imagery in the first four texts. In all of them the desire of the two lovers remains unsatisfied: while the trees interweave their branches, the depicted couple is not able to mingle with each other; although the trees embrace each other tightly, there is no embrace for the two lovers; no matter how urgently the narrating voice asks Eros to unite the two lovers, in none of these epigrams is their erotic longing fulfilled. The only exception is the final text, where the narrating voice addresses the two trees, asking them to finally bear fruit in the marriage of these lovers.

62–66. To a Garden

A cycle of five poems filled with various metaphorical messages, all of which are based on the diverse meanings of the garden.[45] As already noted in the introduction, the poem could have been used as a preface to an anthology of works,

---

[43] For the text, see D. A. Russell and N. G. Wilson, *Menander Rhetor, edited with Translation and Commentary* (Oxford 1981), 140, lines 7–10; cf. also the notes on p. 314.
[44] Russell and Wilson, *Menander Rhetor*, 152, 15–16.
[45] It should be emphasized that the garden seems to be a 'protean' motif, since it assumed various meanings across various Byzantine works: see I. Nilsson, 'Nature Controlled by Artistry: The Poetics of the Literary Garden in Byzantium', in: H. Bodin and R. Hedlund (eds), *Byzantine Gardens and Beyond* (Uppsala 2013), 14–29, which also includes a discussion of these five poems.

while its structure and content resemble that of *Songs of Songs*.⁴⁶ The five texts form a dialogue between the narrating voice and the imaginary beholder of a garden, speaking in the following sequence: narrating voice; beholder; narrating voice; beholder; narrating voice. Each epigram offers a slightly different description of the garden's allegorical connotations. In the first poem, the I-person induces the beholder to partake of the garden's beauty, but in appropriate moderation. Moreover, the garden assumes the role of a mirror of the mortal life: just like the garden, mortals are born, flourish, and die. In the second epigram, the fear of the beholder reaches its peak, because the garden reminds him of the Tree of Knowledge, which led to his expulsion from the Garden of Eden. The third epigram resembles the first, as the narrating voice incites the beholder once more to partake of the garden's gifts, but with self-control. In the fourth epigram, the beholder has succumbed to the invitation of the garden and its pleasures. The narrating voice in the final epigram reminds the beholder that good things in life are not free from hardships.

Poem 62

4. χλόη: this is the object of τρύφησον, just as κρίνον is the object of τρύγησον (line 3) and ὕδωρ the object of ῥόφησον (line 5). For the use of the dative after τρυφῶ, see *Historical poems*, 71.61 and *Iambic calendar*, 3 July (p. 130).

Poem 63

2. It is difficult to choose between ἀγάλλομαι and ἐκπλήττομαι. The latter reading would also suit the meaning of the line: 'I am overwhelmed in my heart at the sight'. However, I have opted for ἀγάλλομαι for three reasons: first, most of the manuscripts offer ἀγάλλομαι (only N, R, and Z read ἐκπλήττομαι); second, the scribe of H corrected ἀγάλλομαι over ἐκπλήττομαι; and third, poems 62 and 65 revolve around the concept of pleasure.

67. On an icon of the most holy Mother of God

A short epigram for an icon of the Holy Virgin owned by Georgios of Antioch, the celebrated admiral in the service of the Norman king Roger II. As with

---

⁴⁶ See p. 18.

poem 25, which was written for another icon of the Virgin, the epigram's vocabulary is associated with the slave trade: Christ gave his life to purchase his mother's freedom. In turn the Virgin is asked to purchase Georgios and set him free from his sins. The circumstances of its production—whether it was a gift or a commission by Georgios of Antioch—and its dating are completely unknown, but it should be dated before 1147, when Corfu was seized by the Norman fleet.[47] It is likely that the icon with the inscription was a gift for Georgios from an embassy dispatched to Palermo by Manuel Komnenos in 1143/44, with the aim of forging an alliance between the Normans and the Byzantines.[48]

5. Georgios was of Antiochene origins, but he had to flee together with his family some time after the capture of the city by the Seljuk Turks in 1084. He was in the service of the Zarid ruler Tanīm in Ifriqiya before defecting to the Normans around 1108. For the life of Georgios of Antioch and a discussion of his Arabic biographies, see J. Jones, *Arabic Administration in Norman Sicily* (Cambridge 2002), 80–88.

6. προὔχοντα instead of 'ἄρχων τῶν ἀρχόντων'. Georgios held various titles. For example, in his anonymous epitaph, he is called πανυπερσέβαστος. For the text of this, see A. Rhoby, *Ausgewählte byzantinische Epigramme in illuminierten Handschriften: Verse und ihre inschriftliche Verwendung in Codices des 9. bis 15. Jahrhunderts* (Vienna 2018), 485, v. 5. For a discussion of the title, see 486-87.—Σικελαρχίας is a *hapax legomenon*, but Prodromos makes use of such compounds (e.g. στραταρχία, στρατοπεδαρχία, φυλαρχία). The word Σικελάρχης (cf. *LBG* s.v.) is used in Manganeios Prodromos as an epithet of Roger II (always with negative connotations).

68. Riddle on the cloud

This poem is a riddle on the cloud and its genesis. As is often the case with this kind of text, the I-person assumes the voice of the object, the identity of which must be discovered by solving linguistic puzzles. The concluding verse is an explicit invitation to the addressee to guess the solution: 'Know me: who I am,

---

[47] P. Rassow, 'Zum byzantinisch-normannischen Krieg 1147–1149', *MiÖG* 62 (1954), 213–18; cf. also P. Magdalino, *The Empire of Manuel I Komnenos, 1143–1180* (Cambridge 1993), 137, and E. Kislinger, 'Giorgio di Antiochia e la politica marittima tra Normanni e Bisanzio', in: M. Re and Cr. Rognoni (eds), *Giorgio di Antiochia: L'arte della politica in Sicilia nel XII secolo tra Bisanzio e l'Islam. Atti del Convegno Internazionale (Palermo, 19–20 Aprile 2007)* (Palermo 2009), 47–63.

[48] A. Acconcia Longo, 'Gli epitaffi giambici per Giorgio di Antiochia, per la madre e per la moglie', *Quellen und Forschungen aus italienischen Archiven und Bibliotheken* 61 (1981), 25–59, at 41–44.

whom I brought forth, who gave birth to me'. The first six verses develop a circular genealogy: the cloud's son is the rain (ὑετός), and the daughter of this son is the sea (θάλασσα), which in turn gives birth to the cloud. The poem does not build on the mythological story of the personified Nephele (=cloud), except perhaps for the combination 'divine daughter' (v. 1), which may be an allusion to the sea more generally, but also to the Hellespont, named after Helle, the mythological character who was drowned in the strait in her attempt to flee from her stepmother Ino with her brother Phrixus on a golden ram.

Even though Prodromos' work does not contain many riddles—in fact this is the only surviving riddle in his output—the genre is well-attested throughout the Byzantine centuries.[49] This also applies to the Komnenian period, with a large number of riddles written by various authors, including Eustathios Makrembolites,[50] Theodoros Aulikalamos,[51] Manuel Karantenos,[52] and Euthymios Tornikes.[53]

2. ἐμπελάω: instead of ἐμπελάζω, cf. Oppian, *Halieutika*, 2.176 and 3.312.

3. υἶιν is a very unusual epic accusative occurring only in Prodromos: see also *Miscellaneous poems*, 70.4, and *Historical poems*, 42.42. Prodromos may have coined it by analogy to the epic dative υἶι, which occurs in Homer and many other authors.

5. λιμοῦ is a better reading than λοιμοῦ. The meaning here is that harvests are ruined without rain, resulting in death from starvation, whereas plagues occur with or without rain.

7. φιλεῖ καὶ ἀπεχθαίρῃσι: note the use of the subjunctive instead of the indicative, probably chosen for the construction of a correct dactylic verse (see also poem 28.3).

69. Hypothetical verses about a dead body without hands washed up by the sea

An ethopoetic monologue from a deceased person relating the details of his death and how he lost both his hands. In the opening verses, the dead person

---

[49] On metrical riddles, see Lauxtermann, *Byzantine Poetry*, vol. 2, 252–56.
[50] M. Treu, *Eustathii Macrembolitae quae feruntur aenigmata* (Breslau 1893), 1–9.
[51] J. F. Boissonade, *Anecdota graeca e codicibus regiis*, 5 vols. (Paris 1829–33; repr. Hildesheim 1962), 3, 453–54 and Treu, *Eustathii Macrembolitae*, 10–14.
[52] U. Criscuolo, 'Altri inediti di Manuele Karanteno o Saranteno', *ΕΕΒΣ* 44 (1979–80), 151–63, at 161.
[53] In total ten riddles: see A. Papadopoulos-Kerameus, *Noctes Petropolitanae: Sbornik vizantijskich tekstov XII-XIII věkov* (St Petersburg 1913), 203–06; N. A. Bees, Τὰ χειρόγραφα τῶν Μετεώρων: Κατάλογος περιγραφικὸς τῶν χειρογράφων κωδίκων τῶν ἀποκειμένων εἰς τὰς Μονὰς τῶν Μετεώρων ἐκδιδόμενος ἐκ τῶν καταλοίπων, 2 vols. (Athens 1967), 685; and S. Zanadrea, 'Enigmistica bizantina: considerazioni preliminari', *Miscellanea Marciana* 2-4 (1987–89), 141–57, at 149 (no. 7).

addresses the beholder, saying that he did not lose his life and his hands because of war. He died in a shipwreck and then the fishes devoured his hands. In verses 11–16, the deceased person asks the beholder to tell his parents to stop eating fish; if they do not do so, they will eventually consume their own son. The two concluding verses repeat the message that if his mother were to eat fish, she would have her son in her belly/womb, just as she did when she was pregnant with him.

The content of the first ten verses resembles *Rhodanthe and Dosikles*, 6.480–491, where Dosikles, full of sorrow, laments the putative death of his beloved Rhodanthe after a turbulent storm wrecked their ship.[54] Dosikles' threnody and his description of the dead body of Rhodanthe is an ethopoetic monologue. Though the phrasing and the metrical form varies between the two works, we see here Prodromos using the same theme both in a self-contained *ethopoiia* and embedded in a large narrative.

Rubric ὑποθετικοί: as we remarked in Chapter 1 (pp. 19–20), this word suggests that this poem is an *ethopoiia*. However, it is worth noting that the word also denotes works intended as exhortation (cf. *LSJ* s.v.). Both this poem and the following three (70–72) address a stranger (see 69.1 and 72.4), showering him with exhortations. As with poems 70–72, which resemble funerary epigrams, poem 69 also reminds us of tomb inscriptions addressed to a passer-by.

1. περὶ ὄμμα πετάσσας: tmesis (περιπετάσσας).

3. The Homeric expression Ἄρης βροτολοιγὸς (cf. *LSJ* s.v.) becomes proverbial in Byzantium, as it is recorded in the *Souda* (3852, 6 and 553, 2).

6. νηὸς ὑγροσκελέος: see above p. 301.

7. εἰναλινήχυτος: 'swimming in the sea' is a *hapax legomenon* not recorded in any lexicon; it is a combination of the words ἐνάλιος ('of the sea') and νήχυτος, which Prodromos, however, apparently does not derive from νη- and χέω ('full-flowing'), but from νήχω ('to swim').

14. ἀλιτρεφέα is not a common epithet. It occurs earlier only in Quintus of Smyrna and Nonnus (*LSJ* s.v.). In the twelfth century, it is used elsewhere in Tzetzes, *Carmina Iliaca*, 2.291, and Eustathios of Thessaloniki, *Commentary*

---

[54] ἐντὸς παρ' αὐτὸν σὺ μένεις τὸν πυθμένα, | ἢ πόντος ἐλθὼν νεκρὰν ἐξέβρασέ σε | καὶ σῶμα γυμνὸν ἐκτὸς ἐξέρριψέ σε, | καί τις παρελθὼν ἢ κατὰ ψάμμον μέσην, | ἢ πρὸς τὸ χεῖλος τῆς θαλάσσης ἐμπλέων | ἀσυγκάλυπτον, ὦ θεοί, δέδορκέ σε; | Ἰχθῦς διεῖλον καὶ διεσπάσαντό σε, | ἢ κῦμα τοῖς κάχληξιν ἐξέθρυψέ σε, | καὶ ταῖς ὑφάλοις τῶν πετρῶν ἤραξέ σε; | πνέεις τι μικρὸν καὶ παρασπαίρεις ἔτι, | ἢ κῆτος ἀρτίπνικτον ἐρρόφησέ σε; (=Do you remain within the deep itself, | Or has the ocean found you and tossed you aside, a corpse, | And thrown you out, a naked body? | And who either passing by along the sandy shore | Or sailing on the edge of the sea | Has seen you, O gods, unveiled? | Have fishes torn you apart and ravaged you | Or have the waves battered you with their pebbles | And dashed you onto submerged rocks? | Or are you breathing a little and still gasping, | or are you recently drowned and swallowed by a sea-monster?); transl. in Jeffreys, *Byzantine Novels*, 110–11.

on the *Odyssey* I.175.29, as an epithet of the sun (Ἡελίοιο ἀλιτρεφέος) and seals (φωκάων ἀλιτρεφέων), respectively.—**Θαλασσοπόρα** also occurs in Prodromos, *Tetrasticha on the Old and New Testaments*, 205b.3: οἳ τόδε λέμβος ἔθεσθε θαλασσοπόρον, καλίγομφον, in *AP* IX.376.2, and in various other texts, as an epithet of a ship. However, this seems to be the only time it is used as an epithet of the word ζῷον.

70-72. Hypothetical verses about Pausanias who was petrified due to the death of his son Peter

As with the previous poem, these three short poems are *ethopoiiai*. While the speaker in the previous poem was a deceased person without hands, the main character speaking here is a tombstone standing over the grave of a certain Peter. In drawing inspiration from funerary epigrams, in which the tombstone is frequently personified to address a wayfarer, the tombstone in all three poems addresses its beholder, recounting the story of Peter's father, called Pausanias. The first poem, by using a number of puns (see below), recounts that Pausanias was turned into stone after the death of his son. The second poem is a comparison between Pausanias and Niobe. The final poem is a dialogue between the tombstone and its beholder.

Rubric ὑποθετικοί: see the discussion of the previous poem and pp. 19-20.

Poem 70

1. Πέτρος ἔχω Πέτρον: there is a wordplay here on the Greek word πέτρος for 'stone' and the name Πέτρος.

1. ἑκατοντάλιθος is a rare epithet of πέτρος. According to *LBG*, before Prodromos it is used only in the *Book of Ceremonies*, as an epithet of λάρναξ and λίθος, but it is worth noting that it denotes the very same words in the *Patria of Constantinople* 206.10 and 207.11.

4. ἔπαυσ' ἀνίην: another pun on the word παυσανίας, 'allayer of sorrow', and the name Pausanias.

Poem 71

1. Νιόβην πολύδακρυν: Niobe was turned into stone by Zeus after the death of her children. The earliest version of this story is found in *Iliad* 24.596-617.

For Niobe as a paradigm of grief in the novel of Niketas Eugenianos and other Byzantine texts, see Roilos, *Amphoteroglossia*, 72–73; cf. also S. Papaioannou, 'Byzantine Mirrors: Self-Reflection in Medieval Greek Writing', *DOP* 64 (2010), 81–102, at 99–100, and Jeffreys, *Byzantine Novels*, 256, esp. note 290. Prodromos refers once more to Niobe in *Historical poems*, 2.70, an oration consoling for Eirene Doukaina on the occasion of the death of her son Sevastokrator Andronikos, saying that her grief exceeded that of Niobe (along with other well-known ancient exempla, such as Iokaste and Hekabe). Note the use of Doric in this poem (for example, the form τὰν used twice in v. 3). It is not clear why Prodromos opted for these forms; they may hint at an imitation of the style of a tragic chorus or an ancient epigram in Doric. In any case, Doric forms occur elsewhere in his corpus (e.g. *Tetrasticha on the Old and New Testaments*, 9b.1 and 92b.1).

73–74. Verses of protest at seeing the disregard of learning

A set of poems on the popular twelfth-century theme of the futility of letters. In the first poem, the I-person addresses his books, bidding farewell to them and asking them to disappear completely from his life. The reason is that he has gained no benefit from his erudition, described in vv. 4–9 by enumerating some of the most celebrated classical authors, including Aristotle, Plato, Empedocles, Homer, and Democritus. The breadth of his learning is further emphasized by references to the study of rhetoric and orthography. In the second poem, the I-person urges his soul to distance himself from his books and stop pursuing a career as an intellectual. He is initially encouraged to go to places which host various kinds of spectacle, where jesters and mimes dance and sing—this is probably a subtle allusion to the 'rhetorical theatra'. But since people are so foolish and at present glorify inferior forms of learning, he is then advised to keep well away from these kinds of gatherings, in which foolish people seek glory through their intellectual achievements. The ideas of the futility of letters and the vanity of life are combined to articulate his wish to withdraw from public life.[55]

Poem 73

2. πρόπαν: an epithet of μελέδημα, although it is also used as an adverb in the late Byzantine period (cf. *LBG* s.v.). For this form and its use, see also Hesiod,

---

[55] For this kind of poem, see Lauxtermann, *Byzantine Poetry*, vol. 2, 156–57.

Theogony, ed. with Prolegomena and Commentary by M. L. West (Oxford 1966), 525.

4-9: The emphasis on learning with references to the entire spectrum of Greek literature and philosophy (Aristotle, Plato, Empedocles, Homer, and Democritus) is intended to contribute to the escalating tone of despair and frustration of the poem. Prodromos also includes excursuses on his education elsewhere. In *Historical poems* 38.50-59, for example, while complaining to Anna Komnene, he offers details about his education. For a discussion of this passage, see pp. 50-1.

6. Empedocles was a pre-Socratic philosopher and author of the Nature poem 'On the origins of the world' and the 'Purifications'. While Empedocles' works are praised here, his cosmological theory is attacked in *Miscellaneous poems*, 76. 53-57.

9-10. Democritus was an atomist philosopher in the second half of the fifth century;—Orpheus was a mythological person, particularly known for his music's magical powers over humans and animals. This reference to Orpheus is intended to emphasize the deep immersion of the I-person in poetry, since, in Byzantium, Orpheus is the symbol *par excellence* of poetry (see *ODB* 3 1538)—in Greek mythology Oeagrus is the father of Orpheus. The form Ύαγρος is rare (instead of the common Οἴαγρος), used elsewhere in a prose monody for Konstantinos Hagiotheodorites (Prodromos, *Orations*, 37.253.31), and before Prodromos only in Arethas, *Scripta Minora*, 17.191.2.

Poem 74

6-9. These verses allude to the competitive intellectual life of Constantinople. As noted above, the entertaining spectacles are an allusion to 'rhetorical theatra', while the mimes and jesters are a subtle attack on intellectual peers.—γελωτοπόνοισι is a *hapax legomenon* (cf. *LBG* s.v.), supplanting the common γελωτοποιός. On jesters and mimes in Byzantium, see P. Marciniak, 'How to Entertain the Byzantines? Mimes and Jesters in Byzantium', in A. Öztürkmen and E. B. Vitz (eds), *Medieval and Early Modern Performances in the Eastern Mediterranean* (Turnhout 2014), 125-48. This is not the first time Prodromos refers to mimes and jesters. In the satirical dialogue *Amarantos, or the erotic desire of an old man* 10.5-14, the protagonist's old teacher of philosophy, Stratocles, resembles a mime during his wedding with a young girl. Similarly, in his work *On those who curse Providence on* *account of poverty*, hideous-looking men who are getting married to young and beautiful girls act like mimes or jesters.[56]

75. Verses of protest regarding Providence

A poem filled with complaints about the social inequality between vulgar craftsmen who are wealthy and highly educated men who suffer dire poverty. Although social inequality is frequently criticized in Byzantine poems before Prodromos' time, the focus on rich craftsmen and poor intellectuals is deeply rooted in the thematic repertoire of twelfth-century poetry.[57] Its complex structure and rich content can be summarized as follows:

vv. 1-6	It is impossible to understand the depths of Providence's judgement.
vv. 7-40	The entire universe is governed by divine providence: the sun, the moon, the entire planet, and even all the climate phenomena.
vv. 41-50	A polemical criticism of Epicureanism, which maintains the absence of divine intervention.
vv. 51-56	The two opening verses of the poem are repeated (with minor differences). Though unaware of the hidden depths of God's will, the I-person is not able to endure the way lives are distributed.
vv. 57-96	A side-by-side description of the vulgar craftsmen of humble origin and hideous countenance and the intellectuals with well-bred manners. The former enjoy a comfortable life, while misfortune and poverty befall the latter.
vv. 97-102	Unlike the poor intellectuals, this throng of uneducated wealthy people is able to buy books and orations.
vv. 103-114	The rich craftsmen are compared to the foolish Meletus and Anytus, the poor intellectuals to the wise Socrates.
vv. 115-127	Diagnosis of the problem: the Greek philosophers were ignorant of wise Providence, resulting in the custom of dividing mankind into slaves and masters.
vv. 128-146	The blame should not be placed on gold, but on the foolish and rapacious nature of humans.

---

[56] For the text, see *PG* 133, col. 1293-1294a. [57] See the references on p. 329.

vv. 147-163   The I-person wishes to be granted a trumpet-like mouth to proclaim injustice and the transience of material riches.

vv. 164-167   The I-person is urged to keep silent, since not even Paul was able to shed light on the inexplicable will of God.

3-4. Habakkuk was an Old Testament prophet waiting at his watch-post for God to reply to his complaints about the injustice in the world.

8-40. In the prose work *On those who curse Providence on account of poverty* (*PG* 133, 1300A), which is a counterpart to this poem (see the discussion on pp. 49-50), there is similar imagery describing Providence regulating the entirety of creation.

20. Since Thales, it was known that the moon receives its light from the sun.— γλαυκοφεγγοῦς is a rare word which occurs elsewhere only in Eugenianos, *Drosilla and Charikles* 8.113 and *Anacharsis* 884.

22-23. These two verses seem to refer to the movement of the moon, which results in tidal effects.

43-44. A rebuke of Epicureanism, which teaches the absence of divine intervention. Attacks on Greek philosophers on these grounds are frequent in Prodromos' work. For example, the pre-Socratic philosophers Democritus and Hippo are scolded in his work *On those who curse Providence on account of poverty*, 1297A: Μὴ γὰρ δὴ τὴν Δημοκρίτου μανίαν νοσήσαιμεν, μηδ' εἰς τὴν Ἵππωνος ἐμπέσοιμεν ἀθεότητα, ὡς τοῦ παντὸς ἐπιχειρεῖν ἀφαιρεῖσθαι τὴν θείαν Πρόνοιαν.

45-48: The imagery of a ship without steersman and a horse without reins is intended to rebut Epicurean doctrine. Similar examples were used by Gregory of Nazianzus in a poem on Providence to refute the theory that the universe was self-generated and automatic: see Gregory of Nazianzus, *Poemata Arcana*, 5.10-13: Τίς δὲ δόμον ποτ' ὄπωπεν, ὃν οὐ χέρες ἐξετέλεσσαν; | Τίς ναῦν, ἢ θοὸν ἅρμα; τίς ἀσπίδα καὶ τρυφάλειαν; | Οὔτ' ἂν τόσσον ἔμεινεν ἐπὶ χρόνον, εἴπερ ἄναρχος, | Καὶ χορὸς ἂν λήξειεν ἀνηγεμόνευτος ἔμοιγε.

57-86. The financial self-sufficiency of workers of a low social status is a popular motif in Prodromos (see *Historical poems*, 38.68-74 or the third (Ptocho)prodromic poem), deriving from Aristophanes' *Wealth* 160-167. Among the many different types of workers, tailors and tanners are mentioned here, both of which are to be found in Aristophanes' *Wealth*. Moreover, the poem has intertextual connections with Lucian's *The Runaways* (12-13), where various craftsmen (such as fullers, joiners, and cobblers) take advantage of philosophy and turn into false philosophers in order to move up the social ladder. Unlike Prodromos' poem, in Lucian they are not financially secure. The motif is also used after Prodromos, in the poetry of Manuel Philes: see Kubina, *Manuel Philes*, 197–98.

58. Βυρσοδέψης: the profession of tanning is associated with low status and usually has negative connotations in Greek literature (see *ODB* 3 2010). The most well-known example is Aristophanes' *Knights*, where Cleon is called a tanner for his seductive demagogic strategies: see H. Lind, *Der Gerber Kleon in den 'Rittern' des Aristophanes: Studien zur Demagogenkomodie* (Frankfurt am Main 1990).—σκυτεύς: As with tanners, cobblers enjoyed a low social status and are often scorned for their social aspirations in ancient literature. For some remarks, see Alexiou, 'Poverty of Écriture', 17.

59. Here the craftsmen are presented as a disorderly crowd of people. There is a similar description of the working class as a chaotic mob in Ephraem, *Chronicle*, 5553–5555: ὁ ξυγκλύδων ὄχλος δὲ καὶ τῶν συρφάκων, | ἀλλαντοπῶλαι, βυρσοδέψαι καὶ ῥάπται, | παλιγκαπήλων ἀλόγιστος φατρία.

63. νῦν δ' ἐξ ἁμάξης ὑβριοῖ: the scribe of Vat. gr. 305 indicates that this line is a proverb by adding the word 'παροιμία' in the margin. For the proverb, see *LSJ* s.v. ἅμαξα.

64–65. The association of women working in public places, and particularly in taverns, with prostitution is common in Byzantine literature: see T. Labuk, 'Aristophanes in the Service of Niketas Choniates: Gluttony, Drunkenness and Politics in the Χρονικὴ διήγησις', *JÖB* 66 (2016), 127–51, at 138, note 82 (with extensive literature).

67–68. A witticism revolving around the low value of timber. The uneducated savages take pride in their origins, although their father is nothing more than 'a "prince of logs" or a timber-merchant', an occupation with very little social value.

69. In Byzantium, shoes are a sign of economic standing and social significance: see P. Koukoules, Βυζαντινῶν βίος καὶ πολιτισμός, 6 vols. (Athens 1948–55), vol. 4, 395–418, and Alexiou, 'The Poverty of Écriture', 18, esp. note 37. The image of craftsmen who, despite their lack of *paideia*, enjoy footwear, features in twelfth-century begging poetry (*Ptochoprodromika* 3.60–61; *Historical poems*, 38.71).

73. Inebriation and its connection with inappropriate performances frequently features in satirically charged scenes in various twelfth-century texts, such as the description of the drunken sleeping Nausikrates at a banquet (*Rhodanthe and Dosikles* 3.19–32) and the drunken dance of the aged Maryllis in honour of Dionysos (Eugenianos, *Drosilla and Charikles* 6.270–289).

74. The gluttony of vulgar craftsmen is compared to that of the 'seleukis' (*pastor roseus*, rosy starling), a bird renowned in Greek literature for its voracity: see W. G. Arnott, *Birds in the Ancient World from A to Z* (New York 2007), 309-10. In the twelfth century, the bird 'seleukis' is mentioned as a symbol of gluttony only in a verse invective by Euthymios Tornikes against an unknown bishop of Seleucia who attempted to take control of the monasteries on Euboia contrary to canon law (Euthymios Tornikes, *Poems* (ed. Hörandner), 4.1-4: Λαίμαργα φασὶ ζῶα τὰς σελευκίδας, | αἳ καὶ κατεσθίουσι πᾶν ζώων γένος | καὶ πτῶμα μυροῦν καὶ σεσηπότα μέλη | ἀκταῖς ῥιφέντα καὶ ῥόθοις θαλαττίοις).

81-82. The most famous horse of antiquity, Alexander's charger Bucephalus, was of Thessalian breeding; this became a popular *topos* in various Greek texts (e.g. Sophocles, *Electra*, 703-706; Euripides, *Andromache*, 1229). Similarly, the quality of Thessalian and Arabian horses becomes proverbial in Prodromos (cf. *Historical poems*, 45.210-211; 59.20-21; and 44.69-71) and in other twelfth-century works (e.g. *Timarion* 7.193: Ἵπποι δὲ τούτοις Ἀραβικοὶ γαυριῶντες ὑπέστρωντο and *Anacharsis* 1144-1145: ἵππον Ἀραβικὸν ὠνησάμενος γαῦρον).

87-96. The description of genteel, poor intellectuals in Prodromos, *On those who curse Providence on account of poverty*, 1293B, is very similar: ὁ δέ τις ἕτερος, Κόδροις μὲν τὸ γένος, Πλάτωσι δὲ τὴν παιδείαν παραβαλλόμενος, μηδὲ μιᾶς εὐποροίη γοῦν ἡμιόνου.

93. Food denotes social class: the complete lack of food is intended to place the intellectuals at the very bottom of the twelfth-century pyramid of economic prosperity, echoing one of the main motifs of the (Ptocho)prodromika (e.g. *Ptochoprodromika* 4.399: ἐκεῖνοι τὴν σεμίδαλαν, ἡμεῖς τὸν πιτυροῦντα).

100. The frustration against these shabby vulgarians escalates even more, as they even snatch away books because of their burgeoning wealth. There seems to be a core of truth behind this complaint, since the same idea is expressed elsewhere in Prodromos: see, for example, *Encomium of Patriarch Ioannes IX Agapetos* 7.312-17. In *The Plato-lover, or the tanner* 124-132, a rustic man who possesses a book of Plato is scorned. The *Sale of political and poetical lives*, moreover, describes the auction of some of the most well-known authors of antiquity (Homer, Hippocrates, Euripides, Aristophanes, Pomponius, and Demosthenes) conducted by Hermes, where all the potential bidders are called ignoramuses, since they are unable to appreciate the qualities of these authors.

107-108. Meletus was the chief prosecutor in the trial of Socrates, which led to the unjust execution of the philosopher.—ἕνδεκα: according to Plato,

Phaedo, 59e–60b, eleven prison officers were chosen by lot to give directions to Socrates regarding his execution.

112. Anytus was a powerful Athenian politician who acted as accuser of Socrates (Plato, *Apology*, 399b; 18c; 29b; 31a) together with Meletus and Lycon.

117-118. The philosophical doctrines of *tyche* and *automaton* are not easily distinguishable. The Byzantines took an interest in their relationship: for example, a section of Psellos' philosophical work *Concise Answers to Various Questions* is entitled Περὶ τύχης καὶ αὐτομάτου. For the text of the work, see L. G. Westerink, *Michael Psellus, De omnifaria doctrina: critical text and introduction* (Utrecht 1949), 59.—Ἑλλήνων δύο: it is not easy to determine the identity of these two Greeks to whom Prodromos refers, but he may mean the two pre-Socratic philosophers Democritus and Hippo, since both are attacked in the prose work *On those who curse Providence on account of poverty* (see above p. 328). However, *tyche* and *automaton* are also essential parts of the Aristotelian and Epicurean doctrines of causality.

128. γῆς τυφλὸν τέκνον: an allusion to the Aristophanic *Plutus*, who is described as a blind beggar distributing wealth in a random manner.

141-144. To emphasize the tragedy and absurdity of the current situation, Prodromos refers to the popular imagery of the weeping Heraclitus and laughing Democritus. For a discussion of this legend and its protean use in literature, see C. E. Lutz, 'Democritus and Heraclitus', *The Classical Journal* 49/7 (1954), 309-14 (with no discussion of the Byzantine tradition).

148. ἀγχίστροφον δὲ γλῶσσαν stands for rhetorical ambidexterity, here metonymically rendered by the image of a tongue able to twist and turn with quick writhing movements. For the term and its use in twelfth-century texts, see Roilos, *Amphoteroglossia*, 29-30, and P. A. Agapitos, 'John Tzetzes and the Blemish Examiners: A Byzantine Teacher on Schedography, Everyday Language and Writerly Disposition', *MEG* 17 (2017) 1-57, at 35-36.

149. Home to the oracle of Delphi, Parnassus was known as the mountain of the Muses and poetry from antiquity. On Parnassus in Byzantine literature, see Rhoby, *Reminiszenzen an antike Stätten*, 216.

76. On Friendship's departure

This poem is an ethopoetic dialogue between Friendship and a stranger about the sufferings the former has undergone because of her husband, and her decision to abandon the world. Prodromos' work heavily depends on Lucian's

Runaways, in which the personified Philosophy leaves the world because of the false philosophers.[58] Its structure and content can be outlined as follows:

1-35	A dialogue between the two main characters. Friendship has left her husband World because she has been beaten and thrown out of their home. Despite her initial hesitation about the details of her story, Friendship agrees to give a full account of it.
36-261	A long monologue by Friendship with many details about her qualities and divine powers:
36-49	She establishes the hierarchy between the numerous celestial beings. Only Lucifer questioned her authority and was therefore cast out of heaven.
50-108	She created the entire universe and continues to govern it.
109-125	The city and its urban life are regulated by her.
126-138	Marriage and erotic affection exist thanks to her.
139-153	She even convinced God to become a mortal and rescue mankind from the yoke of evil.
154-193	Despite her qualities and her superiority over Animosity, she has been thrown out of her house by her husband, with the assistance of Folly.
194-198	Even though her husband has chosen Animosity, Friendship does not have feelings of hatred towards him.
199-221	She firmly maintains that the accusations against her husband are not unfounded, emphasizing that Animosity is the source of all kinds of tensions.
222-228	Friendship continues to demonstrate her virtues over the vices of Animosity with two examples from Greek drama.
231-245	Friendship helped the Greeks to win the Trojan war. It was she who reconciled the Greeks and summoned Achilles to fight against Hector.
246-261	Following her departure from the world, all good things have vanished and Animosity together with her six evil children have caused great tumult.
262-297	Another dialogue between Friendship and the stranger. The stranger asks Friendship to share her life with him and enter his hut. Though initially reluctant, she eventually accepts his invitation. The stranger swears that he will remain faithful to her.

---

[58] See the discussion on p. 23.

rubric: in the edition by Gesner, there is a brief summary of the poem between the title and the main text of the poem:

> κύρου Θεοδώρου τοῦ Προδρόμου ἐπὶ ἀποδήμου τῇ φιλίᾳ.
> Περιοχή τοῦ δράματος.
> Φιλία ὑπ᾽ ἀνδρὸς αὐτῆς τοῦ κόσμου ἤτοι βίου ἀνθρωπίνου
> ἐκβέβληται· συνεζεύχθη δ᾽ αὐτῷ ἡ μαχλὰς ἔχθρα,
> συμβουλευσάσης Μωρίας τῆς θεραπαινίδος αὐτοῦ.
> Τὰ πρόσωπα.
> Ξένος καὶ Φιλία.

However, this title is Gesner's invention, which, in turn, was copied in later editions, such as that of Dübner.

2–14. The description of Friendship's appearance resembles that of Rhodanthe in *Rhodanthe and Dosikles* 6.291–304, where Dosikles laments for her after their separation.

6. βλαυτίον: The poor condition of Friendship's shoes and girdle is intended emphasize the hardship of her long wanderings. Similarly, in *Historical poems*, 79.19–20, Prodromos focuses on his ruined shoes in order to highlight the long distances that he has covered, as a poet in the service of the court (οἷς ἔπι πόλλ᾽ ἐμόγησα καὶ ἄρβυλα πλεῖστα δάμαξα | πολλῆς ἡματίῃσι καὶ ἐννυχίοισι κελεύθοις).

11. ἀρβυλίδες: For shoes as a sign of financial self-sufficiency, see above p. 329.

32–34. Friendship summons the stranger to come and sit with her next to a pine tree; only then will she start talking about her torments. The choice of the setting has some intertextual connections with earlier works: in Plato, *Phaedros*, 229a, Socrates asks Phaedros to sit with him next to a plane tree and repeat a speech of Lysias he had just heard; in Achilles Tatius' novel, Clitophon asks the anonymous narrator to do the same thing (cf. *Leucippe and Klitophon* 1.2.3, 4).

36–39. Friendship is united with the Holy Trinity and the incorporeal intellects, which stands for the angels of different ranks. Similar imagery is used for the personified Chastity in poem 2 for Gregory of Nazianzus, where Chastity is united with the Holy Trinity, angels, and men of unblemished soul.

39–41: Prodromos derives the hierarchical status of the celestial beings from Ps. Dionysios Areopagites, *De caelesti hierarchia*, (chapter VI) 26, 1–27, 2 for

Ps. Dionysios distinguishes the triads of the Cherubim, Seraphim, and Thrones from the other celestial beings.

45. Friendship places a chain between the celestial beings to hold them together. Prodromos is alluding to the Homeric 'golden chain' (*Iliad* 8.19) via its Neoplatonic allegorical interpretation, which associated it with ideas of love and friendship that shaped Byzantine understanding of this motif. For this motif in the twelfth century, see Roilos, *Amphoteroglossia*, 176–77.

53–54. Empedoclean cosmogony as expressed in the Nature poem is here lambasted for claiming that the world was fashioned because of strife (νεῖκος), the very opposite of love (φιλότης). Discussions of Empedocles' philosophical theories seem to be fashionable in twelfth-century literature, and particularly in Prodromos' milieu: a letter of Michael Italikos about Empedocles' poem on strife and love was written at the request of an unknown addressee (*Michael Italikos, Letters*, 29.193-197).

53–57. Friendship questions the credibility of Empedocles' theory by referring to the well-known story that he hurled himself into the flames of Mount Etna to prove his godlike nature.

58–61: A reference to the theory that the world was formed into a geometrical sphere because of φιλότης [Empedocles, *Fragments*, 27.28, 29 (p. 237–38 Diels-Kranz)], which becomes standard from Plato onwards, e.g. Plato, *Timaeus*, 33b; Aristotle, *De Caelo*, 290b/I 2; Aristotle, *De Coloribus*, 280A.

95–96. An image of the personified seasons as four weaving maidens. This has similarities with *Historical poems*, 1.81-83, where the coronation of Alexios—the first son of emperor Ioannes II Komnenos—is celebrated, with the Graces presented as tender maidens weaving a rhythmic dance around the Empress Piroska-Eirene of Hungary, wife of Ioannes II. For the various personifications of the four seasons in Byzantium, see *ODB* 3 1861.

102. τετρακτὺς: An allusion to the Pythagorean doctrine of 'four-ness' comprising the sequence 1, 2, 3, 4, whose sum (1 + 2 + 3 + 4) resulted in the perfect number 10—τετρακτὺς τῶν χυμῶν stands for the four bodily fluids (blood, yellow bile, black bile, and phlegm) and their well-balanced coexistence.

127-136. To visualize Friendship's control over erotic desire, Prodromos juxtaposes a number of traditional novelistic motifs: the intertwining tree branches between the date palms; the eel which comes to the shore to mate with the viper; and the attraction between the magnet and iron. All these motifs are drawn from Achilles Tatius' novel, but they become particularly popular in the Komnenian novels and Palaeologan romances (cf. also the apparatus).

142. τὸ παμφαὲς φῶς echoes *John* 8.12, where Jesus refers to himself as 'the light of the world', sent to earth by his Father to triumph over evil and sin.

156-157. As indicated both in the text and by the scribe of V in the margins of these two verses, Friendship here makes use of two popular maxims. Despite her acts of kindness, her husband is unable to appreciate them—it is like sprinkling fragrant scents on a corpse and playing the lyre for witless asses. It is worth noting that these maxims appear together elsewhere only in two works, which draw extensively upon Prodromos' work: in *Anacharsis* 776-777 (ἀλλ' εἰς νεκροὺς τὰ μύρα, κατὰ τὴν παροιμίαν, καὶ πρὸς ὄνους κανθηλίους τὸ λύρισμα), and in Euthymios Tornikes, *Poems* (ed. Hörandner), 4.182-183: ὡς εἰς νέκυν ἔραινον εὐώδη μύρα, | ὡς εὐμελῆ δ' ἔπληττον εἰς ὄνον λύραν.

163-165. The slave girl Folly (Μωρία) assisted Animosity in throwing Friendship out of her own house. The personification of Folly is another connection between the poem and its hypotext, Lucian's *The Runaways* (14, 8-14), where the lady Folly (Ἀπόνοια), with the help of Boldness, Ignorance, and Impudence, serves sham philosophers by making them even more aggressive.

178-179. There seems to be a witty remark here, but I have not been able to decode it.

180-181. The food imagery and the contrast between luxurious and simple food (sesame cakes and salt, respectively) is intended to highlight the moderate character of Friendship. Moreover, the use of the word 'πλακοῦντες' seems to have Aristophanic overtones (Aristophanes, *Acharnians*, 1092 and 1125).

194. *Βίος*: For most of the poem Friendship's husband is called 'Κόσμος', but from this verse on, Prodromos switches to 'Βίος'. It is hard to explain this change, but both words are translated as 'World' for the sake of consistency.

205. πνέεις δὲ πῦρ is a standard expression denoting rhetoric prowess. For example, in *Miscellaneous poems*, 53, the personified Rhetoric states Ἐγὼ πνέω πῦρ κατὰ τῶν ἀντιθέτων.

207. ἀντιπροθοίμην is rare, occurring elsewhere only in the work of Dio Cassius, in the *Epitome* of Dio Cassius by Ioannes Xiphilinos, and in Zonaras' *Epitome historiarum* (cf. *TLG*). Probably Prodromos borrowed the word directly from Dio Cassius, whose work he seems to have been familiar with. For example, in the prose work *On those who curse Providence on account of poverty* 1292B, he quotes verbatim an extract from Dio Cassius, while in Prodromos, *Orations*, 31.177.99-101, a work addressed to Alexios Aristenos, he says: καὶ πάλαι μὲν ὁ Ἀθηναῖος ἔφη σοφὸς ἐν ἐπιστολῇ τὴν οἰκουμένην ὅλην εἰς μόνον ἀποβλέπειν τὸν Δίωνα. Ἐγὼ δὲ καὶ Δίωνα μὲν θαυμάζω τοῖς ἱστορικοῖς βιβλίοις ἐντυγχάνων (=the wise man of Athens said once in a letter that the world kept his gaze on Dion and no other. I too admire Dion when I am reading his history books).

210. δοῦλον...δεσπόταις: 'servants are hostile to their masters' is a proverb first attested in the Hermogenian corpus (cf. *app. Font.*). It is wrongly ascribed to Euripides in Prodromos, *Bion Prasis*, 301 (see also the comments in Migliorini, *Teodoro Prodromo*, 163), and in Arsenios Apostoles' collection of proverbs, ed. Leutsch, XVIII.4b.1 (p. 716).

211. λυσιγάμου is another rare word, attested only twice before Prodromos: Gregory of Nazianzus, *Poems*, I.2.29 [898] 186, and *AP* V.302.14.

222-224. The feud between Eteocles and Polyneices over the throne of Thebes resulted in a battle during which the two brothers killed each other. The story appears in the *Iliad* 4.376-398, but it is a common theme in the works of writers of Greek Tragedy.

225-228. The strong friendship between Orestes and Pylades becomes prominent in Euripides. The relationship between them is a frequent motif in twelfth-century texts concerned with the theme of friendship: in a poem on friendship, Manuel Karantenos notes that a loyal friend is willing to travel to the underworld, as did Pylades (Karantenos, *Poems*, 2.5-6: ἄλλος Πυλάδης Ὀρέστῃ φιλουμένῳ | ῥᾴστως θελήσας συγκατελθεῖν 'εἰς Ἅιδου'), while in Niketas Choniates, *Orations*, 18.196.13, a prose oration on friendship, Orestes and Pylades are also used as paradigms of steadfast friendship.

231-232. Achilles refused to help the Greeks further against the Trojans when Agamemnon took away his mistress Briseis (cf. *Iliad* 1.182ff).

233. Πριάμου παῖς: Priam's son is Hector, who was very successful on the third day of the battle, before Achilles' return to the battle.

236. Ajax was a hero renowned in Homer for his gigantic size (*Iliad* 2.768-769).—τῷ πελωρίῳ is used of Ajax from Homer onwards (*Iliad* 17.174), and this is also found in twelfth-century texts, e.g. in Euthymios Tornikes, *Poems* (ed. Hörandner), 4.96.

240-245: The account of Achilles dragging Hector's dead body is in *Iliad* 22.395-405.

254-255. Animosity has six children: three sons (Phthonos, Ambush, Murder) and three daughters (Vice, Wrath, Battle). These six personifications seem to be inventions by Prodromos to accentuate the world's critical situation resulting from the absence of Friendship. The personification of *Phthonos* is particularly interesting since this emotion plays an instrumental role in Prodromos and twelfth-century literature more generally: see M. Hinterberger, *Phthonos*:

Mißgunst, Neid und Eifersucht in der byzantinischen Literatur (Wiesbaden 2013), 425–41.

270. τὴν καλύβην εἴσελθε: according to Hesychios, the word has a twofold meaning: 'hut' and 'marriage chamber' (κ 523 [ed. Latte 1953–2009])—both meanings suit the content of the verse. The word is used with the same ambiguity in Prodromos' novel: see Jeffreys, *Byzantine Novels*, 143.

279–297. Friendship asks the stranger to take an oath before he receives her. This is reminiscent of Rhodanthe's oath of everlasting love to Dosikles (*Rhodanthe and Dosikles* 7.111–112). For oath-taking in Byzantium, see Koukoules, Βυζαντινῶν βίος καὶ πολιτισμός, vol. 3, 346–75.

288. διπλόας is used elsewhere in the epigrammatic cycle 'On Virtues and Vices' (poem 53) to denote the ambivalent nature of rhetoric.

Bibliography

Primary Sources

1. Texts by Theodoros Prodromos

Admonitory poem/Against envy (Hörandner 157), ed. W. Hörandner, 'Visuelle Poesie in Byzanz: Versuch einer Bestandaufnahme', *JÖB* 40 (1990), 1–43

Amarantos, or the erotic desire of an old man (Hörandner 146), ed. T. Migliorini, 'Teodoro Prodromo: Amaranto', *MEG* 7 (2007), 183–247

Bion Prasis, Theodoros Prodromos, ed. E. Cullhed, in P. Marciniak, Taniec w roli Tersytesa: Studia nad satyrą bizantyńską [A Dance in the Role of Thersites: Studies on Byzantine Satire] (Katowice 2016)

Calendar in tetrasticha, ed. C. Giannelli, 'Tetrastici di Theodoro Prodromo sulle feste fisse e sui santi del calendario bizantino', *AnBoll* 75 (1957), 299–336 371 = *SBN* 10 (1963), 255–89

Commentary on Aristotle's Posterior Analytics 2 (Hörandner 134), ed. M. Cacouros, *Le commentaire de Théodore Prodrome aux Analytiques postérieurs, livre II d'Aristote: Texte (editio princeps, tradition manuscrite), étude du commentaire de Prodrome*, unpublished PhD thesis (Paris IV–Sorbonne 1992)

Dedicatory poem for the novel, ed. P. A. Agapitos, 'Poets and Painters: Theodoros Prodromos' Dedicatory Verses of His Novel to an Anonymous Caesar', *JÖB* 50 (2000), 173–85

Encomium of Patriarch Ioannes IX Agapetos (Hörandner 84), ed. K. A. Manaphis, 'Θεοδώρου τοῦ Προδρόμου Λόγος εἰς τὸν πατριάρχην Κωνσταντινουπόλεως Ἰωάννην Θ΄ τὸν Ἀγαπητὸν', *ΕΕΒΣ* 41 (1974), 223–42

Epigram on the Last Supper (Hörandner 126), ed. W. Hörandner, 'Zu einigen religiösen Epigrammen', in: U. Criscuolo and R. Maisano (eds), *Synodia. Studia humanistica Antonio Garzya septuagenario ab amicis atque discipulis dicata* (Naples 1997), 431–42

Exegesis on the canons of Kosmas and Ioannes of Damascus, ed. H. M. Stevenson, praefatus est I. B. Pitra, *Theodori Prodromi Commentarios in Carmina Sacra Melodorum Cosmae Hierosolymitani et Ioannis Damasceni* (Rome 1888)

Fifth Ptochoprodromic poem (Hörandner 213), ed. A. Maiuri, 'Una nuova poesia di Theodoro Prodromo in greco volgare', *BZ* 23 (1914–19), 397–407

Grammar (Hörandner 138), ed. C. G. Goettling, *Theodosii Alexandrini Grammatica* (Leipzig 1822)

Historical Poem 78, ed. M. Tziatzi-Papagianni, *Theodoros Prodromos, Historisches Gedicht LXXVIII, BZ* 86–87 (1993–94), 363–82

Historical Poems (Hörandner 1–79), ed. W. Hörandner, *Theodoros Prodromos: Historische Gedichte* (Vienna 1974)

Iambic calendar (Hörandner 119), ed. A. Acconcia Longo, *Il calendario giambico in monostici di Teodoro Prodromo* (Rome 1983)

Katomyomachia (Hörandner 139), ed. H. Hunger, *Der byzantinische Katz-Mäuse-Krieg* (Graz/Vienna/Cologne 1968)

Letters and Orations (Hörandner 80-83, 85-111), ed. M. D. J. Op de Coul, *Théodore Prodrome: Lettres et Discours. Édition, Traduction, Commentaire*, 2 vols., unpublished PhD thesis (Paris 2007)
On those who curse Providence on account of poverty (Hörandner 151), ed. J. P. Migne, *PG* 133, 1291-1302
Ptochoprodromika (Hörandner 209-12), ed. H. Eideneier, *Ptochoprodromos: Einführung, Kritische Ausgabe, deutsche Übersetzung, Glossar* (Cologne 1991); cf. also H. Eideneier, Πτωχοπρόδρομος (Herakleion 2012)
Rhodanthe and Dosikles, ed. M. Marcovich, *Theodori Prodromi Rhodanthes et Dosiclis amorum libri IX* (Stuttgart/Leipzig 1991)
Satirical Works (Hörandner 141-42 and 144-51), ed. T. Migliorini, *Gli scritti satirici in greco letterario di Teodoro Prodromo: introduzione, edizione, traduzione, comment*, PhD thesis (Pisa 2010)
Schede, ed. S. D. Papadimitriou, *Feodor Prodrom*, Odessa 1905; I. D. Polemis, 'Προβλήματα τῆς βυζαντινῆς σχεδογραφίας', *Hell* 45 (1995), 277-302; I. Vassis, 'Graeca sunt, non leguntur. Zu den schedographischen Spielereien des Theodoros Prodromos', *BZ* 86/87 (1993/94), 1-19
Tetrasticha for Basil of Caesarea/Tetrasticha for John Chrysostom, ed. H. Guntius, *Cyri Theodori Prodromi epigrammata ut uetustissima, ita pijssima, quibus omnia utriusq(ue) testamenti capita felicissime comprehenduntur: cum alijs nonnullis, quae Index uersa pagella singillatim explicat* (Basel 1536)
Tetrasticha for Gregory of Nazianzus, ed. M. D'Ambrosi, *I tetrastici giambici ed esametrici sugli episodi principali della vita di Gregorio Nazianzeno, Introduzione, edizione critica, traduzione e commento* (Rome 2008)
Tetrasticha for the great martyrs Theodoros, Georgios, and Demetrios (Hörandner 117), ed. C. Giannelli, 'Epigrammi di Teodoro Prodromo in onore dei senti megalomartiri Teodoro, Giorgio e Demetrio', in: *Studi in onore di Luigi Castiglioni* (Florence 1960), 333-71 = *SBN* 10 (1963), 349-78
Tetrasticha on the Old and New Testaments, ed. G. Papagiannis (Hörandner 115), *Theodoros Prodromos: Jambische und hexametrische Tetrasticha auf die Haupterzählungen des Alten und des Neuen Testaments*, 2 vols. (Wiesbaden 1997)
To the caesar or for the colour green (Hörandner 145), ed. J. A. Cramer, *Anecdota græca e codd. manuscriptis bibliothecarum oxoniensium*, 4 vols. (Oxford 1835), vol. 3, 216-21

2. Texts by other authors

A. Apostoles, Γέρας εἴ μ' ὀνομάσειας σπάνιον τῶν σπουδαίων, οὐκ ἂν ἁμάρτοις δηλαδή, τῆς ἀληθείας φίλε (Rome c. 1519)
A. Apostoles, Ἀποφθέγματα φιλοσόφων καὶ στρατηγῶν, ῥητόρων τε καὶ ποιητῶν συλλεγέντα παρὰ Ἀρσενίου ἀρχιεπισκόπου Μονεμβασίας (Rome c. 1519)
Achilleid, ed. O. L. Smith, *The Byzantine Achilleid: The Naples Version* (Vienna 1999)
Anacharsis, ed. D. Christidis, Μαρκιανὰ ἀνέκδοτα (Thessaloniki 1984)
Andronikos Palaiologos, *Kallimachos and Chrysorroe*, ed. M. Pichard, *Le Roman de Callimaque et de Chrysorrhoé* (Paris 1956)
Anna Komnene, *Alexias*, ed. A. Kambylis and D. R. Reinsch, *Annae Comnenae Alexias*, 2 vols. (Berlin/New York 2001)
Anonymous poem on St Nicholas, ed. S. G. Mercati, 'Vita giambica di S. Nicola di Mira secondo il codice Messinese greco 30', in: *Collectanea Byzantina*, 2 vols. (Rome 1970), 44-65
Arethas, *Scripta Minora*, ed. L. G. Westerink, *Arethae archiepiscopi Caesariensis scripta minora*, vol. 1-2 (Leipzig 1968/1972)

Arsenios, *Metrical Preface to Ionia*, ed. C. Walz, *Arsenii violetum: Ἀρσενίου Ἰωνίαν* (Stuttgart 1832)
Basil of Caesarea, *Oratio ad adolescentes*, ed. M. Naldini, *Basilio di Cesarea. Discorso ai Giovani (Oratio ad adolescentes)* (Florence 1984)
Christodoulos Hagioeuplites, *Poem on St Barbara*, ed. C. Gallavotti, 'Nota sulla schedografia di Moscopulo e suoi precedenti fino a Teodoro Prodromo', *Bolletino dei Classici* III.4 (1983), 3–35
Ephraem, *Chronicle*, ed. O. Lampsides, *Ephraem Aenii Historia Chronica* (Athens 1990)
Eustathios Makrembolites, ed. M. Treu, *Eustathii Macrembolitae quae feruntur aenigmata* (Breslau 1893)
Eustathios Makrembolites, *Hysmine and Hysminias*, ed. M. Marcovich, *Eustathius Macrembolites: De Hysmines et Hysminiae amoribus libri XI* (Munich/Leipzig 2001)
Eustathios of Thessaloniki, *Commentary on the Odyssey*, ed. G. Stallbaum, *Eustathii Archiepiscopi Thessalonicensis Commentarii ad Homeri Odysseam*, vols. 1–2 (Leipzig 1825/1826)
Euthymios Tornikes, *Poems*, ed. A. Papadopoulos-Kerameus, *Noctes Petropolitanae: Sbornik vizantijskich tekstov XII–XIII věkov* (St Petersburg 1913)
Euthymios Tornikes, *Poems*, ed. W. Hörandner, 'Dichtungen des Euthymios Tornikes in Cod. gr. 508 der Rumänischen Akademie', in P. Odorico, A. Rhoby, and E. Schiffer (eds), *Wolfram Hörandner: Facettes de la littérature byzantine. Contributions choisies* (Paris 2017), 93–140
Gregory of Nazianzus, *Poems*, ed. J. P. Migne, *PG* 37
Gregory of Nazianzus, *Poemata Arcana*, ed. D. A. Sykes and C. Moreschine, *St Gregory of Nazianzus, Poemata Arcana* (Oxford 1997)
Ioannes Mauropous, ed. P. de Lagarde, *Iohannis Euchaitorum Metropolitae quae in Codice Vaticano Graeco 676 supersunt* (Göttingen 1882)
Ioannes Tzetzes, *Letters*, ed. P. A. M. Leone, *Ioannis Tzetzae epistulae* (Leipzig 1972)
Ioannes Tzetzes, *Carmina Iliaca*, ed. P. A. M. Leone, *Ioannis Tzetzae Carmina Iliaca* (Catania 1995)
Ioannes Tzetzes, *Histories*, ed. P. A. M. Leone, *Ioannis Tzetzae Historiae* (Galatina ²2007)
Isaak Komnenos, *Kosmosoteira Typikon*, ed. L. Petit, 'Typikon du monastère de la Kosmosotira près d'Aenos (1152)', *IRAIK* 13 (1908), 17–75
Joseph Bryennios, ed. N. Tomadakis, 'Ἰωσὴφ μοναχοῦ τοῦ Βρυεννίου ἐπιστολαὶ λ'', *ΕΕΒΣ* 46 (1983–86), 279–360
Konstantinos Manasses, *Funerary oration on the death of Nikephoros Komnenos*, ed. E. Kurtz, 'Εὐσταθίου Θεσσαλονίκης καὶ Κωνσταντίνου Μανασσῆ μονῳδίαι περὶ τοῦ θανάτου Νικηφόρου Κομνηνοῦ', *VV* 17 (1910), 302–22
Konstantinos Manasses, *Aristandros and Kallithea*, ed. O. Mazal, *Der Roman des Konstantinos Manasses: Überlieferung, Rekonstruktion, Textausgabe der Fragmente* (Vienna 1967); ed. E. Th. Tsolakis, Συμβολὴ στὴ μελέτη τοῦ ποιητικοῦ ἔργου τοῦ Κωνσταντίνου Μανασσῆ καὶ κριτικὴ ἔκδοση τοῦ μυθιστορήματός του 'Τὰ κατ' Ἀρίστανδρον καὶ Καλλιθέαν' (Thessaloniki 1967)
Manganeios Prodromos, *Poems*, ed. S. Bernardinello, *Theodori Prodromi De Manganis* (Padova 1972)
Manuel Karantenos, *Poems*, ed U. Criscuolo, 'Altri inediti di Manuele Karanteno o Sarànteno', *ΕΕΒΣ* 44 (1979–80), 151–63
Manuel Philes, *Poems*, ed. E. Miller, *Manuelis Philae carmina*, 2 vols. (Paris 1855–57)
Manuel Philes, *Poems*, ed. M. Gedeon, 'Μανουὴλ τοῦ Φιλῆ ἱστορικὰ ποιήματα', *Ekklesiastike Aletheia* 3 (1882–83), 215–20, 246–50, 655–59

Manuel Philes, *Poems*, ed. E. Braounou-Pietsch, *Beseelte Bilder: Epigramme des Manuel Philes auf bildliche Darstellungen* (Vienna 2010)

Michael Choniates, *Poems*, ed. Sp. Lambros, Μιχαὴλ Ἀκομινάτου τοῦ Χωνιάτου τὰ σωζόμενα, vols. 1–2, Athens 1879–80

Michael Haploucheir, ed. P. Leone, 'Michaelis Hapluchiris versus cum excerptis', *Byz* 39 (1969), 251–83

Michael Italikos, *Letters*, ed. P. Gautier, *Michel Italikos, Lettres et discours* (Paris 1972)

Michael Psellos, ed. L. G. Westerink, *Michael Psellus, De omnifaria doctrina: critical text and introduction* (Utrecht 1949)

Michael Psellos, *Theologica*, ed. P. Gautier, *Michael Psellus Theologica*, vol. 1 (Leipzig 1989)

Michael Psellos, *Poems*, ed. L. G. Westerink, *Michael Psellus: Poemata* (Stuttgart/Leipzig 1992)

Michael Psellos, *Letters*, ed. S. Papaioannou, *Michael Psellus: Epistulae* (Berlin/Boston 2019)

Nikephoros Basilakes, *Orations*, ed. A. Garzya, *Nicephorus Basilaca, orationes et epistolae* (Leipzig 1984)

Niketas Choniates, *Orations*, ed. I. A. van Dieten, *Nicetae Choniatae orationes et epistulae* (Berlin 1972)

Niketas Eugenianos, *Funerary Oration on the Death of Theodoros Prodromos*, ed. L. Petit, 'Monodie de Nicétas Eugénianos sur Théodore Prodrome', *VV* 9 (1902), 446–63

Niketas Eugenianos, *Funerary poems*, ed. C. Gallavotti, 'Novi Laurentiani Codicis Analecta', *SB* 4 (1935), 203–36

Niketas Eugenianos, *Drosilla and Charikles*, ed. F. Conca, *Nicetas Eugenianus, De Drosillae et Chariclis amoribus* (Amsterdam 1990)

Nikolaos Mesarites, *Epitaphios for John Mesarites*, ed. A. Heisenberg, *Neue Quellen zur Geschichte des lateinischen Kaisertums und der Kirchenunion I. Der Epitaphios des Nikolaos Mesarites auf seinen Bruder Johannes*, Sitzungsberichte der königlich bayerischen Akademie der Wissenschaften, philosophisch-philologische und historische Klasse (1922), 5, 16–72

Nikolaos Mesarites, *Narrative of the coup of John the fat*, ed. A. Heisenberg, *Nikolaos Mesarites, Die Palastrevolution des Johannes Komnenos* [Programm des K. Alten Gymnasiums zu Würzburg für das Studienjahr 1906–1907] (Würzburg 1907), 19–49

Nikolaos of Otranto, ed. A. Acconcia Longo and A. Jacob, 'Une anthologie salentine du XIVe siecle: le Vaticanus Gr. 1276', *RSBN* 17–19 (1980–82), 149–228

Patria of Constantinople, ed. Th. Preger, *Scriptores originum Constantinopolitanarum* (Leipzig 1901–07)

Poem on the Reconquest of Dorylaion, ed. F. Spingou, 'A Poem on the Refortification of Dorylaion in 1175', *Symm* 21 (2011), 137–68

Ps. Dionysios Areopagites, *De caelesti hierarchia*, ed. G. Heil and A. M. Ritter, *Corpus Dionysiacum, De coelesti hierarchia, de ecclesiastica hierarchia, de mystica theologia, epistulae* (Berlin 1991)

Ps. Gregorios Korinthios, *On the Four Parts of the Perfect Speech*, ed. W. Hörandner, 'Pseudo-Gregorios Korinthios: Über die vier Teile der perfekten Rede', *MEG* 12 (2012), 87–131

Schede tou Myos, ed. J.-T. Papadimitriou, 'Τὰ σχέδη τοῦ μυός: New Sources and Text', *Classical Studies presented to B. E. Perry by his students and colleagues at the University of Illinois, 1924–1960*, Illinois Studies in Language and Literature 58 (1969), 210–22; cf. also M. Papathomopoulos, 'Τοῦ σοφωτάτου Θεοδώρου τοῦ Προδρόμου τὰ σχέδη τοῦ μυός', Παρνασσός 21 (1979), 377–99

Seven Anonymous Byzantine Epigrams, ed. G. Tserevelakis, 'Ἑπτά ἀνέκδοτα βυζαντινά ἐπιγράμματα ἀπό τον κώδικα Marcianus Graecus 524', *Βυζαντινός Δόμος* 17-18 (2009-10), 265-92

Theodoros Aulikalamos, ed. J. F. Boissonade, *Anecdota graeca e codicibus regiis*, 5 vols. (Paris 1829-33, repr. Hildesheim 1962)

Theodoros Metochites, *Poems*, ed. I. D. Polemis, *Theodori Metochitae Carmina* (Turnhout 2015)

Theodoros Stoudites, *Poems*, ed. P. Speck, *Theodoros Studites:. Jamben auf verschiedene Gegenstände* (Berlin 1968)

Timarion, ed. R. Romano, *Pseudo-Luciano, Timarion* (Naples 1974)

Secondary Sources

A. Acconcia Longo, 'Gli epitaffi giambici per Giorgio di Antiochia, per la madre e per la moglie', *Quellen und Forschungen aus italienischen Archiven und Bibliotheken* 61 (1981), 25-59

A. Acconcia Longo, *Il calendario giambico in monostici di Teodoro Prodromo* (Rome 1983)

A. Acconcia Longo and A. Jacob, 'Une anthologie salentine du XIVe siecle: le Vaticanus Gr. 1276', *RSBN* 17-19 (1980-82), 149-228

P. A. Agapitos, 'Poets and Painters: Theodoros Prodromos' Dedicatory Verses of His Novel to an Anonymous Caesar', *JÖB* 50 (2000), 173-85

P. A. Agapitos, 'Grammar, Genre and Patronage in the Twelfth Century: Redefining a Scientific Paradigm in the History of Byzantine Literature', *JÖB* 64 (2014), 1-22

P. A. Agapitos, 'Anna Komnene and the Politics of Schedographic Training and Colloquial Discourse', *Νέα Ῥώμη* 10 (2013 [2014]), 89-107

P. A. Agapitos, 'Karl Krumbacher and the History of Byzantine Literature', *BZ* 108 (2015), 1-52

P. A. Agapitos, 'New Genres in the Twelfth Century: The *Schedourgia* of Theodore Prodromos', *MEG* 15 (2015), 1-41

P. A. Agapitos, 'John Tzetzes and the Blemish Examiners: A Byzantine Teacher on Schedography, Everyday Language and Writerly Disposition', *MEG* 17 (2017), 1-57

P. A. Agapitos, 'The Politics and Practices of Commentary in Komnenian Byzantium', in: B. van den Berg, D. Manolova, and P. Marciniak (eds), *Byzantine Commentaries on Ancient Greek Texts, 12th-15th Centuries* (Cambridge 2022), 41-60

P. Agapitos and D. Angelov, 'Six Essays by Theodore II Laskaris in Vindobonensis Phil. Gr. 321: Edition, Translation', *JÖB* 68 (2018), 39-75

N. Agiotis, 'Tzetzes on Psellos revisited', *BZ* 106 (2013), 1-8

G. Agosti and F. Gonnelli, 'Materiali per la storia dell' esametro nei poeti cristiani greci', in: M. Fantuzzi and R. Pretagostini (eds), *Struttura e storia dell' esametro greco*, 2 vols. (Rome 1995), vol. 1, 289-434

M. Alexiou, 'The Poverty of Écriture and the Craft of Writing: Towards a Reappraisal of the Prodromic Poems', *BMGS* 10 (1986), 1-40

M. Alexiou, 'Ploys of Performance: Games and Play in the Ptochoprodromic Poems', *DOP* 53 (1999), 91-109

M. Alexiou, 'Of Longings and Loves: Seven Poems by Theodore Prodromos', *DOP* 69 (2015), 209-24

M. Angold, *Nicholas Mesarites: His Life and Works (in Translation)* (Liverpool 2017)
G. Anrich, *Hagios Nikolaos*, 2 vols. (Leipzig 1913-17)
T. Antonopoulou, *Leonis VI Sapientis Imperatoris Byzantini Homiliae* (Turnhout 2008)
T. Antonopoulou, 'On the Reception of Homilies and Hagiography in Byzantium: The Recited Metrical Prefaces', in: A. Rhoby and E. Schiffer (eds), *Imitatio—Aemulatio— Variatio: Akten des internationalen wissenschaftlichen Symposions zur byzantinischen Sprache und Literatur* (Vienna 2010), 57-79
T. Antonopoulou, 'Ἀνώνυμο ποίημα για την αγία Βαρβάρα από τον κώδικα Barocci 197', in: T. Korres, P. Katsoni, I. Leontiadis, and A. Goutzioukostas (eds), *Φιλοτιμία: Τιμητικός τόμος για την ομότιμη καθηγήτρια Αλκμήνη Σταυρίδου-Ζαφράκα* (Thessaloniki 2011), 69-74; repr. in *Βυζαντινή Ομιλητική, Συγγραφείς και κείμενα* (Athens 2013), 480-85
D. Arnesano, *La minuscula 'barocca': Scritture e libri in Terra d'Otranto nei secoli XIII e XIV* (Galatina/Congedo 2008)
W. G. Arnott, *Birds in the Ancient World from A to Z* (New York 2007)
P. Augustin, 'À propos d'un catalogue récent: Remarques philologiques et historiques sur quelques manuscrits grecs conservés à la Bibliothèque de la Bourgeoisie de Berne ou ayant appartenus à Jacques Bongars', *Script* 63 (2009), 121-41
A. M. Bandini, *Catalogus codicum manuscriptorum Bibliothecae Mediceae Laurentianae*, 3 vols. (Florence 1764-70)
K. Barzos, *Η Γενεαλογία των Κομνηνών*, 2 vols. (Thessaloniki 1984)
A. Basilikopoulou-Ioannidou, *Ἡ ἀναγέννησις τῶν γραμμάτων κατὰ τὸν ΙΒ΄ αἰῶνα εἰς τὸ Βυζάντιον καὶ ὁ Ὅμηρος* (Athens 1971)
C. Baur, *Der heilige Johannes Chrysostomus und seine Zeit*, 2 vols. (Munich 1929-30)
M. Bazzani, 'The Historical Poems of Theodore Prodromos, the Epic-Homeric Revival and the Crisis of Intellectuals in the Twelfth Century', *BSl* 65 (2007), 211-28
M. Bazzani, 'Theodore Prodromos' Poem LXXVII', *BZ* 100 (2007), 1-12
R. Beaton, 'Rhetoric of Poverty: The Lives and Opinions of Theodore Prodromos', *BMGS* 11 (1987), 1-28
H.-G. Beck, *Geschichte der byzantinischen Volksliteratur* (Munich 1971)
N. A. Bees, *Τὰ χειρόγραφα τῶν Μετεώρων: Κατάλογος περιγραφικὸς τῶν χειρογράφων κωδίκων τῶν ἀποκειμένων εἰς τὰς Μονὰς τῶν Μετεώρων ἐκδιδόμενος ἐκ τῶν καταλοίπων*, 2 vols. (Athens 1967)
A. Beihammer, *Griechische Briefe und Urkunden aus dem Zypern der Kreuzfahrerzeit: Die Formularsammlung eines königlichen Sekretärs im Vaticanus Palatinus Graecus 367* (Nicosia 2007)
A. Ben-Tov, *Lutheran Humanists and Greek Antiquity: Melanchthonian Scholarship between Universal History and Pedagogy* (Leiden/Boston 2009)
B. van den Berg, 'John Tzetzes as Didactic Poet and Learned Grammarian', *DOP* 74 (2020), 285-302
F. Bernard, 'Gifts of Words: The Discourse of Gift-Giving in Eleventh-Century Byzantine Poetry', in: F. Bernard and K. Demoen (eds), *Poetry and Its Contexts in Eleventh-century Byzantium* (Farnham/Burlington 2012), 37-51
F. Bernard, *Writing and Reading Byzantine Secular Poetry, 1025-1081* (Oxford 2014)
F. Bernard, 'Rhythm in the Byzantine Dodecasyllable: Practices and Perceptions', in: A. Rhoby and N. Zagklas (eds), *Middle and Late Byzantine Poetry: Texts and Contexts* (Turnhout 2018), 13-41
F. Bernard and K. Demoen, 'Byzantine Book Epigrams', in: W. Hörandner, A. Rhoby, and N. Zagklas (eds), *A Companion to Byzantine Poetry* (Leiden/Boston 2019), 404-29
D. Bianconi, '"Piccolo assaggio di abbondante fragranza": Giovanni Mauropode e il Vat. gr. 676', *JÖB* 61 (2011), 89-103

P. M. Blowers, *Drama of the Divine Economy: Creator and Creation in Early Christian Theology and Piety* (Oxford 2012)

L. Bossina, 'Psello distratto: Questioni irrisolte nei versi In Canticum', in: V. Panagl (ed.), *Dulce Melos: La poesia tardoantica e medievale. Atti del III Convegno internazionale di Studi, Vienna, 15–18 novembre 2004* (Alessandria 2007), 337–60

C. Bouras, 'Ἀλληγορικὴ παράσταση τοῦ βίου-καιροῦ σε μια μεταβυζαντινὴ τοιχογραφία στὴ Χίο', Ἀρχαιολογικὸν Δελτίον 21, Αʹ, 1966 (1967), 26–34

E. C. Bourbouhakis, '"Political" Personae: The Poem from Prison of Michael Glykas: Byzantine Literature between Fact and Fiction', *BMGS* 31 (2007), 53–75

E. C. Bourbouhakis, *Not Composed in a Chance Manner: The Epitaphios for Manuel I Komnenos by Eustathios of Thessalonike* (Uppsala 2017)

R. Browning, 'Unpublished Correspondence between Michael Italicus, Archbishop of Philippopolis, and Theodore Prodromos', *Byzantinobulgarica* 1 (1962), 279–97

R. Browning, 'Il codice Marciano Gr. XI 31 e la schedografia bizantina', in: *Miscellanea Marciana di Studi Bessarionei* (Padua 1976), 21–34 (repr. in Idem, Studies on Byzantine History, Literature and Education. London 1977, no. XVI) = transl. in Greek in: Idem, "Ὁ Μαρκιανὸς ἑλληνικὸς κώδικας XI.31 καὶ ἡ βυζαντινὴ σχεδογραφία", Παρνασσὸς 15 (1973), 506–19

R. Browning, 'Homer in Byzantium', *Viator* 8 (1978), 15–33 (repr. in R. Browning, *Studies on Byzantine History, Literature and Education* (London 1977), no. XVII)

R. Browning, *The Byzantine Empire* (London 1980)

B. Bydén, 'Imprimatur? Unconventional Punctuation and Diacritics in Manuscripts of Medieval Greek Philosophical Works', in: A. Bucossi and E. Kihlman (eds), *Ars Edendi Lecture Series*, 2 vols. (Stockholm 2012), vol. 2, 155–72

M. Cacouros, *Recherches sur le commentaire inédit de Théodore Prodrome sur le second livre des Analytiques Postérieurs d'Aristote* (Naples 1990)

M. Cacouros, *Le commentaire de Théodore Prodrome aux Analytiques postérieurs, livre II d'Aristote: Texte (edition princeps, tradition manuscrite), étude du commentaire de Prodrome*, unpublished PhD thesis (Paris IV–Sorbonne 1992)

M. Cacouros, 'La tradition du commentaire de Théodore Prodrome au deuxième livre des Seconds Analytiques d'Aristote: quelques étapes dans l'enseignement de la logique à Byzance', Δίπτυχα Ἑταιρείας Βυζαντινῶν καὶ Μεταβυζαντινῶν Μελετῶν 6 (1994–95), 329–54

A. Cameron, *The Greek Anthology from Meleager to Planudes* (Oxford 1993)

P. Canart, 'À propos du Vaticanus graecus 207: Le recueil scientifique d'un érudit constantinopolitain du XIIIe siècle et l'emploi du papier "à zig-zag" dans la capitale byzantine', *Illinois Classical Studies* 7 (1982) [= *Studies in Memory of Alexander Turyn (1900–1981)*, part Four], 271–98

P. Canart, 'Les palimpsestes en écriture majuscule des fonds grecs de la Bibliothèque Vaticane', in: S. Lucà (ed.), *Libri palinsesti greci: conservazione, restauro digitale, studio. Atti del Convegno internazionale, Villa Mondragone—Monte Porzio Catone—Università di Roma 'Tor Vergata'—Biblioteca del Monumento Nazionale di Grottaferrata, 21–24 apr. 2004* (Rome 2008), 71–84

P. Cesaretti and S. Ronchey, *Eustathii Thessaloncensis Exegesis in Canonem iambicum pentacostolem* (Munich/Boston 2014)

M. Chatzidakis, 'Χρονολογημένη βυζαντινὴ εἰκόνα στη Μονὴ Μεγίστης Λαύρας', in: N. A. Stratou (ed.), *Byzantium: Tribute to Andreas N. Stratos*, 2 vols. (Athens 1986), 225–40

K. Chryssogelos, 'Theodore Prodromos' Βίων πρᾶσις as a Satire', *MEG* 21 (2021), 303–12

M. M. Colonna, 'Il ms. Neapolitanus gr. III AA 6', *Nicolaus* 5 (1977), 325–64

F. Conca, *Nicetas Eugenianus, De Drosillae et Chariclis amoribus* (Amsterdam 1990)
C. N. Constantinides, *Higher Education in Byzantium in the Thirteenth and Early Fourteenth Centuries* (Nicosia 1982)
C. N. Constantinides and R. Browning, *Dated Greek Manuscripts from Cyprus to the Year 1570* (Washington DC/Nicosia 1993)
A. B. Cook, *Zeus: A Study in Ancient Religion*, 2 vols. (Cambridge 1926)
H. O. Coxe, *Bodleian Library Quarto Catalogues, I. Greek Manuscripts* (Oxford 1969; repr. with corrections from the edition of 1853)
A. Crugnola, *Scholia in Nicandri Theriaca cum glossis* (Milan–Varese 1971)
E. Cullhed, 'The Blind Bard and "I": Authorial Personas and Homeric Biography in the Twelfth Century', *BMGS* 38 (2014), 49–67
E. Cullhed, 'Editing Byzantine Scholarly Texts in Authorized Manuscripts', in: E. Göransson, G. Iversen, and B. Crostini (eds), *The Arts of Editing Medieval Greek and Latin: A Casebook* (Toronto 2016), 72–95
E. Cullhed, 'To the Caesar or For the Color Green', in: F. Spingou (ed.), *The Visual Culture of Later Byzantium (c. 1081–c. 1350)*, 2 vols. (Cambridge 2022), vol. 1, 337–89
M. Cunningham, 'Divine Banquet: The Theotokos as a Source of Spiritual Nourishment', in: L. Brubaker and K. Linardou (eds), *Eat, Drink, and Be Merry (Luke 12:19): Food and wine in Byzantium* (London 2007), 236–44
C. Cupane, 'Das erfundene Epigramm: Schrift und Bild im Roman', in: W. Hörandner and A. Rhoby (eds), *Die kulturhistorische Bedeutung byzantinischer Epigramme: Akten des internationalen Workshop (Wien, 1.–2. Dezember 2006)* (Vienna 2008), 19–28
E. R. Curtius, *Europäische Literatur und lateinisches Mittelalter* (Bern 1948)
S. Cyrillus, *Codices Graeci mss. Regiae Bibliothecae Borbonicae descripti*, 2 vols. (Naples 1832)
M. D'Ambrosi, *I tetrastici giambici ed esametrici sugli episodi principali della vita di Gregorio Nazianzeno, Introduzione, edizione critica, traduzione e commento* (Rome 2008)
M. D'Ambrosi, 'Un monostico giambico di Teodoro Prodromo per i ss. Tre Gerarchi', *Bollettino dei Classici* 33 (2012), 33–46
M. D'Ambrosi, 'The Icon of the Three Holy Hierarchs at the Pantokrator Monastery and the Epigrams of Theodore Prodromos on Them', in: S. Kotzabassi (ed.), *The Pantokrator Monastery in Constantinople* (Boston/Berlin 2013), 143–51
K. Dapontes, *Καθρέπτης Γυναικῶν*, 2 vols. (Leipzig 1766)
K. Dark and A. Harris, 'The Orphanage of Byzantine Constantinople: An Archaeological Identification', *BSl* 66 (2008), 189–201
G. de Andrés, *Catálogo de los códices griegos de la Real Biblioteca de El Escorial*, 3 vols. (Escorial 1968)
P. F. de Cavalieri, *Bibliotecae Apostolicae Vaticanae codices manu scripti recensiti: Codices Graeci Chisiani et Borgiani* (Rome 1927)
M. de Groote, 'The Metre in the Poems of Christopher Mitylenaios', *BZ* 103 (2011), 571–94
M. de Groote, *Christophori Mitylenaii, Versvvm variorvm, collectio crypte* (Turnhout 2012)
O. Delouis, 'La Vie métrique de Théodore Stoudite par Stéphane Mélès (*BHG*1755m)', *AnBoll* 132 (2014), 21–54
K. A. de Meyier, *Bibliotheca Universitatis Leidensis. Codices manuscripti. VI. Codices Vossiani graeci et miscellanei* (Leiden 1955)
K. A. de Meyier (with the assistance of E. Hulshoff Pol), *Codices bibliothecae publicae graeci: Codices manuscripti/Bibliotheca Universitatis Leidensis, VIII* (Leiden 1965)
K. Demoen, '*Phrasis poikilê*: Imitatio and Variatio in the Poetry Book of Christophoros Mitylenaios', in: A. Rhoby and E. Schiffer (eds), *Imitatio—Aemulatio—Variatio: Akten*

des internationalen wissenschaftlichen Symposions zur byzantinischen Sprache und Literatur (Vienna 2010), 103-18

K. Demoen and E. M. van Opstall, 'One for the Road: John Geometres, Reader and Imitator of Gregory Nazianzen's Poems', in: A. Schmidt (ed.), *Studia Nazianzenica II* (Turnhout 2010), 223-48

J. Diethart and W. Hörandner, *Constantinus Stilbes, Poemata* (Munich 2005)

E. Dionysatis, 'Συμπληρωματικὸς κατάλογος ἑλληνικῶν χειρογράφων Ἱερᾶς Μονῆς Διονυσίου Ἁγίου Ὄρους', *ΕΕΒΣ* 27 (1957), 233-71

I. Drpić, 'Chrysepes Stichourgia: The Byzantine Epigram as Aesthetic Object', in: B. Bedos-Rezak and J. F. Hamburger (eds), *Sign & Design: Script as Image in a Cross-Cultural Perspective (300-1600 CE)* (Washington DC 2016), 51-69

I. Drpić, *Epigram, Art, and Devotion in Later Byzantium* (Cambridge 2016)

H. Eideneier, *Ptochoprodromos: Einführung, Kritische Ausgabe, deutsche Übersetzung, Glossar* (Cologne 1991) [H. Eideneier, *Πτωχοπρόδρομος* (Herakleion 2012)]

H. Eideneier, 'Tou Ptochoprodromou', in: M. Hinterberger and E. Schiffer (eds), *Byzantinische Sprachkunst: Studien zur byzantinischen Literatur gewidmet Wolfram Hörandner zum 65. Geburtstag* (Berlin/New York 2007), 56-76

S. Eustratiades, *Catalogue of the Greek Manuscripts in the Library of the Laura on Mount Athos, with Notices from other Libraries* (Cambridge, MA 1925)

S. Eustratiades, *Ἡ Θεοτόκος ἐν τῇ ὑμνογραφίᾳ* (Paris 1930)

A. Faulkner, 'Theodoros Prodromos' Historical Poems. A Hymnic Celebration of John II Komnenos', in: A. Faulkner, A. Vergados, and A. Schwab (eds), *The Reception of the Homeric Hymns* (Oxford 2016), 261-74

E. Feron and F. Battaglini, *Codices manuscripti Graeci Ottoboniani Bibliothecae Vaticanae* (Rome 1893)

N. Festa, 'Nota sui versiculi in vitia et virtutes', in: *Miscellanea Ceriani: Raccolta di scritti originali* (Milan 1910), 569-76

M. R. Formentin, *Catalogus codicum Graecorum Bibliothecae nationalis Neapolitanae*, 2 vols. (Rome 1995)

C. Gallavotti, 'Novi Laurentiani Codicis Analecta', *SB* 4 (1935), 203-36

C. Gallavotti, 'Nota sulla schedografia di Moscopulo e suoi precedenti fino a Teodoro Prodromo', *Bolletino dei Classici* III.4 (1983), 3-35

A. Garzya, 'Literarische und rhetorische Polemiken der Komnenenzeit', *BSl* 34 (1973), 1-14

A. Garzya, 'Literarische Gebrauchsformen: Testi letterari d'uso strumentale', *JÖB* 31 (1981), 263-87

C. Gastgeber, 'Manuel Meligalas: Eine biographische Studie', in: C. Gastgeber (ed.), *Miscellanea codicum Graecorum Vindobonensium 1, Studien zu griechischen Handschriften der Österreichischen Nationalbibliothek* (Vienna 2009), 51-84

T. Gelzer, 'Bemerkungen zu Sprache und Text des Epikers Musaios', *Museum Helveticum* 24 (1967), 129-48

D. Getov, *A Catalogue of Greek Manuscripts in the Scientific Archives of the Bulgarian Academy of Sciences* (Sofia 2010)

C. Giannelli, 'Tetrastici di Theodoro Prodromo sulle feste fisse e sui santi del calendario bizantino', *AnBoll* 75 (1957), 299-336

C. Giannelli, 'Epigrammi di Teodoro Prodromo in onore dei senti megalomartiri Teodoro, Giorgio e Demetrio', in: *Studi in onore di Luigi Castiglioni* (Florence 1960), 333-71

C. Giannelli, 'Un altro "calendario metrico" di Teodoro Prodromo', *ΕΕΒΣ* 25 (1955), 158-69 = *SBN* 10 (1963), 203-213

C. Giannelli and P. Canart, *Codices Vaticani graeci 1684-1744* (Rome 1961)

A. Giannouli, 'Eine Rede auf das Akathistos-Fest und Theodoros II. Dukas Laskaris (BHG3 1140, CPG 8197)', *JÖB* 51 (2001), 259–83

A. Giannouli and E. Schiffer, *From Manuscripts to Books: Vom Codex zur Edition: Proceedings of the International Workshop on Textual Criticism and Editorial Practice for Byzantine Texts (Vienna, 10–11 December 2009)* (Vienna 2011)

P. L. Gilbert, *On God and Man: The Theological Poetry of St. Gregory of Nazianzus* (Crestwood NY 2001)

C. G. Goettling, *Theodosii Alexandrini Grammatica* (Leipzig 1822)

F. Gonnelli, *Giorgio di Pisidia, Esamerone* (Pisa 1998)

V. Grecu, 'Die Darstellung des Καιρός bei den Byzantinern', *SBN* 6 (1940), 147–54

M. Grünbart, 'Prosopographische Beiträge zum Briefcorpus des Ioannes Tzetzes', *JÖB* 46 (1996), 175–226

M. Grünbart, 'Byzantinisches Gelehrtenelend—oder wie meistert man seinen Alltag?', in: L. M. Hoffmann and A. Monchizadeh (eds), *Zwischen Polis, Provinz und Peripherie: Beiträge zur byzantinischen Geschichte und Kultur* (Wiesbaden 2005), 413–26

M. Grünbart, *Formen der Anrede im byzantinischen Brief vom 6. Bis zum 12. Jahrhundert* (Vienna 2005)

M. Grünbart, ''Tis Love That Has Warm'd Us: Reconstructing Networks in 12th-Century Byzantium', *Revue Belge de Philologie et d'Histoire* 83/2 (2005), 301–13

J. P. Gumbert, 'Codicological Units: Towards a Terminology for the Stratigraphy of the Non-Homogeneous Codex', *Segno e Testo* 2 (2004), 17–42

M. Hagen, Ἠθοποιΐα: *Zur Geschichte eines rhetorischen Begriffs* (Erlangen 1966)

F. Halkin, 'Les manuscrits grecs de la Bibliothèque Laurentienne à Florence: Inventaire hagiographique', *AnBoll* 96 (1978), 5–50

I. Hardt, *Catalogus codicum manuscriptorum graecorum bibliothecae Regiae Bavariae*, 5 vols. (Munich 1806–12)

F. Hieronymus, Ἐν Βασιλείᾳ πόλει τῆς Γερμανίας. *Griechischer Geist aus Basler Pressen. Ausstellungskatalog Universitätsbibliothek Basel 4. Juli bis 22. August 1992* (Basel 1992)

I. Hilberg, 'Kann Theodoros der Verfasser des Χριστὸς πάσχων sein?', *WSt* 8 (1886), 282–314

M. Hinterberger, *Phthonos: Mißgunst, Neid und Eifersucht in der byzantinischen Literatur* (Wiesbaden 2013)

W. Hörandner, 'Theodoros Prodromos und die Gedichtsammlung des Cod. Marc. XI 22', *JÖB* 17 (1967), 91–99

W. Hörandner, 'Prodromos-Reminiszenzen bei Dichtern der Nikänischen Zeit', *BF* 4 (1972), 88–104

W. Hörandner, *Theodoros Prodromos: Historische Gedichte* (Vienna 1974)

W. Hörandner, 'Review of A. Kazhdan and S. Franklin (eds), *Studies on Byzantine Literature of the Eleventh and Twelfth Centuries* (Cambridge 1984)', *JÖB* 38 (1988), 468–73

W. Hörandner, 'Customs and Beliefs as Reflected in Occasional Poetry: Some Considerations', *BF* 12 (1987), 235–47

W. Hörandner, 'Visuelle Poesie in Byzanz: Versuch einer Bestandaufnahme', *JÖB* 40 (1990), 1–43

W. Hörandner, 'Ein Zyklus von Epigrammen zu Darstellungen von Herrenfesten und Wunderszenen', *DOP* 46 (1992), 107–15

W. Hörandner, 'Autor oder Genus? Diskussionsbeiträge zur "Prodromischen Frage" aus gegebenem Anlass', *BSl* 54 (1993), 314–24

W. Hörandner, 'A Cycle of Epigrams on the Lord's Feasts in Cod. Marc. gr. 524', *DOP* 48 (1994), 117–33

W. Hörandner, 'Beobachtungen zur Literarästhetik der Byzantiner: einige byzantinische Zeugnisse zu Metrik und Rhythmik', *BSl* 11 (1995), 279–90

W. Hörandner, 'Zu einigen religiösen Epigrammen', in: U. Criscuolo and R. Maisano (eds), *Synodia: Studia humanistica Antonio Garzya septuagenario ab amicis atque discipulis dicata* (Naples 1997), 431–42

W. Hörandner, 'Zur kommunikativen Funktion byzantinischer Gedichte', in: I. Ševčenko and G. G. Litavrin (eds), *Acts, XVIIIth International Congress of Byzantine Studies, Selected Papers* (Shepherdstown 2000), IV, 104–18

W. Hörandner, 'Epigrams on Icons and Sacred Objects: The Collection of Cod. Marc. gr. 524 Once Again', in: M. Salvadore (ed.), *La poesia tardoantica e medievale: Atti del I Convegno Internazionale di Studi, Macerata, 4–5 maggio 1998* (Alessandria 2001), 117–24

W. Hörandner, 'Court Poetry: Questions of Motifs, Structure and Function', in: E. Jeffreys (ed.), *Rhetoric in Byzantium* (Aldershot 2003), 75–85

W. Hörandner, 'Musterautoren und ihre Nachahmer: Indizien für Elemente einer byzantinischen Poetik', in: P. Odorico, P. A. Agapitos, and M. Hinterberger (eds), *'Doux remède...' Poésie et poétique à Byzance: Actes du IVe colloque international philologique, Paris, 23-24-25 février 2006* (Paris 2009), 201–17

W. Hörandner, 'Weitere Beobachtungen zu byzantinischen Figurengedichten und Tetragrammen', *Nea Rhome* 6 (2009), 291–304

W. Hörandner, 'Theodore Prodromos and the City', in: P. Odorico and Ch. Messis (eds), *Villes de toute beauté: L'ekphrasis des cités dans les littératures byzantine et byzantino-slaves. Actes du colloque international, Prague, 25–26 novembre 2011* (Paris 2012), 49–62

W. Hörandner, 'The Byzantine Didactic Poem—A Neglected Literary Genre? A Survey with Special Reference to the Eleventh Century', in: F. Bernard and K. Demoen (eds), *Poetry and Its Contexts in Eleventh-Century Byzantium* (Farnham/Burlington 2012), 55–67

W. Hörandner, 'Teaching with Verse in Byzantium', in: W. Hörandner, A. Rhoby, and N. Zagklas (eds), in: *A Companion to Byzantine Poetry* (Leiden/Boston 2019), 459–86

H. Hunger, *Katalog der griechischen Handschriften der Österreichischen Nationalbibliothek, Teil 1. Codices historici, Codices philosophici et philologici* (Vienna 1961)

H. Hunger, *Der byzantinische Katz-Mäuse-Krieg* (Graz/Vienna/Cologne 1968)

H. Hunger, *Die hochsprachliche profane Literatur der Byzantiner*, 2 vols. (Munich 1978)

H. Hunger, 'Byzantinische Namensdeutungen in iambischen Synaxarversen', Βυζαντινά 13 (1983), 1–16

H. Hunger, 'Gregorios von Korinth, Epigramme auf die Feste des Dodekaorton', *AnBoll* 100 (1982), 637–51

H. Hunger (with the collaboration of W. Lackner and Ch. Hannick), *Katalog der griechischen Handschriften der Österreichischen Nationalbibliothek, Teil 3/2. Codices historici, Codices Theologici 201-337* (Vienna 1992)

H. Hunger (with the collaboration of Ch. Hannick), *Katalog der griechischen Handschriften der Österreichischen Nationalbibliothek, Teil 4. Codices Supplementum Graecum* (Vienna 1994)

H. Hunger, 'Aus der letzten Lebensjahren des Johannes Chortasmenos: Das Synaxarion im Cod. Christ Church gr. 56 und der Metropolit Ignatios von Selybria', *JÖB* 45 (1995), 159–218

D. F. Jackson, 'Janus Lascaris on the Island of Corfu in A.D. 1491', *Script* 57 (2003), 137–39

M. C. Janssen and M. D. Lauxtermann, 'Authorship Revisited: Language and Metre in the Ptochoprodromika', in: T. Shawcross and I. Toth (eds), *Reading in the Byzantine Empire and Beyond* (Cambridge 2018), 558–84

B. Janssens, *Maximi Confessoris ambigua ad Thomam una cum epistula secunda ad eundem* (Turnhout 2002)

E. Jeffreys, 'The Labours of the Twelve Months', in: E. Stafford and J. Herrin (eds), *Personification in the Greek World: From Antiquity to Byzantium* (Aldershot 2005), 309-23

E. Jeffreys, 'Why Produce Verse in Twelfth-Century Constantinople?', in: P. Odorico, P. A. Agapitos, and M. Hinterberger (eds), *'Doux remède...': Poésie et poétique à Byzance. Actes du IVe colloque international philologique, Paris, 23-24-25 février 2006* (Paris 2009), 219-28

E. Jeffreys, 'The Sebastokratorissa Irene as Patron', in: L. Theis, M. Mullett, and M. Grünbart (eds), *Female Founders in Byzantium and Beyond* (Vienna 2014), 177-94

E. Jeffreys, *Four Byzantine Novels* (Liverpool 2012)

E. M. Jeffreys, 'The Song of Songs and Twelfth-Century Byzantium', *Prudentia* 23 (1991), 36-54

E. and M. Jeffreys, *Iacobi Monachi Epistulae* (Turnhout 2009)

M. Jeffreys, 'The Nature and Origin of the Political Verse', *DOP* 28 (1974), 141-95

M. Jeffreys, 'Rhetorical Texts', in: E. Jeffreys (ed.), *Rhetoric in Byzantium* (Aldershot 2003), 87-100

J. Jones, *Arabic Administration in Norman Sicily* (Cambridge 2002)

E. Kaltsogianni, *Το αγιολογικό και ομιλητικό έργο του Ιωάννη Ζωναρά: εισαγωγική μελέτη, κριτική έκδοση* (Thessaloniki 2013)

A. Kambylis, *Prodromea* (Vienna 1984)

D. K. Karathanasis, *Sprichwörter und sprichwörtliche Redensarten des Alterturms in den rhetorischen Schriften des Michael Psellos, des Eustathios und des Michael Choniates sowie in anderen rhetorischen Quellen des XII. Jahrhunderts*, unpublished PhD thesis (Munich 1936)

A. Kazhdan, 'Theodore Prodromus: A Reappraisal', in: A. Kazhdan and S. Franklin (eds), *Studies on Byzantine Literature of the Eleventh and Twelfth centuries* (Cambridge 1984), 87-114

A. P. Kazhdan and A. Wharton Epstein, *Change in Byzantine Culture in the Eleventh and Twelfth Centuries* (Berkeley 1985)

U. Kenens and P. van Deun, 'Some Unknown Byzantine Poems Preserved in a Manuscript of the Holy Mountain', *MEG* 14 (2014), 111-18

E. Kiapidou, 'Critical Remarks on Theophylact of Ohrid's Martyrdom of the Fifteen Martyrs of Tiberiopolis: The Editorial Adventure of a Text from the Middle Ages', *Parekbolai* 2 (2012), 27-47

E. Kislinger, 'Giorgio di Antiochia e la politica marittima tra Normanni e Bisanzio', in: M. Re and Cr. Rognoni (eds), *Giorgio di Antiochia: L'arte della politica in Sicilia nel XII secolo tra Bisanzio e l'Islam. Atti del Convegno Internazionale (Palermo, 19-20 Aprile 2007)* (Palermo 2009), 47-63

S. Klementa, 'Vom bequemen Luxusdasein zur vergänglichen Lebenszeit. Die Personifikation des Bios', in: G. Brands and H. Gabelmann (eds), *Rom und die Provinzen: Gedenkschrift für Hanns Gabelmann* (Mainz 2001), 209-14

S. Kotzabassi, *Die handschriftliche Überlieferung der rhetorischen und hagiographischen Werke des Gregor von Zypern* (Wiesbaden 1998)

V. Koufopoulou, 'Δύο ἀνέκδοτα ποιήματα τοῦ Θεοδώρου Στυππειώτη', *Βυζαντινά* 15 (1989), 351-67

P. Koukoules, *Βυζαντινῶν βίος καὶ πολιτισμός*, 6 vols. (Athens 1948-55)

O. Kresten, 'Zum Sturz des Theodoros Styppeiotes', *JÖB* 27 (1978), 49-103

K. Krumbacher, *Geschichte der byzantinischen Litteratur von Justinian bis zum Ende des Oströmischen Reiches (527–1453)* (Munich ²1897)

K. Kubina, 'Manuel Philes and the Asan Family. Two Inedited Poems and Their Context in Philes' Œuvre (Including Editio Princeps)', *JÖB* 63 (2013), 177–98

K. Kubina, 'Manuel Philes: A "Begging Poet"? Requests, Letters, and Problems of Genre Definition', in: A. Rhoby and N. Zagklas (eds), *Middle and Late Byzantine Poetry: Texts and Contexts* (Turnhout 2018), 147–81

K. Kubina, *Die enkomiastische Dichtung des Manuel Philes: Form und Funktion des literarischen Lobes in der Gesellschaft der frühen Palaiologenzeit* (Berlin/Boston 2020)

K. Kubina and N. Zagklas, 'Greek Poetry in a Multicultural Society: Sicily and Salento in the 12th and 13th Centuries', in: K Kubina and N. Zagklas (eds), *Why Write Poetry? Transcultural Perspectives from the Later Medieval Period*, Medieval Encounters 2024 (forthcoming)

J. Kucharski and M. Marciniak, 'The Beard and Its Philosopher: Theodore Prodromos on the Philosopher's Beard in Byzantium', *BMGS* 41 (1) (2017), 45–54

M. Kulhánková, 'Figuren und Wortspiele in den Byzantinischen Bettelgedichten und die Frage der Autorschaft', *Graeco-Latina Brunensia* 16 (2011), 29–39

M. Kulhánková, '"…For Old Men Too Can Play, Albeit More Wisely So": The Game of Discourses in the *Ptochoprodromika*', in: P. Marciniak and I. Nilsson (eds), *Parody and Satire in Byzantium* (Leiden/Boston 2020), 304–23

E. Kurtz, *Die Gedichte des Christophoros Mitylenaios* (Leipzig 1903)

M. J. Kyriakis, 'Professors and Disciples in Byzantium', *Byz* 43 (1973), 108–19

M. J. Kyriakis, 'Theodoros Prodromos and His Adversities', Δίπτυχα Ἑταιρείας Βυζαντινῶν καὶ Μεταβυζαντινῶν Μελετῶν 4 (1986/1987), 58–93

T. Labuk, 'Aristophanes in the Service of Niketas Choniates: Gluttony, Drunkenness and Politics in the Χρονικὴ διήγησις', *JÖB* 66 (2016), 127–51

E. Lamberz, *Katalog der griechischen Handschriften des Athosklosters Vatopedi, Codices 1–102*, 1 vol. (Thessaloniki 2006)

S. Lambros, *Catalogue of the Greek Manuscripts on Mount Athos*, 2 vols. (Cambridge 1895–1900)

S. Lambros, 'Κατάλογος κωδίκων τῆς βιβλιοθήκης τῆς Βουλῆς', *NE* 3 (1906), 113–21

S. Lambros, 'Κατάλογος τῶν κωδίκων τῆς Ἱστορικῆς καὶ Ἐθνολογικῆς Ἑταιρείας', *NE* 7 (1910), 83–84

S. Lambros, 'Ἡ βιβλιοθήκη τῆς Ἑλληνικῆς κοινότητος Βουδαπέστης καὶ οἱ ἐν τῇ πόλει ταύτῃ σωζόμενοι ἑλληνικοὶ κώδικες', *NE* 8 (1911), 70–79

S. Lambros, 'Ὁ Μαρκιανὸς κῶδιξ 524', *NE* 8 (1911), 3–59, 123–92

O. Lampsides, "Ἕνα ἀνδριακὸ χειρόγραφο στὴ Βιβλιοθήκη τοῦ Λονδίνου', Θεολογία 60 (1989), 167–75

O. Lampsidis, 'Les "Gnomologia" tirés de la Chronique de K. Manassès', *Byz* 55 (1985), 118–45

O. Lampsidis, *Constantini Manassis Breviarium Chronicum*, 2 vols. (Athens 1996)

O. Lampsidis, 'Die Entblößung der Muse Kalliope in einem byzantinischen Epigramm', *JÖB* 47 (1997), 107–10

M. D. Lauxtermann, 'The Velocity of Pure Iambs: Byzantine Observations on the Metre and Rhythm of the Dodecasyllable', *JÖB* 48 (1998), 9–33

M. D. Lauxtermann, 'Book Review of Gr. Papagiannis, Theodoros Prodromos: Jambische und hexametrische Tetrasticha auf die Hauptzerzälungen des Alten und des Neuen Testaments', *JÖB* 49 (1999), 367–70

M. D. Lauxtermann, *The Spring of Rhythm: An Essay on the Political Verse and Other Byzantine Metres* (Vienna 1999)

M. D. Lauxtermann, *Byzantine Poetry from Pisides to Geometres: Texts and Contexts*, 2 vols. (Vienna 2003-19)

M. D. Lauxtermann, 'His, and Not His: The Poems of the Late Gregory the Monk', in: A. Pizzone (ed.), *The Author in Middle Byzantine Literature: Modes, Functions, and Identities* (Berlin/Boston 2014), 77-86

M. D. Lauxtermann, 'Tomi, Mljet, Malta: Critical Notes on a Twelfth-Century Southern Italian Poem of Exile', *JÖB* 64 (2014), 155-76

M. D. Lauxtermann, 'Of Cats and Mice: The *Katomyomacha* as Drama, Parody, School Text, and Animal Tale', in: B. van den Berg and N. Zagklas (eds), *Byzantine Poetry in the Twelfth Century (1081-1204)* (forthcoming)

I. N. Lebedeva, *Opisanie rukopisnogo otdela biblioteki Akademii Nauk SSSR* (St Petersburg 1973)

E. L. von Leutsch and F. G. Schneidewin, *Corpus Paroemiographorum Graecorum*, 2 vols. (Göttingen 1839-51)

H. Lind, *Der Gerber Kleon in den 'Rittern' des Aristophanes: Studien zur Demagogenkomödie* (Frankfurt am Main 1990)

C. Litzica, *Catalogul manuscriptelor grecești* (Bucharest 1909)

M. Loukaki, 'Ekphrasis Earos: Le topos de la venue du printemps chez des auteurs byzantins', *Parekbolai* 3 (2013), 77-106

M. Loukaki, 'Dating Issues: The Defection of Sebastokrator Isaakios Komnenos to the Danishmendid Turks, the Death of His Brother Andronikos Komnenos, and the Death of Their Mother Empress Irene Doukaina', *Symm* 32 (2022), 11-16

A. Ludwich, *Aristarchs homerische Textkritik nach den Fragmenten des Didymos dargestellt und beurteilt, nebst Beilagen* (Leipzig 1885)

C. E. Lutz, 'Democritus and Heraclitus', *The Classical Journal* 49/7 (1954), 309-14

M. J. Luzzatto, *Tzetzes lettore di Tucidide: note autografe sul codice Heidelberg Palatino greco 252* (Bari 1999)

P. Maas, 'Der byzantinische Zwölfsilber', *BZ* 12 (1903), 278-323

L. S. B. MacCoull, 'Mathousala Macheir and the Melkite Connection', *Script* 50 (1996), 114-16

P. Magdalino, *The Empire of Manuel I Komnenos, 1143-1180* (Cambridge 1993)

P. Magdalino, 'Cultural Change? The Context of Byzantine Poetry from Geometres to Prodromos', in: F. Bernard and K. Demoen (eds), *Poetry and Its Contexts in Eleventh-Century Byzantium* (Farnham/Burlington 2012), 19-36

H. Maguire, 'The Depiction of Sorrow in Middle Byzantine Art', *DOP* 31 (1977), 123-74

H. Maguire, *Image and Imagination: The Byzantine Epigram as Evidence for Viewer Response* (Toronto 1996)

H. Maguire, 'The Profane Aesthetic in Byzantine Art and Literature', *DOP* 53 (1999), 189-205

P. Marciniak, 'Theodore Prodromos' Bion Prasis: A Reappraisal', *GRBS* 53 (2013), 219-39

P. Marciniak, 'How to Entertain the Byzantines? Mimes and Jesters in Byzantium', in: A. Öztürkmen and E. B. Vitz (eds), *Medieval and Early Modern Performances in the Eastern Mediterranean* (Turnhout 2014), 125-48

P. Marciniak, 'Prodromos, Aristophanes and a Lustful Woman: A Byzantine Satire by Theodore Prodromos', *BSl* 73 (2015), 23-34

P. Marciniak, 'It Is Not What It Appears to Be: A Note on Theodore Prodromos' *Against a Lustful Old Woman*', *Eos* 103 (2016), 109-15

P. Marciniak, 'Teaching Lucian in Middle Byzantium', *Antiquitas Perennis* 14 (2019), 267-79

P. Marciniak and K. Warcaba, 'Theodore Prodromos' Katomyomachia as a Byzantine Version of Mock-Epic' in: A. Rhoby and N. Zagklas (eds), *Middle and Late Byzantine Poetry: Texts and Contexts* (Brepols 2018), 97–110

M. Marcovich, *Theodori Prodromi Rhodanthes et Dosiclis amorum libri IX* (Stuttgart/Leipzig 1991)

B. Markesinis, 'Janos Lascaris, la bibliothèque d'Avramis à Corfou et le Paris. Gr. 854', *Script* 54 (2000), 302–06

B. Markesinis, 'Les extraits de S. Maxime le Confesseur transmis par le Parisinus gr. 854 (13e s.)', *Orientalia Lovaniensia Periodica* 31 (2000–05), 109–17

A. Martini and D. Bassi, *Catalogus codicum graecorum Bibliothecae Ambrosianae*, 2 vols. (Milan 1906; repr. Hildesheim/New York 1978)

C. M. Mazzucchi, 'Uno sconosciuto codice greco di lessicografia', *Aevum* 83 (2009), 411–23

J. A. McGuckin, 'Gregory: The Rhetorician as Poet', in: J. Børtnes and T. Hägg (eds), *Gregory of Nazianzus: Images and Reflections* (Copenhagen 2006), 193–212

I. Mercati and P. F. de' Cavalieri, *Vaticani Graeci: Codices 1–329* (Vatican City 1923)

S. Mergiali-Falangas, 'L'école Saint-Paul de l'orphelinat à Constantinople: bref aperçu sur son statut et son histoire', *REB* 49 (1991), 237–46

W. Meyer, *Die Handschriften in Göttingen*, vol. 1 (Berlin 1893)

T. Migliorini, 'Teodoro Prodromo: Amaranto', *MEG* 7 (2007), 183–247

T. Migliorini, 'Un epigramma inedito di Giorgio Cabasila nel Laur. S. Marco 318', *MEG* 8 (2008), 1–29

T. Migliorini, *Gli scritti satirici in greco letterario di Teodoro Prodromo: introduzione, edizione, traduzione, comment*, PhD thesis (Pisa 2010)

T. Migliorini and S. Tessari, "Ῥεῖτε δακρύων, ὀφθαλμοί, κρουνοὺς ἡματωμένους: Il carme penitenziale di Germano II patriarca di Constantinopoli", *MEG* 12 (2012), 155–80

E. Miller, 'Poésies inédites de Théodore Prodrome', Annuaire de l'Association pour l'encouragement des études greques en France 17 (1883), 18–64

T. S. Miller, *The Orphans of Byzantium: Child Welfare in the Christian Empire* (Washington DC 2003)

T. S. Miller, 'Two Teaching Texts from the Twelfth-Century Orphanotropheion', in: J. W. Nesbitt (ed.), *Byzantine Authors: Literary Activities and Preoccupations, Texts and Translations Dedicated to the Memory of Nicolas Oikonomides* (Leiden/Boston 2003), 9–22

E. Mioni, *Bibliothecae divi Marci Venetiarum codices graeci manuscripti*, 2 vols. (Rome 1981–85)

B. Mondrain, 'Les écritures dans les manuscrits byzantins du XIVe siècle, quelques problématiques', *RSBN* 44 (2007), 157–96

M. Mullett, 'Aristocracy and Patronage in the Literary Circles of Comnenian Constantinople', in: M. Angold (ed.), *The Byzantine aristocracy IX to XIII Centuries* (Oxford 1984), 173–201

M. Mullett, 'The Madness of Genre', *DOP* 46 (1992), 233–43

A. Muñoz, 'Le rappresentazioni allegoriche della vita nell'arte bizantina', *L'Arte* 7 (1904), 130–45

R. Nares, A Catalogue of the Harleian Manuscripts in the British Museum, 3 vols. (London 1808–12)

P. Ş. Năsturel, 'Prodromica', Βυζαντινά 13(2) (1985), 761–70

I. Nesseris, Η Παιδεία στην Κωνσταντινούπολη κατά τον 12ο αιώνα, unpublished PhD thesis (Ioannina 2014)

L. Neville, 'Lamentation, History, and Female Authorship in Anna Komnene's Alexiad', *GRBS* 53 (2013), 192–218

D. Z. Nikitas, *Eine byzantinische Übersetzung von Boethius' 'De hypotheticis syllogismis'* (Göttingen 1982)

I. Nilsson, 'Nature Controlled by Artistry: The Poetics of the Literary Garden in Byzantium', in: H. Bodin and R. Hedlund (eds), *Byzantine Gardens and Beyond* (Uppsala 2013), 14-29

I. Nilsson, *Raconter Byzance: la littérature du 12e siècle* (Paris 2014)

I. Nilsson, *Writer and Occasion in Twelfth-Century Byzantium: The Authorial Voice of Constantine Manasses* (Cambridge 2020)

I. Nilsson and N. Zagklas, '"Hurry Up, Reap Every Flower of the *Logoi!*": The Use of Greek Novels in Byzantium', *GRBS* 57 (2017), 1120-48

J. Noret, 'L'accentuation byzantine: en quoi et pourquoi elle diffère de l'accentuation savante actuelle, parfois absurde', in: M. Hinterberger, *The Language of Learned Byzantine Literature* (Turnhout 2014), 96-146

E. Nyström, *Containing Multitudes: Codex Upsaliensis Graecus 8 in Perspective* (Uppsala 2009)

P. Odorico and Ch. Messis, 'L'anthologie Comnène du cod. Marc. gr. 524: Problèmes d'évaluation', in: W. Hörandner and M. Grünbart (eds), *L'épistolographie et la poésie épigrammatique: projets actuels et questions de méthodologie* (Paris 2003), 191-213

H. Omont, *Inventaire sommaire des manuscrits grecs de la Bibliothèque nationale et des autres bibliothèques de Paris et des Départements*, 4 vols. (Paris 1886-98; repr. 4 vols., Hildesheim/Zurich/New York 2000)

H. Omont, 'Catalogue des manuscrits grecs des Bibliothèques Suisse: Bâle, Berne, Einsiedeln, Genève, St. Gall, Schaffhouse et Zürich', *Centralblatt für Bibliothekswesen* 3 (1886), 385-452

M. D. J. Op de Coul, *Théodore Prodrome: Lettres et Discours. Édition, Traduction, Commentaire*, 2 vols., unpublished PhD thesis (Paris 2007)

P. Orsini, *Musée, Héro et Léandre* (Paris 1968)

C. Palau, 'Mazaris, Giorgio Baiophoros e il monastero di Prodromo Petra', *Nea Rhome* 7 (2010), 367-97

S. D. Papadimitriou, 'Ὁ Πρόδρομος τοῦ Μαρκιανοῦ κώδικος XI 22', *VV* 10 (1903), 102-63

S. D. Papadimitriou, *Feodor Prodrom*, Odessa 1905

A. Papadopoulos-Kerameus, Κατάλογος τῶν ἐν ταῖς βιβλιοθήκαις τῆς νήσου Λέσβου ἑλληνικῶν χειρογράφων (Μαυρογορδάτειος Βιβλιοθήκη I/2 = Ὁ ἐν Κωνσταντινουπόλει Ἑλληνικὸς Φιλολογικὸς Σύλλογος 15, Παράρτημα) (Istanbul 1884)

A. Papadopoulos-Kerameus, Ἱεροσολυμιτικὴ Βιβλιοθήκη ἤτοι κατάλογος τῶν ἐν ταῖς βιβλιοθήκαις τοῦ ἁγιωτάτου ἀποστολικοῦ τε καὶ καθολικοῦ ὀρθοδόξου πατριαρχικοῦ θρόνου τῶν Ἱεροσολύμων καὶ πάσης Παλαιστίνης ἀποκειμένων ἑλληνικῶν κωδίκων, 5 vols. (St Petersburg 1894-1915)

A. Papadopoulos-Kerameus, 'Εἷς καὶ μόνος Θεόδωρος Πρόδρομος', *Lětopis Istoriko-Filologičeskago Obščestva pri Imperatorskom Novorossijskom Universitetě, VII, Vizantijskij Otdelenie IV* (Odessa 1898), 385-402

A. Papadopoulos-Kerameus, 'Δύο κατάλογοι ἑλληνικῶν κωδίκων ἐν Κωνσταντινουπόλει, τῆς Μεγάλης τοῦ Γένους Σχολῆς καὶ τοῦ Ζωγραφείου', *IRAIK* 14 (1909), 33-85

A. Papadopoulos-Kerameus, *Noctes Petropolitanae: Sbornik vizantijskich tekstov XII-XIII věkov* (St Petersburg 1913)

G. Papagiannis, *Theodoros Prodromos: Jambische und hexametrische Tetraticha auf die Haupterzählungen des Alten und des Neuen Testaments*, 2 vols. (Wiesbaden 1997)

G. Papagiannis, *Philoprodromica: Beiträge zur Textkonstitution und Quellenforschung der historischen Gedichte des Theodoros Prodromos* (Vienna 2012)

S. Papaioannou, 'Language Games, Not the Soul's Beliefs: Michael Italikos to Theodoros Prodromos, on Friendship and Writing', in: M. Hinterberger and E. Schiffer (eds), *Byzantinische Sprachkunst: Studien zur byzantinischen Literatur gewidmet Wolfram Hörandner zum 65. Geburtstag* (Berlin/New York 2007), 218-33

S. Papaioannou, 'Byzantine Mirrors: Self-Reflection in Medieval Greek Writing', *DOP* 64 (2010), 81-102

S. Papaioannou, *Michael Psellos: Rhetoric and Authorship in Byzantium* (Cambridge 2013)

S. Papaioannou, 'Voice, Signature, Mask: The Byzantine Author', in: A. Pizzone (ed.), *The Author in Middle Byzantine Literature: Modes, Functions, and Identities* (Berlin/Boston 2014), 21-40

S. Papaioannou, *Michael Psellus, Epistulae*, 2 vols. (Berlin/Boston 2019)

C. Pasini, *Inventario agiografico dei manoscritti greci dell'Ambrosiana* (Brussels 2003)

E. Passamonti, 'Dell' Ἀπόδημος φιλία Di Teodoro Prodromo', *Rendiconti della Reale Accademia dei Lincei, Classe di scienze morali, storiche e filologiche* I (1892), 361-70

M. Patedakis, 'Μια επιγραφή με ηγεμονική διάσταση. Επίγραμμα του Θεοδώρου Προδρόμου στο Βίβλος γενέσεως (ευαγγ. Ματθαίου 1.1) από την Παναγία στον Μέρωνα', in: M. S. Patedakis and K. D. Giapitsoglou (eds), Μαργαρίται. Μελέτες στη Μνήμη του Μανόλη Μπορμπουδάκη (Sitia 2016), 328-59

W. R. Paton, *The Greek Anthology*, 5 vols. (Cambridge, MA/London 1918; 6th reprint 1979)

A. Paul, 'Dichtung auf Objekten: Inschriftlich erhaltene griechische Epigramme vom 9. bis zum 16. Jahrhundert: Suche nach bekannten Autorennamen', in: M. Hinterberger and E. Schiffer (eds), *Byzantinische Sprachkunst: Studien zur byzantinischen Literatur gewidmet Wolfram Hörandner zum 65. Geburtstag* (Berlin/Leipzig 2007), 234-65

S. M. Pelekanides, Οἱ θησαυροὶ τοῦ ἁγίου Ὄρους (Εἰκονογραφημένα χειρόγραφα. Παραστάσ εἰς-ἐπίτιτλα-ἀρχικὰ γράμματα), 4 vols. (Athens 1991)

L. M. Peltomaa, *The Image of the Virgin Mary in the Akathistos Hymn* (Leiden 2001)

I. Pérez Martín, 'Les Kephalaia de Chariton des Hodèges (Paris, BNF Gr. 1630)', in: P. Van Deun and C. Macé (eds), *Encyclopedic Trends in Byzantium?* (Leuven/Paris/Walpole, MA 2011), 361-81

A. Pignani, *Niceforo Basilace, Progimnasmi e monodie* (Naples 1983)

A. Pizzone (ed.), *The Author in Middle Byzantine Literature: Modes, Functions, and Identities* (Berlin/Boston 2014)

A. Pizzone, 'The Historiai of John Tzetzes: A Byzantine "Book of Memory"?', *BMGS* 41.2 (2017), 182-207

I. D. Polemis, 'Μία ὑπόθεση γιὰ τὴν προέλευση τῆς σχεδογραφικῆς συλλογῆς τοῦ κώδικα Vaticanus Palatinus graecus 92', in: E. Karamalengou and E. D. Makrygianni (eds), Ἀντιφίλησις: *Studies on Classical, Byzantine and Modern Greek Literature and Culture. In Honour of John-Theophanes A. Papadimitriou* (Stuttgart 2009), 558-65

L. Politis, 'Δύο χειρόγραφα ἀπὸ τὴν Καστοριά', *Hell* 20 (1967), 29-41

L. Politis and M. L. Politi, Βιβλιογράφοι 17ου-18ου αἰῶνα: Συνοπτικὴ Καταγραφή (Athens 1994)

F. Pontani, *Sguardi su Ulisse* (Rome 2005)

F. Pontani, 'The First Byzantine Commentary on the *Iliad*: Isaac Porphyrogenitus and His Scholia in Par. gr. 2682', *BZ* 99 (2006), 559-604

F. Pontani, 'Dodecasillabi anonimi su Michele VIII nel Conv. Soppr. 48', in: *Filologia, papirologia, storia dei testi. Giornate di Studio in Onore di Antonio Carlini, Udine, 9-10 dicembre 2005* (Pisa/Rome 2008), 63-82

F. Pontani, V. Sarris, and V. Katsaros (eds), *Reading Eustathios of Thessalonike* (Berlin/Boston 2017)

F. J. G. La Porte du Theil, 'Notice d'un manuscrit de la bibliothèque du Vatican, coté CCCV, parmi les manuscrits Grecs', *Notices et extraits des manuscrits de la Bibliothèque Nationale et d'autres bibliothèques* 8/2 (1810), 249ff

K. Praechter, 'Beziehungen zur Antike in Theodoros Prodromos' Rede auf Isaak Komnenos', *BZ* 19 (1910), 314-29

G. Prato, 'La produzione libraria in area Greco-Orientale nel periodo del regno Latino di Constantunopoli (1204-1261)', in: G. Prato (ed.), *Studi di Paleografia Greca* (Spoleto 1994)

P. Rassow, 'Zum byzantinisch-normannischen Krieg 1147-1149', *MiÖG* 62 (1954), 213-18

D. R. Reinsch, *Michaelis Pselli Chronographia*, 2 vols. (Berlin/Boston 2014)

A. Rhoby, *Reminiszenzen an antike Stätten in der mittel und spätbyzantinischen Literatur: Eine Untersuchung zur Antikenrezeption in Byzanz* (Göttingen 2003)

A. Rhoby, 'Aspekte des *Fortlebens* des Gregor von Nazianz in byzantinischer und postbyzantinischer Zeit', in: M. Grünbart (ed.), *Theatron: Rhetorische Kultur in Spätantike und Mittelalter/Rhetorical Culture in Late Antiquity and the Middle Ages* (Berlin/New York 2007), 409-17

A. Rhoby, *Byzantinische Epigramme in inschriftlicher Überlieferung*, 4 vols. (Vienna 2009-18)

A. Rhoby, 'Verschiedene Bemerkungen zur Sebastokratorissa Eirene und zu Autoren in ihrem Umfeld', *Nea Rhome* 6 (2009), 305-36

A. Rhoby, 'Ioannes Tzetzes als Auftragsdichter', *Graeco-Latina Brunensia* 15/2 (2010), 167-83

A. Rhoby, 'Zur Identifizierung von bekannten Autoren im Codex Marcianus Graecus 524', *MEG* 10 (2010), 167-204

A. Rhoby, 'Vom jambischen Trimeter zum byzantinischen Zwölfsilber: Beobachtung zur Metrik des spätantiken und byzantinischen Epigramms', *WSt* 124 (2011), 117-42

A. Rhoby, 'On the Inscriptional Versions of the Epigrams of Christophoros Mitylenaios', in: F. Bernard and K. Demoen (eds), *Poetry and Its Contexts in Eleventh-Century Byzantium* (Farnham/Burlington 2012), 147-54

A. Rhoby, 'Labeling Poetry in the Middle and Late Byzantine Period', *Byz* 85 (2015), 259-83

A. Rhoby, *Ausgewählte byzantinische Epigramme in illuminierten Handschriften: Verse und ihre inschriftliche Verwendung in Codices des 9. bis 15. Jahrhunderts* (Vienna 2018)

A. Rhoby and N. Zagklas, 'Zu einer möglichen Deutung von Πανιώτης', *JÖB* 61 (2011), 171-77

M. Rizou-Kouroupou and P. Gehin, *Catalogue des manuscrits conservés dans la Bibliothèque du Patriarcat Oecuménique, Les manuscrits du monastère de la Panaghia de Chalki*, 2 vols. (Turnhout 2008)

R. H. Robins, *The Byzantine Grammarians: Their Place in History* (Berlin/Boston 1993; reprint Berlin 2011)

P. Roilos, *Amphoteroglossia: A Poetics of the Twelfth-Century Medieval Greek Novel* (Washington DC 2005)

R. Romano, *Nicola Callicle, Carmi* (Naples 1980)

D. A. Russell and N. G. Wilson, *Menander Rhetor, edited with Translation and Commentary* (Oxford 1981)

J. Sajdak, *Historia critica scholiastarum et commentatorum Gregorii Nazianzeni, Pars I* (Krakow 1914)

I. A. Sakkelion, Κατάλογος τῶν χειρογράφων τῆς Ἐθνικῆς Βιβλιοθήκης τῆς Ἑλλάδος (Athens 1892)

I. A. Sakkelion, Πατμιακὴ Βιβλιοθήκη, ἤτοι ἀναγραφὴ τῶν ἐν τῇ βιβλιοθήκῃ τῆς κατὰ τὴν νῆσον Πάτμον γεραρᾶς καὶ βασιλικῆς μονῆς τοῦ Ἁγίου Ἀποστόλου καὶ Εὐαγγελιστοῦ Ἰωάννου του Θεολόγου τεθησαυρισμένων χειρογράφων τευχῶν (Athens 1890)

F. Scheidweiler, 'Studien zu Johannes Geometres', *BZ* 45 (1952), 277–319

P. Schreiner, *Die byzantinischen Kleinchroniken*, 3 vols. (Vienna 1975–79)

N. P. Ševčenko, *The Life of Saint Nicholas in Byzantine Art* (Turin 1983)

N. P. Ševčenko, 'The Vita Icon and the Painter as Hagiographer', *DOP* 53 (1999), 149–65

N. Patterson Ševčenko, 'Kosmosoteira: Typikon of the sebastokrator Isaac Komnenos for the monastery of the Mother of God *Kosmosoteira* near Bera', in: *Byzantine Monastic Foundation Documents: A Complete Translation of the Surviving Founders' Typika and Testaments edited by John Thomas and Angela Constantinides Hero with the assistance of Giles Constable* (Washington DC 2000)

C. Simelidis, *Selected Poems of Gregory of Nazianzus: I.2.17; II.1.10, 19, 32: A Critical Edition with Introduction and Commentary* (Göttingen 2009)

A. Skarveli-Nikolopoulou, Τὰ μαθηματάρια των ελληνικων σχολείων της Τουρκοκρατίας: Διδασκόμενα κείμενα, σχολικά προγράμματα, διδακτικές μέθοδοι· συμβολή στην ιστορία της νεοελληνικής παιδείας (Athens 1993)

E. Skouvaras, Ὀλυμπιώτισσα: Περιγραφὴ καὶ ἱστορία τῆς Μονῆς. Κατάλογος τῶν χειρογράφων-Χρονικὰ Σημειώματα. Ἀκολουθία Παναγίας τῆς Ὀλυμπιωτίσσης. Ἔγγραφα ἐκ τοῦ Ἀρχείου τῆς Μονῆς (1336–1900), 2 vols. (Athens 1967)

V. Somers, *Histoire des collections complètes des Discours de Grégoire de Nazianze* (Louvain-la-Neuve 1997)

V. Somers-Auwers, 'Les collections byzantines de xvi discours de *Grégoire* de Nazianze', *BZ* 95 (2002), 102–35

P. Sotiroudis, Ἱερὰ Μονὴ Ἰβήρων: Κατάλογος ἑλληνικῶν χειρογράφων. ΙΑ΄ (1387–1568) (Mount Athos 2007)

K. Spanoudakis, 'Nonnus and Theodorus Prodromus', *MEG* 13 (2013), 241–50

J. Spier, *Late Byzantine Rings, 1204–1453* (Wiesbaden 2013)

F. Spingou, 'A Poem on the Refortification of Dorylaion in 1175', *Symm* 21 (2011), 137–68

F. Spingou, 'Byzantine Collections and Anthologies of Poetry', in: W. Hörandner, A. Rhoby, and N. Zagklas (eds), *A Companion to Byzantine Poetry* (Leiden/Boston 2019), 381–403

F. Spingou, *Words and Artworks in the Twelfth Century and Beyond: Twelfth-Century Poetry on Art from MS. Marcianus Gr. 524* (Tolworth, Surrey 2021)

V. Stanković, 'A Generation Gap or Political Enmity? Emperor Manuel Komnenos, Byzantine Intellectuals and the Struggle for Domination in Twelfth Century Byzantium', *ZRVI* 44 (2007), 209–26

R. S. Stefec, 'Die Synaxarverse des Nikephoros Xanthopoulos', *JÖB* 62 (2012), 145–61

R. S. Stefec, 'Zu einigen zypriotischen Handschriften der Österreichischen Nationalbibliothek', *RBNS* 49 (2012), 53–78

L. Sternbach, 'Spicilegium Prodromeum', *Rozprawy Akademii Umiejętności, Wydział filologiczny*, ser. II, 24 (1904). 336–68 (also published separately: Krakow 1904)

H. Stevenson, *Codices manuscripti Palatini Graeci Bibliothecae Vaticanae* (Rome 1885)

H. Stevenson, *Codices manuscripti Graeci Reginae Svecorum et Pii PP. II Bibliothecae Vaticanae* (Rome 1888)

G. Stickler, *Manuel Philes und seine Psalmenmetaphrase* (Vienna 1992)

C. Stornajolo, *Codices Urbinates Graeci Bibliothecae Vaticanae descripti* (Rome 1895)

P. Stotz, 'Heinrich Bullinger (1504–1575) and the Ancient Languages', in: E. Campi, S. De Angelis, A.-S. Goeing, and A. Grafton (eds), *Textbooks in Early Modern Europe* (Geneva 2008), 113–38

W. Studemund and L. Cohn, *Verzeichnisse der griechischen Handschriften der Königlichen Bibliothek zu Berlin*, 2 vols. (Berlin 1890)

M. Trizio, 'Socrates in Byzantium', in: C. Moore (ed.), *Brill's Companion to the Reception of Socrates* (Leiden/Boston 2019), 592–615

A. Turyn, *Codices graeci Vaticani saeculis XIII et XIV scripti annorumque notis instructi* (Vatican City 1964)

A. Turyn, *Dated Greek Manuscripts of the Thirteenth and Fourteenth Centuries in the Libraries of Great Britain* (Washington DC 1980)

M. Tziatzi-Papagianni, 'Theodoros Prodromos Historisches Gedicht LXXVIII', *BZ* 86-87 (1993-94), 363-82

P. Tzivara and S. Karydis, *Ἡ βιβλιοθήκη τῆς μονῆς Πλατυτέρας Κέρκυρας, Χειρόγραφα—Ἔντυπα—Ἀρχεῖο* (Athens 2010)

E. van Opstall, 'Verses on Paper, Verses Inscribed? A Case Study, with Epigrams of John Geometres', in: W. Hörandner and A. Rhoby (eds), *Die kulturhistorische Bedeutung byzantinischer Epigramme: Akten des internationalen Workshop (Wien, 1.-2. Dezember 2006)* (Vienna 2008), 55–60

E. M. van Opstall, *Jean Géomètre: Poèmes en hexamètres et en distiques élégiaques. Editions, traduction, commentaire* (Leiden/Boston 2008)

M. van Raalte, *Rhythm and Metre: Towards a Systematic Description of Greek Stichic Verse* (Leiden 1986)

I. Vassis, 'Graeca sunt, non leguntur: Zu den schedographischen Spielereien des Theodoros Prodromos', *BZ* 86/87 (1993/94), 1–19

I. Vassis, '*Τῶν νέων Φιλολόγων Παλαίσματα. Ἡ συλλογὴ σχεδῶν τοῦ κώδικα* Vaticanus Palatinus gr. 92', *Hell* 52 (2002), 37–68

I. Vassis, *Initia Carminum Byzantinorum* (Berlin/New York 2005)

I. Vassis, 'Das Pantokratorkloster von Konstantinopel in der byzantinischen Dichtung', in: S. Kotzabassi (ed.), *The Pantokrator Monastery in Constantinople* (Boston 2013), 203–49

I. Vassis and I. Polemis, *Ἕνας Ἕλληνας ἐξόριστος στὴν Μάλτα τοῦ δωδέκατου αἰώνα* (Athens 2016)

M. Vogel and V. Gardthausen, *Die griechischen Schreiber des Mittelalters und der Renaissance* (Leipzig 1909; repr. Hildesheim 1996)

S. J. Voicu, *Note sui palinsesti conservati nella Biblioteca Apostolica Vaticana*, in: *Miscellanea Bibliothecae Apostolicae Vaticanae XVI* (Vatican City 2009)

P. L. Vokotopoulos, *Byzantine Illuminated Manuscripts of the Patriarchate of Jerusalem [Μικρογραφίες τῶν βυζαντινῶν χειρογράφων τοῦ Πατριαρχείου Ἱεροσολύμων]*, translated from the Greek by D. M. Whitehouse (Athens 2002)

K. von Tischendorf, *Apocalypses Apocryphae* (Leipzig 1866; repr. Hildesheim 1966)

H. G. Wackernagel, *Die Matrikel der Universität Basel 1460-1818*, 5 vols. (Basel 1951–80)

R. Webb, *Ekphrasis, Imagination and Persuasion in Ancient Rhetorical Theory and Practice* (Farnham 2009)

M. E. Welti, 'Der Gräzist Simon Grynaeus und England', *Archiv für Kulturgeschichte* 45 (1963), 232–42

N. Zagklas, 'A Byzantine Grammar Treatise Attributed to Theodoros Prodromos', *Graeco-Latina Brunensia* 16 (2011), 77–86

N. Zagklas, 'Theodore Prodromos and the Use of the Poetic Work of Gregory of Nazianzus: Appropriation in the Service of Self-Representation', *BMGS* 40 (2016), 223–42

N. Zagklas, 'Astrology, Piety and Poverty: Seven Anonymous Poems in Vaticanus gr. 743', *BZ* 109.2 (2016), 895–918

N. Zagklas, 'Experimenting with Prose and Verse in Twelfth-Century Byzantium: A Preliminary Study', *DOP* 71 (2017), 229–48

N. Zagklas, 'Metrical *Polyeideia* in Twelfth-Century Poetry: Multimetric Poetic Cycles as a Medium for Generic Innovation', in: A. Rhoby and N. Zagklas (eds), *Middle and Late Byzantine Poetry: Texts and Contexts* (Brepols 2018), 43–70

N. Zagklas, '"How Many Verses Shall I Write and Say?": Writing Poetry in the Komnenian Period', in: W. Hörandner, A. Rhoby, and N. Zagklas (eds), *A Companion to Byzantine Poetry* (Leiden/Boston 2019), 237–63

N. Zagklas, 'Satire in the Komnenian Period: Poetry, Satirical Strands and Intellectual Antagonism', in: P. Marciniak and I. Nilsson (eds), *Satire in the Middle Byzantine Period: The Golden Age of Laughter?* (Leiden/Boston 2020), 279–303

N. Zagklas, 'Epistolarity in Twelfth-century Byzantine Poetry: Singing Praises and Asking Favours *in Absentia*', in: K. Kubina and A. Riehle (eds), *Epistolary Poetry in Byzantium and Beyond: An Anthology with Critical Essays* (New York 2021), 64–77

S. Zanandrea, 'Enigmistica bizantina: considerazioni preliminari', *Miscellanea Marciana* 2–4 (1987–89), 141–57

B. Zeitler, 'Ostentatio Genitalium: Displays of Nudity in Byzantium', in: L. James (ed.), *Desire and Denial in Byzantium* (Aldershot 1999), 185–91

A. Zervoudaki, 'Hymnography in a Form of Rhetoric: An Interesting "Marriage" of Genres in a late Byzantine Hymnographic Ethopoiia', *REB* 69 (2011), 49–79

Index Locorum

This *index* contains references to works in the *apparatus fontium et locorum parallelorum* of the critical edition. The editions of the Byzantine texts are fully indicated only when they are not included in the bibliography.

I) Biblica Sacra

Vetus Testamentum

Genesis (Gen.)
  18, 1–16 7/8
  22, 1–13 19.1–2
  2, 8 63.2
  2, 9 63.8
  1, 6 75.24–25
  1, 26 76.153

Exodus (Ex.)
  19, 16/19 75.147

III Regnorum (III Regn.)
  18, 17–40 16.1–2

Psalmi (Ps.)
  35, 7 75.2

Ecclesiastes (Eccl.)
  5, 14 55.5

Iob
  1, 21 55.5
  1, 21 69.17
  1, 3 75.87

Ioel
  3, 13 15

Habacuc (Hab.)
  2, 1 75.3–4

Isaias (Is.)
  26, 18 14.3–5

Novum Testamentum

Matthaeus (Matth.)
  28, 11–15 10
  13, 24–30 15
  27, 35 26.1–2

Marcus (Marc.)
  15, 24 26.1–2

Iohannes (Ioh.)
  19, 29/34 27
  19, 26 28
  5, 19 75.140

Actus Apostolorum (Act.)
  9, 15 1.2
  15, 2 1.6

Ad Romanos (Rom.)
  11, 20 55.4
  11, 33 75.6

I ad Corinthios (I Cor.)
  9, 22 1.17

Ad Ephesios (Eph)
  5, 16 1.16

II ad Thessalonicenses (II. Thess.)
  2, 16 56.9

Apocalypsis (Apc.)
  14, 15–16 15

II) ALII AUCTORES

Achiles Tatius (Achil.Tat.)
  Leucippe et Clitophon (L&C)
  1, 16, 2.1 76.33
  1, 18, 3–5 76.129–134
  1, 17, 2 76.135–136

Aeschylus (Aesch.)
  Persae (Pers.)
  165 10.8
  Prometheus vinctus (Prometh.)
  870 76.34

Aesopus (Aesop.)
Proverbia (Prov.)
51, 1 14.1-2

Anacharsis sive Ananias (Anacharsis): ed. Christidis
1325 74.11
707-709 75.55
754 75.147

Andronicus Ducas Sgouros (Andron. Duc. Sgouros)
Carmina (Carm.): ed. Tzivara and Karydis
9 (p. 94) 6.5

Anthologia Graeca (Anthol. Gr.): ed. Beckby
8 91, 4 2.3
5 272, 4 2.10
8 6, 1 3.1
8 4, 3 3.4
8 10, 1-2 3.10
8 91, 4 4.12
9 361, 3 6.9
1 26, 2 6.23-24
8 246, 2 13.6
8 247, 1 13.6
12 97, 4 21.1
16 275, 2 25.2
1 44, 2 68.3
1 10, 68 74.4
5 259, 3 76.3
5 259, 4 76.4
10 87, 1 76.158-159
16 380, 2 76.258

Anthologia Graeca Appendix (Anthol. Gr. App.): ed. E. Cougny, *Epigrammatum anthologia Palatina cum Planudeis et appendice nova epigrammatum veterum ex libris et marmoribus*, vol. 3 (Paris 1890)
6 268, 2 6.20
3 133, 4 25.2
1 370, 2 27.4
2 522, 1 69.17
3 255, 1 73.1
1 131, 4 74.10

Apollinaris (Apoll.)
Metaphrasis psalmorum
2,118, 101 6.9

Apollonius Rhodius (Apoll. Rhod.)
Argonautica (Arg.)
4, 1359-1360 1.10
4, 360 4.17

Aristoteles (Arist.)
Politica (Pol.)
1291a1 76.120-125

Bacchylides (Bacchyl.)
Epinicia
13, 168 25.2

Canones in *AHG*: ed Schirό
Canones Maii, can. 6, od. 8, trop. 5, 179-180, p. 56 10.15
Canones Augusti, can. 5 (2), od. 9, trop. 2, 250, p. 70 69.1
Canones Iulii, can. 35, od. 8, trop. 4, 243-244, p. 468 76.152
Canones Decembris, can. 5, od. 8, trop. 7, 368, p. 73 76.152

Christophorus Hagioeuplites (Christ. Hagioeupl.): ed. Gallavotti
Carmina (Carm.)
p. 31, 24 13.6
p. 31, 3 20.1

Christophorus Mitylenaeus (Christ. Mityl.): ed. de Groote
Carmina (Carm.)
13, 1 75.1

Christus Patiens: ed. A.Tuilier, *Grégoire de Nazianze, La Passion du Christ* (Paris 1969)
2500-2503 9.2-5

Constantinus Manasses (Const. Manass.)
Aristandros et Callithea (A&K): ed. Mazal
9 160, 1-2 55.9-10
1 21a 76.127-128

Breviarium Chronicum (Breviar. Chron.): ed. O. Lampsides, *Constantini Manassis Breviarium Chronicum* (Athens 1996)
5008 74.7
5259 76.13

Vita Oppiani (Vit. Opp.): ed. A. Colonna, 'De Oppiani vita antiquissima', *Bollettino del Comitato per la preparazione della edizione nazionale dei classici greci e latini* 12 (1964) 33-40
p. 38, 28 25. 2

Diogenes Laertius
  (Diog. Laert.)
  Vitae philosophorum
  6, 41, 251 76.24
Etymologicum Magnum (Etymol.
  Magnum): ed. T. Gaisford,
  Etymologicum magnum (Oxford 1848;
  repr. Amsterdam 1967)
  321, 45 75.128
Eudocia Augusta (Eud.)
  Homerocentones (Homeroc.)
  1, 1198 2.19
  1, 895 3.19
  1, 1638 6.9
  3, 55 6.13
  1, 1791 6.16
  1, 1962 27.3
  3, 97 28.4
Euripides (Eurip.)
  Bacchae (Bacch.)
  244 et 594 12.3
  Hecuba (Hecub.)
  1128 13.1
  Orestes (Orest.)
  633 10.8
  Supplices (Suppl.)
  1011 12.3
Eustathius Macrembolites (Eust.
  Macremb.)
  Hysmine et Hysminias (H&H): ed.
  Marcovich
  10, 10, 2.3 71.1
  10, 3, 2.10–14 76.127–128
Eustathius Thessalonicensis
  (Eust.Thessal.)
  Sermones: ed. P. Wirth, *Eustathii
  Thessalonicensis opera minora (magnam
  partem inedita)* (Berlin 1999)
  2, p. 38, 13–14 4.4
  Commentarii ad Homeri Iliadem
  (Comm. In Hom. Il.): ed M. van der
  Valk, *Eustathii Archiepiscopi
  Thessalonicensis commentarii ad
  Homeri Iliadem pertinentes ad fidem
  codicis Laurentiani editi*, 4 vols.
  (Leiden 1971–1987)
  16, 14 (III p. 797, 30–31) 74.7

Euthymius Tornices (Euth. Torn.)
  Carmina (Carm.): ed. Hörandner
  4, 42 75.100
  Carmina (Carm.): ed.
  Papadopoulos-Kerameus
  1, 53 (p. 190) 74.4
Georgius Pisides (Georg. Pisid.)
  De vita humana: ed. F. Gonnelli, 'Il De Vita
  Humana di Giorgio Pisida', *Bollettino dei
  Classici* 12 (1991) 118–38
  50 4.12
Gregorius Antiochus (Gregor. Antioch.)
  Oratio (Or.): ed. A. Sideras, *Gregorii
  Antiochi opera: orationes et epistulae*,
  vol. 2 (Vienna 2021)
  3, 234–235 (p. 642) 76.24
Gregorius Nazianzenus (Greg.Naz.)
  Carmina (Carm.): ed. *PG* 37
  II.1, 34 [515] 8–10 2.8–11
  II.2, 1 [1460] 115–117 2.11
  II.1.89 [1442] 3 62.7–8
  II.1 [559] 490 68.1
  II.2.3 [1495] 211 73.1
  I.1.26 [503] 61 74.10
  I.2.2 [609] 388 74.10
  Orationes
  Or. 43 (in Basilium): ed. J. Bernardi,
  *Grégoire de Nazianze. Discours 42–43.
  Introduction, texte critique, traduction
  et notes* (Paris 1992)
  23, 15, p. 174 2.3
  1, 1, p. 116 2.24
Gregorius Nyssenus (Greg. Nyss.)
  De sancto Theodoro: ed. J.P. Cavarnos, in:
  Gregorii Nysseni Sermones, vol. 2
  (Gregorii Nysseni Opera, 10.1) (Leiden/
  New York/Copenhagen/Cologne 1990)
  p. 68, 21 76.5
  In Canticum canticorum homiliae (in
  cant. cant.): ed. H. Langerbeck,
  *Gregorii Nysseni In Canticum
  canticorum* (Leiden 1960)
  Hom. 5, p. 154, 1–3 62.1–5
Himerius (Himer.)
  Fragmenta ex incertis orationibus
  1, 20–21 1.19

Hesiodus (Hes.)
  Theogonia (Theog.)
  867 3.18
  575 28.4
  131 69.4
  Scutum
  59 3.18
Hesychius (Hesych.)
  Lexicon (Lexic.)
  μ 275 13.1
  ε 2425 27.6
Hermogenes (Hermog.)
  Corpus Rhetor. (Corpus Rhetor.): ed. M. Patillon, *Corpus rhetoricum II: Hermogène, Les états de cause*, vol. 2 (Paris 2009)
  III, 4, 11–12 (p. 21) 76.210
Homerus (Hom.)
  Ilias (Il.)
  1, 290 1.1
  9, 443 1.19
  17, 557 1.7
  12, 242 2.19
  8, 563 3.18
  1, 286 3.19
  2, 214 4.17
  3, 59 5.3
  18, 570 5.23
  10, 83 6.9
  8, 13 6.13
  5, 439 6.16
  12, 273 6.17
  8, 328 21.8
  10, 373 27.3
  5, 725 28.4
  5, 816 70.1
  13, 85 74.4
  8, 141 74.10
  6, 202 74.11
  1, 490 74.12
  8, 19 76.45
  23, 115 76.45
  18, 478–608 76.234
  16, 116–117 76.235–236
  Odyssea (Od.)
  1, 263 1.1
  9, 552 2.19
  2, 251 3.19
  3, 138 4.17
  9, 143 6.9
  3, 298 6.17
  6, 306 28.4
  4, 350 70.1
  10, 289 74.4
  8, 233 74.4
  3, 57 74.10
  17, 233 76.27
Hymnus Acathistus (Hymn. Acath.): ed. C. A. Trypanis, *Fourteen Early Byzantine Cantica* (Vienna 1968)
  13, 16 (p. 35) 24.3
Hymni Homerici (Hymn. Hom.)
  In Cererem
  310–311 68.4–5
  113 73.2
Inscriptio metrica (Inscr.metr.)
  Me83, 2 (ed. Rhoby, Byzantinische Epigramme auf Ikonen und Objekten der Kleinkunst, II, p. 258) 27.4
  IT, 1 (ed. Rhoby, Byzantinische Epigramme auf Stein, III, p. 406) 33.2
Iohannes Chrysostomus (Ioh. Chrys.)
  Contra eos qui subintroductas habent virgine: ed. J. Dumortier, *Saint Jean Chrysostome. Les cohabitations suspectes. Comment observe la virginité* (Paris 1955)
  7, 17 (p. 67) 74.7
  De sancto Melet. (De sancto Meletio Antiocheno): ed. *PG*
  50, 519 76.5
  Expositiones in Psalmos (Expos. in Ps.): ed. *PG*
  55, 497 4.4
  Fragmenta in Jeremiam (Fr.in Jer.): ed. *PG*
  64, 856D 76.13
  In Ioannem: ed. PG
  59, 211 35.1
  In epistulam ad Romanos (in ep. ad Rom.): ed. *PG*
  60, 674 74.7
Iohannes Damascenus (Ioh. Damasc.)

Laudatio sanctae martyris Barbarae
(Laud. S. Barb.): ed. P.B. Kotter, *Die
Schriften des Johannes von Damaskos,
Opera homiletica et* hagiographica,
vol. 5 (Berlin/New York 1988)
12, 23–25   11.1–2
16, 36   11.3–4
11, 4–5   11.4
18, 20–22   12.1–2
9, 21–22   20.1
19, 20–21   20.2–4
18, 16–17   21.8

Sacra Parallela: ed. *PG*
95, 1124D   55.10

Iohannes Geometres (Ioh. Geom.)

Carmina hexametrica et elegiaca (Carm.
hex. et el.): ed. van Opstall
300, 57   4.3

Iohannes Mauropus (Ioh. Maurop.): ed.
F. D'Aiuto, *Tre canoni di Giovanni
Mauropode in onore di santi militari*
(Rome 1994)

Canones
III, 96–102 (p. 126)   11.3–4
III, 236–7 (p. 134)   27.4

Iohannes Stobaeus (Ioh. Stob.)

Anthologium (Anthol.)
1.40.1.227   75.39–40

Iohannes Tzetzes (Ioh.Tzetz.): ed. Leone

Chiliades (Chil.): ed. Leone
7, 868   74.11

Epistulae (Epist.): ed. Leone
19 p. 37, 2   74.11
14 p. 26, 21–22   75.84–85
67 p. 97, 16–17   75.84–85

Iohannes Zonaras (Ioh. Zonar.)

Epitome historiarum (Epitome Histor.):
ed. L. Dindorf, *Ioannis Zonarae Epitome
Historiarum*, vol. 2 (Leipzig 1869)
II 445, 1   76.5

Iosephus Bryennios (Ios.Bryennius)

Epistulae (Epist.): ed. Tomadakis
20, 62   62.2
20, 98–99   62.7–8

Libistrus et Rhodamne: ed. P. A. Agapitos,
Ἀφήγησις Λιβίστρου καὶ Ῥοδάμνης.
Κριτικὴ ἔκδοση τῆς διασκευῆς α
(Athens 2006)
173–175   76.127–128
179–181   76.129–134

Lucianus (Lucian.)

Prometheus (Prom.)
10, 9   76.24

Fugitivi (Fugit.)
3, 2–3   76.2–3

Manuel Philes (Man. Philes)

Carmina (Carm.): ed. Miller
App. 43, 1(II p. 349)   10.1
cod. Florent., 66, 4 (I p. 241)   25.7
cod. Florent., 211, 114 (I p. 387)   44.2
cod. Paris., 168, 6 (II p. 192)   55.1
cod. Florent., 107, 3 (I p. 295)   76.258

Carmina (Carm.): ed. A. E. Martini,
Manuelis Philae Carmina Inedita
(Naples 1900)
92, 87   76.13

Carmina (Carm.): ed. Braounou-Pietsch
23, 15–16   76.146–147

Meletios Galesiotes (Melet. Galesiot.)

Alphabetalphabeton: ed. Th. N. Simopulos,
Μελέτιος ὁ Γαλησιώτης (1230–1307),
ὁ ἄγνωστος, Θεολόγος, Ὅσιος,
Ὁμολογητής, Λόγιος, Συγγραφεύς
(Athens 1978)
131, 24   73.2

Michael Glycas (Mich. Glyc.)

Quaestiones in sacram scripturam II: ed.
S. Eustratiades, Μιχαὴλ τοῦ Γλυκᾶ
εἰς τὰς ἀπορίας τῆς Θείας Γραφῆς
κεφάλαια, vol. 2 (Alexandria 1912)
II 59, 10, p. 133   74.7

Michael Haploucheir (Haplouch.)

Dramation (Dram.): ed. Leone
67–69   75.57–59
69   75.64
71   75.77
73–74   75.84–85
76   75.87
77   75.92
78–79   75.100
110   75.128

Michael Italicus (Mich. Italic.)
  Orationes (Or.): ed. Gautier
  41 236,6 4.4
Marinus
  Vita Procli: ed. R. Masullo, *Marino di Neapoli. Vita di Proclo* (Naples 1985)
  697 6.20
Michael Choniates (Mich. Chon.)
  Carmina (Carm.): ed. Sp. Lambros, Μιχαὴλ Ἀκομινάτου τοῦ Χωνιάτου τὰ σωζόμενα, vol. 2 (Athens 1880)
  7, 15 (p. 395) 43.1
Michael Psellus (Mich. Psell.)
  Theologica (Theol.): ed. P. Gautier, *Michael Psellus Theologica*, vol. 1 (Leipzig 1989)
  I, 7, p. 28, 15–18 5.13–16
  I 17, p. 69, 13 74.7
  Orationes hagiographicae (Orat. Hagiogr.): ed. E. A. Fisher, *Michaelis Pselli orationes hagiographicae* (Stuttgart 1994)
  3b, 155–156 27.2–3
Musaeus Grammaticus (Mus. Grammat.)
  Hero et Leander
  8 71.3
Nicephorus Basilaces (Nic.Basilac.)
  Progymnasmata (Progymn.): ed. Pignani
  26, 123 6.11
  5, 11–12 20.1–4
Nicephorus Ouranos (Niceph. Ouran.)
  Carmina (Carm.): ed. S. G. Mercati, 'Versi di Niceforo Uranos in morte de Simeone Metafraste', AnBoll 68 (1950), 126–34
  34, p. 131 10.13
Nicetas Choniates (Nic.Choniat.)
  Historia (Histor.): ed. I. A. van Dieten, *Nicetae Choniatae Historia* 2 vols (Berlin 1975)
  p. 645, 71 74.11
Nicetas Eugenianus (Nic.Eugen.)
  De Drosillae et Chariclis amoribus (D&C): ed. Conca
  6, 398 12.1
  3, 78 29.1

5, 19 75.38
6, 105 75.115–116
4, 139–142 76.127–128
4, 217 76.214
5, 97 76.214
4, 137–138 76.135–136
Monodia in Theodorum Prodromum (Mon. in Theod. Prodr.): ed. Petit
456,17 20.1–4
456, 13–14 75.108–112
Epitaphius in Theodorum Prodromum (Epit. in Theod. Prodr.): ed. Gallavotti
222, 1 76.7
Nicolaus Callicles (Nic.Callic.) Carmina (carm.): ed. Romano
9, 21 26.3–4
Nonnus (Nonn.)
  Dionysiaca (Dion.)
  1, 112 69.4
  5, 443 69.15
  18, 263 71.3
  46, 124 76.193
  46, 276 76.244
Oppianus (Opp.)
  Halieutica (Hal.)
  2, 282 4.17
  4, 551 27.3
  3, 1 74.4
Orphica (Orph.)
  Argonautica (Argon.)
  819 6.16
  Hymni
  39 1.13
  Lithica
  5 4.5
Petrus Argivus (Petr.Argiv.)
  Encomium ad magnam martyrem Christi Barbaram (Barbar.): ed. K. Th. Kyriakopoulos, Ἁγίου Πέτρου ἐπισκόπου Ἄργους βίος καὶ λόγοι. Εἰσαγωγή, Κείμενον, Μετάφρασις, Σχόλια (Athens 1976)
  p. 206, 384–385 12. 1–2
Pindarus (Pind.)
  Fragmenta (Fragm.)
  52f, 97 3.18

Photius (Phot.)
  Bibliotheca (Biblioth.): ed. R. Henry, *Photius, Bibliothèque* 8 vols (Paris 1959–1977)
  Cod. 243, 369a 39, p. 103 Henry VI 1.19
  Lexicon (Lexic.): ed. C. Theodoridis, *Photii patriarchae lexicon (E–M)*, vol. 2 (Berlin/New York 1998)
  μ 109 13.1
  ε 1049, 105 76.24
Plato (Plat.)
  Phaedrus (Phaedr.)
  227a 76.2
  229a 8 76.33
Plutarchus (Plutarch.)
  Alcibiades (Alc.)
  8.1, 3 76.24
  An seni respublica gerenda sit
  795E, 8 1.19
  Brutus (Brut.)
  9.3, 1 76.24
Posidonius
  Fragmenta (Fragm.)
  337a, 24 75.39–40
Proclus (Procl.)
  Homilia in sanctum apostolum Thomam (Hom. Thom.): ed. F. J. Leroy, *L'homilétique de Proclus de Constantinople* (Vatican City 1967)
  33 VII, 20 9.2–5
Ps. Aristoteles (Ps. Arist.)
  De Mundo
  394b35–36 75.39–40
Ps. Epiphanius (Ps. Epiph.)
  Hom. in divini corporis sepulturam: *PG* 43, 452B 43.1
Ps. Iohannes Chrysostomus (Ps. Ioh. Chrys.)
  In illud: Memor fui dei: ed. *PG* 61, 698 43.1
Ps. Phocylides (Ps. Phoc.)
  Sententiae
  44 75.128

Ps. Prodromus (Ps. Prodr.)
  carm.hist., Epitaphius in Alexium.: ed. Hörandner
  22 75.2
Ps.Zonaras (Ps-Zonar.): ed I. A. H. Tittmann, *Ioannis Zonarae Lexicon*, 2 vols (Leipzig 1808)
  Lexicon
  χ 1842, 2 75.128
Ptochoprodromica (Ptochoprodr.): ed. Eideneier
  4, 305 75.84–85
Rhetorica Anonyma (Rhet. Anon.), ed. C. Walz, Rhetores Graeci, vols 8, Stuttgart: Cotta, 1835 (repr. Osnabrück: Otto Zeller, 1968): 402–413
Problemata rhetorica in status 8 403, 17 35.1
Rogerius Hydruntinus (Rog. Hydr.)
  Carmina (Carm.): ed. C. O. Zuretti, 'Ἰταλοελληνικά II: Il contrasto fra Taranto e Otranto', in Centenario della nascita di Michele Amari: Scritti di filologia e storia araba, di geografia, storia, diritto della Sicilia medievale, 2 vols. (Palermo 1910): 173–83
  174, 4–9 20.1–4
Romanus Melodus (Roman. Mel.)
  Cantica (Cant.): ed. J. Grosdidier de Matons, *Romanos le Mélode. Hymnes*, 5 vols (Paris 1964–1981
  42, 16, 5, IV p. 474 9.8–9
  40 11, 8, IV p. 398 69.1
  17, 12, 1, II p. 284 76.5
Quintus Smyrnaeus (Quint. Smyrn.)
  Posthomerica (Posthom.)
  1, 824 6.17
  7, 181 69.4
Simonides (Simon.)
  Fragmenta (Fragm.)
  26, 5 25.2
Suda: ed. A Adler, *Suidae Lexicon, I. A-Γ; II. Δ-Θ; III. K-O. Ω; IV. Π-Ψ; V Index* (Leipzig 1928–1938; Stuttgart 1967–1971)
  μ 186 13.1

Sophocles (Sophoc.)
Oedipus Tyrannus (OT)
1424-1425 5.19
Oedipus Coloneus (Oedip. Colon.)
1207 74.4-5
Strabo (Strab.)
Geographica (Geograph.)
IX 5, 5, p. 608, 8 1.19
Theocritus (Theocr.)
Idyllia (Id.)
15, 41 4.17
Theodorus Balsamon (Theod. Bals.)
Carmina (Carm.): ed. K. Horna, 'Die Epigramme des Theodoros Balsamon', WSt 25 (1903) 165-217
29, 35 43.1
Theodorus Prodromus (Prodr.)
Amarantus: ed. Migliorini
71, 13 76.24
Carmina Historica (Carm. Hist.): ed. Hörandner
56b, 14 1.13
8, 2 2.2
38, 3 3.18
8, 6 3.19
8, 213 5.3
74, 80 7.1
63, 15 7.8
64a, 17 12.1
74, 29 12.1
16, 196 15.2
33b, 9 15.2
16, 102 15.6
17, 229 15.6
45, 47 17.3
74, 59 17.3
17, 180 17.5
4, 106 19.2
4, 287 19.2
59, 76 19.2
75, 112-113 20.10-11
57, 9-10 24.6-7
73, 6 25.9
2, 53 27.3
8, 46 28.2
6, 87 28.4
8, 121 28.4

17, 124 31.1
1, 59 55.2
1, 59 56.2
21, 21 62.12
46, 45 68.5
6, 53 69.1
61, 12 69.1
6, 149 70.1
38, 23 70.1
2, 70 71.5
77, 12-13 73.1
38, 84 74.13-14
42, 38 74.4
3, 88 74.10
6, 33 75.27
30, 395 75.80
40, 19 75.122
19, 74 76.40
74, 92 76.47
43c, 16 76.127-128
50, 19 76.141
63, 1 76.142
43c, 17 76.135-136
Carmina miscellanea (Carm.misc.): ed. Zagklas
71, 6 6.12
69, 4 25.14
76, 205 53.1
12, 14 67.4
6, 12 69.6
76, 272 75.93
75, 50 76.51
75, 22 76.69
53, 1 76.205
75, 93 76.272
Catomyomachia (Catomyom.): ed. Hunger
364 76.29
327 76.2
In eos qui ob paupertatem providentiae conviciantur: ed. *PG*
133, 1294A 75.75
In Illud: ed. *PG*
133, 1301C-1302B 75.6
Rhodanthe et Dosicles (R&D): ed. Marcovich
1, 67 5.6
2, 300 6.22
6, 370 7.8
1, 19 19.4

4, 281   26.4
8, 525   42.1
7, 333   74.9
6, 208   75.39–40
3, 422   75.93
2, 156   76.2
7, 340   76.4
6, 293   76.9
1, 279   76.47
1, 43   76.104–105
5, 450   76.131
8, 94   76.168
2, 51   76.273
2, 92   76.273
9, 62   76.273

Tetrasticha in Vetus et Novum
   Testamentum (Tetrast.): ed. Papagiannis
113b, 2   6.9
219b, 3   6.9
263a, 1–4   9.2–5
24a, 4   19.2
97b, 2–3   26.3–4
229a, 3   27
238b, 1   28.2
127b, 3   28.4
165b, 1–2   73.1
6b, 3   74.4
162b, 4   74.10
23b, 4   75.128
5a, 2   76.70

Tetrasticha in Sancti Gregorii Nazianzeni
   vitam (tetrast.Greg.Naz.): ed.
   D'Ambrosi
14b, 4   2.1–2
2a, 1   2.3–4
8b, 1   2.3–4
11b, 1   5.12
10b, 1–2   6.20

Tetrasticha in Sancti Basilii Caesariensis
   vitam (tetrast.Basil.): ed. Guntius
1b, 1   2.13

Tetrasticha in sancti Iohannis Chrysostomi
   vitam (tetrast.Chrysost.): ed. Guntius
κ7r, 1a, 4; λv, 12a, 1   4.5

carmen contra anum adulteram: ed.
   Migliorini
9   10.4
89   76.161

Opera (Oper.): ed. J. A. Cramer,
   *Anecdota græca e codd. manuscriptis
   bibliothecarum oxoniensium*, vol. 3
   (Oxford 1835), 216–21
p. 217, 25   76.112

Vita sancti Meletii Junioris (Melet.): ed.
   C. Papadopoulos, Ὁ Ὅσιος Μελέτιος
   ὁ Νέος (Athens 1935)
41   75.161

Theodorus Studites (Theod. Stud.)
   Epistulae (Epist.): ed. G. Fatouros, *Theodori
   Studitae Epistulae*, vol. 2 (Berlin 1992)
   477, 12   74.7

Theophylactus Ochridensis (Theoph.
   Ochr.): ed. P. Gautier, *Theophylacte
   d'Achrida: Discours, Traités, Poésies*,
   vol. 2 (Thessaloniki 1980)
   Carmina (Carm.)
   14, 70   4.5

Tragica Adespota (Trag. Adesp.)
   Fragmenta (Fragm.)
   208   27.6

Vitae et Miracula Nicolai Myrensis:
   ed. Anrich
   Vita compilata
   I 222, 21–27   6.9–10

Index of Works

This *index* contains references to works discussed in the introduction and the commentary.

Achilleid
  767: 299

Achilles Tatius
  Leucippe and Clitophon
  1.2.3, 4: 333
  1.15, 2: 318
  1.17, 3–5: 318

Alcman
  Fragments
  30.1: 297

Anacharsis
  776–777: 335
  884: 328
  1144–1145: 330

Anna Komnene
  Alexias
  IV.7.2, 7: 301
  XV.7.9, 18–32: 47 n.67

Andronikos Palaiologos
  Kallimachos and Chrysorroe
  810–11: 299

Anthologia Marciana
  no. 43, vv. 3–4: 312
  no. 60: 315

AP
  IV.1: 19 n.85
  V.302.14: 336
  VIII.28.6: 293
  VIII.4.3–5: 295
  IX.214: 127
  IX.376.2: 324
  IX.524.19: 294
  XV.28: 313
  XV.40.40: 313

Apollonius of Rhodes
  Argonautica
  4.892: 297

Arethas
  Scripta Minora
  17.191.2: 326

Aristophanes
  Acharnians
  1092 and 1125: 335
  Ecclesiazusae
  974: 295
  Wealth
  160-167: 328

Aristotle
  De Caelo
  290b/I 2: 334
  De Coloribus
  280A: 334
  Politica
  1326b.6–7: 293

Arsenios Apostoles
  Collection of proverbs
  XVIII.4b.1 (p. 716): 336

Basil of Caesarea
  Oratio ad adolescentes
  IV.35–52: 295

Bible
  Genesis
  18.1-16: 302
  22.1–13: 308
  Leviticus
  9.4: 307
  Judges
  11.30–40: 308
  1 Kings
  21.1-16: 297
  3 Kings
  17.1: 307

18.17-40: 307
Song of Songs
7.6.2: 298
Isaiah
14.12: 316
Matthew
9.9-13: 316
28.11-15: 303
Mark
2.14: 316
Luke
2.2: 310
18.9-14: 316
5.27: 316
19.1-10: 316
16.19-31: 316
John
8.12: 335
19.26: 312
19.29: 312
19.34: 312
2 Corinthians
11.25: 290
Acts
22.22-29: 291
27.39-44: 290

Christodoulos Hagioeuplites
Poem on St Barbara: 65 n.133

Empedocles
Fragments
27.28, 29 (p. 237-38 Diels-Kranz): 335

Euripides
Andromache
1229: 330

Eustathios of Thessaloniki
Commentary on the Odyssey
I.175.29: 324

Ephraem
Chronicle
5553-5555: 329

Eustathios Makrembolites
Hysmine and Hysminias
1.4.1: 299

Euthymios Tornikes
Poems (ed. Hörandner)
4.1-4: 330
4.96: 336
4.182-183: 335
Poems (ed. Papadopoulos-Kerameus)
1b.49: 292
3.9: 317 n.39

Fifth Ptochoprodromic poem
21-23: 39 n.36
21-27: 40
33: 46 n.63
47: 38

Gregory of Nazianzus
Poems
I.2.29 [898] 186: 336
II.1.13 [1228] 5: 293
II.1.45 [1369-72] 229-270: 292
II.1.44 [1359] 76: 301
II.1.55: 21 n.93
II.2.3 [1495] 211: 21 n.93

Poemata Arcana
5.10-13: 328

Herodianus
De prosodia catholica
3.1: 297

Hesychios
κ 523: 337

Homer
Iliad
2.768-769: 336
5.785-786: 293
8.19: 334
8.97: 290
9.443: 291
13.31: 295
16.549: 293
17.174: 306
18.569-572: 300
24.596-617: 324

Odyssey
5.171: 291
12.39-54: 297
23.97: 306
23.121: 87

Ioannes Tzetzes
- *Carmina Iliaca*
  - 2.291: 323
- *Histories*
  - VI.709: 297
  - VIII.200: 317 n.37
  - X.322: 317 n.37
  - X.323: 317 n.37
- *Letters*
  - 70: 317 n.37

Isaak Komnenos
- *Kosmosoteira Typikon*
  - 106.5–8: 79 n.44

Konstantinos Manasses
- *Aristandros and Kallithea*
  - 160: 318
- *Funerary oration on the death of Nikephoros Komnenos*
  - 60–62: 294

Libanius
- *Letters*
  - 672.1.4: 301

Lucian
- *The Runaways*
  - 12–13: 328
  - 14, 8–14: 335

Lycophron
- *Alexandra*
  - 1174: 306

Manganeios Prodromos
- *Poems*
  - 10.21–32: 34

Manuel Karantenos
- *Poems*
  - 2.5–6: 336

Manuel Philes
- *Poems* (ed. Braounou-Pietsch)
  - 102.2: 297
- *Poems* (ed. Miller)
  - vol. 1, 32, poem 67: 317 n.40

Michael Italikos
- *Letters*
  - 1.64.1–6: 40 n.37
  - 1.64.25–29: 70 n.150
  - 7.9: 307
  - 29.193–197: 334
- *Orations*
  - 15.146–147.1–4: 40 n.38

Michael Psellos
- *Letters*
  - 107.4: 307
- *Poems*
  - 2.291: 300
- *Theologica*
  - 61: 295

Nicander
- *Theriaka*
  - 608: 299

Nikephoros Basilakes
- *Orations*
  - 1.24.21–22: 297

Niketas Choniates
- *Orations*
  - 18.196.13: 336

Niketas Eugenianos
- *Funerary Oration on the Death of Theodoros Prodromos*
  - 456.8–9: 299
  - 452.1–12: 36 n.20
- *Funerary poems*
  - 2. 35–140, 150–159, and 251–259: 36–8
- *Drosilla and Charikles*
  - 3.263–288, 297–320 and 6.205–235: 77 n.36
  - 6.270–289: 329
  - 8.113: 328

Nikolaos Mesarites
- *Epitaph for John Mesarites*
  - 46.8: 315
  - 28.15: 57 n.108
- *Narrative of the coup of John the fat*
  - 48.4: 311–12

Nikolaos of Otranto
- *Poems*
  - 193: 133 n.63

INDEX OF WORKS 373

Nonnus
Dionysiaca
26.86: 299

Oppian
Halieutika
2.176: 322
3.312: 322

Orphic Hymns
45.7 and 11.4-5: 294

Patria of Constantinople
206.10 and 207.1: 324

Pindar
Olympia
10.4: 316
Fragments
204: 316

Plato
Apology
399b; 18c; 29b; 31a: 331
Phaedo
59e-60b: 331
Timaeus
33b: 334

Ps. Dionysios Areopagites
De caelesti hierarchia
(chapter VI) 26, 1-27, 2: 333

Ps. Gregorios Korinthios
On the Four Parts of the Perfect Speech
102: 295
108, 162-6: 12 n.60
108, 162-65: 66 n.142

Ps. Menander
152, 15-16 and 140, 7-10: 319

Ptochoprodromika
3.60-61: 329
4.399: 330

Quintus of Smyrna
Posthomerica
14.10: 295

Sappho
Fragments
135-136: 296

Seven Anonymous Byzantine Epigrams
280: 295

Sophocles
Antigone
1170: 318
Electra
703-706: 330
Fragments
155: 295
Philoktetes
94: 318

Souda
553, 2 and 3852, 6: 341

Theodoros Metochites
Poems
18.364: 313

Theodoros Prodromos
Against a lustful old woman
93: 293
Amarantos, or the erotic desire of an old man
10.5-14: 326
Bion Prasis
301: 336
Calendar in tetrasticha
35: 310
50.199-200: 300
Encomium of Patriarch Ioannes IX Agapetos
7.312-17: 330
Historical poems
1.81-83: 334
6.101: 298
8.51 and 228: 313
15.48: 301
17.60: 300
17.291-300: 307
38.49-55: 46-7
38.52: 292
38.50-59: 326
38.68-74: 328
38.71: 347
38.116-18: 45
42.38: 292
42.42: 322
44.69-71: 330
45.210-211: 330

Theodoros Prodromos (*cont.*)
  56a.4: 56 n.104
  56a.34: 290
  56c.12: 292
  57.9-10: 311
  59.20-21: 330
  59.80-81: 307
  59.168-82: 66 n.138
  63: 38
  69.5: 297
  71.7-10: 58
  71.61: 320
  71.96-99: 45
  72.8-9: 307
  79.18-20: 33
  79.19-20: 333
  79.40-41 and 45: 41-2

Iambic calendar
  10 January (p. 110): 300
  27 January (p. 111): 298
  3 July (p. 130): 320

Miscellaneous poems
  6.12: 295
  21.2: 311
  28.1: 17
  70.4: 322
  71.5: 295
  75.5: 290
  75.9: 292
  76.32-34: 23
  76. 53-57: 326
  76.109-110: 315

On those who curse Providence on account of poverty
  1292B: 335
  1293B: 348
  1297A: 328
  1297A-B: 50
  1296B: 50

Orations
  31.177.99-101: 335
  33.199.40: 27 n.114
  36.239.24: 297
  37.253.31: 326
  38.267.82-84: 59 n.114

Rhodanthe and Dosikles
  3.19-32: 329

4.69: 315
4.377: 298
5.144-162: 304
6.291-304: 333
7.111-112: 337
9.196-204: 3 n.11

Schede
  16, 16-17: 28

Tetrasticha on the Old and New Testaments
  9a: 66 n.139
  9b1: 325
  24: 308
  71b.1: 291
  92b1: 325
  97a: 66 n.139
  100: 308
  171a-b: 307
  185a.2: 303
  197: 316
  205b.3: 324
  206a: 66 n.139
  208b.3: 297
  248: 316
  249: 316
  263a.4: 303
  264b.3: 296
  278a.4: 290
  284b.1: 290
  292a: 291
  289b.4: 297

Tetrasticha for Basil of Caesarea
  15b.2 ($\kappa 6^r$): 310

Tetrasticha for Gregory of Nazianzus
  3a.2: 295
  5: 292

Tetrasticha for John Chrysostom
  22a.3 ($\lambda 4^r$): 296
  16 ($\lambda 2^v$-$\lambda 3^r$): 297
  18 ($\lambda 3^r$): 298

The Plato-lover, or the tanner
  124-132: 330

Theodoros Stoudites
Poems
  67.3-4: 294

Timarion
  7.193: 330

General Index

Ablabius, eparch 301
Abraham 16, 63, 133, 136, 185, 199, 302, 308
Achilles 23, 40 n.37, 285, 291, 318, 332, 336
Adonis 299
Ajax 285, 336
Akakios, hieromonachos 101
Alexios I Komnenos, emperor 56
Alexios, scribe 115
Allatius, Leon, scholar 117, 118
Alopos, Konstantinos 302
Anagnostes, Konstantinos, scribe and poet 120
Anagnostes, Romanos, scribe 120
Anastasios Quaestor 313
Angelos, Demetrios (Ἄγγελος, Δημήτριος), scribe 113
Antioch 179
Anytus, accuser of Socrates 49, 265, 327, 331
Apollonius of Rhode 297
Apostoles, Arsenios 11, 13, 18–19, 95, 96, 115, 137, 139 n.85, 157, 159, 170
Arabia 263
Archangel Gabriel 310
Archangel Michael 125, 129
Ares 249
Argyropoulos Ioannes (Ἀργυρόπουλος, Ἰωάννης), scribe 121
Aristenos, Alexios 3, 56, 129, 297, 299, 335
Aristides, orator 50
Aristophanes 3 n.13, 295, 328–30, 335
Aristotle 6, 37, 50, 60, 255, 307, 325, 326
Arius 175
Asan, Andreas 134
Asan, Manuel 134
Athanasios of Alexandreia 299
Athanasios, monk 129
Athens 37
Atlantic Ocean 189
audience 20 n.91, 21, 23, 42, 52, 67
Aulikalamos, Theodoros 322
authority 11, 35, 42, 51, 332
authorship 4, 7 n.34, 9, 11–15, 31, 34, 85, 137, 160, 303, 312

Baal 195, 307
Bacchante 283
Bacchylides 311
Balsamon, Theodoros 125
Barakis, Michael 129
Barbara, saint 16, 63–5, 74, 133, 148, 160, 161, 190–201, 305–9
Bartholomeo de Columnis, Nicola 119
Barys, accuser of Theodoros Prodromos 24, 27
Basel edition 25, 78 n.40, 140 n.87, 155–8, 162–4
Basil of Caesarea 8, 9, 24–5, 27–8, 61, 73 n.6, 78, 128, 134, 146, 160, 177, 181, 290, 295–6, 297, 298, 304, 311
Basilakes, Nikephoros 44
Batrachomyomachia 22
begging poetry 44, 48–53, 329
Bios 16, 139, 160, 316–18
Bosporus 189
Bryennios, Joseph, monk 135
Bryennios, Nikephoros, 48 v.70 67
Byzantium 1–2, 6, 15, 18, 20, 24, 32, 41, 53, 57, 67, 75, 78 n.43, 82, 131, 133, 155, 166, 179, 294, 296, 302 n.3, 318, 323, 326, 329, 334, 337

Cappadocia 177
Cassius, Dio, historian 335
Chalcedon 291
Cherubim 273, 334
Chios 137–9
Choniates, Michael 77 n.36
Chortasmenos, Ioannes 22, 134–5 n.96
Chrysippos, philosopher 37
Chrysostom, John 8, 9, 24–5, 27, 61, 78, 128, 179, 205, 290, 296–8, 310–11
classroom 32, 53–70
clitics 163–6
cloud 247, 321–2
commissions 2, 5, 17, 26, 30, 33, 39–43, 53, 60, 66, 127, 302, 321
Constantine the Great, emperor 301

Constantinople 2, 5, 33–4, 37, 42–3, 48, 89, 90, 107, 109, 122, 126–8, 130, 133–4, 292, 296, 298, 326
Corbinelli, Antonio, book collector 108
Corfu 92, 135, 321
correption
  Attic 85–6
  epic 86
court 7, 31–70, 77–8, 333
cycle (of poems) 7, 9–10, 12–14, 16–19, 24–30, 57, 61–3, 65–6, 74–5, 79, 128–9, 131, 133, 135–6, 139 nn. 83 and 85, 148, 152, 155, 160–1, 167, 290, 305, 306 n.16, 309, 312, 314, 316, 319, 337
Cyprus 120

dactylic hexameter. *see* hexameter
dactylic pentameter. *see* pentameter
Darmarios, Andreas, scribe 97
David 300
death 2, 8, 19, 33, 35 n.19, 37–41, 46, 56, 58, 98, 108, 109, 134, 298, 302, 312, 318, 322–5
demes 33, 41, 75
Democritus, philosopher 255, 267, 325–6, 328, 331
Demosthenes, orator 292, 330
Devil 183, 301–2
dialogue 18, 20 n.89, 22, 51, 72, 74, 292, 302, 320, 324, 326, 331–2
didactic function/poems 43, 51, 52, 60 n.122, 65 n.133, 69, 72, 134, 299
Dionysus 294
Dioscorus, father of saint Barbara 305
Dioskoros of Aphrodito 309
discursive mode 20 n.90, 52
dodecasyllable 1, 3, 22, 29, 35 n.19, 60 n.122, 66, 71–3, 77, 83, 84 n.65, 87, 163, 167 n.33
  caesura 72–3
  stress 74–5
Dodekaorton 14, 62, 133, 309–10
donors 16–17, 24–5, 28, 30, 60, 63, 66, 69, 290, 310–11
Doukas Sgouros, Andronikos, writer 135

Eden 18, 241, 320
education 2, 22, 37, 42, 46–51, 57–8, 60, 265, 314, 326–7
Eirene Doukaina, empress 38–41, 56, 68, 325
Eirene, Sevastokratorissa 6, 11, 15, 56, 67, 131, 135, 300

ekphrasis 17, 52, 130, 296
Elijah, prophet 195, 307
Empedocles, philosopher 255, 273, 325–6, 334
encomium 2, 29 n.123, 52, 55, 59–60, 78–9, 129, 292, 300
envy 2, 8, 213, 239, 287, 289
Eparchos, Antonios (Ἔπαρχος, Ἀντώνιος), scholar 94, 115
epigrams 8–9, 12–19, 24, 26–30, 33, 36, 38, 54, 62–3, 65–6, 72, 74–5, 78, 90, 95, 97, 104, 109, 127–9, 134–7, 139 nn.83 and 85, 152, 155, 157, 160, 167, 290, 295, 297, 302, 305, 309–21, 324–5, 337; *see also* inscriptions
epistolography, *see* letters
Eros 2, 235, 237, 314, 319
Eteocles, king of Thebes 285, 336
ethopoiia 20, 22, 53, 65, 68, 112, 160, 322–4, 331
Eudoxia, empress 297
Eugenianos, Niketas 16, 19, 29, 35, 37–8, 43, 66, 68, 77 n.36, 82 n.54, 83, 131, 299, 325
Eunomius of Cyzicus, bishop 177, 181, 296, 298–9
Euphrates 304
Euripides 22, 336
Eusebius of Caesarea 299
Eustathios of Thessaloniki 59, 79
Eustathios, manuscript collector 93
experiments
  literary 2, 5, 54
  metrical 78, 80, 83

fiction 43–53
flowers 18–19, 243
fortune 22, 49, 132, 205, 267, 310
friendship 2, 22–3, 26, 31, 33–5, 41, 42 n.47, 271–89, 315, 331–7

Galaktion, hieromonachos 98, 116
garden 17–19, 24, 135, 160, 167, 181, 239–43, 298, 314, 318–20
Gebrauchstext 18–19
genre 2–3, 5, 7, 9, 15–24, 28, 31, 47, 51–2, 54, 56, 74, 131, 322
Geometres, Ioannes 77, 81–2, 137 n.80, 292, 313
George, Count of Corinth 96
Georgios of Alexandreia 297
Georgios of Antioch, *amiratus amiratorum* 17, 245, 320–1

Georgios thytes (Γεώργιος ὁ θύτης), scribe 89
Gerasimos, monk 100
Ghislain de Busbecq, Augier, manuscript collector 89, 90
gift 30, 46, 60-1, 281, 289, 320, 321
gluttony 241, 330
Glykas, Michael 52
God 2 n.9, 22, 37, 136, 173, 175, 177, 181, 183, 185, 187, 189, 193, 195, 197, 205, 207, 211, 219, 223, 227, 245, 259, 265, 269, 271, 273, 279, 290, 299, 308, 310, 311, 312, 319, 320, 323 n.54, 327-8, 332
grammar competition 27
grammatikos 38, 43-4, 48
Greek Anthology 127
Gregorios of Corinth 309
Gregory of Nazianzus 8-9, 12, 21-2, 24, 27-9, 60-1, 78, 81-2, 128, 134-5, 160, 290, 291-5, 296, 300-1, 306, 311, 313, 328, 333
Gregory of Nyssa 16, 24-5, 27, 61, 89, 128 n.39, 181, 290, 296-8
Grynaeus, Simon, scholar 156
Guntius, Hieronymus, scholar 155-7, 160, 164

Habakkuk, prophet 259, 328
Hades 45-6, 183, 211
Hagar 63, 185, 302
Hagioeuplites, Christodoulos, poet 63-5
Haploucheir, Michael 22, 51, 131-2
Hector 285, 332, 336
Helle 322
hemistichs 76-7, 79
Heraclitus, philosopher 123, 125, 267, 331
Hermes 330
Hesiod, poet 300
hexameter 1, 3, 16, 21-2, 29, 35, 48 n.71, 60 n.122, 66, 71-2, 77-84, 87, 292, 312-13
   caesura 82-4
   stress 83-4
   verse patterns 80
hiatus 87
hierarchs 8 n.44, 9, 16, 24 n.106, 27, 61, 66, 296
Hippo, presocratic philosopher 328, 331
Hippocrates 330
Holobolos, Manuel 110
Holy Spirit 62, 98, 203

Holy Trinity 135, 136, 162, 185, 273, 302, 333
Homer 2 n.9, 3 n.13, 21, 22, 29, 51 n.81, 53, 57, 78-84, 127, 255, 290-1, 297, 300, 313, 322, 325-6, 330, 336
honey 34, 175, 181, 243, 294-5, 299
Honter, Ioannes, humanist 156
horse 261, 263, 295, 301, 328, 330
Hymettus 34, 181, 299
hymn 28-30, 33, 41, 61, 72, 75-6, 78, 132, 290
hymnography 20 n.89, 303, 308

iamb 8, 13, 16, 24, 35, 57, 70 n.155, 71-2, 130, 137, 152, 160, 300, 305, 309 n.18, 312 n.29, 314, 320
iconography 16-17, 27, 63, 309, 312-13, 317
icons 12, 17, 29 n.127, 36-7, 66, 134, 207, 245, 301-2, 320-1
Ignatios 111
Ignatios Magistor 309
imitation 53, 132, 135, 306, 325
in Ifrīqiya, Tanīm, Zarid ruler 321
inscriptions 16-17, 62-3, 65-6, 75, 136-9, 312 n.29, 314 n.33, 321, 323
intellectual circle 26, 39, 48 n.70, 84, 129, 131, 135
Ioannes II Komnenos, emperor 4, 33, 38-9, 41, 44-5, 66 n.137, 130, 307, 334
Ioannes IX Agapetos, patriarch 59, 330
Ioannes of Damascus 6, 137 n.80, 306
Ioannes, *diakonos*, scribe 104
Ioannikios, monk 18, 34-5, 38-9, 43, 57, 68, 71, 131, 134
Isaac 199, 302, 308
Isaac, monk, scribe 101
Isaiah, prophet 193, 307, 316
Ishmael 63, 185, 302
isometry 72
isosyllaby 72-3, 80, 83
Italikos, Michael 26, 40, 70, 307, 334

Jephthah, judge 197, 308
Jesus Christ 16-17, 21, 24, 120, 173, 187, 191, 203, 211, 261, 265, 309-10, 312-13, 316, 321
Jews 187, 303
John the Forerunner, prophet 34
John, saint 312-13
Justin II, emperor 26

GENERAL INDEX

Kabbades, Mathousalas, monk 89
Kairos, Lysippean statue 317–18
Kallikles, Nikolaos 14–15, 42–3, 74, 77, 130, 156, 160, 312
Kalliope 59
Kallistos of Vatopedi, hieromonachos 106
Kallistou Xanthopoulos, Nikephoros 156, 310
Kalophrenas, Michael, scholar 98
Kamateros, Andronikos, eparch 311
Kamateros, Gregorios, logothetes ton sekreton 297
Kamytzes, Konstantinos, sevastos 15
Komana 179, 298
Komnene, Anna 45–8, 59, 79, 326
Komnenos, Alexios, son of Ioannes II Komnenos 39, 41, 334
Komnenos, Andronikos, sevastokrator 38, 40, 56, 135, 325
Komnenos, Isaak, sevastokrator 79, 130
Konstantinos IX Monomachos, emperor 67
Kosmas, hymnographer 6
Kosmoteira Monastery 130

laments 21–2, 32, 48, 52, 60, 267, 323, 333
Lazarus of Bethany 62, 203, 309, 316
Leo of Rhodes, metropolitan 27
Leo the Philosopher, poet 21, 109, 127
Leo tou Megistou 59
Leo X, pope 18, 95, 139 n.85
Leon, scribe 108
letters 2, 6, 40 n.37, 51–2, 55, 60, 72, 78, 122–3, 129, 130, 132, 156, 161–2, 291, 300, 307, 317, 334, 336
Libanius 123, 125
Lignos, Germanos, monk 93, 132
Likinios, Ioannes, monk 114
lion 201
literati 42, 44, 50, 59, 68
logos 315
Lopadius, Ludwig, writer 156
Lucian 23, 328–9, 331–2, 335
Lucianic style 3, 66, 69
Lucifer 273, 316, 332
Lycia 183
Lycon, accuser of Socrates 331
lyre 179, 183, 281, 300, 335
Lysias, orator 333

Macheir, Mathousalas, writer 100
Makedonios, bishop 175
Makrembolites, Eustathios 314, 322

Manasses, Konstantinos 7 n.34, 11, 13, 15, 31, 42, 52 n.89, 68 n.151, 130, 134
Manganeios, Prodromos 3–4, 34, 39 n.35, 41–2, 77, 130–1, 304, 321
Manuel I Komnenos, emperor 26, 33, 38–41, 45, 51 n.81, 321
Manuel Karantenos, patriarch 322
mathemataria 135–6
Matthew, evangelist 303, 316
Mauropous, Ioannes 10, 14, 24 n.106, 77, 130, 156, 296, 309
Meleager 19 n.85
Meles, Stephanos, logothetes tou dromou 59, 297
Meletios, hieromonachos 113
Meletus, accuser of Socrates 49, 265, 327, 330–1
Meligalas, Manuel 123, 125, 129
Menander 29 n.123, 125
Mesarites, Nikolaos 57
Metaphrastes, Symeon 137 n.80, 297
metre 1, 3–5, 10, 15, 19, 29, 49, 56–8, 63, 66, 70 n.155, 71–87, 101, 119, 130, 137, 156, 164, 229, 299, 303, 323
Michael IV the Paphlagonian, emperor 46
Michael V Kalaphates, emperor 58
Michael VII Doukas, emperor 67
mimes 257, 325–7
misfortune 37, 267, 327
Mitylenaios, Christophoros 10, 14–15, 21, 58, 77, 82, 137 n.80, 312
Monachos, Iakovos 300
monody 2, 26, 33 n.11, 35 n.19, 38, 56, 59, 77 n.36, 326
monologue 20, 22, 322–3, 332
Monotropos, Philippos 22
moon 259, 275, 327–8
Muses 37, 59, 255, 294–5, 331

Naxos 135, 313 n.29
Neilos of Ankyra, abbot 299
Nephele 322
Nicaea 93, 128, 132
Nicander 123, 125–6
Niccoli, Niccolò, humanist 109
Nicholas, saint 15–16, 24–5, 27–8, 30 38, 55, 61, 135, 183, 205, 290, 300–2, 310–1
Nikephoros I, patriarch of Constantinople 90, 99
Nikolaos of Otranto, abbot 108, 133
Niobe 251, 324–5
Nonnus of Panopolis 80–3, 323
nudity 318

GENERAL INDEX 379

occasional literature 10, 17–19, 23, 24–30, 31–70
Oeagrus, king of Thrace 255, 326
Oppian, poet 112
orations 2, 6, 27, 52, 59 n.115, 104, 106, 108, 175, 265, 293–5, 299–300, 305, 311, 325, 327, 336
Orestes 285, 336
Origen, theologian 299
Orphanotropheion of St. Paul 24–30, 59 n.119, 60, 61, 290, 291, 304
Orphanotrophos 3, 51, 56
Orpheus 255, 326

Palaiologos Doukas Komnenos, Georgios, *megas hetairiarches* 59
panegyrics 16, 19, 29–30, 35–8, 45, 56, 58–9, 294
Paniotes, author 13, 15
Paradise 221
Parnassus 269, 331
Paul the Silentiary 80
Paul, saint 16, 24–30, 49, 59 n.119, 60–1, 160, 173, 259, 269, 290–1, 297, 304, 328
patronage 31, 42, 60–1
Pausanias 19, 251, 253, 324
Pediasimos, Ioannes, scholar 62 n.129
Peleus, king of Phthia 285
pentameter 3, 71–2, 77–9, 83, 85, 87
performance 6, 16, 29, 32, 53–6, 60, 63, 65, 68–9, 74, 120, 329
persona 5, 50, 53–4
personification 22–3, 57, 132, 137, 160, 161, 162, 292, 308, 314, 316–17, 322, 324, 332–6
Peter (son of Pausanias) 251
Peter of Argos, saint 306
Peter, monk 131
Peter, saint 14, 16, 19, 26, 98, 209, 297, 312
Philes, Manuel 7 n.36, 14, 45 n.60, 51 n.85, 128 n.42, 160, 310, 317, 329
Phrixus 322
Pinelli, Gian Vincenzo, humanist 110
Piroska-Eirene, princess of Hungary 334
Pisides, Georgios 12, 21, 80, 309
Pius IX, pope 122
Plato 23, 37, 49–50, 59, 122, 255, 325–6, 330–1, 333–4
pleasure 2, 17, 37, 70, 175, 243, 292, 317, 320
political verse 1, 60 n.122, 71–2, 75–7, 83
Polyneices, brother of Eteocles 285, 336
Pomponius, author 330

Porphyry, philosopher 123, 125, 127
Priam 285, 336
progymnasmata 57, 119
Proklos, saint 298
prose 2–3, 5, 14, 35, 47 n.67, 49–52, 55–6, 67 n.147, 70 n.155, 78, 122, 128–9, 132, 135–6, 175, 298
prosody 58, 72, 78, 84–6, 129, 137, 166, 303
Prosouch, Byzantine general of Turkish origin 119
Providence 48–50, 59, 131–3, 259–9, 327–31, 335
Ps. Dionysios Areopagites, theologian 333–4
Ps. Herodotus, writer 125
Ps. Menander 319
Psellos, Michael 12–13, 15, 46, 67, 77, 137, 152, 156, 162 n.16, 299–300, 331
(Ptocho)prodromos 3–5, 8, 11, 14, 56
Pylades, prince of Phocis 285, 336

readers 12, 15, 17–19, 31, 53, 69–70, 167–8
reality 32, 43–4, 52, 161
recipient 17, 54, 61, 65, 67, 69, 79
recycling 58–9, 68 n.151, 162
rhetoric of poverty 44, 48, 52–3
riddle 19, 62, 68, 247, 321–2
Ridolfi, Niccolò, cardinal 92
ring 17, 63, 160, 235, 237, 318–19
Roger II, Norman king 320–1
Rome 173, 175, 179, 291

Sabellios, theologian 175, 293
Saponopoulos, Nikephoros, protonotarios 125, 128
Saponopoulos, Theophylaktos 126–9, 167
Sarah 63, 136, 185, 302
satire 2–3, 6–7, 9, 42, 59, 66, 69, 128, 293, 326, 329
schedographer 35, 38
schedos 2–3, 6, 7 n.34, 18, 24, 27–8, 34–5, 38–40, 47–8, 54–60, 63–5, 68–9, 71, 84, 120, 134, 301
schedourgia 21 n.92, 56
self-deprecation 2
self-referentiality 21
self-representation (or self-fashioning) 23, 32, 43, 53, 130
Seraphim 273, 334
Serblias, Nikephoros, judge 43
Sicily 245
Simeon, prophet 203
Simonides, lyric poet 311

sirens 179, 296–7
Skylitzes, Stephanos 26, 33, 41, 59–60
social inequality 21–2, 48–9, 51, 327
Socrates 49, 265, 327, 330–1, 333
Sodom 191, 305
Solomon 181, 300
Sophos, Konstantinos, scribe 99
Sosthenes 314
Southern Italy 13 n.67, 74, 133–4
Stilbes, Konstantinos, author 123, 125
Stobaeus, Ioannes, author 14
Stoudites, Theodoros 292
Stratocles, character in Prodromos' work Amarantos 3 n.12, 326
style 2–3, 5, 15, 17, 53, 63, 66, 69, 133, 325
Styppeiotes, Theodoros, grammatikos 26, 38, 45–6, 48, 55, 58, 307
sun 290, 324, 328
swallow 34, 179, 296
sylloge 128, 131–2
Symeon the New Theologian, monk 101

Tabor 203
Taronites, Ioannes, sevastos 43
Tarsus 173, 291
Tatius, Achilles, writer 23, 69, 318, 333–4
tetrastichs 7–8, 24, 61, 65–6, 106, 131–3, 155, 292–3
Thales of Miletus, astronomer 328
theatron 40–1, 53–70, 131, 325–6
Thebes 336
Theodoret of Cyrrhus, bishop 302
Theodoros II Laskaris, emperor 132
Theodoros of Trimithous, bishop 297
Theodoros Prodromos
   Against a lustful old woman 9, 131
   Against a man with a long beard 9
   Amarantos, or the erotic desire of an old man 3, 326
   Bion Prasis (Sale of the political and poetical lives) 3, 59
   career of 3, 10, 32–42, 68, 155, 325
   Commentary on Aristotle's Posterior Analytics 2, 6, 60
   Encomium of Patriarch Ioannes IX Agapetos 59, 330
   Exegesis on the canons of Kosmas and Ioannes of Damascus 6
   Grammar 6, 67, 69
   Historical poems 7, 10, 12, 29 n.122, 58, 60, 69, 74–6, 78–9, 88, 139, 140

   Katomyomachia 7, 11, 22, 72, 74, 157
   On those who curse Providence on account of poverty 49–51
   Orations 6, 27, 299
   Rhodanthe and Dosikles 2–3, 41, 67–8, 72, 75, 135, 323, 329
   Tetrasticha on the Old and New Testaments 8, 24, 66 n.139, 74–5, 87 n.73, 128, 133–4
   Tetrasticha for Basil of Caesarea, Gregory of Nazianzus and John Chrysostom 8–9, 73 n.6, 78, 128, 134
   Tetrasticha for the great martyrs Theodoros, Georgios, and Demetrios 7, 61, 78
   To the caesar or for the colour green 48 n.70, 67 n.147
Theotokos. *see* Virgin Mary
Thessaly 263
Thomas, saint 309
Thrones 273, 334
topos 51–2, 67 n.147, 132, 294, 296, 299, 303, 318, 330
Tornikes, Euthymios 292, 317, 322, 330
Trebizond 33, 41, 60
tree 16, 23, 235–7, 241, 273, 318–20, 333–4
trivium 47, 314
Turks 33, 321
Tzetzes, Ioannes 5, 13, 15, 42, 43, 59, 77 n.36, 79, 134, 317

Valens, emperor 298
van Lennep, Johannes Daniel 113
vanity 2, 21, 325
variation (rhetorical) 5, 63
Vergikios, Angelos (Βεργίκιος, Ἄγγελος), scribe 94, 113, 149
vernacular poetry 3–5, 8, 11, 53, 72
verse-filling asyndeton 62–3
Virgin Mary 16–17, 134, 308, 310–2, 320–1
Vlachos, Gerasimos, scholar 105

Xiphilinos, Ioannes, monk 335

Zacchaeus 316
Zeus 251, 316, 324
Zonaras, Ioannes 335
Zotikos, saint 26
Zwingli, Jakob, son of Ulrich 156
Zwingli, Ulrich, leader of the Reformation 156

Index of Manuscripts

Athens, Βιβλιοθήκη τῆς Βουλῆς τῶν
  Ἑλλήνων
  Cod. 57: 99–100, 136
Athens, Ἐθνικὴ Βιβλιοθήκη τῆς Ἑλλάδος
  Athen. EBE 1183: 100
  Athen. EBE 1264: 100
  Athen. EBE 3104: 100–1
  Metoch. S. Sep. 797: 101
Athens, Ἱστορικὴ καὶ Ἐθνολογικὴ Ἑταιρεία
  Athen. Hist. – Ethn. Het. 66: 101, 135
Athos
  Athous. Dionys. 594: 102
  Athous. Doch. 108 (2782): 103, 136
  Athous. Hag. Paul. 9: 103
  Athous. Iber. 161: 160
  Athous. Iber. 509 (olim 4629): 103–4
  Athous. Iber. 765: 104
  Athous. Iber. 1418: 28, 104
  Athous. Kar. Chart. 79: 104
  Athous. Meg. Laura B 43: 131–2
  Athous. Meg. Laura Λ 62
    (1552): 105, 136
  Athous. Meg. Laura Ω 34 (1844): 105
  Athous. Pantel. 683: 105–6
  Athous. Vatop. 56: 28, 106, 160
  Athous. Vatop. 95: 106

Bern, Burgerbibliothek
  Bern 48 B: 115–16, 161
Bucharest, Biblioteca Academiei Române
  Cod. 601 (214): 114
  Cod. 646: 114
Budapest, private collection of
    Philippos Tialos
  Cod. 3: 107

El Escorial, Biblioteca Real
  Cod. y-III-9 (gr. 332): 88, 115
Elassona, Μονὴ τῆς Ὀλυμπιωτίσσης
  Cod. 80: 102
  Cod. 83: 102

Florence, Biblioteca Medica Laurenziana
  Laurent. Conv. Soppr. 2: 60

Laurent. Conv. Soppr. 48: 14, 107–8
Laurent. Conv. Soppr. 121 (C. 558):
  108, 161
Laurent. Plut. V 10: 108–09, 161
Laurent. Acq. e Doni 341: 109, 161
Laurent. San Marco 318: 13, 109–10

Göttingen, Niedersächsische Staats- und
    Universitätsbibliothek
  Cod. 4: 96
  Cod. 29: 14, 96–7

Heidelberg, Ruprecht-Karls-Universität
  Cod. 43: 67, 95–6, 161
  Cod. 356: 96

Istanbul, Πατριαρχικὴ Βιβλιοθήκη
  Constantin.mon. Pan. Camar. in Chalce
    insula 165: 116
Istanbul, Γραφεῖα τῆς ἐκκλησίας Παναγίας
    (τῶν Εἰσοδίων)
  Cod. 27: 116–17
  Cod. 32: 117

Jerusalem, Πατριαρχικὴ Βιβλιοθήκη
  Hierosolymitanus Nikod. 14: 107
  Hierosolymitanus Sab. gr. 462: 107

Leiden, Universiteitsbibliotheek
  B.P.G. 88: 113
  Voss. gr. Q 26: 113
  Voss. gr. Q. 42: 113–14, 136
Lesbos, Ἱερὰ Μονὴ Λειμῶνος
  Cod. 219: 101–2
London, British Library
  Lond. Add. 10014: 97–8
  Lond. Harl. 5624: 88, 98
Lyon, Bibliothèque municipale
  Cod. 122 (52): 92

Milan, Biblioteca Ambrosiana
  Ambr. H 22 sup. (426): 110
Munich, Bayerische Staatsbibliothek
  Cod. 306: 97, 318

Naples, Biblioteca Nazionale
  Neapol. Branc. IV A 5: 7 n.34
  Neapol. II D 4: 111–12
  Neapol. II D 22: 112
  Neapol. III AA 6: 112

Oxford, Bodleian Library
  Bodl. Barocc. 197: 98–9
  Bodl. Roe 18: 14, 99

Paris, Bibliothèque Nationale de France
  Paris. gr. 554: 28, 92, 134, 160
  Paris. gr. 854: 14, 92–3, 136
  Paris. gr. 997: 93, 132
  Paris. gr. 1277: 93–4
  Paris. gr. 1630: 94
  Paris. gr. 2831: 25, 94, 160
  Paris. gr. 2870: 94–5
  Paris. gr. 3019: 95
  Paris. gr. 3058: 13, 18, 95, 137, 139 n.85, 157, 161
  Paris. Suppl. gr. 501: 95
Patmos, Μονὴ τοῦ Ἁγίου Ἰωάννου τοῦ Θεολόγου
  Cod. 407: 106

Rovereto, Biblioteca Civica
  Cod. 28: 113

St Petersburg, Rossijskaja Akademija Nauk, Biblioteka (BAN)
  Petropol. AN RAIK 181 (B 28): 114–15

Sofia, The Scientific Archives of the Bulgarian Academy of Sciences
  Sofien. Cen. 'Ivan Dujčev' gr. 12: 91, 134

Vatican, Biblioteca Apostolica Vaticana
  Vat. gr. 207 (olim 1100): 117
  Vat. gr. 305 (olim 218): 10, 14–15, 25, 88, 117–18, 122–30, 133, 160–7, 329
  Vat. gr. 306 (olim 989): 118
  Vat. gr. 307 (olim 668): 14, 118, 136
  Vat. gr. 1126 (olim 887): 14, 89, 118–19
  Vat. gr. 1702: 119, 148, 163, 165, 170, 190–8
  Vat. gr. 2363: 119
  Vat. Pal. gr. 92: 39 n.129, 40, 57, 65 n.132, 67, 69, 134
  Vat. Pal. gr. 367: 120, 133
  Vat. Reg. Gr. Pii II 54: 63–5, 120, 161
  Vat. Chis. gr. R.IV.11: 13, 120–1, 133
  Vat. Ottob. gr. 324: 121, 134
  Vat. Urb. gr. 134: 121–2
Venice, Biblioteca Nazionale Marciana
  Marc. gr. Z 436: 110
  Marc. gr. Z 512: 111
  Marc. gr. Z 524: 11, 111
Vienna, Österreichische Nationalbibliothek
  Vindob. Histor. gr. 106: 14, 62 n.129, 89
  Vindob. Philol. gr. 110: 89–90
  Vindob. Philol. gr. 149: 90, 311
  Vindob. Philol. gr. 321: 132
  Vindob. Suppl. gr. 125: 91
  Vindob. Theol. gr. 249: 90–1